Straley's Guide to Programming with CA-Realizer®

Stephen J. Straley

Addison-Wesley Publishing Company
Reading, Massachusetts • Menlo Park, California • New York
Don Mills, Ontario • Wokingham, England • Amsterdam
Bonn • Sydney • Singapore • Tokyo • Madrid • San Juan
Paris • Seoul • Milan • Mexico City • Taipei

Many of the designations used by manufacturers and sellers to distinguish their products are claimed as trademarks. Where those designations appear in this book, and Addison-Wesley was aware of a trademark claim, the designations have been printed in initial capital letters or all capital letters.

The authors and publishers have taken care in preparation of this book, but make no expressed or implied warranty of any kind and assume no responsibility for errors or omissions. No liability is assumed for incidental or consequential damages in connection with or arising out of the use of the information or programs contained herein.

Library of Congress Cataloging-in-Publication Data
Straley, Stephen J.
   [Guide to programming with CA-Realizer]
   Straley's guide to programming with CA-Realizer / Stephen J. Straley.
     p.   cm.
   Includes index.
   ISBN 0-201-40944-5 (pbk.)
   1. Object-oriented programming (Computer science) 2. CA-Realizer (Computer program language)   I. Title. II. Title: Guide to programming with CA-Realizer.
QA76.64.S75 1995
005.265—dc20
                                                                                               95-3960
                                                                                                 CIP

Copyright © 1995 by Stephen J. Straley

All rights reserved. No part of this publication may be reproduced, stored in a retrieval system, or transmitted, in any form or by any means, electronic, mechanical, photocopying, recording, or otherwise, without the prior written permission of the publisher. Printed in the United States of America. Published simultaneously in Canada.

Sponsoring Editor: Kathleen Tibbetts
Project Manager: Sarah Weaver
Project Coordinator: Erin Sweeney
Cover design: Courtesy of Computer Associates International, Inc.
Set in 11 point Times Roman by Gex

1 2 3 4 5 6 7 8 9 -MA- 9998979695
First printing, April 1995

Addison-Wesley books are available for bulk purchases by corporations, institutions, and other organizations. For more information please contact the Corporate, Government, and Special Sales Department at (800) 238-9682.

There is a group of people to whom I would like to dedicate this book. Most have graced my life with insights and wisdom. Some, due to a variety of inexcusable reasons, are no longer with us. But, to the living, I'd like to thank the people of Hotel New York (Anne, Fernando, Dick, Mize, and Philip), Avert, Bill Hungerford and John Lutjes, Joop Pecht and Ernst Peter Tamminga of CDGN (Clipper Developer's Group of the Netherlands), and Martin Band, Bill Hattfield, and Ron Maldon. Finally, to the great people of The Netherlands. It is said that home is where the heart is, and based on the amount of heart and warmth these and others have shown, my home is indeed here.

Acknowledgments

There are many people to acknowledge on this project. First, my editor: Essor Maso. He has been with me from the early Clipper days as well as into these new and uncharted waters. Also, to Kathleen Tibbetts and the great people at Addison-Wesley, who took a chance on this book. There are no finer people in the publishing business than they. Additional recognition goes to Marc Sokol of Computer Associates, who first planted in my head the seed to write a book on Realizer, and to Jack Kraimer for watering that seed. Also, I need to thank the people at Computer Associates for their help and assistance: Christine Glynn and Philip Williams. And finally, special recognition goes to the people on CompuServe and those in technical support who guided me through this arduous task: Gary Zimak, Michael Massaro, and on CompuServe, David Ullrich. To you all, my deepest and sincere thanks!

Contents

Foreword		ix
How to Use This Book		xi
Chapter 1	Programming Concepts and Ideas	1
Chapter 2	Menus of an Application	44
Chapter 3	More Programming Concepts	98
Chapter 4	Simple Forms for Data Entry and Data Validation	158
Chapter 5	More Complex Forms and User Interface	249
Chapter 6	Boards, Charts, and Sheets	322
Chapter 7	Simple File Manipulation and String Parsing	371
Chapter 8	Reusable Code and Subsystems	418
Chapter 9	Output, Help, and Errors	447
Chapter 10	The Animator, Importing/Exporting, and DDEs	491
Chapter 11	External Routines, Windows API, and User-Defined Types	538
Chapter 12	Frequently Asked Questions	566
Epilog		575
Appendix	Libraries, Add-On Products, and Third-Party Services	577
Index		593

Foreword

The history of CA-Realizer is an interesting one. The brainchild of a group of Princeton graduates, it made its debut at Windows World in 1991, where it won a "Best of Show" award. About one year later, it was acquired by Computer Associates. Since then, CA-Realizer has seen a successful 2.0 release on both the Windows and OS/2 platforms.

Steve Straley's new book, *Straley's Guide to Programming with CA-Realizer*, is the newest turn in the history of CA-Realizer. It offers the CA-Realizer developer everything he or she needs to know—from understanding the basic concepts of programming in CA-Realizer, to building complex user interfaces, to tapping into the power of CA-Realizer's programmable application tools—and is complete with extensive code examples and demo programs. This is a "must buy" for all CA-Realizer developers, new or experienced.

Marc Sokol
Vice President, Product Strategy
Computer Associates International, Inc.

How to Use This Book

When I began this task, my goal was to provide three things to the Realizer programmer. The first was to give a general overview of the Realizer language. In this, my approach has been to use Realizer as a tool toward application development; to understand not just the various tools and the environment, but to look at the language and the nuances. To me, the language makes or breaks the product. A programmer cannot just blindly use the tools and expect to know the product; source code must be studied. As a result, I focus on source code examples, written either by hand or by the FormDev Utility program. I look at language theories and postulates, code structures and foundations, fragments and examples.

The second focus is not a replacement to the manuals or a regurgitation of the functions or procedures; rather it attempts to augment the documentation by looking at how the individual pieces of the language are put together. In learning the language, I found that I had to have three or four of the manuals open simultaneously while programming. Therefore, I wanted to make this book the glue that brings those books together and tries to make sense of not just some of the undocumented features, but also of those documented in scattered fashion.

Finally, the last focus has been to provide the experienced Realizer programmer hope and evidence of a growing Realizer market, as well as to give confidence to this expanding market. I also wanted to give those programmers some additional insights and views on not just application development (which, as a Clipper programmer, I have focused on for the past ten years), but on some of the unique and powerful tools and features of the language. I wanted to look at application development and to see how Realizer fits in the puzzle of an exponential demand by end-users for Windows-based applications.

So, as you go through this book, think of the end results, the goal, the product. It has been a complete and utter joy, and I hope that you find not just the information you need to accomplish your immediate task, but also the same joy as I found as I *realized* what could be done.

Steve Straley
Sirius Press, Inc.

Chapter 1

Programming Concepts and Ideas

Much of this chapter is about general programming techniques, although these will pertain exclusively to Realizer. Many of the ideas and topics contained within this chapter appear throughout the book, in various ways. When you have finished this chapter, you will understand terms like parameters, parameter passing, data types, scoping, and operators. In addition, I will stress the importance of these concepts to overall good programming skills. These concepts are like the structures of a sentence. We may know all of the words in the English language, but without knowing what a noun, pronoun, verb, clause, or phrase is, we might as well communicate using some other means. The concepts that follow are the keys to unlocking how a program can be built and are vital to success. This chapter is broken down into four separate areas: Variables, Operators, Program Structure, and Procedures with Parameter Passing. There are many other concepts, such as using external operations, the operating system, and working with Realizer System Variables. However, these four basic topics must be mastered before moving on. No matter which area you feel the most comfortable in, you must keep in mind three basic questions about any language:

- What types of data are there?
- What is the value of the data?
- How is data stored?

Answer these three questions, and all else will fall into place.

First, we'll throw out a great deal of terminology. There is no simple way to do this. It is like trying to explain an automobile to someone who has never seen one. As soon as we start to talk about wheels and an engine, then come new questions concerning these related objects. Eventually, after all of the individual components are explained, we can go back to the beginning and reassemble the car. Programming any language is the same. As soon as we talk about programs, we have to talk about variables. From there, commands, functions, procedures, statements, declarations, operators ... all are a part of the overall puzzle we call programming. Even to do this:

```
print "Hello"
```

there are several concepts in front of us: a Realizer command, a literal constant, the structure of a line of code. Suppose we expand that line:

```
sSaying = "Hello"
print sSaying
```

Now we have several new concepts, including operators and variables. And going one step further, if we placed this in a file all by itself and gave it a special name, we would then be talking about procedures, functions, and subroutines. So, talking about one element leads to talking about the others. There is no way to avoid this. So, in the beginning, just place yourself in the source code editor, as shown in Figure 1-1.

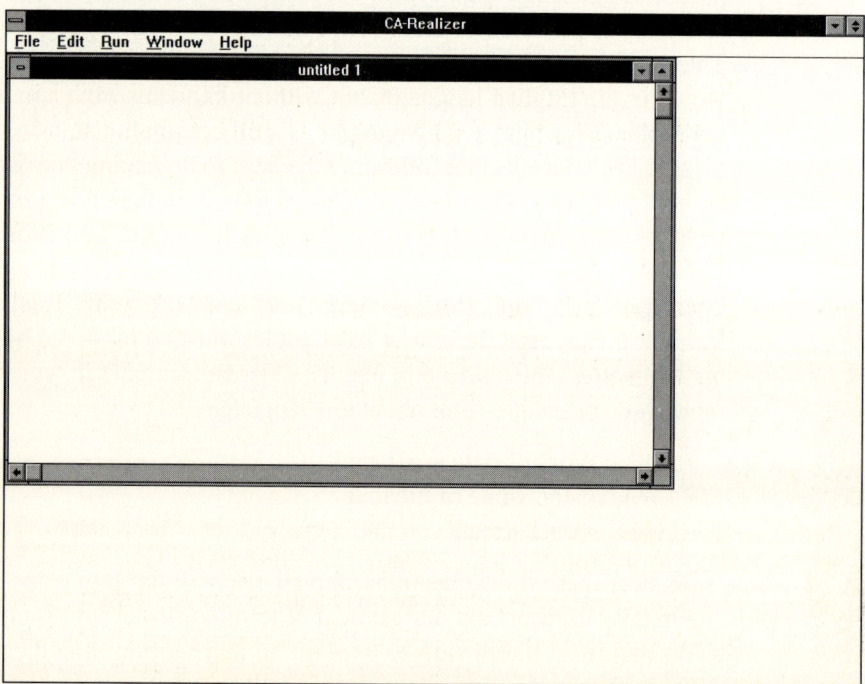

Figure 1-1. Untitled new source code window.

If you have the optional source code disk, you can load any of these files and run them as they are being talked about. Or, you can type them in and follow along as you want. If you are new to programming or new to Realizer, you may want to follow along with windows open other than the source code editor. For example, you may want to open the Print Log window as well as the Debugger window. If you do, give yourself plenty of room, as your screen might look something like Figure 1-2.

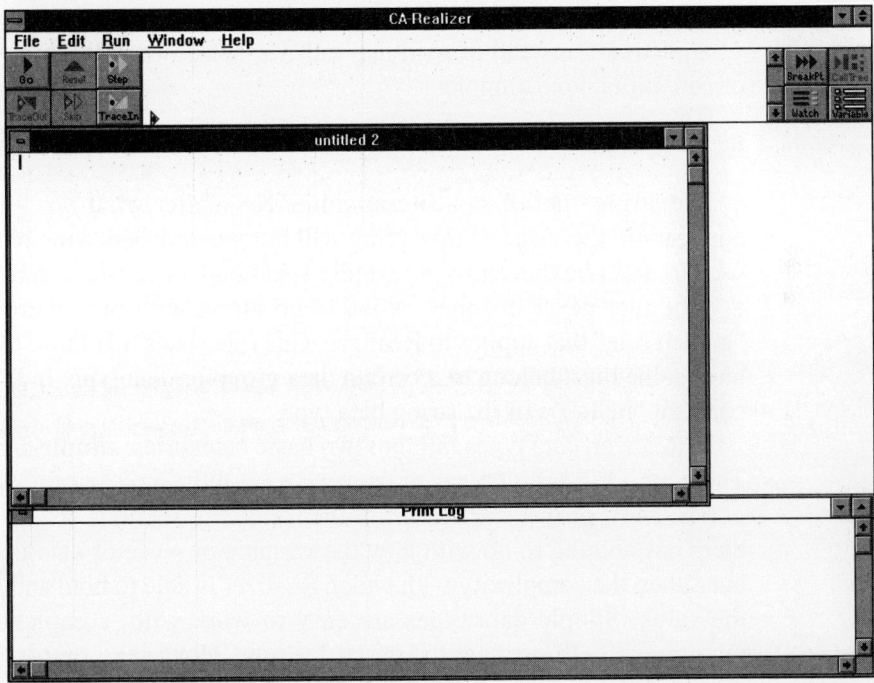

Figure 1-2. Untitled new source code window with DEBUG and PRINT LOG windows open.

Variables

Variables are a basic part of the language that we use to hold values, to compare with other values or constants, to be joined with other variables or values, or to be displayed to the screen or even to the printer. These are holding bins for us to use in the flow of an application. Even in high school, when learning algebra, we learned that unknowns were often referred to as *X*. This is a variable, and often we had to find the value of *X* for such mathematical expressions as *2x + 4y = 64*. However, in programming, we turn the tables slightly. Instead of solving for *X*, we use *X* to solve other problems. Variables all hold values or, to put it another way, variables all hold data. In Realizer, there are different types of data, such as numerics or strings. The **data type** of a variable depends on its value; that is, on what type of data a variable represents. For example, consider the following phrase:

```
store "Hello" to a variable named Greeting.
```

The name of the variable is *Greeting* and its value is the string "Hello." Since the value of the variable is a string, we often refer to that data type as being a **character data type** or a **string data type**.

Sometimes, instead of working with variables, we will work with literals or **constants**. For example:

```
print "hello"
```

The string "hello" is a literal value. No matter what takes place in an application, the value of this string will not change; hence the term constant used to describe this entity. Generally speaking, all constants have a value—a value that never changes. Now, to go along with this, there is another "golden rule" that applies to Realizer. This rule states that those things which have value must belong to a certain data group or data type. In this case, the constant "hello" is of the string data type.

In Realizer, data types fall into two basic categories: **simple** and **complex**. There are 11 different types of data and each falls into one of these two categories. Most of these are listed in the following sections. The category for them has nothing to do with how the variable or piece of data is to be used, but rather, the complexity with which Realizer is able to hold and manipulate the value. Simple data types are easy to work with; complex data types require extra effort to get the desired results. However, complex data types offer greater flexibility to the programmer, and often they offer speed enhancements or massive data opportunities with which simple data types cannot compete. Knowing the differences between simple and complex data types can enhance and improve any application.

Variable Names

A variable name may consist of any alphanumeric character, including the underscore character (_) and the @, $, !, and ? symbols. In addition, variable names must meet these requirements:

1. Variable names cannot contain spaces or start with a number.
2. Variable names cannot exceed a maximum length of 240 characters.

Programming Concepts and Ideas

3. Variable names cannot be the same as any reserved word in the Realizer environment.
4. Variable names are *not* case sensitive.

Elsewhere in this section, a programming convention is defined to help name variables and to identify the data type of each variable within the source code editor. It is important to develop a style of programming, document that style, and then stick with it. Conventions are needed not for the sake of the end user running the application; rather, for the developer who has the dubious task of maintaining the source code for fixes, enhancements, and upgrades.

Simple Data Types

There are three kinds of simple data types: numeric, string, and date-time. Each data type has different aspects. For example (see below), there are eight flavors of numerics and two styles of string data. However, there is only one date-time data type. We need all these data type categories because in Realizer, as in most programming languages, it is important to tell the environment as much information about the variables as possible. In addition, the different categories allow the language to deal with the various parts code more efficiently. For example, when there is a distinction between variables that have decimal places and those that do not, then the language can use certain internal math routines to handle decimals in some cases and not in others. It would be inefficient for the language to use math routines for dealing with decimal places on values that never have decimal places. If not specifed, a numeric data type will be a Numeric Long.

Numeric Byte This data type is a 1-byte unsigned integer ranging from 0 to 255. (Do not confuse it with the Numeric Integer type, which is a 2-byte signed integer.) Numeric Byte variables deal primarily with single bytes of information found on the disk. For example, if a byte with the value of 131 ASCII or 83 Hex was the first byte in the header of a .DBF file, we could then say that there is an associated .DBT file. That first position in the .DBF file is a numeric value containing 1 byte of information.

Numeric Word This data type is a 2-byte unsigned integer ranging from 0 to 65,535 (or 64K). This 2-byte numeric is often used in binary files to represent a greater number. For example, 2 bytes of data on the disk can represent an entire range of color choices, where each unique color combination is given a single value. With this in mind, there could be up to 64K worth of combinations.

Numeric Dword This data type is a 4-byte unsigned integer that can range from 0 to 4,294,967,295. It can be used to hold a variety of information including pointers to blobs (binary large objects), pictures and images, or sounds. While this is categorized as a simple data type, the "D" stands for double, and the large size of the number may hint at complexity in using this data type.

Numeric Char This data type is a 1-byte, signed integer. This means that acceptable values for this type of data can range from –128 to 127. Its range is similar to that of Numeric Byte; however, Numeric Char will accept negative values.

Numeric Integer This data type is a 2-byte signed integer that can range in value from –32,768 to 32,767. Its range is similar to that of Numeric Word; however, Numeric Integer will accept negative values.

Numeric Long This data type is a 4-byte signed integer that can range in value from –2,147,483,648 to 2,147,483,647. Its range is similar to that of Numeric Dword; however, Numeric Long will accept negative values.

Numeric Single This data type is a 4-byte floating pointer value that can range from approximately 1.4E–45 (scientific notation) to 3.4E+38 for either positive or negative numbers.

Numeric Double This data type is an 8-byte floating pointer value that can range from approximately 4.94E–324 to 1.8E+308 for either positive or negative numbers.

String–Variable Length This data type is a variable-length character string that can range from 0 to 65,500 characters. (Don't confuse it with the Numeric Char data type; later on, I'll show you a way in notating your code to avoid confusion.)

String–Fixed Length This data type is a fixed-length string, where a preassigned number will tell Realizer the maximum length. If Realizer encounters a string with a greater number of characters than the specified number, that string will be truncated. If Realizer encounters a string with fewer characters than the specified number, then the string is padded on the end with blank spaces.

DateTime A special data type that holds both date and time information and can range from 01/01/1900 to 12/31/2099. There are many conversion functions and notations available for this data type.

Difference in the Numerics

To make things a bit more complicated, there are two basic types of numerics: **integers** and **reals**. Here, there are only two real numbers. The rest are integers. The best way to look at an integer is as a **whole number**, either positive or negative. Real numbers are not whole numbers. They contain decimal points and what is commonly referred to as **precision**. As we discussed, there are two types of precision: **single precision** and **double precision**. The difference between the two is in the number of decimal places they can accurately hold. For the most part, single-precision numbers are accurate up to 7 decimal places, while double-precision numbers are accurate up to 15 decimal places. In Realizer, all real numbers conform to the IEEE floating-point standards.

Names and Variable Conventions in Source Code

One of the key things to keep in mind when looking at source code is to know what classification a certain variable has at the time it is declared and used. This is handled in what has been called **Hungarian notation**. It is a coding convention that helps the programmer know what each variable is at any given time without having to run the program to find out. We will use this again in the following chapter as we begin to build an application by constructing a menu. Table 1-1 outlines the coding conventions.

Table 1-1. Meta Symbols for Simple Data Types.

Meta Symbol	Data Type	Characteristic
b	byte	1-byte unsigned integer
w	word	2-byte unsigned integer
dw	dword	4-byte unsigned integer
c	char	1-byte signed integer
i	integer	2-byte signed integer
l	long	4-byte signed integer
f	floating	4-byte floating point number
fd	float-double	8-byte floating point number
s	string	variable-length string
s!	fixed-string	fixed-length string
dt	string-date	8-byte string in date format

A **meta symbol** is a one- or two-letter symbol that is used to signify the data type of a particular variable. For example, if a variable is *iItem*, you know that its data type is numeric integer. The real name of the variable is "Item," which is designed to tell us more about what that variable represents.

Note: It is important to choose names for variables wisely. Well-named variables can help tell you in the future what is going on within a particular section of code or what that variable is intended to represent.

For example, a variable named *iAge* is appropriate, because it is mnemonic whereas *iX* is not (unless *X* is a generic throw-away variable).

Examples

The best way to see how these various variables work is to either type in the program *SimpVar.rlz* while in the source code editor or load the file from the optional source code disk. Once the source code editor's window is open,

Programming Concepts and Ideas 9

the next thing to open is the Debugger window. To do this, select the Show Debugger option from the Window option on the main menu. You can also press the CTRL-D key combination to toggle this state (to show and to hide the Debugger window). In either case, you should get the following screen:

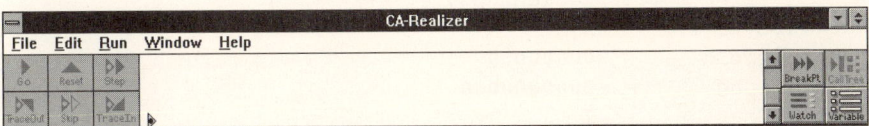

Next, open the Print Log window. This is another menu option off of the Window option on the main menu. As with the Debugger window, Printer Log may be opened using the CTRL-P key combination. Now, the Realizer environment should look like the following screen:

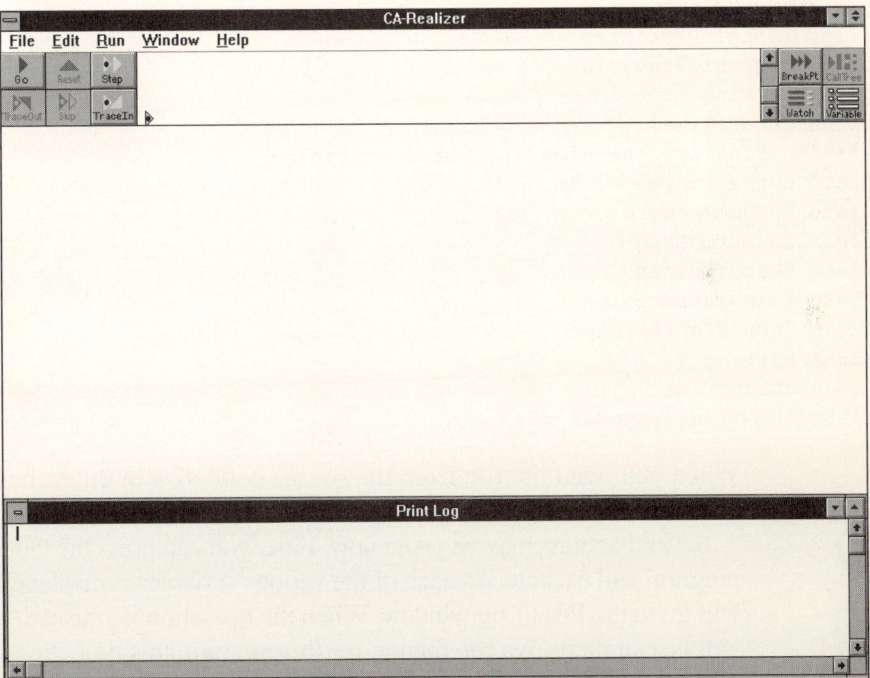

With both of these windows open, select either the New option or the Open option from the file menu. In either case, the `SimpVar.rlz` file should contain the following code:

```
'* Application ... : Simpvar.rlz
'* Authors ....... : Steve Straley
'* Notice ........ : Copyright(c) 1994 - Sirius Press, Inc.
'* ............... : All Rights Reserved
'* Date .......... : January 1, 1994
'* Description ... : THis shows how some simple variables can be assigned.
'*
'*****  First the assignment phase *******
bNumericByte        = &H1A
dwNumericWord       = 300000000
lNumericLong        = -2000000000
cNumericChar        = -2
fSinglePrecision    = 3.22
dsDoublePrecision   = -2.123412
sString             = "Hello"
dtDateTime          = &D("01/21/61")
'*****  Now, the displaying phase *******
print bNumericByte
print dwNumericWord
print lNumericLong
print cNumericChar
print fSinglePrecision
print dsDoublePrecision
print sString
print dtDateTime
'*****  Finally, the clearing phase *******
clear bNumericByte
clear dwNumericWord
clear lNumericLong
clear cNumericChar
clear fSinglePrecision
clear dsDoublePrecision
clear sString
clear dtDateTime
'* End of File: SimpVar.rlz
```

When you open the file from the source code disk or enter the code in the source code editor window, the screen should look like Figure 1-3.

Several actions may be taken now. First, you can press the Go icon and the program will execute. As each of the various variables is displayed, the output will go to the Print Log window. When the operation is finished, the program will just sit there. We can then re-try the program, this time pressing the Step icon. This will execute the program one line at a time. As each line is executed, the variable assignments, one at a time, will appear on the line next to the little arrow in the window, as shown in Figure 1-4.

Programming Concepts and Ideas

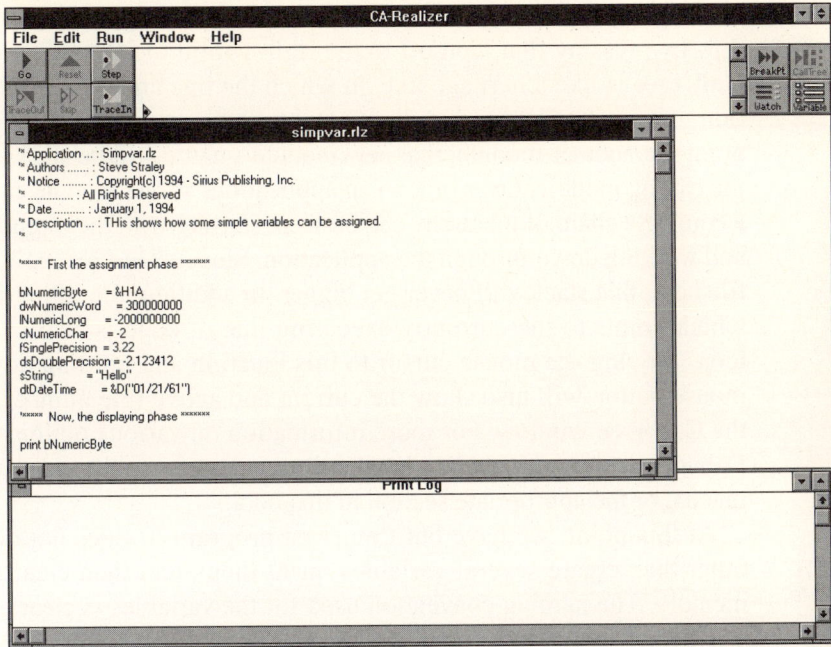

Figure 1-3. Source code loaded with DEBUG and PRINT LOG open.

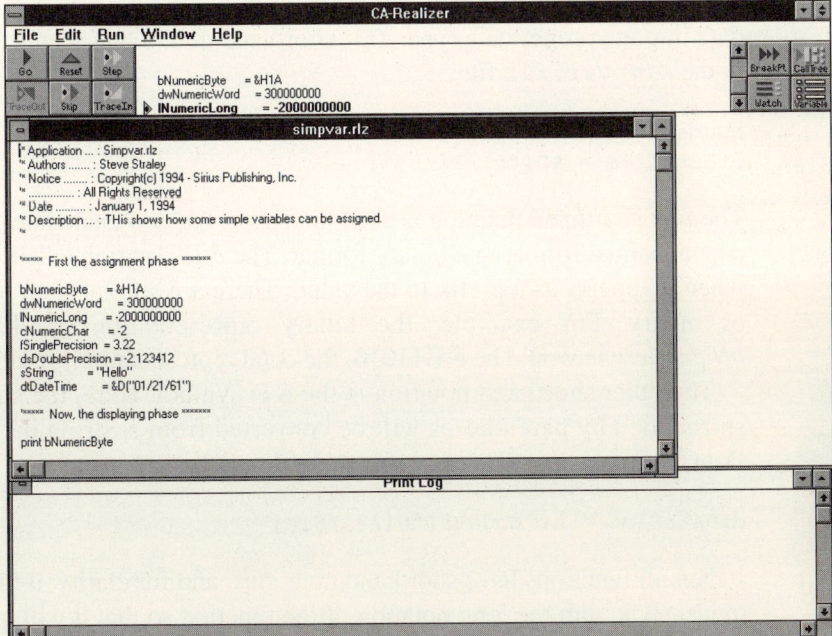

Figure 1-4. Line-by-line execution in DEBUG window.

We can resize the source code window and then open the Call Tree window by pressing that icon off to the right within the Debugger window. A **Call Tree** is like a heritage tree, in which the line and source file of execution will appear in the window area as the program executes. Should a program run another module, that new module's name will be stacked on top of the calling module. Over time in an application, as one module calls another, a complete chain of hierarchy can be seen, starting with the topmost program and working down through the application. Since *SimpVar.rlz* is only one file here, this stack will never get bigger. In addition, the little triangle icon which points to the currently executing line of code is also an activation icon. Moving the mouse cursor to this location and holding down the left mouse button will also show the current and active line number, similar to the Call Tree window. For more information on various options within the Debugger window, including breakpoints and tracing, please consult the user manual or the appropriate section in this book.

At this point, we have built our first program. It does not do anything other than create several variables, print them, and then clear them from memory. The naming convention used for the variables is clear and simple. The names you choose should follow suit.

Binary, Octal, Hexadecimal and Other Notations

In this first program, there is a new convention that may be used to convert data into the proper data type. This shorthand notation is seen in two places in the *SimpVar.rlz* file:

```
bNumericByte = &H1A
dtDateTime = &D("01/21/61")
```

The first shorthand notation is used to convert the two characters "1A" from a hexidecimal format to a binary format. The &H notation tells Realizer this when it appears as a prefix to the value. There are similar prefixes for octal or binary. For example, the binary representation of the variable *bNumericByte* would be &B11010; the octal representation would be &O32.

The other shorthand notation is the &D symbol. Here, the string that is surrounded by parentheses will be converted from a String data type to a DateTime data type. This is the same as doing the following:

```
dtDateTime = strtodate("01/21/61")
```

Not all functions have shorthand notations, and for clarity, it may be wise to just stick with the long notation of the function so that it will not get confused with the other notational options.

We have now built, tested, and observed a simple program. Without knowing it, we've learned something about operators ... namely, the assignment operators. We've also learned a couple of new command and functions, such as the PRINT and CLEAR commands and the STRTODATE() function. And all of this involves, in one way or another, the concept of a variable: something that has a value and an associated data type. It does not take much to begin to see how these key parts play off one another to make a greater whole.

Complex Data Types

When there is a section in a book on "simple data types," you might suppose that there is another section on "not-so-simple data types." This is that section. Basically, these types of data all deal with the notion of storing related pieces of data together in a single variable. Database records and arrays are nothing more than collections of similar data and structures. Individual components within these data types are often simple data types; however, it is possible to have a complex data type refer to another complex data type. There are four complex data types, as follows:

Array fixed This data type is an array with a fixed number of elements all of the same data type.

Array This data type is an array that has a dynamic number of elements all of the same data type.

Record This data type may be seen as an array with a fixed number of elements that may be of different data types. This type of an array is sometimes referred to as a collection.

Family This data type may be seen as array with a dynamic number of elements that may be of different data types. This type of an array is sometimes referred to as a dynamic collection.

So, in all of these descriptions, the term array is used to define itself. This may seem confusing at first, but in theory, an array is simply a collection or a gathering. For example, a multiplication table is an array, consisting of rows and columns with slots or cells holding the values of certain expressions. In other words, an array is something like a table, or even a spreadsheet. A **matrix** is similar to an array in that all matrixes are arrays; however, not all arrays are matrixes. A matrix is a rigid union of structures, whereas in some cases, an array is more flexible. For example, if one member of an array is an integer, all of the other members in that structure must be integers if that array is to be considered a matrix. When the data types of individual members within the structure can vary, then that structure is no longer a rigid entity and as such, cannot be a matrix. In some programming languages, such as C, this type of structure is often referred to as a union.

Differences

Arrays are used to hold collections. Arrays are involved in many items in Windows, in Realizer, in databases, and certainly in spreadsheets. The real question is when to use an array, a record, or even a family, as opposed to working with individual memory variables. To some, working with arrays are far easier than working with individual memory variables, while to others, the complexities of an array seem intimidating. Once, at another time, and in another language, I became so enthralled with arrays, their power, and the implications of their importance in applications, that I began to create unnecessarily complicated arrays that required unnecessarily complex code to manipulate them. Please refer to the chapter on arrays, families, and records for examples and an extended discussion.

Names and Variable Conventions in Source Code

Just because these data types are considered complex does not mean that they need not follow the rules of Hungarian notation as laid out for the simple data types. Consistency in coding is extremely important. Use the conventions outlined in Table 1-2.

Table 1-2. Meta Symbols for Complex Data Types.

Meta Symbol	Data Type	Characteristic
m	Array/Matrix	A fixed array of elements with same data types
a	Array	A dynamic array of elements with same data type
r	Record	A fixed collection of fields of different data types
fam	Family	A dynamic collection of members of different data types

Declaring a Data Type

There are two basic (no pun intended) ways in which a variable may be initialized to a specific data type: implicitly and explictly. The implicit way is the easiest. In essence, when a variable is assigned a value, the data type of

Programming Concepts and Ideas 15

the value becomes the implied data type of the variable. An implicit data type is commonly called **weak typing** because you are relying on the environment to decide the data type of a variable. Relying on the language to determine what data type a particular variable should be may produce unnecessary sluggishness in the application. For example, in a counting loop in which a variable is to be incremented, and do nothing else, it's inefficient to force the language to "figure out" what data type is to be associated with that counting variable. So, the other way in which a variable can be declared is via explicit declarations. This is commonly called **strong typing**. Here, you tell the language in advance of any assignment operation what the data type of the variable is to be. Here, you will need the DIM command as well as the key word representing the data type. In order to strongly type a variable, we need to use the various key words for the data types in the following manner:

DIM <variable> AS <data type>

There are many possible combinations to this command. Please refer to the appropriate section for additional support, since not all will be covered in this section. Here, in the following program example, many ideas are combined:

```
'* Application ... : Var1.rlz
'* Authors ....... : Steve Straley
'* Notice ........ : Copyright(c) 1994 - Sirius Press, Inc.
'* .............. : All Rights Reserved
'* Date .......... : January 1, 1994
'* Description ... : This Shows how variables can be strongly typed in an
'*                   application, how variables can be assigned, printed,
'*                   cleared, and swapped.
'* strongly typed variables should be declared at the top of any
'* routine.  They can be on multiple lines or on individual lines

dim iSteveAge          as integer     '* Holds Steve's age, unfortunately
dim dsSteveBirthdate   as datetime    '* Yes, it's real: just send money
dim cName              as string, \\
    fAmount            as single      '* this is not on the one line

iSteveAge         = 33
dsSteveBirthdate  = strtodate("01/21/64")
cName             = "Steve"
fAmount           = 89.45

print iSteveAge
print dsSteveBirthdate
print cName
print fAmount
```

```
clear iSteveAge,          \\
      dsSteveBirthdate,   \\
      cName,              \\
      fAmount

'* End of File: Var1.rlz
```

Here, four variables are strongly typed, assigned values, printed, and then cleared. Note that two of the variables are strongly typed on the same line, using the comma (,) character to separate the variables as well as the double backslash characters.

Note: The double backslash characters are used for line continuation. Sometimes they are used only to lend visual clarity to a program file, as opposed to cramming several instructions on a single line.

The other two variables are strongly typed in individual lines. This offers more clarity to the program file. In addition, the in-line comments appearing at the end of the statements for the variables *iSteveAge* and *dsSteveBirthdate* are possible only because there are separate DIM statements for each. Since there is line continuation for the *cName* and *fAmount* variables, there cannot be an in-line comment appearing after the end of each clause. This is why, for stylistic reasons, we recommend that you type variables one after another on separate lines. This allows you to provide additional comments on the same line with the declaration.

Note: If you run a program that does not clear the variables and then re-run that same program, you will get an error indicating that the variable is in the Realizer environment and it is "already declared at this level."

Once a variable is strongly typed, it must remain that data type unless the variable is cleared using the CLEAR command. Here, in this test program, the four variables are cleared at the end of the program. They now may be used again and set to different data types. You will get an error: if you attempt to assign a variable to a data type other than that which is strongly typed, as shown in the following code:

Programming Concepts and Ideas 17

```
dim sSteve as char
sSteve = "First Name"
```

The Char data type is not a character string, and if these two lines are executed, the Error Log window will display the error message shown in Figure 1-5.

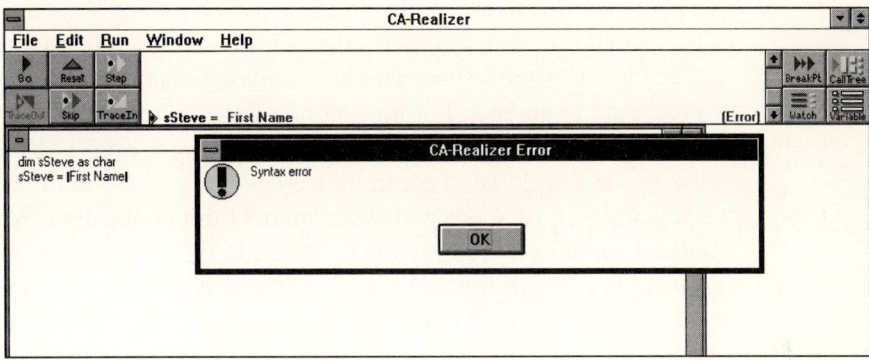

Figure 1-5. Default error dialog.

Once the program is loaded into the system, we should expand the Realizer system so that the Debugger window and the Print Log window can appear on the screen at the same time with the source code window.

Now, select the Go option off of the main menu or press the Go icon. As we do, the value of 33 will be displayed in the Print Log window. Once finished, we can rerun the program or step through the program by pressing the Step icon.

> **Note**: Variables in Realizer will remain in the environment unless cleared. Sometimes, the only way to do this completely is to exit Realizer and then re-enter the system. Otherwise, erroneous errors will persist, even if you select the Reset Program option from the main screen.

Run the sample program a couple of times to see how variables are created, assigned, and displayed.

Scoping Considerations

The term "scoping" means how the variable is stored in memory as opposed to being stored in a file on the disk. In most cases, variables are used temporarily to hold values within a subroutine. These variables should not be seen outside of the domain of those subroutines. In general, variables that need to be seen in other parts of an application should get explicitly passed as a parameter from one routine to another. Those variables that are not to be passed should be seen only within the domain of the creating routine. This will be clearer when I show you how to pass parameters from one function or procedure to another. For now, think of an application as a house and the furniture in the house as variables. We do not want everyone outside of our house to see what type of furniture we have, especially at my house, unless we physically move a piece of furniture out through the door. When the door is closed and no one can see the furniture in the house, we can say that the furniture is *local* to the walls of the house. No one else can see it unless inside of the house or if I grant access to any one piece by moving it through a door. The word LOCAL is important and can be used in conjunction with the DIM command. The format is:

DIM LOCAL <variable> AS <data type>

This means that a variable which is declared as a local variable should not be seen outside of the scope of a function, procedure, or program file. For example, consider the following example program, *Var2.rlz*:

```
'* Application ... : Var2.rlz
'* Authors ....... : Steve Straley
'* Notice ........ : Copyright(c) 1994 - Sirius Press, Inc.
'* .............. : All Rights Reserved
'* Date .......... : January 1, 1994
'* Description ... : This shows the violation of scoping considerations
'*
'*********************
'* Name:    PrintIt()
'* Purpose: To print out the contents of a variable
proc PrintIt
  print iSteveAge
end proc
'* strongly typed variables should be declared at the top of any
'* routine.  They can be on multiple lines or on individual lines
dim iSteveAge as integer       '* Holds Steve's age, unfortunately
iSteveAge = 33
PrintIt()
clear iSteveAge
'* End of File: Var2.rlz
```

Programming Concepts and Ideas 19

Here, the variable *iSteveAge*, which is in the main body of the program file and after the procedure named *PrintIt()*, is declared as a regular variable. While this is legal, it violates tight scoping considerations. It is considered this way because there is no formal announcement within the *PrintIt()* procedure that tells it something about the variable *iSteveAge*. In other words, we are using the variable *iSteveAge* in a location that really should know nothing about it. Now, while this is a simple PRINT instruction, we could also (and often unintentionally) alter the value of the variable. This is the main reason we want to avoid situations like this and stick to a tightly scoped variable scenario. It would do us no good to have a variable like *iSteveAge* in one part of the application when in another program module, the variable is altered without our consent or knowledge. This happens all the time on large programming projects or in large development teams. Modularity is a key factor to good programming skills in any language.

If the LOCAL clause is used, then that variable is considered visible only within the confines of the program module, or if defined within a procedure or a function, then it will be visible only on that level. The lifespan of a LOCAL variable is again within the confines of the procedure, function, or program module making the call. To see this better, consider the file `Var3.rlz`. It is a modified version of `Var2.rlz`:

```
'* Application ... : Var3.rlz
'* Authors ....... : Steve Straley
'* Notice ........ : Copyright(c) 1994 - Sirius Press, Inc.
'* .............. : All Rights Reserved
'* Date .......... : January 1, 1994
'* Description ... : This shows the scoping use of the LOCAL statement
'*
run "C:\Realizer\sirius\samples\var3a.rlz"
'* strongly typed variables should be declared at the top of any
'* routine.  They can be on multiple lines or on individual lines
dim local iSteveAge as integer      '* Holds Steve's age, unfortunately
iSteveAge = 33
PrintIt()
clear iSteveAge
'* End of File: Var3.rlz
```

This file contains a RUN command and the LOCAL statement, along with the strongly typed variable *iSteveAge*. At the top of `Var3.rlz`, the *PrintIt()* routine is defined within the file `Var3a.rlz`, as follows:

```
'* Application ... : Var3a.rlz
'* Authors ....... : Steve Straley
'* Notice ........ : Copyright(c) 1994 - Sirius Press, Inc.
'* .............. : All Rights Reserved
```

```
'* Date .......... : January 1, 1994
'* Description ... : This shows the scoping use of the LOCAL statement
'*********************
'* Name:    PrintIt()
'* Purpose: To print out the contents of a variable
proc PrintIt
  print iSteveAge
end proc
'* End of File: Var3a.rlz
```

This PrintIt() routine will not work since the variable here, *iSteveAge*, is not visible to this program file. This is because it was declared a LOCAL variable within the original file `Var3.rlz`.

Most of the time you will create strongly typed, LOCAL variables in order to protect values within an application or to build reusable modules and functions.

Values: Altering, Exchanging, or Clearing

Once a variable is explicitly assigned a specific data type only its value can change, not its data type. However, if a variable is declared and/or assigned within the DIM statement, then both its value and data type can be altered. This is another good reason why strongly typed variables within an application should be the rule of the day. For example, the following coding extract will generate an error when if the Go option is selected (seen earlier as well). On the other hand, the value of the variable as well as its data type can be altered at any time. For example, the following code would be acceptable:

```
sName = "Hello there"
print sName
sName = 1
```

Although acceptable, this code actually violates good programming practice and thwarts the purpose of using Hungarian notation for variable names. In the first line, the "S" meta symbol tells us that the variable *sName* holds a string, but in the third line, that variable is changed to an integer.

You can avoid this trap by using strongly typed variables and the DIM instruction. For example, an error message would appear if you strongly typed the *sName* variable, as follows:

```
dim sName as string
sName = "Hello there"
print sName
sName = 1
```

The Error Log window will generate a message as soon as we attempt to alter the data type of the *sName* variable. However, altering the value of a variable to the same data type is perfectly legal and quite useful. For example, the following variation on same four instructions is acceptable, since both values assigned to the *sName* variable are of the String data type:

```
dim sName as string
sName = "Hello there"
print sName
sName = "Good-bye"
```

Sometimes, we have to exchange the value of two variables. To do this, we have in the past needed a temporary variable to hold a value. For example, in simple math, if we had the following two variables:

x = 1
y = 2

and the goal is to exchange the two values between the variables, we would have to do something like this:

z = x
x = y
y = z

The variable *z* would temporary hold the value of *x*. Then *x*, would be assigned the value of *y*, and then the value of *z* would be placed into *y*.

However, in Realizer, there is a simpler solution: the SWAP instruction. The basic format of this command is as follows:

SWAP <var1>, <var2>

If either of the two variables are strongly typed, and are of different data types, the Error Log window will display an error message when this command begins its operation. If the two variables are neither strongly typed nor of the same data type, we can use this command and avoid the need to bring in a temporary variable. So, in the Realizer environment, we could express our math problem like this:

```
swap x, y
```

It is that simple. The SWAP command becomes very important if we want to sort items in an array or exchange items in a group. We'll explore SWAP at more depth when we begin to look at records, arrays, and families. For now, it is best to just see the ease with which two items can be swapped.

> **Note**: There are sometimes errors with the SWAP command in relation to individual array elements. In cases where the SWAP command seems to perform incorrectly, use temporary variables to hold the swapping values.

Sometimes, as we've seen in several example programs so far, a variable needs to be cleared from the system and the environment. Obviously, the command to do this is the CLEAR command.

CLEAR <variable>

This command works not only with variables, but also with other items, such as procedures and functions. We will look at that possibility later on. In the meantime, think of the CLEAR command as a way to remove a variable from the Realizer environment. You need to do this in order for the DIM instruction not to bomb out every time a program runs. If a variable is not cleared, for example, the second pass through a program file will produce an error message like the the one in Figure 1-6. Therefore, it is always a good idea to close off an application by clearing the memory variables involved.

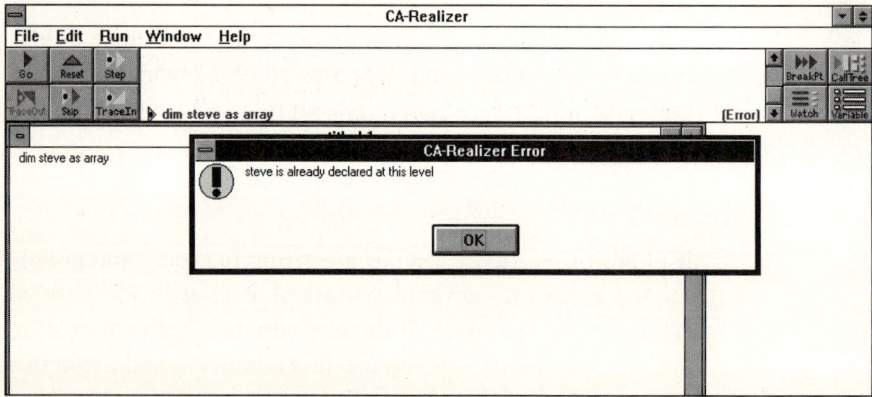

Figure 1-6. Another error dialog.

Acquiring Information on a Variable

Once a variable is assigned, information on that variable can be obtained at any point in the flow of a program. Sometimes, we simply need to find out if the variable exists, and sometimes we need to see if it is of a particular data type before performing some data type–specific operation (like attempting to add a number to a string ... not a good idea on an empty stomach). So, without looking to the actual value of a variable, there are ways to discover information on that variable. There is a function that we can use to help us out:

QVAR(<variable> [, <query>])

In this function, <variable> specifies the name of the variable, and <query> identifies the internal variable you want to know about. See Table 1-3 for a list of internal variables.

Table 1-3. Internal Variables for the QVAR() Function.

Internal Variable	Function
_DEFINED	Yields 1 if <variable> is not defined; otherwise, 0
_ALPHA	Yields 1 if <variable> is string scalar or string array; otherwise, 0
_REAL	Yields 1 if <variable> numeric scalar of numeric array; otherwise, 0
_DATETIME	Yields 1 if <variable> is date-time scalar or date-time array; otherwise, 0
_RECORD	Yields 1 if <variable> is a record; otherwise, 0
_FAMILY	Yields 1 if <variable> is a family or a family array; otherwise, 0
_ARRAY	Yields 1 if <variable> is an array; otherwise, 0
_SCALAR	Yields 1 if <variable> is scalar; otherwise, 0
_NAME	Yields the string representing the name of the variable. It will return the original name of the variable if queried on a single parameter.
_NUMDIMS	Yields the number of dimensions (or number of elements) in an array <variable> or 0 if <variable> is scalar.
_MEMBERS	Yields an array of strings indicating the number of members of a family or the fields of a record. If <variable> is not a family or a record, a 0 will be returned.

> **Note:** When using the _NAME, _NUMDIMS, or _MEMBERS internal variable to query a variable, no other internal variable may be used in conjunction with other internal variables.

Except in the case of _NAME, _NUMDIMS, and _MEMBERS (see note), some of the internal variables may be used in conjunction with one another. For example, we can use the _SCALAR internal variable in conjunction with the _REAL internal variable to find out if a variable is either a numeric-real scalar or a numeric-real array.

> **Note:** When you need to combine internal variables when querying an array, specify the sum of the internal variables, as in _REAL + _SCALAR.

So how do we use the QVAR command in a program? The sample program named *QuVar.rlz* shows just some of the various data types being initialized, assigned, and then queried using the QVAR() function.

```
'* Application ... : QVar1.rlz
'* Authors ....... : Steve Straley
'* Notice ........ : Copyright(c) 1994 - Sirius Press, Inc.
'* .............. : All Rights Reserved
'* Date .......... : January 1, 1994
'* Description ... : This shows how some of the ways in which the QVAR()
'*                   function may be called
print qvar( sName, _DEFINED )         '* RETURNS 0 or false
clear sName                           '* The QVAR() function inits variable
dim sName as string                   '* Declares the variable
print qvar( sName, _DEFINED )         '* RETURNS 1 or true
print qvar( sName, _ALPHA )           '* RETURNS 1 or true
sName = "Steve"                       '* Simple assignment
print qvar( sName, _DEFINED )         '* RETURNS 1 or true
print qvar( sName, _ALPHA )           '* RETURNS 1 or true
print qvar( sName, _ALPHA + _ARRAY )  '* RETURNS 0 or false
print qvar( sName, _NAME )            '* RETURNS sName
clear sName
'* End of File: QVar1.rlz
```

Programming Concepts and Ideas

```
'* Application ... : QVar1.rlz
'* Authors ...... : Steve Straley
'* Notice ....... : Copyright(c) 1994 - Sirius Publishing, Inc.
'* ............. : All Rights Reserved
'* Date ......... : January 1, 1994
'* Description ... : This shows how some of the ways in which the QVAR()
'*                  function may be called

print qvar( sName, _DEFINED )   '* RETURNS 0 or false

clear sName                     '* The QVAR() function inits variable

dim sName as string             '* Declares the variable

print qvar( sName, _DEFINED )   '* RETURNS 1 or true
print qvar( sName, _ALPHA )     '* RETURNS 1 or true

sName = "Steve"                 '* Simple assignment

print qvar( sName, _DEFINED )          '* RETURNS 1 or true
print qvar( sName, _ALPHA )            '* RETURNS 1 or true
print qvar( sName, _ALPHA + _ARRAY )   '* RETURNS 0 or false
```

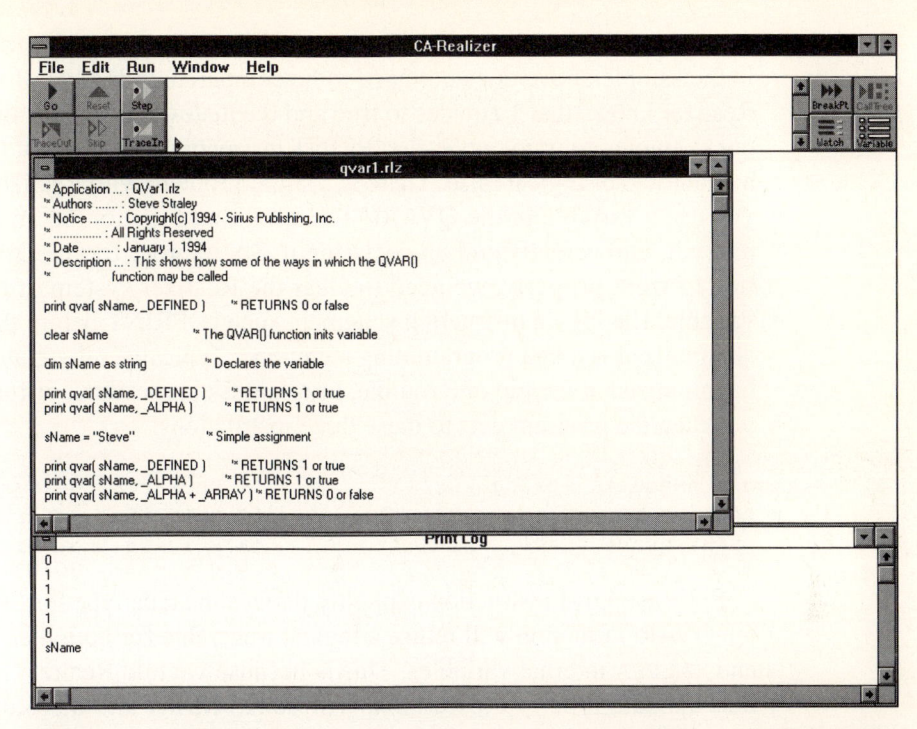

Print Log:
```
0
1
1
1
1
0
sName
```

Figure 1-7. QVAR1.RLZ in source code window with DEBUG and PRINT LOG open.

If typing in this program from scratch, select the New option from the File menu or, if you use the source code disk for this, select the Open option from the File menu. Once the program is loaded in the source code editor, we can either select Go to run the program or Step to step through the program line by line. Before you run this program, make sure that you are at a startup point within Realizer, and have the Debugger window open as well as the Print Log window, as shown in Figure 1-7.

When this program executes, the value of the QVAR() function will be passed off to the Print Log window. Typically, this is not what takes place in an application. More typical is the following piece of code.

```
if qvar( sName, _DEFINED ) then
 print( sName )
end if
```

When the function QVAR() returns a numeric 1, this actually is the standard for a logical true (.T.) value. If QVAR() returns a numeric 0, then this represents a logical false (.F.). This is why the value of the QVAR() function in the sample above does not need to be compared with a literal value of 1. Realizer knows that 1 equates to true and 0 equates to false. Turning back to our example program, in the first PRINT instruction, the value of QVAR() is a numeric 0 or logical false. There is a slight problem with Realizer in that if you use a variable in the QVAR() function, that function, in an attempt to query it, will actually end up declaring it. So, in order for the DIM instruction to work properly, we need to clear the Realizer system of the *sName* variable. Having an instruction statement such as PRINT before the variable is initialized is a bad programming technique. Typically, all variables should be initialized at the top of a routine, program file, procedure, or function.

When the program gets to these three instructions:

```
dim sName as string              '* Declares the variable
print qvar( sName, _DEFINED )    '* RETURNS 1 or true
print qvar( sName, _ALPHA )      '* RETURNS 1 or true
```

Since the DIM instruction explicitly defines the data type for the variable, the QVAR() function will return a logical true value for both the `_DEFINED` and `_ALPHA` internal variables. This is because we told Realizer in advance that the data type of the variable will be AS String and therefore will be alphabetic. But the `_ALPHA` internal variable checks to see if the variable is a String data type or an array of strings. In either case, the QVAR() function will continue to return a numeric 1 or logical true. At this point, we now are ready to see the the sum of two internal variables:

```
print qvar( sName, _ALPHA + _ARRAY ) '* RETURNS 0 or false
```

Here, we are testing to see if the *sName* variable is exclusively a string and an array. Since the QVAR function now returns a numeric 0 or a logical false, we can conclude that *sName* is of the String data type and is not an array of String data types. This is how we can use some of the internal variables together. Keep in mind that some of the internal variables will not work in combination with other internal variables (see earlier note). We'll revisit this function when we look into the relevance of array technology.

Constants

In some languages, such as CA-Clipper, a preprocessor (or a glorified translator) will scan through a source file before execution and change certain variables to predefined values. These constants or predefined values are sometimes referred to as manifest constants. Constants never change and in many ways are useful for clarity. As we've seen in previous examples, including the QVAR function, Realizer uses internal variables or internal constants to tell certain functions what to do and what we expect from then.

For example, in an application that deals with the commonly known value of pi, we might have the constant value of 3.1415926 all over the place. In Realizer, we can use the CONST function to assign that value as a constant to a specially declared variable.

CONST <var> = <value>

The value assigned to the variable may be a literal value or it may be the value found in another variable. Unless specified by the assignment statement, the data type of a constant is typically either a Long, Double, String, or DateTime. In addition, to follow our present coding conventions, constants should be given their own format. Internal variables or internal constants are always seen in uppercase letters with an underscore character in front. We can follow this format, but omit the underscore character. The sample program *Constant.rlz* shows the use of the CONST command.

```
'* Application ... : Constant.rlz
'* Authors ....... : Steve Straley
'* Notice ........ : Copyright(c) 1994 - Sirius Press, Inc.
'* .............. : All Rights Reserved
'* Date .......... : January 1, 1994
'* Description ... : The shows how a constant can be assigned
'*
const PI = 3.1415926      '* Assign the constant
print PI                  '* Print the constant
print cint(PI)            '* Perform operations with the constant
print PI / 2
print atn(1)
clear PI                  '* Clear the constant
'* Constant.rlz
```

When you open or type this file into the source code editor and open the Print Log window and the Debugger window, your screen should look like Figure 1-8.

Here, the constant PI is in uppercase letters and can be used in assignment statements, output statements, and as a parameter of a function such as the ATN() function (or the arctangent or inverse tangent function).

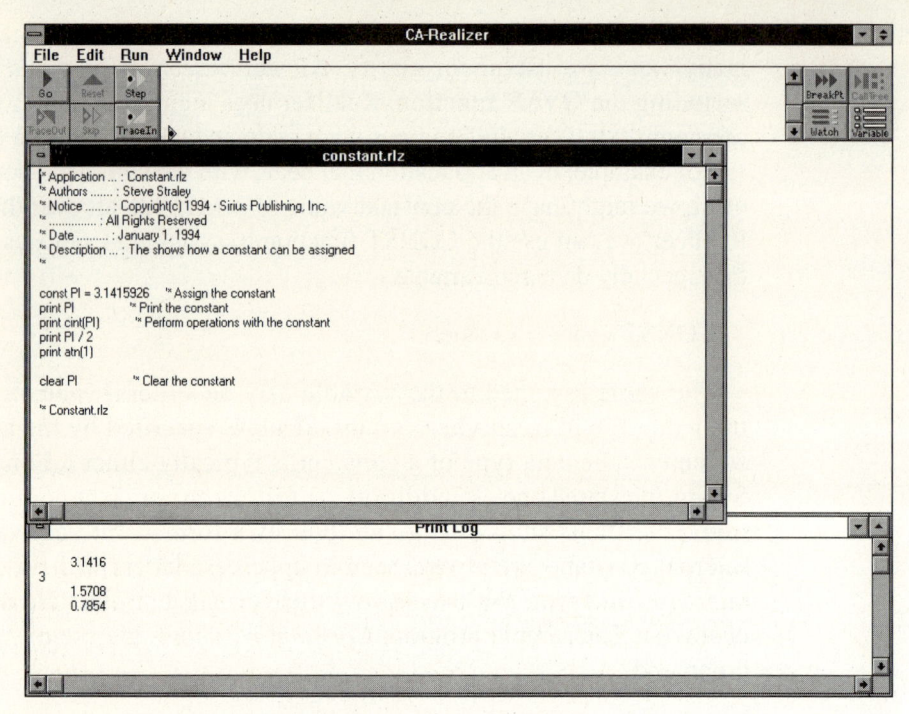

Figure 1-8. Output of CONSTANT.RLZ in window.

Note: Once a constant is defined, it cannot be assigned a new value or be used as a name in an array, record, or family unless the variable is first removed via the CLEAR command.

When building an application, a good practice is to create a separate file that contains nothing but constants for the entire application. This would work similarly to a header file that a preprocessor might use in the translation of the source code.

Operators

Operators are as vital to the language as variables are. As a matter of fact, very little can get accomplished without them. So what are they? Operators are, simply, symbols that tell a program to perform a mathematical or logical operation.

For example, the expression $x + y = 5$ contains two operators. One operator tells you to add x to y. The other operator tell you to compare the value of that to the literal value of 5. That combination returns an expression whose value might be a logical true or a logical false, depending on the individual values of x and y.

Burned into the Realizer language are rules of how to treat operators based on how the code is laid out. For example, a slight variation of the previous example would be the following:

$x = 5$

Even though this expression contains the same equal sign (=), we know that this is an assignment (or replacement) statement, not a comparison statement. Again, depending on how the code is laid out and what items are contained in relation to what operators are used will tell the tale on what the results will be.

There are different operators for strings than for numbers, and even a different set for arrays. As we have just shown, some operators look the same but have different meanings based on what is being evaluated at the time. For example, the <= symbol is the less-than-or-equal-to operator. If the code looked like this:

```
print 1 <= 2
```

Realizer would determine if the value of 1 is less than or equal to the value of 2 and if so, print a 1 to the Print Log window. But what if the expressions on either side of the operator were strings rather than numbers:

```
print "Steve" <= "Straley"
```

This expression would yield a 0 or a logical false. Strings mean something different to the <= operator than do numbers. The rules for strings are as follows:

- The ASCII value of the characters follows alphabetical order from A to Z.
- Uppercase letters have smaller ASCII values than do lowercase letters.
- Evaluations go from left to right within each string.
- The left side of the operator is compared to the right.

Generally speaking, the mathematical operators available are those listed in the following table.

Operator	Function
+	Addition or Unary plus
–	Subtraction or Unary minus
*	Multiplication
/	Division
^	Exponentiation
MOD	Remainder or Modulus
\	Truncated division
=	Equal to or assign
<>	Not equal to
<	Less than
<=	Less than or equal to
>	Greater than
>=	Greater than or equal to

DATETIME variables can accept + (plus) and – (minus) operations.

Now, in these is another item called the **expression**. It is very important and works just as things did back in your favorite classes like algebra. An expression is signified by a set of parentheses. The rule with an expression is to evaluate the innermost expression first and expand outward. In conjunction with expression, there are also six basic logical operators:

Operator	Function
NOT	Logical Negation
AND	Logical And
OR	Logical Or
XOR	Logical Exclusive or
EQV	Logical Equivalence
IMP	Logical Implication

To help explain logical operators, consider the following line of code:

```
print A <operator> B
```

Using the same table, let's look at what this could mean:

Operator	Expression Value
AND	If both A and B are logical true values, then the expression will be a logical true value. Otherwise, the expression will be considered false.
OR	If either A or B is a logical true value, then the expression will be a logical true value. Otherwise, the expression will be considered false.

NOT	This returns the logical inverse of the expression
XOR	If A is a true and B is false OR if A is a false and B is true, then this will return a true value. Otherwise, this will return a false.
EQV	If either A and B are true or A and B are false, then this will return a true value. Otherwise, this will return a false.
IMP	If A is false or B is true, then true is returned. Otherwise, false is returned.

Statements / Program Structure

Statements are like operators in that the language knows about them and expects our code to follow certain patterns. I like to say that statements are intrinsic to the language. We do not need to define them; the language knows. Quite often, it is the instrinsic nature of these statements and operators that distinguish one language from the next. For example, in CA-Clipper, there is what is known as the CASE statement; in C, it is the SWITCH statement.

There are only a few statements to any language, and everything else is built on them.

Operators are like statements in that they make up the crux of the language. For example, we do not need to tell Realizer what "addition" means ... it just knows it. Variable declaration and memory allocation are also predefined within the language. In other languages like C, memory is often a concern to the programmer; in Realizer, however, that concern is removed. Statements are another part of the language. Key words like FUNCTION, RETURN, or SELECT CASE are neither operators nor variable assignments. These, too, are a part of the language. Like operators and how variables are held by the language, there is no easy way to learn what the statements are other than just sitting down and memorizing them.

When you want to test a condition between two values, the IF statement comes into play. If the test is simple and non-branching, then the structure of your code should look like this:

```
IF <condition> THEN
 <operation>
END IF
```

Earlier in this chapter we saw a piece of code that looked like this:

```
if qvar( sName, _DEFINED ) then
  print( sName )
end if
```

Here is a perfect example. If the value of QVAR( ) is a true value, then the operation of PRINT will be performed. However, in some cases, we need a balancing operation in case the value of <condition> should be false. In this case, the code structure should look like this:

```
IF <condition> THEN
  <operation>
ELSE
  <new operation>
END IF
```

Later on in this chapter, you'll see the following example of this code structure:

```
if qvar( iCount, _REAL ) then
  sReturn = ucase$( left$( sItem, iCount ) )
else
  sReturn = sItem
end if
```

Here, if the value of QVAR( ) is a true value, then the value of the variable *sReturn* will be one thing. But, if the value of QVAR( ) is a false value, then the value of *sReturn* will be the value of *sItem*.

However, this is still not the limit to our conditional testing. Sometimes, when we need to test a multitude of conditions, we need to build a series of tests. Rather than nesting a series of IF..ELSE..END IF statements, we can stack the tests using the ELSE IF statement. The structure of this looks like this:

```
IF <condition 1> THEN
  <operation 1>
ELSEIF <condition 2> THEN
  <operation 2>
ELSEIF <condition 3> THEN
  <operation 3>
ELSE
  <concluding operation>
ENDIF
```

Similar to this is the SELECT statement that looks something like this:

```
SELECT CASE <condition 1>
  <operation 1>
CASE <Range1>
  <operation 2>
```

Programming Concepts and Ideas

```
    CASE <Range2>
    <operation 3>
    CASE LSE
    <concluding operation>
END SELECT
```

Look for an example of this coding construct in the next chapter when a menu is built and the selections from that menu are evaluated at each CASE clause.

The GOTO statement allows for a sudden break in the flow of a program. This works in conjunction with a name, chosen by the programmer, that represents a label. The structure for this is:

GOTO <name>

and the section of code that begins this jumping effect looks like this:

<name>:

A label may be any legal name but must appear on a line by itself and must appear with a colon.

> **Note:** It is not a wise practice to rely on the GOTO statement. This provides an unstructured approach to problem solving and can cause trouble during the debugging and maintenance stages of application development.

Looping is also a possibility with Realizer. There are three basic code structures for looping. One is a sequential type of a loop using the FOR…NEXT code structure, which looks like this:

```
FOR <variable> = <starting point> TO <ending point> [STEP <value>]
   <operation>
NEXT
```

A sample of this can be seen further on in this chapter, in a piece of code that looks like this:

```
for iTemp = iStart to (iStart + iRange)
   iStart = iStart + 1
next
```

Here, the variable *iTemp* starts off as the value of *iStart*. When the NEXT instruction is processed, the value of *iTemp* is incremented by one. If the new value of *iTemp* is still within the specified range, the looping process continues. As soon as the value of *iTemp* is greater than the expression *(iStart + iRange)*, the FOR…NEXT loop will stop.

The direction of the loop can be set as well as the amount to increment. If the STEP clause is used, then the value used in the clause will be the incrementing amount. The default will be 1. In addition, the direction of the process may be determined by flipping the ranges and offering a STEP clause. Using the same structure, the code might look something like this:

```
for iTemp = (iStart + iRange) to iStart step -1
    iStart = iStart - 1
next
```

Another type of looping process involves the LOOP statement itself. Here, a loop can go on forever until an EXIT LOOP statement is processed. Here is the code structure for a LOOP:

LOOP
 <instruction>
IF <condition>
 EXIT LOOP
 END IF
END LOOP

Applied to the same code fragment, the code fragment might look like this:

```
iTemp = 1
 loop
   if iTemp > 5
     exit loop
    end if
   iTemp = iTemp + 1
end loop
```

The third and final looping structure uses the WHILE statement. It looks similar to LOOP, except that the testing condition is a part of the loop structure and not within the code fragment. So, this structure would look like this:

WHILE <condition>
 <instruction>
END WHILE

Programming Concepts and Ideas

Again, applied to that same code fragment, the outcome would look something like this:

```
iTemp = 1
 while iTemp <= 5
   iTemp = iTemp + 1
end while
```

It is important to denote program flow within the loops. In all of these last few programming examples, indentation is used to show levels of program flow. Within the Realizer program editor, this might be seen as a single tab stop. (In some text editors, two or three blank spaces can be used instead.)

There are many other types of statements. For example, the FUNC...END FUNC or PROC...END PROC statements define the area in the source file for user-defined procedures or functions as outlined in the next section. In addition, there is the ON ERROR GOTO statement that allows for a sudden branch from the normal program flow to handle an existing error. The point is this: know your statements and operators. Memorize them and rely on them throughout the development of an application.

Procedures, Functions, and Parameters

As we mentioned at the beginning of this chapter, it is difficult to discuss any particular concept out of context, whether it's variables, statements, or procedures. But all languages, have certain rules that must be followed, and these differ from language to language, which is why it is important to know what they are before you begin.

Procedures

Talking about this subject is no different than talking about program files or even functions. A procedure is nothing more than a series of instructions with an associated name. Typically, the format for this is as follows:

```
proc <name>
    <instructions>
end proc
```

All procedures must end with the END PROC statement. The instruction set contained within this bound area is called a **subroutine** and has with it an associated name. It is a good coding practice to indent the levels of code. This means that the PROC and END PROC statements are on one level of code while the instructions contained within are on another. Indenting is a good habit to get into but can be carried away and taken to extremes.

Naming a procedure is similar to naming a variable. You choose a name that comes as close as possible to describing the action taken within. For example, if we want to clear all the menu items that appear at startup in the Realizer environment, we might collect several menu-oriented function calls into a procedure called, perhaps, ClearMenus. Such a procedure might look something like this:

```
proc ClearMenus()
    menuselect(_FILEMENU)      'Refer to the FILE menu on the top
    menucontrol(_HIDE)         '... and hide it
    menuselect(_EDITMENU)      'Refer to the EDIT menu on the top
    menucontrol(_HIDE)         '... and hide it
    menuselect(_RUNMENU)       'Do the same with the RUN menu
    menucontrol(_HIDE)         '
    menuselect(_HELPMENU)      'And the HELP menu
    menucontrol(_HIDE)         '
    menuselect(_WINDOWMENU)    'And the WINDOW menu
    menucontrol(_HIDE)         ' and hide it as well
end proc
```

Defining a procedure is half of the operation. Calling it, or getting it to execute, is the other half. This is handled simply by making a reference to the name specified after the PROC statement; in this case, *ClearMenus()*.

Procedures help compartmentalize operations and help make modular, reusable code. You may think of a program file like a procedure as well. The name of the procedure is like the name of the file, and the call to the procedure is like the Execute or Go command within the Realizer environment. Procedures are nothing more than smaller routines contained within larger files. Libraries are nothing more than collections of these individual routines, and applications are nothing more than a series of routines that collectively perform a specific set of tasks.

Terminating a Procedure

A golden rule of program flow, concerning the proper structure of a procedure (or a function), suggests that there only be one natural exit point to a function or a procedure. In a function, this is handled by the RETURN statement, which we'll discuss in a moment. The natural end of a procedure is determined by the END PROC statement. However, it is possible to prematurely terminate a procedure with an EXIT PROC statement. This will stop the flow of a program at that point and return control of the application to the calling point.

> **Note:** EXIT PROC commands may not exit from a conditional or an iterative statement started outside of the procedure. A balance between the various levels must be maintained at all times.

Finally, consider the concept of value with regard to subroutines. In most languages, everything has a value, whether we need the value or not. In Realizer, there is a distinction between a series of instructions that merely do something and a series of instructions that not only do something, but also yield a value. This distinction is at the heart of what constitutes a function.

> **Note:** A major programming challenge is to see that functions have a value (and therefore a data type), while procedures do not.

Functions

Functions are similar to procedures except for one main difference: they return a value. The programming structure of a function is as follows:

```
func <name>
   <instructions>
   return <value>
end func
```

The big difference here, other than the words used to define the operation, is the RETURN statement.

A good rule to follow when working with procedures or functions is this:

One entry point (the call) and one exit point (the return value, if applicable)

It is not always possible to follow this rule, but it should be a worthy goal to strive for. Why? Well, for example, imagine trying to debug a function with several exit points (RETURN instructions). It would be tedious in the extreme to have to check every RETURN statement within the function. However, if the function observed the one-exit rule, you could easily follow the flow of the function or procedure until the very end of that routine to draw a conclusion.

> **Note**: Keep in mind that since there is a RETURN statement, there cannot be an END FUNC instruction.

Making a call to a function is similar to that of a procedure. All it takes is a reference to the name defined in the function declaration, as shown in these instructions:

```
func SiriusPublishing()
    return "Makes this book"
end func
print SiriusPublishing()
```

The string "Makes this book" would be printed to the Print Log window. Moreover, we might say that the value returned by this function is of the String data type. Now, when the program flows from top to bottom in a source code file, the declaration of the function is seen first. Following the END FUNC statement, the call to that function is made from within the PRINT instructions. The value of the function is passed back from the function to the PRINT command for output. These values could be assigned to other memory variables, used in a computation, or used in conjunction with other functions. Nesting function calls is an important aspect of good programming.

Now, since functions can perform actions as well as have value, it is possible to make a call to a function without regard to what the return value of that function might be. This is solely at the discretion of the programmer. Often, programmers will opt to program functions exclusively since they can both act as a procedure and also have a return value. What we do with that return value is often more important than the operation contained within the function itself.

> **Note:** Both functions and procedures must be defined before they can be executed. This means that a function or a procedure must precede, in the source file, the calling instruction. If a procedure or a function resides in another source file, then that file must be brought into the Realizer environment via the RUN command before any of those functions or procedures can be called.

Parameters

Regardless of whether you are working with a function or a procedure, there is the potential that either may receive additional information via the use of one or more **parameters**. Earlier, in the discussion of the LOCAL clause in the DIM command, I said that no one could see the furniture in the house unless the pieces of furniture inside the house were passed through the door to the outside world. This "passing through" concept is exactly what a parameter is all about. It is a porthole, a way in which data from one routine may be passed to another. Sometimes, we will write functions and/or procedures to be more generic in nature and that they will take on new values and perform different operations based on the values found at any given moment within an application. These values are what can trigger this behavior change. These values, or parameters, give information to a generic subroutine in order for it to do a specific and expected task.

When a function or a procedure is called, a series of values may be passed from the calling routine into the subroutine. Then, on the receiving side of the problem, parameters may be accepted from the calling routine into the subroutine. When a parameter is passed down into a subroutine, the call might look like this:

```
print Count( 24, 5 )
```

The values 24 and 5 are both constants, and both are passed to the *Count()* function. The *Count()* function needs to resolve or evaluate to a value in order for the PRINT instruction to complete its task. Now suppose the function *Count()* looked like this:

```
func Count( iStart, iRange )
   dim iTemp as integer
   for iTemp = iStart to (iStart + iRange)
      iStart = iStart + 1
   next
   return iStart
end func
```

Here, the function would assign the value of 24 to the variable *iStart*. Even though *iStart* is a parameter, it is still a variable and should follow the appropriate coding conventions. The same can be said for the constant 5 passed as well. Here, the function will process through the FOR...NEXT loop, incrementing the value of *iStart* along the way. Then, when the operation is finished, the function will return the new value of *iStart* (which should be 29), which, in turn, will be passed on to the PRINT command for processing.

In this example, the function passes literal values; however, this is not always the case. Often, we need to pass variables to a function, or even to pass the value of another function to a function or procedure. The example program *params1.rlz* illustrates a couple of ways in which a parameter may be passed from the main routine to a function:

```
'* Application ... : Params1.rlz
'* Authors ....... : Steve Straley
'* Notice ........ : Copyright(c) 1994 - Sirius Press, Inc.
'* .............. : All Rights Reserved
'* Date .......... : January 1, 1994
'* Description ... : This show basic parameter passing and receiving.
'* Name:          FirstPass()
'* Params:        <sString>       String that will get evaluated
'* Purpose:       To print out the length of the passed parameter and to
'*                display the name of the original variable.
proc FirstPass( sString )
  print len(sString)
  print qvar( sString, _NAME )
end proc
'* Name:          SecondPass()
'* Params:        <sItem>         String that will get parsed
'*                <iCount>        Position to parse by
'* Returns:       <sReturn>       string of results
'* Purpose:       To show how skipping parameters with dummy values is
'*                possible, how to have a conditional test within a
'*                function, how to use several nest call to Realizer
'*                functions.
func SecondPass( sItem, iCount )
  if qvar( iCount, _REAL ) then
    sReturn = ucase$( left$( sItem, iCount ) )
  else
    sReturn = sItem
  end if
  return( sReturn )
end func
'***************   The Main Processing area *************
dim sName as string
sName = "Steve Straley"
FirstPass( sName )                                '* Normal call
print SecondPass( "Steve Straley", 5 )            '* Regular call
print SecondPass( sName, "DUMMY ITEM" )           '* With dummy passing
FirstPass( SecondPass( sName, 5 ) )               '* Nested calling
clear sName
'* End of Params1.rlz
```

When this program executes, the Print Log window should look something like this:

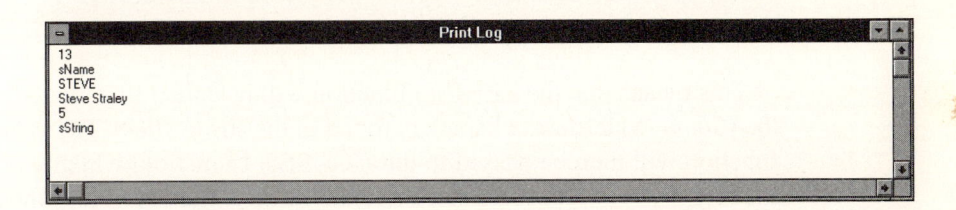

```
                              Print Log
13
sName
STEVE
Steve Straley
5
sString
```

In this program, a procedure named *FirstPass()* and a function named *SecondPass()* are defined before the beginning of the program. The variable *sName* is declared to be a string and is eventually passed to the *FirstPass()* procedure. There is no distinction between Realizer functions and user-defined functions. Here, in the *FirstPass()* procedure, calls to the LEN() and QVAR() functions are made in conjunction with the PRINT command. Since the name of the variable is *sName* which holds the original string and was passed to the procedure, the value of QVAR() when used in conjunction with the _NAME internal variable will return the name not of *sString* (which is the name of the receiving parameter), but of *sName* (which is the name of the passing parameter).

> **Note**: It is a good idea to generate small mini-headers in front of all procedures and functions. These mini-headers should contain the name of the routine, the parameters, the purpose of the routine, the purpose of the parameters, and if applicable, the return value of the function.

After the call to the *FirstPass()* procedure, the value of the *SecondPass()* function is eventually handed off to the PRINT command, as well. Here, a literal string and a literal value are passed to a function. Within the *SecondPass()*, function, the QVAR() function is called again, but this time in a conditional test. The IF...ELSE...END IF command structure is testing to see if the variable *iCount* is a numeric real number. In this first call to the function, it is (it has a value of 5), so the value of *sReturn* will be the dual function call of UCASE$() and LEFT$().

> **Note:** When there are nested function calls, it is important to go to the innermost function and resolve it before expanding outward.

This means that the LEFT$( ) function will be called first, which will take the *iCount* (5) leftmost characters found in the string *sItem*. The value of that function will then be passed to the UCASE$( ) function, which will convert the result to all uppercase letters. That value is then stored to the *sReturn* variable. It is important to see that regardless of the value of the test, the value of *sReturn* will be established and this variable will be the expression passed back by the RETURN command. This is how a one-entry-point, one-exit point function should look. We could have placed a RETURN command to look like this:

```
if qvar( iCount, _REAL ) then
   return ucase$( left$( sItem, iCount ) )
else
   return sItem
end if
```

But consider an extensive code construct in which the RETURN instruction might appear anywhere within that subroutine. By sticking to the notion that there should be only one exit location within a function, you will find a program easier to maintain.

In the second PRINT command to the *SecondPass()* function, a unique call is made. It is unique due to this rule:

> **Note:** It is vitally important that no parameter is skipped. This means that if a defined function is able to accept 2 parameters, then when that function is called, 2 parameters must be passed.

The function *SecondPass()* is defined to receive two parameters; therefore, every time the function is called, two parameters must be passed. Here, in the second call, the literal string "DUMMY ITEM" is passed instead of the literal value of 5. Within the *SecondPass()* function, the data type of the passed parameter is checked and in this case, the data type is *not* a real number. Therefore, the value of this Item is directly passed to the return value of *sReturn*. This one simple program example shows the complexity and power of parameter passing, function calls, procedures, and a combination of them all.

In Chapter 3, we'll explore two methods of passing parameters: **passing by value** and **passing by reference**, but for now, just accept the notion that some piece of information may be passed from one routine to another.

Conclusion

Without a doubt, this is the most complex, yet the most fundamental chapter in this book. It is complex because the concepts outlined within are so important to the structure and power of the Realizer language. Reports, menus, database files, graphs, communications, and animation all mean absolutely nothing without a firm handle on these key topics.

Chapter 2

Menus of an Application

The objective of this chapter is to show how to create an application using either the language or the various tools that come with Realizer. Many of these steps may be accomplished faster using the tools; however, those aids may get in the way of understanding how the language works within the Windows environment. Make no mistake about this, Realizer is a programming language and this book aims to teach it to you.

Conventions

One of the first things that we have to recognize is a need for coding standards using the Realizer language. With another language that I am familiar with, Clipper, it took more than seven years before the majority of Clipper programmers coded in the same style. This made for easy development of large applications, especially within a team environment. Programming standards make it easy to share code and ideas, and easy to maintain applications in future generations. Toward that end, this book uses the following conventions:

- Realizer functions and commands in code are exclusively in lowercase letters. In text, they are set in all caps to be easily distinguishable.
- User-defined procedures and functions are a combination of uppercase and lowercase letters, depending on pronunciation. However, the first letter is always capped.
- Realizer internal variables and values preceded by an underscore character (_) are in all uppercase letters, set in the monospace font.
- Variables assigned by the programmer follow Hungarian notation as outlined in Chapter 1. These variables are set in italics.

In this section, we'll look at code and begin to build an application from the very beginning. This is the best way to learn about a programming language and environment such as Realizer.

Menus

The first things that an end user of an application sees are the opening screen shot and the menus. The proper layout of a menu can be crucial to the user's acceptance of that application. There are many ways to build a menu within Realizer, and some specialized tools can cut the coding time considerably. The manuals and documentation that come with Realizer outline these tools, but none of them helps the programmer to understand the language or shows how to build an application from the ground up. To do that, we need to jump in and get our hands dirty by using coding fundamentals to put together a finished application. In most cases, we will be looking at source code, since Realizer is not just an interpretive environment, but also a language. In some cases, we will use the tools that come with the package. We have to know it all, use it all, in order to use it well.

In the previous chapter, we looked at some language fundamentals. We have to crawl before we can walk, or more appropriate in this case, we have to know the structure of the language before we can build a simple menu. Why start with a menu? For one thing, every application needs a menu; for another, menu-building is an easy task in Realizer, and you'll be able to accomplish something in the language with a fair amount of ease.

Our First Step

The application we are going to build is unique and specialized, and it will use most of the features in the Realizer language. To start, let's look at the opening screen of the Realizer environment.

In addition to the source code editor, you also want to have the Debugger window and the Print Log window open, as shown in Figure 2-1. To open these windows, press `CTRL_D` and then `CRTL_P`. This is a typical start-up condition when working in Realizer. There are several ways to start, including the FormDev utility program that is an option on the Run menu, as shown in Figure 2-2.

Here, a main menu can be quickly built from scratch. Another way to start this application is via the program editor. In this book, we use a combination approach.

Now, our applications will use the Realizer menu, as well as other applications, as a guide to how our menus should look in a Windows environment.

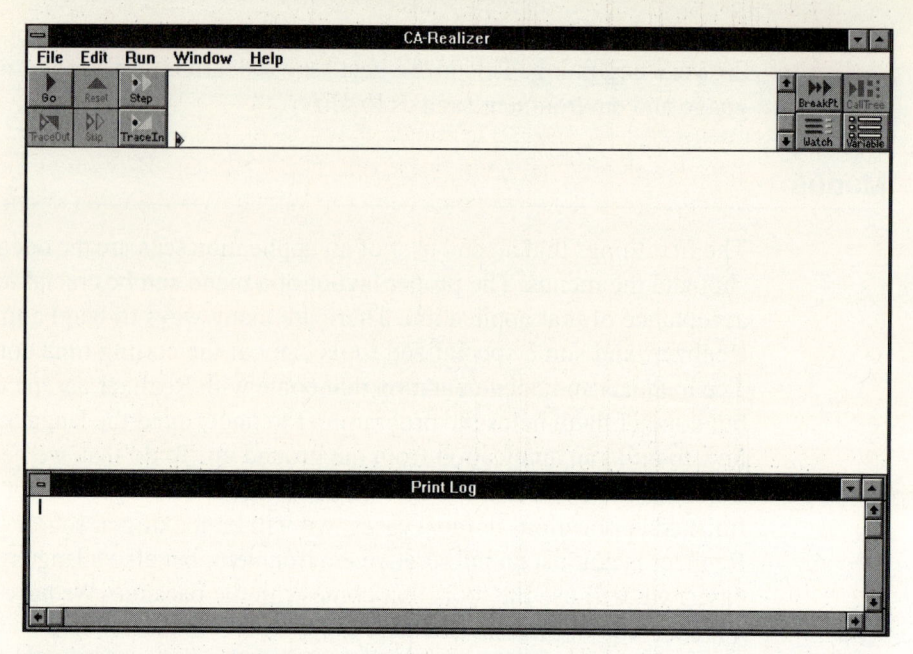

Figure 2-1. Open DEBUG and PRINT LOG windows with no source code loaded.

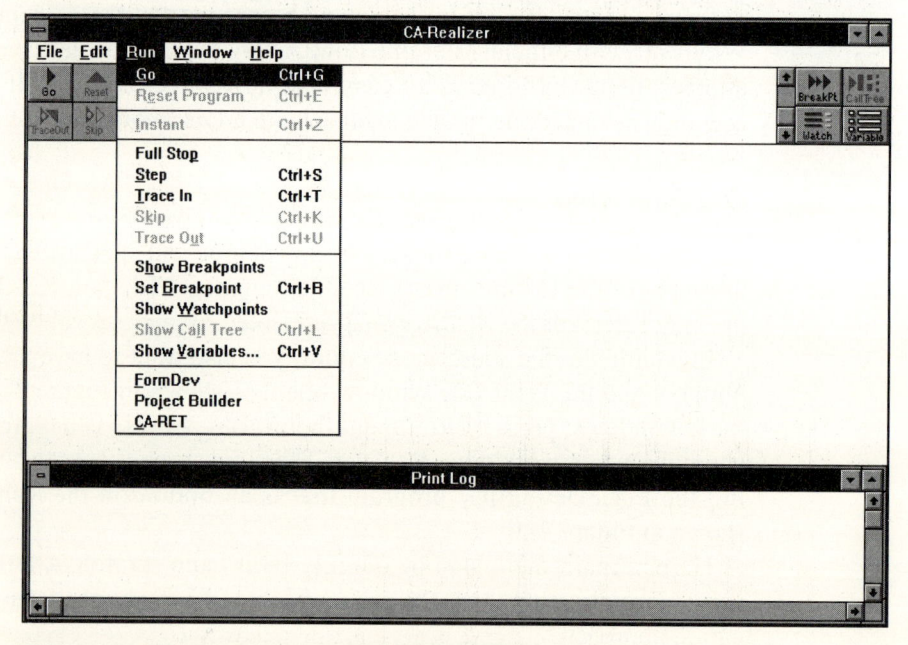

Figure 2-2. The main menu and the GO option.

As you can see in Figures 2-1 and 2-2, there are two types of menus. The first layer of menu options, which appears across the top of the application, is commonly referred to as a **bar menu**. From this menu option, **pull-down menus** appear. Each pull-down menu menu contains other menu items and prompts in a boxed area. Some options within a pull-down menu may open up another pull-down menu. This is a Windows convention, often referred to as a CUA (Common User Access) type of menu: a standard now accepted in the industry.

Each menu item, in the bar menu and in the pull-down menus should have an **accelerator**. This means that the letter that is an underlined letter that represents the Accelerator key. This letter, when pressed in conjunction with the `ALT` key, activates that menu item without the assistance of the mouse. In Figure 2-2, for example, the letter "H" is underlined in the show Breakpoints option, which means that you can press `ALT-H` to select that menu option. In other languages or applications, the Accelerator may be highlighted in a different color, or even blinking. Here, the simple underlining of a letter will suffice. It also should be noted that it is not a requirement that all menu options have an accelerator. The default in Realizer is not to have them unless specifically written into the code.

> **Note:** Not every end user will have a mouse; therefore, accelerator keys and/or "hot keys" may be very important to the end user who relies on a keyboard.

Another bar menu standard is that the first menu option is always File, and in most cases, the last menu option is Help. Try to observe this convention when building your applications.

To get into this language and begin building the first application, select the File option from the main menu, then the New option. When you do, the screen will look like Figure 2-3.

This will be the opening file that we will code in.

Now we need to create a standard header for each file. For this, the code should look like this:

```
'*  Application ... : Test1.rlz
'*  Authors ....... : Steve Straley
'*  Notice ........ : Copyright(c) 1994 - Sirius Press, Inc.
'*  .............. : All Rights Reserved
'*  Date .......... : January 1, 1994
'*  Description ... : The main module of the program
'*
```

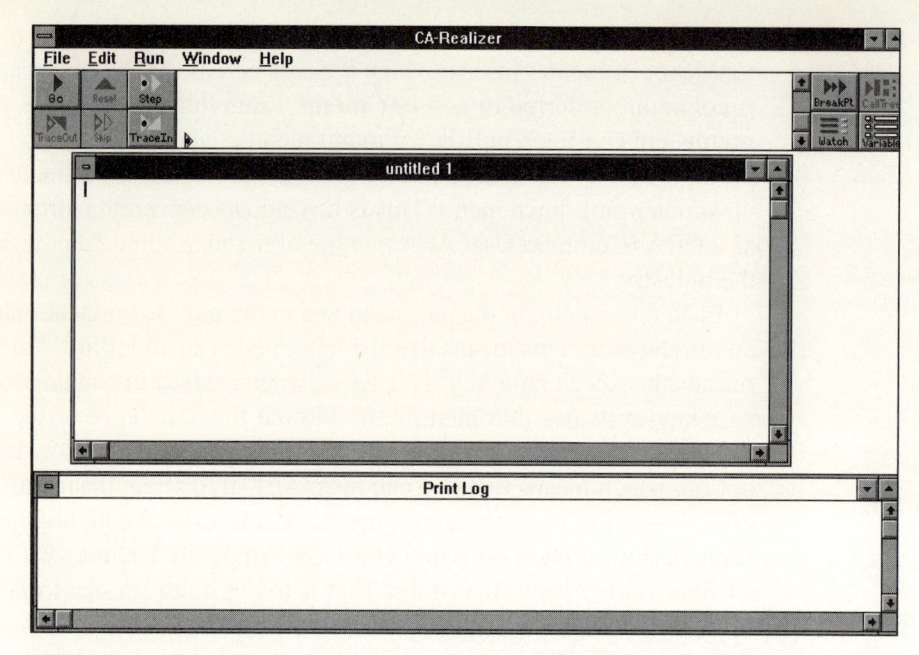

Figure 2-3. Open NEW program opened after DEBUG and PRINT LOG windows open.

Every source code file should begin with a header that contains information about the program, the author(s), date of starting, and any other related information. The file extension of a source code module in Realizer is .RLZ. Whenever you want to make a remark, either on a line by itself or within a line that contains running source code, precede the remark with an apostrophe. In our header, each line starts off with this character. The REM command statement could be used as well; however, this is a matter of style and in this case, convenience.

Once you install the opening header, you can start to build the structure of the menus. Every menu needs some type of structure; we will build this structure into a **procedure**. As a review from the previous chapter, a procedure is nothing more than a name given to a group of actions. A **function** is similar to a procedure except it will have a return value. To start, let's build a simple procedure that loads a single menu item:

```
'* Name:         LoadMenus
'* Purpose:      Loads the basic menu structure for this application
'* Returns:      N/A
```

Menus of an Application

```
proc LoadMenus

    iMainMenu = menuqunique            ' Generate a new menu pointer
    menunew( iMainMenu; "&File" )      ' Add a FILE option to seed menu pointer
    menusetcmd(1, "&New" )             ' Add "NEW" as option with id number 1
    menusetcmd(2, "&Old" )             ' Add "Old" as option with id number 2
    menusetcmd(3, "&Exit" )            ' Add "Exit" as option with id number 3
    menusetproc( MainMenu )            ' Set the procedure
    menucontrol(_SHOW)                 ' Turn on the menu and show it

end proc
```

There is a great deal of information within this short space, so let's take it step by step. To start, the variable *iMainMenu* will hold an integer. This number will act like a pointer—a numeric value representing a greater whole—to a new and unique menu. This is created via the MENUQUNIQUE command. Every menu, window, file, or tool has associated numbers. This is similar in concept to a DOS File Handle. DOS does not recognize elements by their names or their types, but by a sequential numbering system that it assigns. Realizer works in the same way.

Here, the MENUQUNIQUE command creates a new and unique menu pointer and assigns it to the *iMainMenu* variable. Then, a new menu is created and attached to that pointer using the MENUNEW() function.

```
menunew( iMainMenu; "&File" )     ' Add a FILE option to seed menu pointer
```

This means that a new menu is created and attached to *iMainMenu,* and the text of the first option in that menu will be "File." This brings up a couple of new points. First, the MENUNEW( ) function creates the pull-down menus that cascade down from the bar menu items.

The second thing to note is the ampersand character (&) appearing in front of the letter F. The letter immediately following the ampersand will be the accelerator key. When this application is running, the letter F will have an underline associated with it. This will tell the end user of the application that the ALT key in conjunction with the letter F (in this case) will open the associated pull-down menu.

There are three options on the pull-down File menu: New, Old, and Exit. Each of these options is added with the MENUSETCMD( ) function. Like the File option in the bar menu, these options have accelerator keys attached to them. Note the numeric value associated with each of these menu options: 1, 2, and 3. This is our own numeric pointing system. In the future, if an option is selected from this menu, Realizer will tell us the number of the selected menu option. We can devise our own numbering scheme. The FormDev Utility program, for example, starts off with tens digits whereas, we are starting with ones digits.

Note also the brief comment line off to the side of each instruction. Again, comments should be used as often as necessary. Here, the comments give each instruction more meaning. As you get more and more accustomed to the syntax and the program flow, comments should be used whenever you want to make a point, to clear up abiguity, to dictate program flow and direction, and to add information to variables and fields.

The next line:

```
menusetproc( MainMenu )            ' Set the procedure
```

attempts to set this menu to another subroutine to be named *MainMenu*. This line and the next one:

```
menucontrol(_SHOW)                 ' Turn on the menu and show it
```

go together and are important. The last instruction displays the menu that we are creating. Once displayed to the screen, only mouse clicks and/or certain key presses can access the menu. For example, the ALT_F key is important to the menu since it will toggle the File option on the a bar menu and open its pull-down menu. Clicking the left mouse button on the File option will also open up this pull-down menu. However, clicking on menu options and moving the mouse cursor is not the issue, even though the MENUCONTROL() function enables this. The real issue is: What will take place should one of these sub-options receive mouse clicks or key presses? Action needs to be taken if one of the other three menu options receives input. This action is determined within the new procedure referenced here as *MainMenu*. In other words, the MENUSETPROC() function attaches program control in the various menu options to the specified procedure.

Finally, the end of the procedure is specified with the END PROC command.

Now, this code, if called, will execute within the Realizer environment. However, if we were to execute this code now, the resulting screen might look like Figure 2-4.

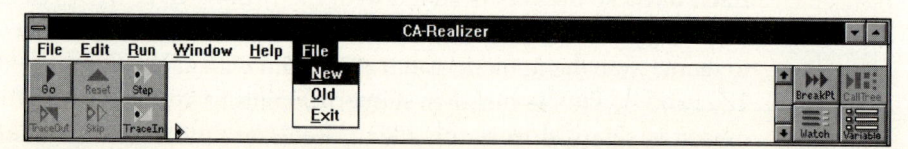

Figure 2-4. The NEW option running in the Menu Editor with DEBUG window open.

Menus of an Application

This is not what we want. We need to clear the standard Realizer menu items before starting our application's menus. To do this, we will create a new procedure called ClearMenus and within it, add the various functions to do the job.

```
'* Name:          ClearMenus
'* Purpose:       To Clear the REALIZER menu routines
'* Returns:       N/A

proc ClearMenus

    menuselect(_FILEMENU)       'Refer to the FILE menu on the top
    menucontrol(_HIDE)          '... and hide it
    menuselect(_EDITMENU)       'Refer to the EDIT menu on the top
    menucontrol(_HIDE)          '... and hide it
    menuselect(_RUNMENU)        'Do the same with the RUN menu
    menucontrol(_HIDE)          '
    menuselect(_HELPMENU)       'And the HELP menu
    menucontrol(_HIDE)          '
    menuselect(_WINDOWMENU)     'And the WINDOW menu
    menucontrol(_HIDE)          ' and hide it as well

end proc
```

The MENUSELECT() function can perform in several ways its function here is to find a reference to the internal Realizer menu named File. This is handled by the internal constant for this function named _FILEMENU. The MENUSELECT() function can also take a numeric in place of an internal constant, but since we do not know the appropriate integer pointer for the menu items that Realizer uses, we need to use internal constants in the ClearMenus procedure. Each Realizer bar menu option is selected with the MENUSELECT() function. Once selected, the MENUCONTROL() function is called. In other languages, this sequence of events might look something like this:

```
iPointer = menuselect(_FILEMENU)
menuHide( iPointer )
```

or

```
iPointer = menuselect(_FILEMENU)
menucontrol( _HIDE, iPointer )
```

When the MENUSELECT() function is called, Realizer moves an internal pointer to that menu (or window, form, or other element), which then is ready for the MENUCONTROL() function. There, that function is called with the internal instruction of _HIDE. This is but one of four possible choices for this function. Within the *ClearMenus* procedure, the five Realizer menus will be, when called, cleared for the application.

The final procedure defined within this test program is the one attached to the menu. This procedure is named *MainMenu*. In this first example, it is the most complicated routine.

```
'* Name:          MainMenu
'* Purpose:       Processes information from the menu selections
'* Returns:       N/A
'* Parameters:    <aParms>

proc MainMenu( aParams )      'Processes the options

  menuselect( aParams[ _MENUNUM ] )     ' Look at the menu selection position
  select case aParams[ _ITEMNUM ]    ' now look at the item number of that
    case 1
    case 2
    case 3
      reset _ALL
      exit program

  end select

end proc
```

When a mouse click or key press is detected and it refers to a menu option, then this procedure kicks in, since it was attached to that main menu structure created earlier. This brings up the first interesting point: parameters. In the previous chapter, we saw the fundamental use of parameters. In future chapters, we will see the various ways in which parameters can be passed and manipulated. In this case, Realizer actually passes the data for us: We do not have to do anything other than write a subroutine able to receive the parameters. This parameter is contained in the variable named *aParams*.

To have Realizer internally select the menu that was clicked on or activated by a key press, the MENUSELECT() function is called, as it was before. This time, however, instead of supplying an internal constant identifier, a numeric integer is passed. The question is, which identifier? The *aParams* array is a complex structure, and the internal constant `_MENUNUM` will find the correct location for the ID marker for the associated menu. Then we need to find out which item was actually chosen. The internal constant `_ITEMNUM` lets us attach branching operations to those various menu items found within a pull-down menu. This is handled with a SELECT CASE command structure. Again, the *aParams* array is used to tell Realizer to look at which item in the selected menu is being activated. If the menu item has an ID number of 3 (the one we assigned to the option Exit), then additional operations are performed.

```
menusetcmd(3, "&Exit" )          ' Add "Exit" as option with id number 3
```

The next line within the SELECT CASE structure says two uses the RESET function along with the internal constant of _ALL to clear everything and return Realizer to its original state.

We could also have offered this:

```
reset( _MENU )
```

which would remove all of our new menus and restore the five hidden menus of Realizer. Following this is a command that needs no explanation: EXIT PROGRAM.

All of these routines are within three procedures: *ClearMenus()*, *LoadMenus()*, and *MainMenu()*. This still does not make a program: These are only small subroutines within the main program. At the bottom of the file, after the END SELECT and END PROC statements, enter the following:

```
'***   Main Body of routine
'
'************************

ClearMenus()
LoadMenus()
```

Here, the first procedure call makes all of the Realizer menus disappear and then, when that has finished, the next procedure call will load the menus and will process in the background for a mouse click or a push button.

The entire file should therefore look like this:

```
'* Application ... : Test1.rlz
'* Authors ....... : Steve Straley
'* Notice ........ : Copyright(c) 1994 - Sirius Press, Inc.
'* .............. : All Rights Reserved
'* Date .......... : January 1, 1994
'* Description ... : The main module of the program
'*

'* Name:         ClearMenus
'* Purpose:      To Clear the REALIZER menu routines
'* Returns:      N/A

proc ClearMenus()

    menuselect(_FILEMENU)      'Refer to the FILE menu on the top
    menucontrol(_HIDE)         '... and hide it
```

```
    menuselect(_EDITMENU)       'Refer to the EDIT menu on the top
    menucontrol(_HIDE)          '... and hide it
    menuselect(_RUNMENU)        'Do the same with the RUN menu
    menucontrol(_HIDE)          '
    menuselect(_HELPMENU)       'And the HELP menu
    menucontrol(_HIDE)          '
    menuselect(_WINDOWMENU)     'And the WINDOW menu
    menucontrol(_HIDE)          ' and hide it as well

end proc

'* Name:        LoadMenus
'* Purpose:     Loads the basic menu structure for this application
'* Returns:     N/A

proc LoadMenus()

    iMainMenu = menuqunique         ' Generate a new menu pointer
    menunew( iMainMenu; "&File" )   ' Add a FILE option to seed menu pointer
    menusetcmd(1, "&New" )          ' Add "NEW" as option with id number 1
    menusetcmd(2, "&Old" )          ' Add "Old" as option with id number 2
    menusetcmd(3, "&Exit" )         ' Add "Exit" as option with id number 3
    menusetproc( MainMenu )         ' Set the procedure
    menucontrol(_SHOW)              ' Turn on the menu and show it

end proc

'* Name:        MainMenu
'* Purpose:     Processes information from the menu selections
'* Returns:     N/A
'* Parameters:  <aParms>

proc MainMenu( aParams )      'Processes the options

    menuselect( aParams[ _MENUNUM ] )       ' Look at the menu selection position
    select case aParams[ _ITEMNUM ]         ' now look at the item number of that
      case 1
      case 2
      case 3
        reset _ALL
        exit program

    end select

end proc

'*** Main Body of routine
'
'*************************
```

```
ClearMenus()
LoadMenus()

'* End of File: Test1.rlz
```

Here is a perfect example of how a testing of values and/or conditions as discussed in the previous chapter. The SELECT CASE command looks to the array named *aParams*. Following this are individual test cases for each of the possible values. One condition that is coded for deals with a CASE 3 value. As the menu grows, so will the array named *aParams*. As that grows, more and more CASE items will be added to this code construct.

Once all of this code is in the first window named "Untitled," we need to save this to the proper directory. Open the File menu and then click on the Save option.

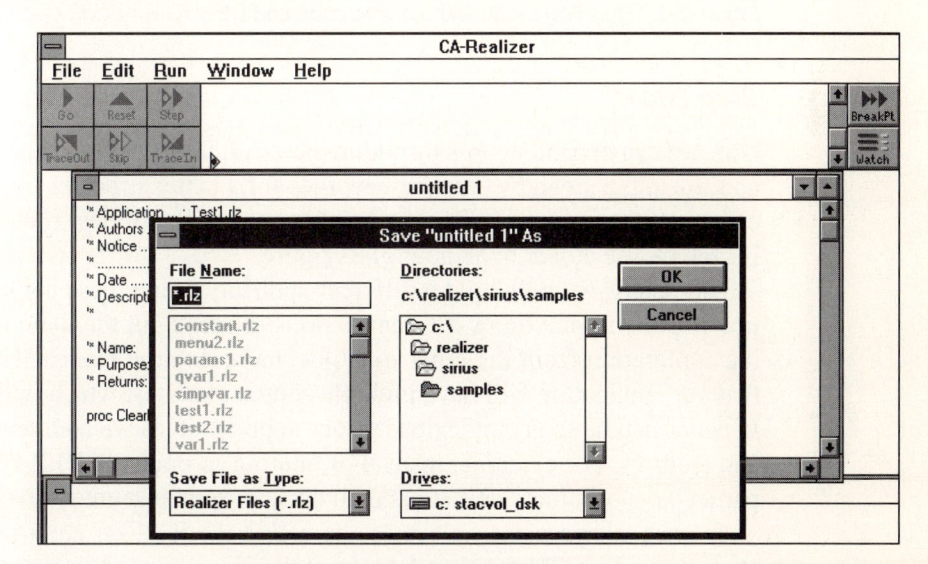

Figure 2-5. Standard SAVE AS dialog window.

In the resulting dialog box, shown in Figure 2-5, move to the appropriate directory (here, *Realizer\Sirius\Samples*) and type in the name `Test1`. To save, click on the OK button. Your screen should look like Figure 2-6.

Once saved, we then can run this simple program. To do this, select the Run option on the main menu bar, then select Go. When you do, the screen should shift a bit as the menu items on the top are cleared, then the new File menu appears. The program is now running. We can open up the File menu and select the Exit option only to watch the menu be cleared and the original Realizer menu reappear, ready for the next operation.

We have built our first Realizer application.

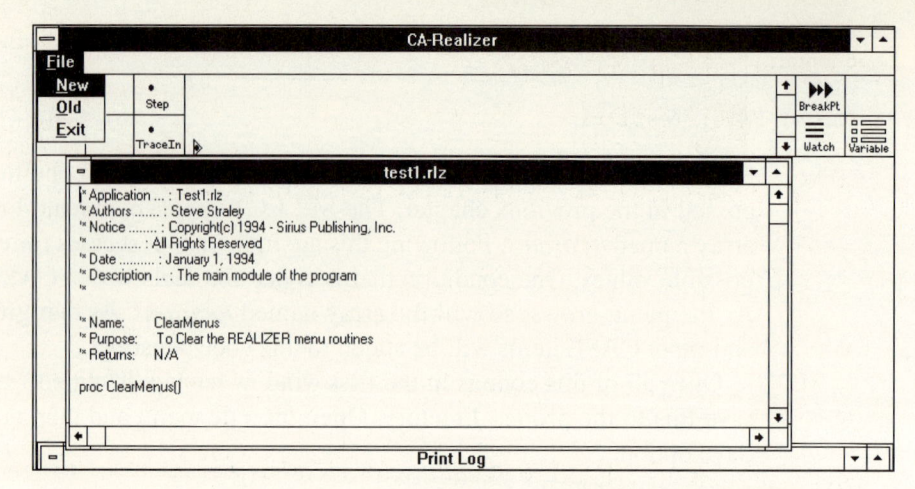

Figure 2-6. Running menu with source code and DEBUG windows open.

Step Two

Now we can expand on this by adding new options or by expanding on what appears in the menu by creating new files for a better structure for the application. We might even add some gratuitous visual pufferies, such as changing the mouse cursor to an hour glass figure.

Ultimately, we will build a different application, but these are good practice steps. The first thing we want to do is to break out the main module of the application from the other modules, including the menus. This means that our application will have multiple source modules, which will allow us to better handle the complexities of our application as we add new modules and features. For example, instead of hunting through an .RLZ file for one particular subroutine, we can open up the appropriate source file.

To start this process, we need to be within the Realizer environment at a start-up position. Then, select New from the File menu to bring up the source code editor in an untitled window, as shown in Figure 2-7.

To import the code from the `Test1.rlz` file, open the File menu again but this time, select Open. This will bring up the standard file **dialog box**, shown in Figure 2-8.

A dialog box can be many things. In this case, it contains a couple of **push buttons** and **drop-down lists** that allow us to search the disk for the desired file. The data-entry portion of this box contains the default file

Menus of an Application

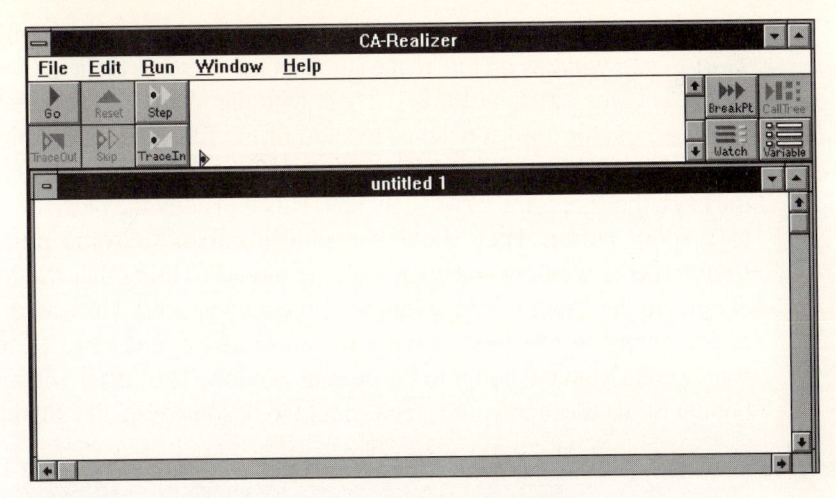

Figure 2-7. Expanded new and untitled program file.

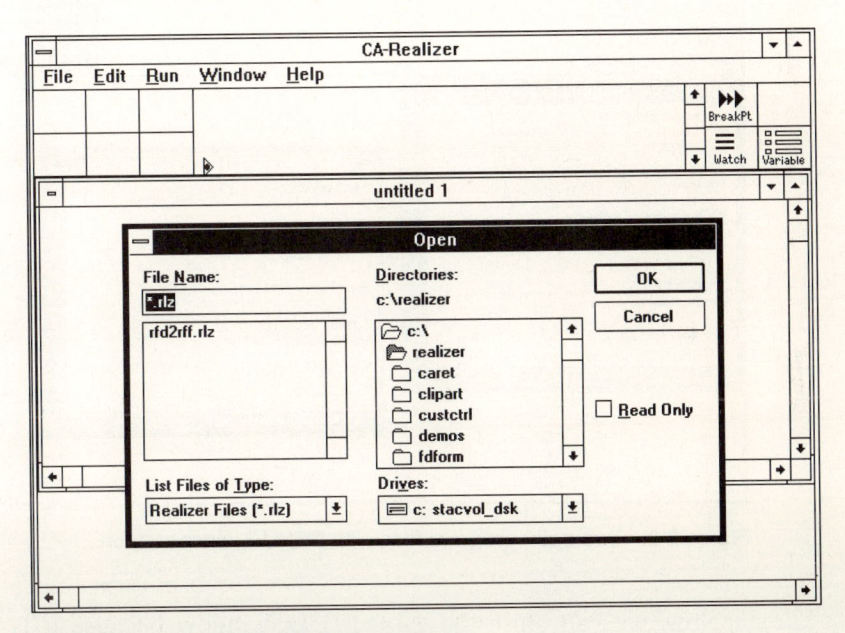

Figure 2-8. Standard OPEN dialog window.

extension of *.RLZ. Our file is in the Samples directory off of the *Sirius* directory off of the *Realizer* directory. Once we find it, the name of the file `Test1.rlz` will appear in the list box on the left side of the dialog box. Select that file. When you click OK a new window will appear for the source code editor, tiled on top of the untitled window previously created.

Moving the source code from one window to the next is simple. With the `Test1.rlz` window on top, make sure that the cursor is at the top of the screen by pressing the CTRL_HOME key. Then, with the LEFT_SHIFT key held down, move the cursor until it reaches the end of the file. As you do this, all of the lines will appear highlighted. When you get to the end of the file, release all of the keys, then press the CTRL_INS key. This will copy the block of source code to a scrap buffer. Then move the mouse cursor to some portion of the `Untitled 1` window and click with the mouse to bring that window forward and move the `Test1.rlz` window to the background. Now, with the cursor inside of the `Untitled 1` window, press LEFT_SHIFT+INS to copy the source code from the buffer to the current window. The cursor will appear at the bottom of the file, and your screen should look something like Figure 2-9.

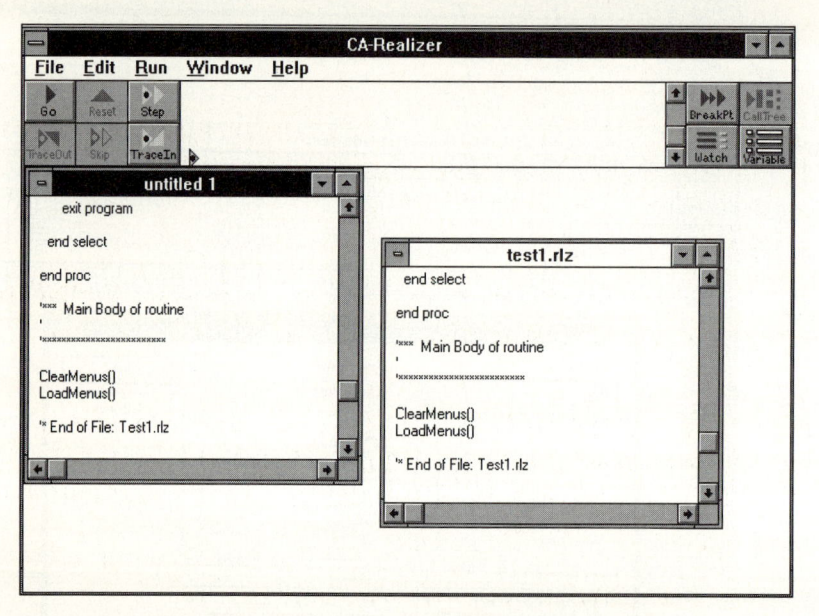

Figure 2-9. Two open program files with DEBUG window open.

Now, we can close the `Test1.rlz` window because it is no longer needed. When you return to the untitled window, change the comment line at the end of the file to refer to `Test2.rlz`.

The next thing we need to do is recognize that the first three subroutines in this source file deal with clearing the standard Realizer menu bar as well as building the menu tree for our application. Finally, the last subroutine deals with selections made from that newly created menu tree. All three of these procedures deal with some aspect of the menu for our application. Therefore, it is appropriate to create a separate file to house all of these routines. To do this, select the File option followed by the New option one more time. This will open up a new window named `Untitled 2`. First, let's copy over the header of the previous file to this new window. To make this easier, reshape the windows so that the first window rests on top of the second to look something like Figure 2-10.

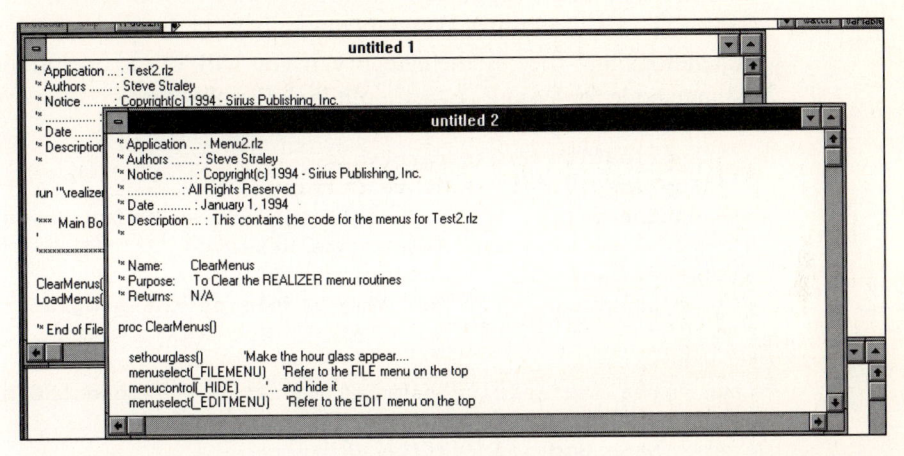

Figure 2-10. Expanded and overlaid two program files.

Now, highlight the header in `Untitled 1`, copy it to the scrap buffer, place the cursor at the top of the other window, and press the `LEFT_SHIFT+INS` keys. Following this, we need to change the name of the application from `Test2.rlz` to `Menu2.rlz`. This way we know that the file contains menu stuff and pertains directly to the `Test2.rlz` file in the other window. Also, we may want to change the description of the file, indicating that this file contains the menu source code for `Test2.rlz`. Once you've copied and altered the header, you can move the source code for the menus over to this new window. In `Untitled 1`, highlight the code starting at the top all the way down to just above the section headed "Main body of routine." Copy it to the scrap buffer, then, selecting the second window, insert the code directly under the header using the `LEFT_SHIFT+INS` key combination. Now, return to the previous window, where the code should still be highlighted, and press the `DEL` key to remove this code from the `Untitled 1` window.

The trick is to have the main file for the application know about the file containing the menus. To do this, we need to insert one line directly above the main body of the code in *Untitled 1*:

```
run "\realizer\sirius\samples\menu2"
```

The RUN command will execute the commands specified in the file. This means that the menu instructions will be loaded into the memory of the Realizer environment, and when the two functions are called at the end of the main program module, *ClearMenus()* and *LoadMenus()*, the program will run as it did before. The advantage here is that we have separated the operations into files by the category, if you will, of the operations. Now, the source code for *Test2.rlz* should look like this:

```
'* Application ... : Test2.rlz
'* Authors ....... : Steve Straley
'* Notice ........ : Copyright(c) 1994 - Sirius Press, Inc.
'* ............... : All Rights Reserved
'* Date .......... : January 1, 1994
'* Description ... : The main module of the program
'*


run "\realizer\sirius\samples\menu2"       ' Load the menu file

'***   Main Body of routine
'
'************************

ClearMenus()
LoadMenus()

'* End of File: Test2.rlz
```

and the source code for the *Menu2.rlz* file should look like this:

```
'* Application ... : Menu2.rlz
'* Authors ....... : Steve Straley
'* Notice ........ : Copyright(c) 1994 - Sirius Press, Inc.
'* ............... : All Rights Reserved
'* Date .......... : January 1, 1994
'* Description ... : This contains the code for the menus for Test2.rlz
'*


'* Name:        ClearMenus
'* Purpose:     To Clear the REALIZER menu routines
'* Returns:     N/A
```

```
proc ClearMenus()

    menuselect(_FILEMENU)         'Refer to the FILE menu on the top
    menucontrol(_HIDE)            '... and hide it
    menuselect(_EDITMENU)         'Refer to the EDIT menu on the top
    menucontrol(_HIDE)            '... and hide it
    menuselect(_RUNMENU)          'Do the same with the RUN menu
    menucontrol(_HIDE)            '
    menuselect(_HELPMENU)         'And the HELP menu
    menucontrol(_HIDE)            '
    menuselect(_WINDOWMENU)       'And the WINDOW menu
    menucontrol(_HIDE)            ' and hide it as well

end proc

'* Name:      LoadMenus
'* Purpose:   Loads the basic menu structure for this application
'* Returns:   N/A

proc LoadMenus()

    iMainMenu = menuqunique            ' Generate a new menu pointer
    menunew( iMainMenu; "&File" )      ' Add a FILE option to seed menu pointer
    menusetcmd(1, "&New" )             ' Add "NEW" as option with id number 1
    menusetcmd(2, "&Old" )             ' Add "Old" as option with id number 2
    menusetcmd(3, "&Exit" )            ' Add "Exit" as option with id number 3
    menusetproc( MainMenu )            ' Set the procedure
    menucontrol(_SHOW)                 ' Turn on the menu and show it

end proc

'* Name:       MainMenu
'* Purpose:    Processes information from the menu selections
'* Returns:    N/A
'* Parameters: <aParms>

proc MainMenu( aParams )     'Processes the options

    menuselect( aParams[ _MENUNUM ] )     ' Look at the menu selection
                                                position
    select case aParams[ _ITEMNUM ]       ' now look at the item number of
                                                that
        case 1
        case 2
        case 3
            reset _ALL
            exit program

    end select
```

```
end proc

'* End of File: Menu2.rlz
```

In two quick sections, we have created a simple menu and separated the code out into unique source files. We can now save both of these windows to their appropriate names. In order to test this application, make certain that the window for *Test2.rlz* is selected. (You can tell when a window is selected because the frame of the window will be lit while the one in the background is not.) Then select Go from the Run menu.

Adding a Menu Separator

In most Windows-based applications, the Exit item in the pull-down File menu is always separated from the other items by either a single or double bar. We can add this feature to our menus using the MENUSETCMD() function. Instead of building a menu item with a unique ID integer for future use, we can use the internal setting of _SEPARATOR. The code in our menu should now look something like this:

```
proc LoadMenus()

   iMainMenu = menuqunique          ' Generate a new menu pointer
   menunew( iMainMenu; "&File" )    ' Add a FILE option to seed menu pointer
   menusetcmd(1, "&New" )           ' Add "NEW" as option with id number 1
   menusetcmd(2, "&Old" )           ' Add "Old" as option with id number 2
   menusetcmd(_SEPARATOR)           ' Add a separator
   menusetcmd(3, "&Exit" )          ' Add "Exit" as option with id number 3
   menusetproc( MainMenu )          ' Set the procedure
   menucontrol(_SHOW)               ' Turn on the menu and show it

end proc
```

Since there is no ID integer associated with this, there is no problem within our SELECT CASE instructions within the *MainMenu* subroutine.

Adding Other "Hot Keys"

In some cases, the accelerator key is not enough. Some end users prefer to use the function keys across the top of the keyboard. To accommodate them, we can add a function key along with the accelerator key. There are a couple of ways in which this can be accomplished. For example, we could assign the F10 key to the EXIT option via the third parameter passed to the MENUSETCMD() function. Also, the menu item text needs to include the function key. The code would look like this:

```
menusetcmd(3, "&Exit.... F10", 10 )   ' Add "Exit" as option
```

The ampersand character (&) remains in the string which has been expanded to include the `F10` key. The third parameter of this function, the number value of 10, tells Realizer that the `F10` key means something. Using values 3 through 12, we can assign the `F3` through the `F12` keys. Ranges from 13 through 22 add the `SHIFT` key to the keystrokes; ranges from 23 through 32 add the `CONTROL+SHIFT` keys to the keystrokes; ranges from 33 through 42 add the `CONTROL+ALT` keys to the keystrokes. There are also other parameter options that we will look at in future examples.

Adding Hour Glasses

During certain operations, such as clearing the menu from the screen, loading a new file from disk, building a new menu structure, acquiring fields from a database, or writing a report, you may need to let the end user know that something is taking place. In the past, folks relied on the little red light on the hard disk; today's end users want more concrete reassurance that all is well with the application.

There are two functions within Realizer that may be called upon to help: SETHOURGLASS() and RESETHOURGLASS(). Strategic locations for these functions depend on the operations being performed. In our text program, it may be advantageous to turn the mouse cursor into an hour glass figure just before the Realizer standard menu items are being removed from the system within the *ClearMenus()* procedure.

```
proc ClearMenus()

sethourglass()                    'Make the hour glass appear....
menuselect(_FILEMENU)             'Refer to the FILE menu on the top
```

Then, just after the new menu is built and placed on the screen within the *LoadMenus()* procedure, the hour glass needs to be converted back to a regular mouse cursor.

```
menusetproc( MainMenu )           ' Set the procedure
menucontrol(_SHOW)                ' Turn on the menu and show it
resethourglass()                  ' Turn back the glass to a cursor
```

Dulling Some Menu Options

At various points within an application, some menu items are not available. For example, a PRINT option would have no relevance if no file were open so this option would be dulled or "grayed out" until a file became visible to the program. This means that the menu item has to be toggled by the program, depending on the status and condition of the application. Fortunately, another option available to the MENUSETCMD() function deals with the style of the menu item being attached. So far, all of the styles have been "normal." Now, we want to gray-out one of the menu options. The code might look like this:

```
menunew( iMainMenu; "&File" )         ' Add a FILE option
menusetcmd(1, "&New" )                ' Add "NEW" as option with id number 1
menusetcmd(2, "&Old"; _GRAY)          ' Add "Old" as option with id number 2
menusetcmd(_SEPARATOR)                ' Add a separator
menusetcmd(3, "&Exit.... F10", 10 )   ' Add "Exit" as option
```

The semicolon following the text of the menu prompt in conjunction with the _GRAY internal variable tells the MENUSETCMD() function that this item is to be grayed out. To switch this menu item back to a normal status, the _NORMAL internal variable may be passed.

Another option for menu items includes toggling a check mark on and off next to a menu item, depending on whether the item is selected. Finally, menu items can even be removed from a pull-down menu using the _REMOVE internal variable.

With all of these changes incorporated, the source code for *Menu2.rlz* should now look like this:

```
'* Application ... : Menu2.rlz
'* Authors ....... : Steve Straley
'* Notice ........ : Copyright(c) 1994 - Sirius Press, Inc.
'* .............. : All Rights Reserved
'* Date .......... : January 1, 1994
'* Description ... : This contains the code for the menus for Test2.rlz
'*

'* Name:       ClearMenus
'* Purpose:    To Clear the REALIZER menu routines
'* Returns:    N/A

proc ClearMenus()

    sethourglass()              'Make the hour glass appear....
    menuselect(_FILEMENU)       'Refer to the FILE menu on the top
    menucontrol(_HIDE)          '... and hide it
    menuselect(_EDITMENU)       'Refer to the EDIT menu on the top
    menucontrol(_HIDE)          '... and hide it
```

```
    menuselect(_RUNMENU)          'Do the same with the RUN menu
    menucontrol(_HIDE)            '
    menuselect(_HELPMENU)         'And the HELP menu
    menucontrol(_HIDE)            '
    menuselect(_WINDOWMENU)       'And the WINDOW menu
    menucontrol(_HIDE)            ' and hide it as well

end proc

'* Name:       LoadMenus
'* Purpose:    Loads the basic menu structure for this application
'* Returns:    N/A

proc LoadMenus()

    iMainMenu = menuqunique              ' Generate a new menu pointer
    menunew( iMainMenu; "&File" )        ' Add a FILE option
    menusetcmd(1, "&New" )               ' Add "NEW" as option with id number 1
    menusetcmd(2, "&Old"; _GRAY)         ' Add "Old" as option with id number 2
    menusetcmd(_SEPARATOR)               ' Add a separator
    menusetcmd(3, "&Exit.... F10", 10 )  ' Add "Exit" as option
    menusetproc( MainMenu )              ' Set the procedure
    menucontrol(_SHOW)                   ' Turn on the menu and show it
    resethourglass()                     ' Turn back the glass to a cursor

end proc

'* Name:        MainMenu
'* Purpose:     Processes information from the menu selections
'* Returns:     N/A
'* Parameters:  <aParms>

proc MainMenu( aParams )     'Processes the options

    menuselect( aParams[ _MENUNUM ] )    ' Look at the menu selection position
    select case aParams[ _ITEMNUM ]      ' now look at the item number of that
      case 1
      case 2
      case 3
        reset _ALL
        exit program

    end select

end proc

'* End of File: Menu2.rlz
```

Before going any further, make sure that these two source code modules (*Test2.rlz* and *Menu2.rlz*) are saved in the same directory along with the *Test1.rlz* file. In the next section, we will see how a stand alone application can be built using these two modules.

Step Three

Making an executable out of these two files is relatively easy. Up to now, we have been working in what is commonly known as an **interpretive** environment. We see this as the Go option is executed: The source code remains on the screen as if the Realizer environment is running through the source code. This is not what we want in the finished product. Can you imagine the shrieks we would hear if end users were forced to view the source code of an application while it was running? So the goal is to build a running, stand-alone executable from the simple menu we have just created. Typically, this is the last step in the application development process; however, since the menu seems to run under the interpretive environment, we can attempt to build the .EXE file immediately. To do this, open Realizer's Run menu and select Project Builder from the pull-down menu, as shown in Figure 2-11. There is no accelerator key associated with this menu option, so select this option with the mouse.

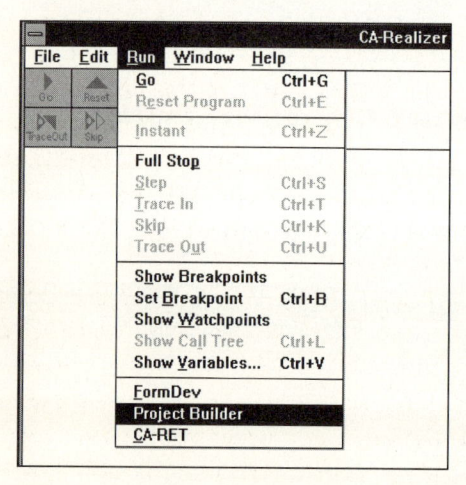

Figure 2-11. Project Builder option off of the RUN menu item.

And then, once this is selected, the following screen should appear:

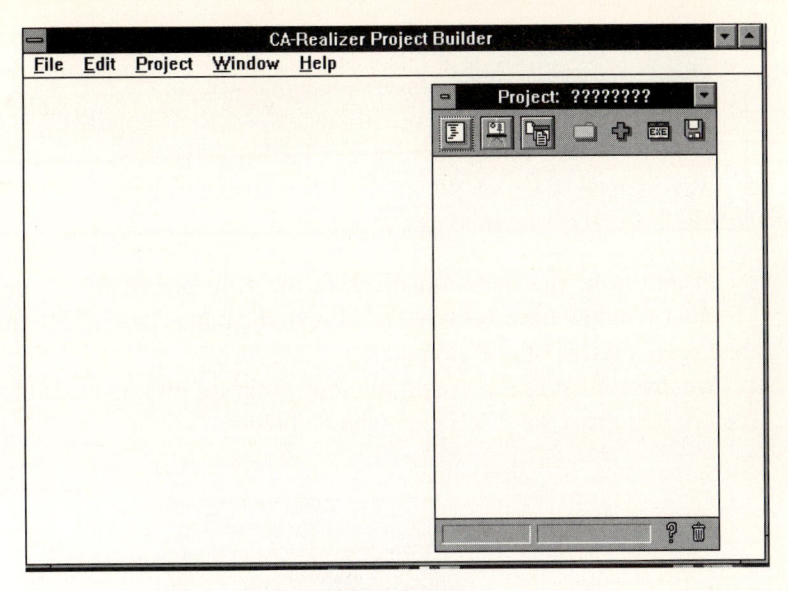

Figure 2-12. Main screen to Project Builder.

In the resulting Project Builder window, shown in Figure 2-12, the Project Builder Toolbar offers a series of icons that will, through the course of this book, begin to make sense. To bring in the source code from the two files, *Menu2.rlz* and *Test2.rlz*, we need to tell the Project Builder that this is to be a new project. To do this, open Project Builder's File menu and select New. In the resulting file-searching dialog box, the default file skeleton of *.RLZ appears in the File Name: box. In the box below there should be a listing of all .RLZ files, including the three files we have created thus far. (More will appear should the source code disk be installed during this instruction.) Select the *Test2.rlz* file.

When the *Test2.rlz* file is selected, the Project Builder Toolbar window will contain a list of the files associated with this application. Realizer will attempt to find all related files and show them in this area of the screen. This means that the RUN command is seen by the system and is able to list the *Menu2.rlz* file along with the selected *Test2.rlz* file. Therefore, it is important to build the application based on the topmost source file in the system.

Note: There are ways you can add dependent source code files for an application that are not explicitly listed as a RUN command to the Project Builder Toolbar screen. For further assistance, please check the user manual or the section in this book concerning the Project Builder.

In addition, the question mark in the title bar of the Project Builder Toolbar window have been replaced with the name `Test2`. Previously, there had been a series of question marks.

We are almost ready to compile our program into an executable file, but before you press the .EXE icon (shown below),

take a quick look at some of the options. To see them, select the Project option from the Project Builder window menu. Halfway down this menu is the EXE Options option; the `F4` key is attached to this selection as well. Choose it (or press the `F4` key), and scan the EXE Options dialog box, shown in Figure 2-13.

The location of the .EXE file, the name or title of the application, as well as start-up options all can be manipulated from this screen. You can even select a different icon for this application. Double clicking on the Icon area of this window opens a dialog box that looks for files with an .ICO file extension. We will take a better look at icons a bit later. For now, either press the `ENTER` key or click on the `OK` button to return to the Project Builder's main window.

Now we are ready to compile the application. Just click on the .EXE icon in the Project Builder Toolbar window. When the compilation is finished, Project Builder will display the message shown in Figure 2-14.

This tells us that the file has been created.

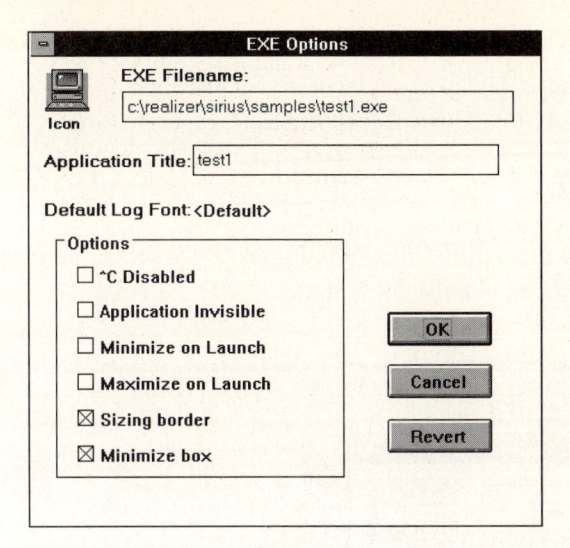

Figure 2-13. Dialog window for Executable Options.

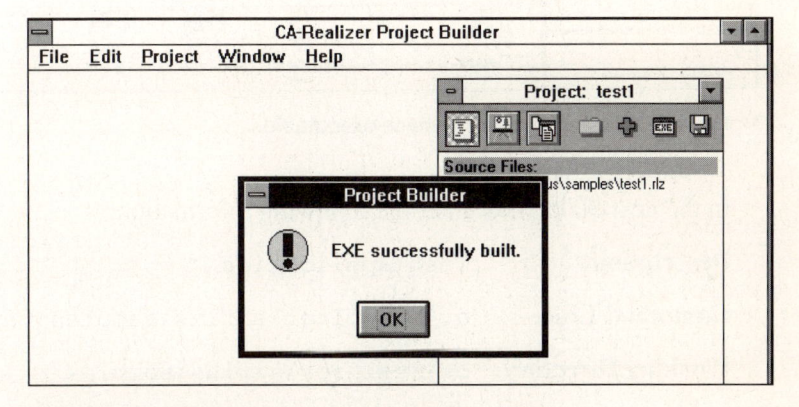

Figure 2-14. Dialog window after successful build.

Step Four

While this seems like the end of the application-building project, there is still one more task. This task is outside of the domain of the Realizer environment, but it needs to be covered. We need to tell Windows' Program Manager of the existence of this new file. This means we have to return to the Program Manager's window, select the File option from the main menu, then select the New option.

> **Note:** When installing an executable in the Windows Program Manager, be sure to activate the appropriate Program Group window *before* you select File - New.

In the resulting dialog box, shown in Figure 2-15, select the Program Item radio button and then click the OK button.

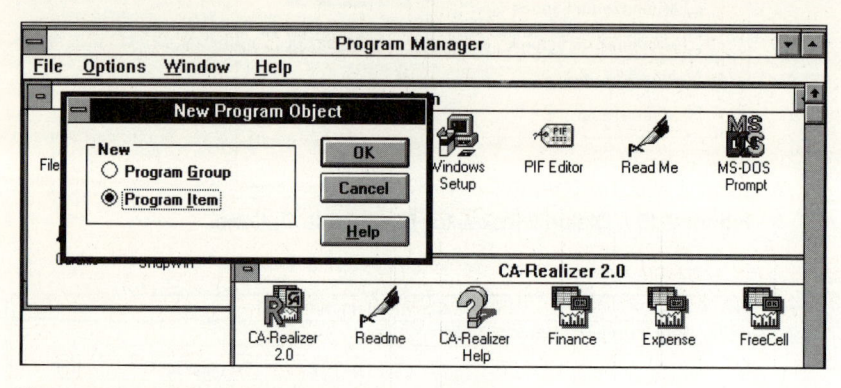

Figure 2-15. Dialog window to place executable.

In the next dialog box enter the following information:

Description: Test Application

Command Line: c:\realizer\sirius\samples\test2.exe

Working Directory: c:\realizer\sirius\samples

Shortcut Key: None

When you click on OK, the associated icon for this application should appear in the proper program group along with the description you entered, as shown in Figure 2-16. To see if this icon will produce the appropriate menu, double-click on it. You should see something like Figure 2-17.

We have now generated a simple menu and installed an icon for the application within the Realizer Program Group. If we were to execute this program, we would see the Realizer system kick in and then clear as the new menu initalizes. When exiting the program, as it stands now, the application would return to the Realizer environment and not to the Realizer program

Menus of an Application 71

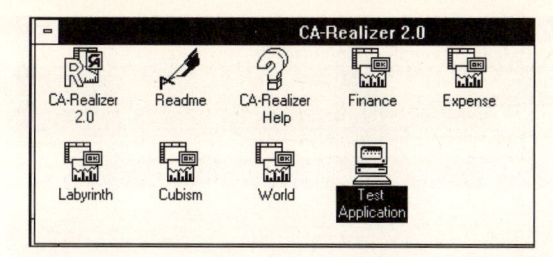

Figure 2-16. Standard Realizer Program Group with new application.

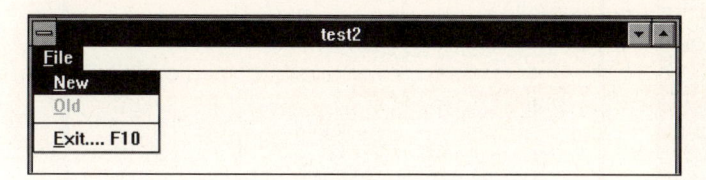

Figure 2-17. Results of TEST2.RLZ being executed.

group within the Windows Program Manager. This is because the command EXIT PROGRAM was used. We could use the command EXIT SYSTEM instead, which would cause the Realizer window to close and control to return to the program group. If EXIT SYSTEM is used in place of EXIT PROGRAM during the Go operation within the environment, the system will not leave Realizer; however, within the executable program, it will.

Step Five

This next step moves us away from the test menus and toward building the menu of an application. We built the text menus by loading program code into the source code editor; this time, we'll use the FormuDev utility program we mentioned earlier. This way, a quick menu can be created without too much hassle. To start, select Run from Realizer's menu bar and choose the FormDev option. Once the logo for the utility is cleared, your screen should look like Figure 2-18.

Keep in mind that we are attempting to build a menu and not a form. The default action for this utility is to build a form; however, we can remove the form from the screen by closing the Form1 window. This will leave just the main menu for the FormDev utility.

To build a menu, open FormDev's Utilities menu and select the Menu Editor option. The resulting Menu Editor dialog box is shown in Figure 2-19.

72   *Chapter 2*

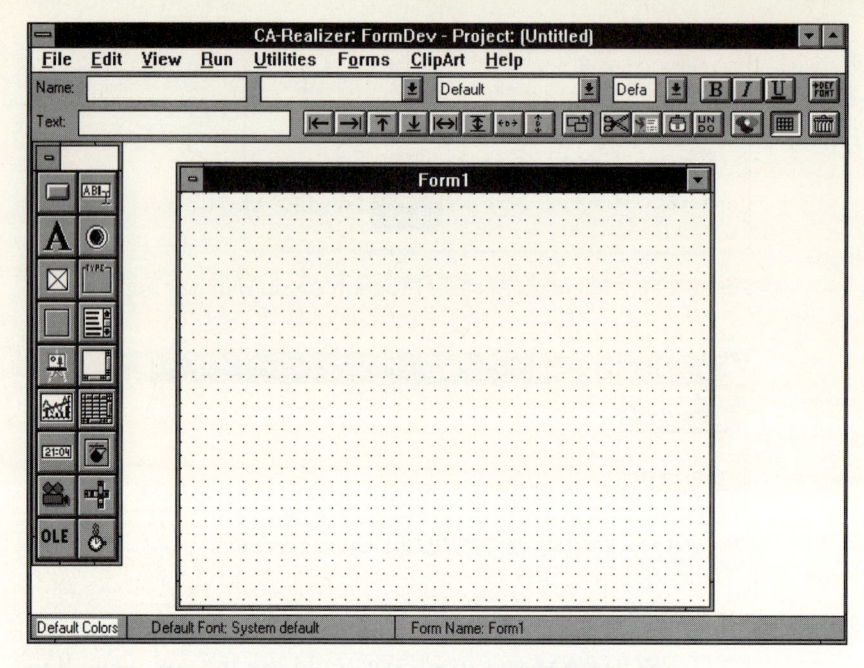

Figure 2-18. Standard opening screen for the FORMDEV utility.

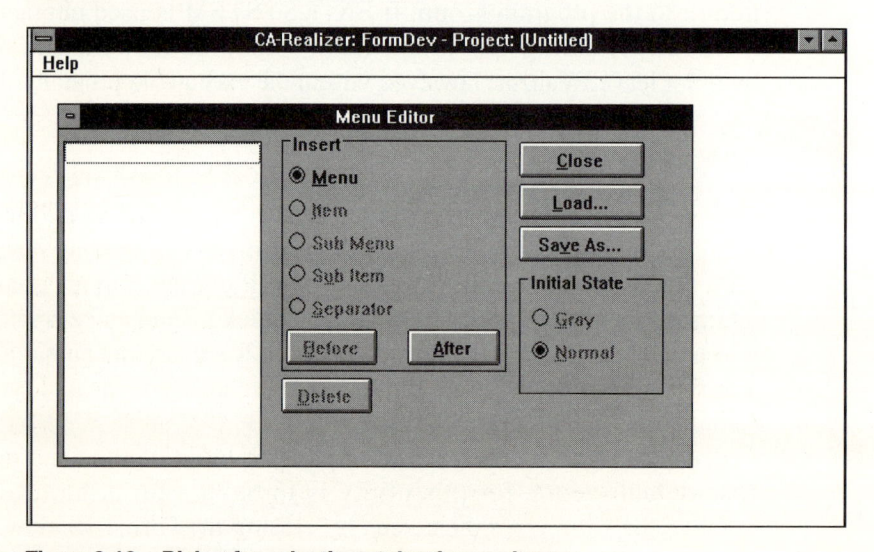

Figure 2-19. Dialog for selection style of menu items.

Menus of an Application

We will start by creating the first layer of menu options—the bar menu that we created earlier using the MENUNEW() function. We will slowly build options interpretively into this editor to create new bar menu options and new pull down menu options. Our goal is to have seven bar menu items in this order: File, View, Edit, Graphs, Tables, Options, and Help. Each of these menu options will offer several other choices that will finish the opening screen for this program. In case you're wondering why we start with a menu item named File, it's a Windows standard. Having a standard look-and-feel to Windows menus cuts down on the learning time for new users of an application. In terms of development, we need to observe the conventions of CUA (Common User Access) menus. To facilitate, let's first look at the menu of a popular word processing program, shown in Figure 2-20.

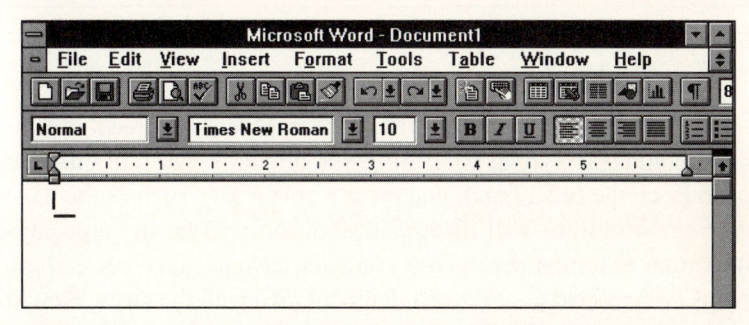

Figure 2-20. Standard Microsoft's Window 6.0 window with menus.

The Windows Program Manager observes this standard, too, as shown in Figure 2-21.

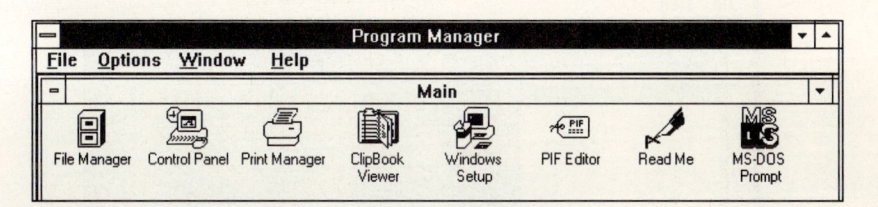

Figure 2-21. Standard menus for Program Manager.

In nearly every Windows application, the first menu option is the File option. To do this in our program, from within the FormDev utility, click on the After button, which will open up the New Menu dialog box, shown in Figure 2-22.

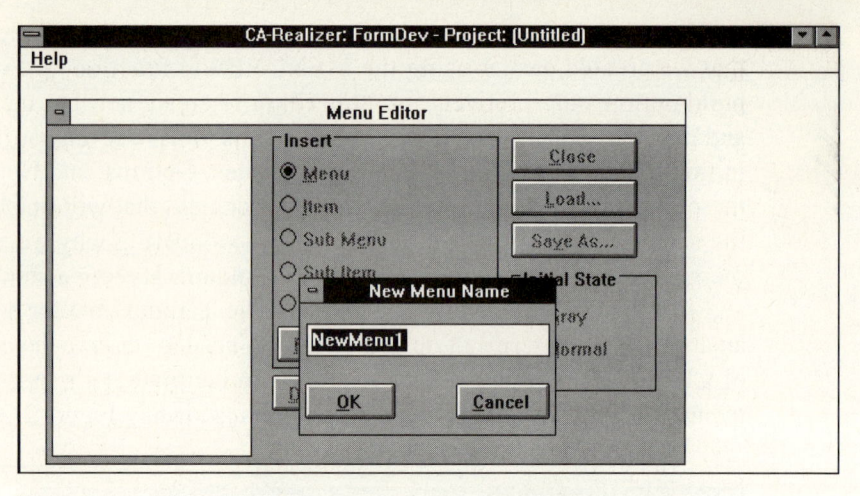

Figure 2-22. Dialog window to create a new menu item.

The default starting menu will be "NewMenu1." Since it is highlighted, the minute you start typing something, the default string will immediately disappear. If, on the other hand, you press a cursor key, such as the RIGHT_ARROW, then the highlight will disappear and you will be in "edit" mode. This is important to remember in case you later have to make corrections to existing items (which, rest assured, will happen). So, with the string NewMenu1 highlighted, type the word File, then either press the ENTER key or click on the OK button. When the text is accepted, it will appear in the empty boxed region on the left side of the Menu Editor dialog box, as shown in Figure 2-23.

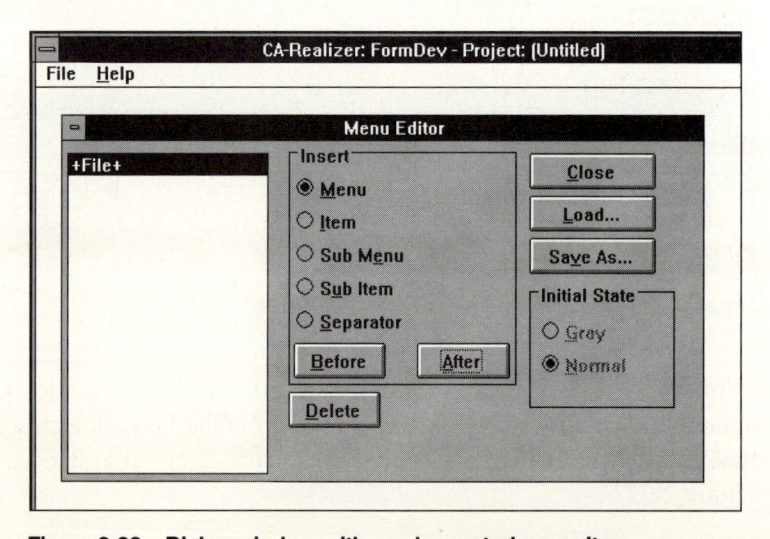

Figure 2-23. Dialog window with newly created menu item.

Menus of an Application 75

This empty region within this dialog box may be called the Menu Stack, for it will contain the tree of menu items that we will be creating. Note that the File menu option now appears in the bar menu. In addition, the Menu Stack is currently highlighting the "+File+" text. Realizer automatically inserts the string delimiters before and after the typed string. Our first menu item has been created. To add the accelerator to the File option, double-click on the "+File+" text. When the Menu Stack contains more menu items, you'll appreciate the ability to scroll through the menu stack and select the menu item to be edited. Once we double-click on this item, we will return to the New Menu Name dialog. Place the mouse cursor just before the letter F, then click the left mouse button once to move the editing cursor into postion. To add the accelerator, type the ampersand character (&). This special character tells Realizer that the letter immediately following will be the accelerator letter. Then press the ENTER key or click on the OK button to return the menu item to the Menu Stack and alter the bar menu at the top of the screen. At this point, your screen should look like Figure 2-24.

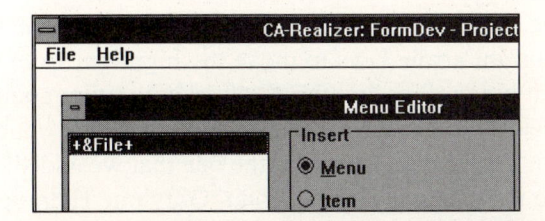

Figure 2-24. Close-up shot of newly created menu item.

Clicking on the AFTER button will allow us to add a new menu item to our bar menu. Clicking the AFTER button tells Realizer that a new menu item is to be added *after* the currently highlighted menu item in the Menu Stack. When there were no menu items, the AFTER button was our way of getting the first menu item into the system. However, now with a menu item in place, the AFTER button means that a new menu item will be added to the stack after the currently highlighted item. You can also use the BEFORE button to add a menu item *before* the currently highlighted item. And by now, you can surely guess what the DELETE button does: It removes the currently highlighted menu item from the stack and from the system.

Now, with all of this in mind, repeat the procedure we just outlined to add the following menu items to the current menu stack: View, Edit, Graphs, Tables, Options, and Help. Each menu item should have as an accelerator the first letter in the string. When you finish, the Menu Editor dialog should look like Figure 2-25.

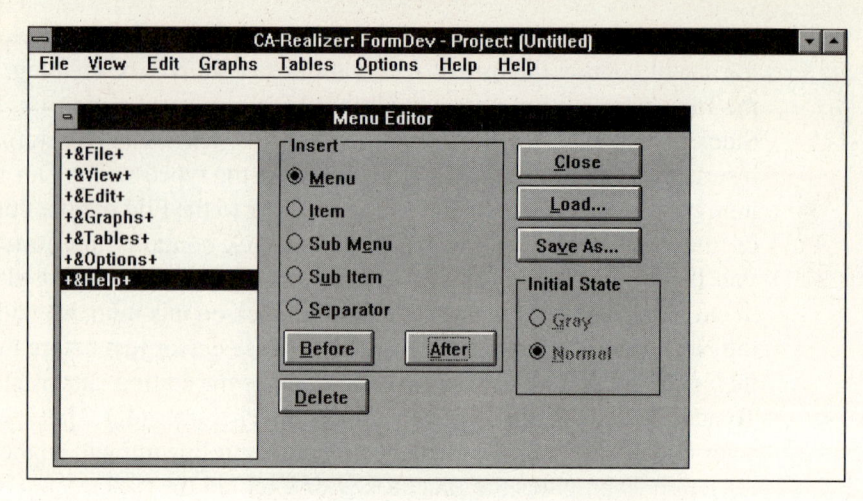

Figure 2-25. Dialog window with several menu items created.

If we press the ALT key, the run-time system of the Menu Editor will execute and the File option across the top of the screen will be highlighted. We can use the left and right arrow keys to move the highlight from option to option across the bar menu. Pressing the ESC key will return control to the Menu Editor. By the way, don't worry about the double Help options at the end of the bar menu. The first Help item is the one that we added; the other Help item is for the FormDev utility program. Only one Help option will appear in the finished application.

So far, we have added only bar menu items. Throughout this exercise, the radio button in the Insert section of the Menu Editor has been on the Menu option. The other Insert options will allow us to create pull-down menus for the bar menu options. As usual, let's start with the File option. Highlight +&File+ in the Menu Stack, Then, click on the Sub Item option in the Insert section.

Before actually inserting a Sub Item under the File option, let me add a brief word on the difference between an Item, a Sub Item, and a Sub Menu. First, a Sub Menu means that the option to be created will have a "child" menu. All of the menu options on the bar menu have Sub Menus stemming from them. This suggests that when a menu item on the bar menu is selected, a pull-down menu will appear. This is what is thought of as a Sub Menu. However, menu items contained within a pull-down menu can lead to other menus. These menus can only be of the pull-down menu type, since there can be only one bar menu and its items exist at the top of the stack. When an item is designated as having another pull-down menu, an ellipsis (...) is added to the end of the menu prompt text. The ellipsis symbol tells the end user that another menu stems from this menu option.

Menus of an Application

An Item and a Sub Item are basically the same thing. They are menu prompts that will stem from either the bar menu or other pull-down menus. These do not lead to other pull-down menus; rather, they suggest specific operations that will take place if selected.

> **Note:** There is no difference between the Item option and the Sub Item option when working off of a menu prompt that is a part of a bar menu. This means that, for example, if the menu option New were created as either an Item or a Sub Item, it would appear no differently on the screen and within the Menu Stack.

Turning back to our example, the highlight should still be on the File option and the Sub Item option within the Menu Editor's Insert section should be selected. Click on the `AFTER` button or press the `ALT-A` key to open the dialog box for adding a menu prompt. Here, we will add the text *Your Cellar*. This item, along with one other, will be special in that they will accept check marks by their names. (This will be explained when we take a look at the generated code.) Click `OK`, then repeat the process to add the &Transaction Files and &Cellar Rack Designer... items.

> **Note:** When there is a Sub Menu item added to the stack, and there is to be a new Sub Item on the same level with that menu item, be careful how the following Sub Item is to be added. One of the tricky items to deal with in this list is Cellar Rack Designer (a Sub Item) added after the Transaction Files (a Sub Menu). The trouble is that even though the radio button for Sub Item is selected, if the `AFTER` button is pressed, Realizer will think that Cellar Rack Designer will be inside of Transaction Files and not on the same level with it.
>
> The solution is simple: Move the highlight to the next item in the Menu Stack list, then click on the `BEFORE` button. This tells Realizer that the next Sub Item (in this case) that is being added will come before the current menu option. This will put the third menu prompt for the Files option on the same level with the Transaction Files option. Once the third menu prompt is added for the Files Sub Menu, then all other prompts can be added using the `AFTER` button instead of the `BEFORE` button.

Now, before adding any more items to this menu prompt, we can imagine that we may want to separate the items in a pull-down menu into categories. So, following this there will be a few more menu prompts; however, these are of a different type or behavior. To help separate items visually within the pull-down menu, we can use a **separator**, a single (or double) bar that appears within the pull-down menu area but cannot be clicked on or highlighted. To add a separator after the &Cellar Rack Designer… item, highlight that item within the Menu Stack, then click on the Separator radio button in the Insert section. Then click on the AFTER button. The screen should now look like Figure 2-26.

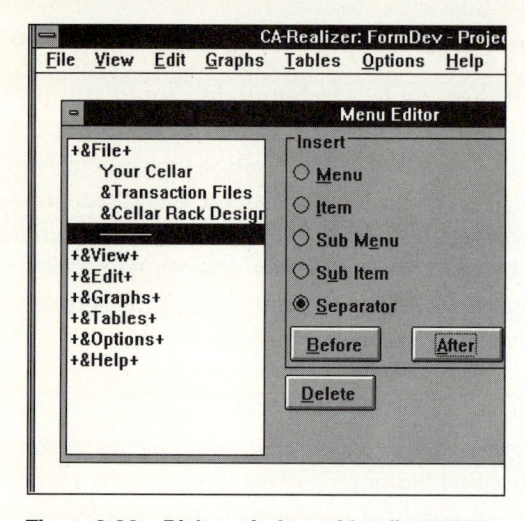

Figure 2-26. Dialog window with adjusted branches of menu items.

As you can see, the stack is being built as each prompt is created.

> **Note:** A Sub-Item or an Item will not have the special "+" characters surrounding the text within the Menu Stack Window. This is normal and tells us that the prompt string we are looking at (the one that is highlighted) does not have a Pull Down Menu stemming from it.

Continue adding the other Sub Items and separators shown in Figure 2-27: Sample Cellar, &Winery Files…, &Make Winery Files, Disclaimer…, &Import && Export, &Backup Data Files…, S&elect Printer…, and Setup &Printer… Sub Items need to be added as well. Note the two ampersands in the middle of

Menus of an Application 79

the &Import&&.Export item. The double ampersands let us tell Realizer to consider the paired ampersands as a single and literal symbol. Within the Menu Stack, both ampersands will appear in the text; however, only one will appear in the pull-down menu. The ampersand at the beginning of the item tells Realizer that the letter I is the accelerator.

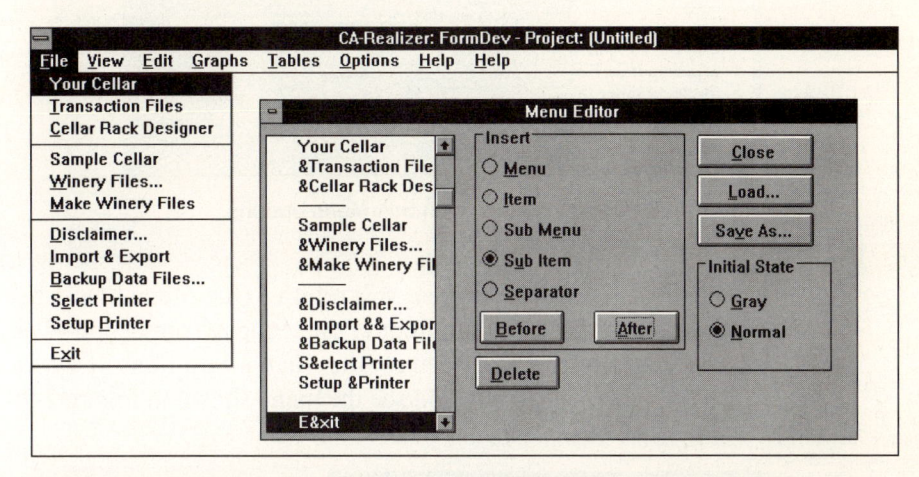

Figure 2-27. Running menu in conjunction with dialog window for menus.

The final menu option, E&xit, is a Sub Item as well. It is common in many applications to assign the `ALT-X` key as the accelerator to exit an application. Even though no other item in this menu stack begins with the letter E, the letter *x* should have the underline character.

Now, up to this point, all of the menu items added off of the File menu selection have been Sub Items. In reality, one of the items needs to be altered from a Sub Item to a Sub Menu. To do this, highlight &Transaction Files in the Menu Stack and click on the `DEL` button. This will remove that item from the stack and move all other items up. The &Cellar Rack Designer option should now be highlighted. Now select the Sub Menu radio button in the Insert section, then either press the `ALT-B` key or click on the `Before` button. Now add the deleted &Transaction Files menu item back into the stack at the proper location (before the &Cellar Rack Designer option), and make it a Sub Menu rather than a Sub Item. The screen should look something like Figure 2-28.

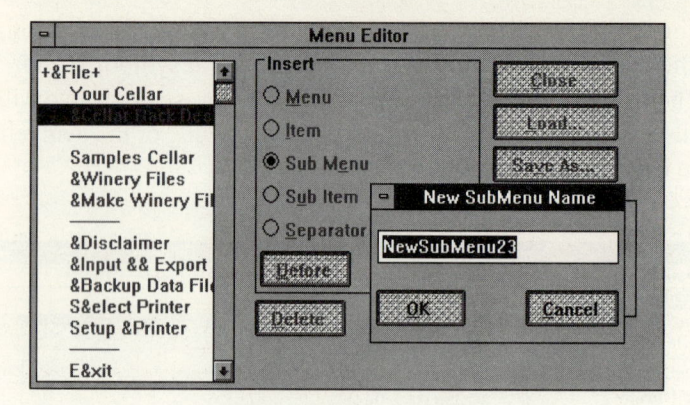

Figure 2-28. Dialog window with Sub Menu options.

When this is added, the item will return to the Menu Stack, but this time, there will be a + character in front of the string &Transaction Files. This tells us that this is now a Sub Menu rather than a Sub Item. If we were to pull down the File menu, we would see the menu shown in Figure 2-29.

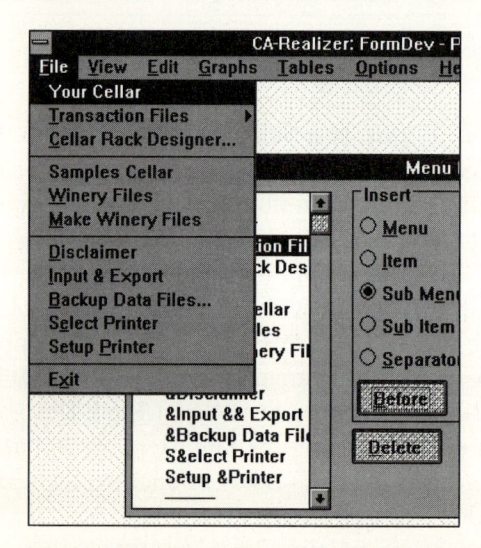

Figure 2-29. Running menu with dialog window in background.

Now, there is a special character to the right of this menu option. This character is automatically added to the item and tells us (a) that this item has been defined as a Sub Menu; and (b) that there will be options stemming from this item.

Menus of an Application

Having completed one pull-down menu, let me add a brief word on the DELETE button. Clicking this button will remove any menu prompt from the menu stack as well as any other nested and associated Sub Menus or Sub Items. Depending on the level of indentation seen within the Menu Stack, you can tell how many items will be deleted when this icon is clicked. In other words, if, for example, +&File+ were highlighted in the Menu Stack when you clicked on the DELETE button, then all of the items under this menu prompt would be removed, including the menu prompt itself.

> **Note:** When the DELETE button is pressed, there is no confirmation dialog box. This means that once the button is pressed, the menu prompt and all subsequent items and menus stemming from that menu prompt will be immediately removed.

Turning back to the several Sub Items within this pull-down menu, there is one more unique feature. Since there is no Sub Menu attached to them (otherwise, there would be a special character appearing to the right of the text), no action can result because there are no additional menu items. Therefore, we will look later on at attaching procedures or subroutines to various menu items.

In the meantime, highlight the Select Printer option in the Menu Stack, then double-click on this item to open the Edit Menu Item dialog box. This time, the box has an added button: Code ..., as shown in Figure 2-30.

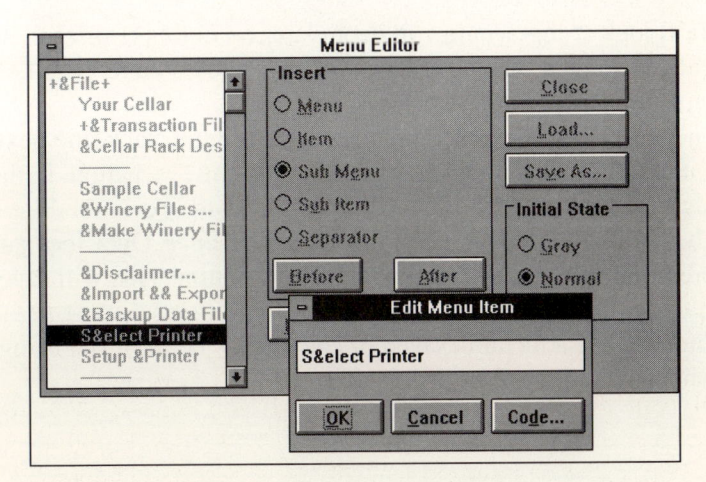

Figure 2-30. Dialog window with editing dialog sub-window.

The `Code` button allows us to attach Realizer code to perform an action should this menu prompt get selected. If you click on the `Code` button, a new window will open, shown in Figure 2-31.

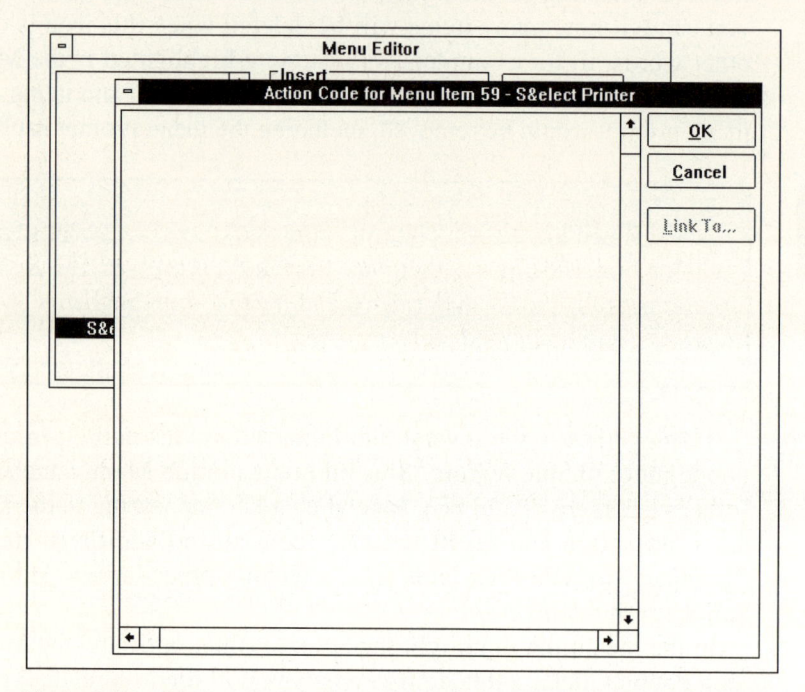

Figure 2-31. Dialog window for action code to be taken with menu items.

We'll look at this window in depth later on in this tutorial as the application begins to take shape. For now, the goal should be to get all of the menu prompts in place.

Once all of the menu prompts are added to the stack, the next task is to save it to a file. To do this, click on the `SAVE AS...` button. In the resulting dialog box, shown in Figure 2-32, the wild-card text in the File Name box will be highlighted. Just type in the string *Decanter*. Once the name is typed in, press the `ENTER` key or click on the `OK` button. This will save the menu form under the name of `Decanter.rfm` into the `C:\REALIZER\FDMENU` directory. Once a menu is saved, it can always be retrieved using the `LOAD` button from the FormDev Utility screen.

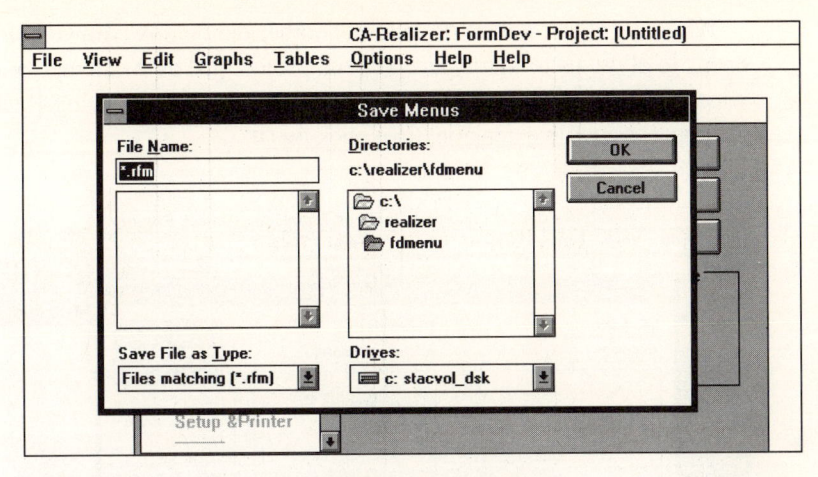

Figure 2-32. Standard SAVE MENU dialog window.

Once the menus are created and saved, we can press the CLOSE button in the Menu Editor to return to the main FormDev window. When we do, the running menu that we are creating for the `Decanter.rfm` file will close and the FormDev Utility menu will take its place. Therefore, the File option that is now on the screen will be that of the FormDev Utility program and *not* the File option that was created for the `Decanter.rfm` program.

We now want to exit. When we exit via the File menu, Realizer will display the dialog box shown in Figure 2-33, asking if we want to save the current project before exiting the FormDev utility.

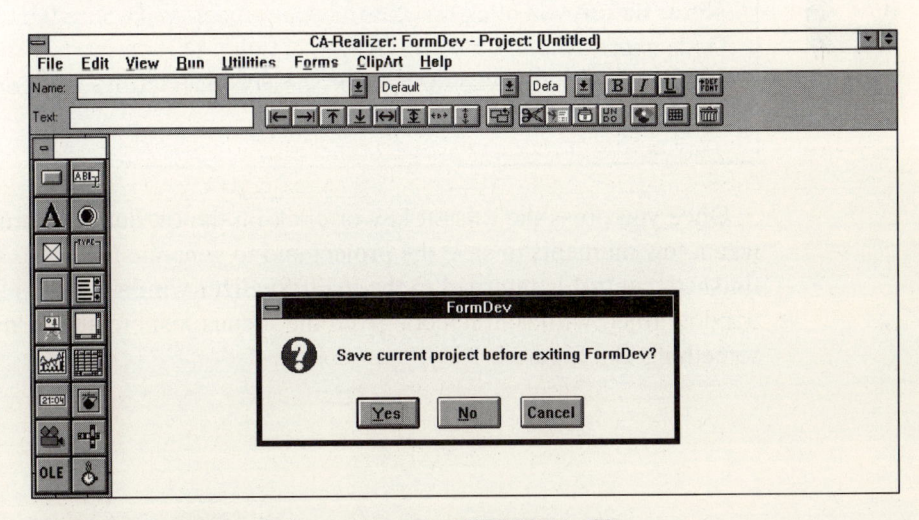

Figure 2-33. Dialog window to leave the FORMDEV utility.

When we click on the YES button, another dialog box (shown in Figure 2-34) opens to allow us to name and save the project just as we named and saved the window. To be consistent, type in the string *Decanter*, allowing Realizer to add the appropriate file extension, then click on OK.

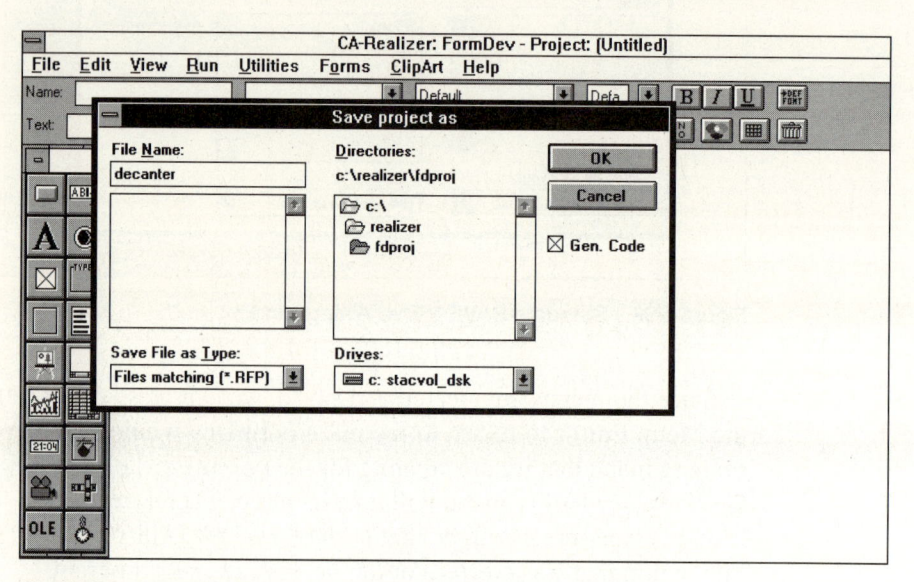

Figure 2-34. Dialog window to SAVE the product to special file.

Note: Before you click on OK to save a project, make sure the Gen. Code check box is turned on (has an X in it). This way, when the project (and menu) is saved to the disk, the FormDev utility will generate the code for this.

Once you press the ENTER key or click on the OK button, FormDev will take a few moments to save the project and to generate the code. When it is finished, control is returned to the main Realizer window, which contains a window filled with source code from the menus just created. It might look something like Figure 2-35.

Menus of an Application 85

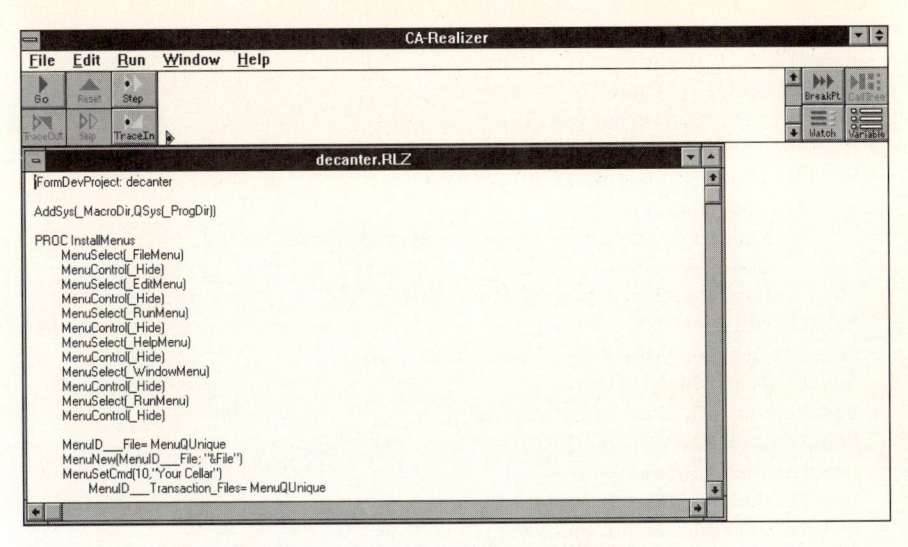

Figure 2-35. Open source code window of generated menu.

Since we did not have a form associated with this project, only one file will be created: *Decanter.rlz*. This file will contain all of the menus that were created using the FormDev Utility program. It looks something like this:

```
'FormDevProject: decanter

AddSys(_MacroDir,QSys(_ProgDir))

PROC InstallMenus
      MenuSelect(_FileMenu)
      MenuControl(_Hide)
      MenuSelect(_EditMenu)
      MenuControl(_Hide)
      MenuSelect(_RunMenu)
      MenuControl(_Hide)
      MenuSelect(_HelpMenu)
      MenuControl(_Hide)
      MenuSelect(_WindowMenu)
      MenuControl(_Hide)
      MenuSelect(_RunMenu)
      MenuControl(_Hide)

      MenuID___File= MenuQUnique
      MenuNew(MenuID___File; "&File")
      MenuSetCmd(10,"Your Cellar")
             MenuID___Transaction_Files= MenuQUnique
             MenuNew(MenuID___Transaction_Files, MenuID___File; "&Transaction Files")
             MenuSetProc(decanterMenuProc)
```

```
        MenuSelect(MenuID___File)
        MenuSetCmd(_Separator)
        MenuSetCmd(20,"&Sample Cellar")
        MenuSetCmd(30,"&Winery Files ...")
        MenuSetCmd(40,"&Make Winery Files")
        MenuSetCmd(50,"&Disclaimer ...")
        MenuSetCmd(_Separator)
                MenuID___Import___Export= MenuQUnique
                MenuNew(MenuID___Import___Export, MenuID___File; "Import && &Export")
                MenuSetProc(decanterMenuProc)
        MenuSelect(MenuID___File)
        MenuSetCmd(60,"&Backup Data Files ...")
        MenuSetCmd(_Separator)
        MenuSetCmd(70,"Se&lect Printer")
        MenuSetCmd(80,"Setup &Printer")
        MenuSetCmd(_Separator)
        MenuSetCmd(90,"E&xit Program")
        MenuSetProc(decanterMenuProc)
        MenuControl(_Show)

        MenuID___View= MenuQUnique
        MenuNew(MenuID___View; "&View")
                MenuID___Index_Listings= MenuQUnique
                MenuNew(MenuID___Index_Listings, MenuID___View; "&Index Listings")
                MenuSetCmd(100,"&All Wines in Cellar")
                MenuSetCmd(_Separator)
                MenuSetCmd(110,"Wines to Drink &Now ...")
                MenuSetCmd(120,"Wines at best in &Future")
                MenuSetCmd(130,"Wines to be &Tasted")
                MenuSetCmd(_Separator)
                MenuSetCmd(140,"Non &Vintage Wine")
                MenuSetCmd(150,"&Young Wines")
                MenuSetCmd(160,"&Improving Wines")
                MenuSetCmd(170,"&Mature Wines")
                MenuSetCmd(180,"Wines in &Danger")
                MenuSetProc(decanterMenuProc)
    MenuSelect(MenuID___View)
                MenuID___Search___Sort_options___ = MenuQUnique
                MenuNew(MenuID___Search___Sort_options___, MenuID___View; \\
                                "&Search and Sort options ...")
                MenuSetCmd(190,"To &Screen ...")
                MenuSetCmd(200,"To &Printer ...")
                MenuSetProc(decanterMenuProc)
        MenuSelect(MenuID___View)
        MenuSetCmd(210,"&Multiple Field Search")
        MenuSetCmd(_Separator)
        MenuSetCmd(220,"&GoldBook for Decanter")
        MenuSetCmd(230,"Winery to &Region ...")
        MenuSetCmd(_Separator)
```

```
        MenuID___Clear_Wine_Rack= MenuQUnique
        MenuNew(MenuID___Clear_Wine_Rack, MenuID___View; "&Clear Wine Rack")
        MenuSetCmd(240,"  1 : -")
        MenuSetCmd(250,"  2 : -")
        MenuSetCmd(260,"  3 : -")
        MenuSetCmd(270,"  4 : -")
        MenuSetCmd(280,"  5 : -")
        MenuSetCmd(290,"  6 : -")
        MenuSetCmd(300,"  7 : -")
        MenuSetCmd(310,"  8 : -")
        MenuSetCmd(320,"  9 : -")
        MenuSetCmd(330,"10 : -")
        MenuSetCmd(340,"11 : -")
        MenuSetCmd(350,"12 : -")
        MenuSetCmd(360,"13 : -")
        MenuSetCmd(370,"14 : -")
        MenuSetCmd(380,"15 : -")
        MenuSetCmd(390,"16 : -")
        MenuSetCmd(_Separator)
        MenuSetCmd(400,"Overall view of Bins 1 .. 256")
        MenuSetCmd(410,"Overall view of Bins 257 .. 512")
        MenuSetProc(decanterMenuProc)
MenuSelect(MenuID___View)
MenuSetProc(decanterMenuProc)
MenuControl(_Show)

MenuID___Edit= MenuQUnique
MenuNew(MenuID___Edit; "&Edit")
MenuSetCmd(420,"&Add a New Wine")
MenuSetCmd(430,"&Edit Existing Wine")
MenuSetCmd(_Separator)
MenuSetCmd(440,"&Global Search and Replace ...")
MenuSetProc(decanterMenuProc)
MenuControl(_Show)

MenuID___Grapsh= MenuQUnique
MenuNew(MenuID___Grapsh; "&Graphs")
MenuSetCmd(450,"&Health Report")
MenuSetCmd(460,"Value and &Stock ...")
MenuSetCmd(_Separator)
MenuSetCmd(470,"&Vintages")
MenuSetCmd(480,"&BestAt for all Wines")
MenuSetCmd(490,"BestAt for &Grape Variety")
MenuSetCmd(500,"&Aging Curve ...")
MenuSetCmd(_Separator)
        MenuID___Distribution_Graphs= MenuQUnique
        MenuNew(MenuID___Distribution_Graphs, MenuID___Grapsh; \\
                                      "&Distribution Graphs")
        MenuSetCmd(510,"&Winery")
```

```
        MenuSetCmd(520,"&Region")
        MenuSetCmd(530,"&Variety")
        MenuSetProc(decanterMenuProc)
MenuSelect(MenuID___Grapsh)
MenuSetProc(decanterMenuProc)
MenuControl(_Show)

MenuID___Tables= MenuQUnique
MenuNew(MenuID___Tables; "&Tables")
MenuSetCmd(540,"&Variety vs Vintage vs Bottles")
MenuSetCmd(550,"Variety vs Best&At vs Bottle")
MenuSetCmd(_Separator)
MenuSetCmd(560,"'Label' vs Vintage vs &Bottle")
MenuSetCmd(570,"'Label' vs Vintage vs &Maturity")
MenuSetCmd(_Separator)
MenuSetCmd(580,"'&TimeLine' of all Wines in Cellar")
MenuSetProc(decanterMenuProc)
MenuControl(_Show)

MenuID___Options= MenuQUnique
MenuNew(MenuID___Options; "&Options")
MenuSetCmd(590,"&Preferences......")
MenuSetCmd(600,"&Fonts ...")
MenuSetCmd(_Separator)
   MenuID___BestAt_Tollerance____= MenuQUnique
   MenuNew(MenuID___BestAt_Tollerance____, MenuID___Options; \\
                        "&BestAt Tollerance")
      MenuSetCmd(610,"&Single")
      MenuSetCmd(620,"&PlusMinus")
      MenuSetCmd(630,"&Auto")
      MenuSetProc(decanterMenuProc)
MenuSelect(MenuID___Options)
MenuSetCmd(640,"&Danger + Decline")
MenuSetCmd(650,"&Resource Monitor")
MenuSetProc(decanterMenuProc)
MenuControl(_Show)

MenuID___Help= MenuQUnique
MenuNew(MenuID___Help; "&Help")
MenuSetCmd(660,"&Using Windows Help")
MenuSetCmd(670,"Decanter &Help")
MenuSetCmd(_Separator)
MenuSetCmd(680,"How to &Register ...")
MenuSetCmd(690,"&Pricing Details ...")
MenuSetCmd(700,"Print Registration &Form ...")
MenuSetCmd(710,"&Customer Support")
MenuSetCmd(720,"I am &Licensed to")
MenuSetCmd(_Separator)
MenuSetCmd(730,"System &Information")
```

```
    MenuSetCmd(740,"&About Decanter")
    MenuSetProc(decanterMenuProc)
    MenuControl(_Show)

END PROC

PROC decanterMenuProc(params)
    MenuSelect(params[_MenuNum])
    SELECT CASE params[_ItemNum]




    END SELECT
END PROC
InstallMenus
'Main Project Code
```

The next step is to move the file to the \Realizer\Sirius\Apps directory. Once there, we can begin to break this code out, just as we did with the Test2.rlz file, or we can use a DOS-based program editor to manage the file for us. In the end, one file named Decanter.rlz should look like this:

```
'* Application ... : Decanter.rlz
'* Authors ....... : Steve Straley
'* Notice ........ : Copyright(c) 1994 - Sirius Press, Inc.
'* .............. : All Rights Reserved
'* Date .......... : January 1, 1994
'* Description ... : This contains the basic Decanter program
'*

addsys(_MACRODIR, qsys(_PROGDIR))

sethourglass()                               ' Change the mouse cursor
run "\realizer\sirius\apps\dmenu.rlz"        ' Load the menus
ClearMenus()                                 ' Clear Realizer Menus
InstallMenus()                               ' Paint Decanter's Menus
resethourglass()                             ' Put back the mouse cursor

'Main Project Code

'* End of File: Decanter.rlz
```

and a new file holding the menus called Dmenu.rlz should look like this (along with some additional modifications):

```
'* Application ... : DMenu.rlz
'* Authors ....... : Steve Straley
'* Notice ........ : Copyright(c) 1994 - Sirius Press, Inc.
'* ..............  : All Rights Reserved
'* Date .......... : January 1, 1994
'* Description ... : This contains the code for the menus for Decanter.rlz
'*

'* Name:          ClearMenus
'* Purpose:       To Clear the REALIZER menu routines
'* Returns:       N/A

proc ClearMenus()

    sethourglass()                  'Make the hour glass appear....
    menuselect(_FILEMENU)           'Refer to the FILE menu on the top
    menucontrol(_HIDE)              '... and hide it
    menuselect(_EDITMENU)           'Refer to the EDIT menu on the top
    menucontrol(_HIDE)              '... and hide it
    menuselect(_RUNMENU)            'Do the same with the RUN menu
    menucontrol(_HIDE)              '
    menuselect(_HELPMENU)           'And the HELP menu
    menucontrol(_HIDE)              '
    menuselect(_WINDOWMENU)         'And the WINDOW menu
    menucontrol(_HIDE)              ' and hide it as well

end proc

'* Name:          InstallMenus
'* Purpose:       To Install the menus for Decanter
'* Returns:       N/A

proc InstallMenus()

   iMenuIDFile = menuqunique
   menunew(iMenuIDFile; "&File")
   menusetcmd(10, "Your Cellar"; _CHECK)
      '* Now create the Transaction sub-menu

      iMenuIDTransaction_Files= menuqunique
      menunew(iMenuIDTransaction_Files, iMenuIDFile; "&Transaction Files")
      menusetproc(decanterMenuProc)

   menuselect(iMenuIDFile)
   menusetcmd(_SEPARATOR)
   menusetcmd(20, "&Sample Cellar")
   menusetcmd(30, "&Winery Files ...")
   menusetcmd(40, "&Make Winery Files")
   menusetcmd(50, "&Disclaimer ...")
```

```
menusetcmd(_SEPARATOR)
  '* Now create the Import/Export sub-menu

  iMenuIDImportExport = menuqunique
  menunew(iMenuIDImportExport, iMenuIDFile; "Import && &Export")
  menusetproc(decanterMenuProc)

menuselect(iMenuIDFile)
menusetcmd(60, "&Backup Data Files ...")
menusetcmd(_SEPARATOR)
menusetcmd(70, "Se&lect Printer")
menusetcmd(80, "Setup &Printer")
menusetcmd(_SEPARATOR)
menusetcmd(90, "E&xit Program")
menusetproc(decanterMenuProc)
MenuControl(_SHOW)

iMenuIDView = menuqunique
menunew(iMenuIDView; "&View")
  iMenuIDIndexListings = menuqunique
  menunew(iMenuIDIndexListings, iMenuIDView; "&Index Listings")
  menusetcmd(100, "&All Wines in Cellar")
  menusetcmd(_SEPARATOR)
  menusetcmd(110, "Wines to Drink &Now ...")
  menusetcmd(120, "Wines at best in &Future")
  menusetcmd(130, "Wines to be &Tasted")
  menusetcmd(_SEPARATOR)
  menusetcmd(140, "Non &Vintage Wine")
  menusetcmd(150, "&Young Wines")
  menusetcmd(160, "&Improving Wines")
  menusetcmd(170, "&Mature Wines")
  menusetcmd(180, "Wines in &Danger")
  menusetproc(decanterMenuProc)

menuselect(iMenuIDView)

  iMenuIDSearchSort = menuqunique
  menunew(iMenuIDSearchSort, iMenuIDView; "&Search and Sort options...")
  menusetcmd(190, "To &Screen ...")
  menusetcmd(200, "To &Printer ...")
  menusetproc(decanterMenuProc)

menuselect(iMenuIDView)
menusetcmd(210, "&Multiple Field Search")
menusetcmd(_SEPARATOR)
menusetcmd(220, "&GoldBook for Decanter")
menusetcmd(230, "Winery to &Region ...")
menusetcmd(_SEPARATOR)
```

```
            iMenuIDClearWineRack= menuqunique
            menunew(iMenuIDClearWineRack, iMenuIDView; "&Clear Wine Rack")
            menusetcmd(240, "  1 : -")
            menusetcmd(250, "  2 : -")
            menusetcmd(260, "  3 : -")
            menusetcmd(270, "  4 : -")
            menusetcmd(280, "  5 : -")
            menusetcmd(290, "  6 : -")
            menusetcmd(300, "  7 : -")
            menusetcmd(310, "  8 : -")
            menusetcmd(320, "  9 : -")
            menusetcmd(330, "10 : -")
            menusetcmd(340, "11 : -")
            menusetcmd(350, "12 : -")
            menusetcmd(360, "13 : -")
            menusetcmd(370, "14 : -")
            menusetcmd(380, "15 : -")
            menusetcmd(390, "16 : -")
            menusetcmd(_SEPARATOR)
            menusetcmd(400, "Overall view of Bins 1 .. 256")
            menusetcmd(410, "Overall view of Bins 257 .. 512")
            menusetproc(decanterMenuProc)

    menuselect(iMenuIDView)
    menusetproc(decanterMenuProc)
    MenuControl(_SHOW)

    iMenuIDEdit = menuqunique
    menunew(iMenuIDEdit; "&Edit")
    menusetcmd(420, "&Add a New Wine")
    menusetcmd(430, "&Edit Existing Wine")
    menusetcmd(_SEPARATOR)
    menusetcmd(440, "&Global Search and Replace ...")
    menusetproc(decanterMenuProc)
    menucontrol(_SHOW)

    iMenuIDGraph = menuqunique
    menunew(iMenuIDGraph; "&Graphs")
    menusetcmd(450, "&Health Report")
    menusetcmd(460, "Value and &Stock ...")
    menusetcmd(_SEPARATOR)
    menusetcmd(470, "&Vintages")
    menusetcmd(480, "&BestAt for all Wines")
    menusetcmd(490, "BestAt for &Grape Variety")
    menusetcmd(500, "&Aging Curve ...")
    menusetcmd(_SEPARATOR)

        iMenuIDDistrib = menuqunique
        menunew(iMenuIDDistrib, iMenuIDGraph; "&Distribution Graphs")
        menusetcmd(510, "&Winery")
```

```
    menusetcmd(520, "&Region")
    menusetcmd(530, "&Variety")
    menusetproc(decanterMenuProc)

menuselect(iMenuIDGraph)
menusetproc(decanterMenuProc)
menucontrol(_SHOW)

iMenuIDTables = menuqunique
menunew(iMenuIDTables; "&Tables")
menusetcmd(540, "&Variety vs Vintage vs Bottles")
menusetcmd(550, "Variety vs Best&At vs Bottle")
menusetcmd(_SEPARATOR)
menusetcmd(560, "'Label' vs Vintage vs &Bottle")
menusetcmd(570, "'Label' vs Vintage vs &Maturity")
menusetcmd(_SEPARATOR)
menusetcmd(580, "'&TimeLine' of all Wines in Cellar")
menusetproc(decanterMenuProc)
menucontrol(_SHOW)

iMenuIDOptions = menuqunique
menunew(iMenuIDOptions; "&Options")
menusetcmd(590, "&Preferences......")
menusetcmd(600, "&Fonts ...")
menusetcmd(_SEPARATOR)

    iMenuIDBestAt = menuqunique
    menunew(iMenuIDBestAt, iMenuIDOptions; "&BestAt Tollerance")
    menusetcmd(610, "&Single")
    menusetcmd(620, "&PlusMinus")
    menusetcmd(630, "&Auto")
    menusetproc(decanterMenuProc)

menuselect(iMenuIDOptions)
menusetcmd(640, "&Danger + Decline")
menusetcmd(650, "&Resource Monitor")
menusetproc(decanterMenuProc)
menucontrol(_SHOW)

iMenuIDHelp = menuqunique
menunew(iMenuIDHelp; "&Help")
menusetcmd(660, "&Using Windows Help")
menusetcmd(670, "Decanter &Help")
menusetcmd(_SEPARATOR)
menusetcmd(680, "How to &Register ...")
menusetcmd(690, "&Pricing Details ...")
menusetcmd(700, "Print Registration &Form ...")
menusetcmd(710, "&Customer Support")
menusetcmd(720, "I am &Licensed to")
```

```
    menusetcmd(_SEPARATOR)
    menusetcmd(730, "System &Information")
    menusetcmd(740, "&About Decanter")
    menusetproc(decanterMenuProc)
    menucontrol(_SHOW)

end proc

proc DecanterMenuProc( aParams )

    menuselect( aParams[_MENUNUM] )

    select case aParams[_ITEMNUM]

        case 10              ' selection on Your cellar
          menusetcmd(20; _UNCHECK)
          menusetcmd(10; _CHECK )

        case 20              ' selection on Sample cellar
          menusetcmd(20; _CHECK)
          menusetcmd(10; _UNCHECK )

        case 90              ' The EXIT option
           reset _ALL
           exit system

    end select

end proc

'* End of FIle: DMenu.rlz
```

There are some things to consider with this modified file. As you can see, the menu information has been separated from the main module created by the FormDev utility. One of the nice features of FormDev is that it will indent the various menus based on the level of the menu item. The results parallels nicely with the list-box display of menu structure within the utility itself.

> **Note:** The FormDev utility does not generate code that follows the standards outlined at the top of this chapter. This means that source code generated by this utility will need modifications if it is to conform.

Again, just as we did for the *Test2.rlz* and *Menu2.rlz* files, here we created a new procedure named *ClearMenus()* which contains all of the instructions to remove the various Realizer menus from the screen. This procedure is then called within the `Decanter.rlz` file. Also, all of the variables in this module were reduced and adjusted to fit our Hungarian notation style of coding.

Within the *DecanterMenuProc()* procedure also created by the FormDev utility, the CASE command tests for a menu selection with a pointer of 90. This value is assigned by FormDev when the various menus items are added using the MENUSETCMD() function. The code looks like this:

```
menusetcmd(90, "E&xit Program")
```

The numbering scheme is automatic within FormDev.

Also, used for the first time in this module, is the case for a sub-menu to be added as an item in another menu. The code looks like this:

```
iMenuIDBestAt = menuqunique
menunew(iMenuIDBestAt, iMenuIDOptions; "&BestAt Tollerance")
menusetcmd(610, "&Single")
menusetcmd(620, "&PlusMinus")
menusetcmd(630, "&Auto")
menusetproc(decanterMenuProc)
```

First, the variable *iMenuIDBestAt* holds the unique pointer to be used by the MENUEW() function. Then, when this function is called, the second parameter is another unique point. This references how the association is to be made. In essence, the menu for BestAt Tollerance will be attached to the Options submenu, and contained within this submenu will be three menu items: Single, PlusMinus, and Auto.

> **Note:** Be careful when using the MENUNEW() function in this manner. There is a semicolon following the second parameter, *not* a comma.

Check Marks

At the start of the program there is unique internal constant used with one of the first menu items available:

```
menunew(iMenuIDFile; "&File")
menusetcmd(10, "Your Cellar"; _CHECK)
```

The internal constant of _CHECK tells the MENUSETCMD() that this menu item will have a check mark to the left of the first letter in the display when the menu is first displayed. Check marks may be toggled.

These menu items have identification numbers associated with them as well. Within the CASE structure, the following code appears:

```
case 10                 ' selection on Your cellar
menusetcmd(20; _UNCHECK)
menusetcmd(10; _CHECK )

case 20                 ' selection on Sample cellar
menusetcmd(20; _CHECK)
menusetcmd(10; _UNCHECK )
```

If the first menu item is selected, then the menu with an ID number of 20 will be told to have an _UNCHECK mark, while the menu with ID number 10 is given a _CHECK mark. The exact opposite holds if the menu with ID number 20 is selected instead of the first.

Finally, the EXIT SYSTEM command is used to return control to the Windows Program Manager should this menu option be selected. As new features and items are added to the application, this SELECT CASE instruction set will continue to grow and evolve.

Terms

We have used many terms in this section. Following is a list of them and their definitions.

Accelerator	A special key or key combination that, when pressed, activates a menu item.
Bar Menu	A type of menu whose prompts appear horizontally across the screen. Other menu items stem from each prompt, typically in a pull-down menu.
Dialog Box	A window screen region that contains several objects, either for display purposes or for acquiring additional information. Typically, it contains at least one Push Button object for confirmation.
Drop-Down List	A graphical user interface device that contains a series of choices visible on the screen and typically connected to some input device.
Hungarian Notation	A style of programming that helps identify various parts of an application, including commands, functions, and memory variables.

Internal Constant	A special key word, always preceded by an underscore character, that gives special instructions to various Realizer functions.
Interpreter	A type of environment that reads and "interprets" each line of code and translates it into machine code. It is the opposite of a compiler.
List Box	A boxed area that contains a series of items that may be selected or de-selected.
Procedure	A series of instructions, such as operations, commands, or functions, that are bound together by a name.
Pull-Down Menu	A type of menu whose prompts appear vertically, usually in a boxed frame. A pull-down menu stems from another menu prompt in either a bar menu or another pull-down menu.
Push Button	A graphical user interface device used to simulate a button being pressed to start an action.
Subroutine	Another name for a procedure.
Toolbar	A series of graphical icons, typically across the top of a screen, that may be used in place of menu items.

Conclusion

Menus are easy to build and modify in Realizer. They are some of the most important aspects of building an application. Choosing the correct wording; establishing the proper layout of the various menus, submenus, and items; and finally, selecting other visual prompts, such as check marks, graying of a menu item, and accelerators all add to the menu and ultimately, end-user acceptance.

Chapter 3

More Programming Concepts

In the previous chapter, we took the basic knowledge of the language to build the beginning of an application by constructing a menu system. While a good menu design is important, it is hardly the total picture. The concept of data is the most important aspect of application development: how to get data, how to manipulate it, and how to format it for output. Before we can even begin to tackle this problem, there are a few more programming fundamentals that we need to consider. In this chapter, we'll expand on our understanding of parameters, as well as data types, and conduct an in-depth examination of arrays, families, and ultimately, records.

Parameters—The Next Step

In Chapter 1 we looked at what makes a parameter, how a function or procedures receives a parameter, and how a parameter can be passed from one calling routine to the next. Now, we need to take a deeper look at parameter passing. Up to this point, we have not cared how a parameter is passed, since parameters have not been important to the overall flow of the application. However, there are times, especially with the use of functions, when how a parameter is passed is just as important as the value or data type of that parameter. There are two ways in which a parameter from one routine may be passed to another: **by value** or **by reference**.

Passing by Reference

This is the default and the most common way in which data is passed from one routine to the next. This means that when a variable is passed as a parameter from one routine to the next, the receiving subroutine can alter the parameter's value and, if applicable, the data type. In essence, the address pointer for the variable—not a copy of the address (or variable)—is passed down into the subroutine. This means that if a variable is passed by reference (and by accident, I may add), then the called subroutine can alter the value, which changes the original variable's value in the original calling routine. This potentially dangerous possibility is another reason for using strongly typed variables. To better understand what might happen, consider the following source code module:

```
'* Application ... : Params2.rlz
'* Authors ....... : Steve Straley
'* Notice ........ : Copyright(c) 1994 - Sirius Press, Inc.
'* ............... : All Rights Reserved
'* Date .......... : January 1, 1994
'* Description ... : This shows how a variable may be passed by reference.

'* Name:               ThisTest()
'* Parameters:         <iVar>
'* Purpose:            To alter the value of the assigned variable

proc ThisTest( iVariable )

   print "Just about to assign a value"    '* Just show that we are here
   iVariable = 23                          '* Assign the new value

end proc

'* This is the main routine of the file
dim iValue as integer          '* Initialize and declare a variable
iValue = 1                     '* Assign a value to the variable
print iValue                   '* Print the value out to the PRINT LOG
ThisTest( iValue )             '* Call procedure, passing by REFERENCE
print iValue                   '* Reprint the value
clear iValue                   '* Ready for the next time through

'* End of File: Params2.rlz
```

When the variable *iValue* is declared an integer data type, it is ready to be assigned the value of 1. After this value is printed to the Print Log window, the *ThisTest()* procedure is called, and the variable *iValue* is passed to it. In its natural state, this variable is passed by reference. (When we look at how items are passed by value, you will see the difference.) Once inside the *ThisTest()* procedure, a new string is printed to the Print Log window, telling us that we are in the subroutine. Following this PRINT statement command, the value of 23 is assigned to the parameter named *iVariable*.

> **Note:** Variables passed as parameters into a function need not have the same names as the receiving parameter. The reverse is also true: The names of the parameters in the called functions or procedures need not have the same names as the variables passed to them.

Since the value of 23 assigned to this variable is the same as the name of the parameter received in the *ThisTest()* procedure, it is connected back to the passed variable named *iValue*. This is the meaning of *by reference*: There is a connection. When something is passed *by value*, there is no such connection. In any event, when the end of the *ThisTest()* routine returns program control to the main part of this example, the last PRINT instruction is encountered. This sends the value of *iValue* out to the Print Log window one more time for viewing. If we were to take a look at the Print Log window for this application, we would see the following:

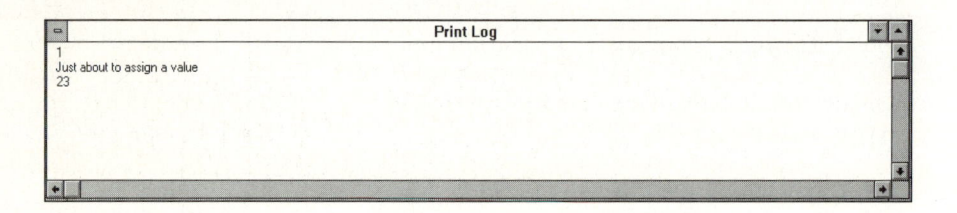

```
                              Print Log
1
Just about to assign a value
23
```

It is clear that the value of *iValue* has been changed from a starting value of 1 to a concluding value of 23.

For a test, let's look at the source code editor for this program module, shown in Figure 3-1.

If we were to change the value assigned to the parameter *iVariable* from 23 to a string like "Hello," we would get an error in the Debugger window and Error Log window (shown in Figure 3-3) after pressing the Go icon:

Since the original variable named *iValue* was declared to be of INTEGER data type, we cannot assign a string value to it. That would be a conflict in data types, which is exactly the kind of error shown in the Error Log window. When this happens, the type of the error is shown in the Error Log window and the violating line is highlighted in red within the Debugger window, as shown in the following figure (and underneath the Error Log window in Figure 3-2).

More Programming Concepts

```
'* Date .......... : January 1, 1994
'* Description ... : This shows how a variable may be passed by reference.

'* Name:          ThisTest()
'* Parameters:    <iVar>
'* Purpose:       To alter the value of the assigned variable

proc ThisTest( iVariable )

    print "Just about to assign a value"    '* Just show that we are here
    iVariable = 23                          '* Assign the new value

end proc

'* This is the main routine of the file

dim iValue as integer      '* Initialize and declare a variable
iValue = 1                 '* Assign a value to the variable
print iValue               '* Print the value out to the PRINT LOG
ThisTest( iValue )         '* Call procedure, passing by REFERENCE
```

Print Log:
```
1
Just about to assign a value
23
```

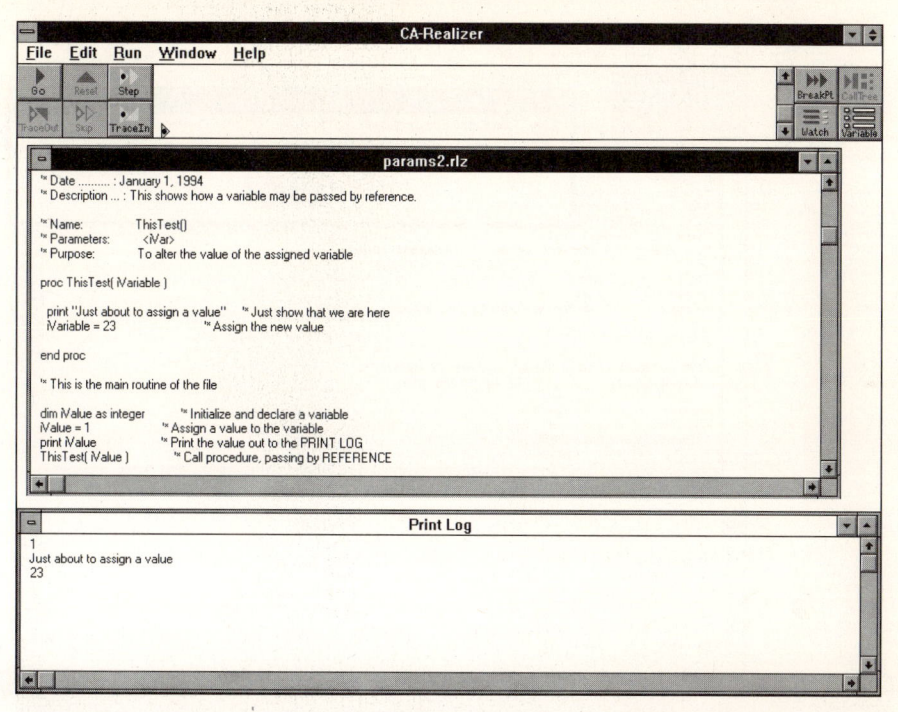

Figure 3-1. Open PARAMS2.RLZ file with DEBUG and PRINT LOG windows open.

This example shows in clear terms why strongly typed variables should be the rule and not the exception. While the value of a strongly typed variable can be changed, the change is limited to a value that is of the same data type. This means that values are not manipulated inadvertently.

Passing by Value

The other way in which variables may be passed from one routine to the next is by value. However, before looking at variables, let me add a brief word on constants and literals (including expressions). Consider the following line of code:

```
ThisTest( "Hello" )
```

Since there is no variable associated with the string "Hello," there is no associated address pointer, which means that this literal string can be passed only by value and not by reference. Think about it. If we were able to pass literal strings by reference and not by value, a subroutine could change a literal string. However, this conflicts with the basic definition of a literal string: A literal string is literal and cannot be changed. Therefore, to work within

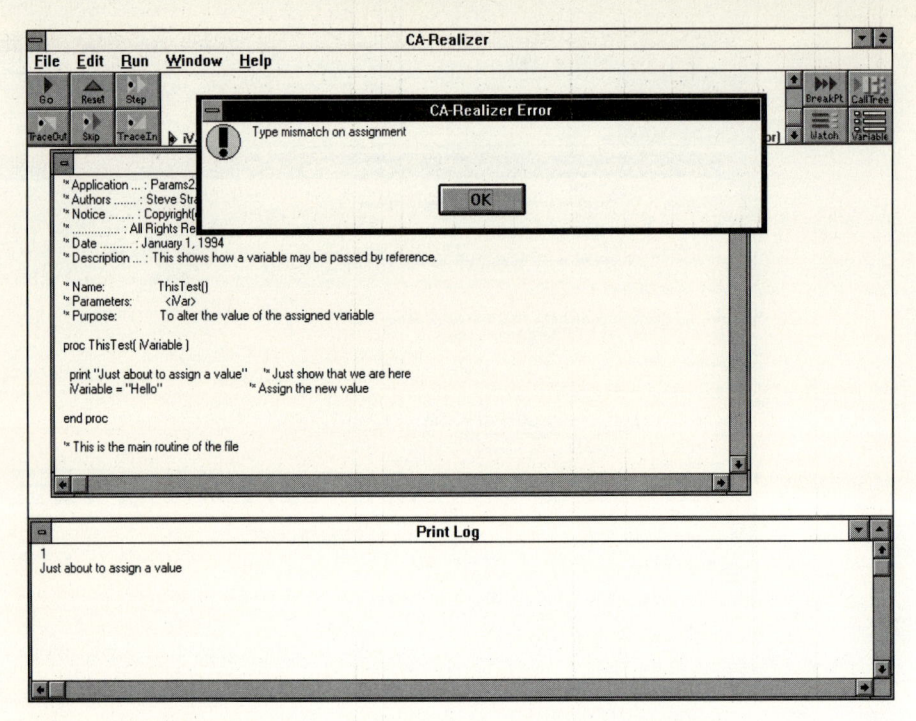

Figure 3-2. Standard error message when program is executed.

their definitions, literals, constants, and expressions are all passed by value and not by reference because a subroutine cannot change their value. So, for some numeric variables, the simple addition of *iVar * 1* turns the variable into an expression, in which case the parameter is not passed by reference but by value.

There are cases where parameters should be passed only by value and not by reference. The way to insure that this happens is to enclose the variable in a set of parentheses. This converts the variable being passed to an expression, which causes it to be passed by value. To see this better, look at the program file named *Params3.rlz*:

```
'* Application ... : Params3.rlz
'* Authors ....... : Steve Straley
'* Notice ........ : Copyright(c) 1994 - Sirius Press, Inc.
'* .............. : All Rights Reserved
'* Date .......... : January 1, 1994
'* Description ... : This shows how a variable may be passed by value
'*                   and by reference.

'* Name:              ThisTest()
'* Parameters:        <iVar1>, <iVar2>
```

More Programming Concepts

```
'* Purpose:              To alter the value of the assigned variables

func ThisTest( iVar1, iVar2 )

   print "Just about to assign a value"   '* Just show that we are here
   iVar1 = 23                             '* Assign the new value
   iVar2 = "Try this out..."              '* Assign the new value

   return( 1 )                            '* In essence, a true value

end func

'* This is the main routine of the file
'*****************************************************

dim iValue1 as integer          '* Initialize and declare 2 variables
dim sValue2 as string

iValue1 = 1                     '* Assign a values to the variable
iValue2 = "Sirius Press"    '* Assign a values to the variable

print iValue1, iValue2          '* Print the values out to the PRINT LOG

ThisTest( iValue1, (iValue2) )   '* Call function w/ both ref. & value

print iValue1, iValue2          '* Print the values out to the PRINT LOG

ThisTest( iValue1, iValue2 )    '* Call function again, both by ref.

print iValue1, iValue2          '* Print the values out to the PRINT LOG

clear iValue1, iValue2          '* Ready for the next time through

'* End of File: Params3.rlz
```

The flow of this program is simple. To start with, two variables are declared and initialized. One is a string and the other is an integer. Both values are printed to the Print Log window via the first PRINT instruction. Following this, both variables are passed to the *ThisTest()* function. The first parameter, *iValue1*, is passed by reference while the second parameter, *iValue2*, is passed by value. Inside the function, the parameters are assigned to *iVar1* and *iVar2*, respectively. The variable *iVar1* is assigned a new value of 23, and *iVar2* is assigned the new string "Try this out...." When the function completes its task and returns control to the main program, the values of *iValue1* and *iValue2* are printed once again to the Print Log window as you can see in Figure 3-3.

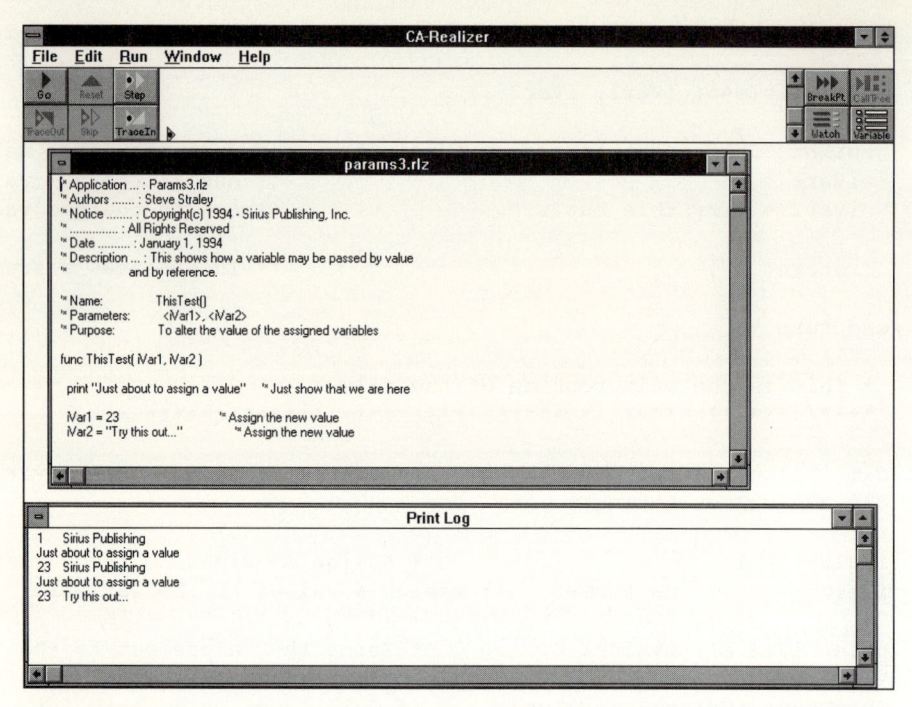

Figure 3-3. Open PARAMS3.RLZ file executing with DEBUG and PRINT LOG windows open.

Then the two variables are passed back to the *ThisTest( )* function, but this time, the second parameter, *iValue2*, is now passed by reference and not by value, since it is not enclosed in parentheses. Then, when the assignment operations inside of the *ThisTest( )* function take place, the values are indeed assigned, which the PRINT instruction at the end of the program sample demonstrates. This example shows how variables can be protected from manipulation in lower function or procedure subroutines.

> **Note:** It may be a safe rule to always pass a variable *by value* rather than *by reference* to avoid the damage of having a variable change in value and/or in data type.

Expressions

In some languages, expressions are almost like valid data types, in that they can take on properties like parameters, functions, and even variables. In Realizer, an expression is more like the traditional mathematical definition:

an operation that results in a value. An expression is identified by a pair of parentheses "()". One is placed at the beginning of the operation and the other, at the end. Expressions are often enclosed in parentheses to control the order of operation. For example, consider the following equations:

```
4 + 3 * 2 - 4 / 3
(4 + 3 * 2 - 4) / 3
(4 + 3) * 2 - 4 / 3
((4 + 3) * 2 - 4) / 3
```

In the first expression, the mathematical order of operation determines the answer: 8.6667. Here, division and multiplication are performed before the other operations, so that the order of operation looks like this:

```
4 + 3 * 2 - 4 / 3
4 + 6 - 1.3333
10 - 1.3333
8.6667
```

In the second example, the parentheses set the following order of the operation, to arrive at a value of 2.0000.

```
(4 + 3 * 2 - 4) / 3
(4+6-4) / 3
6 / 3
2.0000
```

The order of operation within the expression is maintained: multiplication and division will come before addition and subtraction.

By shifting the parentheses again, we achieve a different result in the third example. The answer here is 12.6667, arrived at by the following order of operation.

```
(4 + 3) * 2 - 4 / 3
7 * 2 - 4 / 3
14 - 1.3333
12.6667
```

And finally, by adding another set of parentheses, we can come up with a result of 3.3333:

```
((4 + 3) * 2 - 4) / 3
( 7 * 2  - 4 ) / 3
( 14 - 4 ) / 3
10 / 3
3.3333
```

When working with integers and dealing with logical values, remember that in Realizer, there is no logical data type. A logical true is considered to be a non-zero number, typically 1. A false value is considered to be 0. Given that, consider the following expression:

```
x = 4 + 3
y = x + 4 + ( 7 = 7 )
print x, y
```

Here, the value of X is 7, and the value of Y is 12. The expression (7=7) results in numeric value of 1 (a logical true), which, added to the value of X and the literal value of 4, makes 12. So, keep all of this in mind with working with values, constants, variables, functions, and of course, expressions.

Modifiers—What Are They?

Modifiers, like parameters, are passed from the calling routine into the called routine. However, their use is geared toward toggles or switches within a function or a procedure. For example, sometimes we will write a function that does a certain operation and returns a certain value, like a function that returns an array of file names. If the code within that function is relatively generic, and if we wanted an array of file dates, we would use the same code that returned file names, but this time, change it to return file dates. This makes more sense than writing new code, but we'd still have two separate functions, one for the names of files and one for the date stamps of files. There is another option: Use a modifier. Think of the modifier as a toggle, or in this case, a conditional test that will return either an array of file names or an array of file date stamps.

On both the calling and defining ends of the function, modifiers are separated from the formal parameter list using a semicolon. We saw an example of this in the previous chapter with the MENUSETCMD() function:

```
func menusetcmd( fIdMarker, sText, iKey; fStyle )
end func
```

The fourth item in the list is separated from the others by a semicolon. In Realizer, the value of *fStyle* can be anything from this list: `_REMOVE`, `_NORMAL`, `_GRAY`, `_CHECK`, or `_UNCHECK`. These internal variables tell the MENUSETCMD() conditions by which to operate. Think of these internal values as numeric constants: 1, 2, 3, 4, or 5. Within the source code for MENUSETCMD(), you might have the following SELECT CASE construct:

```
select case fStyle
   case 1         '* To _REMOVE the menu item
   case 2         '* To make the menu item _NORMAL
   case 3         '* To make the menu item _GRAY
   case 4         '* To place a _CHECK in the menu item
   case 5         '* To remove the check from the menu item
end select
```

The programmer using the MENUSETCMD(), knows only that to do something to a particular menu item, the MENUSETCMD() is in order. The *fStyle* modifier tells Realizer what is to happen to the menu item that has an identifier passed as *fIdMarker*.

This example should suggest that constants, as outlined in Chapter 1, can come in handy when working with user-defined functions or procedures that use a modifier list as well as a parameter list. For example, consider the following source code:

```
'* Application ... : Modif1.rlz
'* Authors ....... : Steve Straley
'* Notice ........ : Copyright(c) 1994 - Sirius Press, Inc.
'* .............. : All Rights Reserved
'* Date .......... : January 1, 1994
'* Description ... : This shows a simple use of a modifier in conjunction
'*                   with constants.

'* A series of constants or MAINFEST CONSTANTS to be used
'* by the application
'***********************************************************
const SHOW_DATE   = 1
const SHOW_NUMBER = 2
const SHOW_STRING = 3

'* Name:      PrintIt(; <fModifier> )
'* Params:    <fModifier>
'* Purpose:   To alter the return value of a function by passing a
'*            modifier instead of a parameter.

func PrintIt( ;fModifier )

   select case fModifier

      case SHOW_DATE
         xReturn = date$

      CASE SHOW_NUMBER
         xReturn = 3.1415926
```

```
     CASE SHOW_STRING
        xReturn = "Hey, this is from Sirius Press!"

   end select

   return( xReturn )

end func

'**************** MAIN BODY ********************

print PrintIt( ; SHOW_NUMBER )
print PrintIt( ; SHOW_DATE )
print PrintIt( ; SHOW_STRING )

'* End of File: Modif1.rlz
```

This example program demonstrates the use of constants and modifiers. The values of *SHOW_DATE*, *SHOW_NUMBER*, and *SHOW_STRING* are used in the *PrintIt()* function itself (in the CASE construct), and in the modifier list when the function is called in conjunction with the PRINT command. In addition, inside the function *PrintIt()*, there is a variable that is defined as *xReturn*. In all of the examples so far, we have used various meta symbols to indicate the data type of the variable. Here, the data type of *xReturn* can differ, depending on the value of the modifier *fModifier* that is passed to the function. Depending on that value, the return value of the function *PrintIt()* can be different. The meta symbol *x* is used to show an unknown or changing data type. Some programmers might prefer to include all of the meta symbols as part of the variables name: *dt_f_sReturn*. This would show that either a date time, floating, or string data type can be returned. This is purely a stylistic decision. For me, the *x* is sufficient.

If you load the program named `Modif1.rlz` in the Realizer environment, open the Print Log window, and select Go, you will see the result shown in Figure 3-4.

The Print Log window displays each of the three values returned from the *PrintIt()* function. This shows how a modifier may be used to change the output of a function.

Later, we will look at the notion of building a separate file containing all of the constants for a particular application. For example, a function can return a true or a false value symbolized by either a 0 or non-0 number. But we can make the return value more apparent by doing the following:

```
const TRUE = 1
const FALSE = 0
```

More Programming Concepts

```
┌─                    CA-Realizer                          ▼ ▲ ┐
  File  Edit  Run  Window  Help
  ┌──┐ ┌───┐ ┌───┐                                    ┌──┐ ┌──┐
  │Go│ │Rst│ │Stp│                                    │BP│ │CT│
  └──┘ └───┘ └───┘                                    └──┘ └──┘
  ┌──┐ ┌──┐  ┌──┐                                     ┌──┐ ┌──┐
  │TO│ │Sk│  │TI│                                     │Wt│ │Vr│
  └──┘ └──┘  └──┘
 ┌─                    modif1.rlz                        ▼ ▲ ┐
 │ '* Application ... : Modif1.rlz                              │
 │ '* Authors ....... : Steve Straley                           │
 │ '* Notice ........ : Copyright(c) 1994 - Sirius Publishing, Inc.
 │ '* ............... : All Rights Reserved                     │
 │ '* Date .......... : January 1, 1994                         │
 │ '* Description ... : This shows a simple use of a modifier in conjunction
 │ '*                   with constants.                         │
 │                                                              │
 │ '* A series of constants or MAINFEST CONSTANTS to be used    │
 │ '* by the application                                        │
 │ '*************************************************           │
 └──────────────────────────────────────────────────────────────┘
 ┌─                     Print Log                         ▼ ▲ ┐
 │ 3.1416                                                       │
 │ 06-13-1994                                                   │
 │ Hey, this is from Sirius Publishing!                         │
 └──────────────────────────────────────────────────────────────┘
```

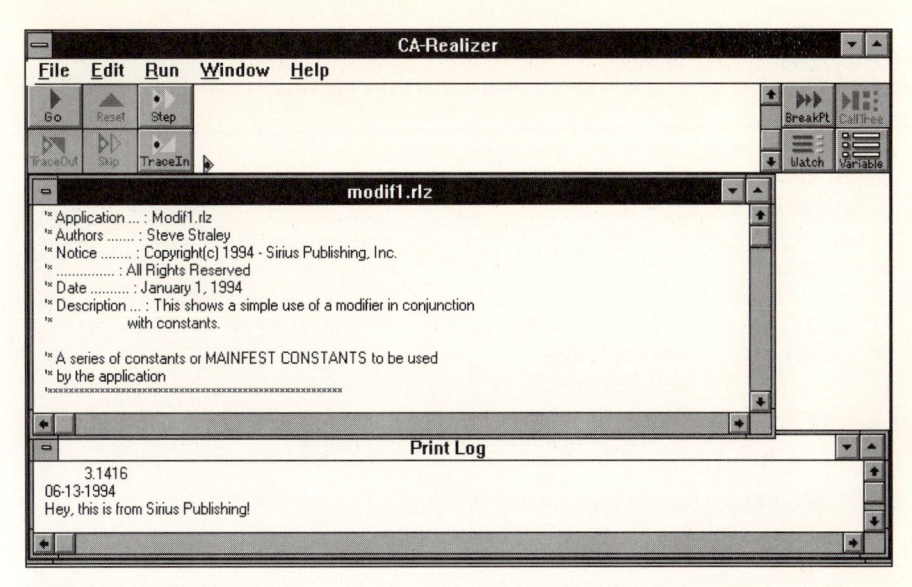

Figure 3-4. Open MODIF1.RLZ file executing with DEBUG and PRINT LOG windows open.

Since we have given meaning to the values, we can use those worded representations to make our code more readable, and thus, more modifiable. Remember, just when you think that an application is finished, the last words of any client or end user will be "But wait... I want one more change... ." So, the advantage of having a file filled with useful constants for values, conditions, and modifiers becomes apparent.

More Rules About Parameters and Modifiers

There is an almost unlimited number of modifiers or parameters that may be passed to a function or a procedure. After the semicolon that separates the modifier list from the parameter list, commas are used to separate individual modifiers as well as individual parameters. In the following example, the *Modif2.rlz* file expands on the previous example program to show how multiple modifiers may be passed to a function or a procedure.

```
'* Application ... : Modif2.rlz
'* Authors ....... : Steve Straley
'* Notice ........ : Copyright(c) 1994 - Sirius Press, Inc.
'* ............... : All Rights Reserved
'* Date .......... : January 1, 1994
'* Description ... : This shows a simple use of multiple modifiers
'*                   in conjunction with constants.
```

110   Chapter 3

```
'* A series of constants or MAINFEST CONSTANTS to be used
'* by the application
'************************************************************

const SHOW_DATE   = 1
const SHOW_NUMBER = 2
const SHOW_STRING = 3
const TRUE        = 1
const FALSE       = 0

'* Name:       PrintIt(; <fModifier>, <nToPrint> )
'* Params:     <fModifier>
'*             <nToPrint>
'* Purpose:    To alter the return value of a function by passing a
'*             modifier instead of a parameter.

func PrintIt( ;fModifier, nCondition )

   select case fModifier

      case SHOW_DATE
         xReturn = date$

      CASE SHOW_NUMBER
         xReturn = 3.1415926

      CASE SHOW_STRING
         xReturn = "Hey, this is from Sirius Press!"

   end select

   if nCondition then                    '* This is a conditional statement
      print "Inside of function:", xReturn   '* looking at the modifier
   end if

   return( xReturn )

end func

'**************** MAIN BODY **********************

print PrintIt( ; SHOW_NUMBER, FALSE )    '* Get the return value
PrintIt( ; SHOW_NUMBER, TRUE )           '* Do the operation

print PrintIt( ; SHOW_DATE, FALSE )      '* Get the return value
PrintIt( ; SHOW_DATE, TRUE )             '* Do the operation
```

```
print PrintIt( ; SHOW_STRING, FALSE )      '* Get the return value
PrintIt( ; SHOW_STRING, TRUE )             '* Do the operation

'* End of File: Modif2.rlz
```

In this example, two new constants have been added to the list, and those constants are used as values to be passed as the second modifiers to the *PrintIt()* function. Inside the *PrintIt()* function there is the simple IF command:

```
if nCondition then
   print "Inside of function:", xReturn
end if
```

Here, the *nCondition* variable holds the value of the constant TRUE or FALSE, which is the second modifier passed. Note how in the function definition and in the call to the function, the semicolon is used to set off the list of modifiers; however, commas are used to separate multiple modifiers. If we were to run this through Realizer, the Print Log window would look something like this:

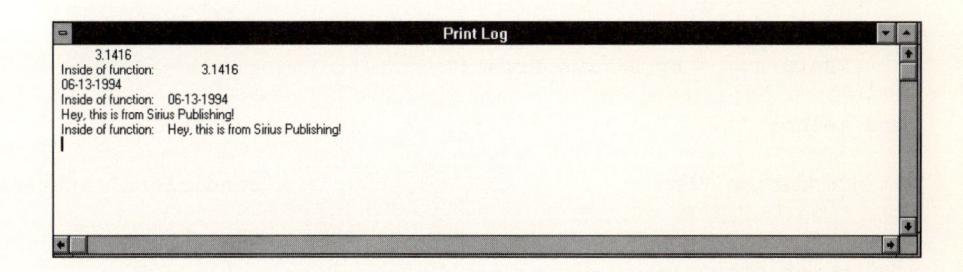

```
                              Print Log
     3.1416
Inside of function:     3.1416
06-13-1994
Inside of function:   06-13-1994
Hey, this is from Sirius Publishing!
Inside of function:   Hey, this is from Sirius Publishing!
```

This next example program, `Modif3.rlz`, includes both parameters and modifiers:

```
'* Application ... : Modif3.rlz
'* Authors ....... : Steve Straley
'* Notice ........ : Copyright(c) 1994 - Sirius Press, Inc.
'* ............... : All Rights Reserved
'* Date .......... : January 1, 1994
'* Description ... : This shows a simple use of multiple modifiers
'*                   in conjunction with constants and with other
'*                   parameters

'* A series of constants or MAINFEST CONSTANTS to be used
'* by the application
'*************************************************************

const ADD_DATE   = 1
const ADD_NUMBER = 2
```

```
const ADD_STRING  = 3
const TRUE        = 1
const FALSE       = 0

'* Name:         PrintIt(<xValue>; <fModifier>, <nToPrint> )
'* Params:       <xValue>         Unkonw data type
'*               <fModifier>      Modifier to tell it something
'*               <nToPrint>       Direction of output
'* Purpose:      To alter the return value of a function by passing a
'*               modifier instead of a parameter.

func PrintIt( xValue ; fModifier, nCondition )

   select case fModifier

      case ADD_DATE
        xReturn = xValue + 10

      CASE ADD_NUMBER
        xReturn = xValue + 3.1415

      CASE ADD_STRING
        xReturn = " by Sirius Press!"

   end select

   if nCondition then                        '* A conditional statement

      if fModifier = ADD_DATE then           '* special test here
        print "The old date was: ", xValue
        print "  and the new is: ", xReturn
        print "*****************************"
      else
        print "==>", xReturn                 '* looking at the modifier
      end if

   end if

   return( xReturn )

end func


'**************** MAIN BODY ********************
PrintIt(    qdate; ADD_DATE,    TRUE )
PrintIt(  10.0000 ; ADD_NUMBER, TRUE )
PrintIt( "This is"; ADD_STRING, TRUE )

'* End of File: Modif3.rlz
```

This time, the QDATE operation is used instead of the string statement DATE$. This way, we can add 10 days to the value without getting a "type mismatch" error. In addition, you can see an example of nested IFs within the *PrintIt()* function. Here, the value of the *xValue* parameters may change in both value and data type. To accommodate the potentially different data types, the constants have been changed and reflect these variances. So, when a datetime data type is passed as the first parameter to the *PrintIt()* function, so is the ADD_DATE modifier, which ensures that the correct code execution takes place. Also, just before the RETURN instruction at the end of the function, a nested IF ... END IF statement compares the modifier *fModifier* with the ADD_DATE constant. Modifiers and constants can be used anywhere a value or a parameter may be used.

When this program executes, the values in the Print Log window should be:

```
Print Log
The old date was:  06/13/94
and the new is:    06/23/94
********************
==>      13.1415
==>  by Sirius Publishing!
```

Missing Parameters and/or Modifiers

In the first chapter, I said that parameters could not be skipped. This is still true; however, there is a way in which an unspecified number of either parameters or modifiers may be added to the definition of a function or a procedure. The same technique holds for both; however, there are different Realizer functions and/or commands that may be used depending on which item we are inquiring about. The basic format for modifiers is the following:

```
func Name( <xParm>; .. )
end func
```

and for parameters it is:

```
func Name( .. ; <xModifier> )
end func
```

In the first example, there is one required parameter and an unspecified number of modifiers that may be passed to this function. In the second example, the exact opposite holds true: there is an unspecified number of parameters and one required modifier. Here's a variation with both required and unspecified parameters and modifiers:

```
func Name( <xPram>, .. ; <xModifier>, .. )
end func
```

In this example, there is one required parameter and one required modifier. After that, there is an optional number of either.

> **Note:** Just because a parameter or modifier is optional, it still may not be skipped in the list.

There are four Realizer functions/commands that may be used on the receiving side of the function/procedure to help work with the unknown parameters/modifiers:

QNOPTMODS Returns the number of optional modifiers found by a function or procedure.

QOPTMOD() Allows the *n*th modifier, specified as a parameter to this function, to be queried and/or altered.

QNOPTPARAMS Returns the number of optional parameters found by a function or procedure.

QOPTPARAM() Allows the *n*th parameter, specified as a parameter to this function, to be queried and/or altered.

The QOPTPARAM() and QOPTMOD() functions may appear on either side of the equal sign (=) to obtain a value:

```
xValue = qoptparam(1)  '* Obtaining the value of the first parameter
```

or on the other side:

```
qoptparam(1) = 23    '* Assign 23 to the first optional parameter
```

> **Note:** Any extra parameters or modifiers passed to a function or a procedure will be ignored by the receiving subroutine.

The techniques involved in using these new features are exactly the same whether we are working with parameters or with modifiers. In the example

More Programming Concepts

file named *Modif4.rlz*, optional modifiers are used, as well as the QNOPTMODS command and the QOPTMOD() function.

```
'* Application ... : Modif4.rlz
'* Authors ....... : Steve Straley
'* Notice ........ : Copyright(c) 1994 - Sirius Press, Inc.
'* .............. : All Rights Reserved
'* Date .......... : January 1, 1994
'* Description ... : This shows how an unknown set of modifiers can be
'*                   looked for in a function or a procedure

'* A series of constants or MAINFEST CONSTANTS to be used
'* by the application
'************************************************************

const TRUE      = 1
const FALSE     = 0
const INCREMENT = TRUE
const DECREMENT = FALSE


'* Name:       TestThis( <nValue>, <nValue2>; .. )
'* Params:     <nValue1>       Starting Value
'*             <nValue2>       Endinf value
'* Purpose:    This will show the various ways in which the QOPTMOD() and
'*             QNOPTMODS function/commands work.

func TestThis( nValue1, nValue2; .. )

  select case qnoptmods              '* check to see how many modifiers
    case 1                           '* One modifier was passed
      if qoptmod(1) = INCREMENT then '* perform incrementing operation
        for nReturn = nValue1 to nValue2
          print nReturn
                next
      else
        for nReturn = nValue2 to nValue1 step -1
          print nReturn
        next
      end if

    case 2                           '* Two modifiers were passed
      if qoptmod(1) = INCREMENT then
        for nReturn = nValue1 to nValue2 step qoptmod(2)
          print nReturn
        next
```

```
      else
        for nReturn = nValue2 to nValue1 step ( -1 * qoptmod(2) )
          print nReturn
        next
      end if

  end select

  return( nReturn )

end func

'**************** MAIN BODY ********************

print "Ready for first test"
TestThis( 1, 10; INCREMENT )

print "Ready for second test"
TestThis( 1, 10; INCREMENT, 2 )

print "Ready for third test"
TestThis( 1, 10; DECREMENT )

print "Ready for final test"
TestThis( 1, 10; DECREMENT, 2 )

'* End of File: Modif4.rlz
```

At the top of the file, we've defined two constants, then used their values to define two more constants. This technique improves the readability of a program. In our program, rather than passing off a TRUE or FALSE constant as a modifier, the constants INCREMENT or DECREMENT are used instead. When we need to revisit this program later, it will be easier to decipher this:

```
TestThis(1, 10; INCREMENT )
```

than to decipher this:

```
TestThis(1, 10; TRUE )
```

In the second example, we would have to remember, perhaps months later, that the first modifier represents the counting direction within the *TestThis()* function. In the first example, this is apparent.

Following this is the definition of the *TestThis()* function, which requires two parameters and an unspecified number of modifiers. Within the function, the SELECT CASE statement uses the value obtained from the QNOPTMODS command. If one modifier is passed to the function, then the code within the CASE 1 executes. If two modifiers are passed to the function, then the code within the CASE 2 command executes. Within the first CASE command, if the value of the first modifier is equal to the constant INCREMENT, then the value of *nReturn* is incremented through the FOR ... NEXT loop. On the other hand, if the value of the first modifier is DECREMENT, then the value of *nReturn* will be decremented and displayed. This is the case in the first and third call to this function from the main body of the file.

If two modifiers are passed to the *TestThis()* function, then the value of QNOPTMODS() will return 2, and the CASE 2 code will execute. Here, again, the value of QOPTMOD(1) is looked at to see if the direction of the FOR ... NEXT loop will be in an incrementing or decrementing order. However, once that is established, the STEP value is obtained via the QOPTMOD(2) function. The value of 2 tells the function to look at the second modifier. To get the value of the last modifier in the list, consider this code:

```
print qoptmod( qnoptmods )
```

In any event, the FOR ... NEXT loop will either increment or decrement by the step value amount, which will be the second modifier passed to the function.

It is also key to note that the constants INCREMENT and DECREMENT set the order of the parameters *nValue1* and *nValue2* within the FOR ... NEXT loop. In other words, when the first modifier is set to INCREMENT, then the order of the parameters will be *nValue1* followed by *nValue2*. However, if the value of QOPTMOD(1) is set to DECREMENT, then the order of the parameters is reversed with *nValue2* coming before *nValue1*. This way, we do not have to alter the order of the parameters when the function is called:

```
TestThis( 1, 10; INCREMENT )
TestThis( 1, 10; DECREMENT )
```

The function handles this for us.

See Figure 3-5 for a complete shot of the Print Log window after the program has executed.

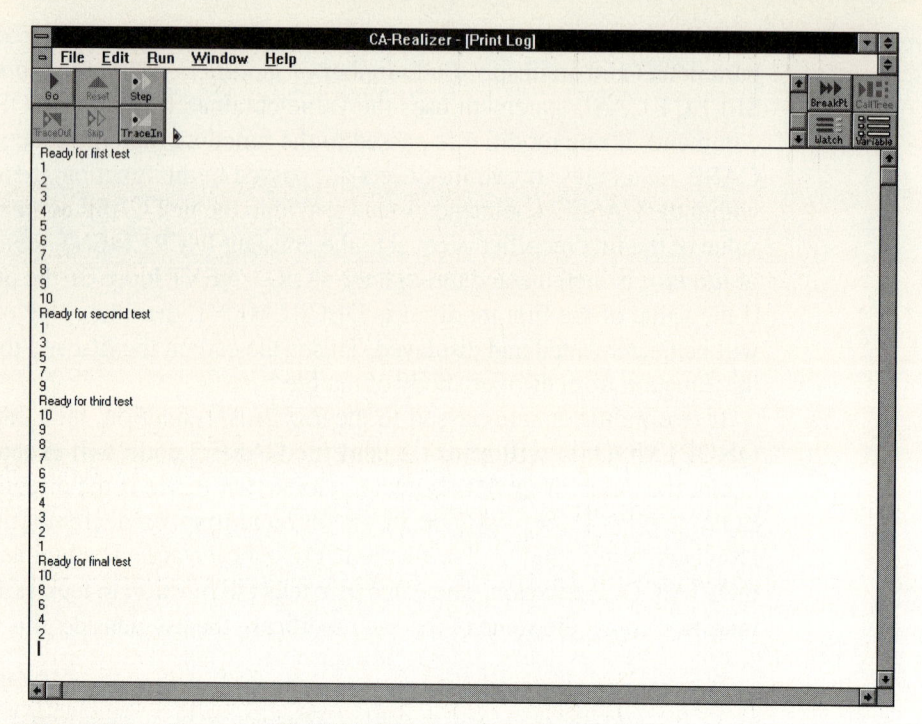

Figure 3-5. Expanded PRINT LOG window with results.

Arrays

Arrays are perhaps the most powerful tools in the Realizer language. In the simplest terms, an array is a grouping of items under the name of a single variable. For example, there are seven days of the week. You might have an array called *aDaysOfWeek,* which contains seven elements, each of the string data type: "Monday," "Tuesday," "Wednesday," and so on. This is an example of a one-dimensional array, also known as a vector. A table, such as the multiplication table, is an example of a two-dimensional array.

Regardless of whether an array is one-, two-, or multi-dimensional, a single variable can represent all the elements in the array. Each element in an array has a subscript position. Turning back to our *aDaysOfWeek* example, if we wanted the first day contained in this variable, we would use square brackets ([]) in conjunction with the array name and the subscript position:

```
print aDaysOfWeek[1]
```

If this were a two-dimensional array (often called a table or a matrix), the same principle holds true for each dimension within the array. So if we wanted the first element of the first dimension of a matrix, the code might look something like this:

```
print aMatrix[1][1]
```

or like this:

```
print aMatrix[1,1]
```

or like this:

```
print aMatrix(1,1)
```

> **Note:** In general, avoid using parentheses for the subscripts of an array. You might confuse them with a function or an expression. Square brackets make a nicer distinction between the two.

> **Note:** Multi-dimensional arrays cannot be ragged. This means that all subscripts will have the same number of elements in them.

Creating an Array

There are several ways to create an array. One way is to create an array as a literal by placing braces (the squiggly brackets) on each side of a list separated by commas:

```
aDaysOfWeek = { "Monday", "Tuesday", "Wednesday", \\
                "Thursday", "Friday", "Saturday", \\
                "Sunday" }
```

You can also build arrays using the INDEX() function:

```
aDaysOfWeek = index(7)
aDaysOfWeek[1] = 15
aDaysOfWeek[2] = 16
aDaysOfWeek[3] = 17
aDaysOfWeek[4] = 18
aDaysOfWeek[5] = 19
aDaysOfWeek[6] = 20
aDaysOfWeek[7] = 21
```

> **Note:** The value of the various subscripts in the array, when created via the INDEX() function, will have the index number as the initial value. This means, in the above example, if the assignments did not take place, then the values for each of the elements would be 1 through 7.

> **Note:** If the INDEX() function is used, then all of the elements in the array will be of a numeric data type. This means that the values within the elements can be changed only to another value of the same data type.

By default, all arrays start at the beginning of a list or at the "base." However, Realizer allows us the flexibility to alter the starting base. Under normal circumstances, when we write the following instruction:

```
aDaysOfWeek = index(7)
```

the first element declared in this array will be *aDaysOfWeek[1]*. However, if we add the command OPTION BASE 0, we can shift the starting base of this array to zero:

```
option base 0
aDaysOfWeek = index(7)
```

Now, the beginning element position will be 0 and not 1. This capability offers flexibility with other languages such as C.

> **Note:** Whatever notional style you use, be consistent. If OPTION BASE 0 is the preferred method, use it throughout an application.

The default for OPTION BASE is obviously 1.

Another way to declare an array is to use the subscript notations directly into the assignment. This is how values other than numerics can be quickly placed into an array. For example, here's how we might declare an array of five (5) elements, all of the String data type:

```
aDaysOfWeek[1:7] = ""
```

More Programming Concepts

This notation tells Realizer to build an array with a beginning subscript position of 1 and an upper bound subscript position of 7 and to assign all the elements the String data type. With this in place, we can list the elements:

```
aDaysOfWeek = index(7)
aDaysOfWeek[1] = "Monday"
aDaysOfWeek[2] = "Tuesday"
aDaysOfWeek[3] = "Wednesday"
aDaysOfWeek[4] = "Thursday"
aDaysOfWeek[5] = "Friday"
aDaysOfWeek[6] = "Saturday"
aDaysOfWeek[7] = "Sunday"
```

Finally, you can use the DIM command to create an array. However, there is a big difference between using the DIM command and using the techniques we've already discussed. The DIM command creates a static array, while the others create dynamic arrays. The difference is that a static array (or matrix) is fixed in length, while the others are not. Another difference in using the DIM command is that you can specify the data type of each element in the array as in the following: For example:

```
dim aBytes(1 to 25) as byte
dim aStrings(1:25) as strings
dim aValues(25) as integer
```

The program named *Array1.rlz* puts some of these techniques to work in the Realizer environment:

```
'* Application ... : Array1.rlz
'* Authors ....... : Steve Straley
'* Notice ........ : Copyright(c) 1994 - Sirius Press, Inc.
'* ............... : All Rights Reserved
'* Date .......... : January 1, 1994
'* Description ... : The show the different ways in which an array may be
'*                   created

'* First, let's build a literal array of strings

aNewDays = { "Monday", "Tuesday", "Wednesday", "Thursday", "Friday" }

print aNewDays                          '* Print the values
print aNewDays[1]                       '* Print only one element
print endvalid(aNewDays), \\
      startvalid(aNewDays)              '* Print the boundaries
```

```
'* Now, develop a blank array w/ proper size and fill it accordingly

aDaysOfWeek[1:5] = ""
aDaysOfWeek[1]   = "Monday"      '* Since all elements are of the
aDaysOfWeek[2]   = "Tuesday"     '* String data type, we can replace
aDaysOfWeek[3]   = "Wednesday"   '* any one of the elements with
aDaysOfWeek[4]   = "Thursday"    '* another string value
aDaysOfWeek[5]   = "Friday"

print aDaysOfWeek                '* Print the values
print endvalid(aDaysOfWeek), \\
      startvalid(aDaysOfWeek)    '* Print the boundaries

'* Now, set the initial option and declare a new array of numerics

option base 0
aDays = {2,4,6}

print aDays
print endvalid(aDays), ubound(aDays), \\
      startvalid(aDays), lbound(aDays)    '* Show the various

'* Now, set the initial option back and use the INDEX() function

option base 1
aDays = index(10)
print aDays
print endvalid(aDays), ubound(aDays), \\
      startvalid(aDays), lbound(aDays)

'* Now declare an array using the DIM instruction.  The default values
'* will be 0 as opposed to the indexed value.

dim x[3:7]
print "This is it", x
print endvalid(x), ubound(x), startvalid(x), lbound(x)

'* Finally, some new assignments as well as fixing the data type
'* that can be associated with these variables.

dim aBytes(1 to 25) as byte
dim aStrings(1:25) as string
dim aValues(25) as integer

print endvalid(aBytes),   startvalid(aBytes)
print endvalid(aStrings), startvalid(aStrings)
print endvalid(aValues),  startvalid(aValues)

clear x, aDaysOfWeek, aDays, aNewDays, \\
      aBytes, aStrings, aValues

'* End of File: Array1.rlz
```

More Programming Concepts

When this code executes, the Print Log window, when expanded, will look like Figure 3-6.

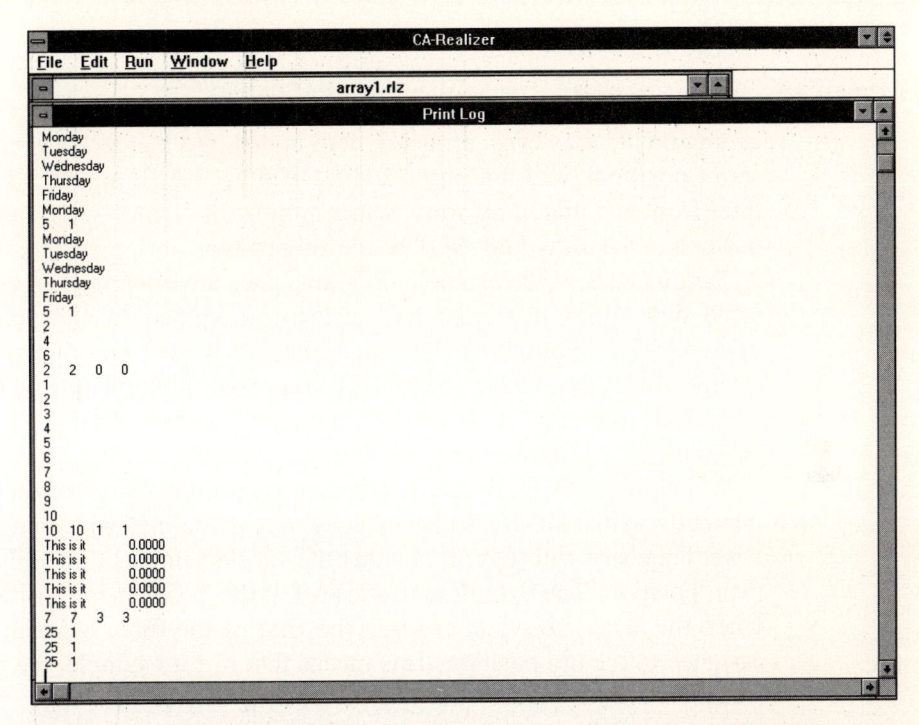

```
CA-Realizer
File  Edit  Run  Window  Help
                    array1.rlz
                    Print Log
Monday
Tuesday
Wednesday
Thursday
Friday
Monday
5    1
Monday
Tuesday
Wednesday
Thursday
Friday
5    1
2
4
6
2    2    0    0
1
2
3
4
5
6
7
8
9
10
10   10   1    1
This is it        0.0000
This is it        0.0000
This is it        0.0000
This is it        0.0000
This is it        0.0000
7    7    3    3
25   1
25   1
25   1
```

Figure 3-6. Expanded PRINT LOG with program window in background.

The program here starts with a literal array stored to the *aNewDays* variable. The PRINT command is powerful enough to print out all the elements in the array, so no FOR...NEXT loop is needed to print out the contents. If an individual element in the array needs to be printed, it can be printed with a subscript specified. Following this are the ENDVALID() and STARTVALID() functions in relation to the *aNewDays* variable. These functions, similar to the UBOUND() and LBOUND() functions (upper bound and lower bound) yield the last and first valid subscript positions in the array. Since the default starting base position for an array is 1, the value of STARTVALID() for the *aNewDays* array is 1. The ending subscript position as returned from ENDVALID() is 5. The same value would be returned from the UBOUND() function.

Following this is a new array, *aDaysOfWeek*, defined with subscripts starting with 1 and ending with 5. The following notation sets up the boundaries of the array:

```
array_name[start:end]
```

Even if the command OPTION BASE 0 is in place, since the beginning and ending boundaries of an array are hard-coded into the declaration, the subscript positions will not observe the OPTION BASE command. We may infer from this that in an array with x number of elements, the last element position in the array may NOT be the xth position.

Turning back to the example program, since an array must have all of the same data types in it, the null string is assigned to each element in *aDaysOfWeek*. Following this, each element is then reassigned to a new string value. Once again, the PRINT command, along with ENDVALID() and STARTVALID(), follows the assignment portion of this section of the program.

When the OPTION BASE 0 command is encountered, Realizer will set it internally so that all arrays that are not explicitly defined with an upper and a lower boundary will start off at either the 1st element position or the 0th element position. The default is to start off at the 1st element position. Now, when the array *aDays* is created, the first of the three elements will be assigned to the 0th position. This means that if, for example, the following statement is encountered shortly after the array is created:

```
print aDays[1]
```

the value displayed in the Print Log window will not be 2 but 4, since 2 is in the 0th element position and 4 is in the 1st element position. This is why it is very important to be consistent with regard to the base value of an array. You want all your arrays to start off at either the 1st element position or the 0th. Mixing the two in an application or even as a standard within a company, unless with specific purpose in mind, is most unwise.

In the next section of this program, the OPTION BASE is returned to 1, and the *aDays* array is reinitialized from an array of three literal values to the return value from INDEX(10). This will create a ten-element array, with each element of numeric data type and having the subscript position in the array as the value. This means that the 1st element in *aDays* will be 1. Should the OPTION BASE remain at 0, then the value of *aDays[0]* will be 0.

> **Note:** When the INDEX() function is used to initialize an array, all of the elements in the array will be of numeric data type. One cannot do the following:
>
> ```
> aData = index(10)
> aData[1] = "hello"
> ```
>
> Since the other elements are set to be of numeric type, and an array cannot yet have a different data type, this will cause a "Type Mismatch" error to appear in the Error Log window.

The next array declaration instruction uses the DIM command. Here, the DIM command creates an array from elements 3 through 7. Unlike the INDEX() function, the values in each of these element positions will be a floating numeric of 0.0000. The ENDVALID(), STARTVALID(), UBOUND(), and LBOUND() functions work as expected.

It is also possible to assign a specific data type to the various elements in an array while it is being declared. Here, in the last three declarations, the DIM <var> AS <data type> instructs Realizer not only to declare an array to a specific dimension, but also to define a specified data type. For example, in the first DIM instruction:

```
dim aBytes(1 to 25) as byte
```

there will be 25 elements in the *aBytes* array, and all will be of a Numeric Byte data type. Following this is another similar convention for initializing an array:

```
dim aStrings(1:25) as string
```

Please observe that the TO part of the command has been replaced with a colon. The effect is the same. Here, the *aStrings* array is declared to contain 25 elements, all of String data type. In the last DIM command:

```
dim aValues(25) as integer
```

The value for OPTION BASE will be used since there is no lower boundary specified. This value is still set at 1. Therefore, this, too, will create a 25-element array, but this time, the elements will be of integer data type.

Functions Returning Arrays

In the previous programming example, we examined several ways to declare an array. However, there is yet another way: An array may be initialized through a user-defined function. Since an array is a valid data type, and since functions can return any valid data type, a function can return an array. In that case, the value of the function is the reference to the array, which means that any variable receiving the value of a function which is an array will have all of the properties and characteristics of that array. Sometimes, a picture or source code is the quickest route to understanding, so the example file *Array2a.rlz* defines two functions:

```
'* Application ... : Array2a.rlz
'* Authors ....... : Steve Straley
'* Notice ........ : Copyright(c) 1994 - Sirius Press, Inc.
'* .............. : All Rights Reserved
'* Date .......... : January 1, 1994
'* Description ... : File containing user defined functions for the
'*                   Test file Array2.rlz

'* Name:          GetIt()
'* Returns:       Array

func GetIt()

  dim aIntern[1:5] as string
  aIntern[1] = "Straley"

  return( aIntern )

end func

'* Name:          GetIt2()
'* Returns:       Array with LOCAL values

func GetIt2()

  dim local aNewOne[1:5] as string
  aNewOne[1] = "Straley"

  return( aNewOne )

end func

'* End of File: Array2a.rlz
```

The first array is called *aIntern* and is DIM'd as an array of strings with a lower subscript boundary of 1 and an upper subscript boundary of 5. The first element is assigned a literal string, leaving the remaining four elements to contain null strings (" "). That variable is the RETURN value of the function. The next function, *GetiT2()*, is similar except that the array named *aNewOne* is DIM'd to be a LOCAL variable. Again, the RETURN value of the function is that array. This file is loaded by another program file named `Array2.rlz` via the RUN command. The `Array2.rlz` file looks like this:

```
'* Application ... : Array2.rlz
'* Authors ....... : Steve Straley
'* Notice ........ : Copyright(c) 1994 - Sirius Press, Inc.
'* .............. : All Rights Reserved
'* Date .......... : January 1, 1994
'* Description ... : This shows how an array can be returned from a function,
'*                   how the array may be seen or not, how the value of
'*                   function takes on the properties of the array, how
'*                   the LOCAL instruction works, and finally, how the
'*                   RESET command works.

run "Array2a.rlz"

aNewArray = GetIt()          '* User defined function in Array2a.rlz file

print endvalid(aNewArray), startvalid(aNewArray), aNewArray[1]
print aNewArray[2]
print endvalid(aIntern), startvalid(aIntern), aIntern[1]

aAnother = GetIt2()                  '* This one is with a local!
print endvalid(aAnother), \\
      startvalid(aAnother), aAnother[1]
print aAnother[2]

if qvar( aNewOne, _DEFINED ) then
  print endvalid(aNewOne), startvalid(aNewOne), aNewOne[1]
else
  print "Not defined!"
end if

reset(_VAR)

'* End of File: Array2.rlz
```

Here, the RUN command at the top of the file loads the `Array2a.rlz` file into the Realizer environment. If both files are loaded, make sure that the active window contains this file and not the `Array2a.rlz` file when you select Go.

> **Note:** It is not important to load the files named in the RUN command into the Realizer environment. When Realizer executes a particular file, it will scan the specified area for the specified files and load them automatically. When this happens, Realizer will create a secondary .RLO (Realizer Object) file.

In the `Array2.rlz` file, the variable named *aNewArray>* receives the value from the *GetIt()* function. Once received, then the ENDVALID(), and STARTVALID() commands and the contents of *aNewArray[1]* will be displayed via the PRINT command. Following this, another PRINT command will print the second element in *aNewArray*. Since this is an empty string, it will appear as a blank line in the Print Log window.

The next PRINT instruction is tricky. Since the variable *aIntern* was declared as a regular variable in the `Array2a.rlz` file within the *GetIt()* function, it is visible to this routine. This violates good modular programming, since a variable created in another routine is being used within this routine. As we will soon see, there is a better way to initialize variables within dependent functions and procedures.

Next, the *aAnother* array receives the value of the *GetIt2()* function. Again, the contents of the two functions and the two elements are displayed to the Print Log window via the two PRINT instructions. After this is a reference to the QVAR() function. This time, we are checking to see if a variable named *aNewOne* is considered _DEFINED or not. Since that was the name of the variable used in the *GetIt2()* function and was DIM'd as a LOCAL variable, the scope of the variable cannot be outside of the domain of the function or program module that defines it. So at this level, the variable is not visible and is considered *not* defined. Therefore, the simple PRINT instruction of "Not defined!" will be cast to the Print Log window.

Finally, this program presents a new function to consider: the RESET command. When running a Realizer program through the interpretive mode (that is, just running the program modules through Realizer and not building an .EXE file), we cannot re-DIM an existing array without getting a run-time error in the Error Log window. Such an error is shown in Figure 3-7.

In this case, the problem is with the code. Reconsider the *GetIt()* function:

```
func GetIt()

    dim aIntern[1:5] as string
    aIntern[1] = "Straley"
```

More Programming Concepts

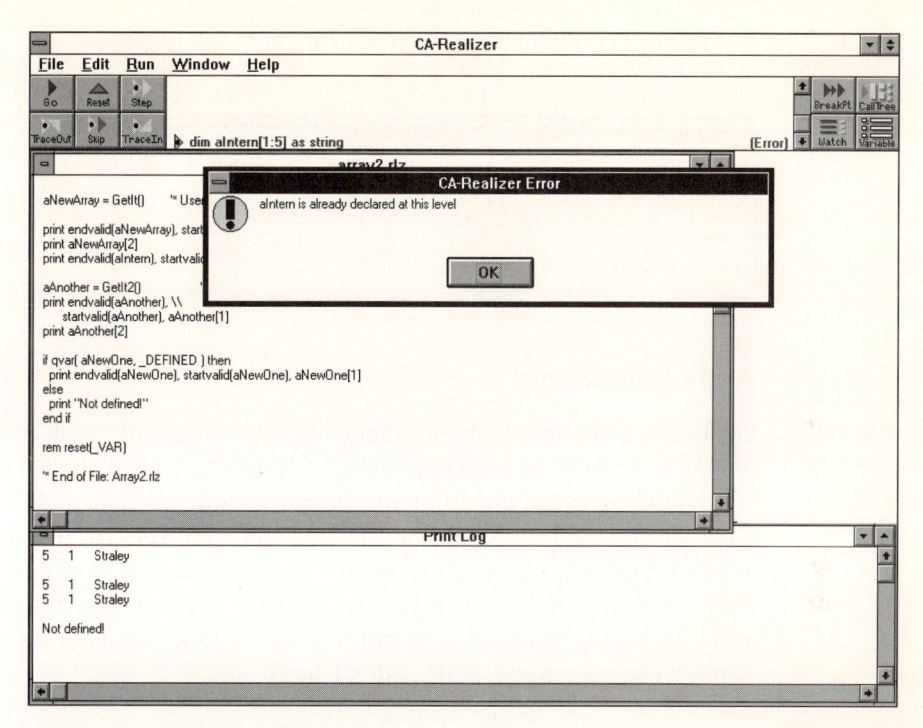

Figure 3-7. Standard CA-Realizer error dialog.

```
    return( aIntern )

end func
```

Here, the value of *aIntern* is the RETURN value of the function, however, in order to remove the DIM from memory, we need to CLEAR the variable. However, we can not do this before the RETURN statement because then the function will return nothing. And, we cannot put the CLEAR command after the RETURN instruction because the program flow will never get to it: once Realizer sees the RETURN instruction, the program will return to the calling routine. So if we were to execute these two programs a second time, as soon as the *GetIt()* function is called from `Array2.rlz`, the DIM instruction will be executed a second time, causing an error.

Fortunately, there is the RESET command. Here, the parameter passed to the function is the internal variable named `_VAR`. This tells Realizer to reset all of the variables within the current environment. Now, when the program concludes, and the RESET command has performed its operation satisfactorily, the two programs can be re-executed within the Realizer environment without fear of a run-time error.

The correct output of this program should look like this:

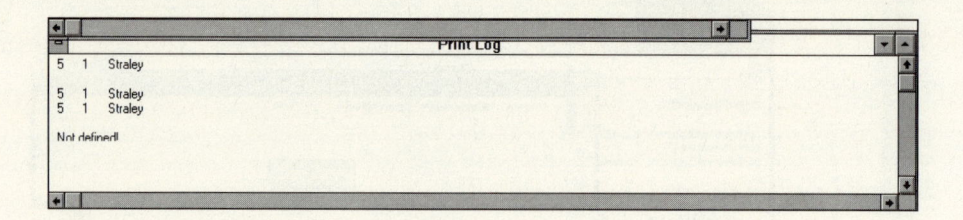

```
Print Log
5  1  Straley
5  1  Straley
5  1  Straley
Not defined!
```

Array Operations

Operators and commands sometimes behave differently with an array than with, for example, a string or an integer. Knowing how to operate on an array efficiently can make the difference between eloquent code and cumbersome code. For example, say we want to store the elements from one array into another. One array is slightly bigger than the other, so we cannot simply assign one array to the other. Instead, we need to iterate through the range of array items. The example program `Array3.rlz` shows how we can do that without resorting to the FOR...NEXT loop.

```
'* Application ... : Array3.rlz
'* Authors ....... : Steve Straley
'* Notice ........ : Copyright(c) 1994 - Sirius Press, Inc.
'* .............. : All Rights Reserved
'* Date .......... : January 1, 1994
'* Description ... : This shows how to process through an array without
'*                   the FOR...NEXT loop

aBaseArray[1:7] = "Monday"       '* Initialize as a string-based array
aBaseArray[2]   = "Tuesday"
aBaseArray[3]   = "Wednesday"
aBaseArray[4]   = "Thursday"
aBaseArray[5]   = "Friday"
aBaseArray[6]   = "Saturday"
aBaseArray[7]   = "Sunday"
print aBaseArray                 '* Show the contents
print "******** END OF ARRAY ********"

aFirstArray[2:5] = ""            '* Make a new array

for iCount = 2 to 5                              '* Iterate through the FOR
   aFirstArray[iCount] = aBaseArray[iCount]      '* NEXT loop, taking from 1
next                                             '* array and assigning to other
```

```
print aFirstArray                         '* And print the results
print "******** END OF ARRAY ********"

aSecondArray[2:5] = ""        '* Make a new array

aSecondArray[2:5] = aBaseArray[2:5]   '* Iterate through!
print aSecondArray                    '* And print results.
print "******** END OF ARRAY ********"

'* End of File: Array3.rlz
```

Here, the initial array on which everything is based is named *aBaseArray*, and it will contain seven elements. Note that initially all of the elements are assigned the string "Monday." This will save an extra step of processing. Then, in elements 2 through 7, the values of the subscripts are altered for the other days of the week. These values are printed to the Print Log window. Following this, a new array named *aFirstArray* is initialized as a string-based array with elements 2 through 5. The *aFirstArray* array will have the same subscript positioning as the main array, *aBaseArray*. The FOR...NEXT loop will increment the counting variable *iCount* beginning at 2 and ending at 5. Then, taking the *iCount* subscript position in *aBaseArray*, the value will be assigned to the *iCount* subscript position in *aFirstArray*. After the FOR...NEXT loop has finished processing, the contents are displayed to the Print Log window.

Finally, a new array named *aSecondArray* is initialized just like *aFirstArray*, however, instead of going through a FOR...NEXT loop, the assignment is made directly from one range in *aBaseArray* (2:5) to another range in *aSecondArray* (2:5). This technique is called **subranging**. If you look at Figure 3-8, you'll see in the Print Log window (which has been adjusted side-by-side with the source file to show all of the output) that everything is as it should be.

The advantages here should be clear: There is no need for an additional memory variable named *iCount* to help with the subscript positions, and processing time is much faster without the FOR...NEXT loop.

More Operators, Unions, and Concatenation

Assigning values from one array to another is not all we can do. Adding or joining arrays together is another valuable possibility. However, using the plus sign (+) will not concatenate two arrays together. If we have two arrays, A and B, and we tried to create a third array with the following:

```
c = a + b
```

```
              array3.rlz                                    Print Log
'* Application ... : Array3.rlz
'* Authors ....... : Steve Straley                 Monday
'* Notice ........ : Copyright(c) 1994 - Sirius Publishing, Inc.   Tuesday
'*               .. : All Rights Reserved          Wednesday
'* Date .......... : January 1, 1994               Thursday
'* Description ... : This shows how to process through an array   Friday
'*              the FOR...NEXT loop                Saturday
                                                   Sunday
aBaseArray[1:7] = "Monday"    '* Initialize as a string-based array   ******** END OF ARRAY ********
aBaseArray[2]   = "Tuesday"                        Tuesday
aBaseArray[3]   = "Wednesday"                      Wednesday
aBaseArray[4]   = "Thursday"                       Thursday
aBaseArray[5]   = "Friday"                         Friday
aBaseArray[6]   = "Saturday"                       ******** END OF ARRAY ********
aBaseArray[7]   = "Sunday"                         Tuesday
print aBaseArray         '* Show the contents      Wednesday
print "******** END OF ARRAY ********"             Thursday
                                                   Friday
aFirstArray[2:5] = ''    '* Make a new array       ******** END OF ARRAY ********

for iCount = 2 to 5        '* Iterate through the FOR
   aFirstArray[iCount] = aBaseArray[iCount]  '* NEXT loop, taking from 1
next                       '* array and assigning to other
print aFirstArray          '* And print the results
print "******** END OF ARRAY ********"

aSecondArray[2:5] = ''     '* Make a new array

aSecondArray[2:5] = aBaseArray[2:5]  '* Iterate through!
print aSecondArray         '* And print results.
print "******** END OF ARRAY ********"

'* End of File: Array3.rlz
```

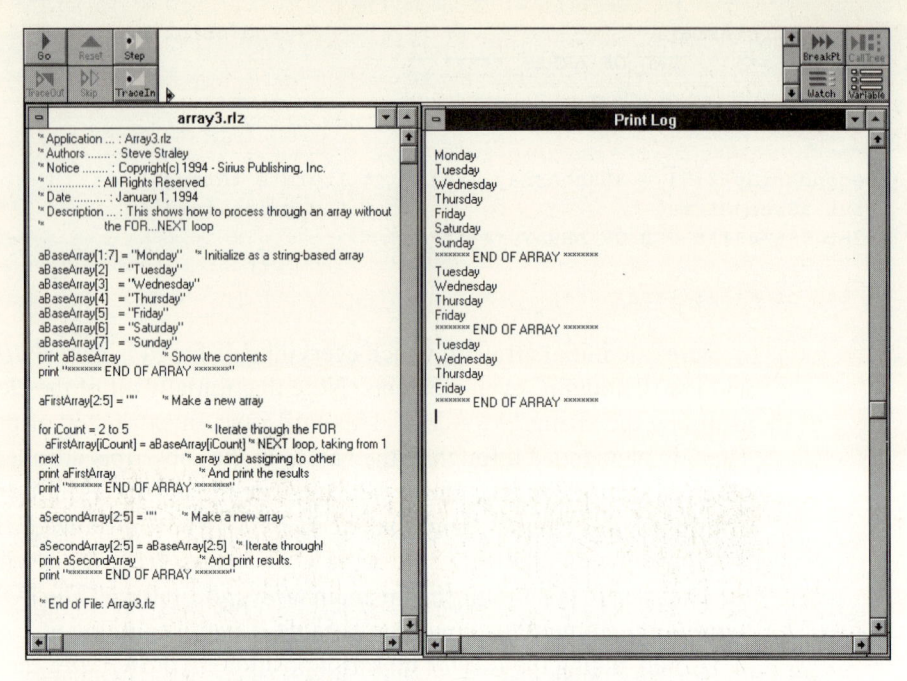

Figure 3-8. Adjusted windows of program and PRINT LOG window with DEBUG window open.

the results would be an array with the length of the smaller of the two arrays A and B, and the elements from both would be added together in each element position in C. This means that the data types of A and B must be the same in order for the elements to be joined together via the plus operator. However, joining two arrays together is not the same as concatenating two arrays. Here, the idea is that the contents of A and B will form a third array in which the number of elements will have the number of elements in A and the number of elements in B. This is different:

```
c = { a, b }
```

In essence, the arrays become subscripts of a literal array assigned to the variable. This is called array concatenation and it is different from the union of arrays. To show this better, here is a program file called `Array4.rlz`, which illustrates both points:

```
'* Application ... : Array4.rlz
'* Authors ....... : Steve Straley
'* Notice ........ : Copyright(c) 1994 - Sirius Press, Inc.
'* ............... : All Rights Reserved
'* Date .......... : January 1, 1994
```

```
'* Description ... : This shows how the + operator works and how to
'*                   concatonate the arrays

'* Build the first array
aBaseArray[1:7] = "Monday"      '* Initialize as a string-based array
aBaseArray[2]   = "Tuesday"
aBaseArray[3]   = "Wednesday"
aBaseArray[4]   = "Thursday"
aBaseArray[5]   = "Friday"
aBaseArray[6]   = "Saturday"
aBaseArray[7]   = "Sunday"

rowprint aBaseArray       '* A new way of output

'* Build the second array
aMonthArray[1:12] = "January"
aMonthArray[2]    = "February"
aMonthArray[3]    = "March"
aMonthArray[4]    = "April"
aMonthArray[5]    = "May"
aMonthArray[6]    = "June"
aMonthArray[7]    = "July"
aMonthArray[8]    = "August"
aMonthArray[9]    = "September"
aMonthArray[10]   = "October"
aMonthArray[11]   = "November"
aMonthArray[12]   = "December"

print (aBaseArray + " - " + aMonthArray)    '* Print the union
print "******** END OF ARRAY ***********"
print (aMonthArray + " - " + aBaseArray)    '* Print the reverse union
print "******** END OF ARRAY ***********"

print { aBaseArray, aMonthArray }           '* Print concatonation
print "******** END OF ARRAY ***********"

'* End of File: Array4.rlz
```

Now, before we discuss how this code works, take a quick look at the output in Figure 3-9. Here, the Debugger window has been closed to show all of the contents in the Print Log window.

The program builds one array with seven string-type elements in it, then uses the ROWPRINT command to print them. This command is similar to the PRINT command except that the contents of the array *aBaseArray* will be printed out to one line within the Print Log window instead of a series of lines. Following this, a new array named *aMonthArray* is built with the names of the 12 months in the year. One array has seven elements, while the other has twelve. The PRINT command of the union looks like this:

```
                                CA-Realizer
File  Edit  Run  Window  Help
                                                Print Log
                                    Monday  Tuesday Wednesday   Thursday Friday   Saturday Sunday
              array4.rlz                        Monday - January
'* Application ... : Array4.rlz                 Tuesday - February
'* Authors ....... : Steve Straley              Wednesday - March
'* Notice ........ : Copyright(c) 1994 - Sirius Publishing, Inc.   Thursday - April
'* .............. : All Rights Reserved         Friday - May
'* Date .......... : January 1, 1994            Saturday - June
'* Description ... : This shows how the + operator works and h   Sunday - July
'*                   concatonate the arrays     ======= END OF ARRAY =======
                                                January - Monday
'* Build the first array                        February - Tuesday
aBaseArray[1:7] = "Monday"    '* Initialize as a string-based ar   March - Wednesday
aBaseArray[2]   = "Tuesday"                     April - Thursday
aBaseArray[3]   = "Wednesday"                   May - Friday
aBaseArray[4]   = "Thursday"                    June - Saturday
aBaseArray[5]   = "Friday"                      July - Sunday
aBaseArray[6]   = "Saturday"                    ======= END OF ARRAY =======
aBaseArray[7]   = "Sunday"                      Monday
                                                Tuesday
rowprint aBaseArray    '* A new way of output   Wednesday
                                                Thursday
'* Build the second array                       Friday
aMonthArray[1:12] = "January"                   Saturday
aMonthArray[2]    = "February"                  Sunday
                                                January
                                                February
                                                March
                                                April
                                                May
                                                June
                                                July
                                                August
                                                September
                                                October
```

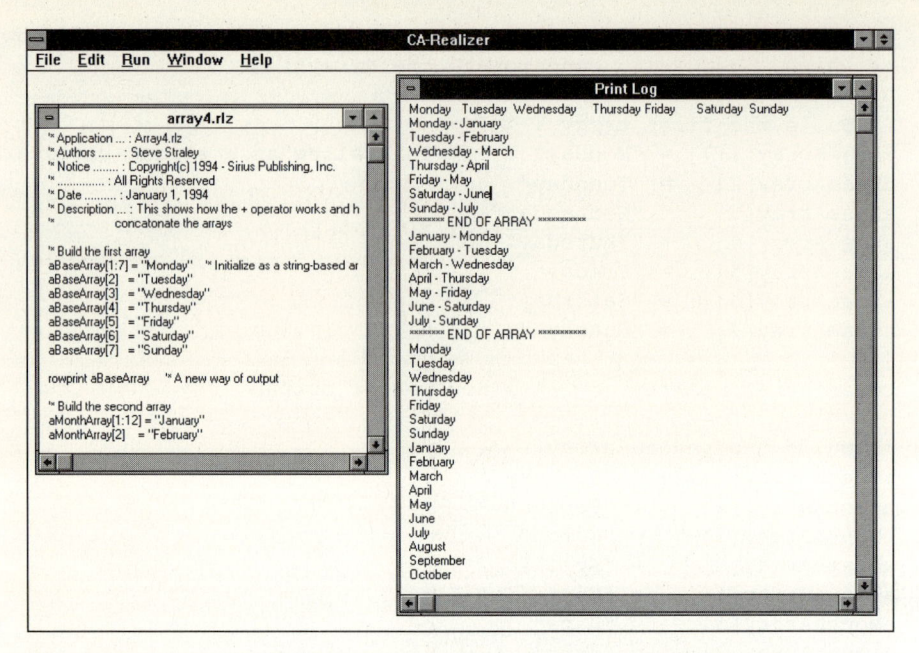

Figure 3-9. Open and adjusted windows of program and PRINT LOG.

```
print (aBaseArray + " - " + aMonthArray) '* Print the union
```

Here, the output will be seven elements, since that is the smaller of the two arrays. In the output, the values found in the array *aBaseArray* will precede the literal string " - " and the contents found in *aMonthArray* will come after it. Two PRINT commands later, this union is reversed:

```
print (aMonthArray + " - " + aBaseArray) '* Print the reverse union
```

Again, only seven elements of this expression will be printed since that is the smaller of the two arrays. However, in this command's output, the contents of *aMonthArray* will appear before the literal string " - " and the contents of *aBaseArray* will appear after it.

Finally, an array concatenation is offered:

```
print { aBaseArray, aMonthArray } '* Print concatonation
```

This command will output nineteen elements, with the first seven elements coming from *aBaseArray* and the last twelve elements coming from *aMonthArray*.

Array Limits

Technically speaking, the limit on an array is bound by two things. The first limit is the amount of memory available for a single entity, which here is roughly 64K. Barring that, the number of elements within an array can contain no more than 65,500 elements—if all the elements are a byte data type. In other words, the maximum number of elements an array is able to hold will vary depending on the data type of the elements. Table 3-1 shows the maximum number of elements based on data type.

Table 3-1. Maximum Number of Elements Based on Data Type.

Data Type	Maximum Number of Elements
Byte	65,500
Word	32,735
Dword	16,368
Single	16,368
Double	8,164
String (variable)	16,368
String * n (fixed)	65,500 / n
DateTime	8,184
Array	16,368
Record	65,500 / (number of fields)
Family	16,368

> **Note:** Although there is a limit to the number of elements within an array, the valid subscript range for elements can be from 0 to 2,147,483,647. The subscript range has nothing to do with the size of the array, it's just the numeric index element position used by the array.

Inserting, Deleting, and Shifting Elements

Deleting elements in an array is easy if you are comfortable dealing with subranging. Basically, to remove an element from an array, the array needs to be reassigned to itself, skipping the subscripts in question with the new subscript range. Inserting array elements works exactly the same way but in reverse. This means that a new range of elements is specified, and the original range is stored into the new.

There are a couple of problems that may crop up when you insert and delete items from an array. For example, consider our standard array of seven elements, each a day of the week. Now, consider the following line of code:

```
aBaseArray[3:5] = aBaseArray[4:6]
```

By subranging the array, all that has taken place is that array elements 4 through 6 have now been placed in element positions 3 through 5. This means that elements 5 and 6 are the same and that the array has not changed in length due to, in this case, the deletion. Instead, we need a more complex expression:

```
aBaseArray = { aBaseArray[ startvalid(aBaseArray) : 2 ], \\
               aBaseArray[ 4 : endvalid( aBaseArray ) ] }
```

This way, the subranging works on just those items below the position to be removed. Then, using the cancatenating technique, the remaining elements can be added back, again using the subranging technique. This way, all of the items have shifted down in the proper order, and the size of the array has been reduced by one.

This is a complex bit of programming that could benefit from a user-defined function or two. You'll find several user-defined functions in *CARTools: A DLL Library for Realizer*. More information is available on CARTools in the back of this book. The file *Array5a.rlz* shows the source code for two of these functions, *AIns()* and *ADel()*. The file that calls it is *Array5.rlz*:

```
'* Application ... : Array5.rlz
'* Authors ....... : Steve Straley
'* Notice ........ : Copyright(c) 1994 - Sirius Press, Inc.
'* ............... : All Rights Reserved
'* Date .......... : January 1, 1994
'* Description ... : Shows how to insert and delete array elements

run "Array5a.rlz"          '* Simple user defined array functions

aBaseArray[1:7] = "Monday"    '* Initialize as a string-based array
aBaseArray[2]   = "Tuesday"
aBaseArray[3]   = "Wednesday"
aBaseArray[4]   = "Thursday"
aBaseArray[5]   = "Friday"
aBaseArray[6]   = "Saturday"
aBaseArray[7]   = "Sunday"

rowprint aBaseArray
```

```
aBaseArray[3:5] = aBaseArray[4:6]       '* This doesn't quite do it!
rowprint aBaseArray

'* Re-set the array again to the correct position!

aBaseArray = {"Monday", "Tuesday", "Wednesday", "Thursday", \\
              "Friday", "Saturday", "Sunday"}

rowprint aBaseArray

aBaseArray = ADel(aBaseArray, 3 )
rowprint aBaseArray

rowprint AIns( aBaseArray, 3, "Wednesday" )

aNew = index(10)

rowprint AIns( aNew, 5, 100 )

'* End of File: Array5.rlz
```

In the beginning of this file, the subranging technique is first used on the *aBaseArray* variable, but we find out with the second occurrence of the ROWPRINT command that the string "Wednesday" has been removed but the string "Saturday" appears twice: once in the fifth position and once in the original sixth position. This is not the goal. When the array is rebuilt, it is then passed off to the user-defined function *ADel()*, which takes two parameters: the array itself and the subscript position to be removed. The value of the *ADel()* function is an array and that value is stored back to the *aBaseArray* variable. The result is then displayed to the Print Log window. The string "Wednesday" has been removed and there is no duplication of elements.

To get the string "Wednesday" back into the array, the *AIns()* function has been created to take three parameters. The source code for this function looks like this:

```
'* Application ... : Array5a.rlz
'* Authors ....... : Steve Straley
'* Notice ........ : Copyright(c) 1994 - Sirius Press, Inc.
'* ............... : All Rights Reserved
'* Date .......... : January 1, 1994
'* Description ... : SPECIAL

'* These functions are part of the CAR Tools created by Sirius Software
'* and published by Sirius Press, Inc.  These tools will be found in
'* part in a .DLL which adds functionality to the Realizer language.  Source
'* code is included where applicable
```

```
'* Name:         ADEL( <aData>, <iElement> )
'* Parameters:   <aData>          Any one-dimensional array
'*               <iElement>       Element position to delete
'* Returns:      <aResults>
'* Purpose:      This function returns an array of <aData> with the
'*               <iElement> removed

func ADel( aData, iElement )
  return( { aData[ startvalid(aData)  : (iElement - 1) ], aData[ (iElement + 1)  : endvalid( aData ) ] } )

end func

'* Name:         AINS( <aData>, <iElement>, <xData> )
'* Parameters:   <aData>          Any one-dimensional array
'*               <iElement>       Element position to insert at
'*               <xData>          Item to be added to array
'* Returns:      <aResults>
'* Purpose:      This function returns an array of <aData> with <xData>
'*               added at the <iElement> position.

func AIns( aData, iElement, xData )

 return( {aData[ startvalid(aData)  : (iElement-1) ], xData, aData[ (iElement)  : endvalid( aData ) ] } )

end func

'* End of File: Array5a.rlz
```

Turning back to the original source file, `Array5.rlz`, the *AIns()* function also works with numerics. In the last few lines of code, a new variable named *aNew* is created with the INDEX() function. Again, the ten elements will have a numeric value of 1 through 10 (assuming that the OPTION BASE command is at its default value of 1). The final call to the ROWPRINT command displays the array returned from *AIns()* in which the fifth element has now a value of 100 and the values of the old fifth through tenth elements have been shifted. The output is shown in Figure 3-10.

It is very important to see that shifting values in an array is not the same thing as removing them, nor is it even close to the same thing as inserting values.

Sorting and Finding Elements in an Array

Sorting elements in an array and finding things in an array are equally challenging tasks. There are several ways to do both. In the program file `Array6.rlz`, a main array is manipulated.

More Programming Concepts

[Figure: CA-Realizer screenshot showing array5.rlz code window and Print Log window]

```
'* Application ... : Array5.rlz
'* Authors ....... : Steve Straley
'* Notice ........ : Copyright(c) 1994 - Sirius Publishing, Inc.
'* ............... : All Rights Reserved
'* Date .......... : January 1, 1994
'* Description ... : Shows how to insert and delete array elements

run "Array5a.rlz"        '* Simple user defined array functions

aBaseArray[1:7] = "Monday"    '* Initialize as a string-based array
aBaseArray[2]   = "Tuesday"
aBaseArray[3]   = "Wednesday"
aBaseArray[4]   = "Thursday"
aBaseArray[5]   = "Friday"
aBaseArray[6]   = "Saturday"
aBaseArray[7]   = "Sunday"

rowprint aBaseArray

aBaseArray[3:5] = aBaseArray[4:6]    '* This doesn't quite do it!
rowprint aBaseArray
```

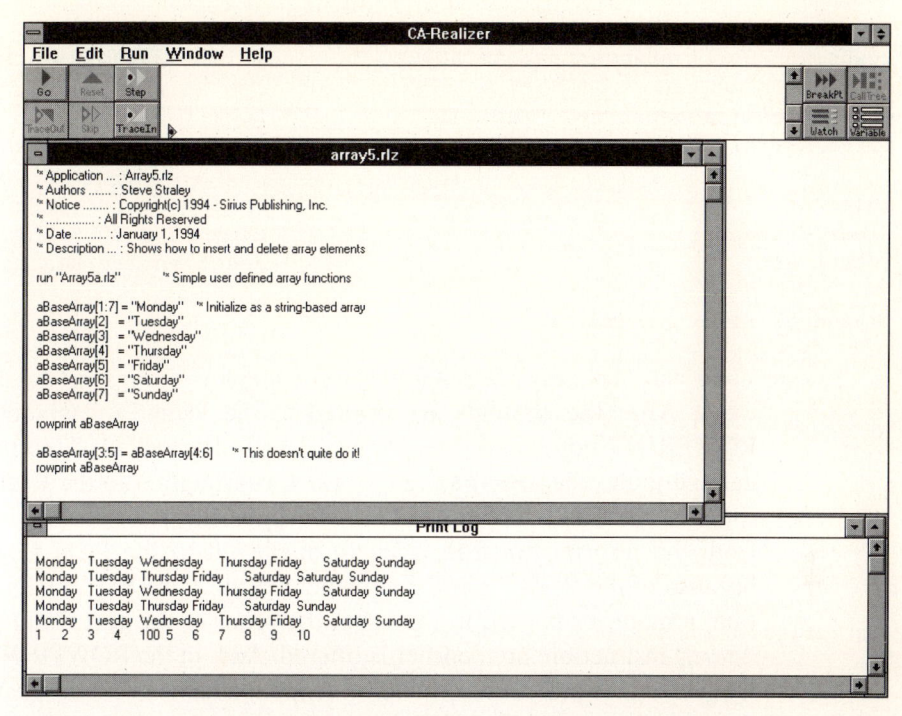

Print Log:
```
Monday  Tuesday  Wednesday  Thursday  Friday   Saturday  Sunday
Monday  Tuesday  Thursday   Friday    Saturday Saturday  Sunday
Monday  Tuesday  Wednesday  Thursday  Friday   Saturday  Sunday
Monday  Tuesday  Thursday   Friday    Saturday Sunday
Monday  Tuesday  Wednesday  Thursday  Friday   Saturday  Sunday
1       2        3          100 5     6        7        8        9        10
```

Figure 3-10.   Executed ARRAY5.RLZ file with PRINT LOG results.

```
'* Application ... : Array6.rlz
'* Authors ....... : Steve Straley
'* Notice ........ : Copyright(c) 1994 - Sirius Press, Inc.
'* ............... : All Rights Reserved
'* Date .......... : January 1, 1994
'* Description ... : This shows the different ways in which an array may
'*                   be sorted and an item may be found.

run "Array6a.rlz"             '* Simple user defined array functions

'* A new array for sorting a seeking

aBaseArray[1:7] = "Monday"       '* Initialize as a string-based array
aBaseArray[2]   = "Tuesday"
aBaseArray[3]   = "Wednesday"
aBaseArray[4]   = "Thursday"
aBaseArray[5]   = "Friday"
aBaseArray[6]   = "Saturday"
aBaseArray[7]   = "Sunday"

rowprint aBaseArray                      '* Print the row of items
rowprint ASort( aBaseArray )             '* Print sorted row of item
```

```
rowprint ASort( aBaseArray; DESCENDING )   '* This is the same as previous
rowprint ASort( aBaseArray; ASCENDING )    '* Print ascending array

print ASeek( aBaseArray, "Wed" )           '* Look for this item
print ASeek( aBaseArray, "Wednesday" )     '* And now look for this item

idle 2                                     '* make wait for 2 seconds
ClearConstants()                           '* Clear the CONSTANTS
reset(_ALL)                                '* Reset entire Realizer!

'* End of File: Array6.rlz
```

To start, the array *aBaseArray* is made up of all strings: all the days of the week. After the contents are printed to the Print Log window via the ROWPRINT command, the *ASort()* function is called. This function is defined in the file `Array6a.rlz`, which is brought into the Realizer environment via the RUN command at the top of this file. The value returned from the *ASort()* function is again displayed to the Print Log window because of the ROWPRINT command. On the third ROWPRINT instruction, a modifier is used to represent the order of the sort. In the previous *ASort()* instruction, no modifier is offered. And, in the ROWPRINT instruction yet to take place, a new modifier is offered named *Ascending*. Where did these modifiers get defined? Let's take a quick look at the `Array6a.rlz` file:

```
'* Application ... : Array6a.rlz
'* Authors ....... : Steve Straley
'* Notice ........ : Copyright(c) 1994 - Sirius Press, Inc.
'* ............... : All Rights Reserved
'* Date .......... : January 1, 1994
'* Description ... : SPECIAL

'* These functions are part of the CARTools created by Sirius Software
'* and published by Sirius Press, Inc.  These tools will be found in
'* part in a .DLL which adds functionality to the Realizer language. Source
'* code is included where applicable

const DESCENDING = 1
const ASCENDING  = 2

'* Name:        ClearConstants()
'* Parameters:  N/A
'* Returns:     N/A
'* Purpose:     This clears the two constants found at the top of the file
'*              and gets executed if the RUN command is experienced

proc ClearConstants()
   clear ASCENDING
```

```
      clear DESCENDING
end proc

'* Name:         ASort( <aData>; <iDirection> )
'* Parameters:   <aData>          Any one-dimensional array
'*               <lDirection>     Direction to be taken
'* Returns:      <aSorted>
'* Purpose:      This sorts a single dimensional array in ascending or
'*               descending order

func ASort( aArray; .. )

  local nBase       as integer
  local xTemp
  local iDirection as integer

  if qnoptmods = 0 then              '* See if a modifier is passed at all
    iDirection = DESCENDING
  else
    if qoptmod(1) = ASCENDING        '* ascending the orders
      iDirection = ASCENDING
    else                             '* descending the orders
      iDirection = DESCENDING
    end if
  end if

  if iDirection = DESCENDING

    nBase = startvalid( aArray )

    while nBase < endvalid( aArray )

      if aArray[ nBase ] <= aArray[nBase+1] then
        nBase = nBase + 1

      else
        xTemp = aArray[nBase]
        aArray[nBase] = aArray[nBase+1]
        aArray[nBase+1] = xTemp

        nBase = startvalid( aArray )

      end if

    end while
  else
    nBase = endvalid( aArray )
    while nBase > startvalid( aArray )
```

```
      if aArray[ nBase ] <= aArray[nBase - 1] then
        nBase = nBase - 1
      else
        xTemp = aArray[nBase]
        aArray[nBase] = aArray[nBase - 1]
        aArray[nBase - 1] = xTemp
        nBase = endvalid( aArray )
      end if
    end while
  end if

  return( aArray )

end func

'* Name:         ASeek( <aData>, <xItem> )
'* Parameters:   <aData>         Any one-dimensional array
'*               <xItem>         Item to be found
'* Returns:      <iPosition>
'* Purpose:      This will return the <iPosition>th in <aData> where <xItem>
'*               may be found. If no item is found, then the function will
'*               return a -1.

func ASeek( aArray, xItem )

  local iCount as integer

  for iCount = startvalid( aArray ) to endvalid( aArray )
    if aArray[iCount] = xItem then
      exit for
    end if
  next

  if iCount > endvalid( aArray ) then
    iCount = -1
  end if

  return( iCount )

end func

'* End of File: Array6a.rlz
```

When this file is loaded into the system, two constants are defined at the top of the file: DESCENDING and ASCENDING. These constants are now available to the system, including the calling file *Array6.rlz*. In addition

More Programming Concepts 143

to being used in the main source file, these constants are also used as the crux of the *ASort( )* function. Within the definition of the *ASort( )* function there are some new declaration statements:

```
local nBase      as integer
local xTemp
local iDirection as integer
```

These variables are now LOCAL to this function and visible to all functions within this file, but not visible to anything outside of the file's domain. With one mandatory parameter named *aArray*, there is an optional modifier. Remember, the two dots (..) mean just that: optional. Therefore, if the modifier is optional, we have to see if it is passed, and if not, we should assume a default condition.

> **Note:** One of the principles of building a robust application, including a robust function or procedure, is that it should work in abnormal conditions. This means that if no parameter is passed or no modifier is offered, the function/procedure should default to an expected behavior.

The code in question looks like this:

```
if qnoptmods = 0 then              '* See if a modifier is passed at all
   iDirection = DESCENDING
else
   if qoptmod(1) = ASCENDING        '* ascending the orders
      iDirection = ASCENDING
   else                             '* descending the orders
      iDirection = DESCENDING
   end if
end if
```

The QNOPTMODS instruction finds out how many modifiers were passed. If none were passed, the value of *iDirection* will be the constant DESCENDING. Also, if anything other than the ASCENDING value is passed as a modifier, the value of *iDirection* is also DESCENDING. If a modifier is passed to this function, the value of the first modifier needs to be retrieved. This is the purpose of the QOPTMOD(1) function. By passing a 1 as a parameter to this function, we are asking for the value of the first modifier, and if it is equal to the constant ASCENDING, then we assign *iDirection* to that value; otherwise, *iDirection* gets the value of the DESCENDING constant. This is a clear case of how modifiers can help a function.

Turning back to our original file, the output from the three sorts should now be obvious. In addition to those, the value of the added *ASeek()* function is printed twice to the Print Log window.

```
print ASeek( aBaseArray, "Wed" )             '* Look for this item
print ASeek( aBaseArray, "Wednesday" )       '* And now look for this item
```

The first call will yield a –1 value. This is default value if the item as the second parameter is not found within the array *aBaseArray*. The second call to *ASeek()* will return a positive 1, which means that the string "Wednesday" is in the first subscript position of the array *aBaseArray*. This is why the return value of –1 is for a no-match situation: We cannot have a –1 subscript position. The *ASeek()* function is defined in the `Array6a.rlz` file, and both it and *ASort()* are a part of *CARTools: A DLL Library for Realizer*.

Here is a snapshot of the Print Log window just before the execution of the last instruction:

```
                            Print Log
Monday   Tuesday  Wednesday  Thursday Friday  Saturday Sunday
Friday    Monday   Saturday Sunday   Thursday Tuesday Wednesday
Friday    Monday   Saturday Sunday   Thursday Tuesday Wednesday
Wednesday Tuesday  Thursday Sunday   Saturday Monday  Friday
-1
1
```

Finally, the last three instructions in this file are:

```
idle 2                    '* make wait for 2 seconds
ClearConstants()          '* Clear the CONSTANTS
reset(_ALL)               '* Reset entire Realizer!
```

The first one introduces the IDLE command, which tells Realizer to wait the specified number of seconds before continuing to process. The *ClearConstants()* procedure call clears the two constants defined in `Array6a.rlz` which were brought into the system via the RUN command. The last command offers a new internal variable in the RESET() function: `_ALL`. This should not only clear the Realizer system of all variables, but also close all files and forms and clear all windows. The only thing it does not do is reset the machine!

Multi-Dimensional Arrays

With the fundamentals of arrays firmly in hand, we now can move on to more-complex structures, such as an item that is sometimes called a table, or a multi-dimensional array, or even a matrix. Databases, spreadsheets—anything with a grid-like formation is a prime example of a matrix. In these cases, there are rows and columns, or fields and records. In Realizer, a matrix is a complex array structure. These items are initialized in the same manner as a simple array and have many of the same properties, including subranging and subscripting. Matrixes must be uniform in dimensions, and individual dimensions can be assigned to individual arrays. In many ways, the rules for individual dimensions are the same as for single arrays.

> **Note:** Realizer does not support the concept of a ragged array. This means that all of the dimensions of a matrix must be consistent and uniform. One dimension of a matrix cannot be of a different format than another.

Again, all of the operations for an array are relatively the same for a matrix, which includes concatenation and joining. Individual elements of a matrix may be specified by referencing the proper dimensional element. For example, consider the following table:

Monday	January	United States
Tuesday	February	Canada
Wednesday	March	Mexico
Thursday	April	The Netherlands
Friday	May	Australia
Saturday	June	Germany
Sunday	July	France
No-day	August	Spain

This table is considered to be a 3-by-8 matrix. This entire entity could be stored to a single variable. That variable could then be printed, manipulated, or even calculated. If we want a single value from this grid, we would refer to its position first down the list, and then over. So if we wanted the 2-by-2 element, which would be the string "Canada," we would note this as [2,2]. The first value in the square brackets is the number of elements down in the grid, and the second value is the number of elements over in the grid: "Canada." Going further, if this entire grid is assigned to a variable named *aGrid*, the code to print the string "Canada" would look like this:

```
print aGrid[2,2]
```

To print an entire row of items, say the row that starts with the string "Sunday", the code would look like this:

```
print aGrid[7,1:3]
```

The subranging in the second dimension limits the scope of the Print command. The variable may also be stored off to another variable for printing:

```
aNewValue = aGrid[7,1:3]
print aNewValue
```

Here, we removed a complete dimension from the *aGrid* variable and assigned it to the variable *aNewValue*. This is now a one-dimensional array, which is printed to the Print Log window. To see all of this in action, here is a sample file called `Matrix1.rlz`, which illustrates many of these concepts:

```
'* Application ... : Matrix1.rlz
'* Authors ....... : Steve Straley
'* Notice ........ : Copyright(c) 1994 - Sirius Press, Inc.
'* ............... : All Rights Reserved
'* Date .......... : January 1, 1994
'* Description ... : This shows the different ways in which a matrix and
'*                   other array-based functions/operations may be
'*                   created.

local aMatrix1[1:3, 1:10] as integer    '* Create the matrix of values
local iXCount              as integer    '* Create a blank value
local iYCount              as integer
local aNew                 as array      '* And now create a blank array

          '* Fill the values appropriately....
for iXCount = 1 to 3
  for iYCount = 1 to 10
    aMatrix[iXCount, iYCount] = iXCount * iYCount
  next
next

print aMatrix    '* The Print command will work on a matrix!
```

More Programming Concepts

```
rowprint aMatrix[1, 1:5]     '* Now print a sub-set of the matrix

aNew = aMatrix[ endvalid( aMatrix ), 2:6 ]  '* Assign the subset
print aNew                                  '* Print the array
print sum( aNew )
print sum( aMatrix[ endvalid( aMatrix ), 2:6 ] )
print product( aNew )
print product( aMatrix[ endvalid( aMatrix ), 2:6 ] )

'* End of File: Matrix1.rlz
```

The output for this example is shown in Figure 3-11.

```
Print Log
1  2  3  4  5  6  7  8  9  10
2  4  6  8  10 12 14 16 18 20
3  6  9  12 15 18 21 24 27 30
1  2  3  4  5
6
9
12
15
18
60
60
174960
174960
```

Figure 3-11. Results in an expanded PRINT LOG window.

The first variable called *aMatrix* is declared to be a 3-by-10 array with all integers to be assigned. After two other variables are declared, a new variable that will be of an array data type, named *aNew*, is also initialized. Then, the FOR...NEXT loop fills the various elements in all of the dimensions of the *aMatrix* array.

> **Note:** Even though a variable may be a matrix, it sometimes is still referred to as an array—an array with multi-dimensions.

After the various positions are filled with values, the entire matrix is displayed with the PRINT command. This command will print out three rows, with ten elements on each row. Following this, the ROWPRINT command will print out the contents of the first dimension, elements 1 through 5. This is how subranging can work with regard to a matrix. We can even assign that subrange of values from any dimension to an array variable. This array will be a one-dimensional array. The *aNew* variable will take the last dimension in *aMatrix*, and from there, we will take elements 2 through 6.

> **Note:** Don't forget that you can use the various functions that return numeric values as part of the subscript position when referencing a particular dimension or element.

The *aNew* array is then printed to the Print Log window, showing that the elements that were once being displayed horizontally across the screen can now be printed vertically.

There are several other functions that can work on an entire array or even a matrix. For example, the SUM() function will sum the values found in the *aNew* array. The next SUM() call, instead of using the *aNew* array as a parameter to this function, references back to the *aMatrix* variable. The results should be identical. The PRODUCT() function works in the same way.

You can also expand existing arrays out to new dimensions. Take the 3-by-10-element array in the previous example. If we were to add the following line of code:

```
aMatrix[4,15] = 100
```

we would extend the matrix to a 4-by-15 matrix with the original subset values, from 1,1 to 3,10, all in place; with the value of *aMatrix[4,15]* set to 100; and everything in between filled with 0.

```
                                 Print Log
1  2  3  4  5  6  7  8  9  10
2  4  6  8  10 12 14 16 18 20
3  6  9  12 15 18 21 24 27 30

1  2  3  4  5  6  7  8  9  10 0  0  0  0  0
2  4  6  8  10 12 14 16 18 20 0  0  0  0  0
3  6  9  12 15 18 21 24 27 30 0  0  0  0  0
0  0  0  0  0  0  0  0  0  0  0  0  0  0  100
```

Realizer offers several functions specifically geared to working with a complex structure like a matrix. These functions are:

MATTRANSPOSE()	Returns the transposition of a given matrix of values
MATINVERT()	Returns the inversion of a given matrix of values. This matrix must be square: 2 by 2, 3 by 3, 4 by 4, and so on.
MATMULT()	Returns the multiplication of two given matrixes

More Programming Concepts 149

In addition, functions such as STATNORM(), STATPERCENT(), STATSORT() and STATRANK() work off of arrays to provide statistical information.

Records and Families

This is the most complex idea within this chapter and it directly relates to the foundations of array technology, data types, expressions, and more.

A Single Record

So far in this chapter, we've touched lightly on the concept of structure, and stressed the idea that only like data can be stored in an array, and not mixed data types. However, sometimes in application development, we need to store pieces of information off to a file, usually a database. In a database, the fields that compose each record of information have something in common with each other, yet the data types for these pieces of information may not be the same. For example, in the database file that we are creating for our wine inventory, each record consists of several fields of information: the name of each bottle of wine, the type, the region from which it comes (appelation), the price we paid for it, the year it was bottled, and so on. These last two pieces of information are of numeric and date data types, which are different from the string data types that could hold the other pieces of data. Since our application needs to be able to work with databases and their constituent records, we need to get Realizer to recognize these database structures.

Before we begin to define the structure for a record, we need to look at what the structure might be for a database. Again, each record in the file will represent one bottle of wine.

Name	Data Type
Winery	String
Style	String
Year	Numeric
Wine Name	String
County	String
State	String
Country	String

Region	String
Composition	String
Bin Number	Numeric
Lot Number	Numeric
Date Purchased	DateTime
Amount	Numeric
Value	Numeric
Date Consumed	DateTime
Date Sold	DateTime
Amount	Numeric
Comments	Array

Now, the *Style* field here might tie into another database containing all of the various wine types available. Additionally, the *Winery* field might also tie into another database containing all of the various wineries around the world. Again, the level of sophistication is limited only by your determination to make a complete, solid, and sound application. It never hurts to add too much help for an end user when it comes to data entry.

With this structure in mind, we can begin to build the RECORD structure in memory. The TYPE command will help us define this structure. Along with the TYPE command must be the name of the structure we are going to build. You can see all of this in action and follow the steps in a sample structure built into the `Record1.rlz` file:

```
'* Application ... : Record1.rlz
'* Authors ....... : Steve Straley
'* Notice ........ : Copyright(c) 1994 - Sirius Press, Inc.
'* ............... : All Rights Reserved
'* Date .......... : January 1, 1994
'* Description ... : This shows how to build a record structure and to use
'*                   it in conjunction with array technology.

'* First, build the structure of the record in memory

type Wine
   Winery          as string * 25
   Style           as string * 20
   Year            as word
   FullName        as string * 40
```

More Programming Concepts

```
    County              as string * 15
    State               as string * 2
    Country             as string * 40
    Region              as string * 20
    Composition         as string * 25
    BinNumber           as byte
    LotNumber           as byte
    DatePurchased       as datetime
    Amount              as single
    Value               as single
    DateConsumed        as datetime
    DateSold            as datetime
    Amount              as single
    Comments            as array
end type

'* Once built, create a variable off of this structure....

dim rWine as Wine           '* create the record in memory
local aStuff as array       '* create a blank array

'* Now, we want to fill the record up with values

rWine.Winery        = "Rodney Strong"
rWine.Style         = "Chardonnay"
rWine.Year          = 1991
rWine.FullName      = "Chalk Hell Vineyard"
rWine.County        = "Sonoma"
rWine.State         = "CA"
rWine.Country       = "USA"
rWine.Region        = "Sonoma"
rWine.Composition   = ""
rWine.BinNumber     = 0
rWine.LotNumber     = 0
rWine.DatePurchased = strtodate("6/1/93")
rWine.Amount        = 14.95
rWine.Value         = 22.50
rWine.DateConsumed  = strtodate("1/1/01")
rWine.DateSold      = strtodate("1/1/01")
rWine.Amount        = 0
rWine.Comments      = {""}

print rWine.Fullname        '* Let's see if we can print...

'* Assign like data types to the array

aStuff = { rWine.Winery, rWine.Style, rWine.FullName, \\
           rWine.County, rWine.State, rWine.Country, \\
           rWine.Region }
```

```
print aStuff          '* And now print the array!
reset( _VAR )

'* End of File: Record1.rlz
```

The record data type is created off of the structure named *Wine* and assigned to the record data type named *rWine*. While in many ways, the *rWine* variable may act like an array where the various field names are the subscripts in that array, it is not the same thing. For example, the PRINT command will not work off of the *rWine* variable. It will, however, print individual members within the *rWine* structure, as shown in the example program. And, we can gather like data types within that structure to build a new array, named *aStuff*, that will eventually be printed off at one time. Keep in mind that while printing or while assigning off to other variables, the prefix name of the record structure—the *rWine* reference—must be used in conjunction with the field name in question. A single period (.) separates the name of the record structure and the name of the field. In addition, to be consistent with our other data types, the lowercase letter "r" is used as a meta symbol for our Hungarian notation style of programming. After this program executes, the Print Log window should look something like this:

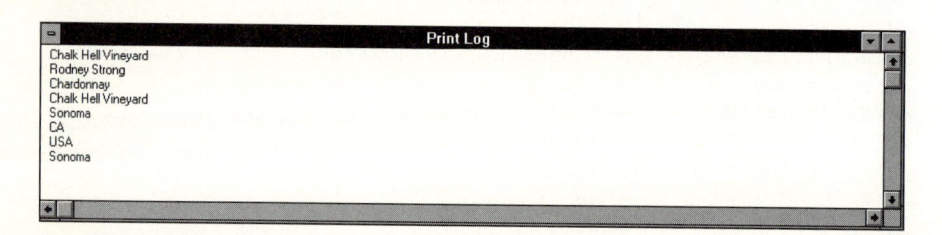

```
                          Print Log
Chalk Hell Vineyard
Rodney Strong
Chardonnay
Chalk Hell Vineyard
Sonoma
CA
USA
Sonoma
```

Groups of Records

The previous example shows one single record stored to the *rWine* variable. Often, we need to gather several records at a time. This is easy to handle in Realizer but requires a strict discipline on your part to keep the various entities straight in your mind. Since a record is like an array, a collection of records can be stored to an array as well. For example, in this file, `Record2.rlz`, in just a few lines of code, many implications can be drawn:

```
'* Application ... : Record2.rlz
'* Authors ....... : Steve Straley
'* Notice ........ : Copyright(c) 1994 - Sirius Press, Inc.
'* ............... : All Rights Reserved
'* Date .......... : January 1, 1994
```

More Programming Concepts

```
'* Description ... : This shows how several records can be built
'*                   from a different routine and how those records can
'*                   be collected in a separate array.

run "Record2a.rlz"              '* Run and load the file

BuildStructures()               '* Build the database structure

local rWines(2) as wine         '* Create an array of records
local aWineries as array        '* Create a dummy array

AddRecord( rWines )             '* Add the records

print rWines[1].Winery, rWines[2].Winery    '* Print them

aWineries = rWines[1:2].Winery              '* Collect them
rowprint aWineries                          '* Print those as well..

'* End of File: Record2.rlz
```

First, the RUN command is executed and, as expected, loads the necessary file. The user-defined procedure named *BuildStructure()* is executed and uses the TYPE command to build the Wine record structure as shown in the previous example. Following this, two variables are declared. One is of a record type and the structure used is *Wine*. In the process of telling what type it is, two records have been created. The array *aWineries* is just an empty array declaration for the time being.

Next, the call to the *AddRecord()* function is unique and special. Since the variable *rWines* is passed to this function by reference, the entire structure is available to this subroutine. The file `Record2a.rlz` shows what takes place:

```
'* Application ... : Record2a.rlz
'* Authors ....... : Steve Straley
'* Notice ........ : Copyright(c) 1994 - Sirius Press, Inc.
'* .............. : All Rights Reserved
'* Date .......... : January 1, 1994
'* Description ... : This builds the structure of the record and creates
'*                   two dummy records.

'* Name:      BuildStructures()
'* Purpose:   Builds the WINE structure

proc BuildStructures()
```

```
    type Wine
        Winery              as string * 25
        Style               as string * 20
        Year                as word
        FullName            as string * 50
        County              as string * 15
        State               as string * 2
        Country             as string * 40
        Region              as string * 20
        Composition         as string * 25
        BinNumber           as byte
        LotNumber           as byte
        DatePurchased       as datetime
        Amount              as single
        Value               as single
        DateConsumed        as datetime
        DateSold            as datetime
        Amount              as single
        Comments            as array
    end type

end proc

'* Name:         AddRecord( <rDataSet> )
'* Parameter:    <rDataSet>      an empty dataset of records for WINE
'* Purpose:      Builds 2 records for the array since it was passed by
'*               reference

proc AddRecord( rDataSet )

    '* Record 1
    rDataSet[1].Winery          = "Rodney Strong"
    rDataSet[1].Style           = "Chardonnay"
    rDataSet[1].Year            = 1991
    rDataSet[1].FullName        = "Chalk Hell Vineyard"
    rDataSet[1].County          = "Sonoma"
    rDataSet[1].State           = "CA"
    rDataSet[1].Country         = "USA"
    rDataSet[1].Region          = "Sonoma"
    rDataSet[1].Composition     = ""
    rDataSet[1].BinNumber       = 0
    rDataSet[1].LotNumber       = 0
    rDataSet[1].DatePurchased   = strtodate("6/1/93")
    rDataSet[1].Amount          = 14.95
    rDataSet[1].Value           = 22.50
    rDataSet[1].DateConsumed    = strtodate("1/1/01")
    rDataSet[1].DateSold        = strtodate("1/1/01")
    rDataSet[1].Amount          = 0
    rDataSet[1].Comments        = {""}
```

```
'* Record 2
rDataSet[2].Winery           = "Schug"
rDataSet[2].Style            = "Pinot Noir"
rDataSet[2].Year             = 1989
rDataSet[2].FullName         = "Napa Valley Pinot Noir (Heinemann Vineyard)"
rDataSet[2].County           = "Napa"
rDataSet[2].State            = "CA"
rDataSet[2].Country          = "USA"
rDataSet[2].Region           = "Napa"
rDataSet[2].Composition      = ""
rDataSet[2].BinNumber        = 0
rDataSet[2].LotNumber        = 0
rDataSet[2].DatePurchased    = strtodate("6/1/93")
rDataSet[2].Amount           = 17.95
rDataSet[2].Value            = 32.50
rDataSet[2].DateConsumed     = strtodate("1/1/01")
rDataSet[2].DateSold         = strtodate("1/1/01")
rDataSet[2].Amount           = 0
rDataSet[2].Comments         = {""}

end proc

'* End of File: Record2a.rlz
```

The parameter in the *AddRecord()* function is called *rDataSet*. Again, the name of the original variable and the name of the parameter do not need to be the same. Now, since there has been an allocation of two records made within the new *rDataSet* variable, we can assign values to individual members within the structure. This will work like a matrix; however, instead of using only subscripts to get at the exact element, here we will use one subscript to point at which record in the structure we want, and then use the name given in that structure.

For example, when the code looks like this:

```
rDataSet[2].Value = 32.50
```

we are assigning the *Value* field in the second record of the *rDataSet* record structure. Now, turning back to the original file, the following lines are left:

```
print rWines[1].Winery, rWines[2].Winery    '* Print them

aWineries = rWines[1:2].Winery              '* Collect them
rowprint aWineries                          '* Print those as well..
```

It is important to see that while the *rWines* variable began as an empty collection of structures, it quickly became filled when it was passed by reference to the *AddRecord()* function. Now with values in the various locations, the PRINT command can print the names of the *Winery* field in both record number 1 and record number 2. Following this, I chose to use the subranging techiques outlined earlier to gather up the contents of the *Winery* field for records 1 through 2. Once collected, I print them to the Print Log window. Both outputs are exactly the same.

Families

Families are similar to records in that the notation between the root name (or the name of the record variable) and the contents (or the fields) are separated by commas. However, unlike records, families do not require the TYPE command to define the structure in advance. This has some advantages as well as some drawbacks. One advantage is that the structure being defined is dynamic and can change based purely on information gathered by the end user. The program can literally grow with the end user as new information becomes available. However, mastering an almost uncontrolled structure is difficult. So, in a twist on the first example program, which illustrated the concept of a record, this file named `Family1.rlz` simply switches the concept from record to family:

```
'* Application ... : Family1.rlz
'* Authors ....... : Steve Straley
'* Notice ........ : Copyright(c) 1994 - Sirius Press, Inc.
'* ............... : All Rights Reserved
'* Date .......... : January 1, 1994
'* Description ... : This shows how to build a FAMILY and to use it in
'*                   conjunction with array technology.

local fWine as family     '* It should be declared!
local aStuff as array     '* And this should be declared as well

'* Now add this record
fWine.Winery         = "Rodney Strong"
fWine.Style          = "Chardonnay"
fWine.Year           = 1991
fWine.FullName       = "Chalk Hell Vineyard"
fWine.County         = "Sonoma"
fWine.State          = "CA"
fWine.Country        = "USA"
fWine.Region         = "Sonoma"
fWine.Composition    = ""
fWine.BinNumber      = 0
fWine.LotNumber      = 0
fWine.DatePurchased  = strtodate("6/1/93")
fWine.Amount         = 14.95
fWine.Value          = 22.50
```

```
fWine.DateConsumed    = strtodate("1/1/01")
fWine.DateSold        = strtodate("1/1/01")
fWine.Amount          = 0
fWine.Comments        = {""}

print fWine.Fullname        '* Let's see if we can print...

'* Assign like data types to the array

aStuff = { fWine.Winery, fWine.Style, fWine.FullName, \\
           fWine.County, fWine.State, fWine.Country, \\
           fWine.Region }
print aStuff                '* And now print the array!

reset( _VAR )

'* End of File: Family1.rlz
```

By simply stating at the beginning that this variable will be of type FAMILY, the structure can be built as we go. This also means that the structure can change as well as the data types contained within. For example, the field-like string values are not set to a fixed length as in the previous example (`Record1.rlz`). In addition, the data type for each of the "family members" can change in value and in type. Note that when items are stored to the *aStuff* variable, other than the meta symbol in front of the family name, there is no difference in output or performance. In other words, without the letter "f" in front of the variable, there would be no way of telling what we are looking at. This same technique could be used in converting the `Record2.rlz` file. We could extend the idea and of a dynamic FAMILY of records, each holding the rigid structure of the RECORD; in essence, the best of both worlds.

These two techniques, along with all of the others outlined so far, will become vital when we begin to talk about data-entry screens and storing these items to a data file. Without the rigid concepts of structure firmly in place, no one should even begin to tackle the concepts of file I/O. So, if you need to, go back and reread this section.

Conclusion

It should be apparent by now that a good fundamental understanding of array technology, family, and record structures, not to mention parameters and user-defined data types, is at the core of the power of this product. Realizer allows you to create flexibility to find data, hold data, merge data, and print data if you are willing to memorize these basic steps. The key to unlocking the power and potential of this product lies in the successful manipulation of array concepts.

Chapter 4

Simple Forms for Data Entry and Data Validation

In this chapter, we will continue to build our wine program, adding such visual elements as start-up screens, data-entry screens, and warning messages. Programmers sometimes call these elements "gratuitous visual pufferies," but they make it possible for end users to interact smoothly with a program. In Realizer, the main tool for creating these elements is the **form**.

The Form

The form is the standard Realizer device for conveying information to the end user and collecting information from the end user. The form is essentially a window without being called a window. Forms are everywhere: data-entry screens with displayed text and push buttons, even a report can be considered a form. Some experts might see a form as a localized event handler, but Realizer is not a true event-driven language. However, to exist in the world of Windows, many of the individual elements within the language have event-like behaviors. We will get more into this as the chapter progresses. Getting back to the main topic, knowing what the form technology is and how it operates in an application is essential in Realizer.

Step One

There are two ways to create a form in Realizer. One is to use the FormDev utility program, as we did to create the menus in Chapter 2. The design of every aspect of the form is handled by this development tool, and we could take that approach here as well. However, in this chapter, we will look at forms from a different angle. Here, we will look at the language of a form, how to make one, how to manipulate one, and how it plays in relation to the application. Once we understand the various pieces of a form, we can turn to the FormDev utility to build quick-and-dirty form "shells" that we can fine-tune and modify to fit our needs. However, before we can walk, we have to crawl; so here are some overall concepts for form development.

Realizer has an internal variable that keeps track of the most current and active form. This internal variable is set when one of two functions are encountered in the language: FORMNEW() or FORMSELECT(). All forms must be created before being selected, and once a form is created, the internal variable for Realizer is set to recognize that particular form. The advantage of this is that we can build forms immediately and activate them for the end user, or we can build our forms in advance and activate them as the need arises, such as in response to a menu selection. The main starting point for a form may look like this:

```
nVar = formnew( ; "Example", _BORDERLESS )
```

Even though the internal variable for Realizer is set to work with this particular form, any other form function will work off of this form unless the **form ID** value is required. The form ID is held in the *nVar* variable, and it is this variable that will be used in some of the other form functions, including FORMSELECT():

```
formselect( nVar )
```

This is how we can tell Realizer to redirect its focus to this particular form. Even though it is not required to have the return value of the FORMNEW() function stored off to a variable, you can now see why it may not be such a bad idea.

When you create a form, you can use any of several internal variables to specify particular characteristics, or styles. In the example above, the _BORDERLESS style was selected when that form was created. Table 4-1 outlines the various styles available.

Table 4-1. Internal Variables and Available Styles.

Internal Variable	Type of Item
_CLOSE	Allows the form to be closed from the form window's system menu or the Realizer FILE CLOSE menu
_FRAME	Places a frame around the form window and may not be used in conjunction with either _TITLE or _SIZE.
_BORDERLESS	Creates the window without any border at all and cannot be used in conjunction with either _TITLE or _SIZE.

(continued)

Table 4-1. *(continued)*

Internal Variable	Type of Item
_SIZE	Places a thin sizing frame around the form window. If the internal variable _TITLE is set as well, a maximize icon is placed in the title bar.
_TITLE	Puts a title bar at the top of the window, which allows the window to be moved.
_MINIMIZE	Allows the window to be minimized from the form window's system menu. If the internal variable _TITLE is also set, a minimize icon is placed in the title bar.
_NOMAX	Prevents the window from being maximized and removes the maximize icon (if present) from the title bar.
_HOTCLICK	Causes mouse clicks in the form to be processed even when the form is not in front (or active). By default, a mouse click in a background window brings only that window forward.
_CONTEXENTER	Controls the behavior of the ENTER key in the form. By default, the ENTER key is the same as object value 1 in the form. If the ENTER key is needed in logs or multi-line controls, the CTRL+ENTER key combination must be used. This internal variable overrides this default in the form, allowing logs and edit control to receive the ENTER key. If this is used, the ENTER key no longer notifies the form as being object number/value 1.
_NONMDI	Creates the form window outside of the Multiple Document Interface (MDI) region. The window is always on top of all MDI windows, and if it is moved outside of the main Realizer window, it will not cause the MDI scroll bars to appear.
_TOOLBAR	A combination of _NONMDI and _BORDERLESS and _HOTCLICK.
_PALETTE	A combination of _NONMDI and _TITLE and _SIZE and _CLOSE and _NOMAX.
_POPUP	Creates a form window completely outside of the main Realizer window.

Unless specified, many of these styles may be combined in a single form. For example, turning back to our first FORMNEW() function call, if we

Simple Forms for Data Entry and Data Validation

wanted a borderless form that could be minimized, we could simply rewrite the first function call as follows:

```
nVar = formnew( ; "Example", _BORDERLESS + _MINIMIZE )
```

Once your program either selects or creates a form, you'll probably want the program to control it in some way, such as showing or hiding the window or establishing its size. The most basic function call would be to show the window:

```
formcontrol( _SHOW )
```

If the form in question is not selected, then the first function call would be to the FORMSELECT() function, followed by the FORMCONTROL() function call. However, if the window you're manipulating is the one that needs to be displayed, then the latter function call is sufficient. Let's take a look at this fragment of code from the *Form1.rlz* sample program.

```
iForm1 = formnew(; "Example Text", _BORDERLESS + _MINIMIZE )

formcontrol( _SHOW )
formcontrol( _MINIMIZE )
formcontrol( _CLOSE )
```

If the Debugger is turned on and we step through the source code, we would see that first, the form is created and an ID reference to that form is stored to the *iForm1* variable. Next, the FORMCONTROL() function is called to show the newly created form. Without any other assignment made to this form, such as position or color, the form will appear as a white, blank area overlaying some of the information in the file, as shown in Figure 4-1.

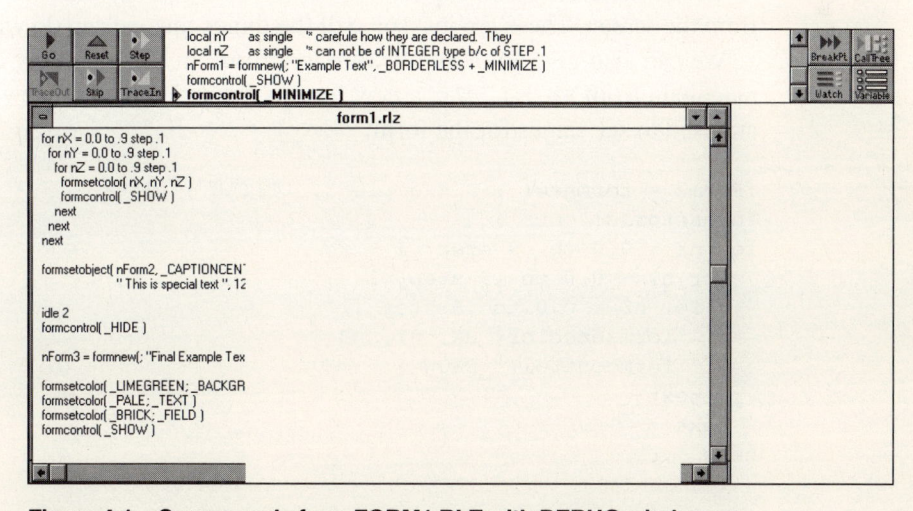

Figure 4-1. Source code from FORM1.RLZ with DEBUG window on.

When the next step executes, that form is reduced to a icon, the white area of the screen is restored, and the "Example Text" string used to identify the form is displayed directly under the icon.

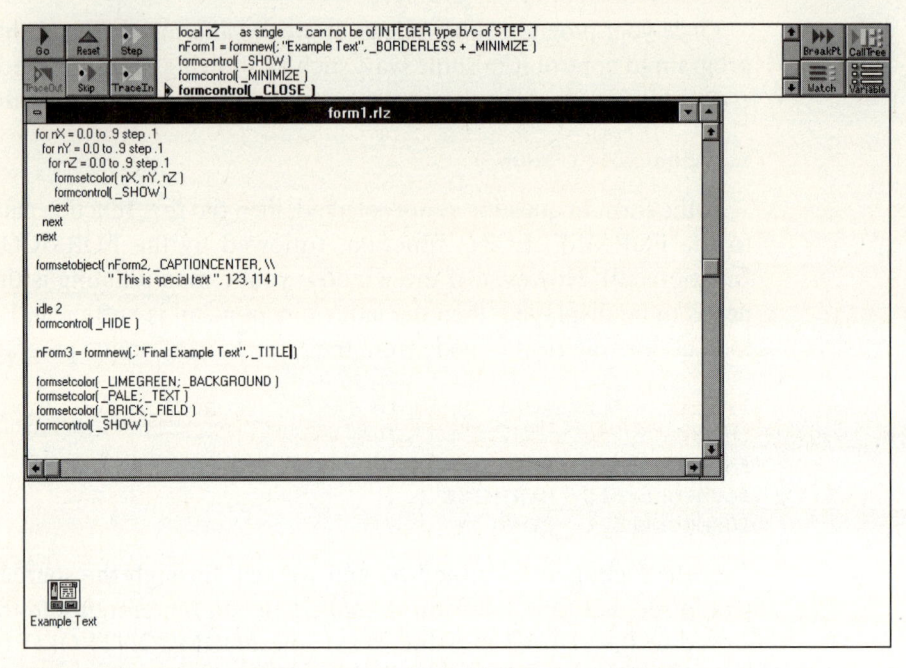

Figure 4-2. Source code from same program with icon loaded.

The last line of this example code will close the form and remove the icon from the screen. These are just some of the things that we can do with a form.

We can also give color and texture to a form. In the following code sample, again from *Form1.rlz*, a new form is created and some new functions are used to set values for the form:

```
iForm2 = formnew( ; " Example ", _TITLE )
formsetgrid( _OFF )
for nX = 0.0 to .9 step .1
  for nY = 0.0 to .9 step .1
    for nZ = 0.0 to .9 step .1
      formsetcolor( nX, nY, nZ )
      formcontrol( _SHOW )
    next
  next
next
```

Simple Forms for Data Entry and Data Validation 163

Now, if we were to run this code with the Debugger Window open and press the GO icon, the colors for the form will be adjusted and the form displayed. For me, this was working to the beat of Beethoven's Fifth, which just goes to further prove the relationship between music and programming. The FORMSETCOLOR() function can take up to three parameters. Each parameter represents a red, green, or blue value and (must range from .0 to 1.0, inclusive). (Of course, this last color pair does nothing to help those individuals—of whom my best friend and editor of this book is one—who are color blind.) In any event, white, for example, would have a value of 1 for all three parameters while black would have a value of 0 for all three parameters. If you do not like working with the incremental changes in the three different settings, there are internal variables available to this function that can set the color of the form just as well. For example,

```
formsetcolor( _TAN )
```

would set the necessary incremental values for red, green, and blue to produce tan. In addition to specifying a color, we have to specify which element of the form needs form to color. An optional modifier, not used in this example, can set the color of either the _BACKGROUND of the form, the _TEXT of the form, or the _FIELD area of the form. If not specified, _BACKGROUND will be the assumed value for the optional modifier. The _TEXT internal variable is for the color of the text displayed within the window and the _FIELD color is the color for the screen area behind the text. In most cases, you'll set all three colors at one time, as shown in the example program *Form2.rlz*. So, using the various modifiers and ignoring the incremental values for the three color selections, our form's colors could be set as follows:

```
iForm3 = formnew(; "Final Example Text", _TITLE + _MINIMIZE )
formsetcolor( _LIMEGREEN; _BACKGROUND )
formsetcolor( _PALE; _TEXT )
formsetcolor( _BRICK; _FIELD )
formcontrol( _SHOW )
```

Note the sum expression _TITLE + _MINIMIZE in the FORMNEW function. Without the internal variable _MINIMIZE, the form's window area is restricted. For example, if we were to open the system menu of such a form (by clicking on the box in the upper-left corner), we might see the following:

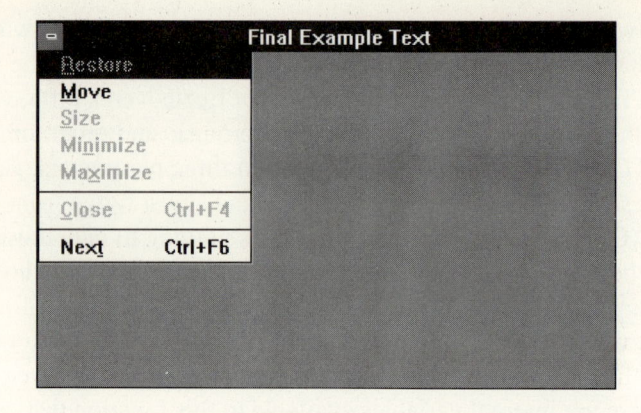

But, the `_MINIMIZE` internal variable adds the minimize icon in the upper-right corner and makes the Minimize option available on the system menu:

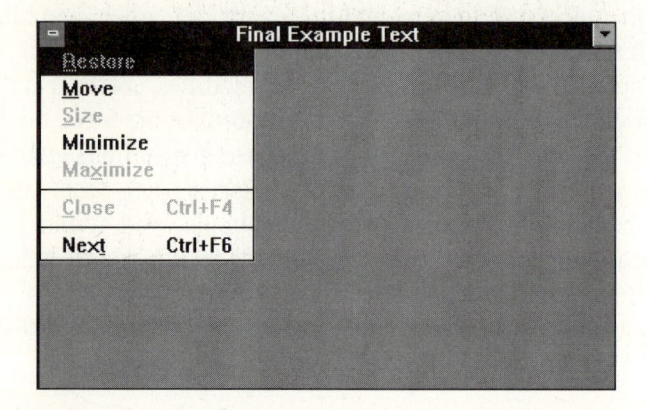

To see all of this in action, here is the entire source to *Form1.rlz*:

```
'* Application ... : Form1.rlz
'* Authors ....... : Steve Straley
'* Notice ........ : Copyright(c) 1994 - Sirius Press, Inc.
'* .............. : All Rights Reserved
'* Date .......... : January 1, 1994
'* Description ... : This shows the beginning steps of how a form may be
'*                   created and manipulated

local iForm1    as integer
local iForm2    as integer
local iForm3    as integer
```

```
local nX        as single     '* These are counting variables, but be
local nY        as single     '* carefule how they are declared.  They
local nZ        as single     '* can not be of INTEGER type b/c of STEP .1

iForm1 = formnew(; "Example Text", _BORDERLESS + _MINIMIZE )

formcontrol( _SHOW )
formcontrol( _MINIMIZE )
formcontrol( _CLOSE )

iForm2 = formnew( ; " Example ", _TITLE )
formsetgrid( _OFF )
for nX = 0.0 to .9 step .1
  for nY = 0.0 to .9 step .1
    for nZ = 0.0 to .9 step .1
      formsetcolor( nX, nY, nZ )
      formcontrol( _SHOW )
    next
  next
next

formsetobject( 1, _CAPTIONCENTER, " This is special text ", 123, 114 )

idle 2
formcontrol( _HIDE )

iForm3 = formnew(; "Final Example Text", _TITLE + _MINIMIZE )

formsetcolor( _LIMEGREEN; _BACKGROUND )
formsetcolor( _PALE; _TEXT )
formsetcolor( _BRICK; _FIELD )
formcontrol( _SHOW )

idle 1
formselect( iForm2 )
formcontrol( _SHOW )
idle 2

reset( _ALL )

'* End of File: Form1.rlz
```

One of the key things to remember, especially when working with the FOR...NEXT code construct and using the STEP clause, the data type of the counting variables *cannot* be of INTEGER data type. Since a step value of −1 is used in each of the three FOR...NEXT loops, the three variables, *nX*, *nY*, and *nZ*, must be declared as something other than a numeric of integer class. This means that they must be real numbers which further dictates that they must be either SINGLE or DOUBLE. So at the top of the file, the three variables are declared to be SINGLE.

> **Note:** If we did not do this, then the STEP.1 incrementing value would have no effect of either one of the three variables and we would find ourselves in an endless loop. This is because the value of the variable would never be incremented.

In addition, there is a new function called FORMSETOBJECT(), which allows new items to be added to the form. This function will be explained in the next section.

Creating Objects

As we've shown so far, building the shell of a form is one part of the programming task and finding the right attributes to give that form (such as color and position on the screen) is another part. A third part of the programming task is to decide what items are to be associated with any given form. For example, let's say that we wanted to build a friendly pop-up message welcoming people to our new wine program. A nice greeting is always welcome, and we can use a form to create one. This form does not need any special properties, such as a title bar or a minimize icon; all that is needed is a simple colored screen containing appropriate text. This form should politely close after a few seconds or if a key press or mouse click is detected.

Most of this is possible with the few commands and functions that we know up to this point; however, adding visible text to the form requires a new function: FORMSETOBJECT(). This function creates a new object and allows us to attach, or associate, that object to a particular form. Objects are individual items that have a distinct characteristic and property. For example, a text message and a push button are both considered objects: They have shape, form, substance, and behavior. (In some cases, the lack of a behavior is all the behavior that is needed.)

The basic format of the function is:

```
formsetobject( <nId>, <sType>, <sText>, <iLeft>, <iRight> )
```

> **Note:** A minimum of five parameters must be passed to FORMSETOBJECT() function. This does not take into account a parameter for the optional font number.

Form1.rlz contains the following FORMSETOBJECT() function:

```
formsetobject( 1, _CAPTIONCENTER, " This is special text ", 123, 114 )
```

The object that is being created is the `_CAPTIONCENTER` object, as specified by the internal variable. This object is given the ID value of 1, and since the currently selected form is that of *iForm2*, then the object is attached to that form. The object will display the literal string "This is a special text," beginning in the column 123 pixels from the left edge of the form window, and the row 114 pixels down from the top of the form window. You may use internal variables such as `_BOTTOM` and `_LEFT` in place of these values, but these are general position items and not as precise as the integers in this example.

Turning back to our pop-up message, we need to create the form, set the colors, add objects to the appropriate locations, and then display the form to the screen. There are 31 different types of objects that may be used with the FORMSETOBJECT() function. In this first example, we want to display text, so our choices are limited to the following:

Internal Variable	Object Type
`_CAPTIONCENTER`	Text captioned center
`_CAPTIONLEFT`	Text captioned, left justified
`_CAPTIONRIGHT`	Text captioned, right justified

In this first example, we will use the `_CAPTIONCENTER` type of object. Just like a form, every object needs a ID value. Any numbering scheme will suffice. Keep in mind that if you use the FormDev utility, that program will keep its own numeric system, similar to the one used in building a menu. When an object is created, it will take on the color attributes most recently assigned. For example, suppose the following FORMSETCOLOR() functions are called early in the program:

```
formsetcolor( _POWDERBLUE )
formsetcolor( _RED; _TEXT )
formsetcolor( _POWDERBLUE; _FIELD )
```

Then, all objects will follow this style until you issue a new set of FORMSETCOLOR functions.

> **Note:** When no modifier is offered, _BACKGROUND is the default value for the FORMSETCOLOR() function.

For example, if you create a new object, and you want it to have new colors, you might write some code that looks like this:

```
formsetobject( 3, _CAPTIONCENTER, \\
                "Published by: Sirius Press, Inc.", \\
                _LEFT, _BOTTOM )

formsetcolor( _TURQUOISE; _FIELD )
formsetcolor( _WHITE; _TEXT )
formmodifyobject(3, _SETCOLOR )
```

> **Note:** Objects in Realizer are not objects as defined in object-oriented programming. They are visual entities that have certain properties like objects (in the true sense of the word) but lack some of the basic principles commonly found in most object-oriented languages (such as construction and destruction, inheritance, and so on).

This code creates the _CAPTIONCENTER object (using whatever color settings are in effect at the time) and attaches it to the currently selected form, then changes the color settings. Here, the colors of object number 3 are reset based on _SETCOLOR. This takes place through the FORMMODIFYOBJECT() function. The complete example is in the *Form2.rlz* program file:

```
'* Application ... : Form2.rlz
'* Authors ....... : Steve Straley
'* Notice ........ : Copyright(c) 1994 - Sirius Press, Inc.
'* .............. : All Rights Reserved
'* Date .......... : January 1, 1994
'* Description ... : This shows how colors and objects may be created and
'*                   modified in a form.

local iForm1   as integer
```

```
iForm1 = formnew(; "Opening Screen", _BORDERLESS )
formsetcolor(_POWDERBLUE )
formsetcolor( _RED; _TEXT )
formsetcolor(_POWDERBLUE;_FIELD)

formsetobject( 1, _CAPTIONCENTER, " Welcome to the Decanter ", 100, 70 )
formsetobject( 2, _CAPTIONCENTER, "          Program          ", 125, 100 )
formsetobject( 3, _CAPTIONCENTER, \\
               "Published by: Sirius Press, Inc.", \\
               _LEFT, _BOTTOM )

formsetcolor( _TURQUOISE; _FIELD )
formsetcolor( _WHITE; _TEXT )
formmodifyobject(3, _SETCOLOR )

formcontrol( _SHOW )
idle 3
formcontrol( _HIDE )

'* End of File: Form2.rlz
```

The positioning of the various objects within the form is critical, and there are some internal variables that may be used to control the direction. Object number 3, for example, is stored to _LEFT corner of the form, on the _BOTTOM—in other words, the lower-left corner of the boxed region.

Prior to this function call, two other FORMSETOBJECT() function calls are made. In the first one:

```
formsetobject( 1, _CAPTIONCENTER, " Welcome to the Decanter ", 100, 70 )
```

the object is placed 100 pixels in from the left edge and 70 pixels down from the top. The second object, the string "Program," is stored 125 pixels from the left edge and 100 pixels down from the top.

> **Note:** If a pixel setting is inappropriate for a given region on the screen, then the object will not be displayed when the form is told to _SHOW.

When all three objects are created, the screen should look like this:

> Welcome to the Decanter
>
> Program
>
> Published by: Sirius Publishing, Inc.

When a form is first created, there is a default size assigned to it. This size roughly places the form in the center of the screen area. After a form is created, the size and location of the form may be adjusted with the FORMCONTROL() function using the _SIZE internal variable. This parameter tells the function to adjust the four coordinates of the screen region to the proper settings. Form position and size and the location of the various objects within the form are specified with pixel settings, not row or column numbers. For example, the following code:

```
formcontrol(_SIZE; 160, 50, 510, 200 )
```

positions the object's upper-left corner 160 pixels from the left edge and 50 pixels from the top and establishes the right edge of the form at pixel 510 (again, from left to right), and the bottom edge of the form at pixel 200. These four are part of the modifier list. The parameter passed to the function is the internal variable _SIZE which sets the function to act appropriately.

To spruce up this opening screen image for the end user let's add a graphic image. This means creating another object, namely the bitmap object, for which we can either use one of the clipart pieces that comes with Realizer or provide one of our own. For this example, I used Corel Draw to create a simple drawing of a grape vine, then I saved it as a bitmap object, moved the object into the directory that holds the source code for the application, and created the form to recognize this object.

Before looking at the code, take a look at the image in Figure 4-3.

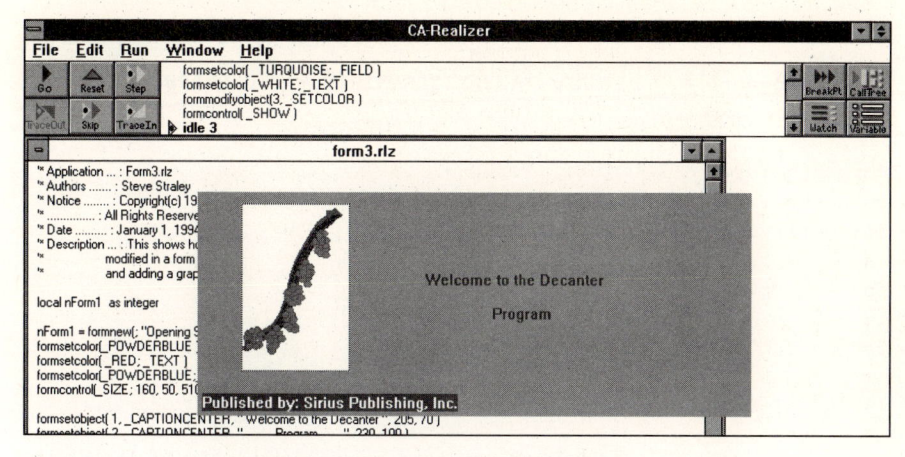

Simple Forms for Data Entry and Data Validation

[Figure 4-3 screenshot showing CA-Realizer debugger with pop-up screen "Welcome to the Decanter Program" published by Sirius Publishing, Inc.]

Figure 4-3. Running of application with pop-up screen.

Keep in mind that this screen shot is seen through the step-by-step process of Realizer's debugger and that the environment controls and source code would not be normally present. It does, however, give you a perspective of the new location of the screen image in conjunction with the video screen's edges. *Form3.rlz* contains the code to make all of that possible:

```
'* Application ... : Form3.rlz
'* Authors ....... : Steve Straley
'* Notice ........ : Copyright(c) 1994 - Sirius Press, Inc.
'* .............. : All Rights Reserved
'* Date .......... : January 1, 1994
'* Description ... : This shows how colors and objects may be created and
'*                   modified in a form as well as the position of the form
'*                   and adding a graphic object.

local iForm1   as integer

iForm1 = formnew(; "Opening Screen", _BORDERLESS )
formsetcolor(_POWDERBLUE )
formsetcolor( _RED; _TEXT )
formsetcolor(_POWDERBLUE;_FIELD)
formcontrol(_SIZE; 160, 50, 510, 200 )

formsetobject( 1, _CAPTIONCENTER, " Welcome to the Decanter ", 205, 70 )
formsetobject( 2, _CAPTIONCENTER, "         Program          ", 230, 100 )
formsetobject( 3, _CAPTIONCENTER, \\
```

```
                    "Published by: Sirius Press, Inc.", \\
                    _LEFT, _BOTTOM )
formsetobject( 4, _BITMAP, "\REALIZER\SIRIUS\APPS\GRAPES.BMP", 40, 10, \\
                    100, 150 )

formsetcolor( _TURQUOISE; _FIELD )
formsetcolor( _WHITE; _TEXT )
formmodifyobject(3, _SETCOLOR )

formcontrol( _SHOW )
idle 3
formcontrol( _HIDE )

'* End of File: Form3.rlz
```

Note that the last four parameters passed to the FORMSETOBJECT() for the bitmapped image contain the coordinates in which the image is to rest. We could also have written the code like this:

```
formsetobject( 4, _BITMAP, "\REALIZER\SIRIUS\APPS\GRAPES.BMP", 40, 10, \\
                    _DEFAULT, _DEFAULT )
```

The `_DEFAULT` internal variable tells Realizer to set the coordinates for the right and bottom edges based on the size of the image saved to disk. If we did this, however, the output would look like Figure 4-4.

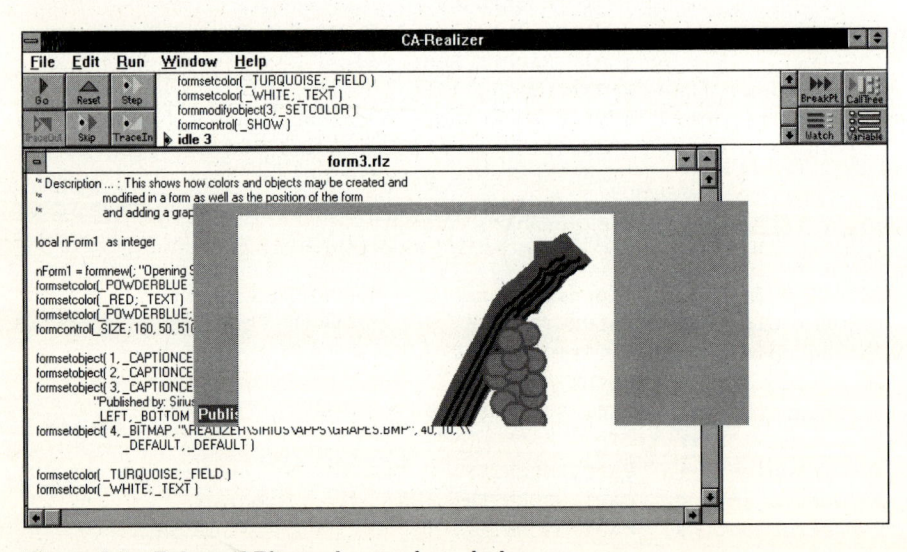

Figure 4-4. Enlarged Bitmap in opening window.

In that figure, the natural size of the image is bigger than the form's viewing area and so the image is truncated. That's why we hard-coded the bottom row and column pixel setting into the function call, instead of using the _DEFAULT internal variable. Noted that even a bitmap image, when brought into the Realizer environment, must have an ID value assigned to it. In this case, the assignment is 4.

Working with the forms and the objects they contain only a part of the issue when it comes to creating a friendly environment for end users. Realizer can also change the font size for any particular piece of text, at any time. To do this, we need to use the FONTQUNIQUE command to assign an ID for the new font.

```
iFont1 = fontqunique
```

We use this ID marker in conjunction with the FONTNEW() function to tap into our fonts loaded in Windows, load the correct one into the environment, and set a reference point for any text that may require it in the future. For example, on my system, I have Microsoft Word 6.0a and many TrueType fonts. One of my favorite fonts is called Arial (similar to Helvetica). To use this font within the application being developed, the FONTNEW() function is required:

```
fontnew(iFont1; "Arial", 20, _BOLD+_ITALICS )
```

The FONTNEW() function has four internal variables associated with it (_UNDERLINE, _STRIKEOUT, _BOLD, and _ITALICS), which like the FORMNEW() function, can be combined when represented as a sum of the variables. In this case, the font is to be Arial in both _BOLD and _ITALICS. The point size for this will be 20. When this table is internally established, the *iFont1* variable will be able to reference this font. We might reference the font in the _CAPTIONCENTER objects we created earlier, for example, by placing an optional parameter immediately after the text and just before the location of the object:

```
formsetobject( 1, _CAPTIONCENTER, " Welcome to the Decanter ", \\
            iFont1, 165, 70 )
```

The pixel location has been altered to allow for the increased size in the text. In this function, the fourth parameter makes the connection to the font that we created. Not all of the objects need to be associated with this font. We can still omit this variable (and font) when creating the objects.

Perhaps we'd like to give a three-dimensional effect to our picture. We could surround it with a frame, but for now, a shadow under it will suffice. There are many ways to achieve this, and one is to use the _GROUPBOX object to create a slightly framed area by specifying a set of coordinates that are a few pixels different from those coordinates used by the _BITMAP object.

In the following code, take a good look at not just the coordinates involved but the order in which the objects are created. The ID values for these objects are not important, but the order in which they are created is important.

```
'* Layer an image behind the shot of the grapes
formsetobject(5, _GROUPBOX, "NewFrame", 38, 8,98,154 )
formsetobject( 4, _BITMAP, "\REALIZER\SIRIUS\APPS\GRAPES.BMP", 40, 10, \\
                 100, 150 )
```

In these two lines of code, the _GROUPBOX object is created before the _BITMAP object. If these two lines were reversed, then the _GROUPBOX object would sit on top of the image:

By reversing the order of the objects when they are created on the form, we get the shadow we're after:

Notice that the words are bigger, bolder, and italic. This typeface is different from the _CAPTIONCENTER object on the lower-left corner of the form because we specified the *iFont1* variable. The code for all of this is contained in the *Form4.rlz* file and looks like this:

```
'* Application ... : Form4.rlz
'* Authors ....... : Steve Straley
'* Notice ........ : Copyright(c) 1994 - Sirius Press, Inc.
'* ............... : All Rights Reserved
'* Date .......... : January 1, 1994
'* Description ... : This shows how colors and objects may be created and
'*                   modified in a form as well as the position of the form
'*                   and adding a graphic object.  In addition, this shows
'*                   how a 3-d effect might look as well as adding fonts
'*                   to the text in the display

local iForm1 as integer
local iFont1 as integer

'* Create a new font and hold it....
iFont1 = fontqunique
fontnew(iFont1; "Arial", 20,  _BOLD+_ITALICS )

'* Create the form
iForm1 = formnew(; "Opening Screen", _BORDERLESS )
formsetcolor(_POWDERBLUE )
formsetcolor( _RED; _TEXT )
formsetcolor(_POWDERBLUE;_FIELD)
formcontrol(_SIZE; 160, 50, 510, 200 )

formsetobject( 1, _CAPTIONCENTER, " Welcome to the Decanter ", \\
               iFont1, 165, 70 )
formsetobject( 2, _CAPTIONCENTER, "          Program          ", \\
               iFont1, 190, 100 )

formsetobject( 3, _CAPTIONCENTER, \\
               "Published by: Sirius Press, Inc.", \\
               _LEFT, _BOTTOM )

'* Layer an image behind the shot of the grapes
formsetobject(5, _GROUPBOX, "NewFrame", 38, 8,98,154 )
formsetobject( 4, _BITMAP, "\REALIZER\SIRIUS\APPS\GRAPES.BMP", 40, 10, \\
                          100, 150 )


formsetcolor( _TURQUOISE; _FIELD )
formsetcolor( _WHITE; _TEXT )
formmodifyobject(3, _SETCOLOR )
```

```
formcontrol( _SHOW )
idle 3
formcontrol( _HIDE )

'* End of File: Form4.rlz
```

At this point, let's place this opening screen in the application, with the menus. Here's how I did it: First, I copied the *Form4.rlz* file to the *\Realizer\Sirius\Apps* directory and renamed the file *DLogo.rlz*. I then modified the file so that the logo screen is now within a procedure named *ShowLogo()*:

```
proc ShowLogo()

   local iForm1 as integer    '* Hold the form
   local iFont1 as integer    '* And hold the font

   '* Create a new font and hold it....
   iFont1 = fontqunique
   fontnew(iFont1; "Arial", 20,  _BOLD+_ITALICS )

   '* Create the form
   iForm1 = formnew(; "Opening Screen", _BORDERLESS )
   formsetcolor(_POWDERBLUE )
   formsetcolor( _RED; _TEXT )
   formsetcolor(_POWDERBLUE;_FIELD)
   formcontrol(_SIZE; 160, 50, 510, 200 )

   formsetobject( 1, _CAPTIONCENTER, " Welcome to the Decanter ", \\
                  iFont1, 165, 70 )
   formsetobject( 2, _CAPTIONCENTER, "         Program         ", \\
                  iFont1, 190, 100 )
   formsetobject( 3, _CAPTIONCENTER, \\
                  "Published by: Sirius Press, Inc.", \\
                  _LEFT, _BOTTOM )

   '* Layer an image behind the shot of the grapes
   formsetobject(5, _GROUPBOX, "NewFrame", 38, 8,98,154 )
   formsetobject( 4, _BITMAP, "\REALIZER\SIRIUS\APPS\GRAPES.BMP", \\
                           40, 10, 100, 150 )

   formsetcolor( _TURQUOISE; _FIELD )
   formsetcolor( _WHITE; _TEXT )
   formmodifyobject(3, _SETCOLOR )

   formcontrol( _SHOW )
   idle 3
   formcontrol( _HIDE )

end proc
```

Simple Forms for Data Entry and Data Validation

Once this is finished, the main source file named *Decanter.rlz* needs to be modified to do two things. First, it needs to load the *DLogo.rlz* file into the Realizer environment. This happens with the RUN command. Second, a call to the *ShowLogo()* function is needed; the location of this code fragment is totally arbitrary. Remember that there is a three-second wait using the IDLE command which may play an important part in when the call to this subroutine should take place. Here's how these modifications look in the main module of the *Decanter.rlz* file.

```
'* Application ... : Decanter.rlz
'* Authors ....... : Steve Straley
'* Notice ........ : Copyright(c) 1994 - Sirius Press, Inc.
'* .............. : All Rights Reserved
'* Date .......... : January 1, 1994
'* Description ... : This contains the basic Decanter program
'*

addsys( _MACRODIR, qsys(_PROGDIR))

sethourglass()                              ' Change the mouse cursor
run "\realizer\sirius\apps\dmenu.rlz"       ' Load the menus
run "\realizer\sirius\apps\dlogo.rlz"       ' Load the logo file
ClearMenus()                                ' Clear Realizer Menus
InstallMenus()                              ' Paint Decanter's Menus
ShowLogo()                                  ' Show the logo
resethourglass()                            ' Put back the mouse cursor

'Main Project Code

'* End of File: Decanter.rlz
```

The call to the logo subroutine is made after the Realizer menu has been cleared and the menus for the Decanter program have been initialized and established.

Step One: Using FormDev to Build a Form

Now that we've used the language to build our first form, let's do the same thing using the FormDev utility. FormDev rarely builds a final product, whether it's a form or a menu. It may come close, or it may only remove the tedious chore of pixel counting and object placement on a screen, but it is important to remember that the utility cannot build a complete application without some degree of programmer modification.

To start building our form in FormDev, open the Run menu and select FormDev.

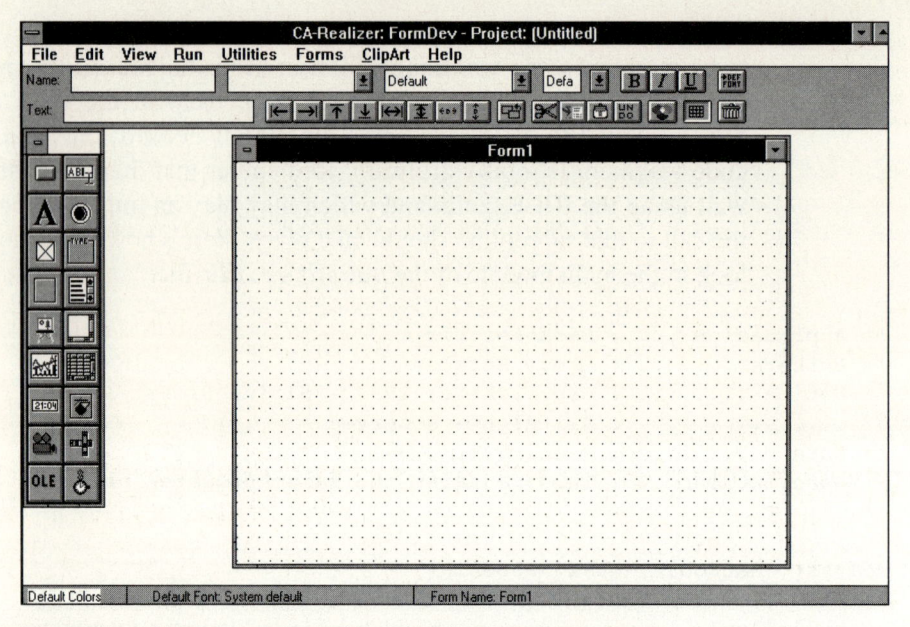

Figure 4-5. Opening screen of the FORMDEV utility program.

In the main screen (shown in Figure 4-5), the form window (here titled "Form1") takes the place of the FORMQUNIQUE command and the FORMNEW() function. In other words, the size and location of the form come later. First, we need to put objects into the form, so let's start the three lines of text.

Click on this icon:

and notice that the text in the toolbar area of the FormDev program now looks like this:

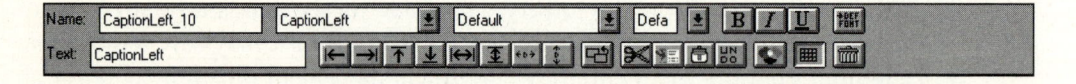

Before we specify the location of the object, we need to modify some of its attibutes. The first thing we need to change is the type of object that is on the form.

The Name of the object starts off at "CaptionLeft_10."

Simple Forms for Data Entry and Data Validation 179

> **Note:** Every new object that is created and stored to a form starts off as "_10" with each subsequent object being incremented by 10. Therefore, the second object will be "_20," the third will be "_30," and so on.

Next to the Name field is a drop-down **Combo box**. Clicking on the down arrow on the right drops down a complete listing of all of the possible objects that may be placed on this form.

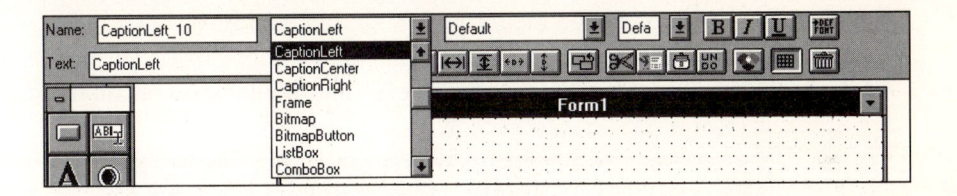

In this list, all of the `_CAPTION`-based objects are grouped together. We need to select CaptionCenter from this list.

Next, we need to change the contents of the Text field. This will be the first text seen on the screen. Highlight the current string of "CaptionLeft" and replace it with "Welcome to the Decanter." Then, once that is entered and WITHOUT striking the ENTER key, open the combo box that contains the string "Default," and select the font to be used by this object (Arial).

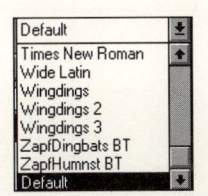

Next we need to set the boldface and italic settings. In the FONTNEW() function, this was represented by the summation of two internal variables: `_BOLD` and `_ITALICS`. As a matter of fact, the code looked like this:

```
iFont1 = fontqunique
fontnew( iFont1; "Arial", 20, _BOLD + _ITALICS )
```

These two choices are on the toolbar as well and look like this:

The last button in this group is for _UNDERLINE. When you click on the Bold and Italic buttons, they will appear to be pushed. This means that they are set for this object.

There remain two more settings that need to be addressed before we can place this object on the form: font size and color.

The font size can be altered in the third combo box on the toolbar. This field originally contained the string "defa," but should now contain the string "10."

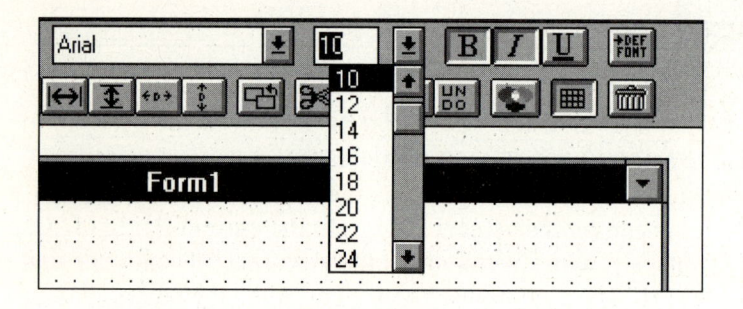

Open this drop-down list and select 20.

This leaves only color. In the program example, the code looked like this:

```
formsetcolor( _RED; _TEXT )
formsetcolor( _POWDERBLUE; _FIELD )
```

To specify color, select this icon from the toolbar:

In the resulting dialog box: the buttons along the bottom allow us to specify colors for text, field, background, and grid.

Simple Forms for Data Entry and Data Validation

All of these have a corresponding internal variable that may be used as well. The first color to be modified will be the text color. Once we choose this option, another dialog box will open, shown in Figure 4-6.

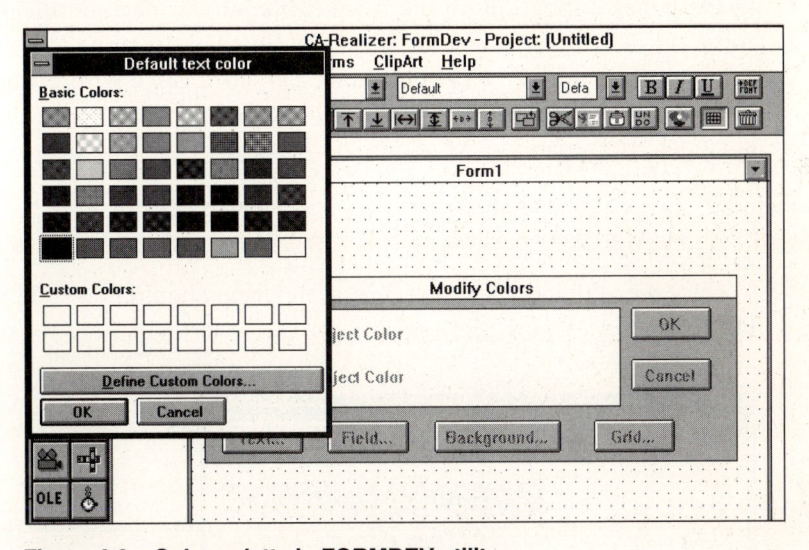

Figure 4-6. Color palette in FORMDEV utility.

In our original example, the text color was _RED, so we need to select the shade that comes closest from the Basic Color palette. Then click on the OK button. This will bring us back to the Modify Colors dialog box. Click on the Field button and repeat the process. Make sure to choose the correct color for the _FIELD region: _POWDERBLUE, then click on OK.

When we make the Text color selection, the Radio Button in the Modify Colors dialog box will reflect the change by showing the string "Current Object Color" in red letters. When we select the Field color, the background area surrounding the text (which is called the "field region") will also be changed.

Now we are ready to move the object to the general location on the form. If we need to, we can expand the form window to the right by moving the mouse cursor to the right edge of the form window, holding down the left button, dragging the window out to the right, and then releasing. This will open up new area for us. We then can move the mouse cursor to our current object.

> **Note:** When there are several objects on the form, the "current" object will be circumscribed by square dots.

When the cursor moves over the currently selected object, the cursor will change from an arrow to crosshairs. We then can hold down the left button and drag this object to the proper location in the form. Once placed in the general location on the form (remember, once an object is on the form, we can adjust its location by selecting and dragging the object), we can now enter a new _CAPTION item. This means we will repeat the basic process for the string "Program" which looked like this in the original example program:

```
formsetobject( 2, _CAPTIONCENTER, "         Program          ", \\
            iFont1, 190, 100 )
```

Once we add and place that object, the form should now look something like this:

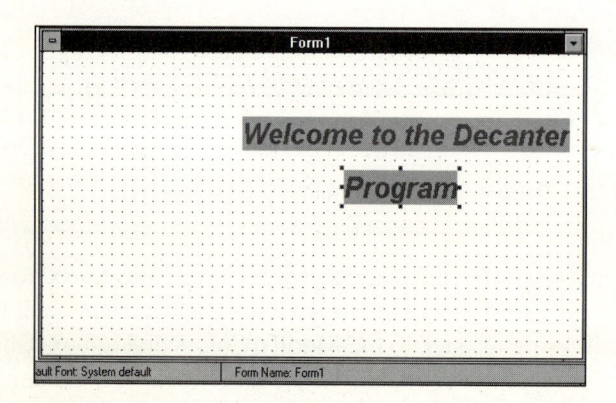

Repeat the process one more time, to add the caption "Published by: Sirius Press Inc." in the bottom-left corner of the form. When finished, the form should now look something like this:

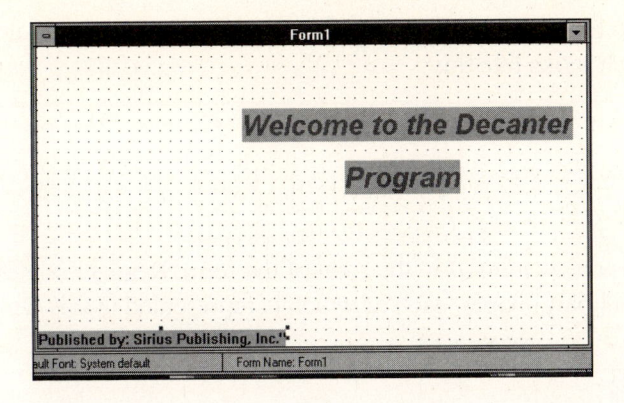

Before moving to the next object, we need to set the general color of the form. In the previous programming example, this was accomplished via the FORMSETCOLOR() function like this:

```
formsetcolor( _POWDERBLUE )
```

Without a modifier, it is assumed to be for the background. To do this in the FormDev utility program, we need to select the color icon again, but this time, choose the Default Object Color radio button, then click on the Background button and select the same `_POWDERBLUE` color we selected for the `_FIELD` color in the other objects on the form. When we click the OK button, the color within the Modify Colors dialog box will change, and so will the background color on the form. Click on the OK button within this dialog box to return to the FormDev utility and the "Form1" screen.

The last two items are the graphic of the grapes and the group box that gives the graphic its 3-D effect. Both are easy in FormDev. However, before we get into how to import the .BMP file, here are a few words on images: They occupy a lot of space.

Like most programs, Realizer has limited memory, so the size of our image file is very important. If we save our image as an entire 1024-by-768-pixel screen, it might be 1MB or more, even if we reduce the dimensions of the image once it's in the form. So when I exported this image in Corel Draw, I set the width of the image to 114 pixels and the height to 195 pixels. This reduced the size of the image to barely 64K, which easily fits in the form and within the FormDev utility.

In order to bring the image into the form, we need to click on the icon for images, which looks like this:

This opens a new *toolbar* to the right of the form. Realizer comes standard with a set of clipart images, each of which is represented in this window:

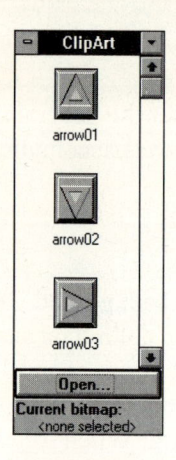

Clicking the Open button at the bottom of the window allows us to select other images that did not come with the Realizer package. In the resulting dialog box, select the file `Grapes.bmp`, which is located in the `\Realizer\Sirius\Apps` directory.

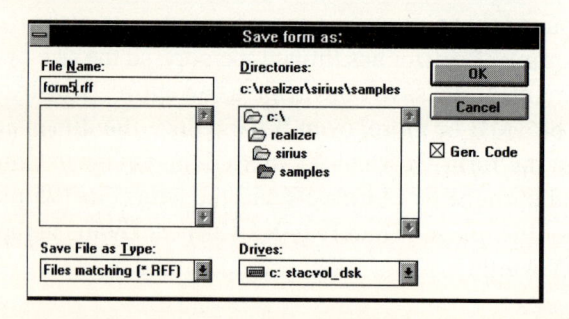

When we select this file, the file name will appear in the ClipArt window, just below the Open button. To place the image on the form, position the

Simple Forms for Data Entry and Data Validation

mouse cursor over the approximate location on the form and click the left button once. The form window should now should look like Figure 4-7.

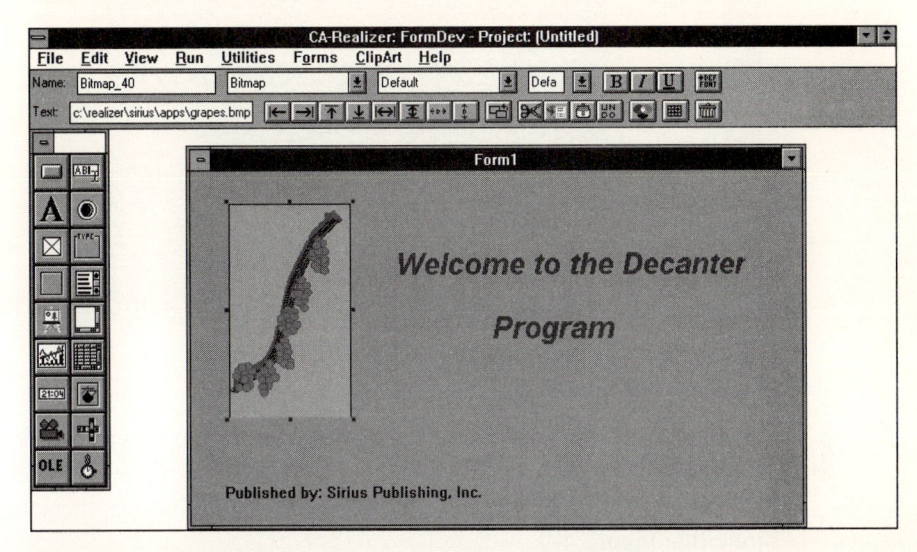

Figure 4-7. Designed pop-up main window of application.

We can now close the ClipArt window. Also, click on the grid icon in the toolbar to remove the little dots from the screen.

The last item to add is the _GROUPBOX object that will give the shadow effect when placed directly underneath the image of the grapes. To add this item, click on this icon:

Once selected, we can place the _GROUPBOX object just beside the image of the grapes. The default size of the group box will not be big enough, so we need to resize the box by dragging the appropriate **selection handle** (the squares around the perimeter). Once the height of the _GROUPBOX looks the same as the image, slide the image over on top of the bitmapped image so that it looks like Figure 4-8.

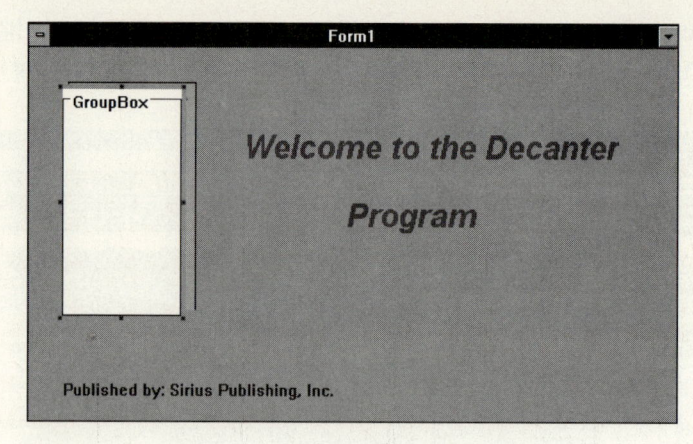

Figure 4-8. Adding a GROUPBOX object fo form.

To get the proper shading, we need to fill this box with black. So select the color icon once again, click the Field button, and select black from the resulting palette. When you click OK to close the dialogs, the screen should look like Figure 4-9.

Figure 4-9. Shading the GROUPBOX object.

The final step is to swap the two items around. On the main toolbar, click on the icon that looks like this:

Simple Forms for Data Entry and Data Validation 187

This will move the currently selected object (which should still be the black box to the back and bring the image of the grapes (`_BITMAP`) up to the front, as shown in Figure 4-10.

Figure 4-10. Bitmap of grapes on shadowed GROUPBOX in background.

If any positioning refinement is necessary, just click on the `_BITMAP` image once to select it, then move it.

Now we are ready to let FormDev generate the source code for this opening screen. From the File menu in the FormDev utility, select Save. In the resulting dialog box:

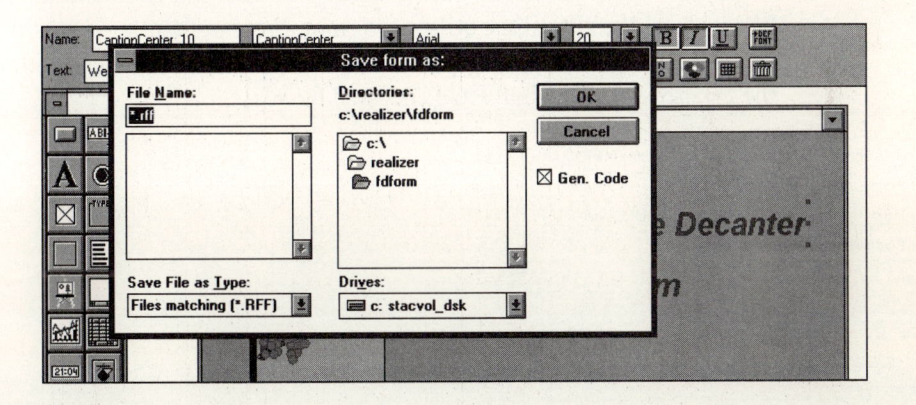

specify the `\Realizer\Sirius\Samples` directory, and enter a file name of `Form5.rff`. The **Check Box** in the right side of this dialog box representing the feature to "Gen Code" check box is marked, as shown in the figure.

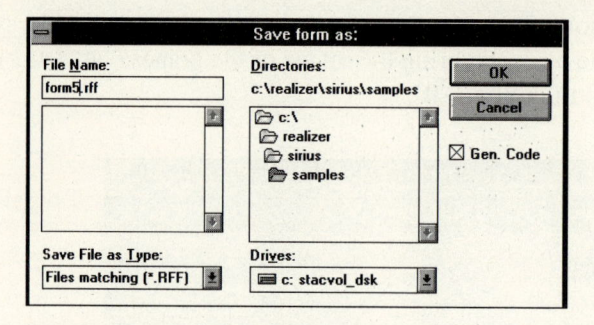

When you click on OK, the following dialog will appear:

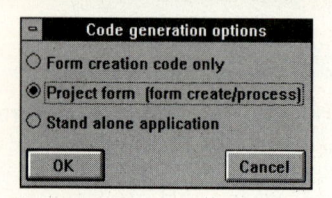

All we want to do is to generate the code for the form. It will have to be modified to fit our application, so generating code for any of the other options does not make sense. Select the radio button for "Form creation code only," then click on the OK button. Once finished, the code and the form will be inside of the FormDev utility program. We can then leave this utility and return to the main Realizer menu. From there, we can take a better look at the *Form5.rlz* file that was generated for us:

```
'****************************************
'FormDevFormName: form5
'FormDev Project Name: Untitled
'FormDev Saveflag: 7
'****************************************

IF QVar(%%flagform5, _Defined) THEN
   EXIT MACRO
END IF
%%flagform5 = 1

PROC Makeform5

  IF QVar(formform5, _Real + _Scalar)
    IF FormQ(_Exists; formform5)
      FormSelect(formform5)
```

```
        EXIT PROC
     END IF
  END IF

  'Define the fonts
  LOCAL font2
  font2 = FontQUnique
  FontNew(font2; "Arial", 20, _Bold + _Italics)


  formform5 = FormQUnique
  FormNew(formform5; "Form1", _Close + _Size + _Title + _Minimize)
  FormSetColor(_Cyan; _Background)
  FormControl(_Size; 134 pxl, 15 pxl, 563 pxl, 300 pxl)
  FormSetColor(_Black; _Field)
  FormSetObject(form5objs.GroupBox_50, _GroupBox, "GroupBox", \\
                                  41 pxl, 27 pxl, 114 pxl, 188 pxl)

  FormSetColor(_Red; _Text)
  FormSetColor(_Cyan; _Field)
  FormSetObject(form5objs.CaptionCenter_10, _CaptionCenter, \\
                                  "Welcome to the Decanter", font2, \\
                                  200 pxl, 60 pxl, _Default, _Default)
  FormSetObject(form5objs.CaptionCenter_20, _CaptionCenter, "Program", font2, \\
                                  300 pxl, 111 pxl, _Default, _Default)
  FormSetColor(_Black; _Text)
  FormSetObject(form5objs.CaptionCenter_30, _CaptionCenter, \\
                                  "Published by: Sirius Press, Inc.", \\
                                  10 pxl, 250 pxl, _Default, _Default)
  FormSetColor(_White; _Field)
  FormSetObject(form5objs.Bitmap_40, _Bitmap, "c:\realizer\sirius\apps\grapes.bmp", \\
                                  46 pxl, 20 pxl, _Default, _Default)
  FormSetProc(formprocform5;_All)

  'Close the fonts
  FontSelect(font2)
  FontControl(_Close)
END PROC

PROC AssignNamesform5
   form5objs.CaptionCenter_10 = 10    'TYPE: CaptionCenter,  TEXT: Welcome to the Decanter
   form5objs.CaptionCenter_20 = 20    'TYPE: CaptionCenter,  TEXT: Program
   form5objs.CaptionCenter_30 = 30    'TYPE: CaptionCenter,  TEXT: Published by: Sirius...
   form5objs.Bitmap_40 = 40           'TYPE: Bitmap,  TEXT: c:\realizer\sirius\apps\grapes.bmp
   form5objs.GroupBox_50 = 50         'TYPE: GroupBox,  TEXT: GroupBox
END PROC

'Main program

AssignNamesform5
Makeform5
```

I have modified the output slightly so that it will fit better on a page. At this point, a couple of comments are needed on the source code that is generated by the FormDev utility. Once again, it is important to remember that the style of coding found in this book is different from that generated by any of the tools in the Realizer system. When FormDev generates code, it creates a family structure for the various objects being attached to the form. Here, the family root name of *form5objs* is used in conjunction with the text found in the Name field within the FormDev Utility. Regardless of what we placed in the Text Title field, the Name field started off with the "_10" suffix attached to the "CaptionCenter" description. That combination, along with the family name, is initialized in the *AssignNamersform5()* procedure:

```
PROC AssignNamesform5
  form5objs.CaptionCenter_10 = 10 'TYPE: CaptionCenter, TEXT: Welcome to the Decanter
  form5objs.CaptionCenter_20 = 20 'TYPE: CaptionCenter, TEXT: Program
  form5objs.CaptionCenter_30 = 30 'TYPE: CaptionCenter, TEXT: Published by: Sirius...
  form5objs.Bitmap_40 = 40        'TYPE: Bitmap, TEXT: c:\realizer\sirius\apps\grapes.bmp
  form5objs.GroupBox_50 = 50      'TYPE: GroupBox, TEXT: GroupBox
END PROC
```

Each of these family members is assigned a numeric integer, starting with the value of 10 (and incremented by 10). These values are used as the ID value for the FORMSETOBJECT() when creating the various objects. So, for example, the first family member is attached to this line of code:

```
FormSetObject(form5objs.CaptionCenter_10, _CaptionCenter, \\
                                "Welcome to the Decanter", font2, \\
                                200 pxl, 60 pxl, _Default, _Default)
```

Personally, I find it a waste of memory to have a variable assigned a constant value which is used not to enhance the program (as would, say, a variable named *TRUE* which makes the code more readable). If anything, this style adds a level of obscurity. So for our coding examples, I chose to use the value of 1 (incrementing by 1 for each new object). Occasionally, I will try to follow the FormDev example by starting with a literal value of 10 and incrementing by 1 or 10 from that point. Again, all of this is left to your decision. In addition, the "pxl" notation after each left and top screen position value is redundant as well. Since the system works consistently in terms of pixels, so these extra tags are not necessary. Finally, notice the use of the internal variable `_DEFAULT` in the previous programming example. If I were to convert that line of code to our standard, I might opt for this:

```
FormSetObject(10 _CaptionCenter, "Welcome to the Decanter", iFont2, \\
                                  200, 60, _Default, _Default)
```

Another difference is in the code that sets up the form initially. Although it is not recommended to mix some of the internal variables with the FORMNEW() function, the FormDev Utility generates code that uses these internal variable combinations.

```
FormNew(formform5; "Form1", _Close + _Size + _Title + _Minimize)
FormSetColor(_Cyan; _Background)
FormControl(_Size; 134 pxl, 15 pxl, 563 pxl, 300 pxl)
```

In our form, the `_TITLE` internal variable is unnecessary, as is the `_MINIMIZE` variable. Since we just want to offer a pop-up screen, there is no need for a title bar in the window, nor will any one need to resize or shrink (minimize) the window; however, these are the standards used by the FormDev utility. In addition, since there are toolbars and other items on display within the FormDev utility, I cannot place the form exactly where I might want it in the application. So, these values need to be altered as well. Perhaps, after the alterations, the previous code example would look something like this:

```
FormNew(formform5; "Opening Screen", _BORDERLESS )
FormSetColor(_Cyan; _Background)
FormControl(_SIZE; 160, 50, 510, 200 )
```

However, one piece of code that differs from our hand-created attempt is the shadow behind the image of the grapes. In the previous version, we barely had the outline of an image behind the grapes. In the FormDev version, we were able to fill the `_GROUPBOX` object with a solid color of black and offset it slightly more than the previous attempt. This gave us a more pronounced shadow. However, even with these minor changes, all in all, it was easier to build the opening screen via the FormDev utility and to modify the results than to do everything by hand. Now, after having said that, I will return to the hard way of doing things to show you more forms, more objects, and the beginning of a data-entry screen.

Step Two: Building a Data-Entry Screen

The next step is to build a data-entry screen for our application. To do this, we need to think for a moment just what type of information we need to gather. If we refer to the previous chapter and look at the structure of a proposed **record** or **family** called *rWine,* we'll have the outline of what a record in a database contains. These items can be the start of our first data-entry screen.

Putting pretty pictures on a screen for an end user to look at is not what application development is all about. These frills help to make the end user feel comfortable with the application; however, now we must address the real business of an application: acquiring data. Data may come into an application directly from a mainframe or via some type of communications interface, or it might arrive in a database file or a spreadsheet table or some other PC-related application. But the most important vehicle by which data can be introduced in an application is human intervention. Ironically, it is this connection that is the weakest link. Errors in reports and calculations can more often than not be traced to user error and the data-entry screen used. This means a couple of things. First, the form that is used for data entry must be simple, straightforward, and clean: no extra visual noise to distract the user. Second, it should be as intuitive as possible. This means that any end user, not just the one who knows the program well needs to be able to understand what you are asking for. And third, use as much non-typing data input as possible: check boxes for logical choices, list boxes for a list of choices, and so on. The less we have the end user typing, the better off the application will be, the better the integrity of the data will be, and the fewer headaches we will have after the application is delivered.

To create a data-entry screen, we need to use a new object: the _TEXTBOX object. A text box is a **modeless** data-entry field. In some languages, all data-entry items must be of like nature, and each data entry item appears on a separate line on the screen and is processed sequentially, one at a time, from top to bottom. Jumping around from, say, the first data entry item to the fifth is not possible. This is known as a modal system. However, with the mouse, the need to jump around is vital. And in a GUI (Graphical User Interface) environment such as this one is, the need to mix different types of data-entry items is equally vital. The use of various visual data-entry techniques makes it easier for an end user to complete the form. Look at a typical data-entry screen—in this case, a dialog box from Microsoft Word, shown in Figure 4-11.

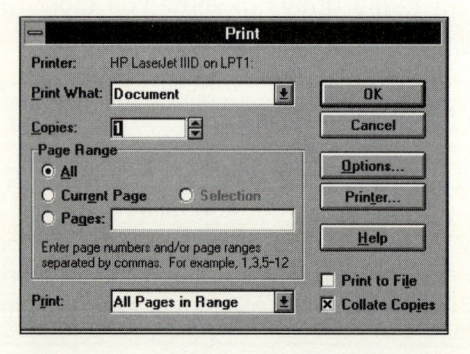

Figure 4-11. Standard PRINT dialog window.

Simple Forms for Data Entry and Data Validation

In this form, a title appears at the top and we can tell that this form can be minimized as well. This might mean, if we were to look at it from Realizer's perspective, that the _TITLE and _MINIMIZE internal variables were used when the FORMNEW() function was called. Since this is not Realizer, this is not the case; however, we should begin to see "reality" in the Windows world and in terms of the Realizer language. On the form are several types of objects: pure text, radio buttons, drop-down boxes, check boxes, and push buttons. With these objects, A great deal of information can be gathered from the end user without requiring a lot of typing. Also, you should decide whether to make the keyboard or the mouse the primary input tool for your application. Once you decide, be consistent. The last thing you need to build is a form that constantly forces the user to switch from keyboard to mouse and back.

Because this is a modeless system, the items can all behave differently, and the user can jump around or use the TAB key to cycle sequentially through the items in the form. This is the style we should be emulating.

Let's begin to examine the _TEXTBOX object. One example might look like this:

```
formsetobject( 2, _TEXTBOX, "            ", 190, 10 )
```

This _TEXTBOX object has an ID value of 2 and will be located at pixel 190 from the left and 10 from the top.

In the next example:

```
formsetobject( 2, _TEXTBOX, "            ", 190, 10; _NOBORDER )
```

the _NOBORDER internal variable overrides the default behavior of a _TEXTBOX object, which is to have a frame around it. There are three possible internal variables for the _TEXTBOX object: _MULTILINE, _NOBORDER, and _NOTIFY.

Keep in mind that this object is only for the data entry point. In order to tell the user what data to enter in it, we may add a _CAPTION object for this _TEXTBOX. The text within the _CAPTION object (typically _CAPTIONLEFT) will be a string telling the end user what you are expecting to have entered into the _TEXTBOX entry point. As you can see in the following example:

```
formsetobject( 1, _CAPTIONLEFT, "Please enter your name:", 10, 10 )
formsetobject( 2, _TEXTBOX, "            ", 190, 10 )
```

the row position for both objects are the same. Another option would be to have additional information on the string passed to the _TEXTBOX object. This might be a simple message like this:

```
formsetobject( 1, _CAPTIONLEFT, "Please enter:", 10, 10 )
formsetobject( 2, _TEXTBOX, "ADDRESS LINE 1", 190, 10 )
formsetobject( 3, _TEXTBOX, "ADDRESS LINE 2", 200, 10 )
```

Here, the strings "ADDRESS LINE 1" and "ADDRESS LINE 2" will appear inside the _TEXTBOX. When the entry point is turned on or "in focus," the text will be highlighted. As soon as the user starts typing, the text in the line will disappear. In other words, these strings are default values and can be used as extra help for the end user. Just because an object is given this string does not mean that that string will appear in a file. This is still controlled by programmers, so have no fear... yet.

Turning back to the behavior of the _TEXTBOX object, we might instead put a variable in this field for display:

```
sLastName = "Straley"
formsetobject( 1, _CAPTIONLEFT, "Please enter your name:", 10, 10 )
formsetobject( 2, _TEXTBOX, sLastName, 190, 10 )
```

In this case, the string "Straley" will be highlighted when the _TEXTBOX is in focus and will immediately disappear as soon as the first key is pressed.

> **Note:** If a cursor key is pressed instead of an alphanumeric key when a _TEXTBOX is first given focus, the highlight will be turned off and the string will remain in the _TEXTBOX. Only when a non-cursor key is pressed will the contents of the _TEXTBOX be removed.

The width of the _TEXTBOX is also important. Even if the string is only 10 bytes long, the data-entry window may be longer. This means that the end user can continue to type. It will be the responsibility of the programmer to format the contents of the data-entry item when stored back to a file or to a variable, especially if it is a fixed-length variable.

> **Note:** The _TEXTBOX object will be as wide as the form unless the width is specified when the object is created.

Sometimes we don't want a default string to appear in the _TEXTBOX; rather, we simply want the cursor to appear as close to the left edge of the _TEXTBOX as possible. To do this, the string parameter within the _TEXTBOX object should be empty:

```
                formsetobject( 2, _TEXTBOX, "", 190, 10 )
```

This means that nothing will be highlighted and the user can start typing immediately.

To show our _TEXTBOX in context, here is a new program file called *Form6.rlz*:

```
'* Application ... : Form6.rlz
'* Authors ....... : Steve Straley
'* Notice ........ : Copyright(c) 1994 - Sirius Press, Inc.
'* .............. : All Rights Reserved
'* Date .......... : January 1, 1994
'* Description ... : This starts to show how data entry can be involved.

local sName as string * 10

sName = string$(10, 32)              '* 32 is the SPACE character

formnew( 100; "First Form", _FRAME )  '* Create a new frame
formcontrol(_SIZE; 100,170,500, 50 )  '* Offer a new size

'* Now, set two objects to it
formsetobject( 1, _CAPTIONLEFT, "Please enter your name:", 10, 10 )
formsetobject( 2, _TEXTBOX, "",  190, 10 )

formwait( _NORMAL )      '* This waits within the form and _SHOWS
formcontrol( _HIDE )     '* Don't _CLOSE!!!!

print formqstr( 1 ), formqstr(2)     '* Show output...

sName = formqstr(2)   '* Same As:   sName = left$( formqstr(2), 10 )

print sName
idle 5                 '* Just wait before resetting system

formcontrol( _CLOSE )
reset(_ALL)

'* End of File: Form6.rlz
```

This example shows how a form can have different objects that cause different effects. To start, a restricted string is initialized to a LOCAL variable at the top of the file. Following this, the STRING$() function stores 10 blank spaces (the ASCII value of a blank space is 10) to the variable *sName*. Then we create a new form of a _FRAME type. After the form is created, it is resized to fit the new position, starting 100 pixels in from the left edge of the monitor and 170 pixels down from the top. The form will be 500 pixels wide and 50 pixels high. Once the form is established, we can start to create objects.

The first object that is created is a `_CAPTIONLEFT` object. This is similar to the `_CAPTIONCENTER` objects we created earlier. Here, the object will be left-justified within the assigned region. After this object, the `_TEXTBOX` object is created. Since the third parameter to this function is a NULL (or empty) string, the `_TEXTBOX`, when granted input focus, will be empty and the cursor will sit on the left edge the box. The `_TEXTBOX` object will appear 190 pixels from the left edge of the active window and 10 pixels down from the top.

Once the object is positioned, we turn on the form and let it engage all of the objects within its domain. This is not accomplished with the following instruction:

```
formcontrol( _SHOW )
```

That line merely shows the form and its contents. The FORMWAIT() function will display the current form and then wait until the user clicks on an item or presses the ENTER or ESC key. This function can take any of four internal variables:

Internal Variable	Purpose
_NORMAL	Instructs the function to wait until an object notifies the form.
_PICK	Instructs the function to wait until the user selects any non-grayed object, then returns the identification of that object.
_PICKDRAG	Allows the user to select and drag any non-grayed object, then returns the identification of that object.
_PEEK	If used after a form procedure is notified by an edit control, then the function will return the identification of the actual item that caused the edit control to lose input focus. Otherwise, the function will return 0 if that item did not notify the form.

In our example, the `_NORMAL` internal variable is used, but since `_NORMAL` is the default mode for the FORMWAIT() function, we could have programmed it this way instead:

```
formwait()
```

Simple Forms for Data Entry and Data Validation

> **Note:** Try to use default values as little as possible. This makes it tougher for people less familar with the language to come behind you, read the code, and understand what you are trying to do.

Once the end user enters something into the _TEXTBOX object and presses the ENTER key, the form is then hidden via the _HIDE internal variable passed to the FORMCONTROL() function.

> **Note:** When editing within a _TEXTBOX, the mouse pointer will automatically change to a text-entry cursor as the mouse crosses the boundary of the object.

> **Note:** You cannot FORMCONTROL(_CLOSE) before you question any of the objects in that form. That means that any FORMQOBJECT() or FORMQ() function that needs to execute must come before the form is closed.

Since the form is not closed, we can now poll the values of the object. The FORMQSTR() function gives us the string that is attached to the object. The first object in the form is easy, since we hard-coded the literal string "Please enter your name:", which will be the value of FORMQSTR(1). However, the value of the string for the _TEXTBOX object came from the end user, so we must print out the value of the FORMQSTR(2) function to see what was typed in the _TEXTBOX. To do so, we can assign that value to the *sName* variable that was initialized at the top of the program. Since this string is restricted in size, no matter what was typed into the _TEXTBOX region, only the first 10 characters will be successfully stored to this variable. We'd get the same result if we were to program the following:

```
sName = left$( formqstr(2), 10 )
```

Once the value of *sName* is printed to the Print Log window, the form is finally closed and after five seconds of waiting, all of the windows and internals are properly reset.

Before you begin to assemble objects into an actual data-entry form, it's important to develop a good mental image of the finished product, with a view toward making data entry as easy as possible for the end user. Think, for example, about what kinds of objects you will use. How will you lay them out on the form? If your form will have a title bar, what title will you give it? When you've formed your mental picture, you might even want to make a rough sketch that you can refer to as you program.

We envisioned the first data-entry form for our Decanter program as a simple dialog box:

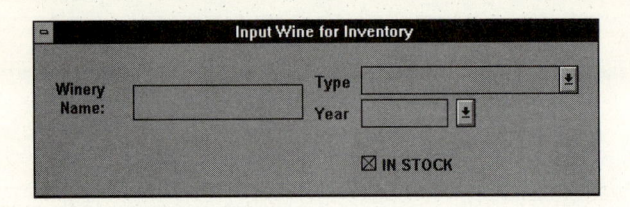

The drop-down Type list allows us to select a type of wine:

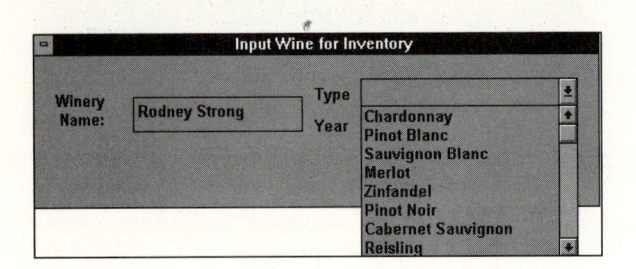

And the drop-down Year list lets us select the vintage year as listed on the label of all wines.

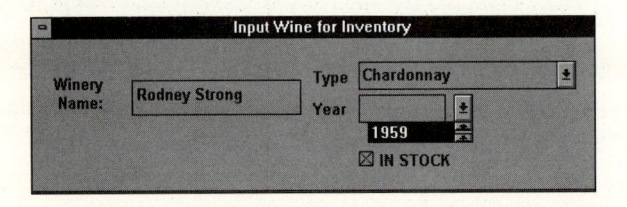

The code for this dialog box is contained in a file called *Form7.rlz*. The code comes in stages, and the main stage looks like this:

Simple Forms for Data Entry and Data Validation

```
'************** MAIN ROUTINE!!! ************

DataEntry()

aItem = formqobject( 4 )

rowprint "            Type is", aItem[ _FQO_ITEMTYPE ]
rowprint "Pixels from top are", aItem[ _FQO_TOP ]
rowprint "       Return value", aItem[ _FQO_VALUE ]

idle 4
reset( _ALL )
```

Obviously, the function that kicks things off is the *DataEntry()* function. We have to see this function before we know what the values could possibly be from the FORMQOBJECT() function. All we know at this point (in part, due to the Hungarian notation used for the variable) is that the return value from this function is an array data type. We also know that the function is looking at an object that has an ID value of 4. Other than that, nothing else can be deciphered, so a look at the *DataEntry()* function is in order:

```
'****************************************************
'* Name:       DataEntry()
'* Params:     N/A
'* Returns:    N/A
'* Purpose:    This procedure draws the form, creates the family structure
'*             updates the values, and prints the results.

proc DataEntry()

   local iFont1 as integer
   local iForm1 as integer
   local fRecord as family

   fRecord = MakeFamily()

   iFont1 = fontqunique
   fontnew( iFont1; "Arial", 10, _BOLD )

   formnew( 100; "Input Wine for Inventory", _TITLE )
   formsetcolor( _CYAN; _BACKGROUND )
   formsetcolor( _CYAN; _FIELD )
   formsetcolor( _BLACK; _TEXT )
   formcontrol(_SIZE; 50,50,500,150 )       '* Offer a new size
```

```
'* Now, field 1
formsetobject( 10, _CAPTIONCENTER, "Winery Name:", iFont1, 10, 30, \\
                                                              70, 40 )
formsetobject( 1, _TEXTBOX, "", iFont1, 90, 35, 150,30 )

'* Field 2
formsetobject( 20, _CAPTIONRIGHT, "Type", iFont1, 250, 25 )
formsetobject(2, _DROPDOWNLIST, "",   iFont1, 290, 20, 190, \\
                                _DEFAULT; _LISTFAMS, WineList() )

'* Field 3
formsetobject( 30, _CAPTIONRIGHT, "Year", iFont1, 250, 52 )
formsetobject( 3, _DROPDOWNCOMBO, "", 290, 48, 100, 50; \\
                                _LISTFAMS, TheYears()  )

'* Field 4
formsetobject( 4, _CHECKBOX, "IN STOCK", iFont1, 290, 90;  1 )

if formwait( _NORMAL ) = 1 then              '* Enter key was pressed
   formcontrol( _HIDE )                      '* Don't _CLOSE!!!!
   UpdateRecord( fRecord, 100 )
end if

print "********** WINE INFORMATION *************"
print fRecord.Winery, fRecord.Year, fRecord.Style
if fRecord.InStock then
   print "IT IS in stock"
else
   print "not available at this time...."
end if

end proc
```

To start, the variable *fRecord* takes the value of the *MakeFamily()* function, which looks like this:

```
'*****************************************************
'* Name:        MakeFamily()
'* Params:      N/A
'* Returns:     <fWine>        A family of structure for WINE
'* Purpose:     This function creates a blank family for data entry
'*              purposes.

function MakeFamily

   local fWine as family
```

```
fWine.Winery       = Space(30)
fWine.Style        = Space(25)
fWine.Year         = "1991"
fWine.InStock      = 0              '* False, it's not in storage

return( fWine )

end func
```

Here, the return value of *fWine* is declared to be a family data type and four members of that family are created and assigned. In the end, the return value of this function will be the empty and fresh family structure. However, in creating that structure, both the *fWine.Winery* and *fWine.Style* members call on the *Space()* function. This function attempts to make it clearer as to what is being accomplished:

```
'*****************************************************
'* Name:         Space( <iNumber> )
'* Params:       <iNumber>         Number of blank spaces to have
'* Returns:      <sValue>          A blank string with a length of <iNumber>
'*               O.k. I'm lazy coming from Clipper.... I wanted to have
'*               a function or two from the old days....

function space( iNumber )

  return( string$( iNumber, 32 ) )

end func
```

Instead of having to remember the value of ASCII 32, the name of the function tells us when looking at the member assignment, just what is being stored to that element: in one case, 30 blank spaces; in another, 25. If the STRING$() function is used, two sets of numbers are used: one for the length of the string to be returned and the other, the ASCII value of the byte to be used. Here, the function has been made simpler to read and understand.

Turning our attention back to the *DataEntry()* routine, a new font is created just after the call to the *MakeFamily()* function call. After the font is created, a new form is generated. This form will have an ID value of 100 and be of the _TITLE type. This means that the name of the form, "Input Wine for Inventory," will be displayed in a title bar, but the form can not be resized, closed, or minimized. The form will remain on the screen until it has completed its task. Stored to this form are two _CAPTION-based objects (one centered and the other right-justified) and one _TEXTBOX object. The height and width of the first two objects are assigned. After this, the fourth object is new and requires an explanation.

A `_DROPDOWNLIST` object is a data-entry item that does not require any typing by the end user; rather, the input will be derived from a list of items. Once the list is open, the end user can press the `DOWN_ARROW` key to scroll through the list one item at a time. The list of items for the Type box is obtained from the function *WineList()*. This modifier, in conjunction with the internal variable `_LISTFAMS`, instructs the `_DROPDOWNLIST` object to display a list of family (or even array) members. Other types of lists may be displayed by altering the internal variable as the first modifier. For example, if the `_LISTFILES` variable is used, a list of files will be displayed, or if `_LISTFONTS` is offered, the names of available fonts will make up the list. Each of these internal variables then dictates what should be the following passed modifier. Here, since the `_LISTFAMS` internal variable is offered, the family of items must be offered. This family is the return value of the *WineList()* function, which looks like this:

```
'*****************************************************
'* Name:       WineList()
'* Params:     N/A
'* Returns:    <aWine>         Array of types of wines
'* Purpose:    To build a quick table of types so that it does not
'*             have to be entered by hand

function WineList()

   local aTypes[18] as string

   aTypes[1]  = "Chardonnay"
   aTypes[2]  = "Pinot Blanc"
   aTypes[3]  = "Sauvignon Blanc"
   aTypes[4]  = "Merlot"
   aTypes[5]  = "Zinfandel"
   aTypes[6]  = "Pinot Noir"
   aTypes[7]  = "Cabernet Sauvignon"
   aTypes[8]  = "Reisling"
   aTypes[9]  = "Port"
   aTypes[10] = "Sparkling"
   aTypes[11] = "Champaign"
   aTypes[12] = "Petite Syrah"
   aTypes[13] = "Barbera"
   aTypes[14] = "Semillon"
   aTypes[15] = "Gewurztraminer"
   aTypes[16] = "Gamay Beaujolais"
   aTypes[17] = "Symphony"
   aTypes[18] = "Madeira"
```

Simple Forms for Data Entry and Data Validation

```
   return( aTypes )

end func
```

This straightforward function creates an 18-element array of strings with each element being assigned a wine type. That array, named *aTypes*, is then the return value of the function to be used by the _DROPDOWNLIST object:

```
formsetobject(2, _DROPDOWNLIST, "",   iFont1, 290, 20, 190, \\
                                   _DEFAULT; _LISTFAMS, WineList() )
```

Also note that the left and top pixel positions are specified, as well as the width of the data-entry item. Here, the width is set to 190 pixels; however, the height of the item is not so certain because the depth (or height) of the list this object will contain is not known. So the internal variable _DEFAULT is used to tell Realizer to calculate the best default fit possible, and use that pixel count.

> **Note:** If a width is offered, a height must be offered as well. Therefore, in cases where you have no clue what might be the best width possible, use the _DEFAULT internal variable.

The next input item is a different type of object, and its height is explicitly offered. Before looking at that, however, a few words on the characteristics of this object are in order. The _DROPDOWNCOMBO object is a combination of data-entry input and drop-down data list. This means that the user can type data into a data-entry point or select from a list of items. The list of items for this input item come from the *TheYears()* function, which looks like this:

```
'*****************************************************
'* Name:       TheYears()
'* Params:     N/A
'* Returns:    <aYears>      An array of 35 string year values
'* Purpose:    To build a quick table of years so that it does not
'*             have to be entered by hand

function TheYears()

   local aYears[35] as string
   local iCount     as integer
```

```
  for iCount = 1 to 35
    aYears[ iCount ] = numtostr( 1958 + iCount )
  next

  return( aYears )

end func
```

This is even simpler than the *WineList()* function. Here, an array of 35 elements is created, with each element containing a 4-character string representing a year, from 1959 through 1994. When the FOR...NEXT loop completes its task, the value of the function will be the array *aYears*. This array is then passed to the `_DROPDOWNCOMBO` object, and that object is told that this is a `_LISTFAMS`, just like the `_DROPDOWNLIST`.

Note the difference in the depth of the input areas between the `_DROPDOWNLIST` object and the `_DROPDOWNCOMBO` object. Here, just like the previous object, a list of items should "drop down" and present themselves for selection. However, since the list of years would be too deep, even if displayed in two columns, Realizer offers a pair of tiny up and down arrows. Here, the years will "spin" in either direction depending on whether the user clicks on the up arrow or down arrow. When the appropriate year appears, double-clicking on it will select that item from the list of *TheYears()*.

The final input object in the *DataEntry()* subroutine is called a `_CHECKBOX` item. This is to be used for logical values that need to be "checked off." The string that is the third parameter to the FORMSETOBJECT() function provides the text directly to the right of the `_CHECKBOX` item. So far, all the other input objects did not use the third parameter, since that parameter in those cases is not used by Realizer as input text. But here, the string "IN STOCK" is necessary to give meaning to the `_CHECKBOX` item. The last parameter used in this function:

```
formsetobject( 4, _CHECKBOX, "IN STOCK", iFont1, 290, 90; 1 )
```

tells realizer to set the `_CHECKBOX` to be "on," or checked, by default. If the value were 0, then the box region would remain empty.

Once all of the input objects are in place, we can activate the form in the following manner:

```
if formwait( _NORMAL ) = 1 then              '* Enter key was pressed
   formcontrol( _HIDE )                      '* Don't _CLOSE!!!!
   UpdateRecord( fRecord, 100 )
end if
```

If the return value of the FORMWAIT() function is 2, then the ESC key was pressed and we do not want to update the family members. However, if the ENTER key is pressed at any time, then the FORMWAIT() function will terminate control, terminate input focus to whichever object is in focus, and return a value of 1. From there, the form is hidden via the FORMCONTROL() function, and the *UpdateRecord()* function is called for the first time. Two parameters are passed to this function. The first parameter is the name of the variable that holds the family structure. This is the *fRecord* variable. The second is a literal value of 100; however, this is the value used when creating this data entry form:

```
formnew( 100; "Input Wine for Inventory", _TITLE )
```

In essence, we are telling the *UpdateRecord()* function the form in which to look to for data and information, and we are giving it the variable that contains the structure and the family members that need to be modified.

```
/*****************************************************
'* Name:         UpdateRecord( fData, iForm )
'* Params:       <fData>         Family name to be modified
'*               <iForm>         ID Integer of form to make sure and select
'* Returns:      N/A
'* Purpose:      This procedure will update the elements in the specified
'*               family

proc UpdateRecord( fData, iForm )

  formselect( iForm )
  fData.Winery  = formqstr(1)
  fData.Style   = formqstr(2)
  fData.Year    = formqstr(3)
  fData.InStock = (formqobject( 4 ) )[ _FQO_VALUE ]

end proc
```

Now, before going into how the UpdateRecord procedure works, some words on the numbering scheme of the various input objects are in order. For a moment, think about using an array data type instead of a family data type. There, instead of names to identify the family members, subscript positions or element numbers are used. So if each input object is incremented, as in this case (review time):

```
formsetobject( 1, _TEXTBOX, "", iFont1, 90, 35, 150,30 )
formsetobject(2, _DROPDOWNLIST, "",  iFont1, 290, 20, 190, \\
                        _DEFAULT; _LISTFAMS, WineList() )
```

```
formsetobject( 3, _DROPDOWNCOMBO, "", 290, 48, 100, 50; \\
                                  _LISTFAMS, TheYears()  )
formsetobject( 4, _CHECKBOX, "IN STOCK", iFont1, 290, 90;  1 )
```

we could use a FOR…NEXT loop to go through the list of objects using the FORMQOBJECT() function. There would be a one-to-one relationship between the numbering scheme for the data-entry object and the subscript position in the array. However, that is an idea for another time. Here, in this example, we are using a family data type and not an array.

In the UpdateRecord procedure, note that the FORMSELECT() function is used to make sure that the internal form pointer inside of the Realizer environment is positioned on the *iForm* field, which has an ID value of 100. Another tidbit of information deals with the family parameter passed. When a family is passed as a parameter, as in this case, all the family members become visible to the subroutine. In addition, any change made to a family member in a subroutine will become visible once that routine has completed its operation. So in this function, three calls to the FORMQSTR() function are made in order to obtain the three string values from the three input data objects. These values are subsequently stored to the first three family members in the structure. The remaining family member, *fData.InStock,* cannot obtain its value from the FORMQSTR() function, since that function returns a string data type and the family member is looking for a logical/integer. In addition, the FORMQSTR(4) function call would only return a value of "IN STOCK," which was the literal string used as prompt text for the `_CHECKBOX` input item. So, instead of the FORMQSTR() function, the FORMQOBJECT() function is used. Here, the function will return an array of values that will tell us all types of information about the desired object in the selected form. In order to obtain the value of the object, the `_FQO_VALUE` subscript position is looked at, but this is accomplished in conjunction with the expression surrounding the FORMQOBJECT(4) function. In essence, the expression becomes an array which is then interpreted as an array. Once that has finished its operation and assignment, the *UpdateRecord()* procedure returns control to the calling routine. This will then bring us back to the PRINT instructions toward the end of the *DataEntry()* function. The output for this entire program file looks like this:

```
************ WINE INFORMATION ************
Rodney Strong 1982      Chardonnay
IT IS in stock
        Type is 4
    Pixels from top are  90
        Return value  1
```

Simple Forms for Data Entry and Data Validation

Once the few print instructions on the *fRecord* family variable are executed, control is returned to the main part of the program file. There, one more look at the FORMQOBJECT() is made. After a few more PRINT instructions, the system is cleared after pausing for four seconds via the IDLE command.

> **Note:** While many of the objects in a form may be positioned with inches rather than pixels but we recommend sticking with pixels. The reason is consistency: The return values from the FORMQOBJECT() function will be an array with pixel values and not inches, even if inches are specified when the object is created.

Step Three: Improving the Data-Entry Screen

The next step is to spruce up the data-entry screen with push buttons and protect it with data validation. Building a better data-entry screen takes practice. The FormDev utility program can help lay out the various objects on the form, but getting into the code, modifying it to work with a record or a family or even an array, adding all sorts of lists and check marks takes time and patience. In the `Form8.rlz` file, I have expanded on the code in `Form7.rlz`. Like the previous example, there is a small main section of code that starts the entire procedure going. However, once that takes over, a series of new concepts are brought into play. In this next example, all of the family members are looked at, new button objects are added, and the FORMWAIT() function gets a new switch/internal variable. We also introduce data-validation and error messages, family values replacement (not to be confused with any political statement), and a new variation on the PRINT command. To start, here is the main code module for the `Form8.rlz` file:

```
'*************** MAIN ROUTINE!!! ************

DataEntry()

idle 4

reset( _ALL )
```

As you can see, there is even less to this than there was before. As a matter of fact, all of this source code running occurs before this could have been stored off to a new file, which could have been loaded into the Realizer environment via the RUN command. Eventually, we will want to do this when we tie this code back into the menu code from Chapter 2. So once again, the *DataEntry()* function is at the heart of everything.

```
'*****************************************************
'* Name:          DataEntry()
'* Params:        N/A
'* Returns:       N/A
'* Purpose:       This procedure draws the form, creates the family structure,
'*                updates the values, and prints the results.

proc DataEntry()

  local iFont1     as integer
  local iForm1     as integer
  local fRecord    as family
  local iSelection as integer

  fRecord = MakeFamily()

  iFont1 = fontqunique
  fontnew( iFont1; "Arial", 10, _BOLD )

  formnew( 100; "Input Wine for Inventory", _TITLE )
  formsetcolor( _CYAN; _BACKGROUND )
  formsetcolor( _CYAN; _FIELD )
  formsetcolor( _BLACK; _TEXT )
  formcontrol(_SIZE; 150,50,500,450 )         '* Offer a new size

  '* Now, field 1
  formsetobject( 10, _CAPTIONCENTER, "Winery Name:", iFont1, 10, 30, \\
                                                              70, 40 )
  formsetobject( 1, _TEXTBOX, "", iFont1, 90, 35, 150,30 )

  '* Field 2
  formsetobject( 20, _CAPTIONRIGHT, "Type", iFont1, 250, 25 )
  formsetobject(2, _DROPDOWNLIST, "",  iFont1, 290, 20, 190, \\
                                      _DEFAULT; _LISTFAMS, WineList() )

  '* Field 3
  formsetobject( 30, _CAPTIONRIGHT, "Year", iFont1, 250, 52 )
  formsetobject( 3, _DROPDOWNCOMBO, "", 290, 48, 100, 50; \\
                                      _LISTFAMS, TheYears() )

  '* Field 5
  formsetobject( 40, _CAPTIONRIGHT, "Full name", iFont1, 4,  110, \\
                                                    79, _DEFAULT )
  formsetobject( 41, _TEXTBOX, "",          iFont1, 85, 105, 170, \\
                                                         _DEFAULT )
```

```
formsetobject( 50, _CAPTIONRIGHT, "County" , iFont1,  4,  145, \\
                                                    79, _DEFAULT )
formsetobject( 51, _TEXTBOX, "",           iFont1, 85,  140, \\
                                                   140, _DEFAULT )

formsetobject( 60, _CAPTIONRIGHT, "State", iFont1,  4,  180, \\
                                                    79, _DEFAULT )
formsetobject( 61, _TEXTBOX, "CA",         iFont1, 85,  175, \\
                                                    40, _DEFAULT )

formsetobject( 70, _CAPTIONRIGHT, "Country", iFont1,  4,  215, \\
                                                      79, _DEFAULT )
formsetobject( 71, _TEXTBOX, "USA",        iFont1, 85,  210, \\
                                                   100, _DEFAULT )

formsetobject( 80, _CAPTIONRIGHT, "Region", iFont1,  4,  250, \\
                                                     79, _DEFAULT )
formsetobject( 81, _TEXTBOX, "",           iFont1, 85,  245, \\
                                                   100, _DEFAULT )

formsetobject( 90, _CAPTIONRIGHT, "Composition", iFont1,  4,  285, \\
                                                          79, _DEFAULT )
formsetobject( 91, _TEXTBOX, "",           iFont1, 85,  280, \\
                                                   200, _DEFAULT )

'* And now the right side of the form.....

formsetobject(100, _CAPTIONRIGHT, "Bin #", iFont1, 295, 110, \\
                                                    51, _DEFAULT )
formsetobject( 101, _TEXTBOX, "0",         iFont1, 350, 105, \\
                                                    40, _DEFAULT )

formsetobject(110, _CAPTIONRIGHT, "Lot #", iFont1, 295, 145, \\
                                                    51, _DEFAULT )
formsetobject( 111, _TEXTBOX, "0",         iFont1, 350, 140, \\
                                                    40, _DEFAULT )

formsetobject(120, _CAPTIONRIGHT, "Amount", iFont1, 295, 180, \\
                                                     51, _DEFAULT )
formsetobject( 121, _TEXTBOX, "0.00",      iFont1, 350, 175, \\
                                                    70, _DEFAULT )

formsetobject(130, _CAPTIONRIGHT, "Retail", iFont1, 295, 220, \\
                                                     51, _DEFAULT )
formsetobject( 131, _TEXTBOX, "0.00",      iFont1, 350, 215, \\
                                                    70, _DEFAULT )

formsetobject(140, _CAPTIONRIGHT, "Quantity", iFont1, 295, 255, \\
                                                       53, _DEFAULT )
```

```
           formsetobject( 141, _TEXTBOX, "0",          iFont1, 350, 250, \\
                                                              40,_DEFAULT )

           '* Field 4
           formsetobject( 4, _CHECKBOX, "IN STOCK", iFont1, 414, 50;  FALSE )

           '* And now, for a series of buttons....
           formsetobject( 5, _DEFBUTTON, "&Accept",  4, 398 )
           formsetobject( 6, _BUTTON, "Cancel", 80, 398 )
           formsetobject( 7, _BUTTON, "History",    iFont1, 424, 345, 70, 20 )
           formsetobject( 8, _BUTTON, "Details...", iFont1, 424, 371, 70, 20 )
           formsetobject( 9, _BUTTON, "Bins",       iFont1, 424, 398, 70, 20 )

           formsetobject( 1000, _DIGITALCLOCK, "", iFont1, _CENTER, _BOTTOM )


           while TRUE

              iSelection = formwait( _NORMAL )

              select case iSelection
              case 2, 6                       '* Both CANCEL or ESC
                exit while

              case 5, 1            '* The ACCEPT button was pushed

                if UpdateRecord( fRecord, 100 )
                  formcontrol( _HIDE )
                  PrintRecord( fRecord )
                  exit while

                else
                  '* Error
                  messagebox("You need to have something in both the first two entries", \\
                            "Update Problems", _MB_OK, _MB_EXCLAMATION )
                end if

              end select

           end while

        end proc
```

There are two parts to this procedure. The first part is designed to set up the form, and the second part works on the FORMWAIT() function within the WHILE loop. The form-generation part of the code could have been separated out from the rest of the code, which would further modularize the components

Simple Forms for Data Entry and Data Validation

of this example file. In this example, more data-entry fields are offered, and the form's coordinates have been expanded to allow for these new fields. Also, most of the text-based objects have now been changed to allow for the _CAPTIONRIGHT object to be used. The way this works is simple:

```
formsetobject(120, _CAPTIONRIGHT, "Amount", iFont1, 295, 180, \\
                                                 51, _DEFAULT )
```

The text "Amount" is one of several strings on the right side of the dialog-box form shown in Figure 4-12.

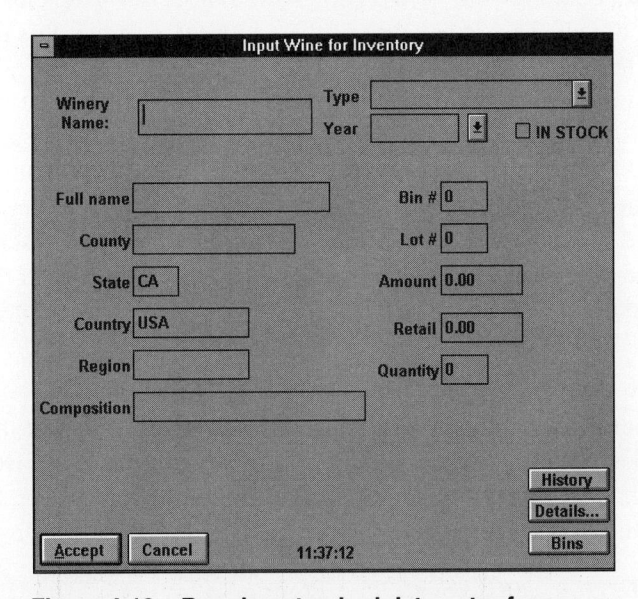

Figure 4-12. Running standard data entry form.

These data-entry items appear to be in line with one another, and as a matter of fact, we can see that they are:

```
formsetobject( 111, _TEXTBOX, "0",    iFont1, 350, 140, 40,_DEFAULT )
formsetobject( 121, _TEXTBOX, "0.00", iFont1, 350, 175, 70,_DEFAULT )
formsetobject( 131, _TEXTBOX, "0.00", iFont1, 350, 215, 70, _DEFAULT )
formsetobject( 141, _TEXTBOX, "0",    iFont1, 350, 250, 40,_DEFAULT )
```

Each item starts pixels 350 from the left, but the strings that are associated with these items are of different lengths. By using the _CAPTIONRIGHT object, we can right-align the text so that the end of the caption should be flush right against the left-aligned data-input boxes. The key here is to define a screen area that would, when flushed right, put the text right up against the _TEXTBOX's. To most of the _CAPTIONRIGHT objects, the region is a width of 51 pixels and a height of _DEFAULT value. Also, you might notice the differences between the pairings when it comes to the row (top) pixel count:

```
formsetobject(120, _CAPTIONRIGHT, "Amount", iFont1, 295, 180, \\
                                                    51, _DEFAULT )
formsetobject( 121, _TEXTBOX, "0.00",       iFont1, 350, 175, \\
                                                    70,_DEFAULT )
```

The top pixel count for the _CAPTIONRIGHT object is 5 pixels less than the _TEXTBOX object. This is because of the _TEXTBOX frame; this difference centers the text vertically with its box.

This example uses three new objects: _DEFBUTTON, _BUTTON, and _DIGITALCLOCK. The latter displays the time in the _CENTER and _BOTTOM of the form. It serves only the cause of gratuitous visual puffery. However, the remaining two additions do serve a purpose.

The _DEFBUTTON object means that this object will be circumscribed with a darker line than all the other buttons, showing that this button is the default action. In addition, there is an **accelerator key** assigned to this object:

```
formsetobject( 5, _DEFBUTTON, "&Accept",  4, 398 )
```

On the button, the letter A will be underlined, indicating that this button can be clicked on or activated via the ALT-A key combination. Both it and the Cancel button, to its right, are of default proportions. However, this is not the case with the other three buttons:

```
formsetobject( 7, _BUTTON, "History",    iFont1, 424, 345, 70, 20 )
formsetobject( 8, _BUTTON, "Details...", iFont1, 424, 371, 70, 20 )
formsetobject( 9, _BUTTON, "Bins",       iFont1, 424, 398, 70, 20 )
```

We can even adjust the height and width of a button. No object is immune trom being shrunk or expanded on the form if the need should arise. The width of each of these buttons will be 70 pixels and the height will be 20 pixels. Now, we may want to offer a different font for these buttons or choose different words so that they will fit better on the button's face.

Once all the objects are created, we come to the main processing loop within this procedure:

```
while TRUE
```

Simple Forms for Data Entry and Data Validation

This means that the form will constantly be active unless we exit out of this loop. Here, the value of the FORMWAIT() function is stored to a new variable:

```
iSelection = formwait( _NORMAL )
```

I chose to do it this way so that I could, during the debugging stage of this example, print the value of *iSelection* to the Print Log window and see what the function returns when the ENTER or ESC keys are pressed, what happens if a new object is selected, or what value is returned if the ALT-A key (attached to the Accept button) is pressed. If the _PICK internal variable was used in place of the _NORMAL internal variable, the ALT_A, ENTER, or ESC keys would be ignored: Only those items which are "picked" by the mouse will cause the function to return a value. Since this is not the case, the accelerator key as well as the ENTER and ESC keys can stop the form and send us into the SELECT CASE statement within the WHILE loop.

In this form, there are two choices to exit the loop:

```
select case iSelection
case 2, 6                              '* Both CANCEL or ESC
   exit while
```

Here, if the value of *iSelection* is 6, this means that the object with an ID of 6 (the Cancel button) was selected. However, if the value of *iSelection* is 2, that will process the EXIT WHILE line of code as well. The value of *iSelection* will be 2 when the ESC key is pressed.

> **Note:** Whenever there is more than one possible value for a SELECT CASE statement, all of the values to be tested need to be separated.

However, if the value of *iSelection* is 1 or 5, then an IF statement will be processed. The 1 value is returned if the ENTER key is pressed; the 5 value is returned if ALT-A was pressed or if the Accept button was clicked on.

If the value of the *UpdateRecord()* function is a logical true, then all is fine. However, if it is not, then a call to a new function is made: MESSAGEBOX(). This function allows us to overlay a form-like structure that consists of a simple message and behaviors, as shown in Figure 4-13. The second parameter of this function is the string that appears in the title bar—here, the string "Update Problems." The text of the message is passed as a literal in the first parameter.

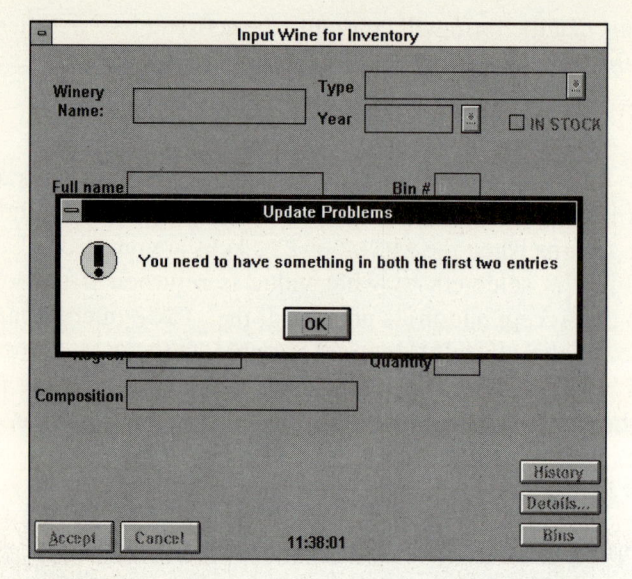

Figure 4-13. Pop-up dialog window with message.

The last two parameters to the MESSAGEBOX() function are simple. The third parameter tells the function what buttons to place inside of the box. Here, only an OK button is needed, since there are to be no other branching choices. This is added to the form/message area via the _MB_OK internal variable. In addition to this button, a special graphical image of an exclamation point will appear to the left of the input string. This image is turned on in the function via the _MB_EXCLAMATION internal variable. There are six possible button combinations that may be added to the MESSAGEBOX() function, and four possible graphical images. Since this is a function, it will have a return value; however, we are not concerned with that value. All this function is designed to do is to inform the user of a problem. This problem is detected in the *UpdateRecord()* function, since it was the function that returned a false value, which led to the call to the MESSAGEBOX() function.

Turning back to the SELECT CASE code construct, if any other object is selected, or if the FORMWAIT() function should return any other value, the WHILE loop will continue to process. The other branches off of this function are either the *UpdateRecord()* function and—if that returns a true value—the *PrintRecord()* function. First, onto the *UpdateRecord()* function:

```
'*****************************************************
'* Name:       UpdateRecord( fData, iForm )
'* Params:     <fData>       Family name to be modified
'*             <iForm>       ID Integer of form to make sure and select
'* Returns:    N/A
```

```
'* Purpose:      This procedure will update the elements in the specified
'*               family

function UpdateRecord( fData, iForm )

  local iUpdate as integer

  iUpdate = FALSE      '* Default value

  formselect( iForm )

  if Empty( formqstr(1) ) or Empty( formqstr(2) ) then
  else

     fData.Winery    = formqstr(1)
     fData.Style     = formqstr(2)
     fData.Year      = formqstr(3)
     fData.InStock   = (formqobject( 4 ) )[ _FQO_VALUE ]

     fWine.FullName     = formqstr(41)
     fWine.County       = formqstr(51)
     fWine.State        = formqstr(61)
     fWine.Country      = formqstr(71)
     fWine.Region       = formqstr(81)
     fWine.Composition  = formqstr(91)

     fWine.BinNumber    = round( strtonum( formqstr( 101 ), 0 ) )
     fWine.LotNumber    = round( strtonum( formqstr( 111 ), 0 ) )
     fWine.Amount       = strtonum( formqstr( 121 ), 0.00 )
     fWine.Value        = strtonum( formqstr( 131 ), 0.00 )
     fWine.Quantity     = strtonum( formqstr( 141 ) )

     iUpdate         = TRUE

  end if

  return( iUpdate )

end func
```

In the previous example program, this was just a procedure that updated the family members with values from the objects, but the *UpdateRecord()* function has now been modified slightly. To start, the default return value of *iUpdate* is set to the CONST value of FALSE, which is initialized at the top of the file:

```
const TRUE  = 1
const FALSE = 0
```

This makes reading the code easier because we don't have to remember how these two values may be used in an expression. Once that is set, the form is selected (precautionary measure). Now, a new function is introduced:

```
if Empty( formqstr(1) ) or Empty( formqstr(2) ) then
```

This is a carryover from my Clipper days. A variable is considered "empty" based mainly on what data type it is. This function right now works only with string data types; however, the version for the *CARTools Library* is slightly different. For example, if a variable is an integer, then 0 would be considered empty. If a variable is a string, as in the cases shown here, then the strings would have to trim themselves down to a length of 0.

```
'*****************************************************
'* Name:         Empty( <xData> )
'* Params:       <xData>         Any data type
'* Returns:      <iEmpty>        Logical true if value is "empty"
'* Purpose:      This function returns a true value should the data passed
'*               is considered to be "empty".

function Empty( xData )

   local iReturn as integer

   iReturn = ( len( ltrim$(xData) ) = 0 )

   return( iReturn )

end func
```

In the *UpdateRecord()* function, if the value of the first or second object in the form is empty, the function will return the logical false value as stipulated at the start of this function. However, if there is an item in both FORMQSTR(1) and FORMQSTR(2), then we can update the family. The update process is as it was before, but with a couple of new hitches. Two of our input items in the form relate to numeric family members, so the values found in the associated objects need to be converted from strings to numerics.

> **Note:** _TEXTBOX objects take only string data types and so, if there is to be a numeric or datetime value associated with these items, the value returned from the FORMQSTR() function needs to be converted.

Simple Forms for Data Entry and Data Validation

Here are the first two update examples:

```
fWine.BinNumber   = round( strtonum( formqstr( 101 ), 0 ) )
fWine.LotNumber   = round( strtonum( formqstr( 111 ), 0 ) )
```

The STRTONUM() function is first used. Here, if the value returned from object 101 or 111 is a string, it will be converted to a numeric. However, the second parameter to the function is 0: This tells the STRTONUM() function that if the value in the first parameter cannot be converted to a numeric, then take the value in the second parameter as a default. In other words, the *fWine.BinNumber* and *fWine.LotNumber* family members will always have default values of 0, regardless of what is entered by the end user.

After the STRTONUM() function returns a value, the ROUND() function removes any decimal places that the STRTONUM() function might insert in the conversion process. Therefore, these two family members will always have whole numbers related to them. Finally, after all the other family members have been updated, the value of the *iUpdate* variable is set to the constant value of true. This is then the return value of the *UpdateRecord()* function.

When the *UpdateRecord()* function returns control to the *DataEntry()* function and returns a logical true value, the form is then hidden via the FORMCONTROL(_HIDE) call, then the *PrintRecord()* function is called. When it is called, the family *fRecord* is passed to the following routine:

```
/*****************************************************
'* Name:        PrintRecord( fRecord )
'* Params:      <fRecord>       Family of values
'* Returns:     N/A
'* Purpose:     This procedure will print out the contents of the family
'*              that is involved.

proc PrintRecord( fRecord )

  print "*********** WINE INFORMATION *************"
  print fRecord.Winery, fRecord.Year, fRecord.Style
  print "- - - - - - - - - - - - - - - - - - -"
  print "  Full name: ", fWine.FullName
  print "     County: ", fWine.County
  print "      State: ", fWine.State
  print "    Country: ", fWine.Country
  print "  Apelation: ", fWine.Region
  print "Composition: ", fWine.Composition
  print " Bin Number: ", fWine.BinNumber
  print " Lot Number: ", fWine.LotNumber
  print using "& $###.##"; "  Purchased: ", fWine.Amount
  print using "& $###.##"; "  Valued at: ", fWine.Value
```

```
if fRecord.InStock then
   print "IT IS in stock and the amount on hand if: ", fWine.Quantity
else
   print "not available at this time...."
end if

end proc
```

What is unique about this subroutine is the new PRINT instruction. Here, we are actually formatting the output with respect to how a numeric value, namely a dollar figure, should appear on the screen (and in a report). To go with the PRINT command is the USING clause. When this clause is used, the PRINT command has two distinct pieces. The first piece contains a string that holds the formatting characters. The second piece becomes a modifier and contains the items that are to be displayed in the Print Log window.

> **Note:** If the USING clause is not used, then the items to be displayed are listed without the use of a semicolon (;). However, if the USING clause is specified, then the string for the format characters and the items to be displayed are separated by a semicolon.

The items in the format string are separated by a space, while the items to be displayed by the PRINT command are separated by a comma. There is a one-to-one relationship between the formatting string and the item to be displayed. In the following line, for example:

```
print using "& $###.##"; " Purchased: ", fWine.Amount
```

the ampersand means "take any alpha input and display it." The literal string " Purchased: " qualifies for this formatting character. Following this is a $###.## formatting string, which is then associated with the numeric family member *fWine.Amount*. This means that the numeric will be displayed as a dollar figure to the Print Log window. There are many other formatting characters that can be used in conjunction with the USING clause of the PRINT command.

Once all of the items are displayed to the Print Log window, control is returned to the *DataEntry()* subroutine, which will then EXIT WHILE out of the loop, return to the main calling routine, and eventually, close the form, wait for four seconds, and then RESET all of the internal states and windows.

Step 4: Setting Up Functions and Procedures

The Realizer language is a powerful language. It can conform to any standard structure of coding practices that you want to employ. It can also work in some less conventional styles of programming. In this next example, I will offer a new way of looking at setting up functions and procedures within a Realizer source file. This will continue to build on the code found in the *Form8.rlz* file.

However, before we start, a few words on code structure are necessary. How a particular function is designed is only part of the scenario. Another issue deals with function location. Unlike other languages in which functions and procedures are complete entities with a beginning and an end, Realizer adds one more twist. A function or a procedure can contain a function or a procedure. For example, consider the rough outline:

```
function DataEntry()

    function UpdateRecord()
    end func

    function MakeFamily()
    end func

    proc MakeForm()
    end proc

end func
```

Any variable, even a LOCAL variable that is defined at the top of the main function (in this case, the *DataEntry()* function), is visible to all of the subfunctions and subprocedures defined within the domain of *DataEntry()*. This means that the LOCAL variables do not have to be passed when these subfunctions and subprocedures are called. So we don't need to do something like this:

```
MakeForm( iFormNumber )
```

because if the variable *iFormNumber* is defined at the top of the routine, it does not need to be passed:

```
function DataEntry()

    local iFormNumber as integer

    function UpdateRecord()
    end func
```

```
            function MakeFamily()
            end func

            proc MakeForm()
            end proc

            '* Main routine
            MakeForm()

        end func
```

There are pros and cons to this structure. One pro may be that the dependent subroutines for the *DataEntry()* function are located near the code of the function, which means that we do not have to search for it if a problem arises with one of the supporting subroutines. On the other hand, for the sake of modularity and maintainability, it is far more difficult to work on the actual code of the *DataEntry()* function when we have to weed through all of the supporting functions contained within. And this issue gets more and more complex: Each of the subfunctions and subprocedures can also contain defined functions and procedures. In addition, by having a LOCAL variable that is not explicitly passed from calling routine to called routine, and having that LOCAL variable visible to those subroutines defined within, we run into the problem of tracking down problems, should that LOCAL variable be accidentally manipulated. One can argue that this is not a difficult task, since all of the code that might be at fault is contained within the main function itself. However, this issue is valid if the code that is involved is tight, confined, and small. In larger systems, I have rarely seen this to be the case. In those cases, passing the LOCAL variable off to a function/procedure, or calling a function that will return a value to be assigned to a LOCAL variable is not only far more modular, but easier to maintain as well. If you are planning to write an application to turn over to someone else, this entire discussion might be moot. In any event, the programming examples in this section offer a different look to the structure and layout of a function, a procedure, and a source code file. To start, here is *Form9.rlz*:

```
'* Application ... : Form9.rlz
'* Authors ....... : Steve Straley
'* Notice ........ : Copyright(c) 1994 - Sirius Press, Inc.
'* ............... : All Rights Reserved
'* Date .......... : January 1, 1994
'* Description ... : This starts to show how data entry can be involved.

run "Form9a.rlz"
run "Form9b.rlz"
```

```
DataEntry()
idle 4
reset( _ALL )

'* End of File: Form9.rlz
```

As you can see, there is not that much involved in this file. Two other source code files are loaded into the Realizer system based on the execution of the RUN command. Following this, the *DataEntry()* function is called. When it completes its task, the program will be IDLE for four seconds, then clear the system of all variables and screens.

Before looking at the file that holds the *DataEntry()* function, take a quick look at the first file that is loaded, `Form9a.rlz`:

```
'* Application ... : Form9a.rlz
'* Authors ....... : Steve Straley
'* Notice ........ : Copyright(c) 1994 - Sirius Press, Inc.
'* ............... : All Rights Reserved
'* Date .......... : January 1, 1994
'* Description ... : Offers supporting functions for the system...

const TRUE  = 1
const FALSE = 0


'***************************************************
'* Name:         TheYears()
'* Params:       N/A
'* Returns:      <aYears>         An array of 35 string year values
'* Purpose:      To build a quick table of years so that it does not
'*               have to be entered by hand

function TheYears()

   local aYears[35] as string
   local iCount     as integer

   for iCount = 1 to 35
      aYears[ iCount ] = numtostr( 1958 + iCount )
   next

   return( aYears )

end func


'***************************************************
'* Name:         WineList()
'* Params:       N/A
'* Returns:      <aWine>          Array of types of wines
```

```
'* Purpose:      To build a quick table of types so that it does not
'*               have to be entered by hand

function WineList()

   local aTypes[18] as string

   aTypes[1]  = "Chardonnay"
   aTypes[2]  = "Pinot Blanc"
   aTypes[3]  = "Sauvignon Blanc"
   aTypes[4]  = "Merlot"
   aTypes[5]  = "Zinfandel"
   aTypes[6]  = "Pinot Noir"
   aTypes[7]  = "Cabernet Sauvignon"
   aTypes[8]  = "Reisling"
   aTypes[9]  = "Port"
   aTypes[10] = "Sparkling"
   aTypes[11] = "Champaign"
   aTypes[12] = "Petite Syrah"
   aTypes[13] = "Barbera"
   aTypes[14] = "Semillon"
   aTypes[15] = "Gewurztraminer"
   aTypes[16] = "Gamay Beaujolais"
   aTypes[17] = "Symphony"
   aTypes[18] = "Madeira"

   return( aTypes )

end func

'*****************************************************
'* Name:         Empty( <xData> )
'* Params:       <xData>         Any data type
'* Returns:      <iEmpty>        Logical true if value is "empty"
'* Purpose:      This function returns a true value should the data passed
'*               be considered "empty".

function Empty( xData )

   local iReturn as integer

   iReturn = ( len( ltrim$(xData) ) = 0 )

   return( iReturn )

end func

'* End of File: Form9a.rlz
```

When this file is loaded, two constants are defined: true and false. These will be used not only by the routines contained in this file, but by all files loaded in the system. The first function defined in this file is *TheYears()*, which will return an array of 35 years to populate the year list. Following this function is the *WineList()* function: It will return an array containing 18 of the most popular styles of wine. The value of this function will be the array used in the _DROPDOWNLIST in the form previously outlined. Finally, after this comes the definition of the *Empty()* function.

In essence, `Form9a.rlz` is nothing more than a generic function library. Rather than having to load each one of these files into the system, this one file will load all three functions to be used by the application. The next file to be loaded is a different story. `Form9b.rlz` contains the *DataEntry()* function and three other unique functions: *MakeFamily()*, *UpdateRecord()*, and *PrintRecord()*. However, within the *DataEntry()* function, four separate functions are defined and maintained: *MakeInputItems()*, *MakeSayItems()*, *MakeForm()*, and *ValidEntries()*. Before showing the entire file, here is the crux of the *DataEntry()* function:

```
proc DataEntry()

   local iForm1      as integer
   local fRecord     as family
   local iSelection  as integer
   local fItems      as family
   local fSays       as family

   fRecord = MakeFamily()
   MakeInputItems()            '* Builds the references to the objects
   MakeSayItems()              '* Builds the references to the SAYs
   MakeForm()                  '* Builds the forms

   loop

      select case formwait( _NORMAL )
      case 2, 6                '* Both CANCEL or ESC
         exit loop

      case 5, 1                '* The ACCEPT button was pushed
         if ValidEntries()
            formcontrol( _HIDE )
            UpdateRecord( fRecord, 100, fItems )
            PrintRecord( fRecord )
            exit loop
         end if

      end select
```

```
    end loop

end proc
```

      Now, if only it could be this simple. Here, the five variables that are defined in this form, even though they are declared as LOCAL variables, will be visible to the functions and procedures defined within the domain of this function. Knowing this, we can see that there is a difference in how we can code. Consider these two lines from the above example:

```
fRecord = MakeFamily()
MakeInputItems()          '* Builds the references to the objects
```

      The *MakeFamily()* function will return the results and store a family of values to the *fRecord* variable. We can draw the conclusion that perhaps the *MakeFamily()* function is not defined within the *DataEntry()* function. If it were, then the *MakeFamily()* function would have access to the *fRecord* variable, even though it is declared to be LOCAL. However, for the sake of this discussion let us say that the *MakeInputItems()* function uses the information stored to the *fRecord* variable. Clearly, that variable is not passed to this function: Realizer does not have to pass the variable. This is the major difference in how these functions work within the system and in relation to the *DataEntry()* function. The *MakeInputItems()* function, in our hypothetical case, would need to be passed the *fRecord* variable if it were defined within the domain of the *DataEntry()* function. Basically, the function *MakeInputItem()* would be on the same level with that of the five LOCAL variables. We do not know for sure that the *MakeInputItems()* function is to be defined in the *DataEntry()* function; however, if the *MakeInputItems()* function could manipulate the various members of the family known as *fRecord* (or any one of the other four variables), then it would have to be defined as such.

      Another feature that I decided to implement in this routine was a concept we first ran across in the FormDev utility program. When a menu or a form is designed, a series of family members are defined to work with the objects. In the previous examples, I hard-coded these values directly into the FORMSETOBJECT() function calls. Now, we are going to offer a new technique. Before showing this, let me show you the structure of the variable *fRecord*. This will hold the various members of "fields" for a particular record:

```
function MakeFamily

  local fWine as family
```

```
fWine.Winery       = space$(30)
fWine.Style        = space$(25)
fWine.Year         = "1991"
fWine.InStock      = 0              '* False, it's not in storage
fWine.FullName     = space$(35)
fWine.County       = space$(20)
fWine.State        = space$(2)
fWine.Country      = space$(10)
fWine.Region       = space$(20)
fWine.Composition  = space$(40)
fWine.BinNumber    = 0
fWine.LotNumber    = 0
fWine.Amount       = 14.95
fWine.Value        = 22.50
fWine.Quantity     = 0

return( fWine )

end func
```

> **Note:** A family member cannot have the same name as a reserved word or a command, function, or clause which is part of the Realizer set. The member named *fWine.Style* was originally named *fWine.Type*, but since the TYPE command is a reserved word, this would give an error message.

Each member of *fRecord* will have an associated data-entry object that will be placed in the form. For example, the *fRecord.Winery* member will have the following _TEXTBOX object:

```
'* Now, field 1
formsetobject( fSays.winery, _CAPTIONCENTER, "Winery Name:", \\
                    iFont1, 10, 30, 70, 40 )
formsetobject( fItems.winery, _TEXTBOX, "", iFont1, 90, 35, 150,30 )
```

Notice how the family member's name is used in two other families: *fSays* and *fItems*. Here, these families will hold the ID markers for creating the objects for the form. Their names are associated with the name of the family member found in *fRecord*. Realizer does not follow this convention when we use the FormDev utility. The idea of attaching a family member's name to another family, one for the objects, is unique and gives us additional continuity.

Before showing the rest of the code for this, it is important to point out that the order in which you create a form's objects is very important. When an end user presses the TAB key to cycle from object to object, the screen location of the object is not important, but the tab sequence will follow the order of creation. For example, the four objects appear in the *MakeForm()* nested function.

```
formsetobject( fItems.winery, _TEXTBOX, "", iFont1, 90, 35, 150,30 )
formsetobject( fItems.typeIt, _DROPDOWNLIST, "", iFont1, \\
                290, 20, 190, _DEFAULT; _LISTFAMS, WineList() )
formsetobject( fItems.year, _DROPDOWNCOMBO, "", 290, 48, 100, 50; \\
                _LISTFAMS, TheYears() )
formsetobject( fItems.FullName, _TEXTBOX, "", iFont1, 85, 105, \\
                170, _DEFAULT )
```

Here, the fourth object is directly under the first object and yet, since it is fourth in the list attached to the form, it will be the forth object processed when the TAB key is pressed.

Here is the complete context of *Form9b.rlz*, as promised:

```
'* Application ... : Form9b.rlz
'* Authors ....... : Steve Straley
'* Notice ........ : Copyright(c) 1994 - Sirius Press, Inc.
'* ............... : All Rights Reserved
'* Date .......... : January 1, 1994
'* Description ... : Builds the record and the main processing routine...


'*****************************************************
'* Name:        MakeFamily()
'* Params:      N/A
'* Returns:     <fWine>        A family of structure for WINE
'* Purpose:     This function creates a blank family for data entry
'*              purposes.

function MakeFamily

   local fWine as family

     fWine.Winery        = space$(30)
     fWine.Style         = space$(25)
     fWine.Year          = "1991"
     fWine.InStock       = 0             '* False, it's not in storage
     fWine.FullName      = space$(35)
     fWine.County        = space$(20)
     fWine.State         = space$(2)
     fWine.Country       = space$(10)
     fWine.Region        = space$(20)
     fWine.Composition   = space$(40)
     fWine.BinNumber     = 0
     fWine.LotNumber     = 0
     fWine.Amount        = 14.95
```

```
   fWine.Value        = 22.50
   fWine.Quantity     = 0

   return( fWine )

end func


'*****************************************************
'* Name:        UpdateRecord(fData, iForm, fItems)
'* Params:      N/A
'* Returns:     <fData>         Family of records items
'*              <iForm>         Holds the integer pointer to form
'*              <fItems>        Family of objects
'* Purpose:     This function updates the members in the family named
'*              <fData> with the values from the form objects obtained
'*              from <fItems> in form <iForm>

proc UpdateRecord( fData, iForm, fItems )

   formselect( iForm )

   fData.Winery      = formqstr(fItems.winery)
   fData.Style       = formqstr(fItems.typeit)
   fData.Year        = formqstr(fItems.year   )
   fData.InStock     = strtonum( formqstr( fItems.quantity ) ) > 0

   fWine.FullName    = formqstr(fItems.Full_Name  )
   fWine.County      = formqstr(fItems.County     )
   fWine.State       = formqstr(fItems.State      )
   fWine.Country     = formqstr(fItems.Country    )
   fWine.Region      = formqstr(fItems.Region     )
   fWine.Composition = formqstr(fItems.Composition)

   fWine.BinNumber   = round( strtonum(  formqstr( fItems.Bin_no ), 0 ) )
   fWine.LotNumber   = round( strtonum(  formqstr( fItems.Lot_no ), 0 ) )
   fWine.Amount      = strtonum( formqstr( fItems.Amount ), 0.00 )
   fWine.Value       = strtonum( formqstr( fItems.Retail ), 0.00 )
   fWine.Quantity    = strtonum( formqstr( fItems.Quantity ) )

end proc


'*****************************************************
'* Name:        PrintRecord( fRecord )
'* Params:      <fRecord>       Family of values
'* Returns:     N/A
'* Purpose:     This procedure will print out the contents of the family
'*              that is involved.

proc PrintRecord( fRecord )
```

```
   print "********** WINE INFORMATION *************"
   print fRecord.Winery, fRecord.Year, fRecord.Style
   print "- - - - - - - - - - - - - - - - - - - -"
   print "  Full name: ", fWine.FullName
   print "     County: ", fWine.County
   print "      State: ", fWine.State
   print "    Country: ", fWine.Country
   print "  Apelation: ", fWine.Region
   print "Composition: ", fWine.Composition
   print " Bin Number: ", fWine.BinNumber
   print " Lot Number: ", fWine.LotNumber
   print using "& $###.##"; "  Purchased: ", fWine.Amount
   print using "& $###.##"; "  Valued at: ", fWine.Value

   if fRecord.InStock then
      print "IT IS in stock and the amount on hand if: ", fWine.Quantity
   else
      print "not available at this time...."
   end if

end proc

'*****************************************************
'* Name:       DataEntry()
'* Params:     N/A
'* Returns:    N/A
'* Purpose:    This procedure draws the form, creates the family structure,
'*             updates the values, and prints the results.

proc DataEntry()

   local iForm1      as integer
   local fRecord     as family
   local iSelection  as integer
   local fItems      as family
   local fSays       as family

      '*****************************************************
      '* Name:       MakeForm()
      '* Params:     N/A
      '* Returns:    N/A
      '* Purpose:    This procedure creates the necessary font, creates
      '*             the form, and designs the various objects for the form.

      proc MakeForm()

         local iFont1     as integer
```

```
iFont1 = fontqunique
fontnew( iFont1; "Arial", 10, _BOLD )

formnew( 100; "Input Wine for Inventory", _TITLE )
formsetcolor( _CYAN; _BACKGROUND )
formsetcolor( _CYAN; _FIELD )
formsetcolor( _BLACK; _TEXT )
formcontrol(_SIZE; 150,50,500,450 )        '* Offer a new size

'* Now, field 1
formsetobject( fSays.winery, _CAPTIONCENTER, "Winery Name:", \\
                            iFont1, 10, 30, 70, 40 )
formsetobject( fItems.winery, _TEXTBOX, "", iFont1, 90, 35, 150,30 )

'* Field 2
formsetobject( fSays.typeIt, _CAPTIONRIGHT, "Type", iFont1, 250, 25 )
formsetobject( fItems.typeIt, _DROPDOWNLIST, "", iFont1, \\
                    290, 20, 190, _DEFAULT; _LISTFAMS, WineList() )
'* Field 3
formsetobject( fSays.year , _CAPTIONRIGHT, "Year", iFont1, 250, 52 )
formsetobject( fItems.year, _DROPDOWNCOMBO, "", 290, 48, 100, 50; \\
                            _LISTFAMS, TheYears()  )
'* Field 5
formsetobject( fSays.Full_Name, _CAPTIONRIGHT, "Full name", \\
                        iFont1, 4, 110, 79, _DEFAULT )
formsetobject( fItems.Full_Name, _TEXTBOX, "", iFont1, 85, 105, \\
                        170, _DEFAULT )
'* Field 6
formsetobject( fSays.County , _CAPTIONRIGHT, "County" , iFont1, \\
                        4, 145, 79, _DEFAULT )
formsetobject( fItems.County,  _TEXTBOX, "", iFont1, 85, 140, \\
                                            140, _DEFAULT )
'* Field 7
formsetobject( fSays.State, _CAPTIONRIGHT, "State", iFont1, \\
                        4, 180, 79, _DEFAULT )
formsetobject( fItems.State, _TEXTBOX, "CA", iFont1, 85, 175, \\
                                            40, _DEFAULT )
'* Field 8
formsetobject( fSays.Country, _CAPTIONRIGHT, "Country", iFont1, \\
                        4, 215, 79, _DEFAULT )
formsetobject( fItems.Country, _TEXTBOX, "USA", iFont1, 85, 210, \\
                                            100, _DEFAULT )
'* Field 9
formsetobject( fSays.Region, _CAPTIONRIGHT, "Region", iFont1, \\
                        4, 250, 79, _DEFAULT )
formsetobject( fItems.Region, _TEXTBOX, "", iFont1, 85, 245, \\
                                            100,_DEFAULT )
'* Field 10
formsetobject( fSays.Composition, _CAPTIONRIGHT, "Composition", \\
```

```
                                      iFont1,   4,   285,  79,  _DEFAULT )
            formsetobject( fItems.Composition,  _TEXTBOX, "", iFont1, 85, 280, \\
                                               200,_DEFAULT )
'* And now the right side of the form.....
'* Field 11
formsetobject( fSays.Bin_no,   _CAPTIONRIGHT, "Bin #", iFont1, \\
                           295, 110, 51, _DEFAULT )
formsetobject( fItems.Bin_no,  _TEXTBOX, "0", iFont1, 350, 105, \\
                                        40, _DEFAULT )
'* Field 12
formsetobject( fSays.Lot_no,   _CAPTIONRIGHT, "Lot #", iFont1, \\
                           295, 145, 51, _DEFAULT )
formsetobject( fItems.Lot_no,  _TEXTBOX, "0", iFont1, 350, 140, \\
                                        40,_DEFAULT )
'* Field 13
formsetobject( fSays.Amount ,  _CAPTIONRIGHT, "Amount", iFont1, \\
                           295, 180, 51, _DEFAULT )
formsetobject( fItems.Amount,  _TEXTBOX, "0.00", iFont1, 350, 175, \\
                                        70,_DEFAULT )
'* Field 14
formsetobject( fSays.Retail ,  _CAPTIONRIGHT, "Retail", iFont1, \\
                           295, 220, 51, _DEFAULT )
formsetobject( fItems.Retail,  _TEXTBOX, "0.00", iFont1, 350, 215, \\
                                         70, _DEFAULT )
'* Field 15
formsetobject( fSays.Quantity , _CAPTIONRIGHT, "Quantity", \\
                           iFont1, 295, 255, 53, _DEFAULT )
formsetobject( fItems.Quantity, _TEXTBOX, "0", iFont1,  350, 250, \\
                                        40,_DEFAULT; _NOTIFY )
'* Field 16
formsetobject( fItems.InStock, _CHECKBOX, "IN STOCK", iFont1, \\
                           414, 50;  FALSE )

'* And now, for a series of buttons....
formsetobject( fItems.accept,    _DEFBUTTON, "&Accept",  4, 398 )
formsetobject( fItems.cancel,    _BUTTON, "Cancel", 80, 398 )
formsetobject( fItems.history,   _BUTTON, "History",    iFont1, \\
                           424, 345, 70, 20 )
formsetobject( fItems.details,   _BUTTON, "Details...", iFont1, \\
                           424, 371, 70, 20 )
formsetobject( fItems.bins,      _BUTTON, "Bins",       iFont1, \\
                           424, 398, 70, 20 )
formsetobject( fItems.Clock, _DIGITALCLOCK, "", iFont1,\\
                           _CENTER, _BOTTOM )

end proc


'*****************************************************
```

```
'* Name:          MakeInputItems()
'* Params:        N/A
'* Returns:       N/A
'* Purpose:       This procedure simply assigns values to the family
'*                members that will be used in the assignment of the
'*                objects in the form.
proc MakeInputItems()

  fItems.winery       = 1
  fItems.typeit       = 2
  fItems.year         = 3
  fItems.InStock      = 4
  fItems.accept       = 5
  fItems.cancel       = 6
  fItems.history      = 7
  fItems.details      = 8
  fItems.bins         = 9
  fItems.Full_Name    = 10
  fItems.County       = 11
  fItems.State        = 12
  fItems.Country      = 13
  fItems.Region       = 14
  fItems.Composition  = 15
  fItems.Bin_no       = 16
  fItems.Lot_no       = 17
  fItems.Amount       = 18
  fItems.Retail       = 19
  fItems.Quantity     = 20
  fItems.Clock        = 21

end proc

'****************************************************
'* Name:          MakeSayItems()
'* Params:        N/A
'* Returns:       N/A
'* Purpose:       This procedure simply assigns values to the family
'*                members that will be used in the assignment of the
'*                SAY/display objects in the form.
proc MakeSayItems()

  fSays.winery       = 101
  fSays.typeit       = 102
  fSays.year         = 103
  fSays.InStock      = 104
  fSays.accept       = 105
  fSays.cancel       = 106
  fSays.history      = 107
  fSays.details      = 108
```

```
        fSays.bins           = 109
        fSays.Full_Name      = 110
        fSays.County         = 111
        fSays.State          = 112
        fSays.Country        = 113
        fSays.Region         = 114
        fSays.Composition    = 115
        fSays.Bin_no         = 116
        fSays.Lot_no         = 117
        fSays.Amount         = 118
        fSays.Retail         = 119
        fSays.Quantity       = 120

end proc

'*****************************************************
'* Name:       ValidEntries()
'* Params:     N/A
'* Returns:    N/A
'* Purpose:    This function returns a logical true or false
'*             based on whether there are proper items in the
'*             various objects in the form
func ValidEntries()

   local iIsOk as integer

   iIsOk = FALSE         '* Default value

   if empty( formqstr( fItems.winery ) ) then
      input "You must enter a name within the form" ;
      formmodifyobject( fItems.winery, _SETFOCUS )

   elseif empty( formqstr( fItems.typeit ) ) then
      input "You must pick a valid type of wine from the list" ;
      formmodifyobject( fItems.typeit, _SETFOCUS  )

   elseif empty( formqstr( fItems.year ) ) then
      input "Every bottle of wine has a year.  Enter it!" ;
      formmodifyobject( fItems.year,  _SETFOCUS )

   elseif strtonum( formqstr( fItems.bin_no ) ) < 0 then
      input "You cannot have a negative number of bins...." ;
      formmodifyobject( fItems.bin_no, _SETFOCUS )

   elseif strtonum( formqstr( fItems.Lot_no ) ) < 0 then
      input "You cannot have a negative number of lots...." ;
      formmodifyobject( fItems.lot_no, _SETFOCUS )
```

```
      elseif strtonum( formqstr( fItems.amount ) ) < 0 then
        input "If the bottle was given, then enter 0!" ;
        formmodifyobject( fItems.amount, _SETFOCUS )

      elseif strtonum( formqstr( fItems.retail ) ) < 0 then
        input "No bottle of wine has a NEGATIVE value!  It's worth something!" ;
        formmodifyobject( fItems.retail, _SETFOCUS )

      elseif strtonum( formqstr( fItems.quantity ) ) < 0 then
        input "You can't have a negative number as quantity....." ;
        formmodifyobject( fItems.Quantity, _SETFOCUS )

      else
        iIsOk = TRUE

      end if

      return( iIsOk )

   end func


'*********************** THIS IS THE MAIN ROUTINE **************`

   fRecord = MakeFamily()
   MakeInputItems()          '* Builds the references to the objects
   MakeSayItems()            '* Builds the references to the SAYs
   MakeForm()                '* Builds the forms

   loop

      select case formwait( _NORMAL )
      case 2, 6              '* Both CANCEL or ESC
        exit loop

      case 5, 1              '* The ACCEPT button was pushed
        if ValidEntries()
          formcontrol( _HIDE )
          UpdateRecord( fRecord, 100, fItems )
          PrintRecord( fRecord )
          exit loop
        end if

      end select

   end loop

end proc

'* End of File: Form9b.rlz
```

The function that does the data validation is called *ValidEntries()*, and it is a subfunction nested within the *DataEntry()* function. This function is called after the user presses the ENTER key (meaning that the FORMWAIT() function will have the value of 1) or presses the ALT-A combination or clicks on the Accept button. The *ValidEntries()* function makes use of the LOCAL variables that are assigned within the domain of the *DataEntry()* function, in particular, the *fItems* family variable. Within this function there is a massive IF ... ELSEIF ... END IF code construct. Here, each of the critical fields/data objects is looked at, one at a time, starting with the *fItems.winery* object. The INPUT command will offer up an error message that looks like this:

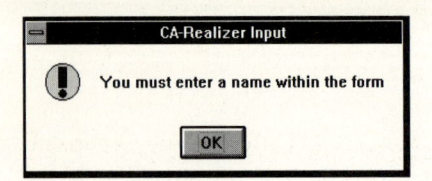

[Dialog box: CA-Realizer Input — "You must enter a name within the form" — OK]

Each of the tests within the branching code will place a different string inside the data-entry box associated with the INPUT command. The OK button is the only choice available to the end user with the INPUT command as it is used. Once the OK button is pressed, the *ValidEntry()* function will then process the FORMMODIFYOBJECT() function following each INPUT command. Turning back to the first item, this code is:

```
formmodifyobject( fItems.winery, _SETFOCUS )
```

Keep in mind that this occurs just after the end user has been told that one of the data-entry items is invalid. The FORMMODIFYOBJECT() function will position the cursor on the appropriate item. Here, it is the data entry object named *fItems.winery*. The _SETFOCUS internal variable is what positions the cursor on that particular field. In other words, regardless of where the cursor was within the form when the user pressed the ENTER key or clicked on the Accept button, if this first field is considered invalid, then the function will return a logical false to the main controlling loop, and position the cursor on the appropriate data entry object, waiting for the correction to be made.

If all the items on the form check out, then the *ValidEntry()* function will return a logical true value, and the main code within the *DataEntry()* function will hide the form, update the family members by making a call to the

UpdateRecord() function, print out the items with the *PrintRecord()* function, and eventually, exit out of the loop. It is important at this point to note that we could just as easily have made the *UpdateRecord()* and *PrintRecord()* functions nested functions within the *DataEntry()* function. That way, the variables used, such as *fRecord* and *fItems*:

```
UpdateRecord( fRecord, 100, fItems )
PrintRecord( fRecord )
```

would not have to be passed to them. Since both variables are still local, they would have been visible to these functions if they, too, were defined within the scope of the *DataEntry()* function.

As a general rule, I prefer to pass parameters rather than rely on the visibility of a variable across several functions or procedures. I do not like the risk that one function can alter the contents of a variable without another function explicitly knowing this. In other words, if I make a variable local, it is not to be shared with any other subroutine unless I explicitly grant that subroutine access. This means that more items will have to be passed and accepted as parameters on both the sending and receiving side of the equation; however, that is a small price to pay. The alternative is to trust that you or someone else could, during future work, ensure the integrity of all of the variables. Quite bluntly, I do not trust myself, especially if I haven't looked at the code for some time.

Step 5: Warning Messages and Notifications

In this section, we will step back from the complexities of the previous example to tackle the issue of on-the-fly warning messages and notifications. In the previous example, the notification of an error within the form takes place at the end of the input flow, when the end user has pressed the ENTER key or clicked on the Accept button. When either of these conditions is met, each of the input items on the form is looked at to see if the data it contains is acceptable. However, another way to provide for field validation (or form validation) is to check each data input item as it is entered. Here, when the user attempts to move off of a field, a quick check of that item's contents is made, and if not valid, then an error message will appear. To accomplish this, the modifier _NOTIFY must be attached to those data-input objects. For example, in the line:

```
formsetobject( 11, _TEXTBOX, "", iFont1, 90, 35, 150,30; _NOTIFY )
```

the `_NOTIFY` internal variable tells the FORMWAIT() function to accept this object's ID value as a possible exit value. This way, if the end user presses the `TAB` key to move to the next data object, the FORMWAIT() function will return this object's value. This means that we can check the value of the object inside of our processing loop:

```
loop
  select case formwait( _NORMAL )
  case 1, 2
    formcontrol( _HIDE )                          '* Don't _CLOSE!!!!
    UpdateRecord( fRecord, 100 )
    exit loop

  case 11
    if Empty( formqstr( 11 ) ) then
      input "You must enter something on this field!" ;
      formmodifyobject( 11, _SETFOCUS )
    end if

  end select
end loop
```

In this small loop, the SELECT CASE on the FORMWAIT(_NORMAL) function tests the object with the ID value of 11. If that data object is empty, the function *Empty()* will return a logical true value which will cause the INPUT command and FORMMODIFYOBJECT() function to process. When finished, control will be returned to the form, and the cursor will be returned to the data item the user just tried to leave.

However, there still remains a small problem. Consider this possible scenario: the first data object is empty, with no value, and the end user presses the `ESC` key. Technically, this should go to the first CASE selection in our code construct. Here, if the value of FORMWAIT() is 1 or 2 (the `ENTER` key or the `ESC` key), the code to *UpdateRecord()* should be processed. However, it is not. Since the contents of object ID number 11 is still *Empty()*, then that code will be processed instead. The trouble is this will cause the INPUT command to appear. Then, when we click on the `OK` button to accept the message from the INPUT command, control is then turned to the CASE 1,2 command and we will leave the loop. We do not want an extra INPUT message to appear if the end user presses the `ESC` key. Yet, as the code stands currently, this is exactly what will take place.

To circumvent the situation, we need to understand better the purpose of the `_NOTIFY` internal variable. This variable tells the FORMWAIT() function that the associated object that has been granted `_NOTIFY` status will trigger the FORMWAIT() function just as if the `ENTER` or `ESC` keys were pressed. However, those two keys constitute true exit actions whereas the one we are building at the moment does not. In essence, we are trying to alter the purpose of the FORMWAIT() function via the _NOTIFY variable. We need to recognize that if the ESC key is pressed, then all _NOTIFY conditions will be processed first before FORMWAIT() will return the value for the ESC key. This means that FORMWAIT() will have two values stacked on top of each other. The first value returned from this function will be that of the data item that has been granted _NOTIFY status. The second value will be either 1 for the ENTER key or 2 for the ESC key. Within the code testing the _NOTIFY data item, we need to check the pending keystroke and see if it is a 2 (or the ESC key). We can do this with the FORMWAIT() function again, but with a different internal variable passed as a parameter:

```
if formwait( _PEEK ) <> 2
```

Here, we are "peeking" into the FORMWAIT() key stack to see if the next pending operation will be the value of 2, and only if it is not will the code under this IF command be processed. So use of the _NOTIFY internal variable is dependent on the use of the _PEEK internal variable as well. To better see this, here is the file *Form10.rlz*, which uses this technique:

```
'* Application ... : Form10.rlz
'* Authors ....... : Steve Straley
'* Notice ........ : Copyright(c) 1994 - Sirius Press, Inc.
'* .............. : All Rights Reserved
'* Date .......... : January 1, 1994
'* Description ... : This shows the use of the _NOTIFY internal variable
'*                   and how fields can be data checked for validity on
'*                   the fly as opposed to the end of the form.

'****************************************************
'* Name:        Empty( <xData> )
'* Params:      <xData>         Any data type
'* Returns:     <iEmpty>        Logical true if value is "empty"
'* Purpose:     This function returns a true value should the data passed
'*              is considered to be "empty".

function Empty( xData )

   local iReturn as integer

   iReturn = ( len( ltrim$(xData) ) = 0 )

   return( iReturn )

end func
```

```
'*****************************************************
'* Name:          TheYears()
'* Params:        N/A
'* Returns:       <aYears>         An array of 35 string year values
'* Purpose:       To build a quick table of years so that it does not
'*                have to be entered by hand

function TheYears()

  local aYears[35] as string
  local iCount     as integer

  for iCount = 1 to 35
    aYears[ iCount ] = numtostr( 1958 + iCount )
  next

  return( aYears )

end func

'*****************************************************
'* Name:          WineList()
'* Params:        N/A
'* Returns:       <aWine>          Array of types of wines
'* Purpose:       To build a quick table of types so that it does not
'*                have to be entered by hand

function WineList()

  local aTypes[18] as string

  aTypes[1]  = "Chardonnay"
  aTypes[2]  = "Pinot Blanc"
  aTypes[3]  = "Sauvignon Blanc"
  aTypes[4]  = "Merlot"
  aTypes[5]  = "Zinfandel"
  aTypes[6]  = "Pinot Noir"
  aTypes[7]  = "Cabernet Sauvignon"
  aTypes[8]  = "Reisling"
  aTypes[9]  = "Port"
  aTypes[10] = "Sparkling"
  aTypes[11] = "Champaign"
  aTypes[12] = "Petite Syrah"
  aTypes[13] = "Barbera"
  aTypes[14] = "Semillon"
  aTypes[15] = "Gewurztraminer"
  aTypes[16] = "Gamay Beaujolais"
  aTypes[17] = "Symphony"
  aTypes[18] = "Madeira"
```

```
     return( aTypes )

end func

'****************************************************
'*  Name:        MakeFamily()
'*  Params:      N/A
'*  Returns:     <fWine>         A family of structure for WINE
'*  Purpose:     This function creates a blank family for data entry
'*               purposes.

function MakeFamily

   local fWine as family

   fWine.Winery     = space$(30)
   fWine.Style      = space$(25)
   fWine.Year       = "1991"
   fWine.InStock    = 0              '* False, it's not in storage

   return( fWine )

end func

'****************************************************
'*  Name:        UpdateRecord( fData, iForm )
'*  Params:      <fData>         Family name to be modified
'*               <iForm>         ID Integer of form to make sure and select
'*  Returns:     N/A
'*  Purpose:     This procedure will update the elements in the specified
'*               family

proc UpdateRecord( fData, iForm )

   formselect( iForm )
   fData.Winery  = formqstr(11)
   fData.Style   = formqstr(12)
   fData.Year    = formqstr(13)
   fData.InStock = strtonum( formqstr( 14 ), 0 )

end proc

'****************************************************
'*  Name:        DataEntry()
'*  Params:      N/A
'*  Returns:     N/A
'*  Purpose:     This procedure draws the form, creates the family structure,
'*               updates the values, and prints the results.
```

```
proc DataEntry()

   local iFont1 as integer
   local iForm1 as integer
   local fRecord as family

   fRecord = MakeFamily()

   iFont1 = fontqunique
   fontnew( iFont1; "Arial", 10, _BOLD )

   formnew( 100; "Input Wine for Inventory", _TITLE )
   formsetcolor( _CYAN; _BACKGROUND )
   formsetcolor( _CYAN; _FIELD )
   formsetcolor( _BLACK; _TEXT )
   formcontrol(_SIZE; 50,50,500,150 )       '* Offer a new size

   '* Now, field 1
   formsetobject( 10, _CAPTIONCENTER, "Winery Name:", iFont1, 10, 30, \\
                                                              70, 40 )
   formsetobject( 11, _TEXTBOX, "", iFont1, 90, 35, 150,30; _NOTIFY )

   '* Field 2
   formsetobject( 20, _CAPTIONRIGHT, "Type", iFont1, 250, 25 )
   formsetobject(12, _DROPDOWNLIST, "",   iFont1, 290, 20, 190, \\
                                   _DEFAULT; _LISTFAMS, WineList() )

   '* Field 3
   formsetobject( 30, _CAPTIONRIGHT, "Year", iFont1, 250, 52 )
   formsetobject( 13, _DROPDOWNCOMBO, "", 290, 48, 100, 50; \\
                                    _LISTFAMS, TheYears()   )

   '* Field 4
   formsetobject( 14, _CHECKBOX, "IN STOCK", iFont1, 290, 90;  1 )

   loop
     select case formwait( _NORMAL )
     case 1, 2
        formcontrol( _HIDE )                      '* Don't _CLOSE!!!!
        UpdateRecord( fRecord, 100 )
        exit loop

     case 11
        if empty( formqstr( 11 ) ) then
           if formwait( _PEEK ) <> 2
              input "You must enter something on this field!" ;
              formmodifyobject( 11, _SETFOCUS )
           end if
        end if
```

```
      end select
   end loop

   print "*********** WINE INFORMATION *************"
   print fRecord.Winery, fRecord.Year, fRecord.Style
   if fRecord.InStock then
      print "IT IS in stock"
   else
      print "not available at this time...."
   end if

end proc

'*************** MAIN ROUTINE!!! ************

DataEntry()

idle 4
reset( _ALL )

'* End of File: Form10.rlz
```

And when this code is processing, if we were to press the TAB key to move off of the first data input item, we would get the following message box:

Step Six: Adding Other Objects to a Form

There are many other types of objects that can appear on a form. One useful type, which we've seen in some FormDev dialog boxes, is the **radio button**. These "buttons" appear in groups of two or more, and only one can be "turned on" at any time. When one button is turned on, the previously selected button is turned off, like the buttons found on car radios of the '60's. Radio buttons are excellent devices to let the user choose among a group of selections, even a group of two choices, as in this next example.

In Realizer, radio buttons are called option buttons, so the internal variable that creates them is _OPTIONBUTTON. The initial state of all buttons is to be off, but you can use a modifier to control the initial state of a button. You can also use the _NOTIFY modifier with these types of objects. Our radio buttons are programmed in the file called *Form11.rlz*:

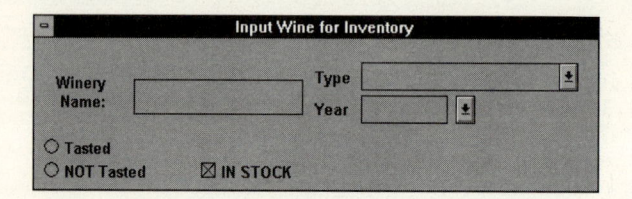

The code for this is identical to the *Form10.rlz* file with the following exceptions:

```
'* Field 4
formsetobject( 14, _CHECKBOX, "IN STOCK", iFont1, 150, 100;  1 )
formsetobject( 15, _OPTIONBUTTON, "Tasted",    iFont1, 10,80 )
formsetobject( 16, _OPTIONBUTTON, "NOT Tasted", iFont1, 10,100 )

loop
  select case formwait( _NORMAL )
  case 1
    if FormValue(15) or FormValue(16)
      formcontrol( _HIDE )                        '* Don't _CLOSE!!!!
      UpdateRecord( fRecord, 100 )
      exit loop
    else
      input "You must select whether this was tasted or not" ;
    end if

  case 2
    exit loop

  case 11
    if empty( formqstr( 11 ) ) then
      if formwait( _PEEK ) <> 2
        input "You must enter something on this field!" ;
        formmodifyobject( 11, _SETFOCUS )
      end if
    end if

  end select
end loop
```

Simple Forms for Data Entry and Data Validation

Just like all of the other objects, the internal variable _OPTIONBUTTON has to have an ID value. Once the object is created, the SELECT CASE command takes over. If the user presses the ENTER key, the value for the CASE command will be 1. At this point, the new function *FormValue()* will be called, looking at objects 15 and 16. The *FormValue()* function makes looking at the object's values easier:

```
'******************************************************
'* Name:          FormValue( iObject )
'* Params:        <iObject>       ID of object
'* Returns:       <xValue>        Value of object
'* Purpose:       This function will return the value of the specified
'*                object

function FormValue( iObject )

  return( formqobject( iObject )[ _FQO_VALUE ] )

end func
```

If a button is not selected, the value of the object will be 0 or FALSE. Here, in this SELECT CASE construct, if both buttons have been selected, the ELSE condition will take effect, causing the INPUT command to be called. This will produce the following screen:

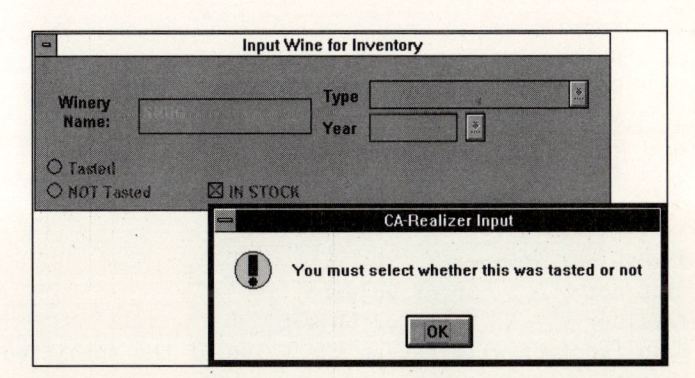

Figure 4-14. CA-Realizer pop-up INPUT dialog window.

So, using option buttons is a real and vital tool in development of a form.

Step Seven: Designing a Custom Button

You are not limited to the types of buttons created by Realizer automatically. You can design a custom button in a drawing package, like Corel Draw and add the bitmapped image (with a .BMP file extension) to a form for use as a button. There are two types, _OPTIONBITMAP and _BITMAPBUTTON, and they differ in both appearance and behavior. In this next program example, we'll place an _OPTIONBITMAP object on a form, which means that the object will have one of two states: on or off. Internally, Realizer will split the custom image in half. The left side will represent a FALSE value, while the right side will represent a TRUE value. I created the following image in Corel Draw and saved it as BUTTONS.BMP:

<pre>
            ┌─────────────────────────────┐
            │   │
            │   Tasted   Not Tasted   │
            │   │
            └─────────────────────────────┘
</pre>

As you can see, it looks as if the two buttons (representing the two states) are joined. The example program that uses this _OPTIONBITMAP looks like this:

```
'* Application ... : Form12.rlz
'* Authors ....... : Steve Straley
'* Notice ........ : Copyright(c) 1994 - Sirius Press, Inc.
'* ............... : All Rights Reserved
'* Date .......... : January 1, 1994
'* Description ... : This shows the use of the _OPTIONBITMAP feature.

'*****************************************************
'* Name:        FormValue( iObject )
'* Params:      <iObject>       ID of object
'* Returns:     <xValue>        Value of object
'* Purpose:     This function will return the value of the specified
'*              object

function FormValue( iObject )

  return( formqobject( iObject )[ _FQO_VALUE ] )

end func


formnew( 100; "sample", _TITLE )
```

Simple Forms for Data Entry and Data Validation

```
formsetobject( 10, _CAPTIONLEFT, "Tasting condition", _CENTER, 20 )
formsetobject( 11, _OPTIONBITMAP, "\realizer\sirius\apps\buttons.bmp", \\
               _CENTER, 60; _NOTIFY )
loop
  select case formwait( _NORMAL )
  case 2, 1
    exit loop

  case 11
    print formqstr( 11 )
    print FormValue( 11 )

  end select
end loop
print FormValue( 11 )
formcontrol( _CLOSE )

'* End of File: Form12.rlz
```

> **Note:** For an object that uses an image, such as an _OPTIONBITMAP, a _METAFILE, a _PICTURE, a _CHECKBITMAP, or a _BITMAPBUTTON, the third parameter to the FORMSETOBJECT() function is not the text to be displayed, but rather the name of the image file. This will also be the value of the FORMQSTR() function.

When the *Form12.rlz* file is executed, the result looks like Figure 4-15.

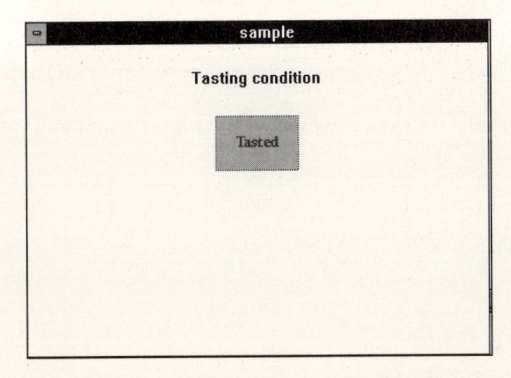

Figure 4-15. Sample form with BITMAP button running.

When we click on the Tasted button, the NOT Tasted part of the button will appear and the value of the object will go from 0 to 1. The _OPTIONBITMAP object is quite different from the _BITMAPBUTTON object. With the latter, each button is a separate image. In this example program, *Form13.rlz*, the image found in *Buttons.bmp* has been broken down into two files: *Tasted.bmp* and *NotTaste.bmp*. The code for this file looks like this:

```
'* Application ... : Form13.rlz
'* Authors ....... : Steve Straley
'* Notice ........ : Copyright(c) 1994 - Sirius Press, Inc.
'* ............... : All Rights Reserved
'* Date .......... : January 1, 1994
'* Description ... : This shows the use of the _BITMAPBUTTON feature.

'*****************************************************
'* Name:          FormValue( iObject )
'* Params:        <iObject>       ID of object
'* Returns:       <xValue>        Value of object
'* Purpose:       This function will return the value of the specified
'*                object

function FormValue( iObject )

   return( formqobject( iObject )[ _FQO_VALUE ] )

end func

local iTasted as integer

formnew( 100; "sample", _TITLE )
formsetobject( 10, _CAPTIONLEFT, "Tasting condition", _CENTER, 20 )
formsetobject( 11, _BITMAPBUTTON, "\realizer\sirius\apps\tasted.bmp", \\
               _CENTER, 60 )
formsetobject( 12, _BITMAPBUTTON, "\realizer\sirius\apps\nottaste.bmp", \\
               _CENTER, 120 )
loop
  select case formwait( _NORMAL )
  case 2, 1
    exit loop

  case 11
    input "You have selected TASTED!";
    iTasted = 1

  case 12
```

```
      input "You have selected NOT TASTED";
      iTasted = 0

  end select
end loop
if iTasted
  print "You have tasted the wine..."
else
  print "You have not, unfortunately, tasted the wine...."
end if

formcontrol( _CLOSE )

'* End of File: Form13.rlz
```

As you can see, there is a difference in approach when using the _BITMAPBUTTON objects. They act just like _OPTIONBUTTONs, in that only one of the _BITMAPBUTTONs can be active at any one time. As each selection is made, the value of the *iTasted* variable switches from logical TRUE to logical FALSE.

> **Note:** The _NOTIFY internal variable cannot be used with the _BITMAPOPTION objects. When a button is selected, the form is automatically notified.

Eventually, when the ENTER or the ESC key is pressed, which will terminate this form, the value of *iTasted* will be looked at and, depending on its value, a PRINT statement will be made.

Conclusion

Form development is at the heart of Realizer. As a matter of fact, almost every Windows element has some form characteristics. These characteristics are bound by the framed region that we call a window. The items that are contained within can range from pure text to graphics, from simple data entry with a keyboard to checking off items in a list. These groupings can move, shrink, close up, or remain on the screen indefinitely. In other words, our entire interface with an application, other than the reports and the menus, comes to us through the use of forms. Data entry and validation is nothing more than form control.

In this chapter we have looked at simple form development using just a few of the object options. All of this is known as a **modal** way of programming. In other words, one item at a time will be processed, and when the form is finished, a corresponding operation will begin. In the next chapter, we will look at **modeless** forms, toolbars, MDI Forms, Palettes and other List Boxes, Sheets, Logs, and Tablets. All of these are other types of user interface options. They are more complex and offer new possibilities.

Chapter 5

More Complex Forms and User Interface

In the last chapter we began to explore forms and form control, the various types of objects that can be placed on a general form, and how variables work with these objects. When we created the example forms, we used what is called a *modal* type of programming. This means that we instructed Realizer to physically wait for something to happen within the form. The FORMWAIT() function did this for us, and we then polled the response from that function. In this chapter, we will program some *modeless* forms. Here, the polling of the form is automatic and constant: We do not have to program any "loop" instructions. As a result, the modeless forms will act differently than forms controlled by a loop. In addition to some new options for some of the objects that we worked with in the previous chapter, we will also examine other user interface techniques, such as toolbars, MDI and non-MDI forms, OBE objects, palettes and other list-box options, scroll bars, and what Realizer calls a **log**. These elements will round out our basic knowledge of form.

Modeless Ideas

A modeless form is created when the FORMSETPROC() function is used instead of the FORMWAIT() function. In previous examples, the FORMWAIT() function sat inside of a LOOP command or code construct. Every time the ENTER or ESC keys were pressed or an object with the _NOTIFY modifier was activated, the FORMWAIT() function stopped processing, returned a value and then checked that value to determine what action needed to be taken. However, it is very important to see that the continual processing of the form happens because the FORMWAIT() function is constantly called from within the LOOP. This is the modal style of operation. However, in a modeless operation, there is no LOOP processing. When a form is created, a procedure is attached to the form. Then, whenever that form experiences an event such as a mouse click or a key press, the designated procedure will be activated. So, the function that is needed in a modeless operation is the FORMSETPROC() function.

```
formsetproc( TestProc; _ALL )
```

Here, the procedure *TestProc( )* is attached to the currently selected form. The modifier _ALL establishes all conditions to exist. It is one of ten possible internal variables for this function, as shown in Table 5-1.

Table 5-1. Internal Variables for FORMSET() Function.

Modifier	Description	When
_SIZE	Form is notified that it has been resized by user.	Specified
_CLICK	Form is modified if user left-clicks the background of form. Most objects generate this message by default or when the _NOTIFY style is used.	Specified
_MIDDLECLICK	Objects in form receive _CLICK message and the form itself receives a _MIDDLECLICK message, indicating that the middle mouse button has been pressed.	Specified
_RIGHTCLICK	Objects in form will receive _CLICK message and the form itself receives a _RIGHTCLICK message, indicating that the right mouse button has been pressed.	Specified
_GETFOCUS	Objects in form receive _GETFOCUS message when user selects them or tabs to them.	Specified
_ALL	Message selects all possible conditions.	Specified
_DRAGNDROP	Form that received the drop of an object receives this message.	Automatic
_CHANGE	A _LISTBOX object created with the _NOTIFY style receives a _CHANGE message every time the selection is changed by the end user.	Automatic
_CUSTOM	Can be generated only by a custom control.	Automatic
_CUSTOMNOW	Can be generated only by a custom control.	Automatic

There are two basic rules to remember when using a procedure attached to a form. First, standard user operations such as a single mouse click or a key press will automatically invoke the attached procedure. Second, a tool inside of a form that has its own set of behaviors will not invoke the procedure attached to the form.

Now, when the assigned procedure is called (the *TestProc( )* procedure, in this example), an array of values is automatically passed to this routine. This array will have certain messages sent from the form down to the procedure. It might, for example, provide information on what caused the procedure to be called: a left mouse click, a right mouse click, and so on. This means that from within the procedure, we need to test certain values of elements of this passed array, such as the ID value of the object within the form on which we are located. This array is commonly called a tool procedure array. Many of the tools, such as charts, boards, logs, and sheets, all have this type of an array passed to the associated procedures. The array can be accessed using internal variables such as those found in Table 5-2.

Table 5-2. Internal Variables for Procedures Attached to Forms.

Constant	Definition of Corresponding Element
_CONTROLHELD	Returns a logical value of 0 or 1, indicating whether the CTRL key was held down during the action that invoked the tool procedure.
_CUSTOMLP	Values used for messages received from the custom controls.
_CUSTOMWP	Values used for messages received from the custom controls.
_DRAGFORM	In a _DRAGNDROP message, if an object being dragged invoked the tool procedure, this will return the ID of the form from which the object was dragged.
_DRAGITEM	In a _DRAGNDROP message, if an item being dragged invoked the tool procedure, this will return the ID of the item that was dragged.
_FORMNUM	If an object in a form invoked the tool procedure, this will return the ID of the form that contains the object.
_INVOKE	Returns a constant that indicates which action invoked the tool procedure. This might include such values as _CLICK or _CLOSE.

(continued)

Table 5-2. *(continued)*

Constant	Corresponding Element Contains
`_ITEMNUM`	If a tool, an object, or a menu item invoked the tool procedure, this will return the ID of the item that was selected.
`_ITEMTYPE`	If a tool, an object, or a menu item invoked the tool procedure, this will return the type of the item that was selected.
`_MENUNUM`	If a menu item invoked the tool procedure, this will return the ID of the menu containing that item.
`_SHIFTHELD`	This will return a logical 0 or 1, indicating whether the `SHIFT` key was held during the action that invoked the tool procedure.
`_USERREALIZER`	This value can be manipulated for special processing.
`_XPOS`	If the tool procedure was invoked by a mouse click, this will return the X position of the mouse cursor, in pixels and relative to the upper-left corner of the tool or object within the form. If the cursor is in a spreadsheet, this number will indicate the column number of the edited or double-clicked cell.
`_YPOS`	If the tool procedure was invoked by a mouse click, this will return the Y position of the mouse cursor, in pixels and relative to the upper-left corner of the tool or object within the form. If the cursor is in a spreadsheet, the number will indicate the row number of the edited or double-clicked cell.

Before I get into code examples, a few more words on the differences between a modal and a modeless system are in order.

Whenever I hear the word "modeless," I think of messages. In the course of our experience, many of us developed traditional, procedural styles of programming: Press a button, and the code goes off to do some process, and when finished, will return us to the location in the program just after the test of the button. All of that back-and-forth processing is actually coded in the application. In many applications, one step can start down a trail of many chained operations, each one hard-coded by the programmer in an attempt to achieve a certain behavior. In a modeless system, there is no such linear trail. Instead, a message from some master control system is sent for us to process, and based on the context of that message, we then respond back with another message or request. This is better known as event-driven programming.

Realizer does not offer a true event-driven system. The closest we get to an event is the relationship between a form and an associated procedure, which is this array that is automatically passed with information on what was pressed, where the mouse cursor was at the time, and what form is involved. In either a modeless or modal form, both the menu and the form will be processing, waiting for a key to be pressed or a mouse button to be clicked. When the Realizer system sees such a trigger, it will call the appropriate routine attached to either the form or the menu and send the procedure a message. This message contains the information we need to figure out what just took place. However, there is no way we can send a message back to the form. In a true event-driven and modeless system, if the end user made a request to close the form, the message to the subroutine would be "User wants to close." The response from the procedure back to the form would be "OK, close yourself." Depending on how detailed a messaging system the programmer wants to develop, a confirming message might be sent or not. However, what is important is that there is two-way communication between form and associated procedure.

In Realizer, messages are one-directional: from form to procedure. This means that control must take place exclusively within the assigned procedure. Moreover, it means that once control is given to the procedure, we can program it to follow another linear trail of functions and procedures, even with the form in question still active. What this means for many of us is a shift in how we design a program to interact with the end user. Do we want a form continually spinning, receiving input while we are processing some action? Do we want not a modeless form, but rather a traditional modal form within our own loop construct? These are questions that I cannot answer for you. There are advantages to both; it all depends on what behavior you want your application to take on.

To start looking at the differences, here is a simple modeless form created in the *Form14.rlz* file. You might want to run this program through with the debugger turned on. It will show you the differences between this program's behavior and, for example, the program in *Form11.rlz*.

```
'* Application ... : Form14.rlz
'* Authors ....... : Steve Straley
'* Notice ........ : Copyright(c) 1994 - Sirius Press, Inc.
'* ............... : All Rights Reserved
'* Date .......... : January 1, 1994
'* Description ... : This shows one possible use of the modeless form.

'*****************************************************
'* Name:        TheYears()
'* Params:      N/A
```

```
'* Returns:      <aYears>        An array of 35 string year values
'* Purpose:      To build a quick table of years so that it does not
'*               have to be entered by hand

function TheYears()

  local aYears[35] as string
  local iCount     as integer

  for iCount = 1 to 35
    aYears[ iCount ] = numtostr( 1958 + iCount )
  next

  return( aYears )

end func


'*****************************************************
'* Name:         WineList()
'* Params:       N/A
'* Returns:      <aWine>         Array of types of wines
'* Purpose:      To build a quick table of types so that it does not
'*               have to be entered by hand

function WineList()

  local aTypes[18] as string

  aTypes[1]  = "Chardonnay"
  aTypes[2]  = "Pinot Blanc"
  aTypes[3]  = "Sauvignon Blanc"
  aTypes[4]  = "Merlot"
  aTypes[5]  = "Zinfandel"
  aTypes[6]  = "Pinot Noir"
  aTypes[7]  = "Cabernet Sauvignon"
  aTypes[8]  = "Reisling"
  aTypes[9]  = "Port"
  aTypes[10] = "Sparkling"
  aTypes[11] = "Champaign"
  aTypes[12] = "Petite Syrah"
  aTypes[13] = "Barbera"
  aTypes[14] = "Semillon"
  aTypes[15] = "Gewurztraminer"
  aTypes[16] = "Gamay Beaujolais"
  aTypes[17] = "Symphony"
  aTypes[18] = "Madeira"

  return( aTypes )
```

More Complex Forms and User Interface   255

```
end func

'*****************************************
'* Name:        DataEntry()
'* Params:      N/A
'* Returns:     N/A
'* Purpose:     This procedure draws the form, creates the family structure, and
'*              updates the values

proc DataEntry()

   local iForm1   as integer

   '* Make Global variables!
   fRecord.Style = space$(25)
   fRecord.Year  = "1994"
   iCounter      = 1
   iFont1        = fontqunique

   '* Make font
   fontnew( iFont1; "Arial", 10, _BOLD )

   '* Make Form
   formnew( 100; "Input Wine for Inventory", _TITLE )
   formsetcolor( _CYAN; _BACKGROUND )
   formsetcolor( _CYAN; _FIELD )
   formsetcolor( _BLACK; _TEXT )
   formcontrol(_SIZE; 50,50,500,150 )       '* Offer a new size

   '* Now, field 1
   formsetobject( 10, _CAPTIONCENTER, fRecord.Style, iFont1, 60, 30 )
   formsetobject( 20, _CAPTIONRIGHT, fRecord.Year, iFont1, 300, 25 )
   formsetobject( 30, _BUTTON, "Next Page (Right Button Special)", \\
                                                   iFont1, 40, 100 )
   formsetobject( 40, _BUTTON, "Goodbye...", 310, 100 )
   formsetproc( TestForm; _ALL )
   formcontrol( _SETMODE; _PICK )

end proc

'*****************************************
'* Name:        TestForm(<aParams>)
'* Params:      N/A
'* Returns:     N/A
'* Purpose:     This procedure accepts input from the active and
'*              attached form

proc TestForm( aParams )
```

```
      formselect( aParams[ _FORMNUM ] )    '* Just in case we moved off of form

   select case aParams[ _ITEMNUM ]
   case 30

      if aParams[ _INVOKE ] = _RIGHTCLICK
         input "About to decrement the counter!" ;
         if iCounter = 1
            iCounter = 15
         else
            iCounter = iCounter - 1
         end if

      elseif aParams[ _INVOKE ] = _CLICK
         if iCounter > 15
            iCounter = 1
         else
            iCounter = iCounter + 1
         end if
      end if
      fRecord.Style = WineList()[ iCounter ]
      fRecord.Year  = TheYears()[ iCounter ]
      formmodifyobject( 10, _SHOW, fRecord.Style )
      formmodifyobject( 20, _SHOW, fRecord.Year )

   case 40
      formcontrol( _CLOSE )

   end select

end proc

'*************** MAIN ROUTINE!!! ************

DataEntry()
input "I'm about to go into the form!" ;
formselect( 100 )
formcontrol( _SHOW )

'* End of File: Form14.rlz
```

At the end of the file are four instructions. The *DataEntry( )* program creates the form that will be used. If we were to step through this program with the debugger active, the *DataEntry( )* function would be called and the form would appear; however, before anything else can happen, the INPUT command is processed. Again, there is no modal processing; it is all modeless. After the INPUT command is activated, the form is selected and shown. This is the end of the program; however, the form is active on the screen, as shown in Figure 5-1.

More Complex Forms and User Interface 257

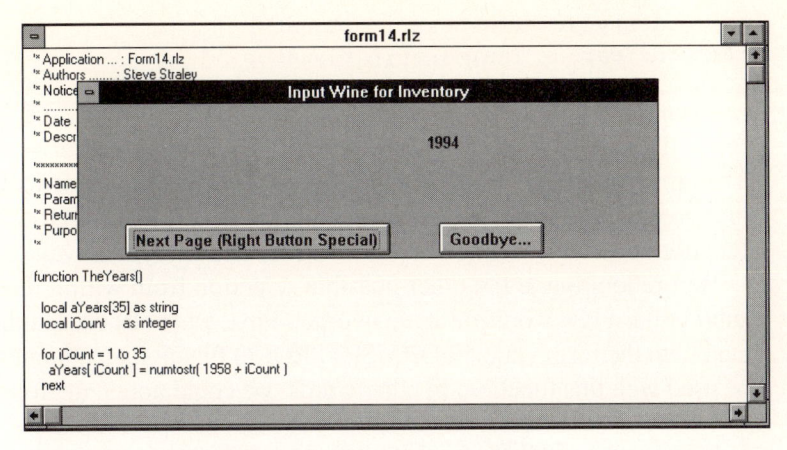

[Screenshot of form14.rlz program window showing "Input Wine for Inventory" with year 1994 and buttons "Next Page (Right Button Special)" and "Goodbye..."]

Figure 5-1. The FORM14.RLZ program running.

Keep in mind that the flow of the program has concluded, and yet, processing will still take place. This is because of the FORMSETPROC( ) function within the *DataEntry()* function. The form is attached to a routine named *TestForm()*. It will take one parameter, which is an array of values. One of the first things that takes place within this routine is that the associated form is reselected. In a modeless environment, selecting forms back and forth is common. We could, for example, have more than one form visible on the screen; however, only one form can be the active and selected form. The FORMSELECT( ) function allows us to select the form via the *aParams[ ]* passed parameter at position _FORMNUM. Once selected, the SELECT CASE code construct takes over, checking to see which object in the form was "selected." The result is stored at the _ITEMNUM position within the *aParams[ ]* array. The first object that is looked at is object ID number 30:

```
formsetobject( 30, _BUTTON, "Next Page (Right Button Special)", \\
                                    iFont1, 40, 100 )
```

At this point within the *TestForm()* routine, we know that this _BUTTON object was selected, but we don't yet know how it was selected. In a modeless scenario, we can test to see which mouse button made the selection. This is held in yet another position of the *aParams* array. The internal variable _RIGHTCLICK and its siblings _CLICK and _MIDDLECLICK cover the mouse-button bases. The way the code is set up, if the right mouse button is pressed, the *iCounter* variable will be decremented, and if the left mouse button is pressed, the *iCounter* variable will be incremented. After each one of these tests is made, the values of the family members of the *fRecord* variable are altered to the following:

```
fRecord.Style = WineList()[ iCounter ]
fRecord.Year  = TheYears()[ iCounter ]
```

Even though these values are used in the objects currently displayed in the form, the values at the time when the objects were created were different. The family members have changed values, but the old values will remain on the screen in the form. We have to call upon the FORMMODIFYOBJECT() function to refresh the objects with the new and associated values.

Before looking at the other possible selection from within the *TestProc()* subroutine, a few words on it are in order. First, when the subroutine is associated with the form via the FORMSETPROC() function, no parameter set may be used with this function. In other words, we could not do the following:

```
formsetproc( TestForm( fRecord ); _ALL )
```

Since Realizer passes a parameter automatically, one cannot be specified within the instruction. This means that any variable that is to be seen within the attached subroutine, such as *TestForm()* in this example, cannot be initialized as a LOCAL variable. If we did that, then the *fRecord* family variable could not be seen within the attached subroutine and could not be used in recreating the appropriate objects. This is why the variables *iCounter* and *fRecord* are initialized within the *DataEntry()* routine but not made LOCAL.

To go along with this, there is another rule to keep in mind. The routine that is specified in the FORMSETPROC() function cannot be defined within the domain of the main subroutine. This means that the code for *TestForm()* must reside outside of the END PROC command associated with the definition of *DataEntry()*. With these two facts in mind, it is difficult to maintain data integrity within this type of programming structure.

In the previous form, there were no pick lists or `_LISTBOX` options on the screen. In addition, there were no data-entry items that the end user could add information to, and further, there were no data-validation checks. In this next example, we will see how we can tell a form to "get" things, or in other words to `_GETFOCUS`, when the form is processing information. And to make things even more spicy, just because a form is considered modeless does not mean that we cannot use the FORMWAIT() function. There is still a valid purpose for this function, as we can see in *Form15.rlz*:

```
'* Application ... : Form15.rlz
'* Authors ....... : Steve Straley
'* Notice ........ : Copyright(c) 1994 - Sirius Press, Inc.
'* .............. : All Rights Reserved
'* Date .......... : January 1, 1994
'* Description ... : This shows another possible use of the modeless form,
'*                   this time with the formwait() function to see what is
'*                   pending for the data entry fields.
```

```
'****************************************************
'* Name:        Empty( <xData> )
'* Params:      <xData>         Any data type
'* Returns:     <iEmpty>        Logical true if value is "empty"
'* Purpose:     This function returns a true value should the data passed
'*              to it be considered as "empty."

function Empty( xData )

  local iReturn as integer

  iReturn = ( len( ltrim$(xData) ) = 0 )

  return( iReturn )

end func


'****************************************************
'* Name:        TheYears()
'* Params:      N/A
'* Returns:     <aYears>        An array of 35 string year values
'* Purpose:     To build a quick table of years so that it does not
'*              have to be entered by hand

function TheYears()

  local aYears[35] as string
  local iCount     as integer

  for iCount = 1 to 35
    aYears[ iCount ] = numtostr( 1958 + iCount )
  next

  return( aYears )

end func


'****************************************************
'* Name:        WineList()
'* Params:      N/A
'* Returns:     <aWine>         Array of types of wines
'* Purpose:     To build a quick table of types so that it does not
'*              have to be entered by hand

function WineList()

  local aTypes[18] as string
```

```
    aTypes[1]  = "Chardonnay"
    aTypes[2]  = "Pinot Blanc"
    aTypes[3]  = "Sauvignon Blanc"
    aTypes[4]  = "Merlot"
    aTypes[5]  = "Zinfandel"
    aTypes[6]  = "Pinot Noir"
    aTypes[7]  = "Cabernet Sauvignon"
    aTypes[8]  = "Reisling"
    aTypes[9]  = "Port"
    aTypes[10] = "Sparkling"
    aTypes[11] = "Champaign"
    aTypes[12] = "Petite Syrah"
    aTypes[13] = "Barbera"
    aTypes[14] = "Semillon"
    aTypes[15] = "Gewurztraminer"
    aTypes[16] = "Gamay Beaujolais"
    aTypes[17] = "Symphony"
    aTypes[18] = "Madeira"

    return( aTypes )

end func

'****************************************************
'* Name:       DataEntry()
'* Params:     N/A
'* Returns:    N/A
'* Purpose:    This procedure draws the form, creates the family structure, and
'*             updates the values

proc DataEntry()

  local iForm1   as integer

  '* Make Global variables!
  fWine.Winery  = space$(30)
  fRecord.Style = space$(25)
  fRecord.Year  = "1994"
  iCounter      = 1
  iFont1        = fontqunique

  '* Make font
  fontnew( iFont1; "Arial", 10, _BOLD )

  '* Make Form
  formnew( 100; "Input Wine for Inventory", _TITLE )
  formsetcolor( _CYAN; _BACKGROUND )
  formsetcolor( _CYAN; _FIELD )
  formsetcolor( _BLACK; _TEXT )
```

```
      formcontrol(_SIZE; 50,50,500,150 )        '* Offer a new size

        '* Now, field 1
      formsetobject( 10, _CAPTIONCENTER, "Winery Name:", iFont1, 10, 30, \\
                                                                   70, 40 )
      formsetobject( 11, _TEXTBOX, "", iFont1, 90, 35, 150,30; _NOTIFY )

        '* Field 2
      formsetobject( 20, _CAPTIONRIGHT, "Type", iFont1, 250, 25 )
      formsetobject( 21, _DROPDOWNLIST, "",  iFont1, 290, 20, 190, \\
                             _DEFAULT; _LISTVARS, _ARRAY, WineList() )

        '* Field 3
      formsetobject( 30, _CAPTIONRIGHT, "Year", iFont1, 250, 52 )
      formsetobject( 33, _DROPDOWNCOMBO, "", 290, 48, 100, 50; \\
                                  _LISTVARS, _ARRAY, TheYears()   )

      formsetobject( 40, _BUTTON, "Confirm...", iFont1, 40, 100 )
      formsetproc( TestForm; _GETFOCUS )

end proc

'****************************************************
'* Name:         TestForm(<aParams>)
'* Params:       N/A
'* Returns:      N/A
'* Purpose:      This procedure accepts input from the active and
'*               attached form

proc TestForm( aParams )

   formselect( aParams[ _FORMNUM ] )    '* Just in case we moved off of form

   select case aParams[ _ITEMNUM ]
   case 11                              '* THE _TEXTBOX field!!!!
     if Empty( formqstr( 11 ) ) then
       if formwait( _PEEK ) <> 0
         input "Winery name must be filled" ;
         formmodifyobject( 11, _SETFOCUS )
       end if
     end if

   case 40                              '* THE _BUTTON
     formcontrol( _CLOSE )

   end select

end proc
```

```
'*************** MAIN ROUTINE!!! ************

DataEntry()
input "I'm about to go into the form!" ;
formselect( 100 )
formcontrol( _SHOW )

'* End of File: Form15.rlz
```

The first real difference with this form is the modifier used with the FORMSETPROC() function. The _GETFOCUS internal variable tells Realizer that the form that is attached to the procedure contains not just pictures, but data-entry items such as _TEXTBOXes or _DROPDOWNLISTs, which require the user to type something. Because regular data-entry items can exist in these forms, data validation is also a concern. In the previous chapter, we saw the _TEXTBOX object working with the _NOTIFY modifier, just as they are used in this example. Here, the procedure created to process keystrokes tests and looks for the object's ID value of 33.

When the TAB key is pressed, or if the mouse cursor is moved to another object, a message is sent to the *TestForm()* procedure. Then, just as in the previous example, we can see which item is involved via the _ITEMNUM internal variable off of the parameter *aParams[ ]*. If the value is 11, then we are working off of the _TEXTBOX object, and just as we did earlier, we use the FORMQSTR() function to see if the data-entry item is "empty" or not. If it is, then we want to see what pending keystroke is coming into the form. This is critical. If we did not offer this test using the FORMWAIT() function, the following INPUT command line would occur twice. In essence, two messages are sent from the form to this procedure: one for the key pressed and one for the mouse click in attempting to leave the form. Typically, the values would be 0 and 2, with 0 being a non-keyed event. So in this example, we will display only the INPUT command if the pending event value coming from the form is not 0. In that case, the INPUT command is processed, and after the message is displayed, the object regains input focus with the _SETFOCUS internal variable via the FORMMODIFYOBJECT() function. So, even if we are in a modeless form, we can still see what keys and mouse messages are being processed and pending. It is important to remember to use the internal variable _PEEK to see what is pending in the form.

Toolbars

Another useful type of data-entry device is the **toolbar**. A toolbar is just what it sounds like: a bar on the screen filled with images of tools. These tools are called not from menu items or data-entry points, but from the images themselves. We learned in the previous chapter that Realizer can place a bit-mapped image in a .BMP file on a form and treat it as a button:

```
formsetobject( 100, _BITMAPBUTTON, <file>, 90, 10 )
```

This function will place a `_BITMAPBUTTON` image to the currently selected form, give it an ID value of 100, and place it 90 pixels from the left and 10 pixels from the top. This should not be new. However, before we can even begin to develop a toolbar, we must create a special form. This form will have unique properties different from those found on a regular data-entry form. As a matter of fact, there is a special internal variable that we can use in conjunction with the FORMNEW() function to create this special form:

```
formnew(; "", _TOOLBAR )              '* Ok.... create the form
```

The `_TOOLBAR` internal variable alerts Realizer that we are about to create a toolbar form. A `_TOOLBAR` form is a combination of a `_NONMDI`, `_BORDERLESS`, and `_HOTCLICK` form. It is `_BORDERLESS` because we want to see just the toolbar, without a border or a frame. It is a `_HOTCLICK` form because we want it to be able to work with existing forms to allow the end user to choose between a tool on the toolbar, and perhaps, a data-entry item. Finally, because the form need not be contained within the **MDI** (multiple document interface) region, it is considered a `_NONMDI` type of form. Among other things, this means that scrollbars will not appear if the toolbar is moved outside of the boundaries of the Realizer window. We will discuss MDI and non-MDI forms in a separate section in this chapter. For now, just remember that the `_TOOLBAR` internal variable is all of these things. Should we want a different type of a toolbar (perhaps one with a border), we will have to combine the internal variables ourselves:

```
formnew(; "", _NONMDI + _HOTCLICK )    '* Ok.... create the form
```

Toolbars do not have to appear on the top of the screen or window. They can appear in any grouped area, and they always contain images of the tools they are attached to. In other words, `_TEXTBOX`es and `_LISTBOX`es are not appropriate data-entry items on a toolbar, not because they will not work, but because it is not the GUI interface standard of all Windows applications. To build our toolbar images, I used a package called ClipWin. It takes images in Windows and clips (or snaps) them to a .BMP file. In building this first toolbar, I took some icons and items from several of my Windows applications and "snapped" them to separate .BMP files located in my *Realizer**Sirius**Apps*\ directory.

> **Note:** Another way of defining MDI is to think of it as the "client" or "end user" visible and working region on the screen.

The final thing to remember with a `_TOOLBAR` form is that we need to set the size of the multiple document interface region. To do this, we need to use the SETSYS() function. There are many internal values that we could use with this function, but the one we want is `_SIZEMDI`: set the size of the MDI region. The others are outlined in Table 5-3.

Table 5-3. Internal Variables for SETSYS().

Internal Variable	Description
`_ALPHAFORMAT`	A string containing the default format string for string values.
`_CASESENSITIVE`	A real scalar that indicates whether lowercase and uppercase letters should be treated the same in string comparisons. A value of 1 indicates case sensitivity; a value of 0 indicates case insensitivity.
`_CENTURYSPLIT`	A real scalar that indicates which dates are for the 20th century and which are for the 21st. Any year entered as a two-digit number that is larger than this value will be considered to be part of the 20th century. Any year smaller than this value is considered to be part of the 21st century.
`_CMDLINE`	The command line parameters passed to Realizer.
`_DATEFORMAT`	A string containing the default format string for date-time values.
`_ERRORLOG`	The ID of the log into which error messages are to be written. The first parameter is the number of the log. If that log is within a form, then the second parameter is the ID of the form. These two values may be passed as a single array.
`_FPERROR`	A numeric scalar that indicates what Realizer does when a floating-point error takes place. If it is not zero, the program will stop and an error will be displayed. If the value is 0, an appropriate value is used for the invalid number.

(continued)

Table 5-3. *(continued)*

Internal Variable	Description
_LOADDIR	A string containing a set of paths. Multiple paths are separated by semicolons. These paths are searched when files are opened or bitmaps are loaded in a form.
_MACRODIR	A string containing a set of paths. Multiple paths are separated by semicolons. These paths are searched when macros are run or external DLLs are loaded.
_OUTPUTWIDTH	A numeric scalar indicating the maximum size, in characters, of an output line to a log. Any line which is set longer than the specified size will wrap.
_PRINTBEST	A numeric scalar that indicates whether Realizer should try to use the best font possible when printing on non-PostScript printers.
_PRINTLOG	The ID value of the log to which the printed output is to be sent. The first parameter passed is the number of the log, and if that log is within a form, the second parameter is the ID of the form. These two values can be passed as a single parameter in array form.
_REALFORMAT	A string containing the default format string used for real values.
_SEPARATOR	A string containing the character used by the FILEIMPORT() and FILEEXPORT() functions to separate columns.
_SIZE	The position and the size of the Realizer window. The first value can be a one-element array set to either _MINIMIZE, _MAXIMIZE, or _RESTORE. It can also be a two-element array indicating the left and top position of the window. It can also be a four-element array indicating all four positions as left, top, width, and height values.
_SIZEINSIDE	Takes a four-element array of numerics indicating position and size of the inside portion of the Realizer window. These will be specified as left, top, right, and bottom pixel positions.
_SIZEMDI	Takes a four-element array of numerics that will set the size of the MDI region. These will be specified as left, top, right, and bottom pixel positions.
_TITLE	Sets the title of the Realizer application window

The `_SIZEMDI` internal variable allows us to control the area on the screen for multiple documents. When used in conjunction with the `_TOOLBAR` internal variable used in the FORMNEW() function, we have some interesting results. The test program, *Tool1.rlz*, is located in the *\Realizer\Sirius\Samples* directory.

```
'* Application ... : Tool1.rlz
'* Authors ....... : Steve Straley
'* Notice ........ : Copyright(c) 1994 - Sirius Press, Inc.
'* ..............  : All Rights Reserved
'* Date .......... : January 1, 1994
'* Description ... : This shows the use of a TOOLBAR type of form


'*****************************************
'* Proc:         TestToolBar()
'* Purpose:      Attached subroutine for toolbar
'*****************************************

proc TestToolBar( aParams )

   select case aParams[ _ITEMNUM ]
   case 11
      input "This will now send something to the printer";
   case 12
      input "We are going to save something to the disk";
   case 13
      input "Now, a new cellar is being opened";
   case 14
      input "Let's cut something to the ClipBoard!" ;
   case 15
      input "Hey, let's get something from the ClipBoard!" ;

   end select

end proc


'*****************************************
'* Proc:         DataTools()
'* Purpose:      Modeless data entry toolbar
'*****************************************

proc DataTools()

   local sLoc as string

   sLoc = "\realizer\sirius\apps\"

   setsys( _sizeMDI, {0,50,0,0} )          '* Must set the background region
```

More Complex Forms and User Interface

```
    formnew(; "", _TOOLBAR )                '* Ok.... create the form
    formsetcolor( _POWDERBLUE; _BACKGROUND ) '* And send the colors
    formcontrol( _SIZE; 0, 0, 100 pct, 50 )
    rem formcontrol( _SIZE; 0, 0, 800, 50 )  '* Set the size of the form

    '* And now, we have to assign the various buttons from the .BMP's
    '* saved to the disk at the <sLoc> location

    formsetobject( 11, _BITMAPBUTTON, sLoc + "printer.bmp", 10, 10, 50, 30 )
    formsetobject( 12, _BITMAPBUTTON, sLoc + "disk.bmp",    90, 10, 50, 30 )
    formsetobject( 13, _BITMAPBUTTON, sLoc + "open.bmp",   170, 10, 50, 30 )
    formsetobject( 14, _BITMAPBUTTON, sLoc + "cut.bmp",    250,10,50,30 )
    formsetobject( 15, _BITMAPBUTTON, sLoc + "paste.bmp",  330, 10, 50, 30 )

    formsetproc( TestToolBar )    '* Set the procedure to do the processing
    formcontrol(_SHOW )           '* Show the form and we're out'a here!

end proc

'****************** MAIN ROUTINE *******************`
'************************* *************************`

DataTools()

'* End of File: Tool1.rlz
```

Note that there are two FORMCONTROL() functions using the `_SIZE` internal variable. They are exactly the same and only one is processed. The other is placed here for comparison purposes only. In the first one, the third modifier uses the 100 pct parameter. This is not a pixel position. In the FORMCONTROL() function that is REM'd out, the same modifier is now set to 800 without the added "pct" characters. Without any qualifier attached to this value, Realizer interprets this value as a pixel count or location. The "pct" represents a percentage of the screen area. This means that 100 percent of the screen area is approximately, the 800th pixel. If you think using "pct" is easier, then do so. Remember, consistency is sometimes a virtue even if it means a little extra work in the beginning. Our toolbar looks like the following:

Again, this is a modeless form, since the FORMSETPROC() function is used to attach the *TestToolBar()* subroutine to this form. A `_TOOLBAR` form can be either modal or modeless. The *TestToolBar()* function will be called when the user clicks one of the icons. Remember that if this form existed in conjunction with other forms, we would have to select this _TOOLBAR form before processing any of the objects contained within. This is accomplished using the FORMSELECT() function. Here, within this subroutine, the parameter *aParams[ ]* is used to see which _BITMAPBUTTON the user clicked on, and based on that, a different INPUT command is displayed to the screen, as shown in Figure 5-2.

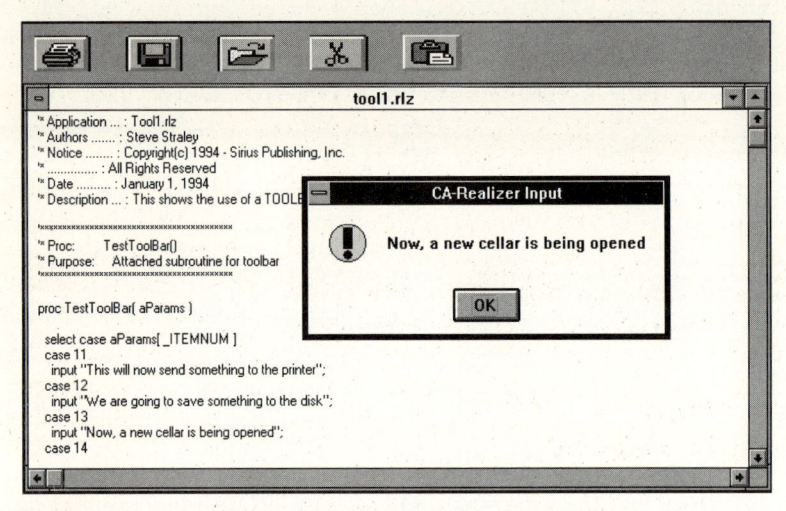

Figure 5-2. Standard CA-Realizer INPUT dialog window.

In a real application, we would have branching operations off each of these CASE commands, rather than a simple INPUT operation.

Within the *DataTools()* function, a LOCAL variable named *sLoc* is created and assigned the literal string of "\Realizer\Sirius\Apps\". This string is the path to the named .BMP files used in the FORMSETOBJECT() functions:

```
formsetobject( 11, _BITMAPBUTTON, sLoc + "printer.bmp",  10, 10, 50, 30 )
formsetobject( 12, _BITMAPBUTTON, sLoc + "disk.bmp",     90, 10, 50, 30 )
formsetobject( 13, _BITMAPBUTTON, sLoc + "open.bmp",    170, 10, 50, 30 )
formsetobject( 14, _BITMAPBUTTON, sLoc + "cut.bmp",     250,10,50,30 )
formsetobject( 15, _BITMAPBUTTON, sLoc + "paste.bmp",   330, 10, 50, 30 )
```

In a moment, I will offer a different way to accomplish this using the SETSYS() function.

In addition to the LOCAL variable, the location and positioning of the bitmapped images are also important. In real life, the images I used are much smaller than they appear in this application. I have, with the FORMSETOBJECT()

function, enlarged each of the images. At the end of each function call with the .BMP files, there are four coordinates. The first two are the left and top pixel locations within the form. The next pair of values deals with width and height of each bit-mapped image. For example, the first image is positioned at pixel location 10, 10. However, the image will be 50 pixels wide and 30 pixels high. We can blow up or shrink any image as we see fit.

In the preceding example, *sLoc* holds the path string to be used in searching for the .BMP files used in the _TOOLBAR. But the SETSYS() function allows us to set this internally to Realizer so that we do not have to either (a) make a constant or variable holding the directory path string; or (b) use the literal path directly into the file name when used in the FORMSETOBJECT() function. To use this new function, we should add the following line just before the call to the *DataTools()* function is made:

```
setsys( _LOADDIR, "\Realizer\Sirius\Apps\;Realizer\Sirius\Samples\" )
```

Now, if we had the RUN command in our code, we would have had the appropriate SETSYS() function situated in the code before those commands are executed. Once this command is in place and executed, we can remove the LOCAL variable found within the *DataTools()* routine. In addition, we need to use only the name of the various .BMP files in the FORMSETOBJECT() function:

```
formsetobject( 11, _BITMAPBUTTON, "PRINTER.BMP", 10, 10, 50, 30 )
formsetobject( 12, _BITMAPBUTTON, "DISK.BMP", 90, 10, 50, 30 )
formsetobject( 13, _BITMAPBUTTON, "OPEN.BMP", 170, 10, 50, 30 )
formsetobject( 14, _BITMAPBUTTON, "CUT.BMP", 250, 10, 50, 30 )
formsetobject( 15, _BITMAPBUTTON, "PASTE.BMP", 330, 10, 50, 30 )
```

This will save memory (for removing the LOCAL variable), speed (for the LOCAL variable assignment and the various string concatenations), and hassle (for not having to remember to use the literal string or the variable). This example program is called *Tools2.rlz*.

In this next example, we will look at the _NONMDI + _HOTCLICK combination. This is similar to the _TOOLBAR internal variable except that a border will appear around the form's edges. As we mentioned earlier, the _TOOLBAR is both of these internal variables plus the _BORDERLESS option. The point is that in concept and functionality, a toolbar is not tied to the internal variable _TOOLBAR: We have other options. There is also no rule that says that a toolbar must appear across the top or bottom of the window or screen. Some toolbars are quite appropriately located on the side of the window. For example, in CorelDraw, here is the opening toolbar screen:

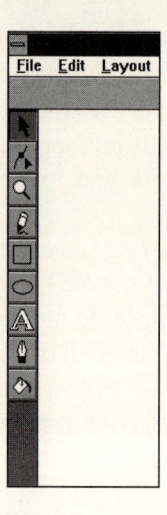

So, toolbar location is something else we will want to consider. In this next example program, the `Tool3.rlz` file holds the solution to these problems.

```
'* Application ... : Tool3.rlz
'* Authors ....... : Steve Straley
'* Notice ........ : Copyright(c) 1994 - Sirius Press, Inc.
'* .............. : All Rights Reserved
'* Date .......... : January 1, 1994
'* Description ... : This shows the use of a _NONMDI+_HOTCLICK combination
'*                   that is like a _TOOLBAR and places the bar in a
'*                   different location.


'*****************************************
'* Proc:          TestToolBar()
'* Purpose:       Attached subroutine for toolbar
'*****************************************

proc TestToolBar( aParams )

  select case aParams[ _ITEMNUM ]
  case 11
    input "This will now send something to the printer";
  case 12
    input "We are going to save something to the disk";
  case 13
    input "Now, a new cellar is being opened";
  case 14
    input "Let's cut something to the ClipBoard!" ;
  case 15
    input "Hey, let's get something from the ClipBoard!" ;
```

More Complex Forms and User Interface 271

```
    end select

end proc

'*******************************************
'* Proc:         DataTools()
'* Purpose:      Modeless data entry toolbar
'*******************************************

proc DataTools()

    setsys( _sizeMDI, {0,0, 0, 0} )        '* Must set the background region
    formnew(; "", _NONMDI + _HOTCLICK )    '* Ok.... create the form
    formsetcolor( _BLUE; _BACKGROUND )     '* And send the colors
    formcontrol( _SIZE; 0, 0, 65, 180 )    '* New size of the form!

    '* And now, we have to assign the various buttons from the .BMP's
    '* saved to the disk at the <sLoc> location

    formsetobject( 11, _BITMAPBUTTON, "printer.bmp", 13, 10, 30, 30 )
    formsetobject( 12, _BITMAPBUTTON, "disk.bmp",    13, 40, 30, 30 )
    formsetobject( 13, _BITMAPBUTTON, "open.bmp",    13, 70, 30, 30 )
    formsetobject( 14, _BITMAPBUTTON, "cut.bmp",     13,100,30,30 )
    formsetobject( 15, _BITMAPBUTTON, "paste.bmp",   13, 130, 30, 30 )

    formsetproc( TestToolBar )    '* Set the procedure to do the processing
    formcontrol(_SHOW )           '* Show the form and we're out'a here!

end proc

'****************** MAIN ROUTINE *********************`
'************************** ************************`

setsys( _LOADDIR, "\Realizer\Sirius\Apps\;\Realizer\Sirius\Samples\" )
DataTools()

'* End of File: Tool3.rlz
```

This file is similar to *Tool1.rlz* but with a couple of important exceptions. First, you can see how the SETSYS() function is used towards the end of the file to set the internal search mechanism within Realizer to the proper directory for the .BMP files. Here, within the FORMNEW() function, the combination of the _NONMDI and _HOTCLICK internal variables creates the border around the toolbar. Next, we want to size the form via the FORMCONTROL() function. Here, the _SIZE internal variable sets the starting position for this form at 0,0 and makes the toolbar 65 pixels wide and 180 pixels long. On the screen, it looks like this:

The MDI region is set to be the entire screen. The first two values in the array used in the SETSYS() function for the `_SIZEMDI` internal variable are for the top region with the last two used for the bottom region. (In the next section, as we begin to look at other options, including palettes and status bars, I will show the difference between MDI and non-MDI forms.) After the region is set, all we have to do is set the various bitmapped objects to the proper screen size and location. Each image will be 30 by 30 pixels, as shown in the last two parameters of each FORMSETOBJECT() function call. And, with the top parameter for each image of these only 30 pixels farther down than the preceding picture, each `_BITMAPBUTTON` will be butted up against its neighbors within the form. Other than that, the behavior of this modeless form is exactly the same as its modal counterpart.

MDI and Non-MDI Forms

Most Windows applications use the term "multiple document interface" (MDI) to mean multiple tasks active on the screen at any one time. This means that within the Realizer screen, many forms may appear. It also means that the code for each form must be coded as an independent unit that can operate independently. For example, the user interface code, the business code, and the database code must all be built so they survive being instantiated multiple times. Typically, all forms start off understanding that they will work with other forms. While only one form can have "focus" active and in control at any one time, they can all appear collectively on the screen. When a form is closed within the MDI region, an icon for the form will appear in the lower-left corner of the screen and might look something like this:

The region in which all MDI forms can exist is, by default, the entire Realizer screen, but we can control the size of the Realizer screen. Like a lens that is closing, the screen region for MDI forms can be "shrunk" using the SETSYS()

More Complex Forms and User Interface

function. This function takes an array of top and bottom coordinates and is squeezed from both directions. For example, the following SETSYS() function:

```
setsys( _SIZEMDI, {0,50,0,0} )
```

establishes the MDI region starting at 0 pixels from the left and 51 pixels down from the top. This leaves the top 50 rows (for lack of a better term) for the non-MDI forms. The last two values in the array establish the in-from-right and up-from-bottom pixel locations. In this case, there is no non-MDI region on the bottom of the screen, but let's create one by flipping the non-MDI area to the last 50 pixels on the screen:

```
setsys( _SIZEMDI, {0,0,0,50} )
```

Think of the four coordinates as creating a frame in which MDI forms can exist. The following SETSYS() function, for example, creates an MDI region that is bordered at the top, bottom, and left:

```
setsys( _SIZEMDI, {55,40,00,60} )
```

These coordinates push the MDI region 55 pixels in from the left, 40 pixels down from the top, and 60 pixels up from the bottom, as shown in Figure 5-3.

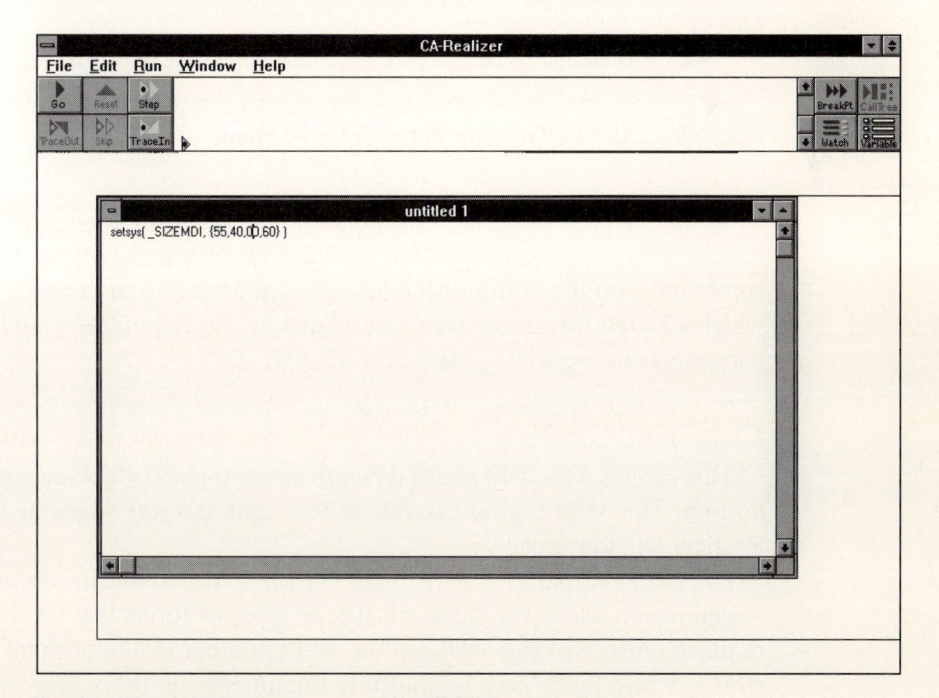

Figure 5-3. Untitled program with DEBUG window open.

If we adjust the third parameter, we can bring the right edge in and create a small non-MDI strip, as shown in Figure 5-4.

```
setsys( _SIZEMDI, {55,40,20,60} )
```

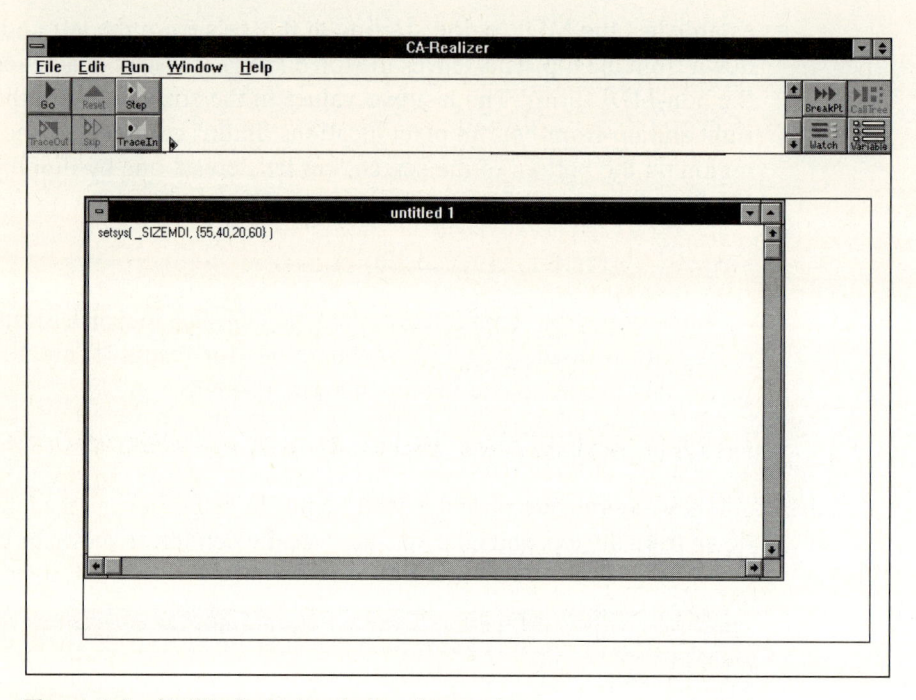

Figure 5-4. Untitled window being dragged open.

We do not have to anchor our toolbar at the right or left edges of the MDI region. Many applications feature toolbars at the top or bottom, depending, sometimes, on the whim of the lead programmer. So to create a region in which all MDI forms can exist surrounded by, for example, a couple of toolbars, we would restrict the size accordingly:

```
setsys( _SIZEMDI, {00, 40, 00, 40} )
```

This creates a strip 40 pixels down from the top and 40 pixels up from the bottom. The MDI region extends to the right and left edges of the entire Realizer window area.

For the most part, we will focus on MDI forms within the prescribed screen region. However, there are special types of forms that we might want to place outside of the MDI region, and a toolbar is one of them. In other words, while there may be multiple documents on the screen within the region, we want a toolbar to remain active within the non-MDI region. Remember, since we can have only one type of form in a non-MDI region, it will be active and will operate on the active and selected form within the MDI region. This association between forms in the two regions is what extends the power of the Windows programming environment.

We've looked at building a toolbar; now, let's explore some other non-MDI forms, such as a status bar. A status bar might display text or even an animated graphic showing the progress of a print job, for example, or a file-save operation. A palette is another type of form that exists in the non-MDI region of the screen. A _PALETTE is like a _TOOLBAR in that it usually contains _BITMAPBUTTONS. However, since a _PALETTE can be moved, whereas a status bar or a toolbar cannot, the items that are placed within a _PALETTE behave differently. In this next example program, we will reduce the size of the MDI area so that both a palette and a status bar can exist on the screen, as shown in Figure 5.5.

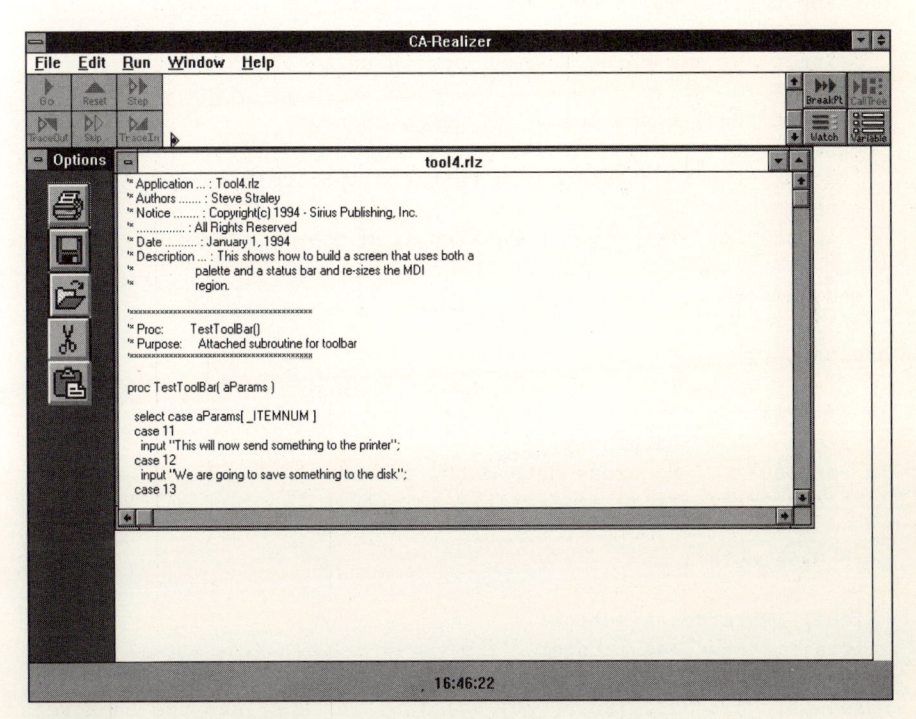

Figure 5-5. Floating toolbar of OPTIONS appear in region.

And now, the file called *Tool4.rlz* looks like this:

```
'* Application ... : Tool4.rlz
'* Authors ....... : Steve Straley
'* Notice ........ : Copyright(c) 1994 - Sirius Press, Inc.
'* ............... : All Rights Reserved
'* Date .......... : January 1, 1994
'* Description ... : This shows how to build a screen that uses both a
'*                   palette and a status bar and resizes the MDI
'*                   region.

'*******************************************
'* Proc:        TestToolBar()
'* Purpose:     Attached subroutine for toolbar
'*******************************************

proc TestToolBar( aParams )

   select case aParams[ _ITEMNUM ]
   case 11
      input "This will now send something to the printer";
   case 12
      input "We are going to save something to the disk";
   case 13
      input "Now, a new cellar is being opened";
   case 14
      input "Let's cut something to the ClipBoard!" ;
   case 15
      input "Hey, let's get something from the ClipBoard!" ;

   end select

end proc

'*******************************************
'* Proc:        DataTools()
'* Purpose:     Modeless data entry toolbar
'*******************************************

proc DataTools()

   local iPalette as integer
   local iStatus  as integer

   setsys( _sizeMDI, {80,0, 20, 37} )      '* Must set the background region

   '* Build a Status Bar..... that just shows a clock!
   iStatus = formnew(; "STATUS", _NONMDI + _BORDERLESS )
   formsetcolor( _POWDERBLUE; _BACKGROUND )
```

```
formsetcolor( _POWDERBLUE; _FIELD )
formcontrol( _SIZE;  0, 460, 100 pct, 40 )
formsetobject( 100, _DIGITALCLOCK, "", _CENTER, _CENTER )
formcontrol( _SHOW )

'* Build the palate form
iPalette = formnew(; "Options", _PALETTE )    '* Ok.... create the form
formsetcolor( _RED; _BACKGROUND )             '* And send the colors
formcontrol( _SIZE; 0, 0, 80, 460 )           '* New size of the form!

formsetobject( 11, _BITMAPBUTTON, "printer.bmp", 18, 10, 40, 40 )
formsetobject( 12, _BITMAPBUTTON, "disk.bmp",    18, 50, 40, 40 )
formsetobject( 13, _BITMAPBUTTON, "open.bmp",    18, 90, 40, 40 )
formsetobject( 14, _BITMAPBUTTON, "cut.bmp",     18,130,40,40 )
formsetobject( 15, _BITMAPBUTTON, "paste.bmp",   18, 170, 40, 40 )

formsetproc( TestToolBar )    '* Set the procedure to do the processing
formcontrol(_SHOW )           '* Show the form and we're out'a here!

end proc

'******************** MAIN ROUTINE ******************`
'************************ ************************`

setsys( _LOADDIR, "\Realizer\Sirius\Apps\;\Realizer\Sirius\Samples\" )
DataTools()

'* End of File: Tool4.rlz
```

To start, we shrink the MDI region to an area whose borders are 80 pixels from the left, 20 pixels in from the right, and 37 pixels up from the bottom. Then we create the first form: a status bar that uses the _NONMDI + _BORDERLESS internal variables. The status bar will display a running clock, so both the _FIELD region and _BACKGROUND region of this area should be the same color: _POWDERBLUE. After the colors are set, we adjust the size of the form to encompass the lower region of the non-MDI area. So, the FORMCONTROL() function is given a few coordinates and told to assume 100 percent of the region:

```
formcontrol( _SIZE; 0, 460, 100 pct, 40 )
```

Finally, after this region is established, the _DIGITALCLOCK object is placed in the center of it.

The next form to be created is the _PALETTE. There is an internal variable for this type of form when using the FORMNEW() function:

```
iPalette = formnew(; "Options", _PALETTE ) '* Ok.... create the form
```

The color of this region will be totally different. Notice that the _PALETTE form actually displays a title in its tiny title bar. A _PALETTE is nothing more that a _NONMDI + _TITLE + _SIZE + _CLOSE + _NOMAX internal variable combination. As you can see, these internal variables are very different from the internal variable combinations that make up a _TOOLBAR.

> **Note:** One of the major differences between a _PALETTE and a _TOOLBAR form is that any object on the form requires a click to first select a form and then a click on the object in order for the object to be activated. In a _TOOLBAR, the object only needs to be clicked upon in order for it to be activated.

To help distinguish this form from any other non-MDI form on the screen, it needs to be assigned a new color and sized to fit the non-MDI area set aside for it. Otherwise, there is no difference in the code: various _BITMAPBUTTON objects populate this form, and the *TestToolBar()* routine is attached to make it a modeless form. And, as expected, the various INPUT commands work as they have in previous examples.

Pop-Up Boxes

Pop-up forms are like other forms created in the Realizer environment, except that the form window resides completely outside of the Realizer window. In other words, a pop-up form will be placed on the task list maintained by the Windows Program Manager. This means that the form is available via the ALT-TAB key combination that cycles through the various forms and activities open in Windows, as you can see in Figure 5.6.

With any other form that is active within the Realizer environment, the prompt to enter into the Realizer system would be in the tagging list (as it would even with a pop-up form). Once the Realizer session is selected, any active form would then be visible. The following code, in the field called *PopUp.rlz*, creates the pop-up form shown in Figure 5-7.

More Complex Forms and User Interface 279

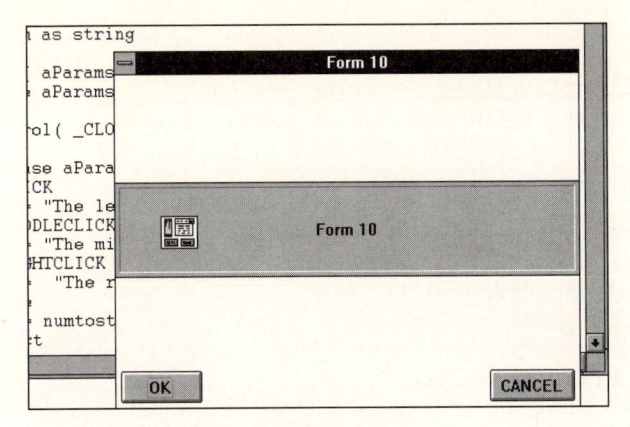

Figure 5-6. Pop-up FORM10 window.

```
'* Application ... : Pop-up.rlz
'* Authors ....... : Steve Straley
'* Notice ........ : Copyright(c) 1994 - Sirius Press, Inc.
'* ............... : All Rights Reserved
'* Date .......... : January 1, 1994
'* Description ... : This shows the use of a pop-up form.
'*

proc PopUpProc( aParams )

  local sItem as string

  formselect( aParams[_FORMNUM] )
  select case aParams[_ITEMNUM]
  case 1, 2
    formcontrol( _CLOSE )

    select case aParams[ _INVOKE ]
    case _CLICK
      sItem = "The left mouse button was pressed"
    case _MIDDLECLICK
      sItem = "The middle mouse button was pressed"
    case _RIGHTCLICK
      sItem =  "The right mouse button was pressed"
    case else
      sItem = numtostr( aParams[_INVOKE] )
    end select

    input sItem, "Closing Pop-up form" ;

  end select
```

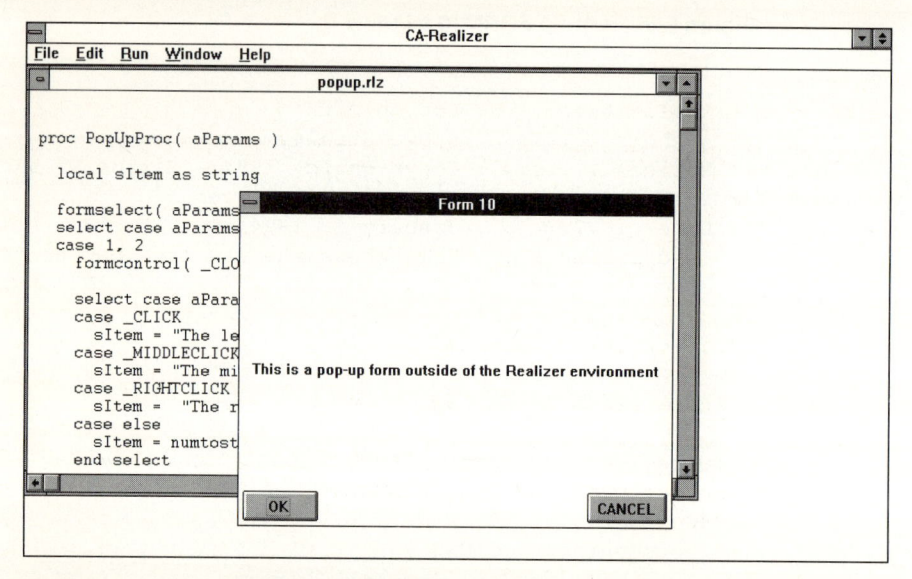

```
end proc

formnew( 10; "", _POPUP + _TITLE )
formsetobject(1, _BUTTON, "OK", _LEFT, _BOTTOM )
formsetobject(2, _BUTTON, "CANCEL", _RIGHT, _BOTTOM )
formsetobject(3, _CAPTIONLEFT, \\
             "This is a pop-up form outside of the Realizer
environment", \\
             _CENTER, _CENTER )
formsetproc( PopUpProc )
formcontrol( _SHOW )

'* End of File: PopUp.rlz
```

Figure 5-7. Pop-up FORM11 application window.

Just like other forms, a `_POPUP` form can have a procedure attached to it. This procedure would behave just like any other procedure attached to a tool, in that it would pass an array of information to the form. Here, if the value of *aParams[_ITEMNUM]* is either 1 or 2, then the associated form is closed and a further test on what invoked the procedure is made. These values are derived from the `_INVOKE` internal variable/element position (outlined later on in this chapter). One of the values obtained at this element position might reveal, for example, whether the left mouse button was pressed. In any event, if the user presses the ENTER or ESC keys to close the form or engages one of the `_BUTTON` objects (which have the same ID value as ENTER and ESC), then the INPUT command within the *PopUpProc()* routine is executed. The message displayed within the window generated by the INPUT command is stored in the LOCAL variable named *sItem*. The title of the INPUT dialog box is the string "Closing pop-up form."

The pop-up form is created by using the internal variable `_POPUP` in the FORMNEW() function. Unless specified, the form will not have a title or any other attribute. So in this example, we use the internal variable `_TITLE` in conjunction with the internal variable `_POPUP`. The form ID value used with the FORMNEW() function is 10. This is the same number that appears in the Program Manager's task list (and when cycling through the open tasks with the `ALT-TAB` key combination) and also in the title bar of the pop-up form.

Logs

Logs are described as windows for text, either to be displayed or to be edited. In the Realizer environment, there are two native logs that often come into play in the development of an application: the Print Log window and the Error Log window. The Print Log window displays the output generated by each PRINT command, and the Error Log window receives the text when an error occurs. We can gain access to either of these logs from within an application, but more important, we can create and manipulate our own logs.

While logs are primarily used for the display of long pieces of text, I like to think of logs as windows for free-form text entry. In many applications, including our wine program, end users may need to annotate certain items within a data file. In dBASE, for example, users can attach an annotation—called a "memo"—to each record in a database. In Realizer, we can have either a standalone log or a log attached to a form. Turning to a practical use for a "memo" log, let's look at the wine program for a moment. Perhaps, in the course of entering a new wine into inventory, we would like to make a couple of comments about its taste and quality. This information will help us in the future to choose from our wine cellars for particular occasions. Notes are important, and a log can help us enter and display them.

As with forms and menus, logs have an ID value. In some cases, there is not only a log ID but also a form ID, which we may need to select the appropriate log. In Chapter 2 we learned that the MENUSELECT() function selects a menu for us; in Chapter 4 we used the FONTSELECT() and FORMSELECT() functions to select those objects; so we might now safely predict there is a LOGSELECT() function used to select the appropriate log, as well as related functions like LOGNEW(), LOGQSIZE(), LOGCONTROL(), LOGQDATA(), and of course, LOGSETPROC(). All of these functions, and log manipulation in general, work on the same principles that govern other Realizer features and components.

To start, we need to look at how a log is created:

```
iVar = lognew(; "Title", _TITLE )
```

This is just one possibility. As usual, several types of logs can be created by mixing and matching the internal variables listed in Table 5-4.

Table 5-4. Internal Variables for LOGNEW().

Internal Variable	Definition
_CLOSE	Allows the log to be closed from the Realizer FILE CLOSE menu or the log window's system menu, or by from pressing the CTRL-F4 key combination.
_FRAME	Places a frame around the log area. This cannot be used with the _TITLE or _SIZE variables.
_SIZE	Places a thin sizing frame around the log window. If _TITLE is used as well, a maximize icon will be placed in the title bar.
_TITLE	Places a title bar at the top of the log window. This makes the window moveable.
_MINIMIZE	Allows the window to be minimized from the log window's system menu. If _TITLE is also used, a minimize icon is placed in the title bar.
_HOTCLICK	Causes mouse clicks in the log window to be processed even if the log is not the active window. By default, a mouse click in a non-active window only activates that window.
_NOMAX	Prevents the log window from being maximized.
_BORDERLESS	Creates the log window without any border and cannot be used in conjunction with the _TITLE or _SIZE internal variables.

Like forms, logs can be resized, use a particular font, and have color. In this next example program, *Log1.rlz*, a simple string is passed to a log for display purposes only:

```
'* Application ... : Log1.rlz
'* Authors ....... : Steve Straley
'* Notice ........ : Copyright(c) 1994 - Sirius Press, Inc.
'* .............. : All Rights Reserved
'* Date .......... : January 1, 1994
'* Description ... : This shows one of the possible uses of the LOG object
```

More Complex Forms and User Interface 283

```
'***************************************************
'*  Name:         CloseLog()
'*  Params:       N/A
'*  Returns:      N/A
'*  Purpose:      Closes the log after the CTRL-F4 key has been pressed.

proc CloseLog( aParams )

   logcontrol( _CLOSE )

end proc

'***************************************************
'*  Name:         DispText()
'*  Params:       N/A
'*  Returns:      N/A
'*  Purpose:      This function builds the form and activates it

proc DispText( cString )

   local iLog  as integer
   local iFont as integer

   iLog = lognew( ; "Wine Notation....", _TITLE + _HOTCLICK + _CLOSE )
   iFont = fontnew( 1000; "Bookman", 12 )

   logcontrol( _SIZE; 400, 100, 300, 100 )
   logcontrol( _SETFONT; iFont )
   logsetproc( CloseLog )

   print #iLog; cString

   logcontrol( _SHOW )

end proc

'*************************** MAIN ROUTINE *********************

DispText( "The taste of a wine is subjective.  Say what you thing!")

'* End of File: Log1.rlz
```

The main part of the program simply passes a literal string off to the *DispText()* function. This function creates both the font to be used and the log that is to display this text. When the string is passed to the function, it is initially kept in the parameter named *cString*. The variable *iLog* holds the pointer to the log being created. This log has the title "Wine Notation...", which will appear in the title bar, since the `_TITLE` internal variable is used. In addition, the variable *iFont* holds a pointer to a new font that is being established—in this case, 12-point Bookman. Once the log is created, we need to specify its size and location, so the `_SIZE` internal variable (along with the four modifiers for left, top, width, and height) is passed to the LOGCONTROL() function. We use that same function to set the font via the `_SETFONT` internal variable. Finally, we attach the procedure named *CloseLog()*. When the log is closed (from the File menu or System menu or by pressing `CTRL-F4`), then control will be sent off to the procedure named *CloseLog()*.

> **Note:** Remember that once the function LOGCONTROL(_SHOW) has been issued, there is no sequential processing to the log and its contents until the log is in control and the attached procedure is called.

To get text into a log window region, the PRINT command may be used:

```
print #iLog; cString
```

The first item passed to this command is the ID associated with the log we want the text to appear in. The contents of *cString* will then appear within the log window identified by the ID in *iLog*. Following the PRINT instruction comes the `_SHOW` internal variable with the LOGCONTROL() function.

The contents of the log can be modified by the end user, but getting the contents of the changes out of the log is a different matter. In this next example, we use some of the other log-manipulation functions to ask the end user to enter some text and then, when the log is to be closed, assign the contents of the log to the appropriate variables. This example program is called *Log2.rlz*:

```
'* Application ... : Log2.rlz
'* Authors ....... : Steve Straley
'* Notice ........ : Copyright(c) 1994 - Sirius Press, Inc.
'* ............... : All Rights Reserved
'* Date .......... : January 1, 1994
'* Description ... : This shows another possible use of the LOG object

local sText      as string
local iTextSize as integer
```

```
'*****************************************
'* Name:         Empty( <xData> )
'* Params:       <xData>         Any data type
'* Returns:      <iEmpty>        Logical true if value is "empty"
'* Purpose:      This function returns a true value should the data passed to
'*               it be considered as "empty."

function Empty( xData )

  local iReturn as integer

  if qvar( xData, _ALPHA )
    if qvar( xData, _ARRAY )      '* array of strings
    else
      iReturn = ( len( ltrim$(xData) ) = 0 )
    end if

  elseif qvar( xData, _REAL )
    if qvar( xData, _ARRAY )      '* array of numbers
    else
      iReturn = ( xData = 0 )
    end if

  end if

  return( iReturn )

end func

proc EditLog( aParams )

  logselect( aParams[ _ITEMNUM ] )
  sText    = logqsize
  iTextSize = logqstr()

  if not empty( iTextSize )
    print sText
    print iTextSize
  else
    print "Nothing in log to show...."
  end if

  logcontrol( _CLOSE )

  logselect( _PRINTLOG )
  logcontrol( _SHOW )
  idle 5
  logcontrol( _CLOSE )

end proc
```

```
'*****************************************************
'*  Name:          DispText()
'*  Params:        N/A
'*  Returns:       N/A
'*  Purpose:       This function builds the form and activates it

proc EnterText()

    local iLog  as integer
    local iFont as integer

    iLog  = lognew( ; "Enter Wine Description", _TITLE + _CLOSE )
    iFont = fontnew( 1000; "Bookman", 12 )

    logcontrol( _SIZE; 400, 100, 300, 100 )
    logcontrol( _SETFONT; iFont )
    logsetproc( EditLog )
    logcontrol( _SHOW )

end proc

'*************************** MAIN ROUTINE ********************

EnterText()

'* End of File: Log2.rlz
```

This is slightly different. Here, in this example, we are wanting the end user to type something into the log and then, when the log is to be closed, we get the value typed into that log and store it to two variables declared at the top of the file.

> **Note:** Remember, a LOCAL variable declared at the top of the file is visible to all functions declared and initialized within the domain of that file.

In this example, everything starts with a call to the *EnterText()* function. As in the previous example, a new log is created, a new font is assigned, and the size of the window is specified. Here, the *EditLog()* function is attached to the log, which is then shown via the _SHOW internal variable with the LOGCONTROL() function.

When the log is closed, the *EditLog()* function is then called. Had we assigned the following modifier to the *EditLog()* function, then the *EditLog()* function would be called every time the end user resizes the window.

```
logsetproc( editlog; _SIZE )
```

Of course, this would mean that _SIZE internal variable would have to be used in conjunction with the LOGNEW() function when creating the log for the first time. However, in this example, this feature is not implemented.

When the *EditLog()* function is called, an array of values is passed from Realizer to the function. Again, this is called a tool procedure parameter array and has all of the values listed in Table 5-2 (page 251).

In this example, this array is held in the *aParams[]* variable. In the function, the LOGSELECT() function is called, passing to it the value of the *aParams[]* variable at the _ITEMNUM element position. The _FORMNUM internal variable can be used as well. As we said earlier, a log can stand alone or be attached to a form. The LOGSELECT() function can accept two parameters: the first is the ID for the appropriate log and the second is the ID for the associated form. This means we can see what is going on inside the form while processing within the confines of the log.

Turning back to the *EditLog()* function, after the log is selected, the value of the LOGQSIZE command is stored to the file-wide LOCAL variable named *iTextSize*. The LOGQSIZE command returns the number of characters found in the selected log. If the value is 0, then the Log is assumed to be empty. This brings us to a new and improved *Empty()* function. This function is a multipurpose operation, in that it can accept a variety of data types. Each data type has its own definition of "empty." To a string, for example, it is a string with a length of 0 or a string with all blank spaces. To a number, it simply means the value of 0. So when the IF command tests to see whether the variable *iTextSize* is "empty", it determines whether there is a value other than 0 in the variable. If there is, then the contents of both *sText* and *iTextSize* will be printed to the Print Log window. If there is nothing in the original and created log, then the string "Nothing in log to show..." will be dumped to the Print Log window. Once either of these expressions is dumped, the current Log is closed. Then the LOGSELECT() function is called again, but this time, instead of passing a log ID as a parameter, it passes the internal variable _PRINTLOG. We can even pass to this function the internal variable of _ERRORLOG; in either case, the appropriate log would be selected. Then, the Print Log window is opened to show the contents of the PRINT commands. Then, after waiting five seconds via the IDLE command, the Print Log window is closed to complete the execution of this example program.

Logs do not usually exist by themselves. They work in conjunction with many other program elements, including forms. A log by itself can be the active window, but a log with a form cannot; the form will always be the active window.

In the following program, a form is created with a push button object in it. When pressed, this object activates a log. The procedure named *LogProc()* will detect the closure of the log. When the log is closed, the procedure will copy the contents of the log to Window Clipboard. This is handled via the MENUDOCMD() function with the `_RLZM_COPYWINDOW` internal variable. Here is how a form and a log can work together:

```
'* Application ... : Log3.rlz
'* Authors ....... : Steve Straley
'* Notice ........ : Copyright(c) 1994 - Sirius Press, Inc.
'* ............... : All Rights Reserved
'* Date .......... : January 1, 1994
'* Description ... : This shows the use of an attached procedure to a
'*                   Log form.

proc LogProc( aParams )

  logselect( aParams[_ITEMNUM] )
  select case aParams[_INVOKE]
    case _CLOSE

      menudocmd( _RLZM_COPYWINDOW )
  end select

end proc

proc FormProc( aParams )

  formselect( aParams[_FORMNUM] )
  select case aParams[_ITEMNUM]
    case 20
      lognew( 10 )
      print #10; "The following information will be copied"
      print #10; "to the clipboard.  If you type something..."
      print #10; "they will come..."
      print #10;
      print #10; "Honestly... type something, then look at the"
      print #10; "clipboard...."
      print #10;
      print #10; "Then close the log and look at the clipboard again..."
      logcontrol( _SHOW )
      logsetproc( LogProc )
  end select

end proc

'* Main body of the routine!
```

```
formnew( 20; "", _TITLE + _CLOSE + _SIZE )
formsetobject( 20, _BUTTON, "Log me, baby!", _CENTER, _CENTER )
formsetproc( FormProc )
formcontrol( _SHOW )

'* End of File: Log3.rlz
```

Keep in mind that while the log is in focus, the form is still open and active. To illustrate this, in this next example, the procedure handling the log's closing will copy the image of the form to the Clipboard rather than copy the contents of the log. Once again, in *Log4.rlz*, the MENUDOCMD() function is used:

```
'* Application ... : Log4.rlz
'* Authors ....... : Steve Straley
'* Notice ........ : Copyright(c) 1994 - Sirius Press, Inc.
'* .............. : All Rights Reserved
'* Date .......... : January 1, 1994
'* Description ... : This shows another use of an attached procedure to
'*                    a Log form.

proc LogProc( aParams )

  logselect( aParams[_ITEMNUM] )
  select case aParams[_INVOKE]
    case _CLOSE
      formselect( 20 )
      formcontrol( _SHOW )
      menudocmd( _RLZM_COPYWINDOW )
  end select

end proc

proc FormProc( aParams )

  formselect( aParams[_FORMNUM] )
  select case aParams[_ITEMNUM]
    case 20
      lognew( 10 )
      print #10; "The following information will be copied"
      print #10; "to the clipboard.  If you type something..."
      print #10; "they will come..."
      print #10;
      print #10; "Honestly... type something, then look at the"
      print #10; "clipboard...."
      print #10;
      print #10; "Then close the log and look at the clipboard again..."
      logcontrol( _SHOW )
```

```
        logsetproc( LogProc )
  end select

end proc

'* Main body of the routine!

formnew( 20; "", _TITLE + _CLOSE + _SIZE )
formsetobject( 20, _BUTTON, "Log me, baby!", _CENTER, _CENTER )
formsetproc( FormProc )
formcontrol( _SHOW )

'* End of File: Log4.rlz
```

Putting It Together

Now, in putting all of this together, let me make a couple of recommendations. First, not every situation is going to immediately warrant a clear path to the end results, especially as it pertains to form development. For some of us, still rooted in a procedural mind-set, a modal form system may be not only comfortable and easy to maintain, but appropriate as well. However, others will feel more at home with the modeless approach. Maintainability is as much of a deciding factor in the layout of a screen and an application as any other issue. To some, it is *the* deciding factor.

I like to address the issue from a different perspective. I ask myself, "Do I want the end user to do anything else while they are doing a specific operation?" If the answer is "yes," I program in a modeless mind set. If, however, I want the end user to pay attention and not veer off onto some other path, then I want to create a modal environment. Being a purist at heart, I tend to opt for the latter, for several reasons: because Realizer is not a true event-driven environment; because the ability to configure user-defined objects is limited, as are the messages passed from form to associated code; and because the Realizer environment, on the whole, does not support the true object-oriented programming you find in other products, such as Visual Objects. This is not to slam Realizer; the program is damn good. However, given my preference, the complete data-entry screen we will be offering in this section is basically a more modeless scenario with whisps of modal programming.

To do this, we need to have an image of what end users will finally see when they begin to enter data. Since Realizer is a graphics-based language, I strongly suggest you take a few moments to draw pictures. That's right; draw, pictures. Visualize what you want to see on the screen, and before you write even one line of code to support that image, draw it on a piece of paper. Then head off to the FormDev utility program and come up with a rough skeleton of the goal. So, before starting this chapter I sat down and drew what I thought the data-entry screen should look like. I will spare you the result of my artistic efforts. Suffice it to say it was enough for me to use as a template within the FormDev utility.

A very important issue to keep in mind relates to using the FormDev utility as a starting point, but then breaking away. This means beginning with the code that the FormDev program generates for our menu system and application, but then modifying it to work with logs, data validation, toolbars, and other related items. In other words, we can go only so far with the FormDev utility, then we have to rely on our coding abilities. At this juncture, it is vital to remember that once you modify a piece of source code generated by the FormDev utility, those changes will not be reflected in FormDev's .FDV file should you later need to edit the form. The .FDV file contains all the properties and attributes associated with the form under construction. From that file, FormDev generates the corresponding .RLZ files that we will use in our applications. If we change the .RLZ files, FormDev knows nothing about these changes. As a result, we could accidentally go back into FormDev, recall an older form, rewrite the source code for that form, and overwrite the changes to the .RLZ file. So to be safe, look at the FormDev utility as a one-shot attempt to handle the tedious part of application development: placing the objects on the forms, assigning the colors and fonts, specifying the size of the form, and so on.

In our form, we just want to get the buttons in place, the text and data-entry points properly situated, the colors and fonts as well as the general size of the form specified. We will add data validation and a couple of other features after we outline the shell.

> **Note:** The following test and example program is created using a screen driver set to SVGA resolution of 800 × 600 pixels. Regular VGA resolutions will not work. Only a Super VGA setting at this resolution or better will be sufficient.

To start, open Realizer's Run menu and select FormDev.

The first thing I always do is remove the dot grid that fills the form window. This grid is supposed to help us line up our objects, but I find the movement of the mouse with the dots very jerky and I do not get the flow that I find necessary when creating a form. This feature is a toggle; you can turn it on and off by clicking on its icon. The icon is in the toolbar right next to the trash can:

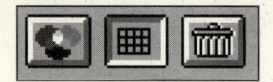

Here, it is the middle icon in this group picture. Once the form is clear of dots, we can select a default color scheme for the form and all of the associated objects. Right next to the icon for the grid dots, on the left, is a color palette icon. This will open the Modify Colors dialog box shown in Figure 5-8.

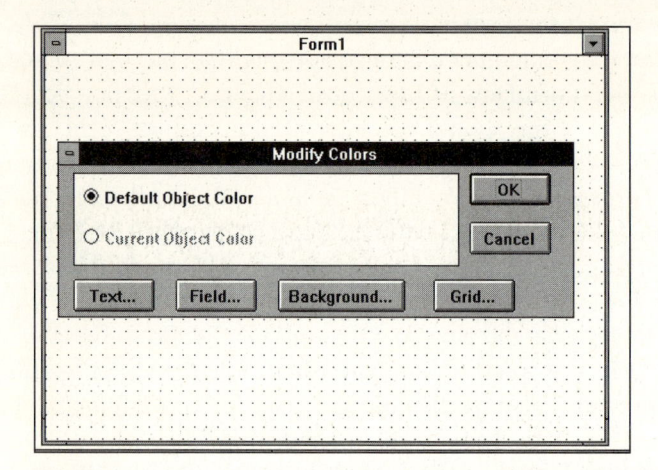

Figure 5-8. Dialog window in FORMDEV utility to change colors.

Now that you have the dialog box open, take a moment to think again about what kind of forms you want to create. Particularly if you're unfamiliar with Windows, observe the Realizer application window and its forms and objects: the menu bar and the tool bar along the top, the status bar along the bottom, the icon palette on the left, and the form window. Look at the open dialog box: the radio buttons, the push buttons, the default sections. You can pick up a lot about the look and feel of Windows applications just by paying attention to what you see in Realizer. (For a sneak peek at the finished version of our form, skip ahead to Figure 5-14.)

In our form, we want to change the background color and the field color, so click on each button in turn—the Background button and the Field button—and in the resulting color palette, select a color that comes as close to `_POWDERBLUE` as possible. Remember, the Field button allows you to make the color of the textbox the same as the background color for all areas not touched by an object. I usually want these two colors to be the same.

More Complex Forms and User Interface

> **Note:** Do not panic when the grid dots reappear on the screen after you've modified the colors of the form. As soon as you click on OK in the Modify Colors dialog box, the grid dots in the form window will revert back to their selected state.

Now we are ready to place objects on the form, and the icons in the palette on the left side of the screen can help. To discover what type of object one of these icons creates, click on it once. The object type will appear in the Name textbox near the top. In other Window applications and languages, a help message or a description of the icon will sometimes appear either directly under the icon or on the bottom edge of the screen. This is a good use of a status bar—an extra help message in a non-MDI region for each of the buttons and icons on a form.

The first thing we want to place on the form are the caption boxes for the data-entry items. Before we do this, however, you might want to enlarge the form window in order to provide more room in which to work, adjust objects, and plan the various heights, widths, and fonts.

In "painting" a screen, I generally try to get all the objects that are similar on the screen at the same time so that I can see how the items will appear in relation to each other and how they should be positioned. So let's select the icon that has an "A" in it on the icon palette, and create the `15_CAPTION` objects shown in Figure 5-9.

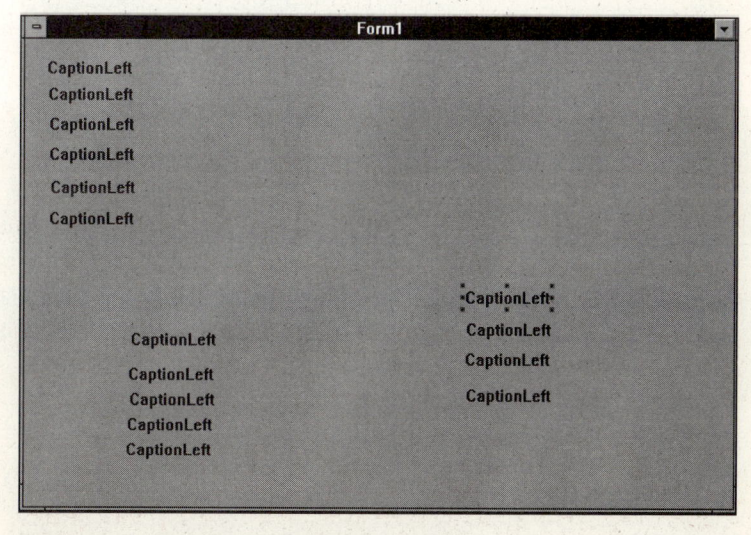

Figure 5-9. Skeleton of FORM1 program.

Now, we can adjust the size, text, location, font, and color, if necessary, for each item. Before doing any of this, let's group together some of the items that ultimately deal with related information. To do this, we need to add two group boxes (which you may remember as the _GROUPBOX internal variable). A group box is nothing more than a frame or a rectangle that is used to delineate items that relate to one another. Typically, a group box surrounds a series of option buttons, or check boxes. However, this does not preclude us from using a group box to surround text or other data entry points that relate to one another.

When we select a group box (use the icon with the word "TYPE" in it), the box will suddenly appear on top of any existing object on the screen. This is expected. We can use the mouse to move the group box to wherever we want it and resize it to whatever size we need, as shown in Figure 5-10.

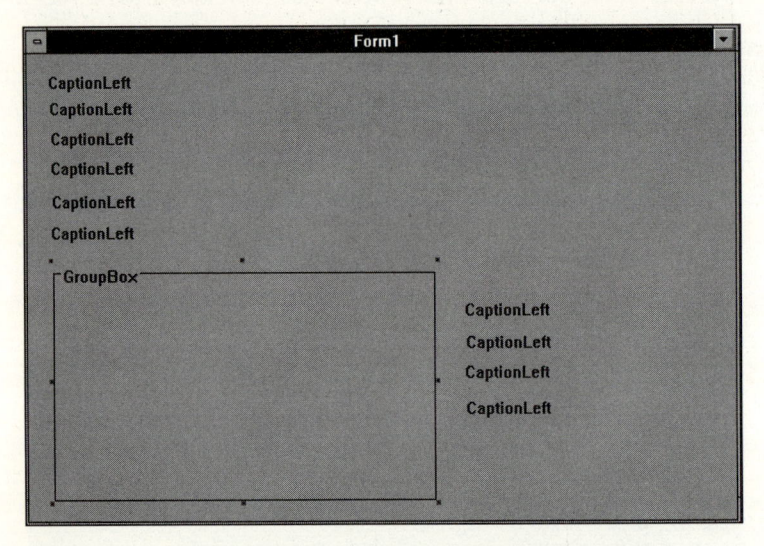

Figure 5-10. GROUPBOX object being attached to FORM1.

We can use the GroupBox title to describe what items are contained within, but first, we have to now "see" the items that the group box has now covered. So, we need to send the group box object to the back and bring forward the individual text objects. On the toolbar at the top of the form is an icon just to the left of the image of the scissors:

This will move the selected item to the background, revealing any object that is underneath.

Add another group box for the items on the right of the form, then add three button objects to the form, resulting in a form that looks like Figure 5-11.

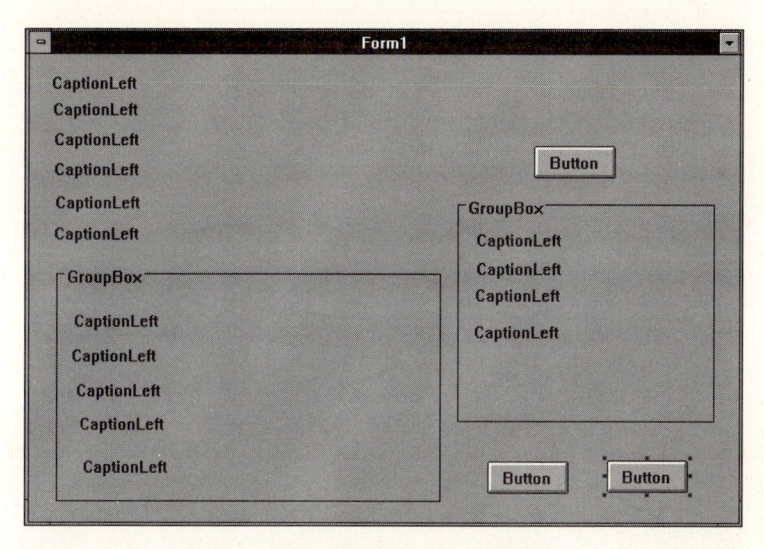

Figure 5-11. Buttons being attached to FORM1.

At this point, we can begin to modify individual objects, which will begin to give more shape to the data-entry form. One at a time, we select an object and make adjustments to the various attributes. For example, all the Caption-Left objects on the form need to be changed to CaptionRight. Remember, we want the text to be flush right against the data-entry objects that have yet to be placed on this form.

> **Note:** When a `_CAPTION` object has been made either `_CENTER`, `_LEFT`, or even `_RIGHT`, you can enlarge the text area by clicking on the left and right corners of the object. If you enlarge a `_CAPTIONRIGHT` object to the right, for example, the text will automatically align flush right within that area.

> **Note:** When you change a text object from a `_CAPTIONLEFT` to a `_CAPTIONRIGHT` and alter its text, the text region will change to fit the next text precisely. This means that if an item is a part of a group, the location or size of the text region may need to be adjusted.

In the second group box object, we do not want a title in the frame itself, so select this object, delete the contents of the text box in the toolbar, and press the ENTER key. In addition to changing the text of the various text items, we also want to change the text in the buttons. To do this, select each button, in turn, and modify the string in the text box, as you did before. We can even add accelerators to the buttons by placing an ampersand in front of the appropriate letter. For example, the text of one of the buttons will be changed to &Accept, which means that the letter A will be underlined and that the ALT-A key will be associated with the button.

Finally, on this screen, we want to add the bitmap option buttons for Tasted and Not Tasted. Find and click on the following icon in the palette area:

From here, we will be able to select any of the icons saved to the `\Realizer\Sirius\Apps` directory; in this case, the `Buttons.bmp` file. When selected, place it on the form near the upper-right corner, as shown in Figure 5-12.

> **Note:** At this point, both sides of the bitmapped image will appear, even though the end user will see only half the image: Tasted or Not Tasted.

So far, we have pretty much completed the text portion of the form, but other than the buttons, we have attached no data input device yet. So the next step is to add the `_TEXTBOX`, `_COMBOLIST`, and `_DROPDOWNLIST` objects as outlined in the previous chapter. Before adding those objects to the form, however, save this form to disk.

More Complex Forms and User Interface

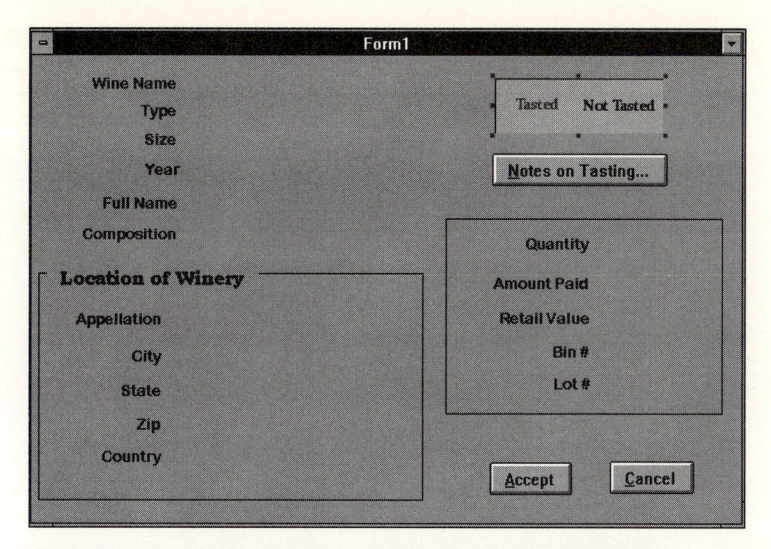

Figure 5-12. BITMAP buttons being attached to FORM1.

> **Note:** Do not generate the source code for the form at this time. That action should be the last operation performed within the FormDev utility program.

Once the form is saved, we can return to the task of adding the remaining objects. The procedure for this will generally be the same. I tend to add all the objects to the form in approximately their final locations, and then go back to make fine adjustments. Don't be alarmed if, as you add objects to the form, they overlap or obscure each other. You can resize or relocate any object or item on the form.

When modifying the values and attributes of the _TEXTBOX objects you just added to the form, give some thought to the default text that will appear in each text box. Most of the text boxes do not need any text, so just delete the contents of the text box in the toolbar for each selected object. When you want a default value to appear in a text box, replace the default contents of the text box in the toolbar with your own default text. For example, we added the default string USA to the Country text box.

After you adjust all of the objects to fit better on the form and in relation to one another, your data-entry form should begin to look like the one in Figure 5-13.

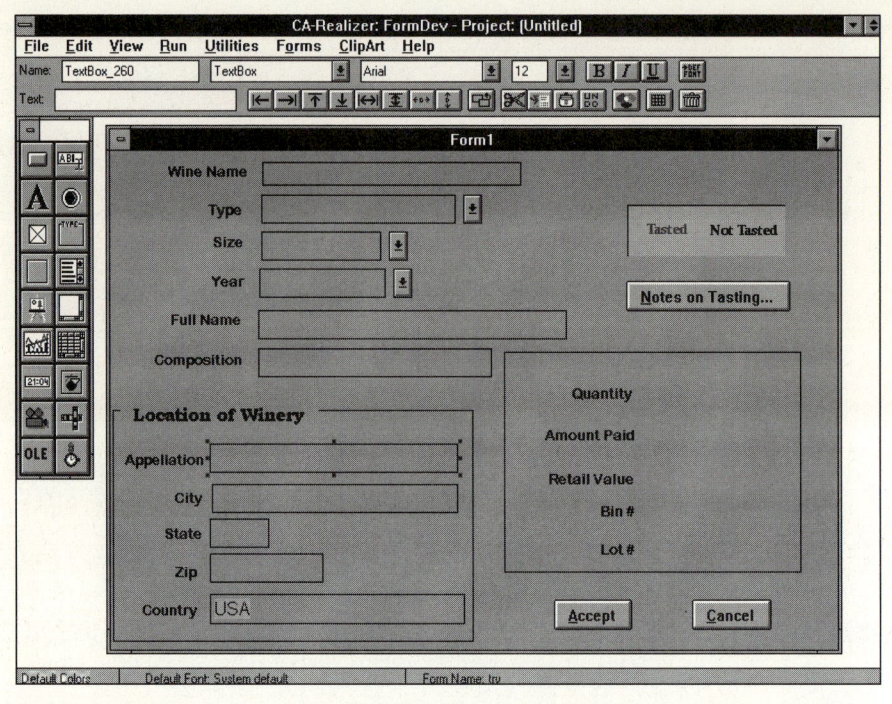

Figure 5-13. Fully executing FORM1 within FORMDEV utility program.

Finally, we need to add a few more _TEXTBOX items for the Quantity, Amount Paid, and other fields in the lower-right group box. Again, the idea is to place the _TEXTBOX objects on the form and then go back and make modifications to each item.

> **Note:** All of the _TEXTBOX, _DROPDOWNBOX, and other data-entry items have been modified to use 12-point Arial as the text font.

Once these items are in place, the final form should look like the one in Figure 5-14.

Now that we've finalized the data-entry items, we can start changing some of the attributes of the form itself. The Form Characteristics option on the View menu opens the dialog box shown in Figure 5-15. This dialog box allows you to modify the form's characteristics. Here, I want to (a) change the name of the form; (b) make the form modal instead of modeless; (c) change the characteristics of the form to remove the frame and to not allow the form to be closed, minimized, or resized.

More Complex Forms and User Interface 299

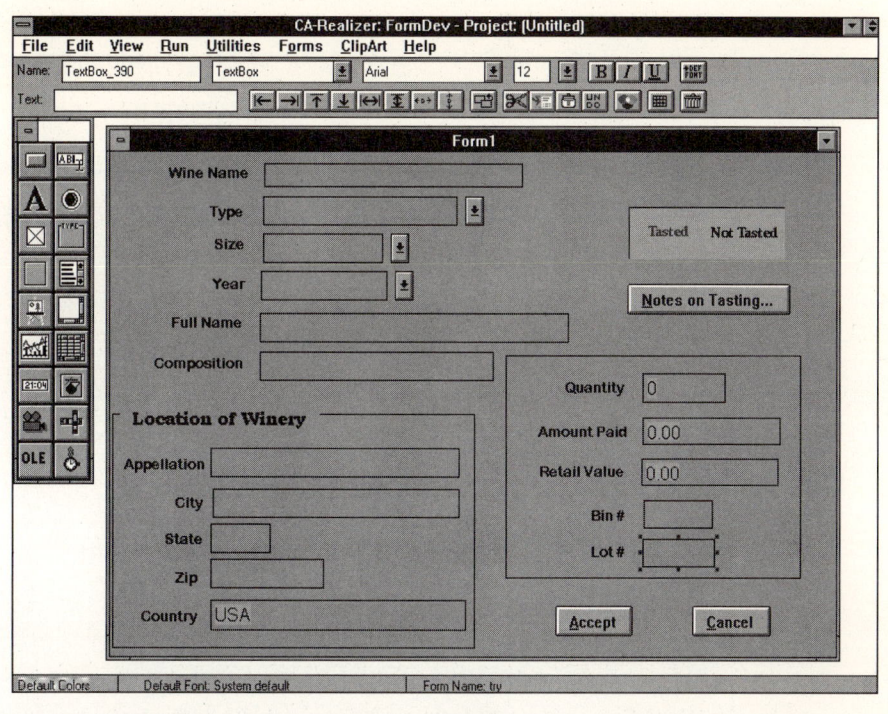

Figure 5-14. Values being entered in FORM1.

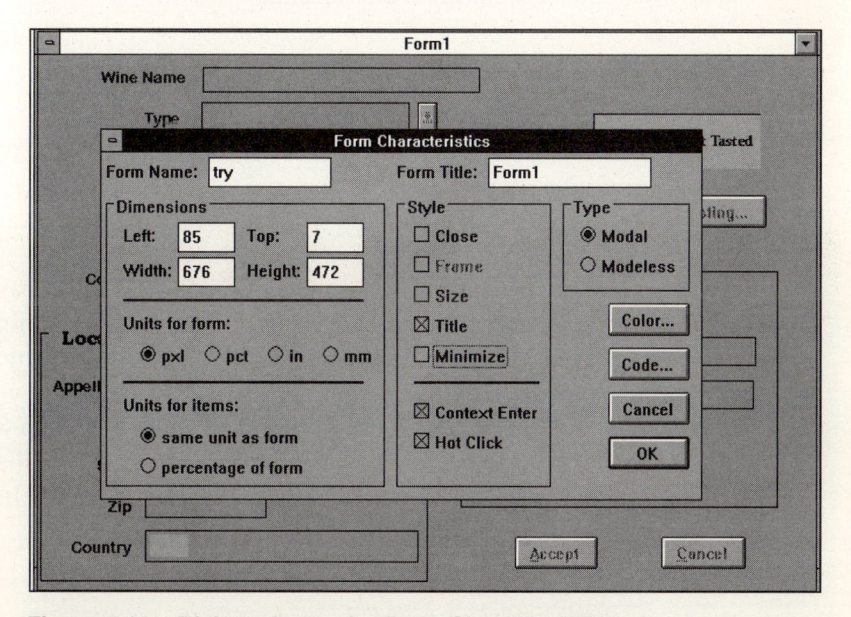

Figure 5-15. Dialog window for Form Characteristics.

If you click on the Code button in this dialog box, you'll open the dialog box shown in Figure 5-16. This dialog box lets you add the search path to be used for the bitmapped objects and other files.

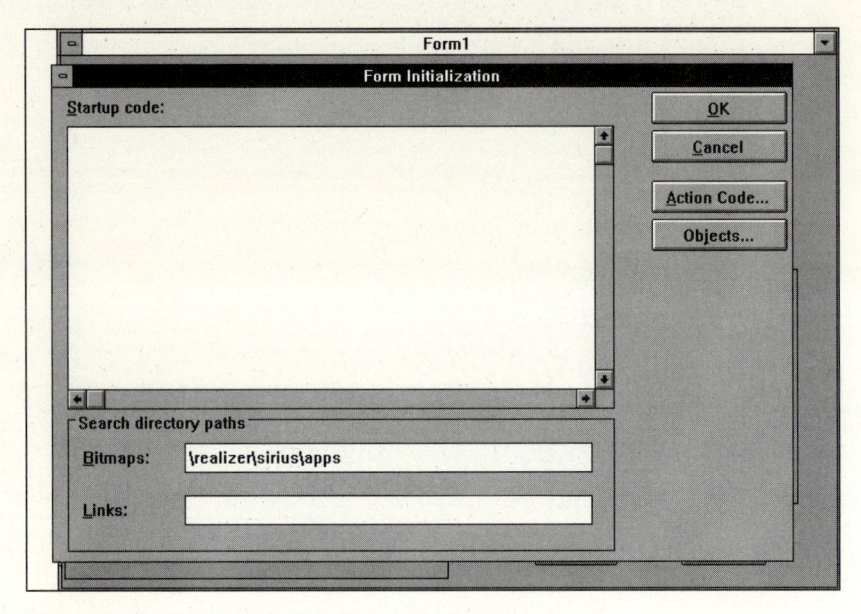

Figure 5-16. Dialog window for startup code.

Remember, the more information we can store into FormDev, the less we will have to code by hand once FormDev generates the source code for this module. Finally, after all of the relevant screens have been opened and looked at and all of the information changed that needs changing, we should save the project/form one more time without generating code just to be safe. Then we can resave, but this time generating the code.

When you save the form and generate the code on the last pass through, you will be faced with three code-generation options. Since this form still needs a great deal of manual intervention, choose the "Form creation code only" option in the Code Generation Options dialog box. When you click on the OK button to begin the operation, you will eventually end up with source code for the form and the various objects. When this finishes, the code will appear in an edit window, which we can modify to fit the application and add the data-validation routines. At this stage, the code looks like this:

```
'*****************************************
'FormDevFormName: try
'FormDev Project Name: Untitled
'FormDev Saveflag: 7
'*****************************************

IF QVar(%%flagtry, _Defined) THEN
        EXIT MACRO
END IF
%%flagtry = 1


AddSys(_LoadDir,"\realizer\sirius\apps")

PROC Maketry

   IF QVar(formtry, _Real + _Scalar)
        IF FormQ(_Exists; formtry)
             FormSelect(formtry)
             EXIT PROC
        END IF
   END IF

   'Define the fonts
   LOCAL font2, font3, font4, font5
   font2 = FontQUnique
   FontNew(font2; "Arial Rounded MT Bold", 10, _None)
   font3 = FontQUnique
   FontNew(font3; "Bookman Old Style", 12, _Bold)
   font4 = FontQUnique
   FontNew(font4; "Arial Rounded MT Bold", 14, _Bold)
   font5 = FontQUnique
   FontNew(font5; "Arial", 12, _None)

   formtry = FormQUnique
   FormNew(formtry; "Winery Input Form", _Title + _ContextEnter + _HotClick)
   FormSetColor(_PowderBlue; _Background)
   FormControl(_Size; 85 pxl, 7 pxl, 676 pxl, 472 pxl)
   FormSetColor(_PowderBlue; _Field)
   FormSetObject(tryobjs.GroupBox_170, _GroupBox, "", font4, 362 pxl, 179 pxl, 273 pxl,
197 pxl)
   FormSetObject(tryobjs.GroupBox_160, _GroupBox, " Location of Winery ", font3, 2 pxl,
222 pxl, 332 pxl, 216 pxl)
   FormSetObject(tryobjs.CaptionRight_10, _CaptionRight, "Wine Name", font2, 21 pxl, 11
pxl, 106 pxl, 20 pxl)
   FormSetObject(tryobjs.CaptionRight_20, _CaptionRight, "Type", font2, 18 pxl, 45 pxl,
104 pxl, 16 pxl)
   FormSetObject(tryobjs.CaptionRight_30, _CaptionRight, "Size", font2, 19 pxl, 74 pxl,
104 pxl, 16 pxl)
   FormSetObject(tryobjs.CaptionRight_40, _CaptionRight, "Year", font2, 17 pxl, 109 pxl,
107 pxl, 19 pxl)
```

```
    FormSetObject(tryobjs.CaptionRight_50, _CaptionRight, "Full Name", font2, 17 pxl, 143
pxl, 104 pxl, 14 pxl)
    FormSetObject(tryobjs.CaptionRight_60, _CaptionRight, "Composition", font2, 18 pxl, 179
pxl, 104 pxl, 16 pxl)
    FormSetObject(tryobjs.CaptionRight_70, _CaptionRight, "Appellation", font2, 13 pxl, 268
pxl, _Default, _Default)
    FormSetObject(tryobjs.CaptionRight_80, _CaptionRight, "City", font2, 9 pxl, 302 pxl, 76
pxl, 17 pxl)
    FormSetObject(tryobjs.CaptionRight_90, _CaptionRight, "State", font2, 13 pxl, 334 pxl,
72 pxl, 16 pxl)
    FormSetObject(tryobjs.CaptionRight_100, _CaptionRight, "Zip", font2, 12 pxl, 368 pxl,
68 pxl, 17 pxl)
    FormSetObject(tryobjs.CaptionRight_110, _CaptionRight, "Country", font2, 14 pxl, 402 pxl,
66 pxl, 16 pxl)
    FormSetObject(tryobjs.CaptionRight_120, _CaptionRight, "Quantity", font2, 375 pxl, 200
pxl, 96 pxl, 19 pxl)
    FormSetObject(tryobjs.CaptionRight_130, _CaptionRight, "Amount Paid", font2, 372 pxl,
239 pxl, 102 pxl, 16 pxl)
    FormSetObject(tryobjs.CaptionRight_140, _CaptionRight, "Retail Value", font2, 372 pxl,
274 pxl, 99 pxl, 16 pxl)
    FormSetObject(tryobjs.CaptionRight_150, _CaptionRight, "Bin #", font2, 373 pxl, 313 pxl,
98 pxl, _Default)
    FormSetObject(tryobjs.Button_180, _Button, "&Notes on Tasting...", 474 pxl, 116 pxl,
_Default, _Default)
    FormSetObject(tryobjs.Button_190, _Button, "&Accept", 408 pxl, 400 pxl, _Default,
_Default)
    FormSetObject(tryobjs.Button_200, _Button, "&Cancel", 534 pxl, 400 pxl, _Default,
_Default)
    FormSetObject(tryobjs.CaptionRight_210, _CaptionRight, "Lot #", font2, 374 pxl, 345
pxl, 97 pxl, 20 pxl)
    FormSetObject(tryobjs.Bitmap_220, _Bitmap, "c:\realizer\sirius\apps\buttons.bmp", 475
pxl, 48 pxl, _Default, _Default)
    FormSetObject(tryobjs.TextBox_230, _TextBox, "", font5, 141 pxl, 10 pxl, 237 pxl, 21
pxl)
    FormSetObject(tryobjs.TextBox_240, _TextBox, "", font5, 137 pxl, 142 pxl, 283 pxl,
_Default)
    FormSetObject(tryobjs.TextBox_250, _TextBox, "", font5, 137 pxl, 176 pxl, 214 pxl, 26
pxl)
    FormSetObject(tryobjs.TextBox_260, _TextBox, "", font5, 92 pxl, 261 pxl, 228 pxl, 26
pxl)
    FormSetObject(tryobjs.TextBox_270, _TextBox, "", font5, 94 pxl, 297 pxl, 226 pxl, 26
pxl)
    FormSetObject(tryobjs.TextBox_280, _TextBox, "", font5, 92 pxl, 328 pxl, 55 pxl,
_Default)
    FormSetObject(tryobjs.TextBox_290, _TextBox, "", font5, 92 pxl, 359 pxl, 104 pxl,
_Default)
    FormSetObject(tryobjs.TextBox_300, _TextBox, "USA", font5, 92 pxl, 395 pxl, 234 pxl, 27
pxl)
    FormSetObject(tryobjs.DropDownCombo_310, _DropDownCombo, "", font5, 140 pxl, 39 pxl,
202 pxl, _Default)
```

```
    FormSetObject(tryobjs.DropDownCombo_320, _DropDownCombo, "", font5, 140 pxl, 72 pxl,
134 pxl, _Default)
    FormSetObject(tryobjs.DropDownCombo_340, _DropDownCombo, "DropDownCombo", font5, 138
pxl, 105 pxl, _Default, _Default)
    FormSetObject(tryobjs.TextBox_350, _TextBox, "0", font5, 488 pxl, 195 pxl, 77 pxl, 26
pxl)
    FormSetObject(tryobjs.TextBox_360, _TextBox, "0.00", font5, 488 pxl, 234 pxl, 128 pxl,
24 pxl)
    FormSetObject(tryobjs.TextBox_370, _TextBox, "0.00", font5, 487 pxl, 270 pxl, 127 pxl,
24 pxl)
    FormSetObject(tryobjs.TextBox_380, _TextBox, "", font5, 489 pxl, 307 pxl, 64 pxl, 25
 pxl)
    FormSetObject(tryobjs.TextBox_390, _TextBox, "", font5, 488 pxl, 341 pxl, 67 pxl, 25
 pxl)
    FormSetColor(_White; _Field)

'Close the fonts
        FontSelect(font2)
        FontControl(_Close)
        FontSelect(font3)
        FontControl(_Close)
        FontSelect(font4)
        FontControl(_Close)
        FontSelect(font5)
        FontControl(_Close)
END PROC

PROC AssignNamestry
    tryobjs.CaptionRight_10 = 10          'TYPE: CaptionRight,   TEXT: Wine Name
    tryobjs.CaptionRight_20 = 20          'TYPE: CaptionRight,   TEXT: Type
    tryobjs.CaptionRight_30 = 30          'TYPE: CaptionRight,   TEXT: Size
    tryobjs.CaptionRight_40 = 40          'TYPE: CaptionRight,   TEXT: Year
    tryobjs.CaptionRight_50 = 50          'TYPE: CaptionRight,   TEXT: Full Name
    tryobjs.CaptionRight_60 = 60          'TYPE: CaptionRight,   TEXT: Composition
    tryobjs.CaptionRight_70 = 70          'TYPE: CaptionRight,   TEXT: Appellation
    tryobjs.CaptionRight_80 = 80          'TYPE: CaptionRight,   TEXT: City
    tryobjs.CaptionRight_90 = 90          'TYPE: CaptionRight,   TEXT: State
    tryobjs.CaptionRight_100 = 100        'TYPE: CaptionRight,   TEXT: Zip
    tryobjs.CaptionRight_110 = 110        'TYPE: CaptionRight,   TEXT: Country
    tryobjs.CaptionRight_120 = 120        'TYPE: CaptionRight,   TEXT: Quantity
    tryobjs.CaptionRight_130 = 130        'TYPE: CaptionRight,   TEXT: Amount Paid
    tryobjs.CaptionRight_140 = 140        'TYPE: CaptionRight,   TEXT: Retail Value
    tryobjs.CaptionRight_150 = 150        'TYPE: CaptionRight,   TEXT: Bin #
    tryobjs.GroupBox_160 = 160            'TYPE: GroupBox,       TEXT:   Location of Winery
    tryobjs.GroupBox_170 = 170            'TYPE: GroupBox,       TEXT:
    tryobjs.Button_180 = 180              'TYPE: Button,    TEXT: &Notes on Tasting...
    tryobjs.Button_190 = 190              'TYPE: Button,    TEXT: &Accept
    tryobjs.Button_200 = 200              'TYPE: Button,    TEXT: &Cancel
    tryobjs.CaptionRight_210 = 210        'TYPE: CaptionRight,   TEXT: Lot #
```

```
      tryobjs.Bitmap_220 = 220           'TYPE: Bitmap,       TEXT: c:\realizer\sirius\apps\buttons.bmp
      tryobjs.TextBox_230 = 230          'TYPE: TextBox,      TEXT:
      tryobjs.TextBox_240 = 240          'TYPE: TextBox,      TEXT:
      tryobjs.TextBox_250 = 250          'TYPE: TextBox,      TEXT:
      tryobjs.TextBox_260 = 260          'TYPE: TextBox,      TEXT:
      tryobjs.TextBox_270 = 270          'TYPE: TextBox,      TEXT:
      tryobjs.TextBox_280 = 280          'TYPE: TextBox,      TEXT:
      tryobjs.TextBox_290 = 290          'TYPE: TextBox,      TEXT:
      tryobjs.TextBox_300 = 300          'TYPE: TextBox,      TEXT: USA
      tryobjs.DropDownCombo_310 = 310    'TYPE: DropDownCombo, TEXT:
      tryobjs.DropDownCombo_320 = 320    'TYPE: DropDownCombo, TEXT:
      tryobjs.DropDownCombo_340 = 340    'TYPE: DropDownCombo, TEXT: DropDownCombo
      tryobjs.TextBox_350 = 350          'TYPE: TextBox,      TEXT: 0
      tryobjs.TextBox_360 = 360          'TYPE: TextBox,      TEXT: 0.00
      tryobjs.TextBox_370 = 370          'TYPE: TextBox,      TEXT: 0.00
      tryobjs.TextBox_380 = 380          'TYPE: TextBox,      TEXT:
      tryobjs.TextBox_390 = 390          'TYPE: TextBox,      TEXT:
END PROC


'Main program

AssignNamestry
Maketry
```

To customize this form to the menu module for the Decanter program, I will add another group box by hand to create a border effect for the bitmapped push button. This Group Box will be black and slightly larger than the push button itself. When placed behind the push button it will give the effect of a border. Also, I want to modify the naming convention for the objects in the form, establishing a family of SAYs as well as a family of GETs: a carryover from my Clipper days. This shows how the SAY information and location of associated objects can work in conjunction with the GET or the data-entry objects. Each of these SAY/GET pairs is tied to the variable that will eventually be used to hold the data which will then be passed off to a database for storage. After all these modifications, the code looks like this:

```
'* Application ... : DWineDat.rlz
'* Authors ....... : Steve Straley
'* Notice ........ : Copyright(c) 1994 - Sirius Press, Inc.
'* .............. : All Rights Reserved
'* Date .......... : January 1, 1994
'* Description ... : This is the main data entry routine for the
'*                   Decanter program
'*
```

More Complex Forms and User Interface

```
iLog = 0    '* Set this in the beginning so that it will not bomb

'* Initialize the record for this routine

fRecord.WineName    = ""
fRecord.WineType    = ""
fRecord.WineSize    = ""
fRecord.WineYear    = ""
fRecord.FullName    = ""
fRecord.Composition = ""
fRecord.Appellation = ""
fRecord.WineCity    = ""
fRecord.WineState   = ""
fRecord.WineZip     = ""
fRecord.WineCountry = ""
fRecord.Notes       = ""
fRecord.Quantity    = 0
fRecord.Amount      = 0
fRecord.Retail      = 0
fRecord.BinNumber   = 0
fRecord.LotNumber   = 0

proc AddData()

   fRecord.WineName    = ucase$( formqstr( fObjs.Get_WineName ) )
   fRecord.WineType    = formqstr( fObjs.Get_WineType )
   fRecord.WineSize    = formqstr( fObjs.Get_Size )
   fRecord.WineYear    = formqstr( fObjs.Get_Year )
   fRecord.FullName    = formqstr( fObjs.Get_Full_Name )
   fRecord.Composition = formqstr( fObjs.Get_Composition )
   fRecord.Appellation = formqstr( fObjs.Get_Appellation )
   fRecord.WineCity    = formqstr( fObjs.Get_City )
   fRecord.WineState   = formqstr( fObjs.Get_State )
   fRecord.WineZip     = formqstr( fObjs.Get_Zip )
   fRecord.WineCountry = formqstr( fObjs.Get_Country )

   if iLog > 0    '* There is a log
     logselect( iLog )
     fRecord.Notes     = logqdata( _LOG_STR )
   else
     fRecord.Notes     = ""
   end if

   fRecord.Quantity    = strtonum( formqstr( fObjs.Get_Quantity ) )
   fRecord.Amount      = strtonum( formqstr( fObjs.Get_Amount ) )
   fRecord.Retail      = strtonum( formqstr( fObjs.Get_Retail ) )
   fRecord.BinNumber   = strtonum( formqstr( fObjs.Get_BinNo ) )
   fRecord.LotNumber   = strtonum( formqstr( fObjs.Get_LotNo ) )
```

```
    input "Ready to print results", INPUT_TITLE ;
    print fRecord.WineName,      fRecord.WineType,      fRecord.WineSize
    print fRecord.WineYear,      fRecord.FullName,      fRecord.Composition
    print fRecord.Appellation,   fRecord.WineCity,      fRecord.WineState
    print fRecord.WineZip,       fRecord.WineCountry,   fRecord.Notes
    print fRecord.Quantity,      fRecord.Amount,        fRecord.Retail
    print fRecord.BinNumber,     fRecord.LotNumber

end proc

proc EditTastedLog( aParams )

    logselect( aParams[_ITEMNUM], aParams[_FORMNUM] )

    aParams[_USEREALIZER] = 0
    fRecord.Notes     = logqdata( _LOG_STR )
    logcontrol( _CLOSE )
    iLog = 0

end proc

proc EnterTastedLog()

    local iFont as integer

    if iLog > 0
      logselect( iLog )
      logcontrol( _SHOW )
    else
      iLog = lognew( ; "Enter Wine Description", _TITLE + _CLOSE + _SIZE)
      iFont = fontnew( 1000; "Bookman", 12 )
      logcontrol( _SIZE; 100, 200, _DEFAULT, 325 )
      logcontrol( _SETFONT; iFont )
      logsetproc( EditTastedLog )
      print #iLog; fRecord.Notes
      logcontrol( _SHOW )
    end if

end proc

proc MakeDataEntryForm_Wine()

    if qvar(iForm1, _REAL + _SCALAR )
      if formq(_EXISTS; iForm1)
        formselect( iForm1 )
        exit proc
      end if
    end if
```

More Complex Forms and User Interface

```
'Define the fonts
local iFont2 as integer
local iFont3 as integer
local iFont4 as integer
local iFont5 as integer

iFont2 = fontqunique
fontnew(iFont2; "Arial Rounded MT Bold", 10, _NONE)
iFont3 = fontqunique
fontnew(iFont3; "Bookman Old Style", 12, _BOLD)
iFont4 = fontqunique
fontnew(iFont4; "Arial Rounded MT Bold", 14, _BOLD)
iFont5 = fontqunique
fontnew(iFont5; "Arial", 12, _BOLD)

iForm1 = FormQUnique
formnew(iForm1; "Winery Input Form", _TITLE + _SIZE + _CLOSE)

formsetcolor( _BLACK; _FIELD )
formsetobject( fObjs.GroupBox_500, _GROUPBOX, "", 474, 47, 76, 50 )

formsetcolor(_POWDERBLUE; _BACKGROUND)
formsetcolor(_POWDERBLUE; _FIELD)
formsetcolor(_BLACK;      _TEXT)
formcontrol(_SIZE; 85, 5, 670, 460)

formsetobject(fObjs.GroupBox_170,   _GROUPBOX, "", iFont4, 362, 179, 273, 197)
formsetobject(fObjs.GroupBox_160,   _GROUPBOX, " Location of Winery ", \\
                            iFont3, 2, 222, 332, 216)

formsetobject(fObjs.Say_WineName,   _CAPTIONRIGHT, "Wine Name",   \\
                            iFont2, 21, 11, 106, 20)
formsetobject(fObjs.Get_WineName,   _TEXTBOX,      "",            \\
                            iFont5, 141, 8, 237, 28; _NOTIFY)
formsetobject(fObjs.Say_WineType,   _CAPTIONRIGHT, "Type",        \\
                            iFont2, 18, 45, 104, 16)
formsetobject(fObjs.Get_WineType,   _DROPDOWNLIST, "",            \\
                    iFont5, 140, 39, 202, _DEFAULT; _NOTIFY, WineList() )
formsetobject(fObjs.Say_Size,       _CAPTIONRIGHT, "Size",        \\
                            iFont2, 19, 74, 104, 16)
formsetobject(fObjs.Get_Size,       _DROPDOWNLIST, "",            \\
                    iFont5, 140, 72, 160, _DEFAULT; _NOTIFY, WineSize() )
formsetobject(fObjs.Say_Year,       _CAPTIONRIGHT, "Year",        \\
                            iFont2, 17, 109, 107, 19)
formsetobject(fObjs.Get_Year,       _DROPDOWNCOMBO, "",           \\
                 iFont5, 138, 105, _DEFAULT, _DEFAULT; _LISTVARS, _ARRAY, Years() )
formsetobject(fObjs.Say_Full_Name,  _CAPTIONRIGHT, "Full Name",   \\
                            iFont2, 17, 143, 104, 14)
```

```
formsetobject(fObjs.Get_Full_Name,    _TEXTBOX,        "",              \\
                                      iFont5, 137, 142, 283, _DEFAULT; _NOTIFY)
formsetobject(fObjs.Say_Composition,  _CAPTIONRIGHT,  "Composition",    \\
                                      iFont2, 18, 179, 104, 16)
formsetobject(fObjs.Get_Composition,  _TEXTBOX,        "",              \\
                                      iFont5, 137, 176, 214, 26)
formsetobject(fObjs.Say_Appellation,  _CAPTIONRIGHT,  "Appellation",    \\
                                      iFont2, 13, 268, _DEFAULT, _DEFAULT)
formsetobject(fObjs.Get_Appellation,  _TEXTBOX,        "",              \\
                                      iFont5, 92, 261, 228, 26)
formsetobject(fObjs.Say_City,         _CAPTIONRIGHT,  "City",           \\
                                      iFont2, 9, 302, 76, 17)
formsetobject(fObjs.Get_City,         _TEXTBOX,        "",              \\
                                      iFont5, 94, 297, 226, 26)
formsetobject(fObjs.Say_State,        _CAPTIONRIGHT,  "State",          \\
                                      iFont2, 13, 334, 72, 16)
formsetobject(fObjs.Get_State,        _TEXTBOX,        "",              \\
                                      iFont5, 92, 328, 55, _DEFAULT)
formsetobject(fObjs.Say_Zip,          _CAPTIONRIGHT,  "Zip",            \\
                                      iFont2, 12, 368, 68, 17)
formsetobject(fObjs.Get_Zip,          _TEXTBOX,        "",              \\
                                      iFont5, 92, 359, 104, _DEFAULT)
formsetobject(fObjs.Say_Country,      _CAPTIONRIGHT,  "Country",        \\
                                      iFont2, 14, 402, 66, 16)
formsetobject(fObjs.Get_Country,      _TEXTBOX,        "USA",           \\
                                      iFont5, 92, 395, 234, 27)
formsetobject(fObjs.Button_Tasted,    _OPTIONBITMAP,  "buttons.bmp",    \\
                   475, 48, _DEFAULT, _DEFAULT; _NOTIFY, 0, 3)
formsetobject(fObjs.Button_Notes,     _BUTTON,        "&Notes on Tasting...", \\
                   474, 105, _DEFAULT, _DEFAULT)
formsetobject(fObjs.Button_Reset,     _BUTTON,        "&Reset Tasted",  \\
                   474, 140, _DEFAULT, _DEFAULT )

formsetobject(fObjs.Say_Quantity,     _CAPTIONRIGHT,  "Quantity",       \\
                                      iFont2, 375, 200, 96, 19)
formsetobject(fObjs.Get_Quantity,     _TEXTBOX,        "0",             \\
                                      iFont5, 488, 195, 77, 26; _NOTIFY)
formsetobject(fObjs.Say_Amount,       _CAPTIONRIGHT,  "Amount Paid",    \\
                                      iFont2, 372, 239, 102, 16)
formsetobject(fObjs.Get_Amount,       _TEXTBOX,        "0.00",          \\
                                      iFont5, 488, 234, 128, 24; _NOTIFY)
formsetobject(fObjs.Say_Retail,       _CAPTIONRIGHT,  "Retail Value",   \\
                                      iFont2, 372, 274, 99, 16)
formsetobject(fObjs.Get_Retail,       _TEXTBOX,        "0.00",          \\
                                      iFont5, 487, 270, 127, 24; _NOTIFY)
formsetobject(fObjs.Say_BinNo,        _CAPTIONRIGHT,  "Bin #",          \\
                                      iFont2, 373, 313, 98, _DEFAULT)
formsetobject(fObjs.Get_BinNo,        _TEXTBOX,        "",              \\
                                      iFont5, 489, 307, 64, 25)
```

```
    formsetobject(fObjs.Say_LotNo,      _CAPTIONRIGHT,  "Lot #",          \\
                                        iFont2, 374, 345, 97, 20)
    formsetobject(fObjs.Get_LotNo,      _TEXTBOX,       "",               \\
                                        iFont5, 488, 341, 67, 25)

    formsetobject(fObjs.Button_Accept,  _BUTTON,        "&Accept",    420, 400,
_DEFAULT, _DEFAULT)
    formsetobject(fObjs.Button_Cancel,  _BUTTON,        "&Cancel",    540, 400,
_DEFAULT, _DEFAULT)

    formsetcolor(_WHITE; _FIELD)
    formsetcolor(_BLACK; _TEXT)
    formmodifyobject(fObjs.Get_WineName, _SETCOLOR )
    formmodifyobject(fObjs.Get_Full_Name, _SETCOLOR )
    formmodifyobject(fObjs.Get_Composition, _SETCOLOR )
    formmodifyobject(fObjs.Get_Appellation, _SETCOLOR )
    formmodifyobject(fObjs.Get_City, _SETCOLOR )
    formmodifyobject(fObjs.Get_State, _SETCOLOR )
    formmodifyobject(fObjs.Get_Zip, _SETCOLOR )
    formmodifyobject(fObjs.Get_WineType, _SETCOLOR )
    formmodifyobject(fObjs.Get_Size, _SETCOLOR )
    formmodifyobject(fObjs.Get_Year, _SETCOLOR )
    formmodifyobject(fObjs.Get_Country, _SETCOLOR )
    formmodifyobject(fObjs.Get_Quantity, _SETCOLOR )
    formmodifyobject(fObjs.Get_Amount, _SETCOLOR )
    formmodifyobject(fObjs.Get_Retail, _SETCOLOR )
    formmodifyobject(fObjs.Get_BinNo, _SETCOLOR )
    formmodifyobject(fObjs.Get_LotNo, _SETCOLOR )

    'Close the fonts
    fontselect(iFont2)
    fontcontrol(_CLOSE)
    fontselect(iFont3)
    fontcontrol(_CLOSE)
    fontselect(iFont4)
    fontcontrol(_CLOSE)
    fontselect(iFont5)
    fontcontrol(_CLOSE)

end proc

proc AssignNamesWine()

    fObjs.Say_WineName    = 10        'TEXT: Wine Name
    fObjs.Say_WineType    = 20        'TEXT: Type
    fObjs.Say_Size        = 30        'TEXT: Size
    fObjs.Say_Year        = 40        'TEXT: Year
    fObjs.Say_Full_Name   = 50        'TEXT: Full Name
    fObjs.Say_Composition = 60        'TEXT: Composition
```

Chapter 5

```
    fObjs.Say_Appellation = 70          'TEXT: Appellation
    fObjs.Say_City         = 80         'TEXT: City
    fObjs.Say_State        = 90         'TEXT: State
    fObjs.Say_Zip          = 100        'TEXT: Zip
    fObjs.Say_Country      = 110        'TEXT: Country
    fObjs.Say_Quantity     = 120        'TEXT: Quantity
    fObjs.Say_Amount       = 130        'TEXT: Amount Paid
    fObjs.Say_Retail       = 140        'TEXT: Retail Value
    fObjs.Say_BinNo        = 150        'TEXT: Bin #
    fObjs.Say_LotNo        = 210        'TEXT: Lot #


    fObjs.GroupBox_160 = 160            'TEXT:   Location of Winery
    fObjs.GroupBox_170 = 170            'TEXT:
    fObjs.GroupBox_500 = 500
    fObjs.Button_Notes  = 180             'TEXT: &Notes on Tasting...
    fObjs.Button_Accept = 190             'TEXT: &Accept
    fObjs.Button_Cancel = 200             'TEXT: &Cancel
    fObjs.Button_Tasted = 220            'TEXT: buttons.bmp

    fObjs.Get_WineName     = 230         'TEXT:
    fObjs.Get_Full_Name    = 240         'TEXT:
    fObjs.Get_Composition  = 250         'TEXT:
    fObjs.Get_Appellation  = 260         'TEXT:
    fObjs.Get_City         = 270         'TEXT:
    fObjs.Get_State        = 280         'TEXT:
    fObjs.Get_Zip          = 290         'TEXT:
    fObjs.Get_WineType     = 310         'TEXT:
    fObjs.Get_Size         = 320         'TEXT:
    fObjs.Get_Year         = 340         'TEXT:
    fObjs.Get_Country      = 300         'TEXT: USA
    fObjs.Get_Quantity     = 350         'TEXT: 0
    fObjs.Get_Amount       = 360         'TEXT: 0.00
    fObjs.Get_Retail       = 370         'TEXT: 0.00
    fObjs.Get_BinNo        = 380         'TEXT:
    fObjs.Get_LotNo        = 390         'TEXT:
    fObjs.Button_Reset     = 400         'TEXT: &Reset Tasted
end proc

proc WineDataEntry( ; iMode )

    AssignNamesWine()
    MakeDataEntryForm_Wine()

    formselect( iForm1 )
    formsetproc( ProcessWineData; _GETFOCUS )
    formcontrol( _SHOW )

end proc
```

```
proc ProcessWineData( aParams )

   local iSelect as integer

   formselect( aParams[ _FORMNUM ] )

   iSelect = aParams( _ITEMNUM )

   if formwait( _PEEK ) = ESC
     ClearWineData()

   else

     select case iSelect
     case fObjs.Button_Cancel            '* Cancel or ESC key
        input "Items to be cleared", INPUT_TITLE ;
        ClearWineData()

     case fObjs.Button_Notes
        if FormObjectValue( fObjs.Button_Tasted )
           input "You can not enter notes on a wine NOT tasted!", INPUT_TITLE ;
        else
           EnterTastedLog()
        end if

     case fObjs.Button_Reset
        formmodifyobject( fObjs.Button_Tasted; 0 )

     case fObjs.Button_Accept
        if Empty( formqstr( fObjs.Get_WineType ) )
           input "You must input a type of wine before you can continue!", INPUT_TITLE ;
           formmodifyobject( fObjs.Get_WineType, _SETFOCUS )

        elseif Empty( formqstr( fObjs.Get_Size ) )
           input "You must enter the size of bottle!", INPUT_TITLE ;
           formmodifyobject( fObjs.Get_Size, _SETFOCUS )

        else
           AddData()
           ClearWineData()

        end if

     case fObjs.Get_WineName
            if formwait( _PEEK ) <> 200   ' THe cancel button was pushed
         if Empty( formqstr( fObjs.Get_WineName ) ) and formwait( _PEEK ) <> 0
            input "You must enter the name of the wine", INPUT_TITLE ;
            formmodifyobject( fObjs.Get_WineName, _SETFOCUS )
```

```
              end if
            end if

        case fObjs.Get_Quantity
          if strtonum( formqstr( fObjs.Get_Quantity ) ) < 0
            if formwait( _PEEK ) <> 0
              input "How can you have a negative number on hand???", INPUT_TITLE ;
              formmodifyobject( fObjs.Get_Quantity, _SETFOCUS )
            end if
          end if

        case fObjs.Get_Amount
          if strtonum( formqstr( fObjs.Get_Amount ) ) < 0
            if formwait( _PEEK ) <> 0
              input "If it was given to you, leave this as 0.00", INPUT_TITLE ;
              formmodifyobject( fObjs.Get_Amount, _SETFOCUS )
            end if
          end if

        case fObjs.Get_Retail
          if strtonum( formqstr( fObjs.Get_Retail ) ) < 0
            if formwait( _PEEK ) <> 0
              input "How can you have a negative retails value?", INPUT_TITLE ;
              formmodifyobject( fObjs.Get_Retail, _SETFOCUS )
            end if
          end if

      end select

   end if

end proc

proc ClearWineData()

   clear AssignNamesWine
   clear MakeDataEntryForm_Wine

   if iLog > 0                  '* Log was created!
     logselect( iLog )
     logcontrol( _CLOSE )
   end if

   formcontrol( _CLOSE )

end proc

run "\realizer\sirius\apps\dfuncs.rlz"
```

```
setsys( _LOADDIR, "\realizer\sirius\apps\" )
setsys( _SIZEMDI, {0,0,0,0} )
WineDataEntry( ; 1 )

'* End of file: DWinedat.rlz
```

One of the first things I added to the source code generated by FormDev is the family called *fRecord* at the top of the file. This holds the basic record structure that will eventually be saved to the disk. Since I declared it at the top of the file, it will be accessible to everything below it. Following this declaration, I also added the procedure named *AddData( )*. This routine will be called when the user clicks on the Accept button and all of the important information is validated. Here, within this routine, the various GET-based objects (those with the *fObjs.Get_* prefix) will be queried, converted (if necessary), and assigned to the various family members in *fRecord*. The function LOGQDATA(), along with the enter variable _LOG_STR, is used to obtain the log's text.

Toward the end of this routine is an INPUT command with the string "Ready to print results." A new parameter, the variable INPUT_TITLE, is passing to this command. This is another user-defined constant that I have created and stored in the *DFuncs.rlz* file. It looks like this:

```
const INPUT_TITLE = "The DECANTER Application"
```

Now, whenever the INPUT command is called, the title bar of the INPUT window will no longer say "CA-Realizer Input," but will now say "The DECANTER Application."

> **Note:** Be aware of various input screens and the context of the objects in the window and the text in the title bar. Some have Realizer default strings.

Following the INPUT command, a series of PRINT commands display the contents of the *fRecord* family.

```
input "Ready to print results", INPUT_TITLE ;
print fRecord.WineName,     fRecord.WineType,      fRecord.WineSize
print fRecord.WineYear,     fRecord.FullName,      fRecord.Composition
print fRecord.Appellation,  fRecord.WineCity,      fRecord.WineState
print fRecord.WineZip,      fRecord.WineCountry,   fRecord.Notes
print fRecord.Quantity,     fRecord.Amount,        fRecord.Retail
print fRecord.BinNumber,    fRecord.LotNumber
```

The next routine in this modified file is the *EditTastedLog()* procedure. This routine will be called if the log that is open and selected and associated with this routine is closed. In that case, the contents of the log need to be stored to the appropriate family member in *fRecord*. Here, the LOGQDATA() function is called again just prior to the LOGCONTROL() function with the `_CLOSE` internal variable.

The *EnterTastedLog()* procedure is called if the Tasted/Not Tasted push button object on the form is activated and given focus. Here, it first checks to see if the value of *iLog* is greater than 0. If it is, the procedure assumes that the log is currently open and probably in the background. In this case, it is selected and brought forward for user input. This is the type of cross-checking that the programmer must do in MDI (multiple document interface) forms. The document we need may already be open but in background, in which case, a new log is not needed. Now, if the value of the variable *iLog*, initialized at the top of this file, is equal to or less than 0, then a new log is created with the LOGNEW() function. The font to be used with this log is also modified and the procedure *EditTastedLog()* is then assigned to the log via the LOGSETPROC() function.

The next line of code troubleshoots a potential problem:

```
print #iLog; fRecord.Notes
```

What if an end user closes the log in the form and then wants to reopen the log? The information previously stored in the log is not attached to the new log, and the value of *iLog* will be lost when the old log is closed and the new log opened using the LOGNEW() function. In essence, the information stored to the *fRecord.Notes* variable needs to get into the log before it is ready for edit. The PRINT command allows us to direct the text found in the variable *fRecord.Notes* to the appropriate log. This "appropriate log" is held in the variable *iLog*, which holds the pointer the new log created by the LOGNEW() function. Since the variable *fRecord.Notes* is initially set to a NULL string byte, the contents of the log when it is first opened up is a blank screen. Since the *EditTestedLog()* function stores the contents of the log back to this variable when the log is closed, it is safe to say that when the log is reopened, the contents of the old log, held directly in the *fRecord.Notes* variable, will be seen.

In the *MakeDataEntryForm_Wine()* function itself, the names of the family members for the various objects on the screen are modified and given uniformity. For example, the `_TEXTBOX` and `_CAPTIONRIGHT` objects that deal with the name of the wine have the same suffixes, while the prefix for the family is slightly different:

```
fObjs.Say_WineName
fObjs.Get_WineName
```

This is a carryover from my Clipper days in which there were SAYs and GETs (the GETs allowed the end user to enter information on the screen). Typically, each GET had an associated SAY (otherwise, an end user would not know what he was looking at). The numeric values for these family members are assigned in the procedure *AssignNamesWine()*. On each assignment, the given comment line with the string "TEXT:" remains.

The *WineDatEntry()* function builds the family members and the data-entry form and sets the entire operation in motion. It also assigns the procedure *ProcessWineDat()* to the form. This procedure takes the parameter *aParams[]*, as passed from Realizer to the form, whenever a key press or mouse click is detected. There are eleven elements found in the variable *aParams[]* and it can have, as an element pointer, any one of the values listed in Table 5-2 (page 251).

If the internal variable `_USEREALIZER` is used in conjunction with the array passed as a parameter, this position will have special meaning. For example, in the preceding `DWineDat.rlz` code, one of these options is used in the procedure attached to the log:

```
proc EditTastedLog( aParams )

  logselect( aParams[_ITEMNUM], aParams[_FORMNUM] )

aParams[_USEREALIZER] = 0
fRecord.Notes      = logqdata( _LOG_STR )
logcontrol( _CLOSE )
iLog = 0

end proc
```

Here, the value of `_USEREALIZER` at this element position is set to 0. This internal variable allows for an alternative behavior to take place based on the type of tool procedure in control. In essence, the tool will not be closed even though the log is. If the value of 1 is passed to this value, then the tool is closed as well. However, if this were a help procedure, the value of a 0 for the `_USERREALIZER` position would tell Realizer not to display its help. If the value is a 1, then Realizer's help will be displayed.

If the `_ITEMNUM` internal variable is used with the array, the value returned at the element position can be any one of three values: −1 (no item was selected), 1 (user pressed ENTER in active form), or 2 (user pressed ESC in active form).

And like the `_ITEMNUM` internal variable, the `_INVOKE` value can return any of the following constants:

`_INVOKE` Constant Value	Definition
`_CHANGE`	Generated when the user either changes the value of a cell in a spreadsheet object or selects a new object in a list box that has the `_NOTIFY` internal variable.
`_CLICK`	Yielded on various actions, depending on the tool in use
`_CLOSE`	Yielded when user attempts to close a tool
`_CUSTOM`	Yielded by custom controls
`_CUSTOMNOW`	Yielded by custom controls
`_DRAGNDROP`	Yielded when a draggable object is moved onto a drag-received object or form.
`_GETFOCUS`	Yielded when a tool window becomes the topmost window, or when an object in a form receives input focus.
`_MIDDLECLICK`	Yielded when an object in a form is selected by pressing the middle mouse button.
`_RIGHTCLICK`	Yielded when an object in a form is selected by pressing the right mouse button.
`_SIZE`	Yielded when the tool window is resized.

The purpose of the SELECT CASE code construct within the *ProcessWineData()* procedure is to evaluate the contents of objects with the `_NOTIFY` internal variable (such as the name of the winery, the amount ordered, and so on), when input focus is moved off the object.

```
case fObjs.Get_Quantity
   if strtonum( formqstr( fObjs.Get_Quantity ) ) < 0
     if formwait( _PEEK ) <> 0
       input "How can you have a negative number on hand???", INPUT_TITLE ;
       formmodifyobject( fObjs.Get_Quantity, _SETFOCUS )
     end if
   end if
```

More Complex Forms and User Interface

For example, if focus was removed from the *fObjs.Get_Quantity* object, and if the value of the object, when converted from string to numeric, is less than 0, then an appropriate INPUT message is displayed to the screen, warning the end user of the problem. When that warning message is acknowledged, control is returned to the appropriate object on the form, using both the FORMMODIFYOBJECT() function and the `_SETFOCUS` internal variable.

Some of the objects do not work like a typical `_CAPTION` box. For example, with regard to the `_DROPDOWNLIST` objects, verification needs to come from the Accept button on the form.

```
case fObjs.Button_Accept
  if Empty( formqstr( fObjs.Get_WineType ) )
    input "You must input a type of wine before you can continue!", INPUT_TITLE ;
    formmodifyobject( fObjs.Get_WineType, _SETFOCUS )

  elseif Empty( formqstr( fObjs.Get_Size ) )
    input "You must enter the size of bottle!", INPUT_TITLE ;
    formmodifyobject( fObjs.Get_Size, _SETFOCUS )

  else
    AddData()
    ClearWineData()

  end if
```

Here, the values in the *fObjs.Get_WineType* and *fObjs.Get_Size* objects are tested if focus is given to the *fObjs.Button_Accept* object. After the appropriate tests are made, messages are displayed if applicable, and focus is returned to the form and to those objects if necessary.

Passwords

Most applications require some sort of a password either to get into the system or to perform certain operations within the application. Everyone has a different idea of what a password entry point should look like; however, most have a few characteristics in common. For example, the password characters, as they are being entered by the end user, do not appear. Instead of the actual letters of the password, asterisks are displayed.

This technique is shown in the next example. Here, the entry field held by the `_TEXTBOX` object will be hidden, while on top of it, the `_CAPTIONLEFT` object will be displayed. In addition, the unique notion about this example program, named *Pass.rlz*, is that it mixes both a loop (modal) and the FORMSETPROC() (modeless) techniques.

```
'* Application ... : Pass.rlz
'* Authors ....... : Steve Straley
'* Notice ........ : Copyright(c) 1994 - Sirius Press, Inc.
'* ............... : All Rights Reserved
'* Date .......... : January 1, 1994
'* Description ... : The shows how a password input box can be created
'*

proc PassWordProc( aParams )

  formselect( aParams[_FORMNUM])
  select case aParams[_ITEMNUM]
  case 2
       formcontrol(_CLOSE)
  case 1
       formcontrol(_CLOSE)
       input "User entered "+chr$(34)+cPassword + chr$(34)+".", "Password";
  end select

end proc

iPassWordLength = 0
iPassWordForm   = formqunique

formnew(iPassWordForm; "Enter Password:", _TITLE+_SIZE+_CLOSE+_HOTCLICK)
formcontrol(_SIZE;_CENTER,_CENTER,.3,.2)

formsetobject(1,_BUTTON, "OK",            _LEFT,  _BOTTOM)
formsetobject(2,_BUTTON, "Cancel",        _RIGHT, _BOTTOM)
formsetobject(10,_TEXTBOX,"",0,0)
formsetobject(20,_CAPTIONLEFT,"",20,15,170,16)
formsetobject(30,_GROUPBOX, "", 18,13,180,20 )
formmodifyobject(30,_SENDBEHIND)
formmodifyobject(10,_HIDE)
formmodifyobject(10,_SETFOCUS)

formsetproc(PassWordProc)
formcontrol(_SHOW)

'* Main Looping part.....

loop

  if formwait(_PEEK) = 1 or formwait( _PEEK) =2 then
    exit loop
  end if

  cPassword  = formqstr(10)
  iNewLength = len(cPassword)
```

```
   if iNewlength <> iPassWordLength then
     iPassWordLength = iNewLength
     formmodifyobject(20, _SHOW, string$(iPassWordLength,42))
   end if

end loop

'* End of File: Pass.rlz
```

At the top of the file is the procedure that will be attached to the form. This procedure will be called automatically. The only action that will take place in this procedure will be if the value of the parameter *aParams[_ITEMNUM]* is equal to 1 or 2. These values can be seen within the form definition itself. They represent the objects in the form. If, for example, the object that has an ID of 1 is selected, the form will be closed via the _CLOSE internal variable with the FORMCONTROL() function, and the INPUT command will be called, showing the contents of the variable *cPassword* in the middle of this dialog box. The CHR$(34) funtion will place quotation marks around the value of the *cPassword* variable.

Following this, the variable *iPassWordLength* is set to a value of 0, and a new form ID value is obtained with the FORMQUNIQUE command. The *iPassWordLength* variable will be used within the control LOOP towards the bottom of the file. There, the LEN() of the password variable *cPassword* is stored to the *iPassWordLength* variable which is in turn, used with the STRING$() function to, in essence, replicate a series of asterisks (ASCII value 42) to the screen. This will become clearer as we step through the rest of the code.

When the form is created with the FORMNEW() function and the size of the form is controlled and adjusted, five objects are placed in the form. Two of the objects are simple: an OK button and a CANCEL button.

```
formsetobject(1,_BUTTON, "OK", _LEFT, _BOTTOM)
formsetobject(2,_BUTTON, "Cancel", _RIGHT, _BOTTOM)
```

These objects have ID values of 1 and 2—the same ID values tested for in the procedure *PassWordProc()* at the top of the file and attached to this form. The three remaining objects on the form are a bit trickier. One object is the actual data-entry point for the password. This is handled by the _TEXTBOX internal variable:

```
formsetobject(10,_TEXTBOX,"",0,0)
```

Because the object will be hidden via the FORMMODIFYOBJECT() function, the location of this object in the form is not very important, although you may want to limit the size of the data-entry point:

```
formmodifyobject(10,_HIDE)
formmodifyobject(10,_SETFOCUS)
```

Clearly, the control is given to this object (the one marked off with an ID value of 10). In addition, the object is hidden via the internal variable `_HIDE`. So, when characters are typed, they will not appear on the screen, since the data-entry `_TEXTBOX` is set to `_HIDE`.

Also in the form is the object that will display the asterisks that represent the password obtained in object number 10. This object, numbered 20, is a `_CAPTIONLEFT` object, and the area within the form is restricted:

```
formsetobject(20,_CAPTIONLEFT,"",20,15,170,16)
```

This object will be used in the main LOOP following the form definition. To add even more visual flair to this form, you can add a framed box for the asterisks. This can be accomplished by building another group box object in the form.

```
formsetobject(30,_GROUPBOX, "", 18,13,180,20 )
```

Of course, this object will obscure anything behind it. Therefore, you must send the `_GROUPBOX` object to the background so that only the line shows and not the contents of the box (which is a blank area). The `_CAPTIONLEFT` object will reside nicely on top of the group box. To do this sending-back operation, the FORMMODIFYOBJECT() function needs to be called one more time:

```
formmodifyobject(30,_SENDBEHIND)
```

The only form definitions needed following this will be to attach the procedure *PassWordProc()* to the form and to `_SHOW` the form on the screen. Once this is out of the way, the main processing LOOP (or the modal part of this example) can be coded. Here, the FORMWAIT() function is used to `_PEEK` to see whether the ENTER or ESC keys were pressed or if either one of the button objects (1 or 2) were pressed. If so, then the EXIT LOOP command takes over and throws us out of the LOOP once the *PassWordProc()* function finishes its operation, which either closes the form or closes the form and displays the contents of the *cPassWord* variable in an INPUT command (at the top of the file).

Within the LOOP, the string contents of object number 10 (which is the `_TEXTBOX` object) is obtained and stored to the *cPassword* variable. This is the variable that appears in the INPUT command attached to the form via the *PassWordProc()* routine. The length of that string, *cPassword*, is then stored to the variable *iNewLength*. Within the LOOP, the IF command tests to see whether the value of *iNewLength* is not equal to the value of *iPassWordLength*. The two values will not be equal if there has been a change in the variable *cPassWord* at any time, either via the `BACKSPACE` key pressed to remove an item from the `_TEXTBOX` or any other character key. If the contents of the variable *cPassWord* should change, then so should the length of that variable, and this is the reason for the test. If there is a change, addition or deletion, then the two variables, the old and the new variable length, will not be the same. Then, the value of *iNewLength* will be assigned to *iPassWordLength* (for the next pass through the loop), and the contents of object number 20 (`_CAPTIONLEFT` object), are then redisplayed via the `_SHOW` internal variable, taking the value of the STRING$( ) function. This function merely replicates ASCII value 42 (which is an asterisk), for the length of the value in *iPassWordLength*. This process repeats until either the OK or Cancel buttons are activated, or the `ENTER` or `ESC` keys are pressed.

Conclusion

Everything, in essence, is a form, and how we manipulate between them, how they maintain focus, how we control the flow of information between tool and procedure, is vital. Logs, hidden forms, hidden objects within forms, and other Windows-related items all come into play when working within the Realizer environment and with a form. It is not so much the notion of doing one thing within the flow of an application, which, in turn, evokes a reaction; rather, it is the notion of having one, two, or several forms working within an environment. Die-hard procedural programmers will have a difficult time adjusting to the concept of an application being built on forms and the way the Realizer environment passes information from form to attached procedure, and then back again. Some argue that this suggests the avoidance of the GOTO command, which implies direct programmer control (as opposed to end-user control and environmental conditions) as well as leads down a path of unstructured, spaghetti-like application code. Barring those two arguments, the GOTO command is the exact opposite of the necessary thinking process for creating active forms, objects, and associated subroutines. Using FormDev will get us only part of the way there, but it does nothing to teach or retrain how our minds should look at application development and the pieces of the puzzle when building such an application.

Chapter 6

Boards, Charts, and Sheets

In this chapter, we will look at some specialized forms and user-interface devices. These items may not appear in every application; however, it is important to know how to work with them, and where in an application they might appear. Every item in every language has a purpose. Some functions and features have more broad-range appeal and as such, appear in many applications. However, there are other features and items that are not only more specific, but more functional in limited ways. Just because something is defined to work in a more narrowed scope does not detract from its usefulness.

Boards

A board is a grid or a table. Within the Realizer language, boards are similar to items such as charts and spreadsheets, but when we look at the other items, we will begin to see the difference. For now, however, think of a board as a grid-like tool used to display families and arrays of data. In the following example, we can see that a series of records is stored to five variables, *fRecord1*, *fRecord2*, *fRecord3*, *fRecord4*, and *fRecord5*, each record containing similar pieces of information:

	The Winery	Type	Vintage
fRecord1	Rodney Strong	Chardonnay	1991
fRecord2	Schug	Pinot Noir	1989
fRecord3	Beringer	Cabernet Sauv	1990
fRecord4	Ridge 1991	Merlot	1991
fRecord5	Whitewood	Petite Sirah	1992

As a matter of fact, the structure of the variables is identical, which suggests that a board is a little less flexible than some other items in what types of data it can receive. A board has two sections: the window itself and the client area that will be used by the various rows and columns. In the preceding example, the window and the client region are the same size.

In the following example, we've enlarged the window to make the distinction between the two more pronounced:

	The Winery	Type	Vintage
fRecord1	Rodney Strong	Chardonnay	1991
fRecord2	Schug	Pinot Noir	1989
fRecord3	Beringer	Cabernet Sauv	1990
fRecord4	Ridge 1991	Merlot	1991
fRecord5	Whitewood	Petite Sirah	1992

To create a board, we use the BOARDNEW( ) function. When created, it becomes the current and selected board on which all subsequent board-like operations will take place:

```
iBoard = boardnew( boardqunique, fDisplay, fRecord1, fRecord2, \\
                                 fRecord3, fRecord4, fRecord5 )
```

The BOARDQUNIQUE function creates a new board ID number. As you can see in the title bar of the preceding illustration, numbering starts off with numeric 1 (the number following the string "Board" is the board's ID value unless specified otherwise). The return value of the BOARDNEW( ) function will be the value of BOARDQUNIQUE, since that is the first parameter in this function. We could have programmed this line as follows:

```
iBoard = boardnew( 10, fDisplay, fRecord1, fRecord2, fRecord3, fRecord4, \\
                                 fRecord5 )
```

Here, the constant 10 is used as this board's ID value, which is passed to the variable *iBoard*. Or, we could have programmed this board the following way:

```
iBoard = boardqunique
boardnew( iBoard, fDisplay, fRecord1, fRecord2, fRecord3, fRecord4, fRecord5 )
```

Use whichever technique is easier to understand; they are all perfectly acceptable.

The BOARDNEW( ) function's second parameter is a variable holding a family of information. This family consists of four basic items. The first item holds a listing of the items to be displayed in the columns of the board. The code might look something like this:

```
fDisplay.member = { "", "Winery", "Style", "Year" }
```

Here, the family item called *fDisplay.member* holds an array. This array references the various family members attached to the board. So, for example, the first column will contain no family reference, the second column will refer to a member called "Winery," the third column will refer to all members called "Style," and so on.

Let's look at the structure of a family that is to be displayed in this board:

```
fRecord5.Winery       = "Whitewood"
fRecord5.Style        = "Petite Sirah"
fRecord5.Year         = 1992
fRecord5.FullName     = ""
fRecord5.County       = "Santa Maria"
fRecord5.State        = "CA"
fRecord5.Country      = "USA"
```

We can see that the first three items to the variable called *fRecord5* are named "Winery," "Style," and "Year." Each data record that is attached to this board must have these names for the various family members. The name of the root variable, *fRecord5*, is not as important as the names of the family members. So the second parameter passed to the BOARDNEW() function must have a structure that tells the board which family members to display in the columns.

After the first item holding reference to the various columns is created, the second parameter to the BOARDNEW() function can stop there; however, there are three other items that can be attached to that family structure. The second item will hold yet another array, this one consisting of the column titles, or field names. If not specified, then the name of the family members will be used in the column. In our example, the column title values are different from the family member values, so the structure of the variable *fDisplay* now looks like this:

```
fDisplay.member = { "", "Winery", "Style", "Year" }
fDisplay.title  = { "", "The Winery", "Type", "Vintage" }
```

> **Note:** There must be a one-to-one relationship between the *.Member* items and the *.Title* items. Otherwise, a run-time error will be generated.

Boards, Charts, and Sheets

We'll look at the two other members of the *fDisplay* family structure in a moment, but first let's examine the next parameter.

The third and subsequent parameters passed to the BOARDNEW() function constitute a list of the board's family variables. Beginning with the third parameter and continuing on until all of the family members have been added, each variable will be passed as a unique parameter. The name of the variable used to hold the family to be displayed in the board will be the name of the family. For example, in the preceding example, the variables *fRecord1*, *fRecord2*, *fRecord3*, *fRecord4*, and *fRecord5* are the headings for the individual rows.

Turning back to the *fDisplay.member* variable, the first element in the stored array is a NULL string (" "). This corresponds with the area used by the names of the variables for the individual rows. In this source file, named `Board1.rlz`, the building of the five variables looks something like this:

```
'* Record 1
fRecord1.Winery   = "Rodney Strong"
fRecord1.Style    = "Chardonnay"
fRecord1.Year     = 1991
fRecord1.FullName = "Chalk Hill Estates"
fRecord1.County   = "Sonoma"
fRecord1.State    = "CA"
fRecord1.Country  = "USA"

'* Record 2
fRecord2.Winery   = "Schug"
fRecord2.Style    = "Pinot Noir"
fRecord2.Year     = 1989
fRecord2.FullName = "Napa Valley Pinot Noir (Heinemann Vineyard)"
fRecord2.County   = "Napa Helena"
fRecord2.State    = "CA"
fRecord2.Country  = "USA"

'* Record 3
fRecord3.Winery      = "Beringer"
fRecord3.Style       = "Cabernet Sauvignon"
fRecord3.Year        = 1990
fRecord3.FullName    = "Knights Valley - Proprietor Grown"
fRecord3.County      = "St. Helena"
fRecord3.State       = "CA"
fRecord3.Country     = "USA"

'* Record 4
fRecord4.Winery   = "Ridge 1991"
fRecord4.Style    = "Merlot"
fRecord4.Year     = 1991
```

```
fRecord4.FullName          = "Santa Cruz Mountains"
fRecord4.County            = "Cupertino"
fRecord4.State             = "CA"
fRecord4.Country           = "USA"

'* Record 5
fRecord5.Winery            = "Whitewood"
fRecord5.Style             = "Petite Sirah"
fRecord5.Year              = 1992
fRecord5.FullName          = ""
fRecord5.County            = "Santa Maria"
fRecord5.State             = "CA"
fRecord5.Country           = "USA"
```

As we can see, each variable has the same member structure. The only thing remaining will be the BOARDCONTROL( ) function and the `_SHOW` internal variable that displays this board to the screen.

Boards, Level 2

We can build on the first example to show how the board might look with a couple of other variations. For example, we need to remove the names of the variables displayed in the first column of the board. In addition, we need to change the name displayed in the title bar of the board's window. Also, why not add a couple of the other family members from the various variables and, while we're at it, adjust the size of both the window and the board.

To add a title to the window's title bar, we add a new modifier to the BOARDNEW( ) function: a string containing the title:

```
fDisplay.member = { "Winery", "Style", "Year", "County" }
fDisplay.title  = { "The Winery", "Type", "Vintage", "Appellation" }
fDisplay.layout = _NOFAMILYHEADERS

iBoard = boardnew( boardqunique, fDisplay, fRecord1, fRecord2, fRecord3, \\
                                 fRecord4, fRecord5 ; "Second Board!")
```

This string will appear in the title bar of the board window:

The Winery	Type	Vintage	Appellation
Rodney Strong	Chardonnay	1991	Sonoma
Schug	Pinot Noir	1989	Napa Helena
Beringer	Cabernet Sauv	1990	St. Helena
Ridge 1991	Merlot	1991	Cupertino
Whitewood	Petite Sirah	1992	Santa Maria

Second Board!

We can remove the names of the family variables from the board by adding the internal variable _NOFAMILYHEADERS to the family structure of *fDisplay* and removing the extra NULL byte ("") from both arrays held by *fDisplay.member* and *fDisplay.title*. The problem remains, then, to allow the end to resize the window without affecting the columns and rows of the board. To remove resizing as an option, we need to add another modifier to the BOARDNEW( ) function:

```
iBoard = boardnew( boardqunique, fDisplay, fRecord1, fRecord2, fRecord3, \\
                   fRecord4, fRecord5 ; "Second Board!", _FRAME)
```

The _FRAME internal variable removes the title bar and the maximize and minimize icons from the window and surrounds the columns and rows—the data-entry area—with a thick frame:

The Winery	Type	Vintage	Appellation
Rodney Strong	Chardonnay	1991	Sonoma
Schug	Pinot Noir	1989	Napa Helena
Beringer	Cabernet Sauv	1990	St. Helena
Ridge 1991	Merlot	1991	Cupertino
Whitewood	Petite Sirah	1992	Santa Maria

The trouble with this arrangement is that the window cannot be moved or closed. However, it is an option. In a few moments, we'll explore some other options for restricting the size of both the board and the window.

Turning back to the third member in the variable *fDisplay*, we can alter the display of the board by flipping, or transposing, the layout of the rows and columns. By default, each row is a new family variable, but in the program *Board3.rlz*, this setup is reversed via the following instruction:

```
fDisplay.layout = _NOFAMILYHEADERS + _FAMILYCOLWISE
```

The summation of the two internal variables yields the following display:

	Second Board!				
The Winery	Rodney Strong	Schug	Beringer	Ridge 1991	Whitewood
Type	Chardonnay	Pinot Noir	Cabernet Sauv	Merlot	Petite Sirah
Vintage	1991	1989	1990	1991	1992
Appellation	Sonoma	Napa Helena	St. Helena	Cupertino	Santa Maria

Note that the titles of the rows (columns, in the previous illustrations) are in bold lettering. Another effect of transposing the rows and columns has to do with a highlighting technique. A special procedure (outlined in a moment) allows the end user to highlight an entire data record at once. For example, in the default mode, where each data record occupies a row, the user can point to a row of information and highlight it with one click. But when we flip the order of the rows and the columns, the highlighting mechanism alters. You still select an entire record, but now each record occupies a column.

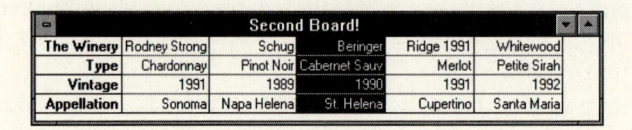

Second Board!				
The Winery	Rodney Strong	Schug	Beringer	Ridge 1991	Whitewood
Type	Chardonnay	Pinot Noir	Cabernet Sauv	Merlot	Petite Sirah
Vintage	1991	1989	1990	1991	1992
Appellation	Sonoma	Napa Helena	St. Helena	Cupertino	Santa Maria

The location of the board is also critical. Using the BOARDCONTROL( ) function, we can set the board's row and column pixel locations. For example, the following instruction:

```
boardcontrol( _SIZE; 55,130 )
```

would place the board 55 pixels in from the left edge of the screen and 130 pixels down from the top. If we want to control the width of the viewing area, we can add two more modifiers:

```
boardcontrol( _SIZE; 55, 130, 400, _DEFAULT )
```

When only one value for each pairing is specified, the `_DEFAULT` internal variable is necessary in order for the third modifier to be recognized. In other words, without the `_DEFAULT` internal variable, any specific value will be considered as "default." When a narrower window is displayed, the window may be enlarged to expose more of the board on the screen, provided that the sizing frame is turned on, and that there is enough physical space on the screen. As discussed earlier, the size of the window can be restricted. The `_SIZETRACK` internal variable allows us to set minimums and maximums to prevent the window from going too far in any direction.

```
iWindowWidth = 465

iBoard = boardnew( boardqunique, fDisplay, fRecord1, fRecord2, fRecord3, \\
                                  fRecord4, fRecord5 ; "Second Board!")
boardcontrol( _SIZE; 55,130, iWindowWidth, _DEFAULT )
boardcontrol( _SIZETRACK; iWindowWidth, 150, iWindowWidth, 160 )
```

Here, the variable *iWindowWidth* holds the basic width of the size of the window, and also restricts the window from being resized vertically. The first modifier in the second BOARDCONTROL( ) function determines the minimum width for the board's window. The third modifier sets the maximum width for the board's window. Both values are expressed in pixels.

> **Note:** Even with minimum and maximum values set to the width (or height) of a board's window, the default start-up size will be maximum width and height, unless there is not enough row or column information in the board, in which case the window will adjust to the size of the board and its contents.

With these settings, we can specify a frame and a title bar without fear of the window restricting the view of the contents of the board.

Modeless Boards

Boards are like forms, in that procedures may be attached to an active board. And like forms, an array that is automatically passed to the attached procedure holds additional information about how the procedure was activated, which board was activated, and what mouse click took place. A variation of the SETPROC idea is used with the board syntax:

```
boardsetproc( boardtest; _SIZE )
```

The _SIZE internal variable is optional and tells the attached procedure if there is a resizing movement within the board's frame. Other than that, the procedure *BoardTest()* is now attached to the currently selected and active form. To remove this association, the BOARDSETPROC() function needs to be called without any parameters.

Within the *BoardTest()* procedure, we can test for a variety of conditions, including what process was used to invoke the procedure and which form was selected in conjunction with the board. With boards, a second parameter is automatically passed to the procedure by the Realizer environment. This second parameter is a reference to the family that was selected within the board. This means that the end user can click on any of the rows or columns, and the associated variable that holds that family's display is then passed, by reference, to the attached procedure.

```
proc BoardTest( aParams, fSelected )

  boardselect( aParams[ _ITEMNUM ] )
```

```
    if aParams( _INVOKE ) = _CLICK
      input qvar( fSelected, _NAME ) ;
    else
      input numtostr( aParams( _INVOKE ) ) ;
    end if

end proc
```

The parameter *fSelected* holds the name of the family variable passed. In our current board, for example, if the first column of information is clicked on, the *fRecord1* family variable is automatically passed to the *BoardTest()* procedure via the second parameter, which is used in conjunction with the QVAR( ) function to tell us the name of that variable. The following will then appear in the INPUT dialog screen:

[CA-Realizer Input dialog showing "fRecord1" with OK button]

Also in this screen is an extra test that engages if there is no selection on a column (or row, depending on how the board is laid out). For example, if the _SIZE modifier is passed to the BOARDSETPROC( ) function, the procedure attached will be notified when the board's window is resized. This is not a row or a column selection; therefore, the value of _INVOKE will not be that of _CLICK. In this case, the ELSE condition takes over and displays the value of _INVOKE in the INPUT window. Resizing the window yields a value of 4; closing the window yields a value of 1. The attached procedure may test for both values.

Turning our attention back to the variable holding the selected family's name, it is important to remember that these variables are passed by reference, which means that we do not need to know the name of the variable directly—only the names of the individual family members. In this case, the parameter called within the *BoardTest()* procedure is the variable *fSelected*, which contains several members, including "Winery," "Style," and "Year." Each of these items may be adjusted:

```
if aParams( _INVOKE ) = _CLICK
  input qvar( fSelected, _NAME ) ;
  fSelected.year   = 1900
```

```
    fSelected.Winery = "Sirius Wines!"
else
  input numtostr( aParams( _INVOKE ) ) ;
end if
```

Here, two of the displayed family members have been modified. Regardless of which column (or row, depending on which side is up) is selected by the mouse, the "year" is now set to 1900, and the name of the winery has been adjusted to "Sirius Wines!" However, adjusting the contents of a family is not the end of the story. The active and associated board is not informed of these changes to the listed family members. Therefore, the board must be "updated" via the BOARDUPDATE() function. Here, the name of the variable holding the updated reference is passed to this function:

```
boardupdate( fSelected )
```

Once this function is called, the board will be updated with new values. Additional features may be attached to the board. For example, let's say we click on a family within the board. This initially tells the board to open up a new row (or column) for another family. The currently highlighted row (or column) is adjusted to this new family, which is added to the board via the BOARDUPDATE() function just as if it existed originally. Then, the selected family is "blanked out," giving the impression that data may now be added. The following code will show this in action:

```
proc BoardTest( aParams, fSelected )

  boardselect( aParams[ _ITEMNUM ] )

  if aParams( _INVOKE ) = _CLICK

    if qvar( fData1, _DEFINED )    '* this is a special case

      input qvar( fSelected, _NAME ) ;

    else
      '* Move the data
      fData1.winery   = fSelected.winery
      fData1.year     = fSelected.year
      fData1.style    = fSelected.style
      fData1.FullName = fSelected.FullName
      fData1.County   = fSelected.county
      fData1.State    = fSelected.State
      fData1.Country  = fSelected.Country
      '* Blank out existing data
```

```
            fSelected.winery    = "Sirius Wines!"
            fSelected.year      = 1900
            fSelected.style     = ""
            fSelected.FullName  = "Sirius Press"
            fSelected.county    = ""
            fSelected.State     = "CA"
            fSelected.Country   = "USA"

            boardupdate( fSelected, fData1 )

        end if

    else

        input numtostr( aParams( _INVOKE ) ) ;

    end if

end proc
```

In this attached procedure, the first test after the mouse click has been detected determines whether the variable *fData1* is defined. On the first pass, this variable is not defined; therefore, the IF condition will fail, causing the *fData1* variable to be defined. In this section of the code, values from the passed parameter *fSelected* are then moved to the newly created *fData1* variable. The individual members within the family variable *fData1* have the same names as all the other families listed in this board. Once the data is moved from the *fSelected* family variable to the *fData1* variable, the values in the *fSelected* family are modified.

> **Note:** Individual items within a family may be modified in attached, or "lower," subroutines if the family is passed by reference. Any adjustment made to a family member in these subroutines will be reflected in the family in the calling routine. This is what is meant by a "calling sequence."

After all the information in the *fSelected* variable has been adjusted, the BOARDUPDATE( ) function is called. Here, the *fSelected* variable is passed to the function (which will refresh the contents of that associated row), and so is the new variable *fData1*. When this function is called, the new family will suddenly appear in the board.

Boards, Charts, and Sheets

> **Note:** When a new family is added to a board, the window is not automatically resized to fit the new constraints brought in by the new family. The BOARDCONTROL() function needs to be called in order to adjust the size.

Also, keep in mind that if the BOARDUPDATE( ) function is called without any parameters like this:

```
boardcontrol()
```

then all of the families within the board will be automatically updated. This does not mean that a new family is suddenly added to the board. That will take place only when the variable holding the family is referenced as a parameter to this function.

If a mouse click is detected a second time within this attached procedure, the variable *fData1* is now defined, and, the QVAR( ) function, along with the _DEFINED internal variable, will return a true value. This will cause the INPUT command to display the name of the family that is being "selected." However, the size of the window still needs to be adjusted, either in advance by the end-user, or within the attached procedure. This example program file, named `Board4.rlz`, illustrates an easy way to enlarge the window:

```
fDisplay.member = { "Winery", "Style", "Year", "County" }
fDisplay.title  = { "The Winery", "Type", "Vintage", "Appellation" }
fDisplay.layout = _NOFAMILYHEADERS

iWindowWidth  = 465
iWindowLength = 150

iBoard = boardnew( boardqunique, fDisplay, fRecord1, fRecord2, fRecord3, fRecord4, \\
                        fRecord5 ; "Second Board!")

boardcontrol( _SIZE; 55,130, iWindowWidth, iWindowLength )
boardcontrol( _SIZETRACK; iWindowWidth, iWindowlength, iWindowWidth, iWindowlength + 100 )
boardsetproc( boardtest; _SIZE )
```

The sizes of the window and board are set in advance to be bigger than really necessary, thus allowing for the potential of a family to be added to the board. Eventually, once the new family is added to the board and a row is reselected, the display of the program might look something like this:

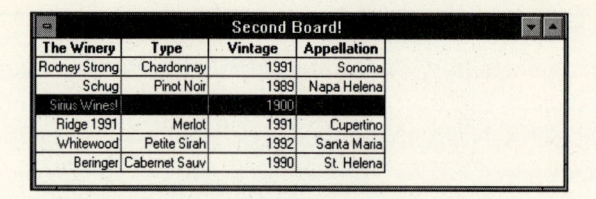

In this picture, the mouse cursor was on the third row. That information was then shifted to the last and newly added row in the board, and the adjusted information for this family redisplayed within the highlighted region. If the mouse button is clicked again, the following message will be displayed:

Since the variable *fData1* is now defined, the INPUT command will take effect. These are just some of the ways in which boards may be used, but remember: Boards provide just one possible solution for displaying records of information. They are convenient for small amounts of data, but the more families that are added, the more adjustments within the board, the window, and the attached procedure will be needed.

Charts

A chart is just another form, but it is a special form, complex with variations and possibilities. In this first example, we'll show how forms and charts can work side by side. If we think of a form as the point of reference between the program and the end user, then the chart is just a vehicle to show information.

To start, the first example program, named *Chart1.rlz*, simply puts a chart and a form next to one another, as shown in Figure 6-1.

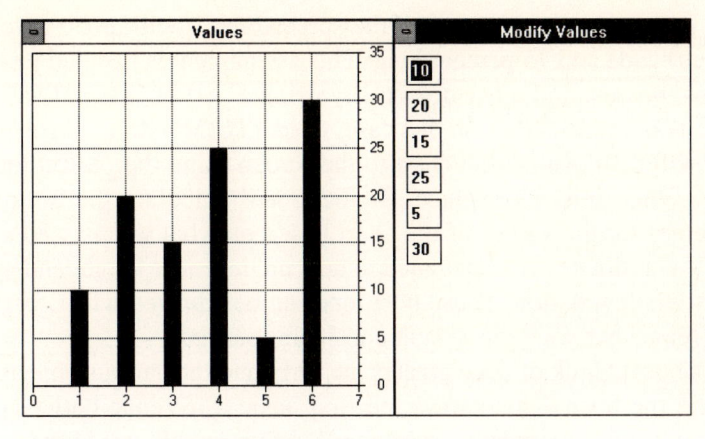

Figure 6-1. Chart with six values to be modified.

```
aValues = {10,20,15,25,5,30}          '* HOLDS THE GOLBAL VALUE

'*  Proc         TESTCHART()
'*  Params       Array of values
'*  Returns      Not used
'*  Purpose      To process the attached form

proc TestChart( aParams )

end proc

'****** [ CREATE the CHART..... ] *******

chartnew( 10; "Values", _TITLE )
chartbar( aValues;15 )
chartcontrol( _SIZE; _LEFT, _TOP, 50 pct, 75 pct )
chartcontrol( _SHOW )
```

In this file, the variable at the top, named *aValues[ ]*, is an array that holds six numeric values. This variable will be used in both the chart and in the associated form. Following this is a dummy procedure named *TestChart()*. This procedure is attached to the form at the bottom of the file and currently, it does nothing.

The first function, CHARTNEW( ), creates the chart and assigns the title of "Values" to be displayed. The ID for this object is 10. Next, the CHARTBAR( ) function associates the array of values with a particular chart. Here, the array *aValues[ ]* is told that the items in the chart will be in bar format (hence the CHARTBAR( ) function as opposed to, say, the CHARTPIE( ) function). In addition, the width of the bars on the chart is set to 15 pixels. Then, the size of the basic chart is calculated and assigned: It will rest in the top-left area of the screen, and it will be 50 percent (of the screen) wide and 75 percent long. This assignment is handled just as it is for forms, boards, and other objects, by using a `_SIZE` internal variable along with a control function; in this case, CHARTCONTROL( ). This same function will then display the chart to the screen using the `_SHOW` internal variable. When this takes place, Realizer will calculate the bottom and top extremes for the values of the chart based on what was passed to it. The X and Y coordinates are calculated to take up the entire height and width of the chart window region. These positions can be adjusted with other functions. Just remember what the default considerations are.

The next block of code creates the form and the various objects contained within the form. This shows the first basic difference between chart and form. Charts contain many subitems, but they are all part of the same object, whereas a form can consist of individual objects, each with a unique characteristic and behavior.

```
formnew( 20; "Modify Values", _TITLE )
formcontrol( _SIZE; _LEFT + 320, _TOP, 40 pct, 75 pct )
formsetobject( 100, _TEXTBOX, numtostr( aValues[1] ), 10,  10, 30, _DEFAULT; _NOTIFY)
formsetobject( 110, _TEXTBOX, numtostr( aValues[2] ), 10,  40, 30, _DEFAULT; _NOTIFY)
formsetobject( 120, _TEXTBOX, numtostr( aValues[3] ), 10,  70, 30, _DEFAULT; _NOTIFY)
formsetobject( 130, _TEXTBOX, numtostr( aValues[4] ), 10, 100, 30, _DEFAULT; _NOTIFY)
formsetobject( 140, _TEXTBOX, numtostr( aValues[5] ), 10, 130, 30, _DEFAULT; _NOTIFY)
formsetobject( 150, _TEXTBOX, numtostr( aValues[6] ), 10, 160, 30, _DEFAULT; _NOTIFY)
formsetproc( TestChart )
formcontrol( _SHOW )
```

Here, our form's ID is 20 with a title (to be displayed) of "Modify Values." Just as in the chart, the form's size is adjusted via the `_SIZE` internal variable, but here it modifies the FORMCONTROL( ) function instead of the CHARTCONTROL( ) function. In a small twist, the `_LEFT` internal variable is used as a base since the chart is already positioned to the `_LEFT` of the window region. Here, the form is positioned 320 pixels from the left. This is the same as passing 320 directly; however, it shows that numeric values and internal variables may be joined together. The width of the form is set to 40 percent of the screen, while the height of the form is exactly the same as the height of the chart (as you can see in the picture).

With the form in place, a series of six `_TEXTBOX` objects are attached to the current form. Each `_TEXTBOX` object is associated with an element in the *aValues[ ]* array; the string of each value is the default value in each data-entry box. The `_NOTIFY` modifier for each object will tell the attached procedure, in a few moments, that something has happened to each of the associated objects. After these six data-entry values are placed on the form, only two steps remain: to attach the *TestChart( )* procedure to the form and to

_SHOW the form. This is all there is to this example program, but it provides a base upon which we can begin to build.

In the next example program, named *Chart2.rlz*, we add a few new modifications, especially to the *TestChart()* procedure attached to the active form:

```
proc TestChart( aParams )

  formselect( aParams[_FORMNUM] )

  if aParams[_ITEMNUM] = 2       '* The ESC key!
    formcontrol( _CLOSE )
    chartselect( 10 )
    chartcontrol( _CLOSE )

  else

    if strtonum( formqstr( aParams[ _ITEMNUM ] ) ) > 0 and \\
       strtonum( formqstr( aParams[ _ITEMNUM ] ) ) < 40

      select case aParams[ _ITEMNUM ]
      case 100
        aValues[1] = strtonum( formqstr( aParams[ _ITEMNUM ] ) )
      case 110
        aValues[2] = strtonum( formqstr( aParams[ _ITEMNUM ] ) )
      case 120
        aValues[3] = strtonum( formqstr( aParams[ _ITEMNUM ] ) )
      case 130
        aValues[4] = strtonum( formqstr( aParams[ _ITEMNUM ] ) )
      case 140
        aValues[5] = strtonum( formqstr( aParams[ _ITEMNUM ] ) )
      case 150
        aValues[6] = strtonum( formqstr( aParams[ _ITEMNUM ] ) )
      end select

      chartselect( 10 )
      chartupdate( 1, aValues; _UPDATE )

    else
      if aParams[_ITEMNUM] <> 1    '* The ENTER key
        formmodifyobject( aParams[_ITEMNUM], _SETFOCUS )
      end if

    end if

  end if

end proc
```

As an added precaution, the FORMSELECT( ) function is called, making sure that we are back on the correct form. Following this, the program tests the _ITEMNUM internal variable in the passed parameter *aParams[ ]* array. If the value is 2, then the ESC key was pressed, and both the form and the chart are closed via the _CLOSE internal variables. However, if the action detected by the form is not the pressing of the ESC key, then the IF condition tests to see if the value of the item in the current _TEXTBOX is greater than 0 and less than 40. These values are in the range seen in the chart and are obtained using a combination of the FORMQSTR( ) function, which returns the string in the appropriate _TEXTBOX object, and the STRTONUM( ) function, which makes the string-to-number conversion. If this holds true, then the SELECT CASE command begins to take shape.

Here, the massive CASE construct tests to see which _TEXTBOX object was modified by polling each one that has an associated element number in the array. We could have opted for a better numbering technique between the ID of the various _TEXTBOX objects and the element index point in the *aValues[ ]* array. As it stands, individual tests of the ID values determine which element in *aValues[ ]* is to receive the new input. So far, all of this is pretty standard. Once the various elements have been updated, the chart to the left of the form needs to be updated as well. This is handled by the CHARTUPDATE( ) function:

```
chartselect( 10 )
chartupdate( 1, aValues; _UPDATE )
```

These two lines are all that is needed. The first instruction simply selects the form. The second function call consists of two parts. The second part is straightforward: It tells the associated and selected chart to _UPDATE itself. However, in order to do this, the CHARTUPDATE( ) function needs to know the plot type and the new values. Since the array *aValues[ ]* is being updated via the CASE statements, this array holds the most current values and will be correct. The first parameter tells the chart that beginning with the plot numbered 1, all values need to be refreshed. This is all that is needed to show the bars move up or down as new values are entered into the _TEXTBOXes in the associated form.

A chart's plot type depends on the function used to create the chart. In the previous two examples, the CHARTBAR( ) function produced a standard vertical-bar plot, but in program file *Chart3.rlz*, the CHARTHBAR( ) function gives us a horizontal-bar plot, as shown in Figure 6-2.

Boards, Charts, and Sheets 339

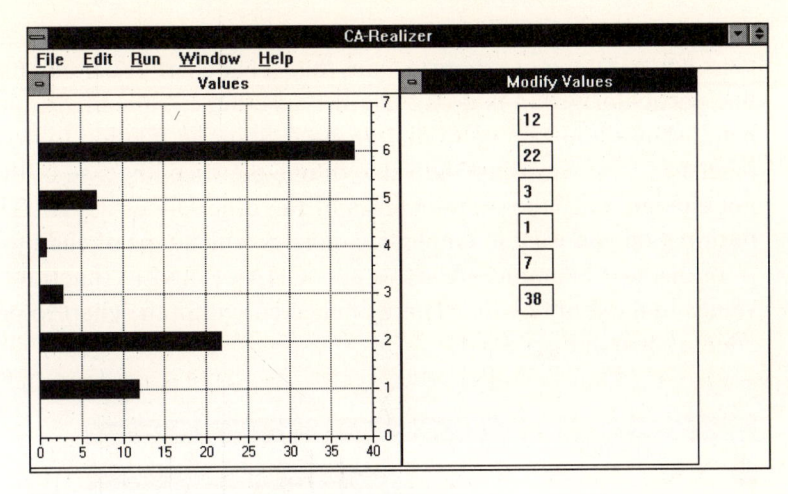

Figure 6-2. Chart with horizontal bars.

Everything else about the example program remains the same and the behavior is exactly what we would expect. The only difference is in how the items are plotted within the chart.

If we wanted a pie chart, we could (as in `Chart4.rlz` and in Figure 6-3) replace the CHARTHBAR( ) instruction with the following:

```
chartpie( aValues )
```

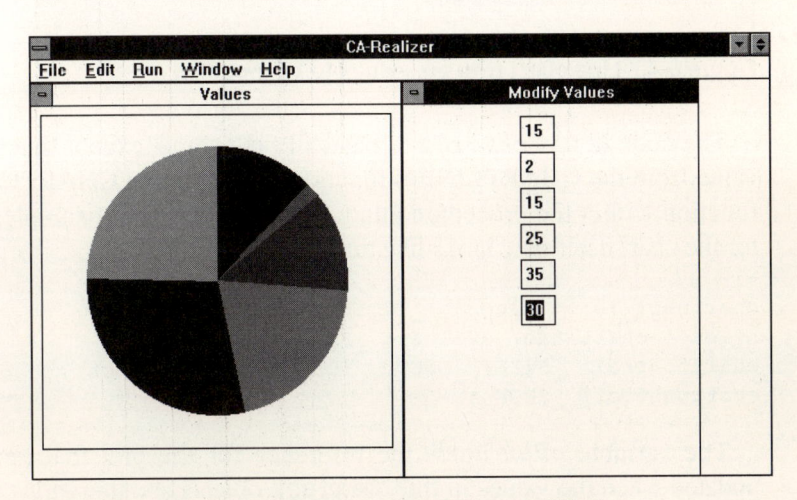

Figure 6-3. Pie chart with six values to be modified.

Each wedge of the pie is represented by a value in the array. A pie chart works on a different set of principles than a bar chart. A bar chart shows how one particular group is doing against all others. A pie chart, on the other hand, shows how one particular group is doing in relation to the whole. In other words, if we adjust the value of one pie slice, the size of the pie does not change; only the relative sizes of the other slices adjust. The type of information you want to emphasize dictates which type of chart to use.

In the next example, we use a new CHARTLINE( ) function. Here, the values in the array *aValues[ ]* are connected within the chart to produce the effect shown in Figure 6-4.

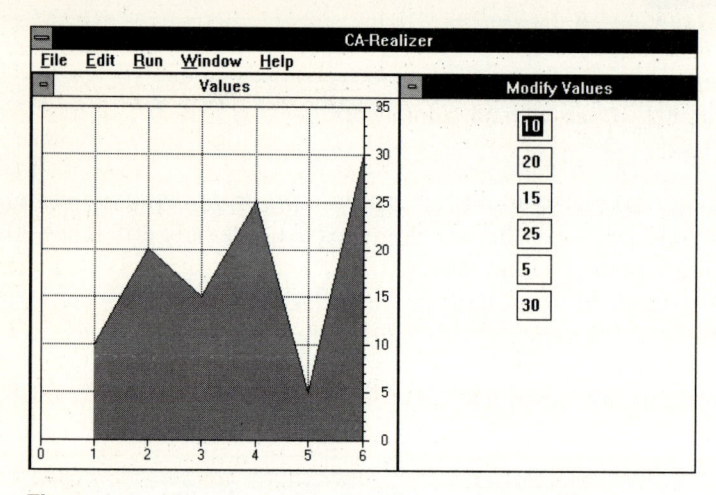

Figure 6-4. Line chart with six values to be modified.

The code in *Chart5.rlz* is basically the same, except that the return value from the CHARTLINE( ) function is used in the CHARTUPDATE( ) function within the procedure attached to the form. For example, the code for the chart itself now looks like this:

```
chartnew( 10; "Values", _TITLE )
nPlot = chartline( aValues; _FILL )
chartcontrol( _SIZE; _LEFT, _TOP, 50 pct, 75 pct )
chartcontrol( _SHOW )
```

The variable *nPlot* holds the reference for the plot that needs to be updated when the values in the _TEXTBOX objects are altered. At the top of the file, the code has been modified to look like this:

```
'* Application ... : Chart5.rlz
'* Authors ....... : Steve Straley
```

```
'* Notice ........ : Copyright(c) 1994 - Sirius Press, Inc.
'* ............... : All Rights Reserved
'* Date .......... : January 1, 1994
'* Description ... : The fifth example of how charts work
'*

nPlot = 0
aValues = {10,20,15,25,5,30}         '* HOLDS THE GOLBAL VALUE
```

When the *nPlot* variable is declared at the top of the file, any change in the lower half of the program file—the section of the code that creates the chart—will be seen at higher levels of the code. The procedure that is attached to the form that holds the various `_TEXTBOX` objects for data manipulation uses the CHARTUPDATE( ) function, and this function needs to know what plot number is to be updated. That ID value is held in the *nPlot* variable. So, when the following function is encountered within the *TestChart( )* procedure:

```
chartselect( 10 )
chartupdate( nPlot, aValues; _UPDATE )
```

all is fine. Each chart function has several options, some of which we will explore in this chapter. For example, in the line chart in Figure 6-4, the fill area from the bottom of the chart to the top of the connected lines can be altered by adding another internal variable to the CHARTLINE( ) function, as seen in *Chart6.rlz*:

```
chartnew( 10; "Values", _TITLE )
nPlot = chartline( aValues; _FILL, _UP )
chartcontrol( _SIZE; _LEFT, _TOP, 50 pct, 75 pct )
chartcontrol( _SHOW )
```

And in *Chart7.rlz*, the CHARTMARK( ) function is used to place unconnected marks on the chart, one for each value:

```
chartnew( 10; "Values", _TITLE )
nPlot = chartmark( aValues)
chartcontrol( _SIZE; _LEFT, _TOP, 50 pct, 75 pct )
chartcontrol( _SHOW )
```

All of these example files, from *Chart2.rlz* through *Chart7.rlz*, are based on the same theme but offer a different graphical presentation of data.

More on Charts

Adding text to charts is as simple as adding data: In the example file named *Chart8.rlz*, another array is created to hold the labels for a chart—in this case, a pie chart:

```
nLog     = 0
nChart   = 0
aValues  = {10,20,15,25,5,30}
aNames   = { "First", "Second", "Third", "Fourth", "Fifth", "Sixth" }
```

When the plotting device is created, both the *aValues[]* array and the *aNames[]* array need to be passed to the function. In addition, the CHARTPIE() function can take a special modifier to specify how the labels are to appear in the chart:

```
nChart = chartnew( chartqunique; "", _FRAME )
nLog   = chartpie( aValues, aNames ;_KEYLABELS )
chartcontrol( _SIZE; _LEFT, _TOP, 50 pct, 75 pct )
chartcontrol( _SHOW )
```

In this example, the CHARTQUNIQUE command generates a new chart ID value, and the CHARTNEW() function passes that value to the *nChart* variable. This variable will then be used in the CHARTSELECT() function within the *TestChart()* procedure attached to the form. Note that the chart no longer shows a title, but has a frame around it. This will anchor the chart to the screen and prevent it from being moved.

The labels in *aNames[]* are not part of either the chart or the array elements, so new _CAPTIONRIGHT objects can be added to the form, along with the corresponding _TEXTBOX objects. These caption objects will display the labels along with the data-entry boxes. For example, here are a couple of items we added:

```
formsetobject( 101, _CAPTIONRIGHT, aNames[1] + " array element", _LEFT, 14 )
formsetobject( 100, _TEXTBOX, numtostr( aValues[1] ), 150, 10, 30, \\
                                                 _DEFAULT; _NOTIFY)
formsetobject( 111, _CAPTIONRIGHT, aNames[2] + " array element", _LEFT, 44 )
formsetobject( 110, _TEXTBOX, numtostr( aValues[2] ), 150, 40, 30, \\
                                                 _DEFAULT; _NOTIFY)
```

These newly added objects give more information to the form and, in turn, to the end user. The final change in this program file is within the *TestChart()* procedure attached to this form. First, if the ESC key is pressed and both the form and the chart need to be closed, a reference to the proper

Boards, Charts, and Sheets

chart is in order: Providing that reference is the *nChart* variable, assigned at the top of the file and then reassigned by the CHARTNEW() function.

```
formcontrol( _CLOSE )
chartselect( nChart )
chartcontrol( _CLOSE )
```

Here, the CHARTSELECT() function uses that variable, instead of a constant, to select the proper chart in order for it to be closed. The other modification within this function deals again with selecting the chart and updating the values. This modification occurs immediately after the extensive SELECT CASE statement:

```
chartselect( nChart )
chartupdate( nLog, aValues, aNames; _UPDATE )
```

You must reuse both the *aValues[ ]* array and the *aNames[ ]* array. If not, then when the chart is updated via the `_UPDATE` internal variable, the values in the chart will be updated, but the labels will be removed from the image. In other words, the chart does not remember that the labels need to be refreshed when the values in the chart are updated.

Finally, the variable *nLog* is used to hold the plot coordinate within the chart that needs to be updated. In the end, the chart and the form should look like those shown in Figure 6-5.

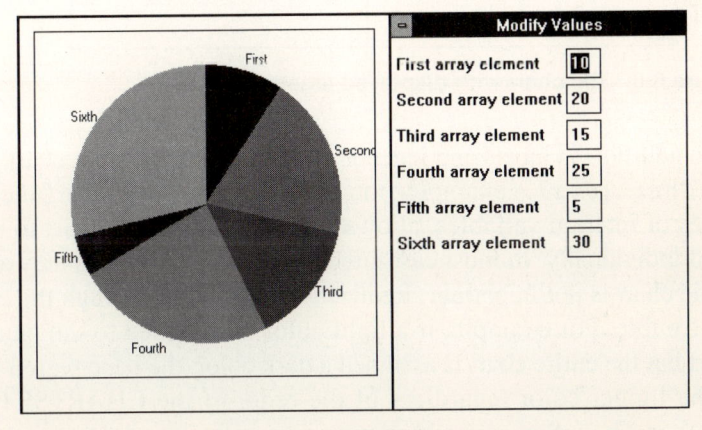

Figure 6-5. Pie chart with labels and text items for input.

If you want your chart to have a legend instead of (or in addition to) labels, you can use the CHARTCONTROLKEY() function. The code would look like this:

```
nChart = chartnew( chartqunique; "", _FRAME )
nLog   = chartpie( aValues, aNames ; _KEYLABELS )
chartcontrol( _SIZE; _LEFT, _TOP, 50 pct, 75 pct )
chartcontrolkey( _SHOW )
chartcontrol( _SHOW )
```

Once again, the _SHOW internal variable does its magic. And on the screen, the new image (as generated by the *Chart9.rlz* file) will look like the one in Figure 6-6.

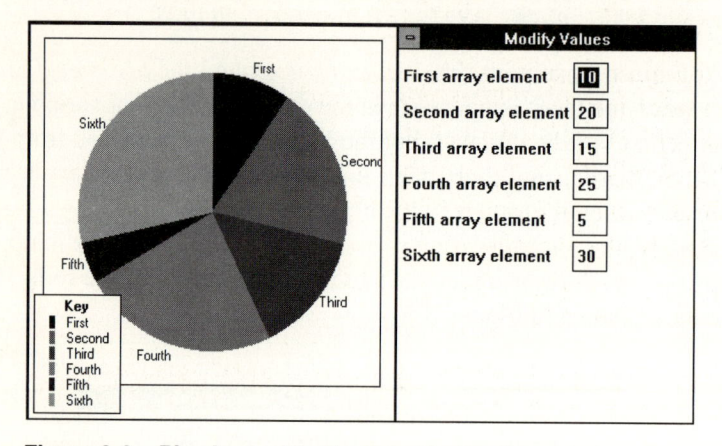

Figure 6-6. Pie chart with displayed legend.

In addition to labels and legends, you can also control a chart's colors. In the *Chart10.rlz* example, the CHARTSETCOLOR() function, via a series of internal variables, allows various parts of the chart to be manipulated individually. In most cases, the order of the colors as they are attached to the chart is not important; Realizer is able to sort through the colors without trouble. For example, if a light color is assigned to the pane area of a chart but the entire chart is assigned a dark color, the pane region will still be in the lighter color regardless of the order of the CHARTSETCOLOR() function. The following code shows some of the retinted pie chart elements:

```
chartsetcolor( _DARKPURPLE; _CHARTBACKGR )
chartsetcolor( _CYAN; _PANEBACKGR )
chartsetcolor( _TAN; _KEYBACKGR )
chartsetcolor( _WHITE; _KEYTEXT )
chartsetcolor( _YELLOW; _KEYBORDER )
```

Boards, Charts, and Sheets   345

The type of the chart can help dictate what colors to choose. Here, trial and error in the run-time environment is the best way to determine color selection.

And as you might expect, colors are not the least of your choices; you can also specify new fonts and chart titles. In this last example in this series, the `Chart11.rlz` file creates two new fonts and three titles, then assigns new colors and fonts to those new titles. The final result looks like Figure 6-7.

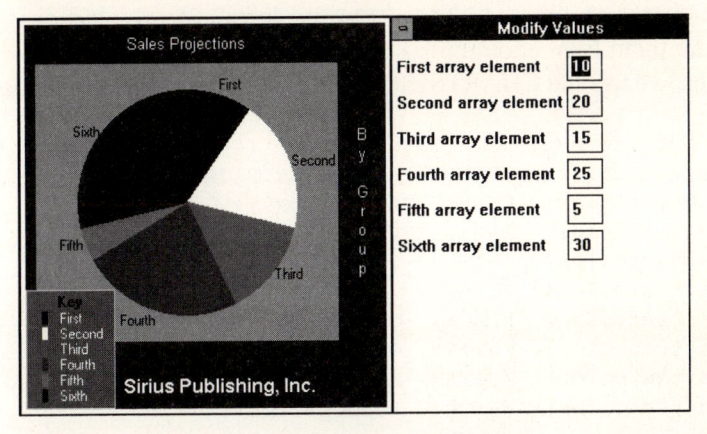

Figure 6-7. Pie chart with new color selections.

At the top of the source file, two new variables are initialized to hold the fonts that are created:

```
nLog       = 0
nChart     = 0
nMainFont  = 0
nCompFont  = 0
aValues    = {10,20,15,25,5,30}
aNames     = { "First", "Second", "Third", "Fourth", "Fifth", "Sixth" }
```

Then, before the chart is created, the two new fonts are created. The order of these instructions is not that important; however, these values will be needed for the CHARTSETFONT() function, so they must be set before using that function. It is also a good idea to keep all like functions grouped together to make debugging easier. We could create the charts, then create the fonts, and then assign the fonts to the proper chart items; however, we don't recommend this type of "skipping." So the first thing we need is to call the FONTNEW( ) function:

```
'******* [ Create the fonts ]*********
nMainFont = fontnew( ; "Arial", 10 )
nCompFont = fontnew( ; "Arial", 12, _BOLD )
```

With the fonts in place and assigned to the proper variables, we can build the chart. The chart titles, which appear at the top, right, and bottom edges of the chart, are on a _DARKPURPLE background, which means we need to make them light enough to show up. To alter the text color for these three titles, we use the CHARTSETCOLOR( ) function with three new modifiers:

```
'* Set the various colors
chartsetcolor( _DARKPURPLE; _CHARTBACKGR )
chartsetcolor( _CYAN; _PANEBACKGR )
chartsetcolor( _TAN; _KEYBACKGR )
chartsetcolor( _WHITE; _KEYTEXT )
chartsetcolor( _YELLOW; _KEYBORDER )
chartsetcolor( _BLACK; _CHARTTEXT )
chartsetcolor( _WHITE; _TOPTITLE )
chartsetcolor( _WHITE; _RIGHTTITLE )
chartsetcolor( _WHITE; _BOTTOMTITLE )
```

The _TOPTITLE, _RIGHTTITLE, and _BOTTOMTITLE internal variables are assigned the white color option. With the color in place, we can add the title text:

```
'* set the various titles
chartsettitle( "Sales Projections", _TOP )
chartsettitle( "By Group", _RIGHT )
chartsettitle( "           Sirius Press, Inc.", _BOTTOM )
```

The internal variables _TOP, _RIGHT, and _BOTTOM correspond to the internal variables used in the CHARTSETCOLOR( ) function and, as we will see in a moment, with the CHARTSETFONT( ) function. Note that in the final call to the CHARTSETTITLE( ) function, the string "Sirius Press, Inc." is indented several spaces. When building a chart, all objects in the chart need to be considered in terms of their visual relationship with one another. The CHARTSETTITLE( ) functions always try to center the text, either at the top, bottom, left or right. The chart legend in the bottom-left corner might obscure the bottom title text. To avoid this, the string for the bottom title needs to be indented.

> **Note:** There is no way to specify how the titles should appear (left-justified, right-justified, and so on) in a specific region. In addition, there is no way to tell in advance which objects will sit on top of which other objects. It is a very good idea to build a chart in run-time mode so that you can make alterations and/or alternative plans on the fly.

With the text positioning adjusted, the final step is to assign the fonts to the various objects in the chart. This is accomplished using the CHARTSETFONT() function:

```
'* set the various fonts that need to be used!
chartsetfont( nMainFont, _TOPTITLE )
chartsetfont( nMainFont, _RIGHTTITLE )
chartsetfont( nCompFont, _BOTTOMTITLE )
```

The variable *nMainFont*, which points to 10-point Arial is used for the `_TOPTITLE` and the `_RIGHTTITLE`, while the variable *nCompFont*, which points to 12-point Arial, boldface, is used for the `_BOTTOMTITLE`.

Multiple Images

So far, we've displayed only one chart at a time, but sometimes end users will want to compare charts. For example, let's say we had three arrays of sales data for our six sales groups. Graphically, it might be nice to see these three pie charts next to one another. To do that, we need to understand the concept of a pane. The pane is the area of the chart that holds a plot, such as a pie chart, a bar chart, or a line chart. Panes dictate the amount of area to be used by a plot, as well as the relative position within the chart area. The size of the finished graph depends totally on the size of the pane. In all of the examples up to this point, the pane area was 100 percent of the chart's area. To plot our three pie charts, we want three panes that take up about 33 percent of the chart area each, for a result that looks like Figure 6-8.

To do this, the code needs to work with each array of information, each element of the chart, and each item within each pane. It may seem like a lot of work for such a small image; however, the ability to display data graphically in a variety of ways is a must-have feature for most business-software users. The code for this example, in *Chart12.rlz*, looks like this:

```
'* Application ... : Chart12.rlz
'* Authors ....... : Steve Straley
'* Notice ........ : Copyright(c) 1994 - Sirius Press, Inc.
```

348 *Chapter 6*

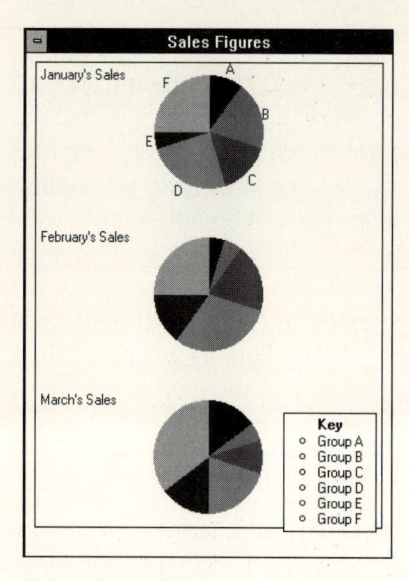

Figure 6-8. Three pie charts in same form.

```
'* .............. : All Rights Reserved
'* Date ......... : January 1, 1994
'* Description ... : The 12th example of how charts work
'*

nChart     = 0
aJanuary   = {10,20,15,25,5,25}
aFebruary  = { 5, 5,20,30,15,25}
aMarch     = {15, 5,10,20,15,35}
aLabels    = {"A","B","C","D","E","F"}

'****** [ CREATE the CHART..... ] *******

nChart = chartnew( chartqunique; "Sales Figures", _TITLE )
chartcontrol( _SIZE; 0, 0, 50 pct, 100 pct )

chartselectpane(1)
chartcontrolpane( _SIZE; 0 pct, 30 pct )
nText1 = charttext(5,10,"January's Sales",_SCREEN,_CTPOS_LEFT)
nPie1  = chartpie( aJanuary, aLabels )

chartselectpane(2)
chartcontrolpane( _SIZE; 35 pct, 30 pct )
nText2 = charttext(5,10,"February's Sales",_SCREEN,_CTPOS_LEFT)
nPie2  = chartpie( aFebruary, aLabels )
```

```
chartselectpane(3)
chartcontrolpane( _SIZE; 70 pct, 30 pct )
nText3 = charttext(5,10,"March's Sales",_SCREEN,_CTPOS_LEFT)
nPie3  = chartpie( aMarch, aLabels )

chartsetkey( "Group A", _MARKER )
chartsetkey( "Group B", _MARKER )
chartsetkey( "Group C", _MARKER )
chartsetkey( "Group D", _MARKER )
chartsetkey( "Group E", _MARKER )
chartsetkey( "Group F", _MARKER )
chartcontrolkey( _SIZE; 225, 300 )
chartcontrolkey( _SHOW )
chartcontrol( _SHOW )

'* End of File: Chart12.rlz
```

The three arrays at the top of the file are the simulated sales values for each group. Each letter in the array *aLabels[ ]* corresponds to a subscript in each of the other arrays and is used as a label for each value. Keep in mind that this example builds only the three panes and places a pie chart in each; each pane could just as easily have a different chart type. Once the data has been entered and the chart built, we need to adjust the size. Here, the CHARTCONTROL() function with the _SIZE internal variable tells us that the top-left position of the chart will be at pixel 0,0. The width of the chart will be 50 percent of the screen and the height will be 100 percent of the screen. In other words, the left half of the window is used.

Next, the CHARTSELECTPANE() function is called for the first time. If there is no pane numbered 1, it will create a pane with this ID value. After a pane has been created, we need to reduce the size of that pane within the associated chart. Here, the CHARTCONTROLPANE() function positions the pie chart that is about to be created and gives it relative size. In this first example, the position will be at the top (0 percent away from the top), while the size of the image will be 30 percent. The CHARTTEXT() function that follows will insert the text "January's Sales" within this pane. Here, the text is to be 5 pixels in from the left and 10 from the top. The text is to be displayed to the _SCREEN at the upper-left position via the _CTPOS_LEFT internal variable. Then the pie chart is created within the pane and is ready for display.

Following this, a new pane is created, again with the CHARTSELECT-PANE() function. This time the value 2 is passed, which creates the new pane. Once again, the size is adjusted. Keep in mind that this adjustment is in terms of the chart's position, not the window. Here, the second pane is located 35 percent from the top of the chart area, and the size of the pane is again 30 percent.

> **Note:** There are three pie charts created in this chart. Each will be in a pane that takes up roughly 30% of the area in that chart region. If one of the panes were set at 45% of the chart region, the total would exceed 100%, and overlap within the area will take place.

After this pane's region is adjusted, a title is set to display. Again, the left and top positions for the text "February's Sales" remain at 5,10; however, since this pane's region is 35 percent down from the top of the chart's area, this 5,10 is based on that relative position within the chart itself. This means that the text will be close to the pie chart in this pane, and not wander toward the previous pane's text of "January's Sales." The same pattern of code is used for the third pane in the chart.

The key or legend for this chart needs to be moved to the right, so the CHARTCONTROLKEY() function is used to move it 225 pixels to the left in the chart area, and 300 pixels down from the top. Again, other positioning variations may be used as well as other Realizer position notations. The CHARTSETKEY() function adds only one more dimension to this example with the use of the _MARKER internal variable.

As we mentioned, you can specify more than one type of a plot in a chart area. For example, we could in one pane have a pie chart, in another have a bar chart, and in the third pane, have a line chart. Using the second pane and the code from `Chart13.rlz`, we might see the following:

```
chartselectpane(2)
chartcontrolpane( _SIZE; 35 pct, 30 pct )
nText2 = charttext(5,10,"February's Sales",_SCREEN,_CTPOS_LEFT)
nBar1  = chartbar( aFebruary; 5 )
```

The only difference in this pane would be the creation of a bar chart as opposed to a pie chart. However, now the axis lines from the bar chart extend up through to our pie chart, so we need to work with yet another chart-based function to "turn off" those axis grid lines.

```
chartselectpane(1)
chartcontrolpane( _SIZE; 0 pct, 30 pct )
chartsetxgrid(0; _LIGHT, _WHITE)
nText1 = charttext(5,10,"January's Sales",_SCREEN,_CTPOS_LEFT)
nPie1  = chartpie( aJanuary, aLabels )
```

The CHARTSETXGRID() function, with the passed modifiers of _LIGHT and _WHITE (seeing that the color of the pane itself is white), effectively "turns off" the grid lines that extend up from the line graph displayed in the third pane, through the bar graph displayed in the second pane, to the pie chart in the first pane. The final output looks like Figure 6-9.

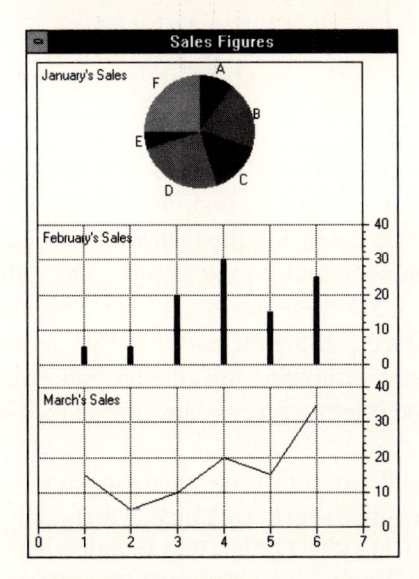

Figure 6-9. Pie chart, bar chart, and line chart in same form.

Printing a Chart

The key thing to remember about printing a chart is that the output of the chart is first dumped to a buffer, which then needs to be "flushed" to the physical device. In a case where colors are used, the program will attempt to use gray-scale colorings to make close approximations. Starting with the pie chart example in *Chart10.rlz*, the file *Chart14.rlz* uses a Print button object to print the pie chart. In order to do this, first the _BUTTON needed to be attached to the controlling form like this:

```
formsetobject( 200, _BUTTON, "Print...", _LEFT, _BOTTOM )
```

Once this object has been attached to the form and given the ID value of 200, that value can then be tested in the attached form procedure called *TestChart( )*. After an initial look at the ESC key, the procedure looks at the value of the object. Here, the _BUTTON has no value, so we would eventually pass through to the following IF command structure:

```
if aParams[ _ITEMNUM ] = 200 ' The BUTTON
   chartselect( nChart )
   chartcontrol( _PRINT )
   lflush
   input "Finished Printing!", "Sirius Press, Inc." ;

elseif aParams[_ITEMNUM] <> 1    '* The ENTER key
   formmodifyobject( aParams[_ITEMNUM], _SETFOCUS )

end if
```

Only the chart will be printed and not the form, since only the CHARTCONTROL( ) function is used in conjunction with the _PRINT internal variable. (Of course, we could add the FORMCONTROL(_PRINT) option as well to give yet another look to the report.) Once the output is printed to the buffer, the LFLUSH command takes over. This causes a message to be displayed on the screen telling the end-user that "page X of Y" is being printed. This is automatic. Following this, the program issues a notice instructing the enduser that the printing process has finished. This is allowed via the INPUT command.

The output need not be confined to just one small section of the page. It can, if you want, take up the entire sheet. This means that additional modifiers need to be passed to the CHARTCONTROL( ) function when used with the _PRINT internal variable. For example, if the CHART CONTROL( ) line in the preceding example were changed to this:

```
if aParams[ _ITEMNUM ] = 200 ' The BUTTON
   chartselect( nChart )
   chartcontrol( _PRINT; _NOHEADER, 80, 150, 80 pct, 40 pct )
   lflush
   input "Finished Printing!", "Sirius Press, Inc." ;

elseif aParams[_ITEMNUM] <> 1    '* The ENTER key
   formmodifyobject( aParams[_ITEMNUM], _SETFOCUS )

end if
```

Boards, Charts, and Sheets   353

the output to the printer is modified so that no header information is printed. This is handled by the `_NOHEADER` internal variable. The next two parameters in this code extract specify that the printed chart will start 80 pixels in from the left and 150 down from the top. Pixels are not part of a piece of paper, of course, but Realizer makes the conversion as best it can to fit the physical output device. The last two parameters indicate the percent of the page to be taken up by the graph. Here, the width of the chart will be 80 percent of the page, while the height of the chart will be 40 percent of the page.

In addition, the following code adds a new button to the form:

```
formsetobject( 200, _BUTTON, "Print...", _LEFT, _BOTTOM )
formsetobject( 2, _BUTTON, "Cancel", _LEFT + 100, _BOTTOM)
```

Here, if the `ESC` key is pressed, the value of *aParams[_ITEMNUM]* will be 2; however, with this `_BUTTON` also assigned the ID value of 2, both the `_BUTTON` and the `ESC` key will terminate the form.

Attaching a Procedure to a Chart

Just like any other Realizer tool, we can assign a procedure to any chart that will be called if the chart is in focus and if it receives a message that something has taken place within its domain. To do this, the CHARTSETPROC() function is called:

```
chartsetproc( TestChar; _SIZE )
```

Here, the procedure *TestChart( )* will be called when the chart is to be closed or if there is a mouse click on the chart, or if the chart is resized in any way. This internal variable of `_SIZE` is optional. If no procedure is specified with this function:

```
chartsetproc()
```

then all association to the previously defined procedure is disengaged.

And, as with all of our other attached procedures, an array will be passed automatically to the attached procedure. This is called a tool procedure parameter array. In essence, Realizer conducts communications between the charts and the program through this array. It holds information that may be useful when building a procedure to be attached to a chart. Now, what this means is that when we create the *TestChart()* procedure (or any other procedure), it should be prepared to receive an array. The shell of the code might look something like this:

```
proc TestChart( aParams )

end proc
```

Within this procedure, we can test values stored to the array named *aParams[ ]*. Those element positions to be tested are made available via the internal variables listed in Table 6-1.

Table 6-1. Internal Variables Allowed in Attached Chart Procedure

Internal Variable	Definition
_CONTROLHELD	A Boolean value (1 or 0) indicating whether the CTRL key was held down during the action that invoked the tool procedure.
_CUSTOMLP	Values used for messages received from custom controls.
_CUSTOMWP	Values used for messages received from custom controls
_DRAGFORM	With the _DRAGNDROP message, if an object being dragged invoked the tool procedure, the ID of the form from which the object was dragged will be returned.
_DRAGITEM	With the _DRAGNDROP message, if an item being dragged invoked the tool procedure, the ID of the item that was being dragged will be the return value.
_FORMNUM	If an object in a form invoked the tool procedure, the ID of that form will be returned.
_INVOKE	Returns a constant indicating what action invoked the procedure.
_ITEMNUM	If a tool, an object, or a menu item invoked the procedure, this will return the ID of the item that was selected.
_ITEMTYPE	If a tool, an object, or a menu item invoked the procedure, this will return the type of the item that was selected.
_MENUNUM	If a menu item invoked the procedure, the ID of the menu containing the item will be returned.
_SHIFTHELD	A Boolean value (1 or 0) indicating whether the SHIFT key was held during the action that invoked the procedure.

(continued)

Table 6-1. *(continued)*

Internal Variable	Definition
_USEREALIZER	A value that can be manipulated for special processing.
_XPOS	If the procedure was invoked by a mouse click, this will return the X position of the mouse cursor, in pixels, relative to the upper-left corner of the tool or object within a form. If the mouse click occurs in a spreadsheet, this value will indicate the column number of the cell.
_YPOS	If the procedure was invoked by a mouse click, this will return the Y position of the mouse cursor, in pixels, relative to the upper-left corner of the tool or object within the form. If a mouse click occurs in a spreadsheet, this value will indicate the row number of the cell.

To use this list with the skeleton of our procedure, let's have the procedure make sure that the item or chart is selected:

```
proc TestChart( aParams )
   chartselect( aParams[ _ITEMNUM ] )

end proc
```

And if an associated form were attached to our chart as well, we could build on this and offer the following:

```
proc TestChart( aParams )

   chartselect( aParams[ _ITEMNUM ] )
   formselect( aParams[ _FORMNUM ] )

end proc
```

Selecting the chart and the form is not that helpful in the larger scheme of things. More useful is the ability to detect a mouse click or how the form was closed:

```
proc TestChart( aParams )

  chartselect( aParams[ _ITEMNUM ] )
  formselect( aParams[ _FORMNUM ] )

  select case aParams[ _INVOKE ]
```

```
   case _CLOSE
     chartcontrol( _CLOSE )

   case _CLICK
     input "O.k.... you can press the mouse!", "Sirius Press, Inc." ;

   case _SIZE
     input "Changing the size on us, eh?" ;

   end select

end proc
```

Obviously, these operations can only do so much. There are two other internal variables that can be used to obtain the position of the mouse click within a chart: _XPOS and _YPOS. These two variables return the row and column position of a mouse click within a chart. So, let's modify one of the earlier example programs to work with an attached procedure. The modified program file, named *Chart17.rlz*, revamps the original line chart to look like Figure 6-10.

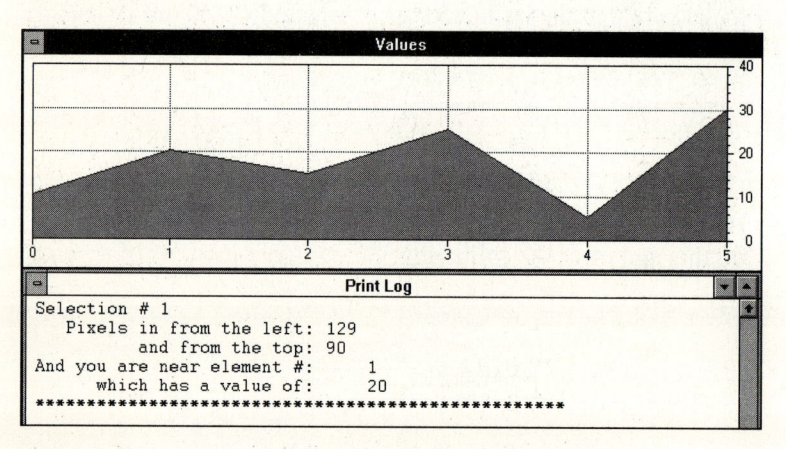

Figure 6-10. Line chart with PRINT LOG window open.

Note that the beginning point on the line is now at pixel 0. This is because the array is adjusted to start with the 0th element. Remember that arrays defined as literals usually start off at the 1st element position. The command OPTION BASE 0 sets the start-off point at 0. Then when the array named *aValues[ ]* is created with the following:

```
option base 0

nSelection = 0
```

```
        nPlot       = 0
        aValues     = {10,20,15,25,5,30}          '* HOLDS THE GOLBAL VALUE
```

the value of 10 is in the 0th element position. So when this array is added to the chart:

```
'* Open the PRINT log
logselect( _PRINTLOG )
logcontrol( _SHOW )

'****** [ CREATE the CHART..... ] *******

chartnew( 10; "Values", _TITLE )
nPlot = chartline( aValues; _FILL )
chartcontrol( _SIZE; _LEFT, _TOP, 100 pct, 45 pct )
chartsetproc( TestChart )
chartcontrol( _SHOW )
```

the line chart will start with the 0th element.

At this point in the source code we see that there are two additions. First, the Print Log is selected and opened. The goal here is that output will be printed within the procedure attached to the chart. That procedure, *TestChart()*, is attached via the CHARTSETPROC() function. All of the major tests for this chart take place within that procedure:

```
proc TestChart( aParams )

  local sXPos as string
  local sYPos as string

  if aParams[_INVOKE] = _CLICK

    nSelection = nSelection + 1

    sXPos = numtostr( floor(aParams[_XPOS]) )
    sYPos = numtostr( floor(aParams[_YPOS]) )
    input "Coordinates selected were (" + sXPos + "," + sYPos + ")", \\
          "Sirius Press, Inc." ;

    rowprint "Selection #", nSelection
    rowprint "    Pixels in from the left:", aParams[_XPOS]
    rowprint "           and from the top:", aParams[_YPOS]
    rowprint "And you are near element #: ", floor( aParams[_XPOS] / 120 )
    rowprint "        which has a value of: ", aValues[floor( aParams[_XPOS] / 120 )]
    rowprint "*****************************************************"

  end if

end proc
```

If a mouse click is detected and invokes this procedure, the value of the comparison between *aParams[_INVOKE]* and _CLICK will be a logical true value. At this point, the value of the global variable *nSelection* is incremented, and the values of both *aParams[_XPOS]* and *aParams[_YPOS]* are converted to strings and assigned to variables. These values are then displayed to the screen via the INPUT command. The screen is 600 pixels wide, and with five separate plots, it is safe to conclude that for every 120 pixels, a new value from the array *aValues[ ]* is plotted. With this in mind, we can take the value of the _XPOS element in the tools procedure array, divide by 120, and pass that to the FLOOR() function. This function always rounds down or truncates. So if the value of *aParams[_XPOS]* /120 is .60, the FLOOR() function will adjust this to be 0. This value can then be used to point to the 0th element in the array *aValues[ ]*. Of course, the problem here is addressing the fifth element in the array. Since the obtained values from the _XPOS position are always rounded down, there is no direct way to get to this position. And if we use the CEIL() function to round all values up to the next highest integer, the problem will exist in reverse. The ROUND() function can take care of those close plots in either direction.

Of course, there are some problems to consider. For example, in the program that holds the pie chart, the bar chart, and the line chart, if we attach a procedure to that main chart ID, there is no way to know via the array passed to the attached procedure which chart the mouse was clicked in. Remember, there are three panes in one chart window, and the _XPOS and _YPOS position are returned from the upper-left corner of the pane's region. Since there is no way to tell which pane was selected, there's no way to tell which chart the _XPOS and _YPOS values belong to. In addition, with the grid coordinates shut off for the pie chart, the values for the _XPOS and _YPOS internal variables would be 0. In essence, attaching the procedure to a chart is useful only for plotting coordinates. In addition, it will work as expected only from single-paned charts. Those multi-paned charts will have to refer to a form-based approach in which that attached procedure can better point to a particular item, select the appropriate chart, and go on from there.

More Complex Procedures

Turning back to `Chart13.rlz`, a simple procedure is attached and, using the values from the parameter passed to that procedure, we can determine which pane a mouse click might occur in. That procedure looks something like this:

Boards, Charts, and Sheets 359

```
proc TestChart( aParams )

  input "Pane number: " + numtostr( chartqptinfo(aParams[_XPOS], aParams[_YPOS])[3]), \\
    "Display Version 1";
  input "Data position X: "+numtostr( chartqptinfo(aParams[_XPOS], aParams[_YPOS])[1]), \\
    "Display Version 2";
  input "Data position Y: "+numtostr( chartqptinfo(aParams[_XPOS], aParams[_YPOS])[2]), \\
    "Display Version 3";

end proc
```

Using the `_XPOS` and `_YPOS` variables in conjunction with the CHARTQPTINFO() function, we can obtain more needed information. This function returns an array of three elements. The third element, displayed in the `INPUT` command, is a pointer to which pane received the mouse click.

> **Note:** In some cases, if there are multiple panes, the first pane visible to the CHARTQPTINFO( ) will have an ID value of 0. However, since every chart has at least 1 pane, and if a mouse click is detected within this chart and causes a call to the tool procedure array, then the return value of 0 must be 1.

So, if a mouse click occurred in the pane holding the pie chart, the return value displayed in the INPUT command would be 0. This would tell us that the user wishes to deal with the array *aJanuary[]*. From here, we could generate a new input form, allowing the end user to select new values for the various sales groups, restore those values back to the array, and update the chart in pane 1 (not pane 0) before returning control to the Realizer environment to detect the next mouse click. The first and second array elements returned from the CHARTQPTINFO() function will return 0 and 0, since the grid coordinates for the pie chart have no relevance. However, these values are important for the other two panes in the chart area, the line plot and the bar plot.

For example, if the mouse click appeared in the second pane, the return value of CHARTQPTINFO()'s third element would be 2, telling us that *aFebruary[]* was involved. If the mouse cursor appeared on the fourth and tallest bar in the chart, the value of the first element returned from this function would be a 4 (giving us the fourth array element), and the value of the second element would be 30 (which is the value of the fourth array element in the *aFebruary[]* array). We could automatically adjust the values in the *aFebruary[]* array by merely pointing to a position on the grid and letting the tool procedure array figure out what new value needs to be entered. Here is the essence of *Chart19.rlz*:

```
'* Application ... : Chart19.rlz
'* Authors ....... : Steve Straley
'* Notice ........ : Copyright(c) 1994 - Sirius Press, Inc.
'* .............. : All Rights Reserved
'* Date .......... : January 1, 1994
'* Description ... : The 19th example of how charts work
'*

nChart    = 0
aJanuary  = {10,20,15,25,5,25}
aFebruary = { 5, 5,20,30,15,25}
aMarch    = {15, 5,10,20,15,35}
aLabels   = {"A","B","C","D","E","F"}

proc TestChart( aParams )

   local nPaneNumer as integer
   local nElement   as integer
   local nNewValue  as integer

   nPaneNumber = chartqptinfo(aParams[_XPOS], aParams[_YPOS])[3]
   nElement    = chartqptinfo(aParams[_XPOS], aParams[_YPOS])[1]
   nNewValue   = chartqptinfo(aParams[_XPOS], aParams[_YPOS])[2]

   if nPaneNumber = 2       '* working with aFebruary
      aFebruary[nElement] = nNewValue
      chartupdate( nBar1, aFebruary; _UPDATE )

   elseif nPaneNumber = 3    '* working with aMarch
      aMarch[nElement] = nNewValue
      chartupdate( nHBar1, aMarch; _UPDATE )
   end if

end proc

'****** [ CREATE the CHART..... ] *******

nFont = chartnew( chartqunique; "Sales Figures", _TITLE )
chartcontrol( _SIZE; 0, 0, 50 pct, 100 pct )

chartselectpane(1)
chartcontrolpane( _SIZE; 0 pct, 30 pct )
chartsetxgrid(0; _LIGHT, _WHITE)
nText1 = charttext(5,10,"January's Sales",_SCREEN,_CTPOS_LEFT)
nPie1  = chartpie( aJanuary, aLabels )
```

```
chartselectpane(2)
chartcontrolpane( _SIZE; 35 pct, 30 pct )
nText2 = charttext(5,10,"February's
Sales",_SCREEN,_CTPOS_LEFT)
nBar1  = chartbar( aFebruary; 5 )

chartselectpane(3)
chartcontrolpane( _SIZE; 70 pct, 30 pct )
nText3 = charttext(5,10,"March's Sales",_SCREEN,_CTPOS_LEFT)
nHbar1 = chartline( aMarch )

chartsetproc( Testchart )
chartcontrol( _SHOW )

'* End of File: Chart19.rlz
```

Within the *TestChart()* function, the return values from the CHARTQPT-INFO() are stored to three variables: *nPaneNumber*, *nElement*, and *nNewValue*. Based on the value of *nPaneNumber* being 2 or 3, we know which array is to be worked on: either *aFebruary[ ]* or *aMarch[ ]*. More important, we also know which plot is being worked on. This is very important when that plot is updated using the CHARTUPDATE() function.

> **Note:** If a mouse click on a coordinate in either the line plot or the bar plot is beyond the range preset by the minimum and maximum values in the array elements, the `_UPDATE` internal variable will adjust the plot to fit the new coordinate.

This technique of using the CHARTQPTINFO() and the `_XPOS` and `_YPOS` internal variables in the passed array parameter to the attached procedure is just one more way in which data may be manipulated in Realizer.

Sheets

The final tool that we will explore in this chapter is the sheet, which might be better called a spreadsheet. Most of the principles outlined with logs, forms, boards, and charts also apply to sheets. A sheet is simply an alternative method to providing an end user with a data-entry interface. Many people, especially those first introduced to computer software through a package like VisiCalc or SuperCalc or even Lotus 1-2-3, relate to data entry in terms of rows and columns.

As with most of the other tools, sheets have their own set of functions. Typically, the prefix of the function tells what type of tool is being created. In the previous two sections, for example, we learned about the BOARDNEW() function and the CHARTNEW() function. Now we will learn about the SHEETNEW() function. To start, the most simple sheet you can create looks like the one shown in Figure 6-11.

Figure 6-11. An empty spreadsheet with visible rows.

And the code that creates it is equally simple:

```
sheetnew( )
sheetcontrol( _SHOW )
```

By default, the title of the sheet includes the ID value. In addition, scroll bars will always appear in the sheet window regardless of the data (or lack of it) in the sheet. On the left of the sheet window are the row numbers. The unnumbered "row" just below the titlebar is an area reserved for the titles of the families of data to be attached to this sheet. This will become clearer as we add data to these two simple lines of code. Under the area reserved for the family is another unnumbered row that will contain what can best be described as column headings. This row will hold either the names of variables or, more commonly, the names of the family members represented in these cells.

To get things going, let's take the array of values seen in the section on Charts and bring it into play for this example:

```
aGroups = {"Group A", "Group B", "Group C", "Group D", "Group E", "Group F" }
aValues = {10,20,15,25,5,30}
```

```
nSheet = sheetnew(sheetqunique, aGroups, aValues)
sheetcontrol(_SHOW)
```

Now, two separate arrays hold parallel information used in previous examples. The first array, *aGroups*, holds the names of the sales groups we plotted in the pie charts. The second array, named *aValues[ ]*, holds the sales percentages for each group. In other words, element one in the array *aGroups[ ]* corresponds to the data found in element one in *aValues[ ]*. When these two arrays are passed to the SHEETNEW( ) function and displayed, the result looks like the window shown in Figure 6-12.

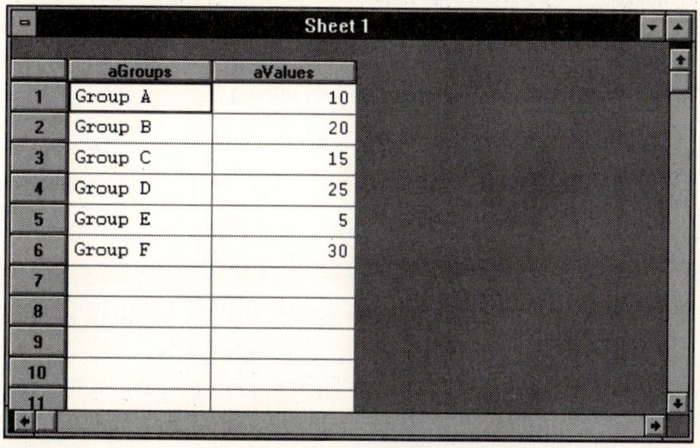

Figure 6-12. Spreadsheet with two columns.

In this image we can see that the names of the arrays, *aGroups[ ]* and *aValues[ ]*, are used as column headings. The area between the column headings and the title bar remains blank.

Labels, Headings, and Widths

Variable names such as these two are not very helpful to an end user, so let's change the titles. To do that, the SHEETSETCOLLABELS( ) function needs to be called:

```
aGroups = {"Group A", "Group B", "Group C", "Group D", "Group E", "Group F" }
aValues = {10,20,15,25,5,30}

nSheet = sheetnew(sheetqunique, aGroups, aValues)
sheetsetcollabels( aGroups; {"Group Names", "%'s"} )
sheetcontrol(_SHOW)
```

Here, the modifier passed to the SHEETSETCOLLABELS() function is the array holding two new literal strings is for the two columns in the sheet. The first parameter tells Realizer at what variable to replace the column labels. Here, the variable *aGroups[]* is specified. Using the SHEETSETCOLLABELS() function without any parameters will return the names of the columns to their original values.

> **Note:** If the modified value of a column label is wider than the format of the column, the text in the column heading may not appear properly. The column needs to be adjusted to fit the column's header, or the text needs to be adjusted to better fit the width of the column.

It is not possible to create a column label by concatenating CHR$(13) + CHR$(10) in hopes that a two-column header will suddenly appear! Instead, two characters and the string of the column's header will appear on one line.

Of course, the number of characters that can fit in the heading of a column depends largely on the size of the font used in that column's label. Fonts can also be manipulated on an individual basis, using the FONTNEW() function in conjunction with the SHEETCONTROL() function:

```
nFont1   = fontnew( fontqunique; "Arial", 12 )
nFont2   = fontnew( fontqunique; "Arial",  8 )
aGroups = {"Group A", "Group B", "Group C", "Group D", "Group E", "Group F" }
aValues = {10,20,15,25,5,30}

nSheet = sheetnew(sheetqunique, aGroups, aValues)
sheetcontrol( _SETFONT; nFont1, nFont2 )
sheetsetcollabels( aGroups; {"Group Names", "Percentages"} )
sheetcontrol(_SHOW)
```

The first modifier used in the SHEETCONTROL() function sets the font for the individual cells in the form. The font held in *nFont2* and passed as the second modifier in this function sets the fonts for the rows and the columns. By increasing the size of the text in the individual cells and reducing the size of the text in the column headers, you can fit more text in each column's header.

The width of a column can be adjusted with a mouse once the data is displayed to the screen; however, why should the end user be forced to do a job that is the responsibility of the programmer? The solution is to "update" the sheet before it is even displayed to the screen. This is possible, since the default width for all columns is 12 characters. Consider this code extract:

```
nFont1   = fontnew( fontqunique; "Arial", 12 )
nFont2   = fontnew( fontqunique; "Arial",  8 )
aGroups  = {"Group A", "Group B", "Group C", "Group D", "Group E", "Group F" }
aValues  = {10,20,15,25,5,30}

nSheet = sheetnew(sheetqunique, aGroups, aValues)
sheetcontrol( _SETFONT; nFont1, nFont2 )
sheetsetcollabels( aGroups; {"Group Names", "Percentages"} )
sheetupdate( aValues; 20 )
sheetcontrol(_SHOW)
```

The SHEETUPDATE() function is called just before the _SHOW instruction is sent to the SHEETCONTROL() function. The first parameter passed to the SHEETUPDATE() function is the name of the column that we want to adjust. Even though the column's label has been adjusted, we still refer to the column via the name of the variable referenced in that column. This is very important. Since no changes have been made to the values in this array, there really is no updating taking place. However, the modifier associated with this function call sets the width of the column to 20. Now the width of the column is properly adjusted before it is even displayed to the screen.

Colors, Display Formats, and Column and Row Restrictions

Color assignments are less flexible for sheets than for the other tools. In fact, only two colors can be adjusted: the color for the text in the cells and the color for the text in the row and column labels. Both colors are manipulated by the SHEETCONTROL() function using the _SETCOLOR internal variable, like this:

```
sheetcontrol( _SETCOLOR; _DARKPURPLE, _BLUE )
```

The first modifier sets the color of the text in the cells; the second modifier sets the text color for the row and column headers. These internal variables could be replaced with an array of three elements. Each element value would range from 0 (darkest) to 1 (lightest) in decimal increments. The three elements represent red, green, and blue hues being mixed to generate the color. For example, the preceding code fragment could have looked like this:

```
sheetcontrol( _SETCOLOR; {.2,.5,.9}, {1,1,1} )
```

That would yield dark blue text in the cells and white text in the row and column headings.

The output of the data in the cells is as important as its color. For example, if we were to add another column to our running example—say, a column holding the actual sales figures of a particular group—the array would look like this:

```
aSales = {28560, 57120,42840,71400,14280,85680}
```

This array would be added to the SHEETNEW() function, and the column headings would be adjusted, like this:

```
nSheet = sheetnew(sheetqunique, aGroups, aValues, aSales)
sheetsetcollabels( aGroups; {"Group Names", "Percentages", "Sales"} )
```

Once the data is in place, the format of that cell is as simple as calling the SETFORMAT() function:

```
setformat( aSales, "$#######.##")
```

The SETFORMAT() function follows the standard printing output options for the PRINT command. Here, this function works just like the SHEETUPDATE() function, in that the name of the array holding the values of the column in question is referenced, rather than the column itself. The SETFORMAT() function works on the same premise. The *aSales[]* array is told that its output will follow the formatting string passed as the second parameter to the function. The output of the column appears in Figure 6-13.

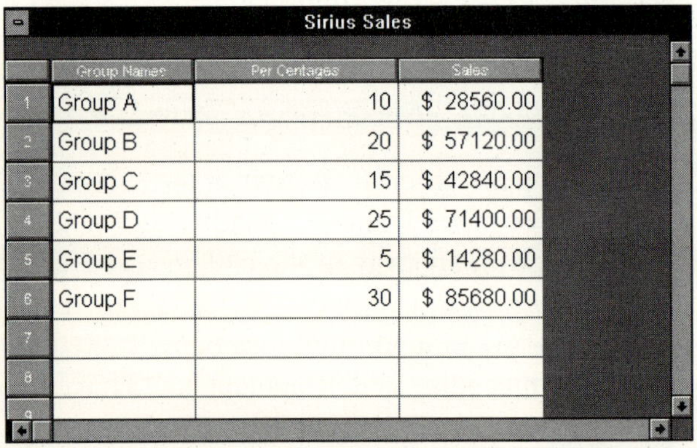

	Group Names	Per Centages	Sales
1	Group A	10	$ 28560.00
2	Group B	20	$ 57120.00
3	Group C	15	$ 42840.00
4	Group D	25	$ 71400.00
5	Group E	5	$ 14280.00
6	Group F	30	$ 85680.00

Figure 6-13. Modified fonts and columns in spreadsheet.

And the source code of *Sheet2.rlz* is as follows:

```
'* Application ... : Sheet2.rlz
'* Authors ....... : Steve Straley
```

Boards, Charts, and Sheets

```
'* Notice ........ : Copyright(c) 1994 - Sirius Press, Inc.
'* ............... : All Rights Reserved
'* Date .......... : January 1, 1994
'* Description ... : This is building on the example program found in Sheet1.rlz

sethourglass()
nFont1  = fontnew( fontqunique; "Arial", 12 )
nFont2  = fontnew( fontqunique; "Arial",  8 )
aGroups = {"Group A", "Group B", "Group C", "Group D", "Group E", "Group F" }
aValues = {10,20,15,25,5,30}
aSales  = {28560, 57120,42840,71400,14280,85680}

nSheet = sheetnew(sheetqunique, aGroups, aValues, aSales; "Sirius Sales", _TITLE)
setformat( aSales, "$#######.##")
sheetcontrol( _SETFONT; nFont1, nFont2 )
sheetcontrol( _SETCOLOR; {.2,.5,.9}, {1,1,1} )
sheetsetcollabels( aGroups; {"Group Names", "Per Centages", "Sales"} )
sheetupdate( aValues; 20 )
resethourglass()
sheetcontrol(_SHOW)

'* End of File: Sheet2.rlz
```

Remember that all the data in a sheet can be modified unless the sheet is told not to allow the data to be modified. Once again, that control lies in the SHEETCONTROL() function in conjunction with the _READONLY internal variable.

```
sheetcontrol( _READONLY; 1)
```

The SHEETCONTROL() function also lets us limit the number of rows displayed in the sheet. In all of the previous examples, there are only six items of data in each of the three arrays, and yet there are more rows in the sheet than there are actual rows of data. We can hide some of those unused rows by using the _ROWRANGE internal variable in conjunction with the SHEETCONTROL() function:

```
sheetcontrol( _ROWRANGE; 1, 6 )
```

This control over the display of the rows and the columns can also extend into those rows and columns that contain data. For example, if the preceding line of code was modified as follows, the result would look like the form shown in Figure 6-14.

```
sheetcontrol( _ROWRANGE; 1, 4 )
```

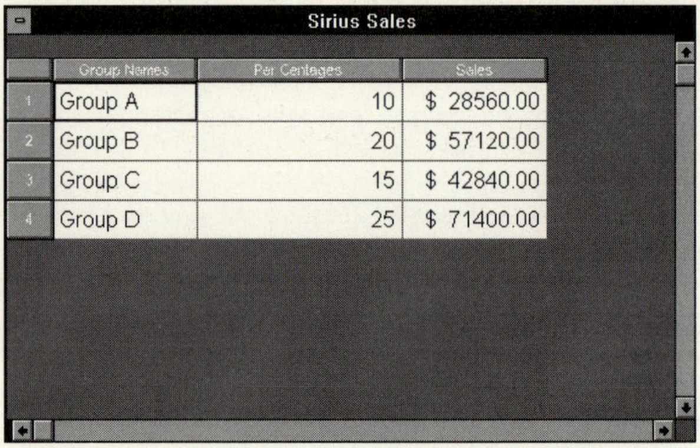

Figure 6-14. Limited row and column focus in spreadsheet.

The same type of control can be made for the columns using the `_COL-RANGE` internal variable instead of the `_ROWRANGE` internal variable.

Special Features: Buttons

The default behavior of a sheet is relatively simple. For example, if you click on the gray button on the upper-left corner of the sheet, the entire sheet is selected. If you click on a column's header (or row's number), then the entire column (or row) is inverted in color, showing that it has been selected. This is the default behavior, but you can assign a special behavior to the columns. To do so, you use the SHEETCONTROL() function and the `_COLBUTTON` internal variable with the `_FORMAT` modifier:

```
sheetcontrol( _COLBUTTON; _FORMAT )
```

The new behavior is that when the user selects a column, a dialog box pops up, allowing the user to modify the display format of that column. For example, the SETFORMAT() function is used to set the display format of the third column in the previous program example. If we add this function to that program example, and if the end user clicks on the header of the third column (the one holding the values from the *aSales[ ]* array), the screen will display the dialog box shown in Figure 6-15.

However, you should avoid this option if you do not plan to apply it to all of the columns.

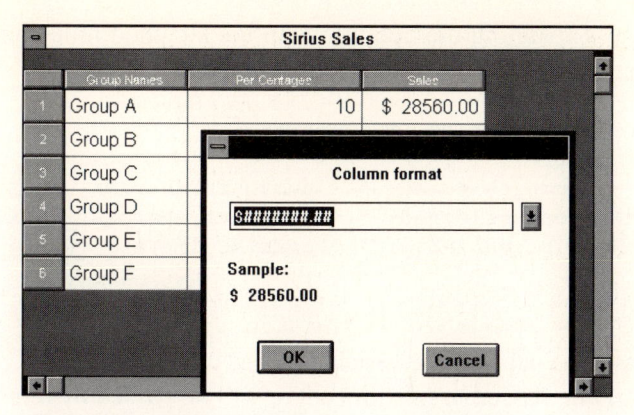

Figure 6-15. Dialog window for column format.

Attaching a Procedure to a Sheet

Attaching a procedure to a sheet follows the same pattern used for all of the other tools. When the procedure is invoked, an array is passed to the procedure. Internal variables can be used to poll any element in that array to obtain values pertaining to the sheet. To start, the skeleton of the attached procedure may look like this:

```
proc TestSheet( aParams, xColumnVar )

end proc
```

and the function that attached this procedure to the current and selected sheet is the following:

```
sheetsetproc( testsheet )
```

This function takes only a few modifiers, such as _SIZE and _CHANGE. If, for example, the _READONLY mode of the sheet is turned off (allowing changes to be made to individual cells directly), the attached procedure would be notified of the change when it takes place. Here, with the _READONLY internal variable in control, you can force the end user to click on a cell in order to modify it. Turning our attention back to the array passed to the attached procedure, the internal variables that can be used are listed in Table 6-1, page 354–355.

However, as we saw in the skeleton of the function, two parameters are automatically passed to the attached procedure: the tool procedure array and the name of the variable of the column or row that was selected by the mouse click. So, by expanding the operations in the attached procedure with the QVAR() function and the _NAME internal variable:

```
proc TestSheet( aParams, xColumnVar )

  input " Column selected: " + numtostr(aParams[_XPOS]) ;
  input "Element selected: " + numtostr(aParams[_YPOS]) ;
  input "Name of variable: " + qvar(xColmnVar, _NAME) ;

end proc
```

we can obtain the name of the variable passed to this function. Keep in mind that any variable passed to this procedure will be passed by reference. This means that any change to any of the elements in the attached procedure will be recognized outside the domain of the procedure. This opens up new possibilities for sheets.

Conclusion

In this chapter we have explored three application-building tools. Proper use of these tools will add more power and punch to an application. The principles of form control and management pertain equally to these tools. Your flexibility in working with combinations of these tools is a key test to tell if you are a Realizer hacker or a Realizer pro. Think of the end user, and constantly ask yourself what best displays the data and what best conveys the message you are trying to share. In some cases, the log is the ideal tool; in other cases, a chart or a sheet will serve the end user better. The choice remains in the hands of the seasoned and experienced programmer, who, regardless of the language, puts himself or herself in the end user's shoes.

Chapter 7

Simple File Manipulation and String Parsing

In the lexicon of programming languages, **parsing** means breaking down a line of code to its most fundamental components. A compiler, for example, needs to be able to do this efficiently and quickly. This is not to say that everyone will want to build a compiler; however, this fundamental ability, mixed with the need to read and write out strings of data efficiently, is at the heart of data manipulation. Realizer itself needs to interpret what part of a line of code is a memory variable and what part is a function; what part is a statement and what part is a parameter or a comment. The better we can think of ways in which to parse data, whether in a program source file or a database, the better we can store it to disk, relate it to other pieces of data, and search for key items within it. Understanding this means understanding not just the language, but the computer as well.

Low-Level File Control

In any language, you'll find a series of functions that work with any type of file directly at the operating-system level. In Clipper and in C, these are the functions that begin with the letter F* (FOPEN(), FREAD(), and so on). In Realizer, a series of FILE* functions have similar behaviors and characteristics. Some pertain to the import and export of data to other data formats, and one deals exclusively with .DBF file. With Realizer's FILE functions, we can work on individual bytes within any given file.

Every file, like every form, font, chart, sheet, board, and so on, needs a numeric ID pointer that refers to that file. This is often called a **file handle**. The FILEQUNIQUE command generates a unique file handle for us to use in conjunction with the FILEOPEN() function.

To begin our exploration of the techniques involved in programming at the operating-system level, let's use the low-level file functions to open a file, to read a file, and to store the contents of a line/record to a specific variable. This simple traversing technique can be seen in the *Parse1.rlz* file:

```
'* Application ... : Parse1.rlz
'* Authors ....... : Steve Straley
'* Notice ........ : Copyright(c) 1994 - Sirius Press, Inc.
'* ............... : All Rights Reserved
'* Date .......... : January 1, 1994
'* Description ... : This begins to show how a parsing routine might work.

'****************************************************
'* Name:        Empty( <xData> )
'* Params:      <xData>        Any data type
'* Returns:     <iEmpty>       Logical true if value is "empty"
'* Purpose:     This function returns a true value should the data passed
'*              be considered "empty".

function Empty( xData )

  return( len( ltrim$(xData) ) = 0 )

end func

'*********************

nFile1 = filequnique
fileopen( nFile1, "parse.prg", _READ )

loop

  fileread( nFile1, sLine )

  if fileeof( nFile1 )
    exit loop
  end if

  if not Empty( sLine )
    print sLine
  end if

end loop

fileclose( nFile1 )    '* <--- Always do this!

'* End of File: Parse1.rlz
```

Simple File Manipulation and String Parsing

Once we have obtained a unique file handle, we use it to open the file named *Parse.prg*. This is a Clipper program file, which I hope, suggests the broad use of this technology. The _READ internal variable tells Realizer that this file can be read but not written to (_WRITE) or both read and written to. Realizer understands more than most languages about how to read data from the disk. For example, the FILEREAD() function will read in only what it understands as a "line": a stream of data terminated by the ASCII carriage return/line feed (CR/LF) combination CHR$(13)/CHR$(10). In Clipper and C, the equivalent function FREAD() will read in a specified number of bytes from the opened file, but it will not automatically read until it encounters the CR/LF combination. Because of this, the FILEREAD() function in Realizer is far easier to use and allows us to have varying line lengths in the opened file. One of the aspects of a database file, specifically a .DBF file, is that the record length (or line length) is preset and fixed. Here, with the intelligence built into the FILEREAD() function, we can simple traverse through the open file, one line at a time. The variable *sLine* will hold the line that is read by the function. Similar to database functions in other languages, the FILEEOF() functions returns a numeric/logical true value when the end-of-file marker is encountered. The internal file pointer is constantly moved as the FILEREAD() function reads in a line of data and stores it to the passed variable. If the end of the file is encountered, the LOOP is exited; if not, and if there is something in the variable *sLine*, the contents are printed to the log. In the Print Log window, the output would look like that in Figure 7-1.

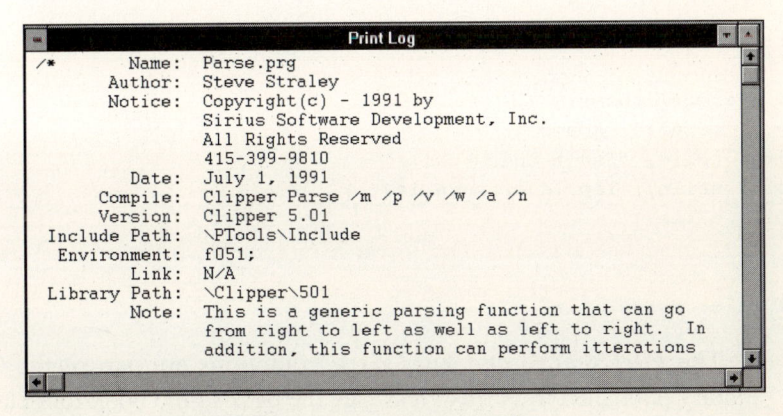

```
                   Print Log
/*        Name:  Parse.prg
        Author:  Steve Straley
        Notice:  Copyright(c) - 1991 by
                 Sirius Software Development, Inc.
                 All Rights Reserved
                 415-399-9810
          Date:  July 1, 1991
       Compile:  Clipper Parse /m /p /v /w /a /n
       Version:  Clipper 5.01
  Include Path:  \PTools\Include
   Environment:  f051;
          Link:  N/A
  Library Path:  \Clipper\501
          Note:  This is a generic parsing function that can go
                 from right to left as well as left to right.  In
                 addition, this function can perform itterations
```

Figure 7-1. PRINT LOG window of read-in-file.

Once we obtain a string of data from the file, we can work with it in a variety of ways. But reading files is only a part of the equation. The file named `Parse2.rlz` shows a technique for writing files and writing strings out to those files:

```
'* Application ... : Parse2.rlz
'* Authors ....... : Steve Straley
'* Notice ........ : Copyright(c) 1994 - Sirius Press, Inc.
'* ............... : All Rights Reserved
'* Date .......... : January 1, 1994
'* Description ... : This begins to show how a parsing routine might work.
func fileCreate( cName )

  local nFileHandle as integer

  nFileHandle = filequnique

  fileopen( nFileHandle, cName, _WRITE )

  return( nFileHandle )

end func

func fileexists( sName )

  return( fileq( sName, _EXISTS ) )

end func

'*****************************

sName = "Steve.ddd"

if not FileExists( sName )
  nFile = FileCreate( sName )
  filewrite( nFile, "Isn't this FUN!!!" )
  filewrite( nFile, "Yep... it sure is!" )
  fileclose( nFile )
end if

'* End of File: Parse2.rlz
```

The *FileCreate()* and *FileExists()* functions are part of the CARTools library published by Sirius Press (see the back of the book for details). Here, the *FileCreate()* function uses the FILEOPEN() function with the _WRITE internal variable. If the file does not exist, it will be created; if it does exist, the contents of that file will be overwritten.

> **Note:** It is important to check for the existence of a file before using the *FileCreate()* function or the FILEOPEN() function. Once a file is overwritten, the process is irreversible.

The language of Realizer is filled with tool-based functions and operations. Most of these alter their behavior via internal variables passed as either parameters or modifiers. The *FileExists()* function combines the FILEQ() function with the `_EXISTS` internal variable. Other internal variables that may be used with the FILEQ() function include `_DATETIME`, `_SIZE`, and `_NAME`. All of these may be better served if used in layered functions that make more intuitive sense.

The variable *sName* in this program example holds a simple file name. If the file exists, nothing will take place; however, if the value returned from *FileExists()* is a numerical true value, then the file is created and the file pointer for that file returned and stored to the variable *nFile*. That variable will be used by the FILEWRITE() function to write out the contents of the two literal strings. Like the FILEREAD() function, the FILEWRITE() function will operate, by default, one line of information at a time. This means that a CR/LF character combination will be attached automatically at the end of the passed line and written to the specified file. Now that we've got Realizer reading and writing a file, we'll introduce the technique of string manipulation.

Parsing

The BASIC language has always been known for its ability to handle and manipulate string information, an advantage that most of the mainstream programming languages have adopted. However, Realizer has a new set of powerful functions geared to make life easier when it comes to strings and expressions. To go along with the RIGHT$(), LEFT$(), and MID$() functions, which return portions of a string from the right, left, or midsection, functions like SUBSTR$(), INSTR(), and STRTOK(), which deal with substrings, give Realizer its new string-based power.

Parsing is the ability to extract subinformation from a string. For example, if we want the middle three characters from the string "Cat in the Hat," the following line:

```
print mid$("Cat in the Hat", 4)
```

would give us the string "in the Hat." Applying from the RIGHT$() function to the same string:

```
print right$("Cat in the Hat", 4)
```

would give us " Hat." And by fine-tuning our MID$() function:

```
print mid$("Cat in the Hat", 5, 6)
```

we could get "in the" in the Print Log window. The function we need use is based on the direction of the search within the string. For left-to-right searches, we can use the LEFT$() and MID$() functions; however, for all string extractions from right to left, only the RIGHT$() function will do. For even finer-tuned searches, you can use the INSTR$() function shown in the file named *Parse6.rlz*:

```
'* Application ... : Parse6.rlz
'* Authors ....... : Steve Straley
'* Notice ........ : Copyright(c) 1994 - Sirius Press, Inc.
'* .............. : All Rights Reserved
'* Date .......... : January 1, 1994
'* Description ... : Using some of the string functions.
'*

local sMainString as string

sMainString = "Cat in the Hat"

input mid$(sMainString, 4),     "MID$(sMainString, 4)" ;
input mid$(sMainString, 4, 5), "MID$(sMainString, 4, 5)" ;
input left$(sMainString, 4),   "LEFT$(sMainString, 4)" ;
input right$(sMainString, 4),  "RIGHT$(sMainString, 4)" ;

input "First occurrence of the letter 't' is at position    " + \\
      numtostr( instr( sMainString, "t" ) ), \\
      "INSTR$(sMainString, 't')" ;
input "Second occurrence of the letter 't' is at position    " + \\
      numtostr( instr( sMainString, "t", 4 ) ), \\
      "INSTR$(sMainString, 't', 4)" ;

'* End of File: Parse6.rlz
```

This program file shows the variations of the three main functions in conjunction with the INPUT command. The INSTR$() function is designed to tell what position within the main string the substring can be found.

Simple File Manipulation and String Parsing

> **Note:** The INSTR$( ) function always returns a number that is the ordinal position of the found substring. This position is always calculated from the left side. Using the return value from this function in conjunction with the RIGHT$( ) function will return bogus results.

If the substring is found within the main string (the first parameter), the function will return a non-zero value indicating the found ordinal position. If a zero is returned, the substring is not contained within the main string. We can also start the search at any position within the main string by passing a third parameter, as shown in the final example program named *Parse6.rlz*. This will tell us the position of any repeated substring search.

This function is slightly modified and enhanced in the CARTools library, as shown in the file named *Parse7.rlz*. Here, we use the modified function to obtain an array of ordinal positions:

```
'* Application ... : Parse7.rlz
'* Authors ....... : Steve Straley
'* Notice ........ : Copyright(c) 1994 - Sirius Press, Inc.
'* ............... : All Rights Reserved
'* Date .......... : January 1, 1994
'* Description ... : Building on some of the string functions.
'*

function AInStr( sMainStr, sSubStr )

  local nPosition as integer
  local aReturn

  nPosition = 1
  aReturn   = {0}     '* Just start the array off...

  loop
    nPosition = instr( sMainStr, sSubStr, nPosition )
    if nPosition = 0
      exit loop
    end if
    aReturn   = { aReturn, nPosition }
    nPosition = nPosition + 1

  end loop

  if endvalid( aReturn ) > startvalid(aReturn) + 1  '* there is more than one
    aReturn = aReturn[startvalid(aReturn)+1:endvalid(aReturn)]
  end if
```

```
        return( aReturn )

end func

local sMainString as string

sMainString = "Cat in the Hat"
print AInStr( sMainString, "t" )
print "******"
print AInStr( sMainString, "$" )

'* End of File: Parse7.rlz
```

And the result in the Print Log window looks like this:

```
3
8
14
******
0
```

Along with the INSTR$() function, there are two other powerful parsing functions to master. The first one is the SUBSTR$() function, which allows for substrings to be inserted, deleted, or even replaced. It is a more flexible function than the STRINSERT$() and the STRDELETE$() functions which, as you can guess by their names, have a more limited focus. Finally, the STRTOK() function is a tokenizing function. Using our *sMainString* variable, the following line of code:

```
print strtok(sMainString)
```

would give us an array of the individual words in the string. In the Print Log window, the array would look like this:

```
Cat
in
the
Hat
```

Now, we can alter the searching criteria within the *sMainString* variable. For example, by passing a secondary array of values to the STRTOK() function, we alter the return value. The following line:

```
print strtok(sMainString, "t")
```

Simple File Manipulation and String Parsing

would now give us:

```
Ca
 in
he Ha
```

Each letter T was searched for and removed from the string, and each subscript position of the returned array shows that substring removal.

> **Note:** Of course, if the return value from the STRTOK() function is an array with only one element, it is safe to say that the parsing substring used as the second parameter was not found in the string. This is similar to a return value of 0 from the INSTR$() function.

The third parameter is the token parameter. Here, an array of additional searching strings may be specified. If the second parameter is specified, then that string will override the internal settings of the STRTOK() function. If the default parsing characters are to be used, then the _DEFAULT internal variable must be specified in order to use the third parameter capabilities:

```
print strtok(sMainString, _DEFAULT, {"t"})
```

Here, the STRTOK() function will return an array of the words found in the *sMainString* variable and will also subparse on those positions of the letter T. The return value is an array that looks like this:

```
Ca
t
in
t
he
Ha
t
```

For a practical example, many of these functions can be seen in `Parse3.rlz` file. In this file, once some of the support functions are defined and in place, the file is opened:

```
nFile1 = filequnique                     '* File pointer
fileopen( nFile1, "Parse3.rlz", _READ )  '* Open file
fileread( nFile1, aLine, 10050, _ALPHA ) '* Read file and create array
fileclose( nFile1 )                      '* Close file
```

A unique feature in this series of function calls is the twist applied to the FILEREAD() function. The variable *aLine* is a new array that will automatically be built by the function. The `_ALPHA` internal variable tells the function that each line is to be stored to the variable passed as the second parameter. The third parameter is the line limit to be read by the function. This may be set to an impractical number, and if there are fewer lines in the file than specified by the third parameter, the function will automatically stop reading the lines. So, this value passed may be a very large number that will cover most of the file read by the function.

Once the array *aLine* is built, it can be used in conjunction with a sheet tool to display the contents, as shown in Figure 7-2.

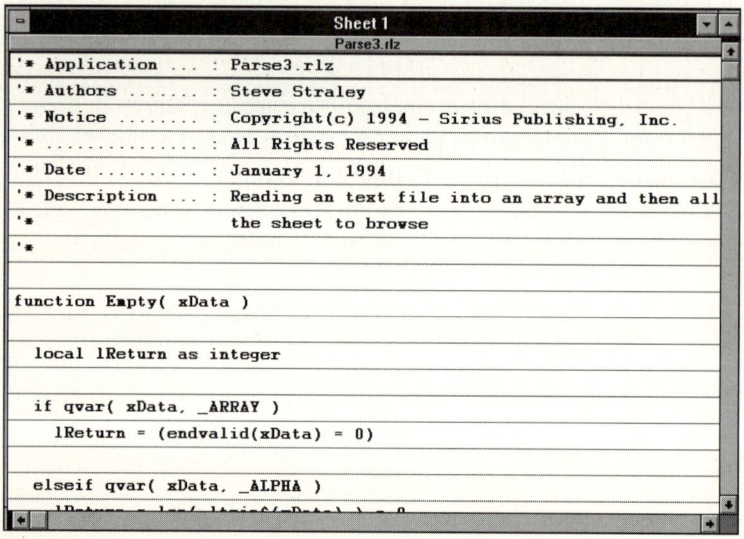

Figure 7-2. Spreadsheet holding parsed in file.

The code for this is as simple as the last fragment of code to read in a file and store it to an array:

```
nSheet = sheetnew( sheetqunique, aLine )
nFont  = fontnew( fontqunique; "Courier", 10, _BOLD )
sheetcontrol( _SIZE; 0,0, 100 pct, 100 pct )
sheetcontrollabels(_HIDE; _ROW )
sheetcontrollabels(_HIDE; _COL1 )
sheetsetcollabels( aLine; "Parse3.rlz" )
sheetupdate( aLine; 100 pct )
sheetsetproc( Testsheet )
```

```
sheetcontrol( _READONLY; 1 )
sheetcontrol( _SETFONT; nFont )
sheetcontrol( _SHOW )
```

Most of the functions called control the output of the screen, the color, the font, and the controls (such as width and display area) of the sheet itself. The browsing ability of the sheet in relation to the array passed to the sheet is built into the Realizer language itself. The attached procedure *TestSheet()* allows the end user to select an individual line in the chart to be parsed. This is our first attempt at parsing the contents of a Realizer source file. If we can parse out the contents of a line, we can build tools and utilities to better document our code, and in doing so, we can better understand the complex logic supporting the Realizer internal operations. In other words, to use the power of the language, we need to see its complexities and subtleties. The *TestSheet()* operation is geared toward this goal. This procedure will be called when the end user clicks on an individual line. If any line within the chart is selected, the following code will be called:

```
proc TestSheet( aParams, xColumnVar )

  sString =  xColumnVar[ aParams[_YPOS] ]
  aVar    =  strtok( sString, chr$(34), {""} )

  nSheet  = sheetnew( sheetqunique, aVar )
  sheetupdate( aVar; 100 pct )
  sheetcontrol( _SIZE; 0,50,100 pct, 100 pct )

  nCount  = cndvalid(aVar)
  nX      = 1

  if not empty( aVar )
    loop
      if not Empty( aVar[nX] )
        if (aVar[nX] = sString)
          exit loop
        end if
        messagebox( ltrim$(aVar[nX]), "Array of string tokens", _MB_OK )
        messagebox( ltrim$(sString),  "The full string", _MB_OK )

        sTemp = ltrim$(aVar[nX] + "*LITERAL*")
        messagebox( "Converted! ->" + sTemp, "Converted string", _MB_OK )

        aVar = strtok( sTemp )
        exit loop
      end if
```

```
      nX = nX + 1
      if nX = nCount
        exit loop
      end if

    end loop

    sheetcontrol( _SHOW )

    messagebox( "That's all folks", "Sirius Press", _MB_OK )

    sheetcontrol( _CLOSE )

  end if

end proc
```

This is our first look at the STDTOK() function, which parses a line into segments known as "tokens." And to make this example program even more complicated, a sheet tool is built within the attached procedure for the array returned from the STRTOK() function. This nesting ability is not only feasible, but vital.

By default, the STRTOK() function will automatically break down each line of code in each line of the array attached to the main sheet into individual pieces. The individual pieces are initially determined as those parts separated by a tab, a carriage return, or even a space. We can modify the behavior of the STRTOK() function slightly by specifying what are actual delimiters and what to ignore. In this program example, the function is called like this:

```
aVar    = strtok( sString, chr$(34), {""} )
```

Here, the function is told to return an array, looking for double quotation marks as the separators. The function will attempt to parse out those literals in the line of code. So, the LOOP command within the *TestSheet()* procedure will go through each element position in the array that was the return value of the STRTOK() function. When a literal string is found (and this will work only on the first one found in the line of code), it will be replaced with the string "*LITERAL*." This, along with the LTRIM$() function becomes the value of the *sTemp* variable. That variable is then passed off to the MESSAGEBOX() function. This function is similar to the INPUT command except that the optional push buttons that appear in the dialog box region may vary. A similar function called *DisplayBox()* acts as a display window for text and is part of the CARTools library.

Once the string has been built, the STRTOK() function is called once again, this time passing to it the variable *sTemp*. The parsed array is then stored to the *aVar* array, which is the same variable that holds the original parsed line of code at the top of the *TestSheet()* procedure. At the bottom of the loop, the SHEETCONTROL() function is called with the _SHOW internal variable. This means that a secondary sheet will be displayed on top of the original. The first sheet showed the various lines of source code from the read-in file. This sheet, displayed within the attached tool procedure *TestSheet()*, shows the various parsed items in the selected line of code. Eventually, one selected line might look like this:

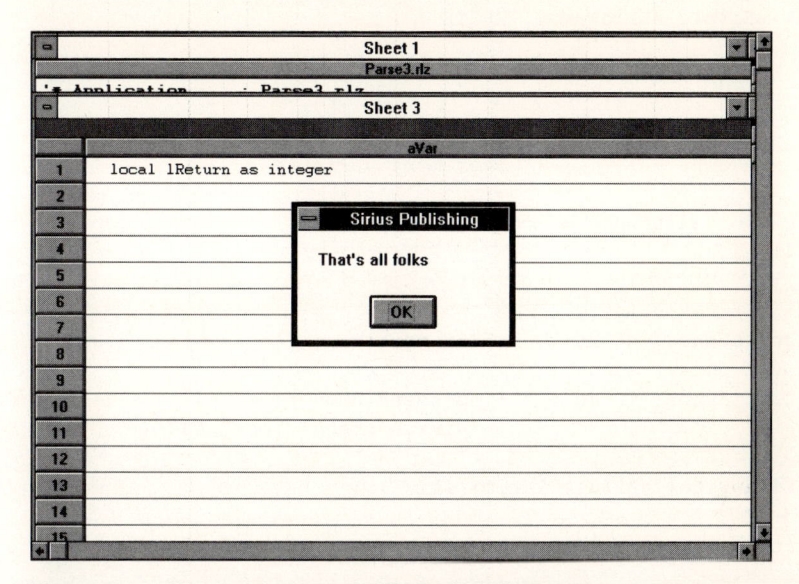

Figure 7-3. Dialog window of MESSAGEBOX() tool.

The call to the MESSAGEBOX() function acts as a temporary hold on the program flow. Clicking on the OK button within this dialog allows the active sheet to be _CLOSEed.

More on Parsing

Literals are only the tip of the iceberg: key words, variable assignments, comments, blank spaces, line continuations, expressions, and evaluations are all key parts of the language. In the next example program, `Parse4.rlz`, the main loop first reads the file in and writes out a temporary file. That file will have in it (or not, as the case may be) blank spaces and comments found on individual lines. In essence, we build a temporary file with our first interpretations. This is commonly known as a "first pass." Some compilers, such as Clipper, are multiple-pass compilers. In the main part of the example program, the first pass begins:

```
nFile1 = filequnique                       '* File pointer
fileopen( nFile1, "parse4.rlz", _READ )    '* Open file
fileread( nFile1, aLine, 10050, _ALPHA )   '* Read file and create array
fileclose( nFile1 )                        '* Close file

nCount    = 1
sFileName = filemakename()
fileopen( nFile1, sFileName, _WRITE )

loop

   sLine  = aLine[nCount]     '* Obtain line from array
   nCount = nCount + 1        '* Increment variable

   '* Check for existence of comment on a line
   '* By itself.

   if left$(ltrim$(sLine), 1) <> "'"
     if asc( sLine ) <> 26    '* Eof marker
       if not empty( sLine )
         Displaybox( "Line : " + numtostr(nCount) + " || " + ltrim$(sLine), \\
                     "Sirius Press, Inc.",400 )

         filewrite( nFile1, ltrim$(sLine) )
       end if
     end if
   end if

   if nCount > endvalid( aLine )
     exit loop
   end if

end loop

DisplayboxClose()
fileclose(nFile1)
```

The start of this code fragment is as expected. The FILEOPEN() function is used to open the source file, and with the FILEREAD() function, the file *Parse4.rlz* is read into the *aLine[]* array. At this point, the variable *nCount* is initialized to a value of 1 and will be used later on in this code segment to show which lines are currently being read into the system. Next comes the function FILEMAKENAME(). This function generates a unique DOS name with a .TMP file extension. This function is ideal for making temporary files to hold new values. The value of this function is then stored to the *sFileName* variable used in the next FILEOPEN() function. The same value for *nFile1* is used, since that file was closed just a few lines earlier and we know that the file pointer is available. After this starts the massive reading loop. The *nCount* variable is used as a subscript pointer for the *aLine[]* array. Once the individual lines are pulled out of the array, the counting variable is incremented. As long as the LEFT$() of the extracted string does not start with an apostrophe (') character, symbolizing the start of a comment line, and as long as the end-of-file marker (which has an ASCII value of 26) is not encountered within the array itself, and as long as the line is not blank (or not *Empty()*), the line is displayed to the screen and written to the file pointer *nFile1* via the FILEWRITE() function.

Note that the user-defined *DisplayBox()* function displays the string of the line to the window. This function is similar to the MESSAGEBOX() function except for a push button in the dialog box. This function is a part of the CARTools package. At the end of the LOOP, the *DisplayBoxClose()* function is called. Since there is no push button to stop the flow of the program and close the dialog box, this function is needed to remove that tool from the screen. Following this, the temporary file is closed. Once reread, the array is attached to a sheet and displayed to the screen via the SHEETCONTROL() function.

After the temporary file is closed, it is reopened and read into the *aLine[]* array. This operation will automatically remove the contents stored previously to that array and fill it with the new stripped and parsed file. The key to this example is the use of the FILEMAKENAME() function to create a temporary file for making a first-pass parse of the contents. The real trick is in the *DisplayBox()* function:

```
proc displaybox( sDisplay, sTitle, .. ; .. )

  proc DisplayMake()
    nDispHandle = formqunique
    nDispObject = 30000
    formnew( nDispHandle; sTitle, _TITLE )
    formcontrol( _SIZE; _CENTER, _CENTER, nDispSize, 100 )
    formsetobject( nDispObject, _CAPTIONLEFT, sDisplay, _CENTER, _CENTER, \\
                                nDispSize - 5, _DEFAULT )

  end proc

  nOldForm = formq(_SELECTED)

  if not Empty( qnoptmods )
    formselect( nDispHandle )
```

```
      formcontrol( _CLOSE )
      nDispHandle = 0
      if not empty( nOldForm )
        if formq( nOldForm; _EXISTS )
          formselect( nOldForm )
        end if
      end if
   else

      if empty( qnoptparams )
        nDispSize = max( len(sDisplay), len(sTitle) ) + 200
      else
        nDispSize = qoptparam(1)
      end if

      if not qvar( nDispHandle, _DEFINED )
        DisplayMake()
      else
        if Empty( nDispHandle )
          DisplayMake()
        else
          formselect(nDispHandle)
        end if
      end if

      formmodifyobject( nDispObject, _SETFOCUS, sDisplay )
      formcontrol( _SHOW )
      if not Empty( nOldForm )
        formselect( nOldForm )
      end if

   end if

end proc

proc displayboxclose( )
  displaybox(1,2;1)
end proc
```

Two parameters are required for this function. Unknown to the programmer, an optional modifier is available. This is used by the *DisplayBoxClose()* function to tell the contents stored in the *DisplayBox()* function to clear out. In Realizer, the programmer applies this same technique by passing internal variables as modifiers to various functions to alter the behavior of various tools, such as _SHOW, _HIDE, and _CLOSE. This example also brings up the topic of reusable code and libraries:

Simple File Manipulation and String Parsing

> **Note:** A generic good tool, function, or procedure will not only be extendable to future applications and compatible with code fragments, but will be robust enough to work in abnormal conditions.

Within the *DisplayBox()* function is a localized function called *DisplayMake()*. This function will be called only by the *DisplayBox()* function and cannot be accidentally called by a programmer. This function attempts to obtain a unique form name for the display region used. It also assigns a very high and unrealistic number for the display object held within the form: 30000. Once the form is created and sized, and the _CAPTION-LEFT object is set to the form, the *DisplayMake()* function terminates.

Within the *DisplayBox()* function itself, the first thing that is accomplished is an attempt to obtain the currently selected form number. In building these types of functions and tools, we have to plan for a variety of scenarios in which they may be called: in conjunction with existing tools and forms, and as standalone tools. If the number of optional modifiers is 0, then the value of the *Empty()* function in conjunction with the QNOPTMODS command will be a logical true numeric. This will eventually close the form region. These same techniques are used throughout this function to achieve the desired effect.

At this point, we can begin to expand on the parsing concepts and see how these techniques can be used to build a valuable tool that will document the patterns found in any Realizer source code. The file that starts this discussion is `Parse5.rlz`. In this program file, the main loop looks like this:

```
if ReadFile()
  BuildArray()

  nCount        = 1
  lLineContinue = FALSE
  nLevel        = 1

  loop

    TopOfLoop:
    if not lLineContinue
      sLine   = aLine[nCount]                '* Obtain line from array
      nCount  = nCount + 1                   '* Increment variable
      if ( right$(sLine,2) = "\\" )          '* Check for line continuation
        sLine = left$( sLine, len(sLine)-2 )
        lLineContinue = TRUE
        goto TopOfLoop                       '* Jump to the label
```

```
      end if
    else
      sLine = sLine + aLine[nCount]
      nCount = nCount + 1
      if (right$(sLine,2) = "\\" )
        sLine = left$( sLine, len(sLine)-2 )
        goto TopOfLoop
      else
        lLineContinue = FALSE
      end if
    end if

    aWords = strtok(sLine, _DEFAULT, {"(", ",", ")", ";"})

    if not lLineContinue

      if instr( "FUNCPROC", ucase$( left$( sLine, 4 ) ) ) > 0
        FuncAndProc( nFile1, sLine, nLevel, aWords )

      elseif ucase$( left$( sLine, 3 ) ) = "END"
        if ucase$( left$( aWords[2], 4 ) ) = "PROC"
          nLevel = nLevel - 1
          filewrite( nFile1, spc(nLevel*2) + "End of Proc" )
          if nLevel > 1
            filewrite( nFile1, "" )
          end if
        elseif ucase$( left$( aWords[2], 4 ) ) = "FUNC"
          nLevel = nLevel - 1
        end if

      elseif ucase$( left$( sline, 6) ) = "RETURN"
        ReturnFound( nFile1, aLevel, aWords )

      else
        RegularLine( aWords, nFile1 )

      end if

    end if

    if nCount > endvalid( aLine )
      exit loop
    end if

  end loop
```

Following this is additional code that closes off the IF command at the top of this program snippet. The first function called is the *ReadFile()* function.

Simple File Manipulation and String Parsing 389

This function allows the end user to select an .RLZ file from the disk. This is accomplished via the following:

```
lReturn   = TRUE
sReadFile = stdopen( "*.rlz", "Sirius Press, Inc" )
```

The STDOPEN() function produces a standard file-opening dialog box, found in practically every Windows application:

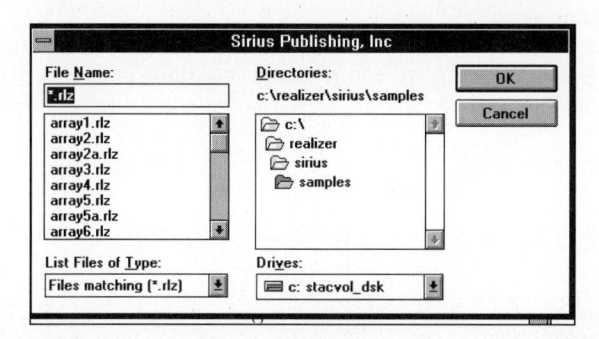

Figure 7-4. Modified dialog window for OPEN operation.

There are other standard functions for writing files, setting the printer, and so on. Knowing these functions can save time and energy and allows you to build a standard interface common with other Windows applications. In this function, if a file is selected from this standard dialog box, the file is opened and read into an array. This operation is the same as seen in previous programming samples. Eventually, the function will return a numerical TRUE value or a FALSE value, allowing the main loop of the program file to continue or not. Once the file is selected and opened, an array is built, along with a few variables. Both *nCount* and *nLevel* are set to 1; *lLineContinue* is set to the global variable FALSE (obtained when the CARTools library was loaded into the system at the top of this example program), the main loop beings.

At the top of the loop is the following line of code:

```
TopOfLoop:
```

This label is used in conjunction with the GOTO command. A label is like a variable without a value and is denoted by the use of the colon attached to its name. While GOTOs are not generally recommended (they support unstructured code which, over time, becomes difficult to manage), they can be very useful in localized, controlled situations, such as the one outlined here. This label is needed because of a new twist in our parsing example:

line continuations. Here, we need to see if the last two characters in a line equal the "\\" combination, and if so, to concatenate the subsequent line to the current line. When this happens, the current line count, held in *nCount*, should remain in place, since we are not going to increment the line position.

```
if not lLineContinue
  sLine  = aLine[nCount]               '* Obtain line from array
  nCount = nCount + 1                  '* Increment variable
  if ( right$(sLine,2) = "\\" )        '* Check for line continuation
    sLine = left$( sLine, len(sLine)-2 )
    lLineContinue = TRUE
    goto TopOfLoop                     '* Jump to the label
  end if
else
  sLine = sLine + aLine[nCount]
  nCount = nCount + 1
  if (right$(sLine,2) = "\\" )
    sLine = left$( sLine, len(sLine)-2 )
    goto TopOfLoop
  else
    lLineContinue = FALSE
  end if
end if
```

If the flag *lLineContinue* is set to a numerical FALSE value, then a line is read into the *sLine* variable and the counting/indexing variable *nCount* is incremented. Then the RIGHT$() function is used to check the right side of the source line to see if there is any indication of a line-continuation scenario. If so, the line *sLine* is stripped of these two characters, the value of *lLineContinue* is set to a logical TRUE numeric value, and Realizer is told to GOTO the *TopOfLoop*. This sets us up for the next possible condition, which occurs if *lLineContinue* is set to a logical TRUE numeric value. In this case, the value of *sLine* is modified to include the value of *aLine[nCount]*. Remember two things about this operation: (1) the "\\" characters have been removed from the back end of the *sLine* variable, and (2) the value of *nCount* has been appropriately incremented prior to the execution of this line of code. Once the line is built, we need to once again increment the *nCount* variable and to recheck to see if that added line contains a line-continuation character combination. Eventually, the value of *sLine* will be one line of code with stripped-out line-continuation markers, ready to be used by the STRTOK() function.

The *aWords[]* variable holds the return value from the STRTOK() function and, one at a time, we check the beginning of this array to see if there are any key words to look for, such as FUNCTION, PROC, END, or

Simple File Manipulation and String Parsing

RETURN. One at a time, the first four characters of the left side of each line are looked at. If, for example, the first four characters of the first word are "FUNC," then the *FuncAndProc()* function is called. This means that some limitations and problems may be encountered along the way (especially if a user-defined function called *FUNCNEW()* is called). Nevertheless, within reason, the loop will look at each of these key words and make some reasonable assertion.

Another point in this parsing routine is the ability to scan for patterns. For example, the operation to search for either a FUNCTION or a PROCEDURE is generally the same. Both statements have the potential of parameters and/or modifiers; therefore, rather than building two functions (one for procedures and one for functions) with the same basic code set, we build only one: *FuncAndProc()*. The test for either key word, FUNCTION or PROCEDURE, is handled by the INSTR() function:

```
if instr( "FUNCPROC", ucase$( left$( sLine, 4 ) ) ) > 0
```

By joining the first four letters of FUNCTION and the first four letters of PROCEDURE to make one eight-letter string, we then can test the first four, uppercase letters from the retrieved line found in *sLine* and if the first four characters can be found in "FUNCPROC," the return value will be greater than 0 (indicating ordinal position). This, however, allows for the first four characters in a line to be "UNCP," or "NCPR," or even "CPRO." These are unlikely possibilities; however, to be on the safe side, we could store the contents of the search to a temporary variable and then see if the ordinal position found is either 1 or 4:

```
nPosFound = instr( "FUNCPROC", ucase$( left$( sLine, 4 ) ) )
if nPosFound = 1 or nPosFond = 4
```

This would insure the search to be at the beginning of the key word "FUNC" or "PROC." Alternatively, we could see if the word itself is a key word. Both "FUNCTION" and "PROC" are key words, so we could use the STRKEYWORD() function:

```
if strkeyword( aWord[ABeg(aWord)] ) and \\
    instr( "FUNCPROC", ucase$( left$( sLine, 4 ) ) ) > 0
```

This, too, would avoid the potential of confusion. With this in mind, here's the complete `Parse5.rlz` file:

```
'* Application ... : Parse5.rlz
'* Authors ....... : Steve Straley
'* Notice ........ : Copyright(c) 1994 - Sirius Press, Inc.
```

```
'* .............. : All Rights Reserved
'* Date .......... : January 1, 1994
'* Description ... : Taking it to the next level of parsing...
'*

run "CARTools.rlz"

'* Func:        ReadFile()
'* Parms:       None
'* Returns:     Logical numeric
'* Purpose      Asks the end user if they want to read in a file using one
'*              of the STD() functions.  If no file is selected from the
'*              standard tool, a numeric false will be returned.  Otherwise,
'*              a numeric TRUE will be returned and the file will be opened,
'*              read into an array, parsed and stored to a temporary file.
'*
'*              The values of TRUE and FALSE are found in the CARTools'
'*              library file.

func ReadFile()

  local lReturn    as integer
  local sReadFile as string

  lReturn    = TRUE
  sReadFile = stdopen( "*.rlz", "Sirius Press, Inc" )

  if empty( sReadFile )
    lReturn = FALSE
  else

    nFile1 = filequnique                    '* File pointer
    fileopen( nFile1, sReadFile,   _READ )  '* Open file
    fileread( nFile1, aLine, 10050, _ALPHA ) '* Read file and create array
    fileclose( nFile1 )                     '* Close file

    nCount   = 1
    sFileName = filemakename()
    fileopen( nFile1, sFileName, _WRITE )

    loop
      sLine  = aLine[nCount]     '* Obtain line from array
      nCount = nCount + 1        '* Increment variable

      '* Check for existence of comment on a line
      '* By itself.

      if left$(ltrim$(sLine), 1) <> "'"
        if asc( sLine ) <> 26
```

```
            if not empty( sLine )
               filewrite( nFile1, ltrim$(sLine) )
            end if
         end if
      end if

      if nCount > endvalid( aLine )
         exit loop
      end if

   end loop

   fileclose(nFile1)

 end if

 return( lReturn )

end func

'* Func:       BuildArray()
'* Parms:      None
'* Returns:    None
'* Purpose     Will open the file stored to the <nFile1> variable and
'*             read the file into the array <aLine>.

proc BuildArray()

   fileopen( nFile1, sFileName, _READ )     '* Open file
   fileread( nFile1, aLine, 10050, _ALPHA ) '* Read file and create array
   fileclose( nFile1 )                      '* Close file
   fileopen( nFile1, sFileName, _WRITE )

end proc

'* Func:       KeyWordBuild( <aData> )
'* Parms:      <aData>        Array of items found on a particular line
'* Returns:    None
'* Purpose     Checks to see if the words in the passed parsed line
'*             of code is a Realizer key word.  And if so, lots of
'*             stuff happens!

proc KeyWordBuild( aData )

   local nStart as integer
   local nEnd   as integer
   local nTemp  as integer

   nStart = ABeg( aData )
   nEnd   = AEnd( aData )
```

```
    for nTemp = nStart to nEnd
      if strkeyword( aWords[nTemp] )
        if instr( "().=", left$(aWords[nTemp],1) ) = 0
          '* Check to see if the key word is in the table and if not, add
          if not qvar( aKeyWords, _DEFINED )
            aKeyWords = { aWords[nTemp] }
          else
            if not firstmatch( aKeyWords, aWords[nTemp] )
              AAdd(aKeyWords, aWords[nTemp])
            end if
          end if
        end if
      end if
    next

end proc

'* Func:      FuncAndProc()
'* Purpose    This function parses out the words FUNCTION and PROC
'*            and checks with optional parameters and modifiers.

proc FuncAndProc( nWriteFile, sData, nPad, aWords )

    local sFirst       as string
    local nTemp        as integer
    local nEndAparams  as integer
    local nCount       as integer
    local aParams

    RemoveComments( aWords )

    '* Just pull out the line to make it easier
    sFirst = ucase$(left$(sLine,4))

    '* Now, write out some prelim stuff
    filewrite( nWriteFile, "" )
    if sFirst = "FUNC"
       filewrite( nWriteFile, spc(nPad*2) + " Function: " + \\
                              ucase$( aWords[2] ) + "()" )
    else
       filewrite( nWriteFile, spc(nPad*2) + "Procedure: " + \\
                              ucase$( aWords[2] ) + "()" )
    end if

    '* Now, look for parameters so we have to re-build the string first
    sData   = BuildString( aWords[3:AEnd(aWords)] )
    aParams = strtok(sLine, _DEFAULT, {"(", ",", ")", ";"})
    nTemp = ABeg(aParams)
```

Simple File Manipulation and String Parsing

```
'*******<< Parse the string into words >>********

loop
   if instr(",().=", aParams[nTemp] ) > 0
      if ALen( aParams ) = 1    '* No more elements to read
         nEndAparams = 0
         nTemp = nTemp + 1
      else
         aParams = ADel( aParams, nTemp )
         nEndAparams = AEnd( aParams )
      end if
   else
      nTemp = nTemp + 1
   end if

   if nTemp > AEnd( aParams )
      exit loop
   end if
end loop

'* So long as there are end-stuff to do...
if nEndAparams > 0
   for nCount = ABeg(aParams) to AEnd(aParams)

      '* Just check the first item in the list!
      if nCount = ABeg(aParams)

         ' There are modifiers
         if aParams[nCount] = ";"

            ' Check to see if there are optional modifiers
            if aParams[nCount+1] = ".."
               filewrite(nWriteFile, " Modifiers: " + \\
                                    "Optional modifiers exist" )
            else
               filewrite(nWriteFile, " Modifiers: " + aParams[nCount+1] )
            end if
            nCount = nCount + 1
         else

            ' No modifiers, just optional PARAMETERS
            if aParams[nCount] = ".."
               filewrite(nWriteFile, " Parameters: " + \\
                                    "Optional parameters exist" )
            else
               filewrite(nWriteFile, " Parameters: " + aParams[nCount])
            end if
```

```
            end if
         else
            if aParams[nCount] = ";"
               if aParams[nCount+1] = ".."
                  filewrite(nWriteFile, "  Modifiers: " + \\
                                      "Optional modifiers exist" )
               else
                  filewrite(nWriteFile, "  Modifiers: " + aParams[nCount+1] )
               end if
               nCount = nCount + 1
            elseif aParams[nCount] = ".."
               filewrite(nWriteFile, "               Optional Parameters exist" )
            else
               filewrite(nWriteFile, "               " + aParams[nCount])
            end if
         end if
      next
   end if

   nPad = nPad + 1

end proc

'* Func:       ReturnFound()
'* Purpose     This function writes out the information found in the
'*             RETURN statement.

proc ReturnFound( nFile1, aLevel, aWords )

   local nEndCount as integer
   local nStart    as integer
   local nEnd      as integer
   local sLine     as string

   ADel( aWords, 1 )
   nEndCount = ABeg(aWords)
   nStart = ABeg(aWords)
   nEnd   = AEnd(aWords)
   loop
     sLine  = aWords[nEndCount]
     if     strkeyword( sLine )
       KeyWordBuild( aWords )
       if ALen( aWords ) = 1   '* Can't delete any more
         aWords[nStart] = ""
         nEndCount = nEnd + 1
       else
         ADel(aWords, nEndCount)
       end if
```

```
      elseif (instr("()", sLine) > 0)
        if ALen( aWords ) = 1   '* Can't delete any more
          aWords[nStart] = ""
          nEndCount = nEnd + 1
        else
          ADel(aWords, nEndCount)
        end if
      else
        nEndCount = nEndCount + 1
      end if

      if nEndCount > AEnd(aWords)
        exit loop
      end if

   end loop

   if not Empty( aWords[ABeg(aWords)] )
     filewrite( nFile1, spc(nLevel*2) + "Returns: " + aWords[ABeg(aWords)] )
   else
     filewrite( nFile1, spc(nLevel*2) + "Unknown trouble..." )
   end if

end proc

'* Func:       RegularLine()
'* Purpose     This function parses out a regular line of Realizer code.

proc RegularLine(aWords, nWrite)

   local nPos         as integer
   local nDataPos     as integer
   local sOutput      as string
   local lDimFound    as integer
   local nNewCount    as integer
   local sAsData      as string
   local lWithLocal   as integer
   local aOldWords

   '* First, check to see if there are any local declarations
   lDimFound   = FALSE
   aOldWords   = aWords
   lWithLocal  = FALSE
   sAsData     = ""
   AUCase$(aOldWords)

   '* The following checks to see if there is a DIM
   '* -----------------------------------------------------------------------
```

```
nPos = firstmatch( aOldWords, "DIM" )
if nPos > 0
  lDimFound = TRUE
  if aOldWords[nPos+1] = "LOCAL"    '* Delete this
    ADel( aWords, nPos + 1 )
    ADel( aOldWords, nPos + 1 )
    lWithLocal = TRUE
  end if
  if lWithLocal
    sOutput = "Dim'd Local: " + aWords[nPos+1]
  else
    sOutput = " Dimmed Var: " + aWords[nPos+1]
  end if
  nDataPos = firstmatch(aOldWords, "AS" )
  if nDataPos > 0
    sOutput = PadRight(sOutput, 35)
    sAsData = "....... " + ucase$(aWords[nDataPos+1])
  end if
  filewrite( nWrite, sOutput + sAsData )

  for nNewCount = nPos+1 to AEnd( aWords )
    if aWords[nNewCount] = ","
      filewrite( nWrite, "              : " + \\
               PadRight(aWords[nNewCount+1], 21) + " " + sAsData )
    end if
  next

end if

'* The following checks to see if there is a LOCAL
'* ----------------------------------------------------------------------

if not lDimFound

  nPos = firstmatch(aOldWords, "LOCAL" )

  if nPos > 0
    sOutput = "   Local Var: " + aWords[nPos+1]
    '* Now check to see if there are any comas
    nDataPos = firstmatch(aOldWords, "AS" )
    if nDataPos > 0
      sOutput = padRight(sOutput, 35)
      sAsData = "....... " + ucase$(aWords[nDataPos+1])
    end if
    filewrite( nWrite, sOutput + " " + sAsData )

    '* Check to see if there are multiple variables
    '* on the same line...
```

Simple File Manipulation and String Parsing 399

```
         for nNewCount = nPos+1 to AEnd( aWords )
           if aWords[nNewCount] = ","
             filewrite( nWrite, "            : " + \\
                     PadRight(aWords[nNewCount+1], 22) + " " + sAsData )
           end if
         next

       end if

     end if

     RemoveLiterals( aWords )
     RemoveComments( aWords )

     '* The following checks to see if there is a LABEL defined
     '* ----------------------------------------------------------------

     for nPos = ABeg(aWords) to AEnd(aWords)
       if right$(aWords[nPos], 1) = ":"              '* This is a label
         print aWords, nPos, len(aWords)
         print "*****"
         sleep 20
         filewrite( nWrite, "Label Found: " + left$(aWords[nPos], \\
                                         len(aWords[nPos])-1) )
       end if
     next

     KeyWordDisp( aWords )

end proc
'* Func:         RemoveComments( <aWords> )
'* Parms:        <aWords>              Array of parsed words
'* Returns:      None
'* Purpose       This function checks to see if there is a comment within
'*               a given and specified line.

proc RemoveComments( aWords )

   local nPos as integer

   for nPos = ABeg( aWords ) to AEnd( aWords )
     if left$( aWords[nPos], 1) = "'"
       asize( aWords, nPos -1 )
       exit for
     end if
   next

end proc
```

```
proc RemoveLiterals( aWords )

  local nPos   as integer
  local nOut   as integer
  local nCount as integer

  for nPos = ABeg(aWords) to AEnd(aWords)
    if aWords[nPos] = chr$(34)
      '* Beginning of a literal
      for nOut = nPos + 1 to AEnd(aWords)
        if aWords[nOut] = chr$(34)
          '* End of a literal
          aWords[nPos] = "Literals"
          for nCount = nPos + 1 to nOut
            print aWords
            print "*******"
            sleep 10
            ADel(aWords, nPos+1)
          next
           nPos = ABeg(aWords)   '* Reset the pointer
          exit for
        end if
      next
    end if
  next

end proc


'* Func:      SheetDo( <aParams>, <aColumn> )
'* Returns:   None
'* Purpose:   This procedure doesn't really use the parameters passed
'*            to it from Realizer.  If the close icon is clicked on within
'*            the attached sheet, then this procedure will be called
'*            which clears out the memory used by the application and
'*            erases the temporary files.

proc SheetDo( aParams, aColumn )

  reset _VAR
  reset _PROC
  reset _SHEET
  kill "*.tmp"

end proc

'***********************[ MAIN ROUTINE ]*********************************
'*************************************************************************
```

```
if ReadFile()
  BuildArray()

  nCount         = 1
  lLineContinue  = FALSE
  nLevel         = 1

  loop

    TopOfLoop:

    if not lLineContinue
      sLine  = aLine[nCount]                '* Obtain line from array
      nCount = nCount + 1                   '* Increment variable
      if ( right$(sLine,2) = "\\" )         '* Check for line continuation
        sLine = left$( sLine, len(sLine)-2 )
        lLineContinue = TRUE
        goto TopOfLoop                      '* Jump to the label
      end if
    else
      sLine = sLine + aLine[nCount]
      nCount = nCount + 1
      if (right$(sLine,2) = "\\" )
        sLine = left$( sLine, len(sLine)-2 )
        goto TopOfLoop
      else
        lLineContinue = FALSE
      end if
    end if

    aWords = strtok(sLine, _DEFAULT, {"(", ",", ")", ";"})

    if not lLineContinue

      if instr( "FUNCPROC", ucase$( left$( sLine, 4 ) ) ) > 0
        FuncAndProc( nFile1, sLine, nLevel, aWords )

      elseif ucase$( left$( sLine, 3 ) ) = "END"
        if ucase$( left$( aWords[2], 4 ) ) = "PROC"
          nLevel = nLevel - 1
          filewrite( nFile1, spc(nLevel*2) + "End of Proc" )
          if nLevel > 1
            filewrite( nFile1, "" )
          end if
        elseif ucase$( left$( aWords[2], 4 ) ) = "FUNC"
          nLevel = nLevel - 1
        end if

      elseif ucase$( left$( sline, 6) ) = "RETURN"
```

```
              ReturnFound( nFile1, aLevel, aWords )

        else
           RegularLine( aWords, nFile1 )

        end if

     end if

     if nCount > endvalid( aLine )
        exit loop
     end if

  end loop

  filewrite( nFile1, "" )
  filewrite( nFile1, "" )
  if qvar( aKeyWords, _DEFINED )
     filewrite( nFile1, "--------------------[ Key Words Used ]--------------------" )
     filewrite( nFile1, "" )
     for nCount = ABeg(aKeyWords) to AEnd(aKeyWords)
        filewrite( nFile1, ucase$(aKeyWords[nCount]) )
     next
  else
     filewrite( nFile1, "No Key Words Used... don't ask me how!" )
  end if

  fileclose( nFile1 )
  fileopen( nFile1, sFileName, _READ )        '* Open file
  fileread( nFile1, aLine, 10050, _ALPHA )    '* Read file and create array
  fileclose( nFile1 )                          '* Close file
  kill sFileName
  nSheet = sheetnew( sheetqunique, aLine )
  nFont  = fontnew( fontqunique; "Courier", 10, _BOLD )
  sheetcontrol( _SIZE; 0,0, 100 pct, 100 pct )
  sheetcontrollabels(_HIDE; _ROW )
  sheetcontrollabels(_HIDE; _COL1 )
  sheetsetcollabels( aLine; sFileName )
  sheetupdate( aLine; 100 pct )
  sheetsetproc( sheetdo )
  sheetcontrol( _READONLY; 1 )
  sheetcontrol( _SETFONT; nFont )
  sheetcontrol( _SHOW )

end if

'* End of File: Parse5.rlz
```

This is the beginning of a utility package especially for Realizer and part of the CARTools library.

Other Files, Other Options

String manipulation is a key element of programming. Its implementation can range from the complex, as we've seen, to the simple, and its usefulness is just as broad. For example, suppose we want our application to accept a string from an end user and encrypt it. In *Parse8.rlz*, we take one of many possible approaches: We find the ASCII value of each character in a string, increase that value by some base amount (in this case, 108), and then flip the string for output. The MID$(), CHR$(), ASC(), and REVERSE$() functions are key in this example:

```
'* Application ... : Parse8.rlz
'* Authors ....... : Steve Straley
'* Notice ........ : Copyright(c) 1994 - Sirius Press, Inc.
'* ............... : All Rights Reserved
'* Date .......... : January 1, 1994
'* Description ... : Simple Encryption and Decryption routines...
'*

function Encrypt( sData, .. )

  local nBase    as integer
  local nCount   as integer
  local sReturn  as string

  sReturn = ""

  if (qnoptparams = 0)
    nBase = 108
  else
    nBase = qoptparam(1)
  end if

  for nCount = 1 to len( sData )
    sReturn = sReturn + chr$( asc( mid$( sData, nCount, 1) ) + nBase )

  next

  return( reverse$(sReturn) )

end func

function Decrypt( sData, .. )
```

```
  local nBase   as integer
  local nCount  as integer
  local sReturn as string

  sReturn = ""

  if (qnoptparams = 0)
    nBase = 108
  else
    nBase = qoptparam(1)
  end if

  sData = reverse$(sData)

  for nCount = 1 to len( sData )
    sReturn = sReturn + chr$( asc( mid$( sData, nCount, 1) ) - nBase )
  next

  return( sReturn )

end func

'****** MAIN ROUTINE *****'

input "Enter any string", "Sirius Press, Inc"; sData

print sData
print Encrypt( sData )
print Encrypt( sData, 0 )
print Decrypt( Encrypt( sData ) )

'* End of File: Parse8.rlz
```

When the INPUT command takes effect, the following dialog box will be displayed:

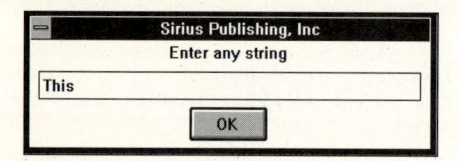

Note: In this example and the next, the text that is entered into the INPUT dialog box will be the string "This."

Simple File Manipulation and String Parsing

The *Encrypt()* function requires at least one parameter passed and, based on the call to the QOPTPARAM() function, only one recognized optional parameter. The second and optional parameter is a numeric value representing the base incrementing value to be applied to the ASCII value of each character in the string *sData*. Within the function, the FOR...NEXT loop goes through each element position in *sData*, extracts one character, and increments the ASCII value of that character by the value of *nBase* (defaulting to an incrementing value of 108). Once incremented, the CHR$() function is called to convert the new ASCII value into a string. This value is then added to the return string *sReturn* (which starts off in this function as a NULL string). The return value of the function will be that string, reversed via the REVERSE$() function.

The *Decrypt()* function performs an operation exactly opposite to the one used in the *Encrypt()* function. It is the programmer's responsibility to use the same base value in both encrypting and decrypting in order to ensure the expected results.

Not needed in this example (and not documented adequately in the manuals), the MID$() function can, as a second parameter, take an array of starting positions. For example, the FOR...NEXT loop in the *Encrypt()* function could have looked like this:

```
function Encrypt( sData, .. )

local nBase    as integer
local nCount   as integer
local sReturn as string
local aData

  sReturn = ""

  if (qnoptparams = 0)
    nBase = 108
  else
    nBase = qoptparam(1)
  end if

  aData = chr$(asc(mid$(sData, index(len(sData)), 1)) + nBase)

  for nCount = 1 to len( sData )
    sReturn = sReturn + aData[nCount]
  next

  return( reverse$(sReturn) )

end func
```

In this function, an array of numerics, 1 through the LEN() of the *sData* variable is passed as a second parameter to the MID$() function. Instead of a string returned from this function, an array is returned. Each value from the array is then converted with the ASC() function, incremented in value by *nBase*, and then converted back to a string using the CHR$() function. Therefore, the new variable *aData* holds an array of single-byte characters that need to be concatenated within the following FOR...NEXT loop. The point of this example (found in `Parse10.rlz`), is that the MID$() function can take, as a second parameter, an array of beginning search points within the string, and the return value of the MID$() function will change accordingly.

Taking this one step further, the encryption can use some of the binary and conversion functions. In the next example, the BIN$(), OCT$(), and HEX$() functions are used to encrypt a string and the BINTONUM(), OCTTONUM(), and HEXTONUM() functions are used to reverse the process:

```
'* Application ... : Parse9.rlz
'* Authors ....... : Steve Straley
'* Notice ........ : Copyright(c) 1994 - Sirius Press, Inc.
'* .............. : All Rights Reserved
'* Date .......... : January 1, 1994
'* Description ... : Simple Encryption and Decryption routines....
'*

_ASC_ENCRYPT = 1
_OCT_ENCRYPT = 2
_HEX_ENCRYPT = 3
_BIN_ENCRYPT = 4

function Encrypt( sData, ..; .. )

  local nBase    as integer
  local nCount   as integer
  local sReturn  as string
  local nIdea    as integer

  sReturn = ""

  if (qnoptparams = 0)
    nBase = 108
  else
    nBase = qoptparam(1)
  end if

  if qnoptmods = 0
    nIdea = _ASC_ENCRYPT
```

```
    else
      nIdea = qoptmod(1)
    end if

    for nCount = 1 to len( sData )
      if nIdea = _ASC_ENCRYPT
        sReturn = sReturn + chr$( asc( mid$( sData, nCount, 1) ) + nBase )
      elseif nIdea = _HEX_ENCRYPT
        sReturn = sReturn + hex$( asc( mid$( sData, nCount, 1) ) + nBase )
      elseif nIdea = _OCT_ENCRYPT
        sReturn = sReturn + oct$( asc( mid$( sData, nCount, 1) ) + nBase )
      elseif nIdea = _BIN_ENCRYPT
        sReturn = sReturn + bin$( asc( mid$( sData, nCount, 1) ) + nBase )
      end if
    next

    return( reverse$(sReturn) )
end func

function Decrypt( sData, ..; .. )

    local nBase    as integer
    local nCount   as integer
    local sReturn  as string
    local nIdea    as integer

    sReturn = ""

    if (qnoptparams = 0)
      nBase = 108
    else
      nBase = qoptparam(1)
    end if
    if qnoptmods = 0
      nIdea = _ASC_ENCRYPT
    else
      nIdea = qoptmod(1)
    end if

    sData = reverse$(sData)

    for nCount = 1 to len( sData )
      if nIdea = _ASC_ENCRYPT
        sReturn = sReturn + chr$( asc( mid$( sData, nCount, 1) ) - nBase )
      elseif nIdea = _HEX_ENCRYPT
        sReturn = sReturn + chr$( hextonum( mid$( sData, nCount, 2) ) - nBase )
        nCount = nCount + 1
      elseif nIdea = _BIN_ENCRYPT
        sReturn = sReturn + chr$( bintonum( mid$( sData, nCount, 8) ) - nBase )
```

```
            nCount = nCount + 7
      elseif nIdea = _OCT_ENCRYPT
         sReturn = sReturn + chr$( octtonum( mid$( sData, nCount, 3) ) - nBase )
         nCount = nCount + 2
      end if
   next

   return( sReturn )

end func

'****** MAIN ROUTINE *****'

input "Enter any string", "Sirius Press, Inc"; sData

print sData
print Encrypt( sData )
print Encrypt( sData ; _BIN_ENCRYPT )
print Encrypt( sData ; _HEX_ENCRYPT )
print Encrypt( sData ; _OCT_ENCRYPT )
print Decrypt( Encrypt( sData ) )
print Decrypt( Encrypt( sData ; _BIN_ENCRYPT ) ; _BIN_ENCRYPT )
print Decrypt( Encrypt( sData ; _HEX_ENCRYPT ) ; _HEX_ENCRYPT )
print Decrypt( Encrypt( sData ; _OCT_ENCRYPT ) ; _OCT_ENCRYPT )

'* End of File: Parse9.rlz
```

At the end of the execution, the Print Log window looks like this:

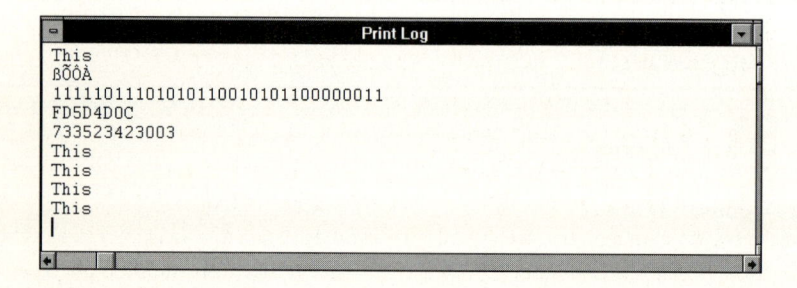

```
Print Log
This
ßÕÒÀ
111110111010101100101011000000011
FD5D4D0C
733523423003
This
This
This
This
```

This code example is a continuation of the previous sample. This version of the *Encrypt()* and *Decrypt()* functions offers the optional modifier that lets you specify how the passed string *sData* is to be encrypted or decrypted. In the previous examples, the conversion technique was pure ASCII-based, meaning that the value obtained was in terms of the ASCII table for each character in the *sData* string. In this example, instead of the CHR$() function, the HEX$(), OCT$(), or BIN$() functions may be used to initially convert the string into hexadecimal, octal, or binary format. That is, the program converts the ASC() value for each character in the string to either hex, oct, or bin format. The return value will be, as expected, the reverse notation of that concatenated string.

The reverse process for the *Decrypt()* function is appropriate. First, the value of the base variable *nBase* is tested and set to a default value as well as the optimal modifier accepted by the function. Second, since the operation of both functions will not change, the use of the modifier is appropriate. The only aspect of the *Decrypt()* function that is not required (but is required in the *Encrypt()* function), is the length of each individual byte in the encrypted string. When we are dealing in pure ASCII terms, each character is represented in a one-to-one relationship; meaning, that for each character passed in the to-be-encrypted string, there is one character in the encrypted string. However, when working in the other three formats, the encrypted string will be longer than the original string. For example, if we are creating a hexadecimal encryption, the return string will be double in length. The return string in an octal encryption will be triple the original string, and in a binary encryption, eight times longer. Keep this in mind when encrypting and converting strings. Make sure the base value of the encryption is the same in both the encrypting and decrypting procedure, and that both procedures have the same expected format. We could build in some special algorithms to guess at the decrypted format; however, it is just as easy for the programmer to supply the appropriate modifier to tell the *Decrypt()* function what to do. Finally, the *Decrypt()* function uses the Realizer functions opposite to the ones in the *Encrypt()* function. For example, if the *Encrypt()* function uses the OCT$() function, the *Decrypt()* function uses the OCTTONUM() function. The same would be true for HEX$() and HEXTONUM() as well as BIN$() and BINTONUM(). This function pattern can be seen in the next programming example `(Parse11.rlz)`, in which converted data is written to the file using special Realizer conversion functions.

For each of the two functions, global and constant variables are initialized at the top of the file and represent a numeric value that the *Encrypt()* and *Decrypt()* functions are expecting. These internal variables along with other functions using same said values will be available in the CARTools library.

Of course, such a simple encryption scheme is easy to break, and most schemes are eventually broken. Just try to keep your average end user from reverse-engineering your logic when it comes to data encryption.

Converting Data and Writing Files

The next step would be to take lines of data, treat them as records, and then write them out to a file using some of the special converting functions found in Realizer.

The `Parse11.rlz` file deals with the issues of writing and reading converted strings of data using functions like MKI$() or MKL$(), as well as the low-level file functions. It also includes an array function called *ASum()*. The SUM() operation in Realizer works only on arrays that have numeric values. This new function takes the first element found in the specified search, assumes that is the initial data type, and allows for summations to take place. This means that an array of string values can be "summed" or joined together using this new *ASum()* function. In previous examples, we saw that the MID$() function can return an array of parsed characters found in a string. *The ASum()* function can reattach those characters. This is extremely useful in encrypting and decrypting a line of text to be saved to a file. Before looking at the source code in `Parse11.rlz`, take a look at its result in the Print Log window:

```
                         Print Log
15
---------
12
---------
5
---------
Steve is here
---------
File has been written...  Look at the file in DOS
|9|9|9|p|w|t|q|+|p|s|||+|z|||+|||||z|+|y
There will be three lines of stuff wrtten out to the file...
```

The code that generates this screen is as follows:

```
'* Application ... : Parse11.rlz
'* Authors ....... : Steve Straley
'* Notice ........ : Copyright(c) 1994 - Sirius Press, Inc.
'* ............... : All Rights Reserved
'* Date .......... : January 1, 1994
'* Description ... : Simple Encryption and Decryption routines....
'*

function asum( aData, .. )

   local nCount as integer
   local nStart as integer
   local nEnd    as integer
   local xReturn     '* we don't know what the return data type will be
```

```
   if qnoptparams = 0
     nStart = startvalid( aData )
     nEnd   = endvalid( aData )

   elseif qnoptparams = 1
     nStart = qoptparam(1)
     nEnd   = endvalid( aData )
     if nStart > nEnd
       nStart = startvalid( aData )
     else
       if nStart < startvalid( aData )
         nStart = startvalid( aData )
       end if
     end if

   elseif qnoptparams = 2
     nStart = qoptparam(1)
     nEnd   = nStart + qoptparam(2) -1

     if nStart < startvalid(aData)
       nStart = startvalid(aData)
     end if
     if nEnd > nStart + endvalid(aData) -1
       nEnd = endvalid(aData )
     end if

   end if

   xReturn = aData[nStart]
   for nCount = nStart+1 to nEnd
     xReturn = xReturn + aData[nCount]
   next

   return( xReturn )

end func

function MkiWrite( sData )

   local nBase    as integer
   local nCount   as integer
   local sReturn  as string
   local nIdea    as integer
   local aData

   nBase   = 1035
   sReturn = ""
   aData   = mki$( asc( mid$( sData, index(len(sData)), 1 ) ) + nBase )
```

```
    return( reverse$( ASum(aData) ) )

end func

function MKIRead( sData )

  local nBase    as integer
  local nCount   as integer
  local sReturn  as string
  local nIdea    as integer
  sReturn = ""
  nBase   = 1035
  sData   = reverse$(sData)

  for nCount = 1 to len(sData) step 2
    sReturn = sReturn + chr$(cvi( mid$(sData, nCount, 2)) - nBase)
  next

  return( sReturn )

end func

'****** MAIN ROUTINE *****'

local sString1 as string
local sString2 as string
local sString3 as string
local nFile    as integer
local sData    as string

sString1 = "There will be three lines of stuff wrtten out to the file..."
sString2 = "With each line representing a specific piece of information"
sString3 = "store to the file like a record of a database."

print asum( {1,2,3,4,5} )
print "------"
print asum( {1,2,3,4,5}, 3 )
print "------"
print asum( {1,2,3,4,5}, 2, 2 )
print "------"
print asum( { "Steve", " is", " here " } )
print "------"

nFile = filequnique
fileopen( nFile, "Special.$$$", _WRITE )
filewrite(nFile, MKIWrite(sString1) )
filewrite(nFile, MKIWrite(sString2) )
filewrite(nFile, MKIWrite(sString3) )
print "File has been written...  Look at the file in DOS"
fileclose(nFile)
```

```
fileopen( nFile, "Special.$$$", _READ )
fileread(nFile, sData)
print left$(sData, 40)
print MKIRead(sData)

'* End of File: Parse11.rlz
```

At the beginning of the main part of the file, a series of PRINT instructions show the various ways in which the new *ASum()* function may be called. The first parameter is naturally, the array to be summed. The second parameter is the starting index or subscript position to begin the summation process, and the third parameter specifies how many subscripts to go through.

> **Note:** It is often a good idea to build testing routines and samples for generic and universal functions. This will ensure stability across a greater range of applications.

Since the *MKIWrite()* function, which is one of the main reasons for this example program file, needs to use a function like *ASum()*, these tests are provided to show the extended use of the function and serve as a test pattern. Once the tests are complete, the *MKIWrite()* function is called, passing to it one of the variables: *sString1*, *sString2*, or *sString3*. The return value of the *MKIwrite()* function will then be written to the file "Special.$$$" held in the file pointer *nFile* and written using FILEWRITE(). The technique within the *MKIWrite()* function is just a minor variation found in the *Encrypt()* function. Here, the values of the individual elements of the array returned from the MID$() function are converted to ASCII via the ASC() function and then increased by the value stored in *nBase*. In previous examples, this value was a potentially optional parameter, whereas in this example, the value is fixed at 1035. This may be altered. Once the ASCII value of the extracted character has been increased, it is then passed to the MKI$() function. This means that the variable aData will hold an array representing an entire line of data in which each individual character of the string has been converted to ASCII, increased by a specified value, and then converted to a two-character string representation in binary format. Since the value of the parameter to the MKI$() function must fall within ±32,768, and since the ASCII characters are well within this range, even with a padded base amount, this conversion should work well. This same type of example could be used for the MKL$() function (converting the individual characters in the data string to four-character string representations), the MKS$() function, the MKDMBF$() function, or the MKSMBF$() function. Each has a similar property and behavior.

The reverse process follows the same logic found in the *Decrypt()* function. Just as there are opposing functions for OCT$(), HEX$() and the others, so there are for MKI$(), MKS$(), and the rest. Here, in the *MKIRead()* function, the CVI() function is used to convert the two-byte integer string into an ASCII value, which will then be decremented by the base value and passed to the CHR$() function to yield the return value/data string.

> **Note:** It is important to match up encrypting functions with decrypting functions. Since the character format varies from, for example, MKI$() to MKDMBF$(), the countering functions must be exact. Otherwise, erroneous data will be returned.

More File Conversions

We can use some of the file functions to convert .ICO files (icons for Windows) to .BMP files (bitmapped files). Typically, the size of the .ICO files should not impede performance within the Realizer environment; therefore, this type of conversion process is quite easy. To see this in action, consider the file *Icofile.rlz*:

```
'* Application ... : IcoFile.rlz
'* Authors ....... : David Ulrich modified by Steve Straley
'* Notice ........ : Copyright(c) 1994 - Sirius Press, Inc.
'* .............. : All Rights Reserved
'* Date .......... : January 1, 1994
'* Description ... : Converting .ICO file to .BMP files
'*

run "Cartools.rlz"

proc BuildDataTypes()

   type icondir
     reserved   as integer
     icontype   as integer
     iconcount  as integer
   end type
```

```
    type icondirentry
      width        as byte
      height       as byte
      colorcount   as byte
      reserved     as byte
      planes       as integer
      bitcount     as integer
      iconsize     as long
      iconoffset   as long
    end type

    type bitmapinfoheader
      size         as long
      width        as long
      height       as long
      planes       as integer
      bitcount     as integer
      compression  as long
      imagesize    as long
      xpelspermeter as long
      ypelspermeter as long
      clrused      as long
      clrimportant as long
    end type

    type bitmapfileheader
      bmptype      as string*2
      size         as long
      reserved1    as integer
      reserved2    as integer
      offset       as long
    end type

end proc

local sIconName  as string
local sBmpName   as string
local nCount     as integer

sIconName = stdopen("*.ico")
if Empty( sIconName )
  exit program
end if

sBmpName = stdsaveas(left$(sIconName,len(sIconName)-3)+"bmp")
if Empty( sBmpName )
  exit program
end if
```

```
BuildDataTypes()

fileopen(10, sIconName, _READ)
clear iconinfo
dim iconinfo as icondir
fileread(10,iconinfo)
clear icondirentryarray
dim icondirentryarray[1:iconinfo.iconcount] as icondirentry
fileread(10,icondirentryarray)

nCount = 1
if iconinfo.iconcount > 1
   input "Which one would you like to extract ss a bmp?","File " + sIconName + \\
        " contains " + numtostr(iconinfo.iconcount) + "icons."; nCount
end if

select case  icondirentryarray[nCount].colorcount
case 2
  bitsperpixel = 1
case 8
  bitsperpixel = 3
case 16
  bitsperpixel = 4
case 256
  bitsperpixel = 256
end select

iconoffset=icondirentryarray[nCount].iconoffset

clear bmpheader
dim bmpheader as bitmapinfoheader
fileseek(10,iconoffset)     '* Position the internal pointer
fileread(10,bmpheader)      '* Read in from this location

bmpheader.height = bmpheader.height/2
clear colortable
fileread(10,colortable,4* icondirentryarray[nCount].colorcount)
clear bmpdata
fileread(10,bmpdata,bmpheader.width*bmpheader.height*bitsperpixel/8)
fileclose(10)

dim bmpfileheader as bitmapfileheader
bmpfileheader.bmptype = "BM"
bmpfileheader.size    = 14+40+len(colortable)+len(bmpdata)
bmpfileheader.offset  = 14+40+len(colortable)

fileopen(10,sBmpName, _WRITE)            '* Open the new file name
filewrite(10,bmpfileheader)              '* Write out the header
filewrite(10,bmpheader)                  '* Write out the info header
filewrite(10,colortable,len(colortable)) '* Write out the color stuff
```

```
filewrite(10,bmpdata,len(bmpdata))        '* Write out the BMP information
fileclose(10)

messagebox( "Operation Completed!", "Sirius Press, Inc.", _MB_OK )

'* End of File: IcoFile.rlz
```

    This example uses user-defined data types, performs file reading and writing, and incorporates some of Realizer's standard windows dialogs, such as STDSAVEAS() and STDOPEN(). Once the entire operation is completed, it calls the MESSAGEBOX() function.

Conclusion

File manipulation and string parsing is an important concept to master. Working with .DBF file structures, .BMP files, and ODBC (Open Database Connectivity) compatibility specs are just a few of the issues involved. Working with some of the conversion functions to encrypt and/or condense a file is also part of the parsing dilemma.

Chapter 8

Reusable Code and Subsystems

This chapter tackles a wide range of issues, all leading to thinking better within the Realizer environment. And one way to think better is to think in terms of reusable code. This means planning how you might use a function or procedure in a variety of applications before even beginning to write the function or procedure. I became an advocate of this concept in my Clipper days, starting with the first Clipper add-on function library. That library showed how the language could be manipulated to work with and for the programmer, and in this chapter, we'll try to bring that versatility to the Realizer environment by exploring many new techniques, tricks, and ideas for reusable subroutines.

Visual Items

An application needs visual contact with the end user as an operation progresses. One of the selling features of the Windows environment was the common "look and feel" of all applications within its domain. More than allowing the end user to point and click on an icon; more than pretty pictures displayed on the screen; the Windows environment offered a new level of standardization.

Within the Realizer language, several tools and functions can help add to the overall consistency of a program. For example, the menus we've built in this book conform to Windows standards, and so do the dialog boxes and message boxes, such as those that follow:

Reusable Code and Subsystems 419

or

or

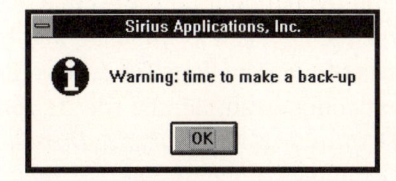

The code that produced those messages is the following:

```
messagebox( "This process cannot be reversed!", \\
            "Sirius Press, Inc.", _MB_OKCANCEL, _MB_STOP, 2 )
messagebox( "Plaid shirts and check pants do not make a good fashion statement.", \\
            "Microsoft Yuk-box", _MB_OK, _MB_EXCLAMATION )
messagebox( "Warning: time to make a back-up", \\
            "Sirius Applications, Inc.", _MB_OK, _MB_INFORMATION )
```

Building on that theme, we need to construct other interface tools that help maintain the universal look and feel, of all Windows applications. One useful tool is to a **display box**, a message-like box that doesn't contain a button or a warning icon but only displays information of something happening without requiring a response. For example, such a box might display a line of text read in from disk and while the next line of text is obtained. This type of visual-reminder technique is important.

Display Boxes

Before we build a generic display box, consider the following series of rules, to which all generic functions must adhere:

1. The limited behavior of the tool or function must be clearly defined.
2. A list of required and optional parameters need to be planned for in advance of the function being called.
3. A list of required and/or optional modifiers need to be planned for in advance of the function being called.
4. A strategy for cleaning up variables and information within the function must be devised.
5. The function or code subset must work in abnormal conditions.
6. The code must work in future, unplanned applications (extendable).
7. The code must work with other generic routines.

These rules are not set in stone and may vary from routine to routine. They are, however, useful guidelines that apply in both procedural environments, such as Realizer, and object-oriented environments, such as Visual Objects. There is no exact formula for building reusable code extracts. The best advice I can give you is practice as much as you can, and build many test examples that try out all types of combinations for every reusable code extract. For example, in this next coded example, the file *DispExam.rlz* holds the source code for the *DisplayBox()* and *DisplayBoxClose()* functions, as well as a couple of test examples of the routine:

```
'* Application ... : DispExam.rlz
'* Authors ....... : Steve Straley
'* Notice ........ : Copyright(c) 1994 - Sirius Press, Inc.
'* .............. : All Rights Reserved
'* Date .......... : January 1, 1994
'* Description ... : This shows how the DisplayBox() function works.

proc displaybox( sDisplay, sTitle, .. ; .. )

  proc DisplayMake()
    nDispHandle = formqunique
    nDispObject = 30000
    formnew( nDispHandle; sTitle, _TITLE )
    formcontrol( _SIZE; _CENTER, _CENTER, nDispSize, 100 )
    formsetobject( nDispObject, _CAPTIONCENTER, sDisplay, _CENTER, \\
                      _CENTER, nDispSize - 5, _DEFAULT )

  end proc

  nOldForm = formq(_SELECTED)
```

```
      if qnoptmods > 0
        formselect( nDispHandle )
        formcontrol( _CLOSE )
        nDispHandle = 0
        if nOldForm <> 0
          if formq( nOldForm; _EXISTS )
            formselect( nOldForm )
          end if
        end if
      else

        if qnoptparams = 0
          nDispSize = max( len(sDisplay), len(sTitle) ) + 200
        else
          if nDispSize < qoptparam(1)    '* Old size is too small and new size specified
            nDispSize = qoptparam(1)
            formcontrol( _SIZE; _CENTER, _CENTER, nDispSize, 100 )
          else
            nDispSize = qoptparam(1)
          end if
        end if

        if not qvar( nDispHandle, _DEFINED )
          DisplayMake()
        else
          if nDispHandle = 0
            DisplayMake()
          else
            formselect(nDispHandle)
          end if
        end if

        formmodifyobject( nDispObject, _SETFOCUS, sDisplay, _CENTER, _CENTER, nDispSize,
_DEFAULT )
        formcontrol( _SHOW )
        if nOldForm <> 0
          formselect( nOldForm )
        end if

    end if

end proc

proc displayboxclose( )
  displaybox(1,2;1)
  clear displaybox
end proc

DisplayBox( "This is a test of a box!", "Sirius Press, Inc." )
```

```
sleep 2
DisplayBox( "Just another test...", "Sirius Press, Inc." )
sleep 3
DisplayBox( "This is another test, after 4 seconds more of waiting", \\
            "Sirius Press, Inc.", 600 )
sleep 4
DisplayBoxClose()
reset

'* End of File: DispExam.rlz
```

At the top of this file is the beginning of the *DisplayBox()* procedure. Here, at least two parameters are required and an unspecified number of optional parameters and modifiers follow. Within the confines of the routine is the beginning of another routine named *DisplayMake()*. This routine cannot be called outside of the *DisplayBox()* procedure; it is a localized subroutine within the explicit domain of the *DisplayBox()* procedure. This is a good way to have code that needs to be repeated several times within the main routine, grouped together, and yet not accessible outside of the main function by another routine. This coding structure makes the subroutine available to the main routine, where it's needed, but protects us from accidentally calling the *DisplayMake()* subroutine in the future.

When working within a form-based environment, you must ask yourself from where this function can be called. To put it another way, if the *DisplayBox()* function requires a form in order to exist, and if a form is present within the application, how do I deselect and remember the original and calling form for the future. Saving environmental values before the code is called is always a standard practice. The first example of this type of housekeeping is with the *nOldForm* variable: It will hold the ID of the currently selected form. This means that the form can be reselected when the *DisplayBox()* function's operation shuts down. At the conclusion of the *DisplayMake()* routine, the testing of both the optional parameters and modifiers is in order. The first test is to discover whether the modifier handled by the QNOPMODS command is passed to this *DisplayBox()* procedure. If so, the subroutine will select itself, close itself, set the internal variable *nDispHandle* to 0, and if an older form existed when *DisplayBox()*'s form was created, then it will reselect that form. This calling convention is streamlined by the *DisplayBoxClose()* procedure located just after the source for the *DisplayBox()* routine. This subroutine calls *DisplayBox()* with the appropriate modifier and follows it up with Realizer's CLEAR instruction of the *DisplayBox()* routine.

> **Note:** It is a good idea to CLEAR out a generic subroutine once it is no longer needed. This will both conserve memory and boost performance.

Turning back to the *DisplayBox()* operation, if there are no modifiers passed to the routine, then focus turns to the optional parameter. This parameter allows for the boxed region of the text to change in width. The variable *nDispSize* defaults to the length of the text string passed as *sDisplay* or the size of the title string, passed as *sTitle*, whichever is longest. However, sometimes a string that comes into the boxed region is larger than originally allotted for, so the form's box needs to be resized. If the value of the function QOPTPARAM(1) is larger than the original size held in *nDispSize*, then the new size is assumed, and the form is re-adjusted with the `_SIZE` internal variable. In this example program, the last call to the *DisplayBox()* routine makes this take place.

Eventually, the dialog box is created and a `_CAPTIONRIGHT` text object is created and redisplayed with the `_SETFOCUS` internal variable. This is important. In the example at the bottom of this file, the first two calls to the routine will pass in two separate display strings; however, within the `_SETFOCUS` internal variable used, only the string passed during the first call will be displayed for both attempts. This means that the first string is attached to the display's text object, and even when a new parameter holding a new string to be displayed comes into the function for the second time, unless the `_CAPTIONCENTER` object is told this, the first string will be redisplayed.

Building Gauges

Another type of display interface is known as a gas-gauge display (sometimes called a fever bar). Here, while operations take place in the background, a graphical display shows the progress. Sometimes, a Cancel push button is also displayed on the screen. The trick is to use the table tool to create the image of an increasing gas gauge; however, that is not all that is needed. The main focus is to have a LOOP of operations based on the contents of an array. The number of iterations within the LOOP depends on the number of items in the array. However, the operation to perform within that LOOP on each of those items is critical and fairly tricky. Here, for the first time, we will look at the use of the EXECUTE command and how, with careful string parsing and manipulation, we can build a useable interface tool. To see the effect of the `GaugExam.rlz` file, open the Print Log window and run the file to yield the following:

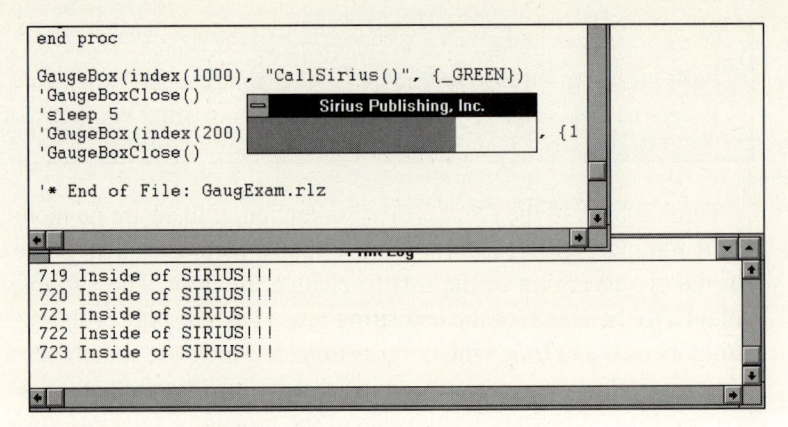

```
end proc
GaugeBox(index(1000), "CallSirius()", {_GREEN})
'GaugeBoxClose()
'sleep 5                        Sirius Publishing, Inc.
'GaugeBox(index(200)                                    , {1
'GaugeBoxClose()

'* End of File: GaugExam.rlz
```

```
719 Inside of SIRIUS!!!
720 Inside of SIRIUS!!!
721 Inside of SIRIUS!!!
722 Inside of SIRIUS!!!
723 Inside of SIRIUS!!!
```

Figure 8-1. GAUGEDEMO program running.

As the array is incremented within the loop, the contents of the individual values are displayed to the Print Log window, and the gas gauge fills. The code for this is as follows:

```
'* Application ... : GaugExam.rlz
'* Authors ....... : Steve Straley
'* Notice ........ : Copyright(c) 1994 - Sirius Press, Inc.
'* ............... : All Rights Reserved
'* Date .......... : January 1, 1994
'* Description ... : This shows the use of a Gas Gauge type of interface.

__CLOSE = 1

proc GaugeBoxClose()
   GaugeBox(index(1), "none"; __CLOSE )
end proc

proc GaugeBox(aData, sCommand, ..; ..)

   local nForm           as integer
   local sTitle          as string
   local nHeight         as integer
   local nWidth          as integer
   local nCount          as integer
   local nPos            as integer
   local sOrigCommand    as string
   local nOldForm        as integer
   local xValue
   local aPositions

   '* Check to see if there is data
```

Reusable Code and Subsystems

```
  if endvalid(aData) = 0
    exit proc
  end if

'* Check the parameters
if qnoptparams = 0
  sTitle     = "Sirius Press, Inc."
  aPositions = {_CENTER, _CENTER, 250, 50, _BLUE}
elseif qnoptparams = 1
  if qvar( qoptparam(1), _ALPHA )
    sTitle = qoptparam(1)
    aPositions = {_CENTER, _CENTER, 250, 50, _BLUE}
  else
    sTitle = "Sirius Press, Inc."
    aPositions = qoptparam(1)
    if endvalid( aPositions ) = 4
      aPositions = {aPositions, _BLUE}
    elseif endvalid( aPositions ) = 1
      aPositions = {_CENTER, _CENTER, 250, 50, aPositions}
    end if
  end if
elseif qnoptparams = 2
  sTitle     = qoptparam(1)
  aPositions = qoptparam(2)
  if endvalid( aPositions ) = 4
    aPositions = {aPositions, _BLUE}
  elseif endvalid( aPositions ) = 1
    aPositions = {_CENTER, _CENTER, 250, 50, aPositions}
  end if
end if

'* Check the modifiers
if qnoptmods = 1
  formcontrol(_close)
  if nOldForm > 0
    formselect( nOldForm )
  end if
  exit proc
end if

nOldForm = formq(_SELECTED)
nForm    = formqunique
formnew(nForm; sTitle, _TITLE + _POPUP + _STAYFRONT)
formcontrol(_SIZE; aPositions[1], aPositions[2], aPositions[3], \\
                   aPositions[4])
formsetobject(10000, _TABLET,"",0,0,1,1)
tabletbrush( aPositions[5] )
tabletpen( aPositions[5] )
nWidth   = formq(_SIZEINSIDE)[3]
```

```
      nHeight = formq(_SIZEINSIDE)[4]
      formcontrol(_show)

      nPos        = instr(sCommand, "(" )   '* See if is funcn call in command
      sOrigCommand = sCommand

      for nCount = startvalid(aData) TO endvalid(aData)
        xValue = aData[nCount]

        if formwait(_peek) = 2      '* The ESC key was pressed
          formcontrol(_close)
          if nOldForm > 0
            formselect( nOldForm )
          end if
          exit proc
        end if
        if sCommand <> ""
          sCommand = sOrigCommand
          if nPos > 0 and right$(sCommand, 1)= ")"    '* Function
            if qvar( xValue, _ALPHA )
              sCommand = substr$(sCommand, "", chr$(34) + xValue + chr$(34), nPos+1 )
            elseif qvar( xValue, _REAL )
              sCommand = substr$(sCommand, "", numtostr(xValue), nPos+1 )
            else
            end if
            execute sCommand
          else
            if qvar( xValue, _ALPHA )
              sCommand = sCommand + chr$(34) + xValue + chr$(34)
            elseif qvar( xValue, _REAL )
              sCommand = sCommand + numtostr( xValue )
            else
            end if
            execute sCommand
          end if
        end if

        tabletrectangle(0,0,nWidth*nCount/endvalid(aData),nHeight)
      next

end proc

'********** Main Test Area *************'

proc CallSirius( xData )
  print xData, "Inside of SIRIUS!!!"
end proc
GaugeBox(index(1000), "CallSirius()", {_GREEN})
```

```
GaugeBoxClose()
sleep 5
GaugeBox(index(200), "print ", "Building array", {100, 40, 200, 60, _RED})
GaugeBoxClose()

aData = {"Steve", "Paul", "Essor", "Don"}
GaugeBox( aData, "CallSirius()", {_CYAN} )
sleep 10
GaugeBoxClose()
GaugeBox( {"Steve", "Paul", "Essor", "Don"}, "print ", {_CYAN} )

'* End of File: GaugExam.rlz
```

At the top of a file is a pseudo-internal variable to be used, more than likely, by one of the two main subroutines. Following this is the simple subroutine named *GaugeBoxClose()*, which calls the *GaugeBox()* routine with that pseudo-internal variable. Again, using the technique outlined in the previous generic function, the use of the optional modifier lets us call the same function or procedure but secure a different behavior. Here, the `_CLOSE` operation is being requested of the *GaugeBox()* operation. This leads us to the crux of this example: *GaugeBox()*.

Just as with the *DisplayBox()* operation, two required parameters are accompanied by an unlimited number of optional modifiers and parameters. The main part of this function, however, looks a little bit different from the previous test. Here, a series of LOCAL variables are defined. Since this subroutine will be in control of the operation, focus will never leave this subroutine; therefore, needed variables may be defined as LOCAL and not kept public. The first required parameter is an array of values that will be processed through the main LOOP in this routine. Near the top of this, the parameter *aData[]* is checked to see if it contains something, and if it does not, the routine exits. The second required parameter is the string to be used as a command. We'll look at this parameter in a moment.

At this point in the code, we come to the section that deals with the optional parameters. Basically, there are two optional parameters. One parameter will eventually be stored to the *sTitle* variable and will contain the title string to be displayed in the gas gauge's title bar. This will be, if specified, the third parameter in the list. The second optional parameter will be the array *aPositions[]*. This can be an array of five elements or an array of one element. The array structure will be the screen region using standard Realizer notation, taking up the first five element positions, with the fifth element in the array the internal variable for the color of the gas gauge itself. If only a four-element array is passed, it will be assumed that `_BLUE` will be the color of the gas gauge, and the color is then added to the array *aPositions[ ]*. If, on the other hand, the array is only one element long, then it will be assumed that the color value was offered, and the screen coordinates for the dialog box need to take on default values. In either case, these are some of the precautionary measures you need to take for reusable code. Think of it as programming for someone else. Not only do you have to program offensively (by building a great subroutine or tool), but you have to program defensively (by building all types of checks and verifications for a variety of items).

> **Note:** There is no rule that says an internal variable for a preexisting Realizer tool, function, or command, cannot exist in an element of an array. It is, like many other data types, a valid item that may be stored there.

Eventually, the code will create the form, held in the variable *nForm*. Once created, the size then is adjusted based on the first four elements in the *aPositions[ ]* array. Following this, a new object is attached to the form. This new object is called a tablet, initiated by the _TABLET internal variable. Once created, we need to set the color for both the paint brush and pen of the tablet: they are created by the TABLETBRUSH() and TABLETPEN() functions. Here, the color is held in the final subscript position in the *aPositions[ ]* array. Once that is in place, we need to figure out the width and height of the inside area of the object, and with that calculated, we know how much to increment the gauge within the form based on the element being processed in the data array *aData[ ]*. The FORMQ() function always returns an array, and the third and fourth element positions hold these values. Before we start in the main processing loop, note a key new development:

```
nPos         = instr(sCommand, "(" )   '* See if is funcn call in command
sOrigCommand = sCommand
```

The first variable is designed to look to the optional parameter *sCommand*. This parameter is a string of an operation that will be performed on each element in the passed data array. And, as that process takes place, the gas gauge grows on the screen. This means that the generic function does the task for the programmer while providing the picture for the end user. In this first value, the variable *nPos* holds the location of the "(" in the string. So, if the following is passed:

```
GasGauge( aData, "Demo", "ShowSirius()")
```

the value of *nPos* will be 11. However, the value of *nPos* will be 0 for the following:

```
GasGauge( aData, "Demo", "Print " )
```

The idea is that the string passed to the *GasGauge()* procedure will be joined with the string representation of each element in the passed array *aData[]*. This will simulate the essence of a code block: the ability to pass executable code to a subroutine. Finally, before starting the loop, the original value of the command string is stored to the *sOrigCommand* variable. Keep in mind that, each time we go through the loop, the command string will be modified. Without the original string as a reference to the second iteration in the loop, the string will constantly be concatenated and not uniquely created for each pass. With this in place, the beginning of the loop will start.

Just because the FOR...NEXT loop is used instead of the LOOP command does not mean that this is not a loop construct; it is. Once starting in the value, the variable *xValue* holds the value of the individual elements in the *aData[]* array. Once we check for the pressing of the ESC key (which is the purpose of the FORMWAIT() function evaluation at the top of the loop), we then check to see the value of *sCommand*. As long as there is a string in *sCommand*, we need to use our acquired parsing techniques to go the next step:

```
sCommand = sOrigCommand
if nPos > 0 and right$(sCommand, 1)= ")"    '* Function
   if qvar( xValue, _ALPHA )
     sCommand = substr$(sCommand, "", chr$(34) + xValue + chr$(34), nPos+1 )
   elseif qvar( xValue, _REAL )
     sCommand = substr$(sCommand, "", numtostr(xValue), nPos+1 )
   else
   end if
   execute sCommand
```

First, the value of the original string is stored to the *sCommand* variable. Next, we need to see if we are working with a function or a command. So, if the value of *nPos* is a non-zero value and if the rightmost character is a ")" character, the assumption is made that a function call is contained within the *sCommand*. Taking this further, if the value of *xValue* is the string "Hello" (which is an element value in the passed *aData[]* array), then the first QVAR() function will be a logical true value. Then the *sCommand* string is modified using the SUBSTR$() function. Here, the value of *xValue* is inserted in the string, immediately after the location of the first "(" character. This means that the string "Hello" will be the first passed parameter. We can assume, based on the code construct, that the value of *sCommand* could even be the following:

```
"ShowSirius(,1;23)"
```

Here, the string "Hello" from the example will continue to be inserted as the first parameter; however, literal values as the second parameter and even modifiers may be specified in the passed string. So, taking this example, the *sCommand* variable will eventually look like this:

```
'CallSirius("Steve")'
```

   or

```
'CallSirius("Paul")'
```

   or

```
'CallSirius("Essor")'
```

   or

```
'CallSirius("Don")'
```

With this modified string, we eventually come to the EXECUTE command. This is a powerful command that has a wide range of uses. In essence, the EXECUTE command parses a string passed to it and "runs" it. So, for example, if the following were issued:

```
execute "x = 1"
```

a new variable named *X* would be assigned the value of 1. Variable-assigning or manipulating, function-calling, and tool-building are all possible with the EXECUTE command. In this example, the user-defined procedure *CallSirius()* will be called for each element in the passed *aData[ ]* array. This will work for functions, user-defined subroutines, and even Realizer commands (as seen in the second test example).

The other feature used in this example were the tablet tools found in Realizer. Like boards, charts, forms, and other tools, these graphical tools can be useful to master. Future documentation and tools in this book will show extended use of the `_TABLET` object as well as the various tablet functions.

Replacing Elements of a Family

In an application in which moving data to and from a database file into a Realizer family or structure is important, generic and reusable code modules that semi-automate this procedure become increasingly more valuable and

Reusable Code and Subsystems

viable. Again, the main technique is to create a string of the field or variable assignment and then, use the EXECUTE command to initiate the process. In other languages, this is known as a scatter and gather process. In Realizer, without a direct database engine, these processes are limited to flat files using the FILEWRITE() function.

In this next example program named *FamRecs.rlz*, there are several generic functions that not only build a string from a family, but replace the contents of that string into a family. In addition, several more broad-based functions are created to add date and time support as well as data-validation support. Sometimes, we can build better generic functions in conjunction with existing generic functions. In essence, we begin to build our programming environment out of these tools so that application development time can be trimmed to a bare minimum. The main crux of the routine looks like this:

```
'****************************** MAIN ROUTINE ************************
'********************************************************************

'* Creates the family first to be used

local fWine as family      '* It should be declared!

'* Now add this record
fWine.Winery           = "Rodney Strong"
fWine.Style            = "Chardonnay"
fWine.Year             = 1991
fWine.FullName         = "Chalk Hell Vineyard"
fWine.County           = "Sonoma"
fWine.State            = "CA"
fWine.Country          = "USA"
fWine.Region           = "Sonoma"
fWine.Composition      = ""
fWine.BinNumber        = 0
fWine.LotNumber        = 0
fWine.DatePurchased    = strtodate("6/1/93")
fWine.Amount           = 14.95
fWine.Value            = 22.50
fWine.DateConsumed     = strtodate("1/1/01")
fWine.DateSold         = strtodate("1/1/01")
fWine.Quantity         = 0
fWine.Comments         = {""}

'* Next, take the record and build a string that may be written out

sData = GatherRecord( fWine )

input sData, "Sirius Press, Inc." ;
```

```
'* Blank out the record so that the values from the stored string may
'* be re-entered into the record.

fWine.Winery         = ""
fWine.Style          = ""
fWine.Year           = 0
fWine.FullName       = ""
fWine.County         = ""
fWine.State          = ""
fWine.Country        = ""
fWine.Region         = ""
fWine.Composition    = ""
fWine.BinNumber      = 0
fWine.LotNumber      = 0
fWine.DatePurchased  = strtodate("01/01/01")
fWine.Amount         = 0.0
fWine.Value          = 0.0
fWine.DateConsumed   = strtodate("1/1/01")
fWine.DateSold       = strtodate("1/1/01")
fWine.Quantity       = 0
fWine.Comments       = {""}

ScatterRecord( fWine, sData )    '* Re-build the record from the string
print "******"                    '* Print a separator
print fWine.Region                '* Print the family member
print fWine.DatePurchased         '* Print the family member
print fWine.Style                 '* Print the family member
```

To start, a LOCAL family is created—the same family used to hold information about our wine collection. Each member in the family has a unique value and data type, ranging from string to numeric to date-time to array. Once the record is built, it is then passed off to one of our generic and reusable functions: *GatherRecord()*. The return value from this function is stored to the variable *sData*, which is then used in the INPUT command to generate this type of output:

```
┌─────────────── Sirius Publishing, Inc. ───────────────┐
│                                                        │
│  ⚠  Rodney Strong[%]Chardonnay[%]1991[%]Chalk Hell    │
│     Vineyard[%]Sonoma[%]CA[%]USA[%]Sonoma[%]          │
│     [%]0[%]0[%]19930106[%]15[%]23[%]20010101[%]20010101[%]0[%]ARRAY!!!! │
│                                                        │
│                      ┌────┐                            │
│                      │ OK │                            │
│                      └────┘                            │
└────────────────────────────────────────────────────────┘
```

Instead of using the INPUT command, we could have implemented the FILEWRITE() function. This would be the initial step of a technique for writing records to a data file. The FILEREAD() function could be used to retrieve a string of data from a file and store it to a variable, such as *sData*.

Reusable Code and Subsystems 433

As seen in the INPUT window, each item in the family is separated by a [%] character combination. This will be our field delimitor. In addition, each family member's data type is checked and appropriately converted to build one large string. This is all part of the *GatherRecord()* function:

```
func GatherRecord( fData )

  local sData    as string
  local sDelim   as string
  local nItems   as integer
  local nCount   as integer
  local aFields  as array

  sData  = ""
  sDelim = "[%]"

  if DataType(fData) <> "F"         '* It is a family
    ErrorTable( 2 )
    sData = "  "

  else
    '* The format of the string will be as follows:
    '*
    aFields = qvar( fData, _MEMBERS )
    nItems  = endvalid( aFields )
    for nCount = startvalid( aFields ) to nItems
       sStatement = "xdata = " + QVAR(fData, _NAME) + "." + aFields[nCount]
       execute sStatement
       if qvar( xData, _REAL )
          sData = sData + numtostr(xData) + sDelim
       elseif qvar( xData, _ALPHA + _SCALAR)
          if xData = ""
             sData = sData + " " + sDelim
          else
             sData = sData + xData + sDelim
          end if
       elseif qvar( xData, _ALPHA + _ARRAY)
          sData = sData + "ARRAY!!!!" + sDelim
       else
          sData = sData + DToS(xData) + sDelim
       end if
    next
  end if

  return( left$(sData, len(sData)-3) )

end func
```

When the family or record of information comes into the function, it is stored to the parameter *fData*. The original name of the family or record is returned using the QVAR() function in conjunction with the _NAME internal variable. Once a series of LOCAL variables is created, we come to the first real test of our reusable theory. Here, a call to the *DataType()* function is issued. This function is similar to Clipper's VALTYPE() function.

```
function datatype( xData )

  local xReturn as string

  xReturn = ""

  if qvar(xData, _ARRAY)
    xReturn = "A"
  else
    if qvar(xData, _DATETIME )
      xReturn = "D"
    elseif qvar(xData, _REAL )
      xReturn = "N"
    elseif qvar(xData, _RECORD )
      xReturn = "R"
    elseif qvar(xData, _FAMILY )
      xReturn = "F"
    elseif qvar(xData, _ALPHA )
      xReturn = "S"
    else
      xReturn = "U"
    end if
  end if

  return( xReturn )

end func
```

Here, the function repeats a massive IF...END IF code construct to tell us what type of data we are looking at. Rather than repeat this massive fragment over and over to check on a specific type of data, it is better to call a reusable function like *DataType()*. Turning back to our other reusable function, *GatherRecord()*, if the test on *DataType()* should fail, another generic function is called: *ErrorTable()*.

```
proc ErrorTable( nError )

  local sError as string

  if    nError = 1
```

```
    sError = "Invalid data type/parameter"
  elseif nError = 2
    sError = "Expecting family data type"
  end if

  input sError, "Sirius Press, Inc. - CARTools" ;

end proc
```

Creating an error table is a good way to maintain standard error messages within an application, and for the CARTool library, this table helps guide the programmer through the debugging process. When programming reusable code keep in mind this key:

Programming is like chess: every move must be both offensive and defensive!

One way to accomplish this is to put yourself constantly in the other guy's shoes: How might another programmer want to use the function, procedure, or tool? How might an end user expect the application to work? Answering these questions will help you make the right decisions in building these utilities.

Back in the *GatherRecord()* function, once all of the tests have been completed, some interesting code fragments begin. First, the array *aField[ ]* holds the individual family members' names. Remember, this is a generic and reusable code fragment, which means that we cannot "hard code" any specific family name or member name. The subroutine has to be able to determine these on its own. The *nTimes* variable holds the ending subscript position of the *aFields[ ]* array, which is used in the FOR...NEXT loop. The first line in that loop begins the extended use of the EXECUTE statement. The string *sStatement* looks like this:

```
"xdata = " + QVAR(fData, _NAME) + "." + aFields[nCount]
```

This means that the string might eventually look like this:

```
"xData = fWine.Winery"
```

The QVAR() function returns the root name of the passed family, while the *aFields[ ]* array at the desired *nCount* position holds the name of the individual family member. In essence, this string will represent an assignment of each family member to the *xData* variable. The proceeding EXECUTE command makes the actual assignment.

With the assignment to the *xData* variable, we can now test what type of data variable it is, and based on its data type, we slowly build the string *sData*, which will be the return value of this function (the same return value seen in the INPUT screen previously displayed). Eventually, in the testing process, one of the family members will be a date-time data type, which requires a special type of conversion. Here, the *DToS()* function is built to assign a date to the stored date-time variable *xData* and convert it into something useful:

```
function Dtos( dDate )

   return( sprint( "D(Y2D1M1)", dDate ) )

end func
```

Instead of forcing us to remember how the SPRINT() function works, with all of the possible formatting keys and strings, this function attempts to simplify the process. Therefore, another good reason to build more generic and reusable code is to better identify what operation is taking place. Here, *DToS()* means "date-time to string," which is a bit more understandable than seeing a SPRINT() function with a funny-looking format string. The formatting characters for the SPRINT() function are outlined in the chapter on reports and output. The point here is that a generic-sounding function may actually be a simple replacement for a Realizer operation with the added benefit of maintainability.

Of course, the reverse process of gathering family members into a string is only part of the problem. Generating values back into a family from a collected string is equally important. This function must know the algorithms used to gather the data together as well as to determine the data type of the family member and to make the proper conversion from the saved and collected string generated by the *GatherRecord()* function.

```
func ScatterRecord( fData, sData )

   local aMembers as array
   local aToks    as array
   local nStart   as integer
   local nEnd     as integer
   local nCount   as integer
   local sDoIt    as string
   local xData

   function Stringify( sData )

      return( chr$(34) + sData + chr$(34) )

   end func
   aToks    = strtok( sData, "[%]" )
```

```
aMember = qvar( fData, _MEMBERS )
nStart  = startvalid( aMember )
nEnd    = endvalid( aMember )

for nCount = nStart to nEnd
  if nCount > endvalid( aToks )
  else
    if aToks[nCount] = "ARRAY!!!!"
      sDoIt = qvar(fData, _NAME) + "." + aMember[nCount] + \\
                               "= {"+ chr$(34) + chr$(34) + "}"
    else
      sDoIt =  "xData = " + qvar(fData, _NAME) + "." + aMember[nCount]
      execute sDoit
      if qvar(xData, _REAL)
         sDoIt = qvar(fData, _NAME) + "." + aMember[nCount] + \\
                                 " = " + aToks[nCount]
      elseif qvar( xData, _ALPHA + _SCALAR )
         sDoIt = qvar(fData, _NAME) + "." + aMember[nCount] + \\
                                 " = " + Stringify(aToks[nCount])
      elseif qvar( xData, _ALPHA + _ARRAY )
      else
         sDoIt = qvar(fData, _NAME) + "." + aMember[nCount] + \\
                 " = SToD(" + Stringify(aToks[nCount]) + ")"
      end if
      execute sDoIt
    end if

  end if
next

return( "" )

end func
```

One of the first tasks of this function is to divide out the various components of the passed string data in *sData*. The STRTOK() function makes this a very simple task by employing one of our parsing techniques. Here, the delimitor will be the string "[%]" and the return array will be the individual string versions of values from the stored family. Since both the root name of the family and the string are passed to this function, we can store back the individual pieces easily enough.

> **Note:** Remember, when an array, a record, or even a family is passed as a parameter, it is automatically passed *by reference*, which means individual family members (or array elements or record members) may be changed within the called subroutine.

The FOR...NEXT loop in this function is actually the same procedure found in *GatherRecord()* but in reverse. If the individual stored item is equal to an array, the string "ARRAY!!!" will be seen, and the appropriate string for *sDoIt* will be built. If not, then the individual family members passed to the function need to be tested for data type. This, in essence, means a double EXECUTE.

```
sDoIt =   "xData = " + qvar(fData, _NAME) + "." + aMember[nCount]
execute sDoIt
```

The first string is another variable assignment to a new variable named *xData*. This is identical to the process seen in *GatherRecord()*. We need to do this to determine the data type of the family member in order to know how to convert the stored string. So if the data type of the family member is numeric, for example, then the following will be considered a true condition:

```
if qvar(xData, _REAL)
   sDoIt = qvar(fData, _NAME) + "." + aMember[nCount] + " = " + aToks[nCount]
```

Here, the *sDoIt* variable has a string of the family name plus the "." literal, plus the name of the family member, plus the assignment literal " = " plus the value of *aToks[]* at the *nCount* position.

> **Note:** It is important to remember the data type of the variable *after* the EXECUTE command takes place and not the value within the string.

It can be difficult to remember the data type of the variable after the EXECUTE command takes place. For example, if we were to examine one possible outcome of this string concatenation, it might look something like this:

```
sDoIt = "fWine.bin = 32"
```

Reusable Code and Subsystems

When the *sDoIt* variable is processed via the EXECUTE command, the 32 will become a numeric 32 and not a string 32, which is what we want. Had we built the *sDoIt* string the following way:

```
sDoIt = "fWine.bin = '32'"
```

then the string of 32 would be assigned to the *fWine.bin* family member, and as that was originally a numeric instead of a string, we could find ourselves in serious trouble.

> **Note:** When building strings to be processed by the EXECUTE command, a good idea is to PRINT them to the Print Log window before continuing on with the operation.

In those cases where the family member is a string data type, then the building of the *sDoIt* variable must include the extra set of quotation marks. This is handled by the locally defined function *Stringify()* which merely makes it easier to work with a piece of data and not to worry about the double CHR$(34) function call. The same type of operation works with the string of the *SToD()* function, which is included in this file and looks like this:

```
function stod( sDate )

  local sBuild as string

  sBuild = mid$(sDate, 5, 2) + "/" + mid$(sDate, 7, 2) + "/" + \\
                               left$(sDate, 4)

  return( strtodate( sBuild ) )

end func
```

In essence, the *SToD()* function is the exact opposite of the *DToS()* function. Eventually, when all finishes successfully, the individual family members used in the PRINT command at the end of the program will have the values of the saved string representations built by the *GatherRecord()* routine.

Turning Off or Graying Items

In this section, we are going to look at the issue of graying (or turning off or disabling) menu items and form objects. Turning a menu item or a button, for example, from a _NORMAL condition to a _GRAY condition tells the end user that the process is either (a) no longer available or (b) being carried out. In either case, the end user maintains a clearer picture of what is taking place. In this next example, we are going to build on a previous source code selection. Using the *GaugeBox()* example, we've built onto it a small form which initiates the gas gauge. In the beginning, the screen might look like this:

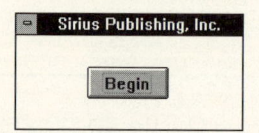

Once the user clicks on the Begin button, the button is grayed and the *GaugeBox()* function takes over, producing the gas-gauge dialog box. The two forms look like this:

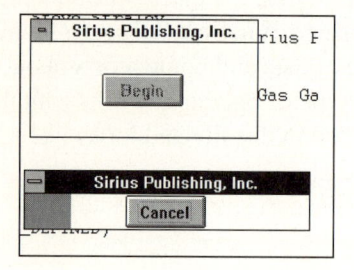

When finished or canceled, the initial form is reselected after the *GaugeBox()* is closed and the Begin button is returned to its _NORMAL state. The example, found in *NewGauge.rlz*, is different from *Gaugexam.rlz* only in the main program area, which looks like this:

```
'********** Main Test Area *************'

proc CallSirius( xData )
  print xData, "Inside of SIRIUS!!!"
end proc

proc Attached( aValues )
  formselect( aValues[_FORMNUM] )
  select case ( aValues[_ITEMNUM] )
  case 10    '* The button
    formmodifyobject( 10, _GRAY )
    GaugeBox(index(1000), "CallSirius()", {_GREEN}; __GAUGEBUTTON)
```

```
      GaugeBoxClose()
      ' FormSelect(params[_Formnum])
      formmodifyobject( 10, _NORMAL )

   end select
end proc

local nForm1 as integer

GaugeBox(index(200), "print ", "Building array", {100, 40, 200, 60, _RED})
GaugeBoxClose()

aData = {"Steve", "Paul", "Essor", "Don"}
GaugeBox( aData, "CallSirius()", {_CYAN} )
sleep 10
GaugeBoxClose()
GaugeBox( {"Steve", "Paul", "Essor", "Don"}, "print ", {_CYAN} )
sleep 5
GaugeBoxClose()

'* Now this is with another existing form in control
'* And shows how to grey out a button!

nForm1 = formqunique
formnew( nForm1; "Sirius Press, Inc.",_TITLE+_CLOSE+_HOTCLICK)
formcontrol(_size;200,50,200,100)
formsetobject(10,_BUTTON,"Begin",_CENTER,_CENTER)
formsetproc( Attached )
formcontrol(_SHOW)

'* End of File: NewGauge.rlz
```

In this example, a form with a Push Button object labeled Begin is generated in the middle of the screen. When the button is clicked on, the procedure *Attached()* is automatically called. Within this routine, the typical passed parameter array *aValues[ ]* allows us to select the correct form and test the correct object. Here, when the Begin button is selected, within the *Attached()* procedure, the FORMMODIFYOBJECT() is called, this time with a reference to object number 10:

```
formmodifyobject( 10, _GRAY )
```

This ties in with the _BUTTON object's ID (used when the form was first created):

```
formsetobject(10,_BUTTON,"Begin",_CENTER,_CENTER)
```

In essence, once the _BUTTON is clicked on, the *Attached()* procedure reselects the object and _GRAYs the button. At this point, the *GaugeBox()* and *GaugeBoxClose()* functions perform their operations. If all works well, the robustness of the the *GaugeBox()* function should be such that when the *GaugeBoxClose()* function performs its task, it will reselect the last form called, preventing us from having to recall Realizer's FORMSELECT() function. If this does work properly, all that is needed is to reselect the correct object (the _BUTTON object) and return the _GRAY color to an active or _NORMAL color.

The techniques are the same in working with menu items. Individual menu items can be grayed by modifying the object with the _GRAY internal variable. However, in most cases, you'll want to gray an entire menu bar. In Realizer (and in Windows), there really is just one menu bar, from which all menu items stem, whether as individual prompts or on pull-down menus. Because of this, only individual menu items can be _GRAYed. The process cannot start at the topmost menu and trickle down until all menus are _GRAYed. We could do it via the Windows API (application programming interface) using the *GetMenu()* function (which obtains the menu handle) and the EnableMenuItem() function (which affects how the entries work). With this and the EXTERNAL command, we could manipulate the menus indirectly.

Another technique, while not quite the same thing, lets us come close. The idea is to build a series of tables when the menu items are created and then, using that table, we can toggle all of the menu items to be either _GRAY or _NORMAL in one quick pass, or we can get fancy and toggle the status of an individual menu item, regardless of where it is on the menu bar stack. This idea, contained in the *Menu3.rlz* file, starts off with the premise that a special function called *AddMenus()* will be called when individual menu items are added:

```
proc LoadMenus()

  iMainMenu = menuqunique                                 ' Generate a new menu pointer
  menunew( iMainMenu; "&File" )                           ' Add a FILE option
  menusetcmd(11, AddMenu("&New", 11) )                    ' Add "NEW" as option with id number 1
  menusetcmd(12, AddMenu("&Old", 12) ; _GRAY)             ' Add "Old" as option with id number 2
  menusetcmd(_SEPARATOR)                                  ' Add a separator
  menusetcmd(13, AddMenu("&Exit.... F10", 13), 10 )       ' Add "Exit" as option
  menusetproc( MainMenu )                                 ' Set the procedure
  menucontrol( _SHOW )

  iNewMenu = menuqunique
  menunew( iNewMenu; "&Gray Out" )
  menusetcmd(14, AddMenu("&Gray Menu", 14) )
```

```
menusetcmd(_SEPARATOR)                          ' Add a separator
menusetcmd(15, AddMenu("&Normal Menu", 15) )
menusetproc( MainMenu )
menucontrol(_SHOW)                              ' Turn on the menu and show it

resethourglass()                                ' Turn back the glass to a cursor

end proc
```

The function *AddMenu()* will always return the string passed as the first parameter. In addition, note that the *AddMenu()* function will be used only on the MENUSETCMD() calls, which add individual menu items, and not on the MENUNEW() function. This trick does not work on the menu items appearing on the main menu bar. The second parameter needed by the *AddMenu()* function is the ID number for that menu item.

This function could have been designed to call the MENUSETCMD() directly rather than jumping through what appears to be a secondary hoop. In other words, the code could have been designed to look like this:

```
iNewMenu = menuqunique
menunew( iNewMenu; "&Gray Out" )
AddMenu(14, "&Gray Menu")
menusetcmd(_SEPARATOR)                          ' Add a separator
AddMenu(15, "&Normal Menu")
menusetproc( MainMenu )
menucontrol(_SHOW)                              ' Turn on the menu and show it
```

Again, this is purely a stylistic decision; however, in the future, you do not necessarily know who will be looking at this piece of code, and the combination of MENUSETCMD() and *AddMenu()* offers more direct insight than just the call to the *AddMenu()* function. However, the *AddMenu()* function could be reprogrammed to act like MENUSETCMD(), and with proper documentation, this overt obstacle could be avoided.

This leads us to the first reusable function for the menus: *AddMenu()*.

```
function AddMenu( sString, nId )

   if not qvar( aMenuIDStack, _DEFINED )
      aMenuIDStack    = {nId}
      aMenuNameStack  = {sString}
      aMenuRoot       = {menuq( _SELECTED )}
   else
      aMenuIDStack    = { aMenuIDStack, nId }
      aMenuNameStack  = { aMenuNameStack, sString }
      aMenuRoot       = { aMenuRoot, menuq( _SELECTED ) }
   end if
```

```
            return( sString )

         end func
```

As we can see, the parameter *sString* is the RETURN() value for this function, which is used directly in the various MENUSETCMD() calls. Here, the function checks to see if at least one of three important arrays exists using the QVAR() function. If *aMenuIDStack[]* has not been _DEFINED, then three array stacks are defined to hold the ID value of the menu passed in as the *nId* parameter, the string passed in as *sString*, and in another stack, the root menu the item is attached to using the MENUQ() function. If, on the other hand, the one array does exist, then it is assumed that all three exist, and in that case, the new items are dynamically added to the three stack arrays. With the three arrays built and in place, another reusable function called *MenusChange()* can be implemented. This function relies on the internal information stored in these three arrays:

```
proc MenusChange(nDirection, ..)

  local nStart as integer
  local nEnd   as integer
  local nCount as integer

  if qvar( aMenuIDStack, _DEFINED )
    nStart = startvalid( aMenuIDStack )
    nEnd   = endvalid( aMenuIDStack )
    for nCount = nStart to nEnd
      menuselect(aMenuRoot[nCount])
      if qnoptparams = 0
        if nDirection = _TO_GRAY
          menusetcmd(aMenuIDStack[nCount], aMenuNameStack[nCount]; _GRAY )
        else
          menusetcmd(aMenuIDStack[nCount], aMenuNameStack[nCount]; _NORMAL )
        end if
      else
        if aMenuIDStack[nCount] = qoptparam(1)
          if nDirection = _TO_GRAY
            menusetcmd(aMenuIDStack[nCount], aMenuNameStack[nCount]; _GRAY )
          else
            menusetcmd(aMenuIDStack[nCount], aMenuNameStack[nCount]; _NORMAL )
          end if
        end if
      end if

    next
  end if

end proc
```

At the top of this routine is the customized declaration of LOCAL variables used to run the function. These are merely variables to hold the positions within the various arrays that will be looked at. The call to the QVAR() function immediately after this is our first test to ensure the procedure's robustness:

> **Note:** Robustness means that a function or procedure will work even in abnormal situations and conditions.

Here, the possibility exists that this function may be called before the *AddMenus()* function is ever called, in which case, the three arrays needed by this function will not even exist. Therefore, to ensure that this function will not bomb when called, a simple test is performed to see if at least one of the three necessary arrays is present before any other operation begins.

Within the FOR...NEXT loop, the subroutine selects the proper menu via the MENUSELECT() function. The top-bar menu ID associated with each menu item is held in the *aMenuRoot[]* array. Following this comes a test of the optional parameter list. If no parameter is passed into the procedure, then the *nDirection* parameter is looked at. This procedure is designed to toggle all menu items in the stack to either the _GRAY or the _NORMAL condition. Which condition to toggle to is held by the *nDirection* parameter. Two pseudo-internal variables declared at the top of the file help make coding for this easier:

```
_TO_GRAY   = 1
_TO_NORMAL = 0
```

If an optional parameter is passed to this procedure, the value of QNOPTPARAMS will not be 0, in which case, it will be assumed that the option parameter passed is a menu ID value. Here, the individual value of QOPTPARAM(1) is tested against the value of *aMenuIDStack[nCount]*, and if they should match, then the normal toggling operation between _GRAY and _NORMAL takes place.

Next we test the new function's ability to _GRAY or make _NORMAL the various menu items:

```
proc MainMenu( aParams )     'Processes the options

  menuselect( aParams[ _MENUNUM ] )    ' Look at the menu selection position
  select case aParams[ _ITEMNUM ]      ' now look at the item number of that
    case 13
      reset _ALL
```

```
      exit system
   case 14
      MenusChange(_TO_GRAY)
      MenusChange(_TO_NORMAL, 15) '* Otherwise, we have problems!
   case 15
      MenusChange(_TO_NORMAL)

end select
```

This procedure is called with each menu selection. The important SELECT CASE statement is for that menu item with an ID value of 14: Gray Menu. Here, the call to *MenusChange()* is made passing to it the pseudo-internal variable of _TO_GRAY. However, following this call is a specific call to ID number 15 to make that menu _NORMAL. That menu option is the menu prompt that allows us to change all of the menu items back to _NORMAL, seen in the following CASE statement. If we do not leave that menu item in a _NORMAL state, then it will not be selectable from the screen which, in turn, effectively keeps our entire menu system "in the dark." This, of course, could have been handled in a variety of other ways, however, it should be noted that if all menu items are turned to _GRAY, and there is a menu item designed to be selected and if so selected, will turn all menu items to _NORMAL, then that menu item needs to remain _NORMAL and not be turned to _GRAY.

Conclusion

Building reusable code means less effort for you during the critical stages of application and tool development. Of course, one key aspect of tool development is source code accessibility. Another is on-line documentation and the ability to use the code and, if neccessary, customize it for your immediate needs. These tools can be the base set of your tool library—a library to be used over and over in all Realizer applications. The routines contained in this chapter form the foundation of the CARTools library. (See the back of this book for more information.)

Chapter 9

Output, Help, and Errors

The three remaining elements of a complete application are the user-oriented help that may be attached to an application, the output of an application, and the programming techniques behind error trapping. First we'll look at a variety of techniques for producing reports. After a tour of the options available for building context-sensitive help, we'll revisit the concept of defensive programming in our discussion of errors and the ON ERROR GOTO command.

Reports

It is commonly said that the best application does not need the best menu interface, the fanciest graphics and charts, or even the most eloquent algorithm for database management. The entire purpose of an application, regardless of the language, is to acquire and hold data for output. Output is the most important issue in application development. No businessperson would ever buy a product that accepts input but produces no manageable, readable, or usable output. Too often, programmers start with the menus or the screens or the log-in scripts and forget about the final outcome until it is too late. In this section, we will look at the various ways in which data may be presented to the end user.

Previous Views

In previous chapters, we have explored various tools to help with the display and output of data. For statistical information, we can use charts and graphs; for string output, we can create and use a log, such as the Print Log window.

In this section, we will look at various controls found in logs and how information may be handled, displayed, and printed within the Realizer environment.

Functions and New Tools

Along with logs and the other tools, there are a series of functions and commands designed to format data for printing. For example, sometimes numerical information needs to be combined with string or date-time information. Formatting the output for maximum readability is an important part of the application-creation process. Typically, the PRINT and ROWPRINT commands send output to the Print Log window, but these commands do nothing to format what is sent, whether the data is a numeric scalar (single value) or an array of date-time values (non-scalar). What we need is the SPRINT() function. This function is not only useful in formatting the output of a report, it can also be used to convert a value in one data type to the format of another.

This function takes at least two parameters. The first is a format string, which we will look at in a moment. The second is the data to be converted. This can be several parameters, especially if there is more than one data type to be printed, based on the contents of the format string.

The format string used in the SPRINT() function is the same as the one used in the PRINT USING command, but the PRINT USING command will actually do the printing operation, while the SPRINT() function returns a formatted string. For this reason, that the SPRINT() function is more versatile and important. Once the string is formatted, it can be concatenated with other strings or even assigned to an array element, which, in turn, is passed off to the PRINT command (this time without the USING clause). The format string consists of two basic parts: literals and template codes. Think of it as a great converter and sieve. For example, there are two ways we can convert a date for a sentence like "Today's date is." One way is to take the SPRINT() function and the date and supply only the codes that will convert the date-time data into a string. That value is then concatenated with the string "Today's date is." The code might look something like this:

```
local sToday as string
local dToday as datetime

sToday = date$
dToday = qdate

print sToday, dToday, "Today's date is" + sprint("D(Y2, M3 D3)", dToday)
```

Output, Help, and Errors

> **Note:** You can use the DATE$ command to convert the date-time data type into a formatted string automatically; however, the format of that string is uniform and constant. In order to obtain a specific format, you must either parse the string from the DATE$ operation or use the SPRINT() function in conjunction with the QDATE operation.

The "D()" operation within the format string is special and important for the SPRINT operation. That same string may be used with the PRINT USING command:

```
print using "D(Y1, M1 D1)"; dToday
```

Now, literals may appear with the format string, which eliminates the need to concatenate the string. This means the same SPRINT() function would look like this:

```
print sprint("Today's date is D(Y1, M1 D1)", dToday )
```

> **Note:** It is sometimes important to avoid concatenation, due to the extra internal functions and memory pointers needed to hold temporary values during the concatenation process.

So, we need to pay special attention to the template functions available within the format string for either the SPRINT() function or the PRINT USING command. Tables 9-1 through 9-4 outline the different template functions based on the data type passed to the function. Each table is followed by an example of how the various template functions might work.

Table 9-1. String Table Templates.

Format String	Definition
&	Includes the complete string.
!	Uses only the first character from the string.
\N\	Prints the first N+2 characters from the string. The backslashes are ignored.
_	Prints the next character exactly as it appears without using it as a formatting command. The underscore allows formatting characters to be used as normal characters.

```
local sName  as string

sName = "Sirius Press, Inc."

print sprint( "!", sName )         '* S
print sprint( "&_!", sName )       '* Sirius Press, Inc.!
print sprint( "\1310\", sName )    '* Sirius
```

Table 9-2. Numeric Table Templates.

Format	Definition
$$	Places a dollar sign to the left of the number.
$#	Places a dollar sign in the leftmost position.
**$	Places a dollar sign to the left of the number and pads it with asterisks.
$**	Puts a dollar sign in the leftmost position and pads it with asterisks.
^^^	Used with any of the # formatting characters to print the number using the exponential notations. At least three ^ characters are required to have one digit in the exponent.
P(x)	Prints the number rounded to the nearest tenth. Leading spaces do not appear.
**	Pads with asterisks instead of spaces.
*#	Places an asterisk in the leftmost position.

```
local nValue as real

nValue = 234.2334234

print nValue, sprint("$$##.##", nValue)       ' 234.2334    $234.23
print nValue, sprint("$###.##", nValue)       ' 234.2334    $234.23
print nValue, sprint("**##.##", nValue)       ' 234.2334    *234.23
print nValue, sprint("*###.##", nValue)       ' 234.2334    *234.23
print nValue, sprint("**$##.##", nValue)      ' 234.2334    *$234.23
print nValue, sprint("$**##.##", nValue)      ' 234.2334    $*234.23
print nValue, sprint("####.####^^^^", nValue) ' 234.2334    234.2334E+00
print nValue, sprint("P(3)", nValue)          ' 234.2334    0
print nValue, sprint("P(2)", nValue)          ' 234.2334    200
print nValue, sprint("P(1)", nValue)          ' 234.2334    230
print nValue, sprint("P(0)", nValue)          ' 234.2334    234
print nValue, sprint("P(-1)", nValue)         ' 234.2334    234.2
```

Table 9-3. Fractional Table Templates.

Format	Definition
W1	Outputs an optional minus sign with the whole part of the number.
W2	Outputs an optional minus sign first. If the whole part is 0, it outputs nothing and skips any literal character up to the next fractional format command.
W3	If the numerator is 0, prints the whole part with an optional minus sign, and ignores all formats until the ending parenthesis.
N1	Outputs the numerator.
N2	Outputs the reduced numerator.
N3	Outputs the numerators padded with 0s.
N4	If the numerator is 0, outputs nothing and skips all formats until the ending parenthesis.
D1	Outputs the denominator.
D2	Outputs the reduced denominator.
_	(the underscore character) Outputs the next character literally, allowing W, D, and N to appear.

```
local nValue as real

nValue = 11.2

print sprint( "F100(D1)", nValue )  '* Output is 100
print sprint( "F100(W1)", nValue )  '* Output is 11
print sprint( "F100(N1)", nValue )  '* Output is 20
```

Table 9-4. Date-Time Table Templates.

Format	Definition
Y1	Yields last two digits of year.
Y2	Yields full four digits of year.
M1	Yields zero-padded two digits for the month.
M2	Yields unpadded two digits for the month.
M3	Yields the three-letter abbreviation for the month.
M4	Yields the full name of the month.
D1	Yields zero-padded number of the day.
D2	Yields unpadded two digits for the day.
D3	Yields the ordinal for the day.

(continued)

Table 9-4. *(continued)*

Format	Definition
D4	Yields the three-letter abbreviation for the day.
D5	Yields the full name of the day.
h1	Yields zero-padded 24-hour hour.
h2	Yields unpadded 24-hour hour.
h3	Yields zero-padded 12-hour hour.
h4	Yields unpadded 12-hour hour.
h5	Yields AM or PM.
m1	Yields zero-padded two digits for the minute.
s1	Yields zero-padded two digits for the seconds.
_	(the underscore character) Yields the next character in the format string as a literal character.

```
sToday = date$
dToday = qdate

print sToday, dToday, "Today's date is " + sprint("D(Y2, M3 D3)", dToday)
print sprint("Today's date is D(Y1, M1 D1)", dToday )
print sprint("D(Y1, M1 D1)", dToday), sprint("D(Y2, M1 D1)", dToday)
print sprint("D(Y1, M2 D1)", dToday), sprint("D(Y1, M3 D1)", dToday)
print sprint("D(Y1, M4 D1)", dToday), sprint("D(Y2, M2 D1)", dToday)
print sprint("D(Y2, M3 D1)", dToday), sprint("D(Y2, M4 D1)", dToday)
print sprint("D(Y1, M1 D2)", dToday), sprint("D(Y1, M1 D3)", dToday)
print sprint("D(Y1, M1 D4)", dToday), sprint("D(Y1, M1 D5)", dToday)
print sprint("D(Y1, M2 D2)", dToday), sprint("D(Y1, M2 D3)", dToday)
print sprint("D(Y1, M2 D4)", dToday), sprint("D(Y1, M2 D5)", dToday)
print sprint("D(Y1, M1 D2)", dToday), sprint("D(Y1, M1 D3)", dToday)
print sprint("D(Y1, M1 D4)", dToday), sprint("D(Y1, M1 D5)", dToday)
print sprint("D(Y2, M2 D2)", dToday), sprint("D(Y2, M2 D3)", dToday)
print sprint("D(Y2, M2 D4)", dToday), sprint("D(Y2, M2 D5)", dToday)
print "------------------------------------------"
print sprint("D(h1 - m1)", dToday )          '* 19 - 05
print sprint("D(h2 - s1)", dToday )          '* 12 - 29
print sprint("D(h3 - h4 in h5)", dToday )    '* 07 - 7 in PM
print sprint("It is D(h4:m1 h5)", dToday )   '* It is 7:05 PM
```

In this code sample, the last four examples depend on what time the program is executed. The output from the SPRINT() function was based on the time this chapter was written (yes, at 7:00 PM!). All of these examples have been combined in the example program named *Print1.rlz*. Also, all of these examples could have worked with the ROWPRINT command just as easily as with the PRINT command. The operations are virtually interchangeable.

Other Uses

The SPRINT() function in particular, is not tied to the concept of printing. For example, sometimes with a date-time data type, we need to convert the format of the string to something a bit more functional. The DATE$ operation formats a date in standard character format, which means that the year portion of the date comes last in the string. For some indexing routines used in conjunction with name fields or other string-based data types, this format for a date string is not acceptable. Instead, the year must come before all other characters in the converted string. In the following example, a wrapper function called *DToS()* (part of the CARTools library) calls the SPRINT() function:

```
function DtoS( dDate )

  return( sprint( "D(Y2D1M1)", dDate) )

end func

function DToC( dDate )

  return( sprint( "D(D1/M1/Y1)", dDate ) )

end func

function DToCcFull(dDate )

  return( sprint( "D(D1/M1/Y2)", dDate ) )

end func
```

Another Function

All of the converting format strings have been used directly with either the SPRINT() function or the PRINT command with the USING clause. Another approach is to use the SETFORMAT() function to set the entire Realizer system to one specific format. The function actually sets the default formatting string to a particular and specified variable. Whenever that variable is used in a PRINT command, the conversion for it is made, as in the following example:

```
local dToday as datetime

dToday = qdate
setformat( dToday, "D(Y2D1M1)")
print dToday        '* 19940920
```

Again, the trouble with this function is that it is variable-specific throughout the entire Realizer system. When working with multiple programmers, it may not be a good idea to set the format of the output to a particular variable, especially without the knowledge of the other programmers on the project.

Other Functions

Using the SPRINT() function to format the output of a data type for the PRINT command is but one possibility. Reports often need headers and footers, and these are controllable within the Realizer command and function set. In some of the tools, such as the sheet or chart, the visual stuff (high-tech term for objects) on the screen can be printed out using CHARTCONTROL() or SHEETCONTROL() and the `_PRINT` internal variable. There is not much the programmer can do once those commands are issued. One of the things that can be controlled are the headers and the footers for the output and to send the output from the buffer to the printer. Most tools' functions have two internal variables that may be used along with one function to do the printing:

`_NOHEADER` Prevents the header from being printed at the top of a page when the `_PRINT` operation is issued.

`_NOFOOTER` Prevents the page number from being printed at the bottom of the page when the `_PRINT` operation is issued.

The command LFLUSH is also very important whenever anything is printed out via the LPRINT or the LROWPRINT commands (similar to the PRINT or the ROWPRINT commands). These operations send the output to the Windows Print Manager. To get the output from the Print Manager to the paper, the LFLUSH command must be issued. This is not necessary if you select the Print option from the File menu.

Other functions available include the various log functions (in which a string is loaded in the log and then printed) and the PRINTERCONTROL() function. The latter has a limited number of options, ranging from changing the orientation of the printer (landscape or portrait), specifying the number of copies to be printed, setting the header and footer of the page, as well as setting the font for the output. The next example program, *Print2.rlz*, shows how this function, along with the STDOPEN() function and the low-level file functions can read in a file, set up a log, and print it to the printer. Note that the LFLUSH command is needed.

```
'*  Application ... : Print2.rlz
'*  Authors ....... : Steve Straley
'*  Notice ........ : Copyright(c) 1994 - Sirius Press, Inc.
'*  .............. : All Rights Reserved
'*  Date .......... : January 1, 1994
'*  Description ... : This shows some of the printing options available in
'*                    a Realizer program.

local nFont    as integer
local cFile    as string
local nSize    as integer
local sLines   as string

nFont = fontnew(fontqunique; "Arial", 10 )

printercontrol( _SETMODE; _LANDSCAPE)
printercontrol( _SETHEADER; "Sirius Press, Inc." )
printercontrol( _SETFONT; nFont )

cFile = stdopen("*.rlz")

fileopen(10, cFile, _read)
nSize = fileq(cFile, _size)

if nSize > 50000
   messagebox( "File is too large. Try something smaller", \\
               "Sirius Press, Inc.", _MB_OK )
   exit program
end if

fileread(10, sLines, nSize)
fileclose(10)
lognew(10)
logsetdata(_log_str, sLines)
logcontrol(_print;500,500)
lflush

messagebox( "The next printing operation is about to engage!", \\
            "Sirius Press, Inc.", _MB_OK )

printercontrol( _SETMODE; _PORTRAIT)
logcontrol(_print; 10, 50 )
lflush

logcontrol(_close)

'*  End of File: Print2.rlz
```

Here, the PRINTERCONTROL() functions set how the output will look to the printer. The file that is selected from the STDOPEN() function is loaded into the log and sent directly out to the printer, bypassing the screen. In the first function call, the margins are set for the top and the left; in the second function call to LOGCONTROL() (using the `_PRINT` internal variable), the margins are changed again, mainly since the orientation will change from `_LAND-SCAPE` to `_PORTRAIT`. However, in both cases the `LFLUSH` command is needed to send the information from the Print Manager to the output device.

CA-RET

This is a standalone, report-writing program that works with either xBASE files or text files. Once a report is finished, and the definitions are available on the disk, the Realizer application can simply send messages to that report definition using the DDE (dynamic data exchange) protocol discussed in the next chapter. The CA-RET() function allows Realizer to access the CA-RET program. There are only four possible options for this function. First, the function needs to be loaded into the system via the `_START` internal variable. The report must already have been created in the CA-RET program. Once loaded, the internal run-time operation of CA-RET may be called using the `_EXECUTE` internal variable along with the CA-RET() function. While the report is printing, the programmer may ask for specific pieces of information from CA-RET using the `_REQUEST` internal variable. And finally, the report can be stopped using the `_STOP` internal variable.

For more information on DDE exchanges, please see the following chapter, and for more detailed information on the CA-RET program itself, please see the separate user guide that comes with the Realizer package.

Help

Even the easiest-to-use applications should have a system of on-line and context-sensitive help. The procedure for building such a system is complicated, and may seem to some like learning a new language altogether. Realizer's Utility subdirectory contains several files whose purpose is to create Windows Help files:

- HC31.EXE   Help 3.1 Compiler
- HC31.ERR   Help 3.1 Error List
- HC.BAT   Batch file to run the Help Compiler
- SHED.EXE*   Hot Spot Editor
- SHED.HLP*   Help file for Hot Spot Editor
- MRBC.EXE   Multiple Resolution Bitmap Compiler

These files may be executed from a DOS shell, running in Windows. They will not work in DOS on their own.

> **Note:** Those files with asterisks can be executed only via the Program Manager's File RUN option.

To start, there are two steps involved with building Help files and working with them in a Realizer program or application. Ironically, the easiest step deals with the Realizer language. Here, only a couple of functions need to be called from within the application, and just a small program snippet sets the context-sensitivity gears in motion. The real challenge, lies in understanding the steps and language of the Windows Help Compiler.

Windows Help Compiler

There are basically three files involved in the compiling process. There is the .MAC file, or the macro file. From this file, we can build the second file, which is an .RTF, or Rich Text Format file. This text file has embedded codes that instruct the compiler how to build the final file: the .HLP file that the Windows Help manager will run. The files `Winhelp.exe` and `Winhelp.hlp` are the "reader" files that execute all .HLP files in Windows.

Before we take the first step in building a help system, we need to create an outline of our help subjects. This outline may mimic the menu structure of our application, along with additional notes and information, or it may reflect a general flow of ideas that we want to cover. For example, using the menu structure in the `Dcanter.rlz` file, we may choose the following outline:

```
Introduction
Credits
Basic Intent
Menu Items
    File
            Your Cellar
            Transaction Files
            Sample Cellar
            Winery Files
            Make Winery Files
            Disclaimer
            Import & Export
            Backup Data Files
            Select Printer
            Setup Printer
            Exit Program
```

```
    View
            Index Listings
            Search and Sort options
            Multiple Field Search
            Goldbook for Decanter
            Winery to Region
            Clear Wine Rack
    Edit
    Graphs
    Tables
    Options
    Help
```

Once a general outline is in place, review it once more with a view toward a key rule of practice: An end user wants to get at information immediately, if not sooner. Each level in the outline will be a page of information. Anything more than four levels deep tends to lose an end user and is more frustrating than helpful.

Once the outline is in place, the next step is to create what are known as **topic tags**. In essence, each item in the outline will be referenced by a single-word "tag." Keep in mind that you can use graphic images or .BMP (bitmapped) files to help explain a topic within the Help file once it is compiled. Also, keep in mind that you can create "jumps" or hypertext links, which means that the flow of the text need not be linear in nature.

Along with the outline will be a reference manual or script. Merging the script with this outline is the crux of making the help file. Go through the user manual or script and circle the words that may need extra clarification or definition. These **terms** will be added to a glossary. There are special markings for these terms, which we will discuss later. For now, remember that there should be a topic tag for each term added to the glossary, and each tag should be unique.

We are now ready to start building the components of our Help System. The system is composed of two sets of files. One file has a .HPJ file extension (referred to as the Help Project File) and contains basic instructions for the Help Compiler about the formatting and other characteristics of that file, and what other text files are involved in creating the Help System. This means that the second set of files holds specific instructions and text that will be displayed on the screen when called. Think of the first file as a make file as well as a general attribute file for the rest of the Help System. This file will point the Help Compiler to other files necessary in the building process.

There are two other files we need to look at. One file is the `HC.bat` file that comes on the optional source code disk. This is a batch file that calls the

Help Compiler. The second file is a .PH file that should hold certain key information found in the mentioned source file. It is not important to the eventual .HLP file (the created Help file); however, should there be problems in the file, this file may be used to provide additional information. Turning back to the `HC.bat` file for a moment, this file may be modified as follows to ensure that the table of information contained in the .PH file is refreshed with each compiled pass:

```
@echo off
if NOT "%1" == "-n" hc30 %1 %2
if NOT "%1" == "-n" del %1.ph
if "%1" == "-n" del %2.ph
if "%1" == "-n" hc31 %2 %3
@echo on
```

In seeing this file, the following syntax may be used within the DOS window:

```
hc -n <file>
```

This will take the name of the file specified and delete the appropriate .PH file.

The .HPJ File

The Help Project file (.HPJ) will be specifically mentioned when the Help Compiler is called from the command line. Several options may be specified in this file that add attributes to the help file. When creating an .HPJ file, remember these basic guidelines:

- The semicolon may be used as a remark in the text file.
- The COMPRESS command should always be used.
- The FILES command needs to be used.

To see these guidelines in action, here is the source for our first .HPJ file:

```
;================================================================
; Name           Help1.hpj
; Author         Steve Straley
; Notice         (C) Copyright 1994 - Sirus Press, Inc.
;                All Rights Reserved
; Purpose        Project file for the first help example
;================================================================
[OPTIONS]
COMPRESS=HIGH

[FILES]
HELP1.TXT

; End of File: Help1.hpj
```

The first [OPTIONS] command is important. There are several optional commands that may be lumped under this heading. Here, the COMPRESS command specifies the compression level to be used when the .HLP file is being built. You can set this command equal to 0 (no compression), MEDIUM (medium compression), or HIGH (high compression).

The second [FILES] command is even more important. Here, the files to be used in the compiling process are specified. The exact subdirectory path may be specified with each file; however, the ROOT command may be used to direct the Help Compiler accordingly. This would be another command in the [OPTIONS] section of the .HPJ file. Also, note that the #INCLUDE option may be used in the [FILES] section. Here, the list of files may be specified outside the domain of the .HPJ file and stored on the disk in a separate file that is "included" in the compiling process.

The Source File

This file has its own series of unique commands and options that guide the Help Compiler in making the appropriate Windows Help file. The first few lines of this file read as follows:

```
{\rtf
...
...
...
}
```

The entire document must be encased in this command construct; otherwise, a compiler error will be generated.

> **Note:** An .RTF file is nothing more than an ASCII file with codes understood by the Help Compiler.

At this point in the file, there are three major things to consider: the use of the \ANSI command, which specifies the character set within the Help file; the fonts to be created; and the color (if applicable) of the various regions within the help screen. The last two settings are not as critical as some others; however, they typically appear at the top of a file's definition, and therefore, need to be mentioned at this time. With these settings established, the file may now look like this:

Output, Help, and Errors   461

```
{\rtf
\ansi
{\fonttbl
    {\f0\froman MS San Serif;}
    {\f1\froman Arial;}
    {\f2\fswiss Courier;}
    {\f3\fdecor Symbol;}
}
...
...
...
}
```

The {\fonttbl command sets up the table of fonts to be used. This table must conclude with the right brace character (or squiggle in high-tech circles). The indention of the font commands is purely stylistic. Each font specified has a corresponding number, with the default being 0. The font numbers created in this table must have corresponding font family members. These are the names immediately following the font number so they are based on the following table:

Family Name	Definition
fnil	Unknown or default
froman	Roman, proportionally spaced serif fonts
fswiss	Swiss, proportionally spaced serif fonts
fmodern	Fixed-pitch serif and sans serif fonts
fscript	Script fonts
fdecor	Decorative fonts
ftech	Technical, symbol, and mathematical fonts

> **Note:** You cannot specify a family member other than those listed in the preceding table; otherwise, a run-time error will be generated.

Following the family member to be assigned comes the name of the typeface, or font. This font should be available from the basic Windows font set. If the font is not available, then Windows Help will choose a font that has the same character set as the one specified. For example, if you specify TrueType fonts in the font table, but an end user doesn't have these fonts, then Windows Help will attempt to select the closest available font when displaying the contents to the screen.

The next step in building a Help file is to create the **footnote**. This important element will be the reference point that connects this file to the topic tags that we made earlier. The \FOOTNOTE command defines topic-specific information, including:

- topic tags
- context string
- titles
- browsing number
- keywords
- execution macros

A special character preceding the \FOOTNOTE command tells the Help Compiler to which category the item belongs. For example, an entry into the table of key words (this will be seen in a moment) would be preceded by the letter K:

```
K{\footnote Contents}
```

This command places the string "Contents" into the key word table. Ultimately, these key words appear as a list in the Search dialog box, shown in Figure 9-1.

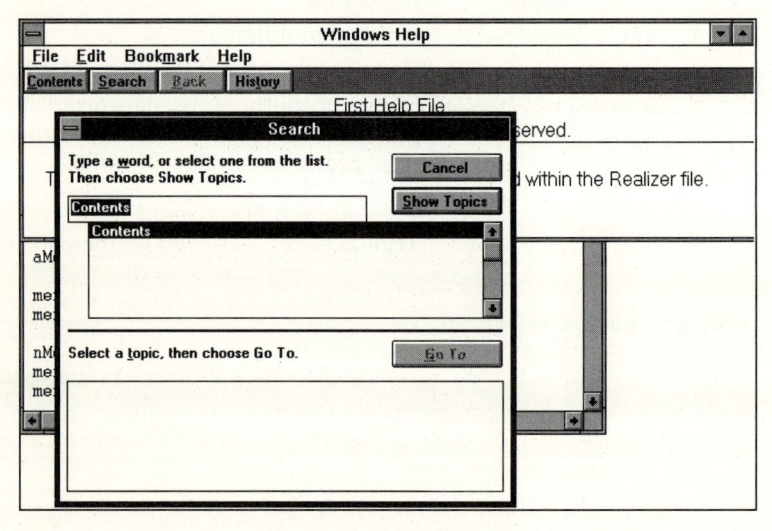

Figure 9-1. Window's HELP Search utility.

Those items that appear in the search listbox also need to be planned for within our outline.

Another type of \FOOTNOTE is the context string. This will be used with another command, the \V option, to create links within the Help System.

Output, Help, and Errors

Initially, our examples will have no links. Links take time to plan and anticipate. The code for the context string is the following:

```
#{\footnote text}
```

Keep in mind that the name of the item following the \FOOTNOTE command may be any combination of letters and numbers, but it may not contain any spaces.

Finally, the last \FOOTNOTE to look at is the topic title:

```
${\footnote New Items}
```

Bringing all of these footnotes together, our file might look like something like this:

```
{\rtf
\ansi
{\fonttbl
   {\f0\froman MS San Serif;}
   {\f1\froman Arial;}
   {\f2\fswiss Courier;}
   {\f3\fdecor Symbol;}
}
#{\footnote main}
${\footnote Table of Contents}
K{\footnote Contents}
...
...
...
}
```

Now, the Search dialog box might look like the one shown in Figure 9-2.

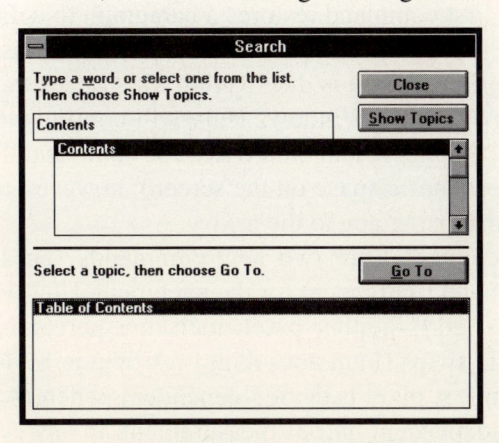

Figure 9-2. Selecting a specific SEARCH topic.

The item that starts with the $ character can be seen in the Go To list box while the text in the item that starts with the K character can be seen in the Show Topics list box.

Finally, you may specify the formatting and attributes for your Help information. For example, the following instructions set the typeface to the first setting, specify a type size of 12 points, and center a line of text between the left and right margins:

```
\f0
\fs24
\qc
First Help File
```

> **Note:** The number specified in the \FS command is double the actual point size of the text.

The first instruction sets the font found in the font table, while the second command sets the font's size. The \QC command centers the following text, "First Help File," within the left and right margins of the screen.

You can also set margins and text paragraphs within the Help file, as shown in the following instructions:

```
\pard
\li180
\ri180
```

These three commands actually appear in the file above the preceding four instructions. The first command restores a paragraph to default values. Once a paragraph is set using various commands and instructions, those settings will continue until a \PARD is discovered. This raises the question, "What is a paragraph?" Text in Windows Help will continue to flow and wrap unless the Help Compiler is told otherwise. The command \PAR makes a paragraph break (or creates a space on the screen); however, the settings are carried over from one paragraph to the next.

After the \PARD command are two new commands. These last two instructions set the left and right indent for the paragraph. However, the unit of measurement specified is neither pixel, inch, nor percent. Paragraph indents are measured in **twips** (I am not joking!). A twip is 1/1440 inch, or 1/20 of a printer's point. A pixel is device-dependent, whereas a twip is a uniform and device-independent unit of measurement. In any event, this is the measuring tool used within the Help system and may be set either by a \PARD instruction or by another \LI or \RI instruction.

With this in place, here are the exact contents of the `Help1.txt` file:

```
{\rtf
\ansi
{\fonttbl
   {\f0\froman MS Sans Serif;}
   {\f1\froman Arial;}
   {\f2\fswiss Courier;}
   {\f3\fdecor Symbol;}
}
\pard
\li180
\ri180
#{\footnote main}
${\footnote Table of Contents}
K{\footnote Contents}
\f0
\fs24
\keepn
\qc
First Help File
\par
\qc
\'a9 1994 Sirius Press, Inc.   All rights reserved
\par
\fs24
\tx540
\pard
\li180
\ri180

\par

This file will show up whenever the HELP button is pressed within the Realizer file.

\par
}
```

This file contains three additional commands at which we need to look. The first is the \TX command, which sets the tab stops, in terms of twips, within the file. The second command is the \' command, used in conjunction with a regular text string. This command tells the Help Compiler that the following two characters are in hexadecimal format and are to be attached to the string. So in this example, the copyright symbol is specified in the text. The final command is the \KEEPN command, which will create a non-scrolling region at the top of the Help window for any given topic. This may be used to set a banner or title for the Help Screen. If the text in the Help window is larger than allowed, scroll bars will appear, but they will not affect this region. There are a few rules with this command:

- If used in a topic, it must be applied to the first paragraph in the topic.
- Do not specify paragraphs before using the command or an error message will be generated.
- Only one non-scrolling region per topic is allowed.
- The \PARD commands resets this region.
- The region fit is based on the text between \PARD instructions.

The commands that we've been examining may be strung together to form one large instruction set. For example, we could create the following code:

```
\par\fs24\tx540
\pard\li180\ri180
```

Sometimes, however, breaking up the instructions makes for easier reading. Whether or not you choose to break up the instructions, they are precisely the commands used to build an .RTF (Rich Text Format) file. For example, these commands would appear in an .RTF file created by Microsoft Word. Other than the special characters, the file looks just like a regular text file.

The Realizer Connection

Once we've complied the .HLP file, we need to get the Realizer application to hook into this specific help file. To do this, there are two basic functions. The HELPSETPROC() function will be called whenever the F1 key is pressed within the Realizer application. The HELP() function calls the Windows Help Manager, specifying the .HLP file and the key word to begin the search. This is how context-sensitive help may be managed, as shown in this brief code sample found in `Htest1.rlz`:

```
'* Application ... : HTest1.rlz
'* Authors ....... : Steve Straley
'* Notice ........ : Copyright(c) 1994 - Sirius Press, Inc.
'* .............. : All Rights Reserved
'* Date .......... : January 1, 1994
'* Description ... : This calls the Help1.hlp file specified in this
'*                   file.  It will be called off of the HELP menu item
```

```
proc MyHelpMenuProc( aParams )

   Help( "help1", "Contents" )

end proc

sethourglass

setsys( _LOADDIR, "\Realizer\sirius\samples" )

menuselect( _HELPMENU )
menucontrol( _HIDE )

menunew( menuqunique; "&Help" )
menusetcmd( 10, "General Help" )
menusetcmd( _SEPARATOR )
menusetcmd( 99, "&Index" )
menusetproc( MyHelpMenuProc )
menucontrol( _SHOW )
resethourglass

'* End of File: Htest1.rlz
```

First, the Realizer Help menu option needs to be selected and hidden. Then a new Help option is added to the menu stack. Added to this option are the "General Help" and "&Index" options. When any menu item is selected, the *MyHelpMenuProc()* procedure will be called. There, the HELP() function is called, specifying the `Help1.hlp` file. Since the SETSYS() function is used to set the search directory, the HELP() function does not need to specify this. The second parameter ties to the text associated with the \FOOTNOTE command and the K option. This is the beginning of context-sensitive help, in that the string "Contents" will be searched for within the specified .HLP file. This completes the connection between Realizer and Windows' Help Manager.

The Next Step

Enhancements to the .HLP file include color, .BMP (bitmap) files, charts, lines, and hypertext connections. To start, we can take a look at the .HPJ (Help Project) file to see what new features can be added. From there, we can begin to experiment with new commands found in the .RTF file format. Again, all of these commands and options appear in the documentation that comes with the Realizer package. To practice this aspect of application development, build a simple Realizer file, such as the *HTest2.rlz* file and have that available in one window. In another window, open a DOS shell in which you can issue and compile the instructions for the Help file. Then, switching from the Realizer window to the DOS window, you can test out the various commands used by the Windows Help Compiler.

Improving on the Main File

To add color to the system, you can use the \COLORTBL and \CF commands. The first one builds a table of colors. Unlike the fonts, in which numeric values may be used, colors are incremented internally, starting with 0. These values will then tie into the \CF command, in which a foreground color may be selected from the table.

> **Note:** Only the foreground color of the text may be selected from within the text or .RTF file. To change the background color, the setting must be assigned in the .HPJ file.

To start, four colors will be assigned:

```
{\colortbl
    \red0\green0\blue0;
    \red255\green0\blue0;
    \red0\green\128\blue0;
    \red0\green0\blue255;
}
```

Each color has a red, green, and blue component. The range of valid numbers for each component is from 0 to 255. Here, the first color is black, the second is red, the third is a medium green, and the fourth is blue. Creating colors this way is, sad to say, a matter of trial and error.

Now, one of the gems about this color-assignment technique is that words may be isolated and turned to a specific color. This technique may be used for almost everything available in the command set. To assign color to a specific word, the word needs to be enclosed in a pair of braces. For example, if in a sentence, to turn a specific word blue, we can do the following:

```
This is a test to see if the word {\sf3 BLUE} is in that color.
```

Here, the \SF command selected the fourth color setting (remember, color settings in the table start off at 0), and the word BLUE will appear in blue letters. The rest of the line will appear in the default or most recent color

Output, Help, and Errors 469

setting made in the file. You can use this same technique for setting a specific word in boldface, in a different font, in a different size, and so on: just surround the word with braces:

```
{\b Boldfacing} words
```

Here, the word "Boldfacing" will be in bold letters in the current font and size.

At this point, a brief word on running text is in order. Since the command \PAR is what separates paragraphs from one another, text within the file can appear on a single line; however, that is too unwieldy to edit. It would be nice, especially when working in a DOS editor, if lines could appear one after another like this:

```
This is the second example of a help file. There will be
{\b three} separate screens in this example. This will be the
first screen. From here there will be two other choices. These
choices will also be able to tie directly into the example
program in Realizer.
```

This paragraph will be joined together on the screen within the margins set in the Help file. Note how, starting on the second line, there is an initial space before the word begins. This is to prevent a run-on from the end of the previous line. Without this, for example, the word "From" and "here" would be joined on the screen as "Fromhere." Adding a space to the end of the line with the "From" will not achieve the proper results. The Help Compiler trims off the line before compiling. Therefore, the space needs to be added at the beginning of the line. However, if you want to make a one-line paragraph extend out to the right of the window, then this technique is not necessary.

When building a Help screen, it is a good idea to tell the end user when the end of the screen has been reached. A user could, of course, look to the scroll bar and see that there is nothing further to scroll down to. Unfortunately, end users often like to be told the obvious, so adding a phrase "End of page" is not too much to ask. If there are multiple pages, then a phrase like "Page 1 of 4" is also reasonable. In this example, the end of the page is duly marked with a line directly under the phrase. This is the \BRDRB command. It looks like this when implemented:

End of page

At this point, the Help file looks like this:

```
{\rtf\ansi
{\fonttbl
    {\f0\froman playbill;}
    {\f1\froman Arial;}
    {\f2\fswiss Courier;}
    {\f3\fdecor Symbol;}
}
{\colortbl
    \red0\green0\blue0;
    \red255\green0\blue0;
    \red0\green128\blue0;
    \red0\green0\blue255;
}
\pard\li180\ri180
#{\footnote main}
${\footnote Contents}
K{\footnote Contents}
\f1
\fs24
\keepn
\b
\qc
Second Help File
\par
\'a9 1994 Sirius Press, Inc.   All rights reserved.
\par\fs24\tx540\plain
\pard\li280\ri280
\f1
\
\par

This is the second example of a help file. There will be {\b three}
 separate screens in this example. This will be the first screen. From
 here there will be two other choices.  These choices will also be able to
 tie directly into the example program in Realizer.
\par\par
The points that we are going to cover here are the following:
\par\par
{\b Boldfacing} words
\par
{\ul Underlining} certain words
\par
{\cf3 Making colors} appear in a line of text
\par
Adding color to the non-scrolling region
\par
```

```
Adding other files to the compiling process
\par
Adding links and context-sensitive help
\par
Other fun stuff
\par\par\par\par\qc\f0\fs36
End of page
\brdrb
}
```

The other file that has been manipulated is the `Help2.hpj` file. Here, we can set the color of the non-scrolling region (which is established by the \KEEPN command). Also, copyright notice and titles for the Help Window may be set. This last may be assigned via the TITLE command, which appears in the [OPTIONS] section of the file:

```
TITLE=Second Example: Sirius Press, Inc.
```

A new section called [WINDOWS] may appear in the .HPJ file as well. Here, the size, location, and colors of the primary Help window and any secondary window may be specified. It works in conjunction with the source file to be compiled. Remember the following:

```
#{\footnote main}
${\footnote Table of Contents}
K{\footnote Contents}
```

The first command is the **type** of the window. This ties in with the [WINDOWS] command option. In the `Help2.hpj` file, the following may be seen:

```
[WINDOWS]
main=,(0,0,1023,700),0,,(0,190,190)
```

These settings are for this type found in the specified source file. For the first window in the Help file, this must be the string "main"—there is no other option. For any secondary window, the TYPE string may be any unique name up to eight characters in length. Keep in mind that there must be a corresponding #{\footnote command in the source file. The first item that may be specified is a caption to be used as a title for the window. Here, there is none, which is why there is a comma right after the equal sign. The title or caption for the first window in the Help system is assigned via the TITLE command in the [OPTIONS] section of the .HPJ file.

The next parameter is a group of four values used to assign the position of the window when Help engages. The first two values in the group are the top and left coordinates of the window. (Windows assumes the screen to be 1024 by 1024.) Here, the top-left corner of the Help window will be at the upper-left corner of the screen. If the first pair had been (512,0), then the window would have started halfway down the screen on the left edge. If the values were reversed, then the window would appear at the top of the screen, halfway in from the left edge.

The next pair in this group deals with width and height. Here, the width of the Help screen is the entire screen, since the value is 1023.

> **Note:** Screen positions, like color and font tables, start off at 0. Therefore, while the maximum width is 1024 pixels, since the starting position of any window is 0, the maximums must be backed off by one pixel.

The final value here is the height of the window starting at the position assigned by the first two values. Here, the Help window will reveal 700 help units worth of information starting at coordinates 0,0.

The next parameter tells the relative size of the secondary window (if any) compared to the first Help window. A 0, as in this case, sets the window to the size specified in the previous group parameter. If a 1 is specified, then the window will be the full screen height and width regardless of the settings.

The next parameter is skipped. It specifies the background color of the window. If not used, then the default window will be the color specified in the Windows Control Panel. Like the final parameter (which is specified), a three-element grouping may be specified here. Each element in the grouping represents the red, green, and blue color settings, similar to the \COLORTBLE command in the main source file. Values may range from 0 to 255.

The last parameter specifies the background color (as outlined in the preceding parameter) of the non-scrolling region (if used) in the Help file. The non-scrolling region is specified via the \KEEPN command, if we activated our help file now, we might see the screen shown in Figure 9-3.

The top part of the window is a different color now, while the rest of the Help window defaults to the background color specified in the Control Panel. Now, the only difference on the Realizer side of this problem is in the *Htest2.rlz* file, in which the file specified is *Help2.hlp*.

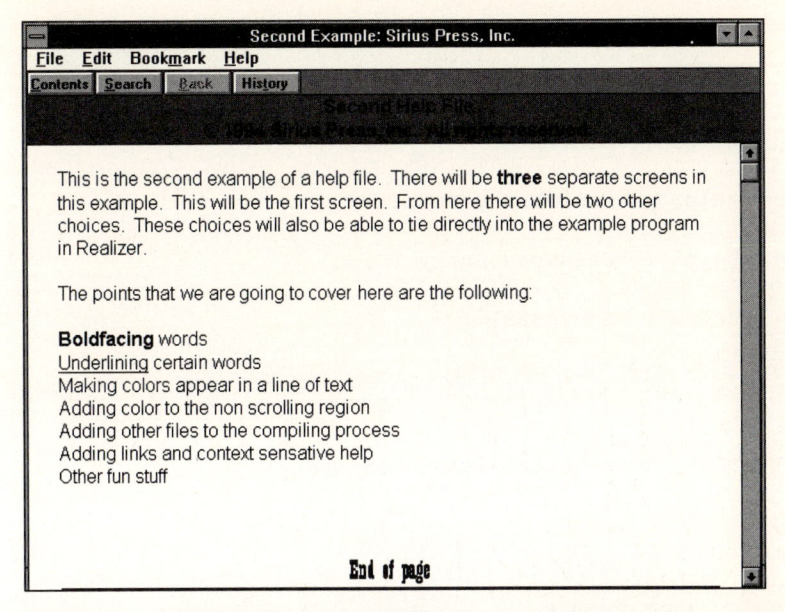

Figure 9-3. Self-generated Help Window for application.

Context-Sensitive Help

Selecting Help from an application's main menu bar is only one way to get help. Sometimes, in data-entry mode, the end user expects to be able to press the F1 key and get specific help for the currently active and focused object. As with the other examples, there is a two-part solution. The Realizer part is the easiest: a simple call to the HELPSETPROC() function. When the user presses the F1 key, this procedure will be automatically called bringing with it the expected array of information, including the in-focus object. As with the previous examples, we can look at which item was in focus when the F1 key was pressed, and then call the HELP() function with the appropriate key words or tags. In the following example, the *Htest3.rlz* file not only changes the HELP menu item, but builds a simple data-entry form with a couple of data-entry objects:

```
'* Application ... : HTest3.rlz
'* Authors ....... : Steve Straley
'* Notice ........ : Copyright(c) 1994 - Sirius Press, Inc.
'* ............... : All Rights Reserved
'* Date .......... : January 1, 1994
'* Description ... : This calls the Help3.hlp file specified in this
'*                   file.  It will be called off of the HELP menu item
'*                   and shows the use of Context-Sensitive Help
```

```
proc MyHelpMenuProc( aParams )

  select case aParams[_ITEMNUM]
  case 10    '* The
    Help( "help3", "Contents" )
  case 11
    Help( "help3", "Name Entry Point" )
  case 21
    Help( "help3", "Password Entry Point" )
  case 99
    Help( "help3", "Contents" )
  end select

end proc

setsys(_LOADDIR, "\realizer\sirius\samples" )

sethourglass

menuselect( _HELPMENU )
menucontrol( _HIDE )

'* set the menus up....
menunew( menuqunique; "&Help" )
menusetcmd( 10, "General Help" )
menusetcmd( _SEPARATOR )
menusetcmd( 99, "&Index" )
menusetproc( MyHelpMenuProc )
menucontrol( _SHOW )

'* Set context sensitive help...

helpsetproc( MyHelpMenuProc )

formnew(100; "Data Entry Example", _TITLE + _CLOSE + _SIZE)
formcontrol(_SIZE;0,0,400,250)
formsetobject(11,_TEXTBOX,"",150,_TOP)
formsetobject(21,_TEXTBOX,"",150,50)
formsetobject(1,_BUTTON,"Save",_LEFT,_BOTTOM)
formsetobject(2,_BUTTON,"Cancel",_RIGHT,_BOTTOM)
formsetobject(10,_CAPTIONLEFT,"Enter Name",_LEFT,_TOP)
formsetobject(20,_CAPTIONLEFT,"Enter Password",_LEFT,50)
formcontrol(_SHOW)

resethourglass

'* End of File: HTest3.rlz
```

Output, Help, and Errors

In this example, the SETSYS() function first tells Realizer where to look for the .HLP file, which is called via the HELP() function contained in the *MyHelpMenuProc()* procedure. Here, if a menu item with an ID of 10 or an ID of 99 is selected, via the MENUSETPROC() function, Realizer will call the HELP() function automatically, passing to the function the search string "Contents."

After the menu functions have been called to set this up, a new function is issued: HELPSETPROC(). This is for the `F1` key. The MENUSETPROC() function, is only for menu items selected; however, no menu is involved in a chart, a form, a log, and so on. Here, the end user will instinctively press the `F1` key on those items on which they want more information. In some cases, the routine for the `F1` / context-sensitive help is a separate procedure from the one used in the MENUSETPROC() function. In any event, the routine associated with the HELPSETPROC() function will be called if the `F1` key is pressed. As with all tool procedures, an array of information will be passed to the attached procedure. In this, we can test for the ID of the object in question. For example, when the user is confronted with the form and data entry points shown in Figure 9-4, pressing the F1 key will produce the help screen shown in Figure 9-5. If the cursor is in the Enter Password field when the user presses F1, the help screen shown in Figure 9-6 appears.

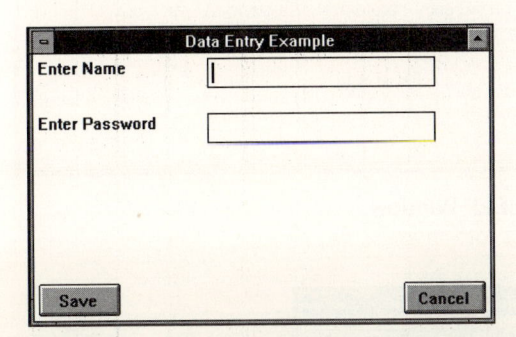

Figure 9-4. Pop-up data entry dialog window.

Even the Search dialog box has all of the key words and search topics or tags listed and available, as shown in Figure 9-7.

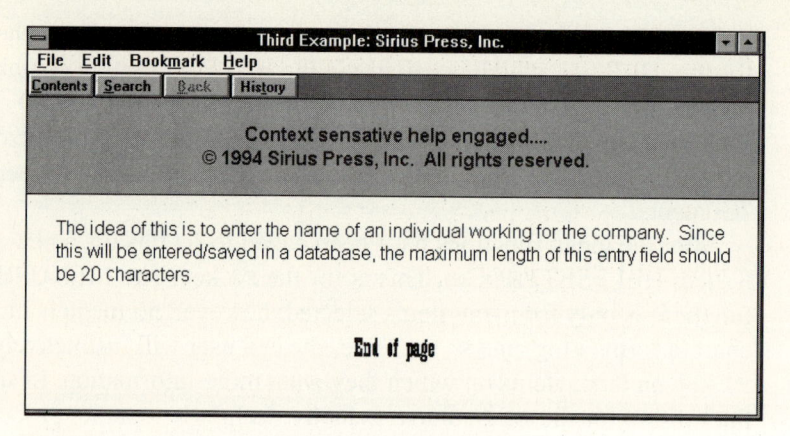

Figure 9-5. Context-sensitive HELP Window.

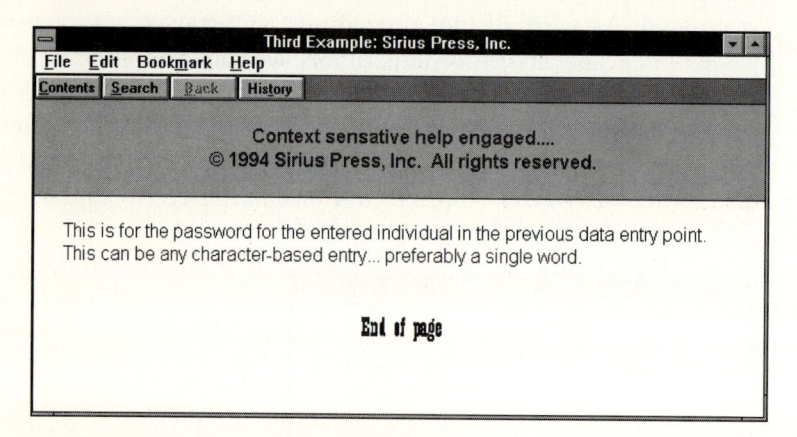

Figure 9-6. Another HELP Window.

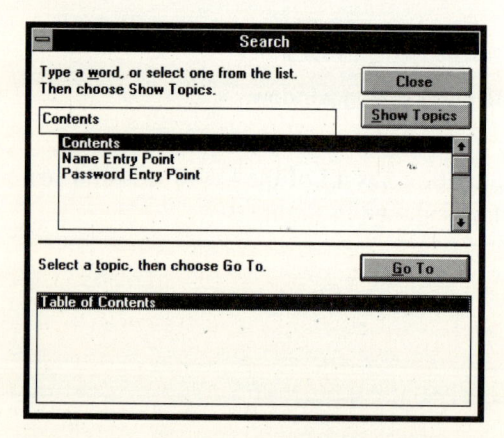

Figure 9-7. HELP Search Dialog Window.

Output, Help, and Errors 477

The text/.RTF file for these two help items offers a new command: \PAGE. First, for the two new pages of information, the *Help3.txt* file now contains the following:

```
\page
\pard

${\footnote Person's Name}
K{\footnote Name Entry Point}

\keepn\f1\fs24\cf3
\b
\qc
\par
Context-sensitive help engaged....
\par
\'a9 1994 Sirius Press, Inc.  All rights reserved.
\par\par\fs24\tx540\plain
\pard\li280\ri280\cf0
\f1
\
\par
The idea of this is to enter the name of an individual working for the
 company. Since this will be entered/saved in a database, the maximum
 length of this entry field should be 20 characters.

\par\par\par\qc\f0\fs36
End of page



\page
\pard

${\footnote Passwords}
K{\footnote Password Entry Point}

\keepn\f1\fs24\cf3
\b
\qc
\par
Context-sensitive help engaged....
\par
\'a9 1994 Sirius Press, Inc.  All rights reserved.
\par\par\fs24\tx540\plain
\pard\li280\ri280\cf0
\f1
\
\par
```

```
This is for the password for the entered individual in the previous
 data-entry point. This can be any character-based entry... preferably
 a single word.

\par\par\par\qc\f0\fs36
End of page
```

The \PAGE command creates a new page for the Help system. At this point, in this new page, we can define a new key word and tag item. So, after the \PARD command resets all of the internal options, the two following \FOOTNOTE commands set up the new page for one of the data-entry objects in the form. Each new page of information can be attached to each item in which the F1 key will be there to yield helpful information. In this code fragment, each new page has a separate non-scroll region with new text. And following that, based on the match made with the tags, the text within the scrolling region fits the data-entry object in question. We could have specified a different position for the second help screens, added pictures, or even tied back to a main table of contents.

The images you add to a Help file may have associated hot spots that link to other operations or even to other pages of help text. In the following example, the first page of help (tied to the menu items) has been modified to hold simple pictures. The bitmap files used in this example come right out of the Realizer package from the *Clipart* directory:

```
\tab\tab\tab\{bmc arrow52.bmp\}     {\b Boldfacing} words
\par
\tab\tab\tab\{bmc arrow52.bmp\}     {\ul Underlining} certain words
\par
```

Here, the \TAB command does just what it implies, and the {bmc <file>\} commands, used in conjunction with the text to be displayed, produce a display that looks like this:

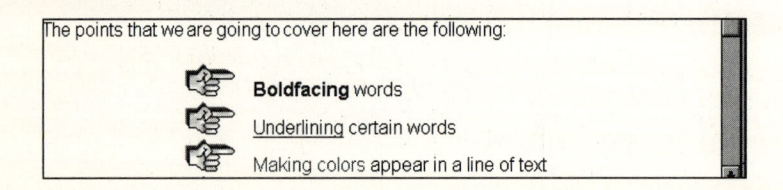

```
The points that we are going to cover here are the following:

    ☞  Boldfacing words
    ☞  Underlining certain words
    ☞  Making colors appear in a line of text
```

However, the location of the .BMP files may be included in the source file or may be listed in the [OPTIONS] section of the .HPJ file using the

BMROOT command. In this example, the directory location for the bitmaps will look like this:

```
BMROOT=C:\REALIZER\CLIPART
```

An entire book could be (and probably has been) written on how to build the perfect help system. We haven't talked about such items as links, hot spots, or the ability to execute code within a Help System. The latter means that demo programs or run-time tutorials can be launched directly from the Help System. Just remember that working with help from the Realizer perspective is relatively simple: Only two functions are involved. It's the issue of building the perfect help system from the Windows Help Compiler that should be the focus of our attention.

Errors

Errors are no joy to deal with in any language, but in this section we will not discuss programmer error. Instead, we will focus on application errors that can be traced to the "human factor." This might mean communication failures with the port, trouble in writing out a file to the disk, or an invalid data-entry field. In these cases, how the program deals with the error, the machine, and the end user is almost as critical as the rest of the application.

There are two basic types of errors: recoverable and non-recoverable. A good error system will be able to handle both situations with little adverse effect on the end user. To begin this discussion, a few good examples will help illustrate the point. The first example shows a very crude error situation and error-recovery plan. There are two main pieces to this example. The first part is with the label—in this case, a tag word followed by a colon. This marks a section of the code to Realizer. When an error is detected, the ON ERROR GOTO command will look for the code immediately following the label.

> **Note:** You cannot have any other text on the same line with a label, including comments preceded by a single quotation mark.

The second part of an error-recovery system works with the ON ERROR GOTO command. Here, the name of the label is used in conjunction with this command to tell Realizer where to "goto" in case of an error. To see this in action, consider the sample program *Error1.rlz*:

```
'* Application ... : Error1.rlz
'* Authors ....... : Steve Straley
```

```
'* Notice ........ : Copyright(c) 1994 - Sirius Press, Inc.
'* ............... : All Rights Reserved
'* Date .......... : January 1, 1994
'* Description ... : This shows how an error message or system may be
'*                   created and used in a Realizer program

'* Prepare the file for the error

logselect( _PRINTLOG )    '* Select the print log
logcontrol( _SHOW )       '* Show the log

TRUE  = (1=1)
FALSE = (1=2)

'************ BEGINNING THE MAIN ROUTINE *******

local nTripped as integer

nTripped = FALSE     '* A False condition

PlacedHere:
if nTripped          '* Test a condition
  input "This is a recovered statement", \\
        "Sirius Press, Inc." ;
  print err, erl, erf     '* Print the errors
  stop
end if
nTripped = TRUE

on error goto PlacedHere

for nCount = 1 to 10
  print nCount, "About to idle..."
  idle 3
  if nCount = 10
    print notDeclared      '* An error!
  end if
next

'* End of File: Error1.rlz
```

    After the _PRINTLOG window is opened and two constant values declared at the top of the routine, the main part of the program begins. Before the actual code with the error is executed, the code for the error recovery is found. The order of the code does not matter so much; however, the technique used to avoid the error system will be slightly different, depending on whether the code extract comes before or after the main program segment. In this example, the key variable named *nTripped* triggers the Error System into action. As Realizer processes this example, the tag *PlacedHere:* will be observed. Just because there is a tag in a piece of code does not mean that Realizer should avoid it. So the IF condition on *nTripped* is vital in order for the following INPUT command to be skipped the first time through the code. At the end of the IF command, the variable *nTripped* is then toggled to the TRUE value which activates the code following the tag.

Following this is the ON ERROR GOTO command, which points Realizer back up to the tagged word *PlacedHere:*. If an error is experienced, the code in that section will execute because the variable *nTripped* was engaged just prior to the execution of the ON ERROR GOTO command. In the FOR...NEXT loop, there is a PRINT command and an IDLE command to be processed through each iteration. When the looping variable *nCount* hits the value of 10, the internal IF condition is processed. At that point, the code attempts to PRINT the variable *notDeclared*. This causes an error, since the variable does not exist, which in turn forces Realizer to break out of the FOR...NEXT loop, look for the tag word *PlacedHere:*, and begin processing the code immediately following the tag. With the variable *nTripped* set to a logical false integer value, the INPUT command will be executed, following one final PRINT command. This command prints three values: ERR, ERL, and ERF. The ERR command value holds the reason for the error. This is a code value. The next command value to be printed, ERL, holds the line of source code that executed the error. Finally, the ERF command holds the value of the source file in which the error took place. If we were to look at the Print Log window, the output might look something like Figure 9-8.

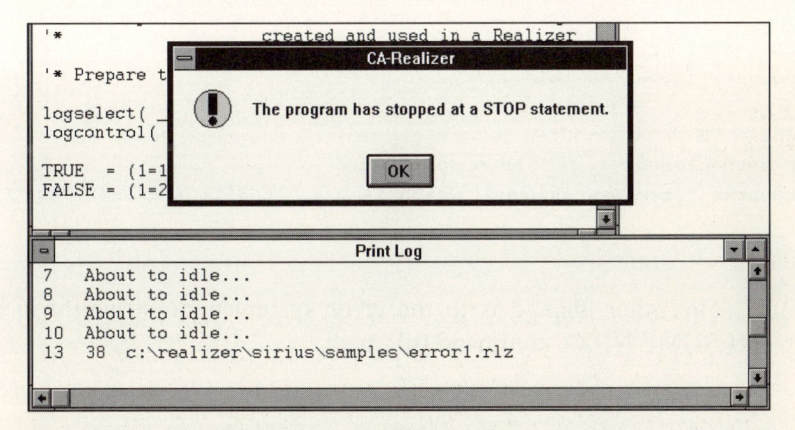

Figure 9-8. Realizer's Error Window for STOP command.

As we mentioned, this is a very crude example. To recover from this error we would need to add new code within the error-recovery section of code and assign a value to the undeclared variable *notDeclared*. Then, the code would use the RESUME command to return to the offending line or, at worst, near the offending line.

There are three possible conditions for the RESUME command. First, we can simply RESUME, which would return to the line that caused the error. The trouble is with this is that if the error is unresolved, an endless loop may be formed, which may require additional counting variables to keep track of the number of times a specified error occurs. However, the advantage of the RESUME command on its own is that it can be reissued. For example, if a file name is misspelled by the end user and is not found on the disk, the RESUME command, after an appropriate warning in the Error System, can retry a condition or situation. The second possibility is to use the NEXT clause in conjunction with the RESUME command. This tells Realizer to resume the execution of the program at the line of code immediately after the offending line. In this case, the problem of an endless loop may be avoided, but the original error may continue to cause other errors throughout an application. The final possibility for the RESUME command is to connect it with another label or tag. In this case, as with the ON ERROR GOTO command, the RESUME command will return to the main application at a specific tagged location in the code.

Now, changing the program, `Error2.rlz` makes use of the NEXT clause with the RESUME command. The first modification is a new MESSAGEBOX() function call following the offending PRINT command in the main program's FOR...NEXT loop. The code looks like this:

```
for nCount = 1 to 10
   print nCount, "About to idle..."
   idle 3
   if nCount = 10
     print notDeclared       '* An error!
     messagebox( "Item was skipped, which is o.k.", "Sirius Press, Inc.", _MB_OK )
   end if
next
```

The other change is in the error system code structure in which the RESUME NEXT command is issued:

```
PlacedHere:
if nTripped            '* Test a condition
   input "This is a recovered statement", \\
         "Sirius Press, Inc." ;
```

```
      print err, erl, erf     '* Print the errors
      resume next
   end if
nTripped = TRUE
```

Everything works as it did in the previous example except that when the PRINT commands for the ERR, ERL, and ERF command values are executed, the control of the program is returned to the line immediately following the offending PRINT command of the *notDeclared* variable. This means that the MESSAGEBOX() command will be executed when the RESUME NEXT command takes effect.

Of course, the other possibility is to assign a value to the *notDeclared* variable and then just RESUME. This would cause Realizer to return control to the original and offending PRINT statement, and this time to actually print a value.

The program example in *Error3.rlz* removes the NEXT clause in the RESUME command and actually makes an assignment:

```
PlacedHere:
if nTripped           '* Test a condition
   input "This is a recovered statement", \\
         "Sirius Press, Inc." ;
   print err, erl, erf     '* Print the errors

   notDeclared = "Ok, it's now assigned a value!"

   resume
end if
nTripped = TRUE
```

This means that the code will make another attempt at the original PRINT command. This also means that the MESSAGEBOX() function call is not needed:

```
for nCount = 1 to 10
   print nCount, "About to idle..."
   idle 3
   if nCount = 10
      print notDeclared      '* An error!
   end if
next
```

The final example, in *Error4.rlz*, uses the RESUME command in connection with another tag or label:

```
'* Application ... : Error4.rlz
'* Authors ....... : Steve Straley
'* Notice ........ : Copyright(c) 1994 - Sirius Press, Inc.
```

```
'* ............. : All Rights Reserved
'* Date .......... : January 1, 1994
'* Description ... : This shows how an error message or system may be
'*                   created and used in a Realizer program

'* Prepare the file for the error

logselect( _PRINTLOG )    '* Select the print log
logcontrol( _SHOW )       '* Show the log

TRUE  = (1=1)
FALSE = (1=2)

'************ BEGINNING THE MAIN ROUTINE *******

local nTripped as integer

nTripped = FALSE     '* A False condition

FinalOne:
if nTripped
   messagebox( "The program will now terminate!", \\
               "Sirius Press, Inc.", _MB_OK )
   reset _all
   exit program
end if

PlacedHere:
if nTripped            '* Test a condition
   input "This is a recovered statement", \\
         "Sirius Press, Inc." ;
   print err, erl, erf      '* Print the errors

   notDeclared = "Ok, it's now assigned a value!"

   resume FinalOne
end if
nTripped = TRUE

on error goto PlacedHere

for nCount = 1 to 10
   print nCount, "About to idle..."
   idle 3
   if nCount = 10
     print notDeclared      '* An error!
   end if
next

'* End of File: Error4.rlz
```

Output, Help, and Errors

The main difference in this example program is that the tag *FinalOne:* is situated along with the *PlacedHere:* tag. Both use the *nTripped* variable to skip the code when first called. The error routine is called via the RESUME *FinalOne* command within the bracketed code tagged by *PlacedHere:*. Within this routine, the RESET command is issued, as well as the EXIT PROGRAM command.

> **Note:** An erroneous error message will be generated if, on the RESUME command, the colon is placed along with the tag name. A line number may not even be given; therefore, debugging will be more tedious.

Note that the EXIT PROGRAM is required in order to leave the system and avoid an endless loop. Without this command, Realizer will repeat and fall back into the error system and bounce, in this case, between the INPUT command in one tagged area and the MESSAGEBOX() function in the other. The only solution at that point would be the familiar three-finger salute: the CTRL-ALT-DEL key combination.

All of the errors so far have been rather mundane. In a more robust error situation/recovery system, we would use the values from ERR to better determine the error experienced and to offer better solutions. Therefore, it is important to be familiar with all of the possible error messages, their numeric values (if you care to know), and the meaning of the code. Table 9-5 shows the internal variables that may be matched against the values returned from ERR.

Table 9-5. Error Codes.

Error Code	Numeric Value	Definition
_ERR_Unclassified	1	Unknown and unclassified error
_ERR_Syntax	3	Syntax error
_ERR_Symbol	4	Variable or symbol error
_ERR_TypeMismatch	5	Data type mismatch error
_ERR_Expression	6	Expression error
_ERR_Function	7	Usage of function error
_ERR_Control	8	Control statement error
_ERR_Command	9	Basic Realizer command error
_ERR_Input	10	INPUT command error

(continued)

Table 9-5. *(continued)*

Error Code	Numeric Value	Definition
_ERR_Run	11	Error in an attempt to RUN a macro
_ERR_Format	12	Error in an attempt to format a value
_ERR_Print	13	PRINT command error
_ERR_DLL	14	Error in an attempt to access DLL
_ERR_Memory	15	Out-of-memory error
_ERR_Array	16	Error in manipulating array
_ERR_Range	17	Value-out-of-range error
_ERR_MatInvert	18	Matrix invert failed error
_ERR_Overflow	19	Value or math overflow error
_ERR_Subscript	20	Array subscript error
_ERR_File	21	General file command error
_ERR_StackOverflow	22	Stack overflow error
_ERR_FileDB	23	FileDB error
_ERR_FileImport	24	File Import or File Export error
_ERR_SerialComm	25	Serial communication error
_ERR_FP	26	Floating point error

Note also that sometimes an error in a file will generate multiple errors. For example, an assignment error may give two separate values in ERR. We can see this in a variation on one of the previous examples, shown in *Error5.rlz:*

```
'* Application ... : Error5.rlz
'* Authors ....... : Steve Straley
'* Notice ........ : Copyright(c) 1994 - Sirius Press, Inc.
'* .............. : All Rights Reserved
'* Date .......... : January 1, 1994
'* Description ... : This starts to show the use of the internal variable
'*                   as a way to better structure the code of the error system

'* Prepare the file for the error

logselect( _PRINTLOG )    '* Select the print log
logcontrol( _SHOW )       '* Show the log

TRUE  = (1=1)
FALSE = (1=2)

'************* BEGINNING THE MAIN ROUTINE *******

local nTripped as integer
```

```
local sMessage as string

nTripped = FALSE      '* A False condition

PlacedHere:
if nTripped           '* Test a condition

  select case err
  case _ERR_TypeMismatch
    sMessage = "There is a type mismatch error"
  case _ERR_Control
    sMessage = "There is a control structure error"
  case _ERR_Print
    sMessage = "There was/is a print error"
  end select

  messagebox( sMessage, "Sirius Press, Inc.", _MB_OK, _MB_Information )

  print erl, erf      '* Print the errors

  notDeclared = "Ok, it's now assigned a value!"

  resume next
end if
nTripped = TRUE

on error goto PlacedHere

for nCount = 1 to 10
  print nCount, "About to idle..."
  if nCount = 10
    print notDeclared                '* An error!
    notDeclared = notDeclared + 1    '* Another error
  end if
next

exit macro

'* End of File: Error5.rlz
```

In this example, the SELECT CASE command is used in conjunction with the ERR command. In addition, each CASE statements works in tandem with the internal variables. For example, the value of ERR is 13 with the first error when the variable *notDeclared*, which does not exist, is passed to the PRINT command. Here, using the internal variable to make the test clearer, the variable *sMessage* is set to the appropriate text message used in the MESSAGEBOX() function. When the RESUME NEXT command is processed, the variable *notDeclared* is assigned to a literal string value.

When Realizer passes control to the NEXT statement in the main program file that began the error process, the assignment of a numeric to what is now a string variable will undoubtedly cause an error. The first error is that the two data types do not match, so the value of ERR will return the internal variable `_ERR_TypeMismatch`. However, when the MESSAGEBOX() function generates the screen for this and control is once again returned, a new error is encountered: `_ERR_Control`. Again, it is important to remember that a single errant command instruction can yield more than one error code. Correcting the topmost error is always the approach to take in these situations. Sometimes, with luck, one correction can fix a string of error messages.

Also in this example, the EXIT MACRO command is used, although it is not necessary in this particular example. If, for example, the order of the code were reversed—that is, if the ON ERROR GOTO command preceded the associated label—the EXIT MACRO command would terminate the main code from the code associated with the label. This is shown in *Error6.rlz:*

```
'* Application ... : Error6.rlz
'* Authors ....... : Steve Straley
'* Notice ........ : Copyright(c) 1994 - Sirius Press, Inc.
'* ............... : All Rights Reserved
'* Date .......... : January 1, 1994
'* Description ... : This starts to show the use of the internal variable
'*                   as a way to better structure the code of the error system

'* Prepare the file for the error

logselect( _PRINTLOG )    '* Select the print log
logcontrol( _SHOW )       '* Show the log

TRUE  = (1=1)
FALSE = (1=2)

'************* BEGINNING THE MAIN ROUTINE *******

local nTripped as integer
local sMessage as string

nTripped = FALSE       '* A False condition
```

```
'******** The error causing routine **********

on error goto PlacedHere

for nCount = 1 to 10
  print nCount, "About to idle..."
  if nCount = 10
    print notDeclared            '* An error!
    notDeclared = notDeclared + 1 '* Another error
  end if
next

exit macro

'*********** The main error handling routine...

PlacedHere:

  select case err
  case _ERR_TypeMismatch
    sMessage = "There is a type mismatch error"
  case _ERR_Control
    sMessage = "There is a control structure error"
  case _ERR_Print
    sMessage = "There was/is a print error"
  end select

  messagebox( sMessage, "Sirius Press, Inc.", _MB_OK, _MB_Information )

  print erl, erf    '* Print the errors

  notDeclared = "Ok, it's now assigned a value!"

  resume next

'* End of File: Error6.rlz
```

> **Note:** To remove an active ON ERROR GOTO statement, the ON ERROR GOTO 0 command may be used. Specifying another tag variable will only cancel the existing ON ERROR statement in favor of the new one.

Conclusion

In this chapter we have looked at three important aspects of application development. Output is always at the top of the list, since output is what most businesspeople want from applications holding critical data about their companies. The design of output is therefore, the most important creative task facing any programmer. Programming for error recovery while an application is running, along with building an on-line help system, are also tasks that make for a more complete application. But where an application can exist without an intuitive error system and on-line help system, it cannot exist without output.

Chapter 10

The Animator, Importing/Exporting, and DDEs

This chapter is a hodgepodge of ideas and techniques that involve some specific functions and tools within the Realizer language. The animator helps bring life, literally, to an application, and the ability to exchange data with other applications brings breadth to an application. Data exchange can range from the simple concept of importing and exporting data from other data formats to the more sophisticated idea of using Windows' DDE (dynamic data exchange) protocol to create a link between two applications. Each function needs only a few words to highlight its importance and purpose.

The Animator

The animator is a special tool in the Realizer language that deals with the display of pictures in such a way that they appear to be in motion. But before we discuss the functions supporting this service, it's important to imagine the images you want to see processed. In essence, you must think like a film director, mentally conceiving each individual frame and how they will be chained together in sequence to make one animation strip, much like a motion picture.

As an example for this chapter, I created an animated strip in which the text box shown in Figure 10-1 turns in a complete circle. I began in Corel Draw (version 4), and created the text box and the two lines of text. This was my base frame. Then, I grouped the three objects together and exported the frame to a .BMP file. In Corel Draw, an image can be saved with a specified number of pixels, so I specified a width of 200 pixels and a height of 50 pixels. This made a 5K .BMP file. For the second image, I rotated the original image 10 degrees to the left and saved it as a new .BMP file. I continued this process until the image had made a complete circle. This resulted in some 48 .BMP files being generated.

A word here about image size and memory: When you run an animation sequence, Realizer loads all of the files for the animation strip into memory. The more files required for the animation, the more memory required. If each file is 80K or more, it takes a few files to bog the system down, and you'll get an error message like the following:

```
                           Error Log
At line 20 in c:\realizer\sirius\samples\animate.rlz.
?-> animatecells("Sirius#.bmp", 1, 41)
AnimateCells failed.
```

While "AnimateCells Failed" is not a very descriptive message, it implies either that there are too many files to load into the system or that the files are too big for the system to handle collectively.

A good drawing package can help you keep your images as small as possible. Try to use a package that, like Corel Draw, allows you to specify the dimensions (in pixels) of the exported image. It also helps if you can export the selected object only. That way, you can avoid saving extraneous borders or white space along with the image.

> **Note:** It is a good idea to keep the .BMP files under 5K in size. Some custom drawing programs allow you to customize the size of the output in terms of pixel height and width.

The unfortunate thing about building a series of pictures for an animation sequence is that you do not know how the total picture will turn out until after all of the images have been created and saved as .BMP files. It is a time-consuming, tedious task that requires not only a keen sense of images, but patience as well.

However, once the files have been built, using them in Realizer is simple. You create a regular form, size it, and place an `_ANIMATE` object in it. This object needs to be sized appropriately based on the images and other objects contained within the form. Then, the various files need to be loaded, the animation process engaged, and the form activated. You can see this in action in the file `Animate.rlz`:

```
'* Application ... : Animate.rlz
'* Authors ....... : Steve Straley
'* Notice ........ : Copyright(c) 1994 - Sirius Press, Inc.
'* .............. : All Rights Reserved
'* Date .......... : January 1, 1994
'* Description ... : This shows how a series of animation cells may be
'*                    created and used in a Realizer program

local aText     as array
local nLooping  as integer
local nCount    as integer
local nTime     as integer

aText = {          "This example shows how an animation program works." }
aText = { aText, "This will loop 10 times before terminating." }
aText = { aText, "There are four separate text lines shown here," }
aText = { aText, "and demonstrate SIRIUS advertising!!!" }

addsys(_LOADDIR, "\REALIZER\SIRIUS\SAMPLES")

formnew(formqunique; "Animate Example", _TITLE + _CLOSE + _MINIMIZE)
formcontrol(_SIZE; _CENTER, _CENTER, 60 pct, 50 pct)

formsetobject(20, _ANIMATE, "", _CENTER, _CENTER, 40 pct, 50 pct)
formsetobject(30, _CAPTIONCENTER, aText[1], _CENTER, _BOTTOM, \\
                                        100 pct, _DEFAULT )

sethourglass
animatecells("Sirius#.bmp", 1, 41)
resethourglass

nTime = 70
for nCount = 1 to 41
  animateframe(nCount, 0, 0, nTime)
next

animatecontrol(_START)
formcontrol(_SHOW)

for nLooping = 1 to 10
  for nCount = 1 to 4
    formmodifyobject( 30, _SHOW, aText[nCount] )
    idle 4
  next
next

reset

'* End of File: Animate.rlz
```

It is a good idea to use the SETHOURGLASS command to change the mouse cursor to an hour glass during any long and tedious process, such as while the various .BMP files are loaded via the ANIMATECELLS() function. Here, a template of the files to be loaded, one at a time, is passed as the first parameter, while the beginning number and ending number for that template character are the second and third parameters to this function. In essence, we are instructing Realizer to load all files beginning with `Sirius1.bmp` and ending with `Sirius41.bmp`.

> **Note:** If you use the SETHOURGLASS command to change the shape of the mouse cursor for the suration of an operation, be sure to use the RESETHOURGLASS command to change the cursor back once the operation has finished.

Once loaded, we need to animate the frames and tell Realizer how long to display each one before moving onto the next screen. This is the purpose of the FOR...NEXT loop. The variable *nTime* holds the pausing factor for each frame; you can increase or decrease this amount. Finally, just like forms and logs and sheets, the ANIMATECONTROL() function is used to _START the animation process. In addition, the form is displayed to the screen using the standard FORMCONTROL() function.

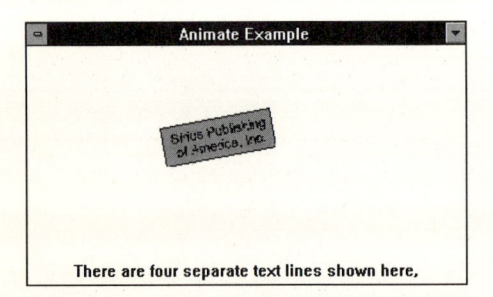

Figure 10-1. Window of animated logo window.

While the animation processes, the nested FOR...NEXT code construct does its magic. Here, the various advertising messages are processed on the form while the image of the floating box continues to be animated. The purpose of this is to show that operations and code processes can perform various duties while the animation strip continues.

Importing and Exporting

In addition to the low-level file functions discussed in a previous chapter, a series of higher-level file functions allows for the import and export of data to and from a variety of file formats. However, before any importing or exporting process takes place, we need to obtain some file-based information. For example, we would have to know if a certain file had enough records in it before we attempted to obtain them. Realizer's querying functions are, therefore, important to the bulletproof-ness of any application.

Database Files

The first of these functions deals exclusively with .DBF files (commonly referred to as xBASE files). This function FILEDB() deals only with the .DBF file and not with .DBT files or index files. For those operations, special database drivers need to be called via the EXTERNAL command. This one function, FILEDB(), can build a database and also read in header information on the file (such as record count, field count, and individual field descriptions), as well as import data from the database directly into a family data type. The basic format of the FILEDB() function depends on whether information is to be obtained (imported) from the .DBF file or stored (exported) to the .DBF file.

Exporting

When data is to be stored to a .DBF file, the calling convention to this function would be the following:

```
filedb(sFile, _DBF, _EXPORT; fInfo, fData)
```

where the variable *cFile* is the name of the file to create, the variable *fInfo* contains the basic file structure of the .DBF file to be created, and the variable *fData* holds the specific data to be exported.

> **Note:** Even though this is the FILEDB() function, the `_DBF` internal variable is still required. Experimentation shows that if, for example, the `_REALIZER` internal variable is used in its place, the operation of the function does not change.

The creation of a file name is nothing special, but the relationship between the variable holding the structure of the database and the variable holding the data is *very* important. The family data type holding the .DBF structure will contain four basic family members: the name of the field, the length of the field, the data type of the field, and the number of decimals for the field.

> **Note:** All database fields must have a value, even if a default value is assumed (such as 0 for the number of decimal places on a character-based field).

The last three items in this family are relatively straightforward:

```
fInfo.lengths   = {20,15,10,8}
fInfo.types     = {"C", "C", "N", "D"}
fInfo.decplaces = {0,0,2,0}
```

In this example, it is obvious that there are four fields involved. The first field will be a character field of 20 characters; the second field will also be a character field 15 characters long. The third field is numeric. It is 10 bytes long and holds two positions on reserve for decimal placement. The last field in this file is a date field, and even though both length and number of decimal places have default values (a date field has to have 8 bytes and no decimal positions), the arrays held in each family member need to be uniform and filled out.

The last item in the family is actually the first item in the list: the names of the fields. In our example, the line of code looks like this:

```
fInfo.fields    = {"lname","fname", "amount", "bdate"}
```

These will be the names of the fields created in the database when the FILEDB() function engages, and they are also the names of the family members found in the *fData* variable talked about earlier.

> **Note:** Since the names of the family members in the *fInfo.fields* family must match the names of the family members in the data family, those names should be assigned the desired names of the fields in advance.

This variable might be an array if the information in each family member will become a field of a database. Consider the following:

```
fData.lname  = {""}
fData.fname  = {""}
fData.amount = {0}
fData.bdate  = {qdate}
```

The Animator, Importing/Exporting, and DDEs 497

Here, the name of the family is *fData* and the names of the family members, regardless of what they are to contain, must be identical to the fields of the database when exported and also to the names listed in the array held in the *fInfo.fields* family. If these pieces of data do not match up, a run-time error will occur. However, if they do match up, then the FILEDB() function can work without hitch, as you can see in the file `FExam1.rlz`:

```
'* Application ... : FExam1.rlz
'* Authors ....... : Steve Straley
'* Notice ........ : Copyright(c) 1994 - Sirius Press, Inc.
'* ............... : All Rights Reserved
'* Date .......... : January 1, 1994
'* Description ... : This shows how to build two families of information and
'*                   how the FILEDB() function may be used to export and
'*                   build the file.

proc MakeData( fInfo )

   local nStart as integer
   local nEnd   as integer

   fInfo.lname  = { fInfo.lname, "Straley", "Maso", "Piko", \\
                                 "Burnclaw", "Mari" }
   fInfo.fname  = { fInfo.fname, "Steve", "Essor", "Paul", "Russ", "Vini" }
   fInfo.amount = { fInfo.amount, 134.34, 20034,22, 1598.00, 987.23, 34.56 }
   fInfo.bdate  = { fInfo.bdate,  strtodate( "01/21/61" ), \\
                                  strtodate( "05/03/25" ), \\
                                  strtodate( "06/23/57" ), \\
                                  strtodate( "10/14/58" ), \\
                                  strtodate( "09/14/64" ) }

   nStart = startvalid(fInfo.lname) + 1
   nEnd   = endvalid(fInfo.lname)

   fInfo.lname  = fInfo.lname[ nStart:nEnd ]
   fInfo.fname  = fInfo.fname[ nStart:nEnd ]
   fInfo.amount = fInfo.amount[nStart:nEnd]
   fInfo.bdate  = fInfo.bdate[nStart:nEnd]

end proc

'************** Main calling routine!!! **************

local fData  as family
local fInfo  as family
local sFile  as string
local sTitle as string
```

```
'* Assign the name of the file to be created!
sFile  = "c:\realizer\sirius\samples\fileout1.dbf"
sTitle = "Sirius Press, Inc."

'* First, set up the data variables w/ blanks
fData.lname   = {""}
fData.fname   = {""}
fData.amount  = {0}
fData.bdate   = {qdate}

'* Second, set up the family of info for the database
fInfo.fields    = {"lname","fname", "amount", "bdate"}
fInfo.lengths   = {20,15,10,8}
fInfo.types     = {"C", "C", "N", "D"}
fInfo.decplaces = {0,0,2,0}

'* Third, make the data
MakeData( fData )

'* Print the data just to be sure!
print fData
logselect(_PRINTLOG)
logcontrol(_SHOW)

messagebox( "About to write out a file!", sTitle, _MB_OK )

if fileq(sFile, _EXISTS)
  filedelete(sFile)
end if

filedb(sFile, _DBF, _EXPORT; fInfo, fData)

messagebox( "File has just been created!", sTitle, _MB_OK )

shell "\realizer\sirius\samples\dbuplus.exe"

'* End of File: FExam1.rlz
```

Note that the family variable *fData* is passed by reference to the *MakeData()* function. When that function builds the various arrays of data and concludes, the arrays in the family variable *fData* are properly assigned and ready to be exported. One of the tricks in this is that the various family members in the variable *fData* begin with, essentially, blank arrays. In each family member, the first element of the array starts off with an empty value based on the data type that is to be stored to it. Inside the *MakeData()* function, the correct data values are appended to the arrays, and before the procedure concludes its operation, the first element in each family member is removed by shifting the contents of the arrays down one position. When the PRINT command completes its operation, the output of the Print Log window should look something like this:

```
              Print Log
Straley    Steve        134.3400    01/21/61
Maso       Essor      20034.0000    05/03/25
Piko       Paul          22.0000    06/23/57
Burnclaw   Russ        1598.0000    10/14/58
Mari       Vini         987.2300    09/14/64
```

This example also contains a SHELL command to a program called *DBUPLUS.EXE*. This is a special utility file found in the Pleiades Software and Training Kit published by Sirius Software Development, but any browsing utility would let you see that the FILEDB() function did its job, as shown in Figure 10-2.

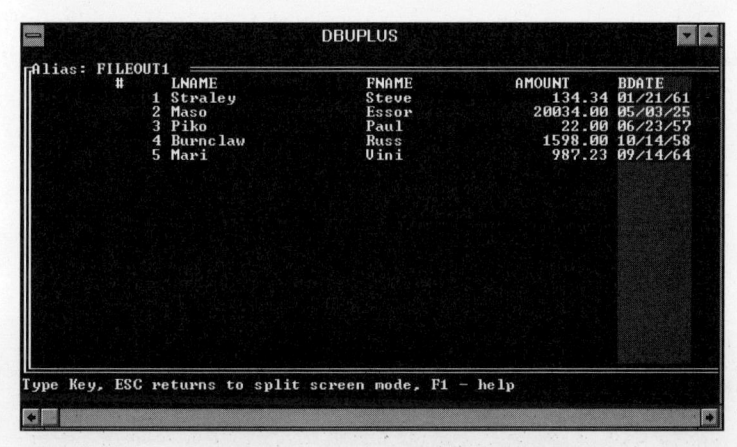

```
                          DBUPLUS
Alias: FILEOUT1
       #      LNAME          FNAME        AMOUNT    BDATE
       1   Straley          Steve          134.34  01/21/61
       2   Maso             Essor        20034.00  05/03/25
       3   Piko             Paul            22.00  06/23/57
       4   Burnclaw         Russ          1598.00  10/14/58
       5   Mari             Vini           987.23  09/14/64

Type Key, ESC returns to split screen mode, F1 - help
```

Figure 10-2. DOS Window shell of DBUPLUS.EXE.

Importing

The inverse of the exporting operation is accomplished with the _IMPORT internal variable used in conjunction with the FILEDB() function. When importing, however, less information is needed in order to get the function to behave properly. This is because all of the information for the .DBF file, such as field names, data types, and lengths, are contained in the header of the file. In fact, you may need to obtain just the header information from the .DBF file rather than the entire file (or even a subset of the file). You can obtain header information with the `_INFO` internal variable. The calling format in either case is pretty much the same:

```
fHeader = filedb(sFile, _DBF, _INFO)
```

or

```
fData = filedb(sFile, _DBF, _IMPORT)
```

In both cases, the variable *sFile* is a string data type that holds the file name to be looked at. In the first example, the family variable *fHeader* holds five family members: *.numRecords*, *.fields*, *.types*, *.lengths*, and *.decPlaces*. The last four family members are arrays of data for each of the various fields in question. If we wanted to see how many data records are in a database, we could use the following instruction:

```
print filedb( "dfile1.dbf", _DBF, _INFO).numRecords
```

The same holds true for the *fData* family members returned by the FILEDB() function with the `_INFO` internal variable.

The example in *FExam2.rlz* uses both techniques to obtain file data and file information and to present that information in the output shown in Figure 10-3.

```
'* Application ... : FExam2.rlz
'* Authors ....... : Steve Straley
'* Notice ........ : Copyright(c) 1994 - Sirius Press, Inc.
'*              .. : All Rights Reserved
'* Date .......... : January 1, 1994
'* Description ... : This shows how to import a file into families using the
'*                   FILEDB() function.

function padRight( sData, nAmount )

  local nLength as integer

  if len(sData) > nAmount
    sData = left$(sData, nAmount)
  else
    if nAmount <> len(sData)
      nLength = nAmount - len(sData)
      sData = sData + spc( nLength )
    end if
  end if

  return( sData )
```

```
end func

'************* Main calling routine!!! **************

local fData    as family
local sFile    as string
local sTitle   as string
local fHeader  as family
local nCount   as integer
local sBanner  as string
local nLength  as integer

'* Assign the name of the file to be created!
sFile  = "c:\realizer\sirius\samples\fileout1.dbf"
sTitle = "Sirius Press, Inc."

if fileq(sFile, _EXISTS)    '* We can procede

  messagebox( "About to read a .DBF file!", sTitle, _MB_OK )
  fData = fileDB(sFile, _DBF, _IMPORT)
  messagebox( "Data obtained!", sTitle, _MB_OK )

  '* Print the data just to be sure!
  logselect(_PRINTLOG)
  logcontrol(_SHOW)
  print fData

  messagebox( "Next display will be of info!", sTitle, _MB_OK )

  print "******** Data information *********"

  print filedb(sFile, _DBF, _INFO)

  print "******** About to get just 3 records ********"

  nEnd   = filedb(sFile, _DBF, _INFO).numRecords
  nStart = nEnd - 2

  messagebox( "About to print out data", sTitle, _MB_OK )

  fHeader = filedb(sFile, _DBF, _INFO)

  sBanner = ""

  for nCount = startvalid( fHeader.fields ) to endvalid( fHeader.fields )
    sBanner = sBanner + PadRight( ucase$(fHeader.fields[nCount]), \\
                          fHeader.lengths[nCount] )
  next
```

```
    rowprint sBanner
    rowprint string$( 70, asc("-") )
    print filedb(sFile, _DBF, _IMPORT, nStart, nEnd)

end if

'* End of File: FExam2.rlz
```

```
-------------------------- Print Log --------------------------
Straley          Steve              134.3400    01/21/6
Maso             Essor            20034.0000    05/03/2
Piko             Paul                22.0000    06/23/5
Burnclaw         Russ              1598.0000    10/14/5
Mari             Vini               987.2300    09/14/6
******** Data information *********
5    lname    C    20   0
5    fname    C    15   0
5    amount   N    10   2
5    bdate    D     8   0
******** About to get just 3 records ********
LNAME            FNAME             AMOUNT      BDATE
-----------------------------------------------------------------
Piko             Paul                22.0000    06/23/5
Burnclaw         Russ              1598.0000    10/14/5
Mari             Vini               987.2300    09/14/6
```

Figure 10-3. PRINT LOG Window of output.

The *PadRight()* function (part of the CARTools library) is used to pad the names of the fields with the right number of spaces based on the width of each field. It does not put the field name at the head of each column; however, it does show how you can use the information obtained from the .DBF file header using the `_INFO` internal variable.

Once the *PadRight()* function is defined, FILEQ() function checks to see if the database file created by `FExam1.rlz` `_EXISTS` on the disk, and if it does, then the following operations will be performed. First, a MESSAGEBOX() will inform us that the file is about to be read by the FILEDB() function with the `_IMPORT` internal variable. Once the file is read and the data is stored to the *fData* variable, another MESSAGEBOX() comes to the screen just before the Print Log window is selected and opened. The variable contents of the *fData* family members are then displayed with the PRINT command.

After another dialog box appears, the header information is sandwiched between two generic PRINT instructions. The next phase is to obtain just the last three records of the database. In order to do that, we need to know how many records are in the file *sFile*. This is where the combination of the `_INFO`

The Animator, Importing/Exporting, and DDEs 503

internal variable and the *.numRecords* family member is used in conjunction with the FILEDB( ) function.

> **Note:** You do not have to store the results of the FILEDB( ) function to a variable in order to obtain a family member. It is important to note that the value of the FILEDB( ) function is the family containing the header of the file and that the *.familyMember* notation is accepted.

Once the last record has been returned and stored to the *nEnd* variable, the appropriate value is stored to the *nStart* variable. Both values are used in another call to the FILEDB( ) function at the end of this example, in which only the last three records will appear on the screen.

Browsing

The fact that you can browse a database and a database header means that a couple of Realizer features can be joined to good effect. *FExam3.rlz* (a limited version of the browsing tool available in the CARTools library) shows how a sheet tool combined with the EXECUTE command can provide an added benefit.

```
'* Application ... : FExam3.rlz
'* Authors ....... : Steve Straley
'* Notice ........ : Copyright(c) 1994 - Sirius Press, Inc.
'* .............. : All Rights Reserved
'* Date .......... : January 1, 1994
'* Description ... : This shows how to browse a database mixing the FILEDB()
'*                   function along with a sheet.  This tool is greatly
'*                   extended for the CARTools Library.

'* Routine      HeaderSheet( <aParams>, <sVar> )
'* Parameters   <aParams>       Array of information for tools
'*              <sVar>          The name of the column selected
'* Purpose      The attached procedure to the second sheet used for the
'*              header information.

proc HeaderSheet( aParams, sVar )

  sheetselect( aParams[_ITEMNUM] )
  select case aParams[_INVOKE]
  case _CLICK
    sheetcontrol( _CLOSE )
    nHeaderSheet = 0
```

```
      end select

end proc

'* Routine       FormBrowse( <aParams> )
'* Parameters    <aParams>       Array of information from the tool
'* Purpose       The tool procedure attached to the form

proc FormBrowse( aParams )

  local fStuff    as family
  local aLabels   as array
  local nFont     as real

  formselect( aParams[_FORMNUM] )
  select case aParams[ _ITEMNUM ]
  case 1010

    if nHeaderSheet > 0
      sheetselect( nHeaderSheet )

    else

      aLabels = {"Stuff", "Field Names", "Data Types", "Lengths", \\
                 "Decimal Places" }

      nFont = fontnew(0; "Arial", 10 )
      nHeaderSheet = sheetnew( 0, fHeader; "", _CLOSE + _FRAME )
      sheetcontrol( _SIZE; _CENTER, _CENTER, 70 pct, 40 pct )
      sheetsetcollabels( fHeader; aLabels )
      sheetcontrollabels( _HIDE; _COL1 )
      sheetcontrollabels( _HIDE; _ROW )
      sheetcontrol( _COLRANGE; 2, 5 )
      sheetcontrol( _SETCOLOR; _BLACK, _RED )
      sheetcontrol( _SETFONT; nFont, nFont )

      sheetcontrol( _READONLY; 1 )
      sheetsetproc( HeaderSheet )
    end if
    sheetcontrol( _SHOW )

  case 1030
    if nHeaderSheet > 0
      sheetselect( nHeaderSheet )
      sheetcontrol( _CLOSE )
    end if
    formselect( aParams[_FORMNUM] )
    formcontrol( _CLOSE )
```

```
      end select

end proc

'* Routine       SheetBrowse( <aParams>, <sColumnVar> )
'* Parameters    <aParams>       Array of information from the tool
'*               <sColumnVar>    The name of the column selected
'* Purpose       The tools procedure attached to the first sheet

proc SheetBrowse( aParams, sColumnVar )

   sheetselect( aParams[_ITEMNUM], aParams[_FORMNUM] )
   select case aParams[_INVOKE]
     case _CLICK
       messagebox( "Uninstalled feature", "Sirius Press, Inc.", _MB_OK )
     end select

   end proc

'* Routine       BrowseDB( <sName> )
'* Parameters    <sName>         The name of the database to be browsed
'* Purpose       The main browsing routine

proc BrowseDb( sName )

   local nCount as integer
   local nStart as integer
   local nEnd   as integer
   local nFont1 as integer
   local nFont2 as integer

   nHeaderSheet       = 0

   if fileq(sName, _EXISTS)

     fHeader = filedb( sName, _DBF, _INFO )
     fData   = filedb( sName, _DBF, _IMPORT )

     nFont1 = fontnew(0; "Arial", 14, _BOLD + _ITALICS )
     nFont2 = fontnew(0; "Times", 6 )

     nStart = startvalid( fHeader.fields )
     nEnd   = endvalid( fHeader.fields )

     sCommand = ""

     for nCount = nStart to nEnd
       if fHeader.types[nCount] = "C"
         fHeader.types[nCount] = "Character"
```

```
      elseif fHeader.types[nCount] = "D"
              fHeader.types[nCount] = "Date"

      elseif fHeader.types[nCount] = "N"
              fHeader.types[nCount] = "Numeric"

      else
         fHeader.types[nCount] = "Logical"

      end if

      sCommand = sCommand + chr$(34) + \\
                 ucase$(fHeader.fields[nCount]) + chr$(34) + ", "

   next

   fHeader.fields   = ucase$( fHeader.fields )

   '* Build the headers of the columns!

   sCommand = "aNames = { " + left$(sCommand, len(sCommand)-2) + " } "
   execute sCommand

   nFormID = formqunique
   formnew( nFormID; ucase$(sName), _TITLE )
   formsetcolor( _CYAN; _FIELD )
   formsetcolor( _CYAN; _BACKGROUND )
   formcontrol( _SIZE; _CENTER, _CENTER, 80 pct, 80 pct )
   formsetobject( 1000, _SHEET, sName, 0, 0, 100 pct, 80 pct )
   formsetobject( 1010, _BUTTON, "Header", _LEFT,   _BOTTOM )
   formsetobject( 1030, _BUTTON, "Close",  _RIGHT,  _BOTTOM )
   formsetobject( 1040, _BUTTON, "Print",  _CENTER, _BOTTOM )

   formsetobject( 1050, _CAPTIONCENTER, "CARTools    Browser", nFont1, \\
                                        _CENTER, 270 )
   formsetobject( 1060, _CAPTIONCENTER, "TM", nFont2, _CENTER+10 , 274 )
   formsetproc( FormBrowse )

   sheetupdate( fData )
   sheetsetcollabels( fData; aNames )
   sheetcontrollabels( _HIDE; _COL1 )
   sheetsetproc( SheetBrowse; _CHANGE )
   sheetcontrol( _READONLY; 1 )
   formcontrol( _SHOW )

  end if

end proc
```

```
'****************** MAIN PROGRAM ****************'

BrowseDb( stdopen( "*.dbf" ) )

'* End of File: FExam3.rlz
```

The program starts by the calling Realizer's STDOPEN() function. The return value of that function is then passed to the *BrowseDB()* function. There, our robust reusable code takes over, using the FILEQ() function and the `_EXISTS` internal variable to check on the existence of the passed file name. Once it is established that the file stored in the *sName* variable exists, the header of the database file is gathered and stored to the *fHeader* variable, while the data is stored in *fData*. Both variables obtain their information via two calls to the FILEDB() function.

After the values of *nStart* and *nEnd* are established (these are the starting and ending element positions for at least one of the arrays stored to the family *fHeader*), a FOR...NEXT loop takes over. One of the goals of this loop is to go through the array stored to the *fHeader.types* family member and change each single-letter value representing a data type to an actual word. These values will be displayed if the user clicks on the Header button on the form, which will reveal the second `_SHEET` on the screen. The variable *sCommand* is important. Instead of using the names of the fields found in the corresponding family member, the goal here is to build a new array of field names. The *sCommand* variable slowly builds a string of uppercase field names enclosed in quotation marks (CHR$(34)). After stripping off the last ", " in the string, a pair of braces ({}) is added to the string, along with an assignment to a variable named *aNames* for the EXECUTE command. When the EXECUTE command takes effect, the variable *aNames* will have the modified headers, which are then used in the procedure with the SHEETSETCOLLABELS() function.

Note that the sheet used in this example is not a standalone sheet, but rather a `_SHEET` object inside of a form. The form contains three buttons and some text. You can see this more clearly in Figure 10-4. The `_SHEET` object has an identification value of 1000 and is placed in the upper-left corner of the form, taking 100 percent of the width of the form, and only 80 percent of the height. The lower 20 percent contains the other objects in the form. Three of those objects are `_BUTTON`s: Header, Close, and Print. The Header button will go to another sheet and show the header of the .DBF file. This sheet will use the family *fHeader* created in this subroutine. The Print button is designed to print for the data in the `_SHEET` or header. And finally, the Close button will close the form. All of these actions are detected by the *FormBrowse()* procedure, which is attached to this form via the FORMSETPROC() procedure.

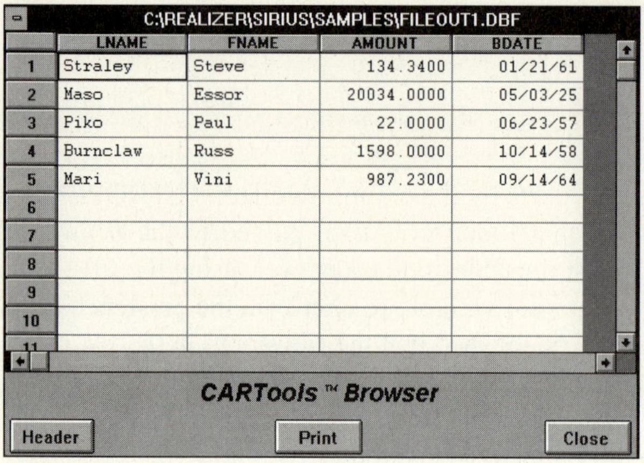

	C:\REALIZER\SIRIUS\SAMPLES\FILEOUT1.DBF			
	LNAME	FNAME	AMOUNT	BDATE
1	Straley	Steve	134.3400	01/21/61
2	Maso	Essor	20034.0000	05/03/25
3	Piko	Paul	22.0000	06/23/57
4	Burnclaw	Russ	1598.0000	10/14/58
5	Mari	Vini	987.2300	09/14/64
6				
7				
8				
9				
10				
11				

CARTools ™ Browser

[Header] [Print] [Close]

Figure 10-4. Window of detailed browser in spreadsheet.

Before we continue, note the way in which the _SHEET is established. In previous examples, when a standalone sheet is created, the SHEETNEW() function asks for the name of the family members or arrays in which data is to be displayed. Here, the _SHEET is an object in the form, and the FORMSETOBJECT() function does not allow a parameter for the family to be attached to the object. Therefore, the SHEETUPDATE() function is needed to join the *fData* family variable to the _SHEET object. Normally, the name of the family (*fData*) will appear in the sheet tool; however, the _HIDE and _COL1 internal variables in the SHEETCONTROLLABELS() function prevents that. In addition, another procedure is attached, not to the form but to the _SHEET object. The *FormBrowse()* procedure checks for the buttons, while the *SheetBrowse()* procedure checks to see if a mouse click occurs within the sheet itself.

The *SheetBrowse()* procedure will be called only if a click is detected within the _SHEET. However, the *FormBrowse()* procedure will be called if the user clicks on one of the buttons. For example, if the user clicks the Header button, which has an ID value of 1010, the screen will look like Figure 10-5.

Taking this slowly, several things happen at the same time. Within the original procedure, *BrowseDB()*, a variable named *nHeaderSheet* is assigned to 0. So within this CASE statement, if the value of *nHeaderSheet* is greater than 0, it is assumed that a secondary sheet tool for the header information has previously been created (the purpose of the Header button) and that the

The Animator, Importing/Exporting, and DDEs 509

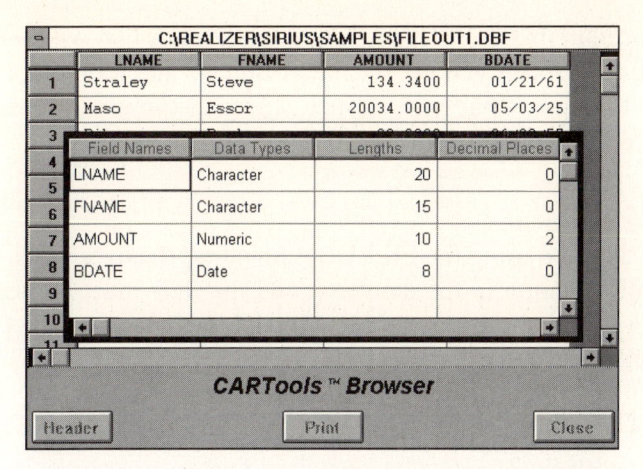

Figure 10-5. Nested spreadsheet window in browser.

sheet can be selected via the SHEETSELECT() function and the SHEET-CONTROLTROL() function with the `_SHOW` setting. If no sheet has been established, then within this IF command (or the ELSE command), the SHEETNEW() function, along with the 0 parameter, assigns a unique number to the *nHeaderSheet* variable. The *fHeader* variable holding the header structure of the .DBF file is also passed along with this function. Remember when browsing the contents of the family generated by the FILEDB() function and the `_INFO` internal variable that the first family member is a single element holding the number of records in the .DBF file. The second, third, fourth, and fifth family members hold the real values. So, to prevent the first column from being displayed in the sheet, the SETCONTROL() function and its `_COLRANGE` internal variable forces the sheet to skip the first column (a single cell holding the number of records). Because there are actually five family members in *fHeader*, even though the first one is skipped, the titles of the columns, if modified, need to be an array of five elements and not four. This is the purpose of the *aLabels* array created earlier.

The first element in *aLabels* is the string "Stuff," which corresponds with the *fHeader.numRecords* family member. The array *aLabels* is told to replace the default names of the family members seen in the *fHeader* variable. This replacement is allowed by the SHEETSETCOLLABELS() function. Then, after the `_ROW` and `_COL1` are hidden, the range of the visible columns in this sheet is set from 2 to 5. After the color of the form and the fonts of the variable elements are set, the sheet is set to be `_READONLY`, and then a new procedure named *HeaderSheet()* is attached to this sheet.

This procedure is simple, but it, too, demonstrates that with the constant reassignment of forms and sheets and of objects and tool procedures, the FILEDB() function, along with other Realizer features, can provide a very powerful front-end tool.

Appending

To append a record using the FILEDB() function, Realizer needs to read in all of the information in the database, add the individual elements to the arrays held in each family, and then write out the data using the FILEDB() function, as shown in the filenamed *FExam4.rlz*:

> **Note:** The FILEDB() function overwrites the file every time. It does not automatically append information to an existing file.

```
'* Application ... : FExam4.rlz
'* Authors ....... : Steve Straley
'* Notice ........ : Copyright(c) 1994 - Sirius Press, Inc.
'* .............. : All Rights Reserved
'* Date .......... : January 1, 1994
'* Description ... : This shows how to append data to a file using the
'*                   FILEDB() function for both _IMPORT and _EXPORT.

proc AddData( fD )

   fD.lname  = { fD.lname,  "Barrett",            "Huffman",            "Valetti" }
   fD.fname  = { fD.fname,  "Mike",       "Gary",        "Joe" }
   fD.amount = { fD.amount, 100.00,       125.00,        150.00 }
   fD.bdate  = { fD.bdate,  strtodate("03/15/55"), strtodate("09/07/59"), \\
                            strtodate("11/01/59") }

end proc

'************** Main calling routine!!! **************

local fData    as family
local sFile1   as string
local sFile2   as string
local sTitle   as string

'* Assign the name of the file to be created!
sFile1 = "c:\realizer\sirius\samples\fileout1.dbf"
sFIle2 =  "c:\realizer\sirius\samples\fileout2.dbf"
sTitle = "Sirius Press, Inc."
```

```
if fileq(sFile1, _EXISTS)     '* We can proceed

   messagebox( "About to read a .DBF file!", sTitle, _MB_OK )

   fData = fileDB(sFile1, _DBF, _IMPORT)

   messagebox( "Data obtained!", sTitle, _MB_OK )

   '* Print the data just to be sure!
   logselect(_PRINTLOG)
   logcontrol(_SHOW)
   print fData

   messagebox( "Now, add a couple of records....", sTitle, _MB_OK )

   AddData( fData )

   messagebox( "Now, about to write out (or append)!", sTitle, _MB_OK )

   '* This is a special combination that REALLY works!
   filedb(sFile2, _DBF, _EXPORT; filedb(sFile1, _DBF, _INFO), fData)

   rowprint string$( 70, asc("-") )
   rowprint "                   And now for the new (or appended) file!)"
   rowprint string$( 70, asc("-") )
   print filedb(sFile2, _DBF, _IMPORT)

end if

'* End of File: FExam4.rlz
```

This code is similar to the code in *FExam2.rlz*, the data obtained from the FILEDB() function from the *FileOut1.dbf* file. With the data held in *fData* and printed to the Print Log window, the variable is then passed to the *AddData()* procedure. There, three additional items, or records, are added to the arrays held in each of the *fData* family members. Remember, when *fData* is passed to the *AddData()* procedure, the parameter *fD* becomes the family of information. This means that data added within the procedure will be seen back in the main routine when the family of records is written back out to a new file.

Before the new file is written out, the FILEDB() function needs to have the structure of the file written, or appended to it. Since the FILEDB() function with the _INFO internal variable can provide that information, could we use it? What of the first family member (the one that holds the total number of database records), which is included as a member of the family of the return value of the FILEDB() function? Because of the way the FILEDB() function works with the `_EXPORT` internal variable, since the variable *fData* has all of the members of that family listed in the *.fields* array held in the `_INFO` return value, no run-time error will occur, and the first family member from the result of the `_INFO` variable will be skipped. The final output of this example looks like Figure 10-6.

```
                           Print Log
Straley           Steve                 134.3400     01/21/6
Maso              Essor               20034.0000     05/03/2
Piko              Paul                    22.0000    06/23/5
Burnclaw          Russ                  1598.0000    10/14/5
Mari              Vini                   987.2300    09/14/6
-----------------------------------------------------------
              And now for the new (or appended) file!
-----------------------------------------------------------
Straley           Steve                 134.3400     01/21/6
Maso              Essor               20034.0000     05/03/2
Piko              Paul                    22.0000    06/23/5
Burnclaw          Russ                  1598.0000    10/14/5
Mari              Vini                   987.2300    09/14/6
Barrett           Mike                   100.0000    03/15/5
Huffman           Gary                   125.0000    09/07/5
Valetti           Joe                    150.0000    11/01/5
```

Figure 10-6. PRINT LOG window of structure.

> **Note:** Since the data from the file to be appended needs to be read into the system before data may be appended to that file, it is important to remember the restriction on the size of arrays and the number of elements. Memory constraints need to be remembered, as well.

FILEIMPORT() and FILEEXPORT()

There are two other functions that provide exporting and importing file support: FILEIMPORT() and FILEEXPORT(). The exact syntax for each is tricky to master and depends on what file format is picked for exporting or importing. With either, there are two basic techniques to remember: `_PLAIN` or `_NAMED`. In the `_PLAIN` format, if the file structure is known (such as `_TEXT`, `_EXCEL`, or `_LOTUS`), then a separate family variable that holds the structure of the file needs to be created. This family variable will have two members: *.variable* and *.format*. The *.variable* family member tells what variables will be written out to the file, while the *.format* member tells the data

The Animator, Importing/Exporting, and DDEs 513

type of that variable. Using this style of output, those variables which may be written out to the specified file may be inside other family variables. For example, consider the following family variable:

```
fInfo.lname   = { "Straley", "Maso", "Piko", "Burnclaw", "Mari", \\
                  "Barrett", "Huffman", "Valetti" }
fInfo.fname   = { "Steve", "Essor", "Paul", "Russ", "Vini", \\
                  "Mike", "Gary",   "Joe" }
fInfo.amount  = { 134.34, 20034.22, 1598.00, 987.23, 34.56, \\
                  100.00,   125.00,  150.00 }
fInfo.bdate   = { strtodate( "01/21/61" ), strtodate( "05/03/25" ), \\
                  strtodate( "06/23/57" ), strtodate( "10/14/58" ), \\
                  strtodate( "09/14/64" ), strtodate( "03/15/55" ), \\
                  strtodate(" 09/07/59" ), strtodate( "11/01/59" ) }
```

Let's suppose that we want the first three family members from the *fInfo* variable to be written out to an Excel spreadsheet. If we want to use the _PLAIN option with the FILEEXPORT() function, we need to create a second variable that holds the names and the data types of these family members. The code might look something like this:

```
fStructure.variable = {"fInfo.lname", "fInfo.fname", "fInfo.amount" }
fStructure.format   = {"A", "A", "R"}
```

> **Note:** The names of the family members in this variable are fixed and important. No other names may be used.

Here, the array stored to the family member *fStructure.variable* contains the names of the family members held in the variable *fInfo*. The array of data types also corresponds with the names of the family members in the array. The following table outlines the possible values in this array:

Data Type Code	Definition
A	Alpha or string
D	Date-time
R	Real or numeric
X	Skip
Z	Format as found

Once both family variables are set up properly, the FILEEXPORT() function may be called:

```
fileexport( "export1.xls", _EXCEL, _PLAIN, fStructure )
```

The first and second parameters are the name and format of the file. The third parameter is the infamous `_PLAIN` type, and the fourth parameter is the variable *fStructure*, with the names and structure previously established. The output of this function might look like the following:

	A	B	C	D
1	Straley	Steve	134.34	
2	Maso	Essor	20034.22	
3	Piko	Paul	1598	
4	Burnclaw	Russ	987.23	
5	Mari	Vini	34.56	
6	Barrett	Mike	100	
7	Huffman	Gary	125	
8	Valetti	Joe	150	
9				
10				

EXPORT1.EXL

If the `_NAMED` format is to be specified, the FILEEXPORT() function is called in a different way. Here, family members cannot be specified in a single parameter. Instead, individual variables need to be created to hold individual family members, and those variables need to be spelled out, one after another. For example, taking three of the values found in the *fInfo* variable, we might come up with the following:

```
local aLName     as array
local aFName     as array
local aBDate     as array

aLName = fInfo.lname
aFName = fInfo.fName
aBDate = fInfo.bdate
```

Once these three arrays are assigned the same values as those found in the individual family members of the *fInfo* variable, we can use the `_NAMED` format. Think of the `_NAMED` format as an explicit listing of variables to the structure. The calling convention of the FILEEXPORT() function looks like this:

```
fileexport( "export2.xls", _EXCEL, _NAMED, aLName, aFName, aBDate )
```

The Animator, Importing/Exporting, and DDEs 515

Here, each array is explicitly listed as a parameter to the function. Notice that we don't need the data type of those variables; they are known by the mere fact that the arrays are being explicitly used. The output for this function looks like this:

	A	B	C	D
1	aLName	aFName	aBDate	
2	Straley	Steve	1/21/61	
3	Maso	Essor	5/3/25	
4	Piko	Paul	6/23/57	
5	Burnclaw	Russ	10/14/58	
6	Mari	Vini	9/14/64	
7	Barrett	Mike	3/15/55	
8	Huffman	Gary	9/7/59	
9	Valetti	Joe	11/1/59	
10				
11				

EXPORT2.XLS

Notice the name of the variables in the first row of the spreadsheet. With the _NAMED format option, the variables named in the exporting operation will be found in the output file, while with the _PLAIN option, only the data of the variables will be in the output. On the other hand, it takes more work to set up the structure of the data parameter for the _PLAIN option than to use the simplifer _NAMED option.

A simple output test can be seen in the *FExamp5.rlz* file:

```
'* Application ... : FExam5.rlz
'* Authors ....... : Steve Straley
'* Notice ........ : Copyright(c) 1994 - Sirius Press, Inc.
'* ............... : All Rights Reserved
'* Date .......... : January 1, 1994
'* Description ... : This shows how the FILEEXPORT() function may work
'*                   with either the _PLAIN or _NAMED option.

local fInfo         as family
local fStructure    as family
local aLName        as array
local aFName        as array
local aBDate        as array

proc MakeData()

   fInfo.lname  = { "Straley", "Maso", "Piko", "Burnclaw", "Mari", \\
                    "Barrett", "Huffman", "Valetti" }
   fInfo.fname  = { "Steve", "Essor", "Paul", "Russ", "Vini", \\
                    "Mike", "Gary",   "Joe" }
   fInfo.amount = { 134.34, 20034.22, 1598.00, 987.23, 34.56, \\
                    100.00,   125.00,  150.00 }
```

```
    fInfo.bdate   = { strtodate( "01/21/61" ), strtodate( "05/03/25" ), \\
                      strtodate( "06/23/57" ), strtodate( "10/14/58" ), \\
                      strtodate( "09/14/64" ), strtodate( "03/15/55" ), \\
                      strtodate(" 09/07/59" ), strtodate( "11/01/59" ) }

end proc

proc MakeStructure

  fStructure.variable = {"fInfo.lname", "fInfo.fname", "fInfo.amount" }
  fStructure.format   = {"A", "A", "R"}

end proc

'******************** MAIN PROGRAM ********************'

MakeData()
MakeStructure()

fileexport( "export1.txt", _TEXT,     _PLAIN, fStructure )
fileexport( "export1.xls", _EXCEL,    _PLAIN, fStructure )
fileexport( "export1.wks", _LOTUS,    _PLAIN, fStructure )
fileexport( "export1.scl", _SUPERCALC, _PLAIN, fStructure )

messagebox( "Four separate files now created!", "Sirius Press, Inc.", \\
                                    _MB_OK )

aLName = fInfo.lname
aFName = fInfo.fName
aBDate = fInfo.bdate

fileexport( "export2.xls", _EXCEL, _NAMED, aLName, aFName, aBDate )
fileexport( "export2.txt", _TEXT,  _NAMED, aLName, aFName, aBDate )

'* End of File: FExam5.rlz
```

A couple of other functions, one of which is SETSYS(), allow you to change the delimiter in the output file (especially if the output is _TEXT). And the FILEIMPORT() function works just like the FILEEXPORT() function, but in reverse.

DDEs

DDE stands for dynamic data exchange, a message sending/receiving protocol that allows data from one running application to be obtained in another. The "dynamic" part is derived from the fact that both programs, the one making the information request and the one sending the information, are running in the Windows environment. If one application is not running (mainly, the one sending back information), the protocol to use would be **ODBC**, (open database connectivity) which we'll save for another time.

This protocol brings a few new terms to the table. To start, the application making the initial request for information is called the **client**. The application receiving the request is called the **server**. The relationship between the client application and the server application can range from a simple "I need this piece of data" to a more complicated updating scenario. When an application makes the initial request for information from another running application, this step is typically called a **DDE SESSION**. You can think of a session like a telephone conversation in which one party has to dial another party. If one party does not have a phone (or in this case, is not currently running), the connection cannot be made. Otherwise, however, a connection is made, and that is called "a session." Using the phone analogy helps because an application, like a person, can do many things while on the telephone. An application with an open line/session to another application can do other operations on the screen while it's busy sending messages in the background. Also, like a telephone call, a DDE session includes an opening greeting, an acknowledgment of the greeting, and a series of requests or messages back and forth between the caller and the receiver.

For testing purposes, we need to be able to start another application from within Realizer, so we'll use the SHELL command to start up our DDE session:

```
shell <command> [, <style> ]
```

The optional <style> parameter can take one of the following internal variables:

Style	Definition
_NORMAL	New application opens in its default size
_MINIMIZE	New application is minimized when opened
_MAXIMIZE	New application is maximized when opened
_INACTIVE	New application is minimized, but not active
_DOS	Command is run in a DOS window

In the following example, *Shell1.rlz*, we open up a second Realizer session from within a Realizer application:

```
'* Application ... : Shell1.rlz
'* Authors ....... : Steve Straley
'* Notice ........ : Copyright(c) 1994 - Sirius Press, Inc.
'* .............. : All Rights Reserved
```

```
'* Date .......... : January 1, 1994
'* Description ... : This shows how the SHELL command may be called.
shell "C:\REALIZER\REALIZER.EXE C:\REALIZER\SIRIUS\SAMPLES\ANIMATE.RLZ", \\
      _INACTIVE
shell "pause", _DOS

'* End of File: Shell1.rlz
```

In the first SHELL command, a second Realizer session is being called from this program. Here, the name of the Realizer program is called and the *Animate.rlz* file is passed as a command-line parameter to it. The _INACTIVE internal variable tells this new application to appear minimized but not in focus. When this command is issued, the Realizer opening screen will appear again, and a Realizer icon should appear in the left corner of the screen. This file should still be in the form window and in front. In the background, the program *Animate.rlz* will be running as expected. Following this command is another SHELL operation. This time, a _DOS command is issued: the PAUSE command. This means that the screen will suddenly switch to a DOS shell window and the words "Press any key to continue..." will appear at the top-left corner. Once a key is pressed, the operation will return to the *Shell1.rlz* file running in the current window.

This is how another running Realizer session can be engaged, but as we said earlier, a session starts off with the caller establishing a connection, or conversation, via a greeting. Every conversation has a unique greeting that is made up of two items: the application name and the topic. In terms of a DDE conversation, the application name is the name of the server, or the receiving end of the conversation. Turning back to our telephone, this would be the phone number we want to dial. The topic, in our telephone analogy, would be the name of the party we want to speak to. Remember, many people can reside at the same phone number or address, so we have to be a bit more specific than just a phone number. To a DDE session, a topic is a general classification of data within which data items will be exchanged in the session or conversation. In Realizer, the function that starts this connection is the DDENEW() function. The basic format for this function is the following:

```
nId = ddenew( 0, <sApplication>, <sTopic> [; <sTitle> [, _ALLFORMATS]] )
```

Here, the first parameter is a 0 although we could have used the following construct:

```
      nId = ddequnique
ddenew( nId ... )
```

The Animator, Importing/Exporting, and DDEs

If 0 is passed as the first parameter, a unique DDE session is generated, which is the same thing as asking the DDEQUNIQUE command to assign a new value to the *nId* variable. If the DDENEW() function cannot start a session, or make a connection, then the return value of the function will be 0. The second and third parameters to this function are for the application name and the topic. The first optional modifier is for an optional title. Only text data can be passed. And finally, the _ALLFORMATS internal variable tells the DDE session that data is to be sent and received in any format and not just one particular data format. To illustrate these beginning steps, here is an example of an attempt to make a DDE connection:

```
'*  Application ... : Client1.rlz
'*  Authors ....... : Steve Straley
'*  Notice ........ : Copyright(c) 1994 - Sirius Press, Inc.
'*  .............. : All Rights Reserved
'*  Date .......... : January 1, 1994
'*  Description ... : This is the first attempt at a client application.

'************ MAIN BODY OF PROGRAM **************

local nSession as integer
local sTitle   as string

sTitle   = "Sirius Press, Inc."
nSession = ddequnique

'Launch the server Realizer session. SERVER is the server program

shell "C:\REALIZER\REALIZER.EXE C:\REALIZER\SIRIUS\SAMPLES\SERVER1.RLZ", \\
      _INACTIVE

messagebox( "First session launched!", sTitle, _MB_OK )

idle 6

'Establish our DDE session and make sure that we have contact

if not ddenew(nSession, "CA-Realizer", "SYSITEMS"; "First Attempt")
   messagebox( "Could Not Initiate DDE Session with Realizer", \\
            sTitle, _MB_OK )
   exit program
else
   messagebox( "Connected to Server Realizer Session", sTitle, _MB_OK )
end if
```

```
logselect(_PRINTLOG)        '* Select the Print Log Window
logcontrol(_SHOW)           '* Open it up

'Print out whether we are a client or server session.

if ddeq(_EXISTS)
  print ddeq(_SELECTED)
  print ddeq(_TITLE)
end if

'* End of File: Client1.rlz
```

To start this program, the SHELL command calls both Realizer and the *Server1.rlz* file and places the latter in an _INACTIVE state. The MESSAGEBOX() function tells us that this has taken place. Following this is an IDLE command to slow down the application.

> **Note:** In some cases, you need to use the IDLE command to allow the Windows environment to "catch up" with all of its internal operations. This command will increase the likelihood of a successful DDE connection. Sometimes, without the IDLE command, a DDE-connection attempt will fail.

Once the second application is up and running, the DDENEW() function is called. The session number, held in *nSession*, is created via the DDEQUNIQUE command. The name of the application will be "CA-Realizer," the importance of which will be seen in a moment. The topic passed to the session will be named "SYSTEMS"; this is unique for Realizer. The modifier passed to the function is the string that is used as the title for the session. Here, the string "First Attempt" can be seen when the DDEQ() function is eventually called. If the connection to the session is successful, then the value returned from the DDENEW() function will be a non-zero number, indicating success. This will, as seen in the code example, call the MESSAGEBOX() function and display the message "Connected to Server Realizer Session."

When the DDENEW() function is called, and well before the MESSAGEBOX() function is activated, the *Server1.rlz* file is sent this message. To see what transpires, take a look at that file:

```
'* Application ... : Server1.rlz
'* Authors ....... : Steve Straley
'* Notice ........ : Copyright(c) 1994 - Sirius Press, Inc.
'* .............. : All Rights Reserved
```

```
'* Date ......... : January 1, 1994
'* Description ... : This is the first attempt at a server application.

proc InitSession(nSession, sMessage, sApplication, xTopic)

  if sApplication = "CA-Realizer"
    if ddenew(nSession, sApplication, xTopic)
      print "Connection has been made....."
    end if
  end if

end proc

'*********************** MAIN PROGRAM MODULE ******************

logselect(_PRINTLOG)              'open up Print Log so we can see our messages
logcontrol(_SHOW)
ddeselect(-1)                     'establish this program as a Server
ddesetproc( InitSession )         'point to the Server Initiator Procedure

'* End of File: Server1.rlz
```

The SHELL command runs this program and gets it ready for the DDE-NEW() function called in the *Client1.rlz* file. Here, this program will open up the _PRINTLOG window. Next, the DDESELECT() function is called, passing to it a –1 value. This tells Realizer, and in particular this program, that this operation will be of a server type and not of a client type. Following that, the procedure *InitSession()* is attached to the server-based protocol. Now, when the DDENEW() function is initiated from the *Client1.rlz* file, it passes the string "CA-Realizer" as the name of the application. That value is then passed to the procedure attached in the server's file; namely, the *InitSession()* procedure. Here, the procedure looks to the parameter *sApplication* and checks to see if it equals the string "CA-Realizer," and if so, a subsequent DDENEW() function is called, which makes the connection. Think of it like this: the first DDENEW() function call in the *Client1.rlz* file is the placing of a phone call. In the *Server1.rlz* file, the specified phone number (the value of *sApplication*) is found in the attached DDE procedure. Since the phone numbers match, the connection will take place when the file *Server1.rlz* "picks up the phone" via the call to the DDE-NEW() function. Once the connection is made, the PRINT instruction in the *Server1.rlz* file is executed, and a message back to the DDENEW() function in *Client1.rlz* informs the file that success has been achieved.

In the *Client1.rlz* file, when a successful connection is made and the appropriate MESSAGEBOX() function is called, the _PRINTLOG of that session is opened as well. Then, a call to the DDEQ() function determines if a session `_EXISTS`, and if so, a couple of PRINT instructions are issued. One of the values returned from the DDEQ() function is the value of `_SELECTED`, which should be the same value as the *nId* variable. The other value printed to the log will be the `_TITLE` of the session, which (based on the DDENEW() call in the `Client1.rlz` file) should be the string "First Attempt."

The output (including the Print Log window) from the Realizer session running the `Client1.rlz` file is shown in Figure 10-7, and the output (including the Print Log window) from the Realizer session running the `Server1.rlz` file is shown in Figure 10-8.

```
'* Application ... : Client1.rlz
'* Authors ....... : Steve Straley
'* Notice ........ : Copyright(c) 1994 - Sirius Pub
'* ............... : All Rights Reserved
'* Date .......... : January 1, 1994
'* Description ... : This is the first attempt at a

'************ MAIN BODY OF PROGRAM ***************

local nSession as integer
local sTitle   as string
```

Print Log:
```
1
First Attempt
```

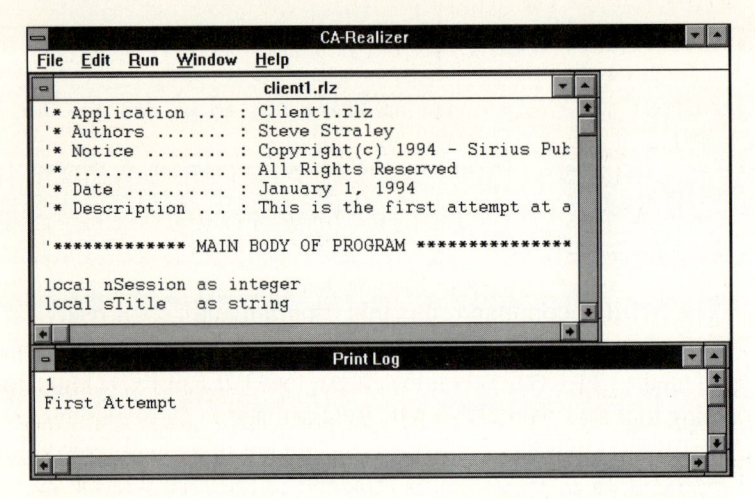

Figure 10-7. CA-Realizer application with Client application.

Print Log:
```
Connection has been made.....
```

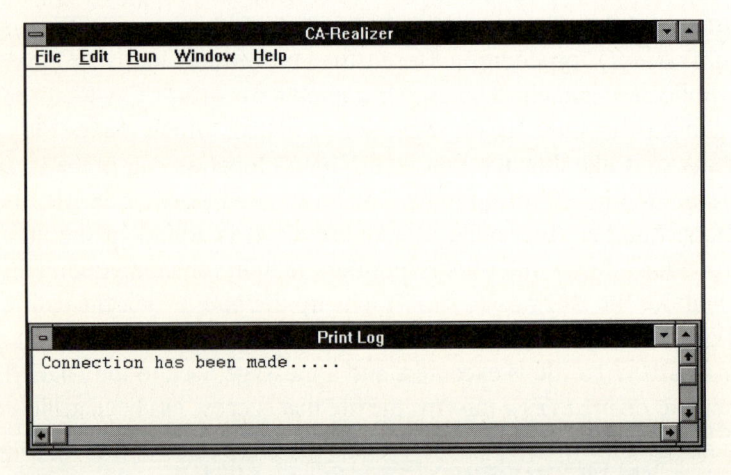

Figure 10-8. CA-Realizer application of Server application.

After the Connection

Another piece of information that may be obtained during the session is the style. For example, we know that in the previous example, the file *Client1.rlz* is the client application while the *Server1.rlz* is the server application. The question is, do the applications know the difference? Well, the DDEQ() function can provide additional and useful information. In *Client2.rlz* and *Server2.rlz*, the following code extract has been added to *Client1.rlz* and *Server1.rlz*:

```
select case ddeq(_STYLE)
case 1
      print "Client Session"

case 2
      print "Server Session"

case else
      print "No Session is selected"

end select
```

The output screen in the client application will display "Client Session," while the running application in the back will display "Server Session." This means that the same program may be executed as both the client application and the server application, behaving differently in each case due to the _STYLE internal variable.

Another interesting programming note is a redirect of the attached DDE procedure. In the previous example, if the name of the application was the string "New-Session," then a PRINT command was issued. Now, in *Server2.rlz*, the code is modified to the following:

```
   proc InitSession(nSession, sMessage, sApplication, xTopic)

 if sApplication = "New-Session"
   if ddenew(nSession, sApplication, xTopic)
     ddesetproc( NewAssignment )
   end if
 end if

end proc
```

In essence, the *InitSession()* function just checks to see if the application name sent by the client application is the proper name. If it is, instead of printing a message, the attached procedure is reassigned via the DDESETPROC()

function. Think of it like this: the procedure *InitSession()* checks to see if the connection is valid, and if it is, the phone is then handed over to another procedure or party. In this case, the *InitSession()* procedure actually reassigns the attached procedure to the *NewAssignment()* procedure, which looks like this:

```
proc NewAssignment( nSession, sMessage, sApplication,
    xTopic )

print "Now in this session..."

end proc
```

Since the connection has been made, verified, and accepted (otherwise, we would not be in the *NewAssignment()* procedure, new tests for the communication between client and server can be made in this procedure.

Looking at the Server Application

On the Server side of the equation, consider the messages coming in from the Client. Once the connection is made and verified, the altered *NewAssignment()* procedure will receive messages directly from the client session. So in the case of the `Client3.rlz` example program, consider the following lines of code:

```
ddecontrol( _ADVISE, "The Variable" )
messagebox( "An _ADVISE message was sent for the 'The Variable' topic", \\
        sTitle, _MB_OK )
ddecontrol( _UNADVISE, "The Variable" )
messagebox( "An _UNADVISE message was sent for the 'The Variable' topic", \\
        sTitle, _MB_OK )
ddecontrol( _REQUEST, "The Variable" )
messagebox( "An _REQUEST message was sent for the 'The Variable' topic", \\
        sTitle, _MB_OK )
ddecontrol( _REQUEST, "The Weather" )
messagebox( "An _REQUEST message was sent for the 'The Weather' topic", \\
        sTitle, _MB_OK )
```

Three messages are sent under the topic of "sVariable": _ADVISE, _REQUEST, and _UNADVISE. When these messages are sent to the server application, a call is made to the attached procedure. Four parameters are passed to the procedure:

```
proc NewAssignment( nSession, nMessage, sTopic, xData )
```

The first parameter, *nSession*, contains the session number. This is always passed by Realizer and should be the same value generated by the original DDEQUNIQUE command. The second parameter is the "message," which is the option toggled by the DDECONTROL() function. In this example, three possible messages are sent: _ADVISE, _UNADVISE, and _REQUEST. There are a limited number of messages that may be sent and received by both the client application and the server application. The second parameter of the DDECONTROL() function deals with the topic that is, in turn, passed as the third parameter to the attached procedure. This message then becomes the variable *sTopic*. In some cases, a fourth parameter is received from the client application via a third parameter passed to the DDECONTROL() function. This parameter holds data specific to the operation and connection. Take a look at the attached procedure in *Server3.rlz*:

```
proc NewAssignment( nSession, nMessage, sTopic, xData )

  select case nMessage
  case _ADVISE
    print "Advise that the message has indeed arrived..."

  case _UNADVISE
    print "Tell the caller: Sorry... no can do!"

  case _REQUEST
    select case sTopic
    case "The Variable"
        print "A request has been issued..."
        ddecontrol( _DATA, sTopic, "Yep... I've got it..." )

    case "The Weather"
        print "Another request, this time for weather...."

    end select

  end select

end proc

proc InitSession(nSession, nMessage, sApplication, xTopic)

  if sApplication = "Server Connect"
    if ddenew(nSession, sApplication, xTopic)
      ddesetproc( NewAssignment )
    end if
  end if

end proc
```

When the initial connection is made, the application name that is stored to the *sApplication* parameter is now the string "Server Connect." Once verified, the DDESETPROC() then turns control over to the *NewAssignment()* procedure. In that procedure, the value of the *nMessage* variable is important, since one of three possible messages is sent from the client application to the server application. If one of the messages or values of *nMessage* is the `_ADVISE` internal variable, then a PRINT instruction in the server application is issued. The same operation takes place if an `_UNADVISE` internal variable is passed. Seen in the code example from `Client3.rlz`, the first two calls to DDECONTROL() are `_ADVISE` and `_UNADVISE`. To review, the last two DDECONTROL() instructions in `Client3.rlz` basically look like this:

```
ddecontrol( _REQUEST, "The Variable" )
ddecontrol( _REQUEST, "The Weather" )
```

In the server application, the value of *nMessage* will be `_REQUEST`, but the value of *sTopic* is different. The connection is still valid as long as a test is made. The second SELECT CASE command performs this test on the parameter *sTopic*. In the first call in the client application, the topic is "The Variable," and in the Server application, if the value of *sTopic* is "The Variable," a PRINT instruction, along with a subsequent DDECONTROL() operation, is issued. This return DDECONTROL() function will be explained in a moment and has nothing to do with the general point of this example. If, on the other hand, the value of the *sTopic* variable is the string "The Weather," as seen in the second call to the DDECONTROL() function in the client application, then a different message is issued using the PRINT command.

Think of the DDECONTROL() function in the client application as calling the assigned procedure in the DDESETPROC() instruction found in the server application. This is the crux of this line of communication. However, not all lines of communication are one-directional. The purpose of the extra DDECONTROL() function in the server application is to suggest that communication is bidirectional. For example, the DDECONTROL() function found in `Server3.rlz` might mean that it has to go to an attached procedure found in the client application. The Print Log window of the server application would look like this:

```
                         Print Log
No Session is selected
Advise that the message has indeed arrived...
Tell the caller: Sorry... no can do!
A request has been issued...
Another request, this time for weather....
```

Looking at the Client Application

Communication is a two-way street, and up to this point in the discussion, the dialog has been in one direction: from the client application to the server application. However, in the preceding example, the procedure attached to the DDE session in the server application has a call to the DDECONTROL( ) function. This is the same function used by the client application to send information to the server application. With the DDECONTROL( ) function in the server application, information is sent back to the client application. When a message is sent back from the server to the client, a procedure on the client side of the communication link needs to be able to respond to the message. The format for this procedure is identical to the procedure used on the server side. In essence, the DDESETPROC( ) function will be called in the client application as well as in the server application. In this next example, *Client4.rlz*, the use of the DDESETPROC( ) function can be seen in the modified code sample:

```
if ddeq(_EXISTS)
  print ddeq(_SELECTED)
  print ddeq(_TITLE)
  ddesetproc( ClientAttached )         'set up the DDE Proc
  ddecontrol( _ADVISE,   "The Variable" )
  ddecontrol( _UNADVISE, "The Variable" )
  ddecontrol( _REQUEST,  "The Variable" )
 ddecontrol( _REQUEST,  "The Weather" )
end if
```

In the client application, if a true value is returned from the DDEQ( ) function with the `_EXISTS` internal variable, two PRINT commands are issued, following which, a call to the DDESETPROC( ) function is made. Here, the procedure *ClientAttached* is attached to the client's DDE session. Once the procedure is attached to this end of the conversation, four calls to the DDECONTROL( ) function are made. There are six possible messages that can be sent from the client application to the server application:

Message from Client	Definition
`_REQUEST`	Asks the server application to send information about the topic. If the server application has the requested information, it responds with a `_DATA` message, which can be processed in the client application by the assigned DDE procedure.
`_ADVISE`	Asks the server application to send information about the topic whenever information with the topic changes.

_UNADVISE	Asks the server application to stop advising on the topic.
_POKE	Sends unrequested data to the server application. The data passed to it relates to the topic in the session.
_EXECUTE	Sends a set of commands, stored in the topic parameter, to the server application to be executed.
_CLOSE	Closes the current DDE session.

Expanding on this, the attached procedure in the server application receives the messages from the client application (found in *Server4.rlz*):

```
proc NewAssignment( nSession, nMessage, sTopic, xData )

   select case nMessage
   case _ADVISE
      ddecontrol( _DATA, "ISSUE 1", "10" )

   case _UNADVISE
      ddecontrol( _DATA, "ISSUE 1", "20")

   case _REQUEST
      select case sTopic
      case "The Variable"
         ddecontrol( _DATA, "REQUEST", "Yep... I've got it..." )

      case "The Weather"
         ddecontrol( _DATA, "REQUEST", "The weather is fine...." )

      end select

   end select

end proc
```

Every DDECONTROL() call in the client application passes a message off to the *NewAssignment()* function in the server application. The parameter *nMessage* is one of the six values in the table listed above. Here, a massive SELECT CASE statement checks the value of the *nMessage* parameter. If the passed message is the _ADVISE internal variable (which is the first DDE-CONTROL() call in the client application), then a DDECONTROL() function is called on the server side. There are only two possible values that may be passed as the first parameter to the DDECONTROL() function from the server's point of view:

Message from Server	Definition
_DATA	Sends data to the client application. The value of the data relates to the specified topic.
_CLOSE	Closes the current DDE session.

The _DATA internal variable tells the DDE session that a return is made back to the client application. The second parameter is the topic of the conversation. Here, if the message from the client is _ADVISE, the DDECONTROL( ) function on the server side returns a _DATA message with the topic of "ISSUE 1." In addition, it sends back the string "10." If the message from the client application is _UNADVISE, then the return topic will also be "ISSUE 1," but the extra piece of data will be the string "20." If the message from the client is _REQUEST, then the value of the parameter *sTopic* will be checked, and if it is equal to the string "The Variable," the return data string will be "Yep… I've got it…." On the other hand, if the _REQUEST message has the topic of "The Weather" (seen as the fourth call to the DDECONTROL( ) function in the client application), then the return data string "The weather is fine…." is passed back.

The next piece of this puzzle is then on the client side, which receives the return message of _DATA from the server application. The procedure set via the DDESETPROC( ) has the same parameter and the same sort of control structure found in the server application:

```
proc ClientAttached( nSession, nMessage, sTopic, xData )

  local sTitle as string

  sTitle = "Sirius Press, Inc."

  select case nMessage        ' process the message from the Client session
  case _DATA                  ' we have a data message
    ddeselect(nSession)       ' make sure the DDE session is selected

    select case sTopic        'check out the topic of the    message
    case "ISSUE 1"            'the topic is "the number"
      if xData = "10"
        messagebox( "A return to _ADVISE has been made..", sTitle, _MB_OK )
      else
        messagebox( "An unrequest has been made <grin>", sTitle, _MB_OK )
      end if

    case "REQUEST"
      messagebox( xData, sTitle, _MB_OK )
```

```
    end select

  end select

end proc
```

Just like the code structure found in the server application, the parameter *nMessage* can be tested for a _DATA internal variable. If found (and it will be, since the server application only returns a _DATA message via the DDECONTROL() function), a test on the topic of the message is performed. In all of the passed messages to the server, it returns one of two topics: "ISSUE 1" or "REQUEST." On the first call to the server, the response for the value of *xData* (which must be a string data type unless specified) is the string "10." On the screen, you'll see the message shown in Figure 10-9.

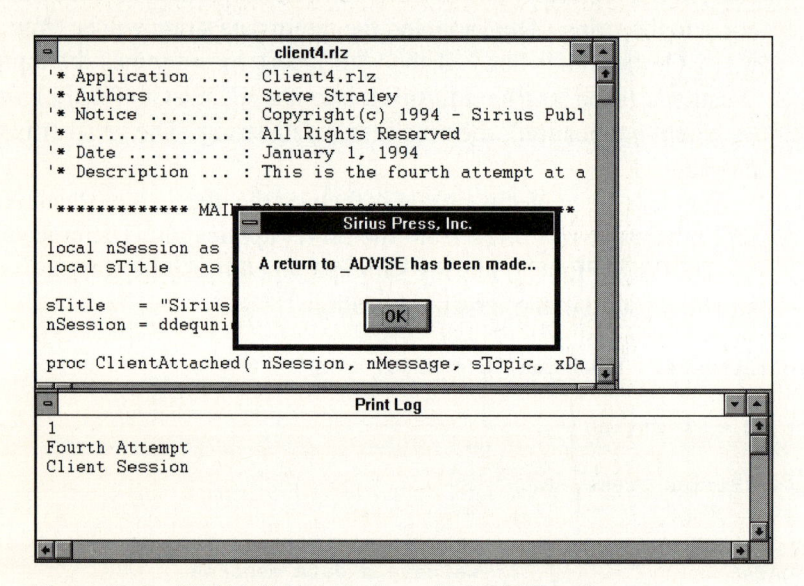

Figure 10-9. INPUT dialog window of _ADVISE notice.

What this means is the following:

Client Application	*Calls*	*Server Application*	*Calls*	*Client Application*
DDECONTROL(_ADVISE, "The Variable")		DDECONTROL(_DATA, "ISSUE 1", "10")		MESSAGEBOX()

This is the exchange and protocol for a Realizer session. And on the last two return messages from the server application, the value of *xData* is passed directly to the MESSAGEBOX() function to produce one of these two messages:

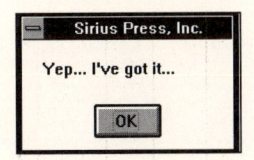

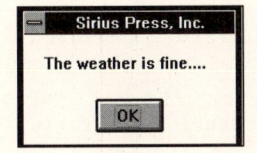

Assigning Values...

In this last session, the goal is to have the `Client5.rlz` file send data over to the `Server5.rlz` and, if the data is proper, assign a variable in that file to the passed information. The client application uses the _POKE internal variable in the DDECONTROL() function. This final setup is shown in the following code for `Client5.rlz`:

```
'* Application ... : Client5.rlz
'* Authors ....... : Steve Straley
'* Notice ........ : Copyright(c) 1994 - Sirius Press, Inc.
'* ............... : All Rights Reserved
'* Date .......... : January 1, 1994
'* Description ... : This is the last attempt at a client application.

local nSession as integer
local sTitle   as string

sTitle   = "Sirius Press, Inc."
nSession = ddequnique

proc ClientAttached( nSession, nMessage, sTopic, xData )

   local sTitle as string

   sTitle = "Sirius Press, Inc."

   select case nMessage          ' process the message from the Client session
   case _DATA                    ' we have a data message
     ddeselect(nSession)         ' make sure the DDE session is selected
     messagebox( xData, sTitle, _MB_OK )

   case _CLOSE
     messagebox( "Other session should be closed", sTitle, _MB_OK )

   end select
```

```
end proc

'************* MAIN BODY OF PROGRAM ***************

'Launch the server Realizer session. SERVER is the server program

shell "C:\REALIZER\REALIZER.EXE C:\REALIZER\SIRIUS\SAMPLES\SERVER5.RLZ", \\
      _INACTIVE

messagebox( "Final Server Session!", sTitle, _MB_OK )

logselect(_PRINTLOG)          '* Select the Print Log Window
logcontrol(_SHOW)             '* Open it up

idle 6

'Establish our DDE session and make sure that we have contact

if not (ddenew(nSession, "Fifth Example", "SYSITEMS"; "Last Attempt")) messagebox(
"Could Not Initiate DDE Session with Realizer", \\
            sTitle, _MB_OK )
  exit program
else
  messagebox( "Connected to Server Realizer Session", sTitle, _MB_OK )
end if

'Print out whether we are a client or server session.

select case ddeq(_STYLE)
case 1
  print "Client Session"

case 2
  print "Server Session"

case else
  print "No Session is selected"

end select

if ddeq(_EXISTS)
  print ddeq(_SELECTED)
  print ddeq(_TITLE)
  ddesetproc( ClientAttached )       'set up the DDE Proc
  ddecontrol( _ADVISE,   "sInformation" )
  ddecontrol( _UNADVISE, "sInformation" )
  ddecontrol( _REQUEST,  "sInformation" )
  ddecontrol( _EXECUTE,  "print 'This is a test with the string', sInformation" )
  ddecontrol( _POKE,     "sInformation", "Passed String!" )
```

```
   ddecontrol( _REQUEST,  "sInformation" )
   ddecontrol( _EXECUTE,  "print 'This is a test with the string', sInformation" )
end if

'* End of File: Client5.rlz
```

In this program, all of the action comes if there is a DDE connection. After the session _TITLE is displayed in the Print Log window, the *ClientAttached()* procedure is assigned in the client application. Following this are a series of calls to the DDECONTROL() function, in which the topic of the session is the string "sInformation." This string is the name of a variable found in the server application. The two new internal variables used here are _EXECUTE and _POKE. The _EXECUTE operation does exactly what we would expect in the server side of the communication. Here, the PRINT command is buried in a string which, when executed, will print the contents of both the literal and the value of the *sInformation* variable. We could press the ALT-TAB key to toggle over to the server side to see this actually happening in the Print Log window:

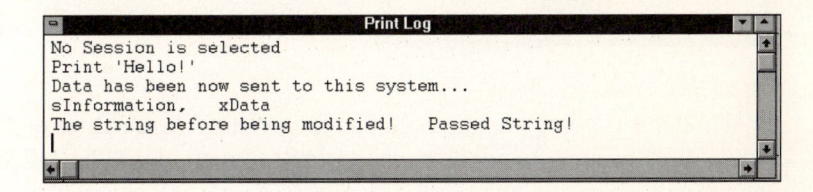

```
                          Print Log
No Session is selected
Print 'Hello!'
Data has been now sent to this system...
sInformation,    xData
The string before being modified!    Passed String!
```

Just before the _EXECUTE internal variable, the _REQUEST variable is used. On the server side, this internal variable causes the following to be issued:

```
case _REQUEST
   ddecontrol( _DATA, sTopic, sInformation )
```

In essence, the value of *sInformation* is sent back from the server to the client. In the procedure *ClientAttached()*, that string will appear as the value of *sTitle* in the call to the MESSAGEBOX() function and will look something like this:

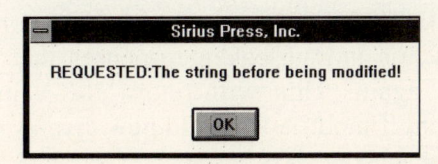

```
          Sirius Press, Inc.
REQUESTED:The string before being modified!
               [ OK ]
```

The line of code following the _EXECUTE instruction is new: It is the _POKE instruction. Here, an unsolicited piece of data is passed from the client application to the server application.

```
case _POKE
   ddecontrol( _DATA, sTopic, "Check the Server sesssion to see the values" )
   print "Data has been now sent to this system..."
   print "sInformation,    xData"
   print sInformation, xData
   if qvar( xData, _SCALAR + _ALPHA )
      sInformation = xData
   end if
```

On the Server side, the _POKE instruction causes a _DATA instruction to be sent back, which produces the following message:

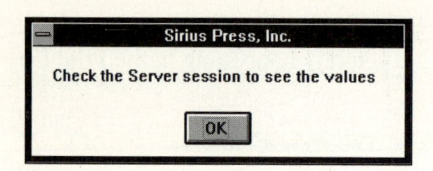

[Dialog box: "Sirius Press, Inc." — "Check the Server session to see the values" — OK]

While this is going on, however, the three PRINT instructions on the server side will be printed. In addition, the QVAR() function will be called, checking to see if the passed parameter from the client's call is both _SCALAR and _ALPHA.

```
ddecontrol( _POKE,    "sInformation", "Passed String!" )
```

Remember, the Client initiated the message with the call of the DDECONTROL() function. The literal string "Passed String!" becomes the parameter *xData* in the *NewAssignment()* procedure found in `Server5.rlz`. The SELECT CASE instruction there tests for the _POKE internal variable as the message and then sends back to the Client the message of _DATA. While that message is being received by the client, these three PRINT instructions are issued and eventually, if all works out well, the literal string "Passed String!" is assigned to the *sInformation* variable. Following the _POKE instruction and subsequent responses, the _REQUEST internal variable is used again. This will return the value of the *sInformation* variable which, if modified, should now display the literal string "Passed String!" in the message box:

The Animator, Importing/Exporting, and DDEs 535

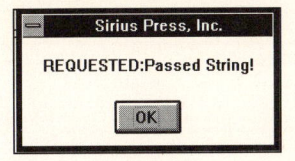

```
Sirius Press, Inc.
REQUESTED:Passed String!
    OK
```

Note what the response to the client would be if the server session should be shut down. To see this, switch over to the server application using the `ALT-TAB` key. If properly selected, the screen should look something like Figure 10-10.

```
CA-Realizer
File  Edit  Run  Window  Help




                    Print Log
No Session is selected
Print 'Hello!'
Data has been now sent to this system...
sInformation,  xData
The string before being modified!    Passed String!
```

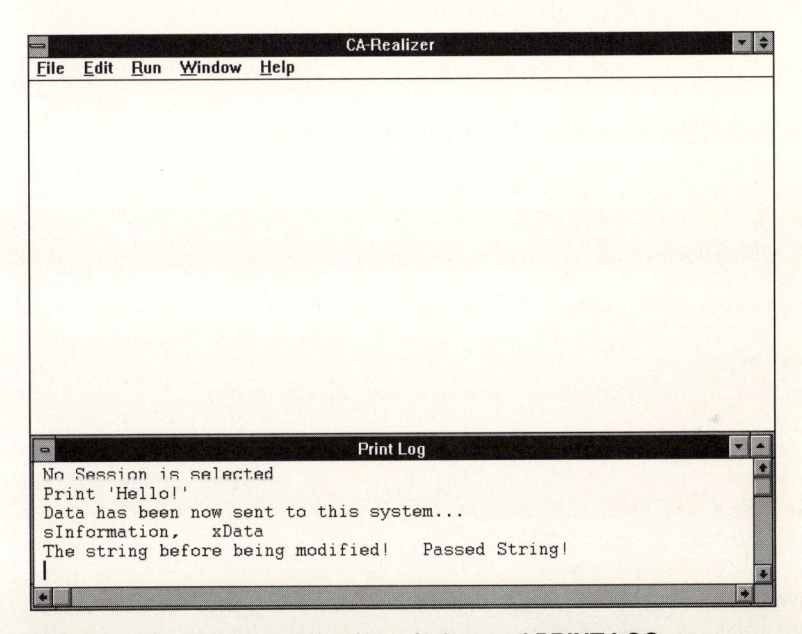

Figure 10-10. Server application window and PRINT LOG.

Now, press the `ALT-F4` key to shut down the session. This will close Realizer and return control to the client application. Since the connection is now lost, a final message is sent to the client application's attached procedure *ClientAttached()*, in which the value of *nMessage* should be *_CLOSE*, which produces the following message box:

[Dialog box: Sirius Press, Inc. — "Other session should be closed" — OK]

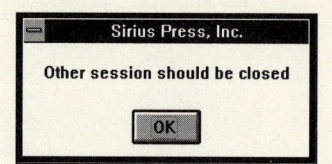

The exact source code for *Server5.rlz* looks something like this:

```
'* Application ... : Server5.rlz
'* Authors ....... : Steve Straley
'* Notice ........ : Copyright(c) 1994 - Sirius Press, Inc.
'* ............... : All Rights Reserved
'* Date .......... : January 1, 1994
'* Description ... : This is the last attempt at a server application.

sInformation = "The string before being modified!"

proc NewAssignment( nSession, nMessage, sTopic, xData )

  select case nMessage
  case _ADVISE
    ddecontrol( _DATA, sTopic, "You are advised!" )

  case _UNADVISE
    ddecontrol( _DATA, sTopic, "You are now un-advised")

  case _POKE
    ddecontrol( _DATA, sTopic, "Check the Server session to see the values" )
    print "Data has been now sent to this system..."
    print "sInformation,   xData"
    print sInformation, xData
    if qvar( xData, _SCALAR + _ALPHA )
      sInformation = xData
    end if

  case _EXECUTE
    ddecontrol( _DATA, sTopic, "The operation is now being performed!")

  case _REQUEST
    ddecontrol( _DATA, sTopic, sInformation )

  end select

end proc

proc InitSession(nSession, nMessage, sApplication, xTopic)
```

```
    if sApplication = "Fourth Example"
      if ddenew(nSession, sApplication, xTopic)
        ddesetproc( NewAssignment )
      end if
    end if

end proc


'************************ MAIN PROGRAM MODULE ******************

logselect( _PRINTLOG)          'open up Print Log so we can see our messages
logcontrol(_SHOW)
ddeselect(-1)                  'establish this program as a Server
ddesetproc( InitSession )      'point to the Server Initiator Procedure

select case ddeq(_STYLE)
case 1
  print "Client Session"

case 2
  print "Server Session"

case else
  print "No Session is selected"

end select

'* End of File: Server5.rlz
```

Other Forms of DDE

The main thing to remember with DDE is that the server application has its own way of receiving data. This means that we could, for example, communicate with Windows Program Manager to create new program groups or make new modules or even run another Windows utility. However, to do this, we have to know the protocol for sending and receiving data between our client application written in Realizer and the server application we want to poll. Information like this is outlined in detail in the Windows Standard Developer's Kit .

Conclusion

Here, we have explored three distinct and unique concepts. On their own merits, you might not give much time to them, or you might consider them as an afterthought. This is a shame, since an application's acceptance by an end user may hinge on such techniques as an engaging animated sequence and the easy exchange of data to and from the application.

Chapter 11

External Routines, Windows API, and User-Defined Types

Sometimes, a need exists for which the solution is not immediately addressable in Realizer. In these cases, relying on resources outside of the Realizer environment is necessary. However, this does mean an extra step of work to achieve the final result. More important than the actual amount of work involved is the time needed to track down the new resource. For example, you know that you need to change title of a form or acquire the name of the currently logged drive, and you know that it "should be" possible, and you also know that the answer is not immediately available in the Realizer basic command set. Such a situation gives rise to two questions: "Where can I find the information I need?" followed by "How do I use the information in Realizer?" These two valid questions typically lead to two answers: (1) the use of .DLL files; and (2) the use of the EXTERNAL command.

.DLLs and External

A .DLL (**Dynamic Linked Library**) file is an executable file that is external to the application and supports some process or processes within the application. Unlike most standard applications, in which the supporting routines are found in a traditional .LIB (or library) file, the .DLL is a separate file at all times and is loaded by Windows when the application is loaded. For this reason, the concept of "dynamic" is appropriate. In DOS-based applications in which a library file is needed in order to resolve the making of an executable file, those modules used by the application are actually pulled out of the library file and attached to the executable file. In Windows, on the other hand, external resources are available and loaded by Windows when the application begins to execute. This means that multiple applications can share the resources in a dynamic linked library without the need for duplicate copies of

External Routines, Windows API, and User-Defined Types 539

those source entries in each executable. Dynamic linked libraries typically have a .DLL file extension; however, this is not a requirement in Windows. For example, all font tables are nothing more than .DLL files, even though they do not have the typical .DLL file extension.

Advantages and Disadvantages

A .DLL file allows programmers to make better use of existing code and to formalize a standard way of doing things within the corporate environment. This is particularly useful in the debugging stages of application development, where the static code (which generally resides in a .DLL file) is not the source of the trouble. In addition, we can take advantage of existing and common interfaces available in the Windows environment, especially those dialogs that are not part of the standard Realizer environment (such as those found in `COMMDLG.DLL`). By using these standards we can reduce the coding effort and ensure that the interface will be similar to other Windows applications.

While those are the benefits of using .DLL files, the down-side risk for using them is in the physical file itself. Since dynamic linked libraries are not explicitly included in the domain of the executable file, their existence needs to be ensured before the application is loaded. Otherwise, the common and ever-so-helpful "Unable to Load Program" message generated from Windows will be the first and only visible action of your application.

Using .DLLs

We can use information stored in a .DLL file as long as we know two things: the names of the functions available to be "called" in the .DLL files and the type (and format) of the data those functions are expecting. Without both pieces of information, using preexisting routines may be a difficult and painful task. However, once you do have this information, Realizer has another command available to bridge the gap between the Realizer application and those preexisting routines: the EXTERNAL command. This command allows the programmer to declare external procedures, functions, and even custom controls that exist in a .DLL. The command makes the "formal" announcement of a routine within the Realizer environment. Typically, when a function or a procedure is declared, it is defined with either the FUNC or PROC command statements. Within the confines of these two commands, source code representing the subroutine exists, allowing Realizer to "know" what is happening and what to expect. However, the source code for EXTERNAL operations is not in the Realizer environment; it is outside of the environment in .DLL files, and we must tell the Realizer system this in advance in order for the system to know where to go whenever a call is made to any one of those internal .DLL routines. The EXTERNAL command makes that declaration, using the following syntax:

```
EXTERNAL <DLL> PROC <name> [( type NAME) ...][ALIAS <newName>]
EXTERNAL <DLL> FUNC <name> [( type NAME) ...] AS <return> [ALIAS <newName>]
```

The format of the calling convention for Windows is known as **prototyping**. It is not Realizer-specific; therefore, the EXTERNAL command adheres to the rules. Here, the name of the subroutine is associated with the appropriate .DLL file. In addition, an unlimited number of parameters may be specified, as long as the data type precedes the name of the parameter being passed. Within the specified .DLL file, Windows searches for the name of the procedure or function and loads the prototype of the function into memory. Sometimes, it is faster to load the subroutine using the ordinal position of the routine within the specified file rather than rely on Windows to search by name. This is where the ALIAS clause comes in.

> **Note:** If the ALIAS clause specifies the exact ordinal position of the routine within the .DLL file, and if that ordinal position should change, then future errors may be experienced; therefore, you may want to avoid using the ALIAS clause with the ordinal position of the routine.

Note that if the routine within the .DLL file is a function, the Realizer environment will expect a return value back. This means that the EXTERNAL command needs to have the AS clause attached. This tells Realizer that the specified function will return a value AS a certain data type.

> **Note:** The location of the .DLL is important and follows a specific order:
> 1. The currently logged directory (which can never be planned)
> 2. The directory in which Windows is located
> 3. The directory in which the application is running
> 4. The path

As with everything else, a good way to start is to look at code example:

```
'* Application ... : Dll1.rlz
'* Authors ....... : Steve Straley
'* Notice ........ : Copyright(c) 1994 - Sirius Press, Inc.
```

```
'*  .............. : All Rights Reserved
'* Date .......... : January 1, 1994
'* Description ... : This routine makes external calls to Realizer's
'*                   Standard.exe file

external "Standard" func GetCurrentDrive () as integer
external "Standard" func DosDiskFreeSpace (integer iDrive) as long
' iDrive is 1 for A:, 2 for B:, and 0 for current drive.

func LoggedDrive()

  return(mid$("ABCDEFGHIJKLMNOPQRSTUVWXYZ", GetCurrentDrive()+1, 1))

end func

func FreeSpace()

  return( DosDiskFreeSpace(GetCurrentDrive()+1 ) )

end func

function CommaFilled( nValue, .. )

  local sValue   as string
  local sReturn  as string
  local nDeci    as real
  local sFormat  as string

  sReturn = ""
  nDeci   = nValue - floor(nValue)

  if nDeci < 1 and nDeci > 0 and qnoptparams = 0
    sFormat = string$(30, asc("#"))
    sValue = ltrim$(sprint(sFormat, floor(nValue)))
    for nCount = 1 to len(sValue) step 3
      sReturn = sReturn + mid$(sValue, nCount, 3) + ","
    next
    sReturn = reverse$(left$(sReturn, len(sReturn)-1)) + "." + \\
              rtrim$(ltrim$(sprint("####", nDeci*1000)))

  elseif nDeci <> 0 and qnoptparams = 1
    sFormat = string$(30, asc("#"))
    sValue = ltrim$(sprint(sFormat, floor(nValue)))
    for nCount = 1 to len(sValue) step 3
      sReturn = sReturn + mid$(sValue, nCount, 3) + ","
    next
    sFormat = string$(qoptparam(1), asc("#"))

    sReturn = reverse$(left$(sReturn, len(sReturn)-1)) + "." + \\
              rtrim$(ltrim$(sprint(sFormat, nDeci*(10^qoptparam(1)) )))
```

```
  else
    sFormat = string$(30, asc("#"))
    sValue = reverse$(ltrim$(sprint( sFormat, nValue )))
    for nCount = 1 to len(sValue) step 3
      sReturn = sReturn + mid$(sValue, nCount, 3) + ","
    next
    sReturn = reverse$(left$(sReturn, len(sReturn)-1))

  end if

  return( sReturn )

end func

'************ MAIN BODY OF THE EXAMPLE PROGRAM ****************'
'**************************************************************'

local sTitle as string

sTitle = "Sirius Press, Inc."

messagebox( "There is " + CommaFilled( FreeSpace() ) + " kb space remaining", \\
            sTitle, _MB_OK )

messagebox( CommaFilled( 123456789.10, 3 ), sTitle, _MB_OK )

messagebox( "Logged Drive is: " + LoggedDrive() + ":", sTitle, _MB_OK )

'* End of File: Dll1.rlz
```

At the top of this file, two EXTERNAL commands are issued, both to the `Standard.exe` file that comes with the Realizer development system. Again, it is important to note that a dynamic linked library need not have a .DLL file extension. By all measuring devices, DLLs are executable files with no beginning point, or no startup code segment. Therefore, the actual file extension is not important. In this case, the function named *GetCurrentDrive()* is located in the `Standard.exe` file. No parameters are expected to be passed and in return, an integer will be passed back. With the *DosDiskFreeSpace()* function, one parameter named *iDrive* will be passed and will be of INTEGER data type. The return value from the function will be a LONG.

Following these two EXTERNAL declarations are two generic functions. The first, *FreeSpace()*, this simply makes the double function call first to *GetCurrentDrive()* and then to *DosDiskFreeSpace()*. This type of a function, though reusable and made only to ease the chore of reading code, is known as a **wrapper function** because it "wraps" itself around other existing functions. The other function, called *LoggedDrive()*, is similar to the *FreeSpace()* function with just a bit more work involved. At the bottom of this file are three calls to the MESSAGEBOX() function just to show some of the results of these EXTERNAL operations. For example, the output of the last function call looks like this:

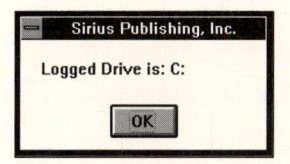

```
┌─ Sirius Publishing, Inc. ──┐
│ Logged Drive is: C:        │
│         ┌────┐             │
│         │ OK │             │
│         └────┘             │
└────────────────────────────┘
```

Eventually, all of the possible functions within all of the possible (and potential) dynamic linked libraries will be in order. That is one large task, but some add-on tools, such as the CARTools library, not only document these operations, but create the series of wrapper functions that call these external operations.

Using Windows API

The EXTERNAL command can also work with the standard interface libraries that come with Windows. Unlike the calls in the previous example, these calls are made to .DLLs which are part of the Windows environment. These are formal calls that every Windows application can make, and since the DLLs are considered a standard feature of the operating system, calls made to these files are known as calls made to the Windows' API (application programming interface). Some API calls deal with the formal presentation of any window in the Window's environment; others deal with messaging between windows or receiving messages from other windows. The API is just another layer of complexity to conquer when working in Realizer and in Windows.

The *User.exe* file (typically located in the *\WINDOWS\SYSTEM* directory) contains some API calls for us to make. In this next example, a wrapper function that is both robust and generic is built around a call to change the text string in a windows title bar, even with that form visible and/or active.

```
'* Application ... : Dll2.rlz
'* Authors ....... : Steve Straley
'* Notice ........ : Copyright(c) 1994 - Sirius Press, Inc.
'* .............. : All Rights Reserved
'* Date .......... : January 1, 1994
'* Description ... : This shows the use of another wrapper function in
'*                   conjunction with another EXTERNAL call.
```

```
TRUE    = (1=1)
FALSE   = (1=0)

_ISFORM   = 1
_ISLOG    = 2
_ISCHART  = 3
_ISSHEET  = 4

external "User" FUNC SetWindowText(INTEGER hwnd, POINTER newwindowtitle) \\
                     AS INTEGER

function SetWindowTitle( sString, ..; .. )

   local iSuccess as integer
   local nHandle  as integer
   local nType    as integer

   if qnoptmods = 0
     nType = _ISFORM
   else
     nType = qoptmod(1)
   end if

   if qnoptparams = 0
     if     nType = _ISFORM
       nHandle = formq(_HWND)
     elseif nType = _ISLOG
       nHandle = logq(_HWND)
     elseif nType = _ISCHART
       nHandle = chartq(_HWND)
     elseif nType = _ISSHEET
       nHandle = sheetq(_HWND)
     else
       return( FALSE )
     end if

     setwindowtext( nHandle, sString )
     iSuccess = TRUE

   else

     if     nType = _ISFORM
       nHandle = formq(_HWND; qoptparam(1) )
     elseif nType = _ISLOG
       nHandle = logq(_HWND; qoptparam(1) )
     elseif nType = _ISCHART
       nHandle = chartq(_HWND; qoptparam(1) )
     elseif nType = _ISSHEET
       nHandle = sheetq(_HWND; qoptparam(1) )
```

```
    else
      return( FALSE )
    end if

    setwindowtext( nHandle, sString )
    iSuccess = TRUE

  end if

  return( iSuccess )

end func

'*********************  EXAMPLE PROGRAM  *********************'

formnew(10; "First and Original Title", _TITLE )
formcontrol(_SHOW)

idle 3

print formq(_HWND)

if SetWindowTitle( "Changed Title" )
  input "The title has been now changed!", "Sirius Press, Inc." ;
else
  input "Error!" ;
end if

idle 3
lognew(11; "And now for a log..." )
logcontrol(_SIZE; 150, 200 )
logcontrol(_SHOW)
idle 3
setwindowtitle( "Changed again..."; _ISLOG )
idle 3
setwindowtitle( "Here again!", 10; _ISFORM )

'* End of File: Dll2.rlz
```

The EXTERNAL command declares the SETWINDOWTEXT() function to be a part of the program and specifies that two parameters are needed. The naming convention for the parameters is not important; however, the declared data is vital. For example, if the wrong name is given for the function, the Error Log window will appear, informing you that the specified function or procedure is not in the listed .DLL file. And if the wrong data type is specified in the parameter list, a run-time error dialog box will appear, offering limited choices for recovery.

Before getting to the wrapper function *SetWindowTitle()*, which makes the official call to the *SetWindowText()* function, the program creates a form, shows it, and waits approximately three seconds. In order to make the Windows API function call work, we need to get Realizer to generate the internal handle, or ID, for the window, whether it is a form, a chart, a log, or a sheet. Each of these tools has an appropriate and corresponding function. For a form, the function is FORMQ(); for a log, the function is LOGQ(). To obtain the ID pointer that the Windows API call will need, the _HWND internal variable is used. This is printed in the Print Log window with the PRINT command, following the three-second IDLE. Then the first call to the *SetWindowTitle()* function is made, which changes the title in the forms window from "First and Original Title" to "Changed Title," at which point the INPUT command takes over:

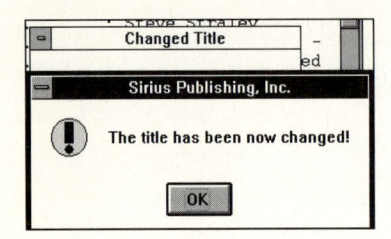

After you press the ENTER key (or click on the OK button) in the INPUT dialog box, three more seconds go by before the next object is created. This new object will be a log using the LOGNEW() function. Once created and sized, it is displayed. Eventually, another call is made to the *SetWindowTitle()* function with a new modifier: _ISLOG. This pseudo-internal variable is declared at the top of the file. The challenge is to match up the appropriate querying function with the current and selected object. In the previous call, a form is created, and since the default condition of this *SetWindowTitle()* function is to assume a form, it makes a call to the FORMQ() function. However, the currently visible and selected item is a log, so the LOGQ() function is required. The _ISLOG internal variable is used as a modifier to tell the function to make this switch. Since the basic behavior of the function remains the same, and only one function call is different, it is appropriate to use a modifier.

Once this new text is changed, the environment is IDLE for three more seconds before the final call to the *SetWindowTitle()* function. Since the currently active window is the log, the *SetWindowTitle()* function needs to be told to go to a specific window that is not active and if necessary, to change that window's title. The form previously created has a Realizer ID value of 10, so that becomes the second parameter passed to the function. With the log

External Routines, Windows API, and User-Defined Types 547

still active and selected, the *SetWindowTitle()* function is told to make a call to the appropriate Windows API function, using the pointer of 10, to find the Windows handle for the specified parameter:

```
nHandle = formq(_HWND; qoptparam(1) )
```

The FORMQ() function does not supply the window handle of the currently selected object (which is not a form but a log), but rather takes the value returned from the QOPTPARAM() function and finds that object's Windows handle. It is this type of robustness, extendability, and reusability that really makes a wrapper function work in tandem with internal Windows API calls.

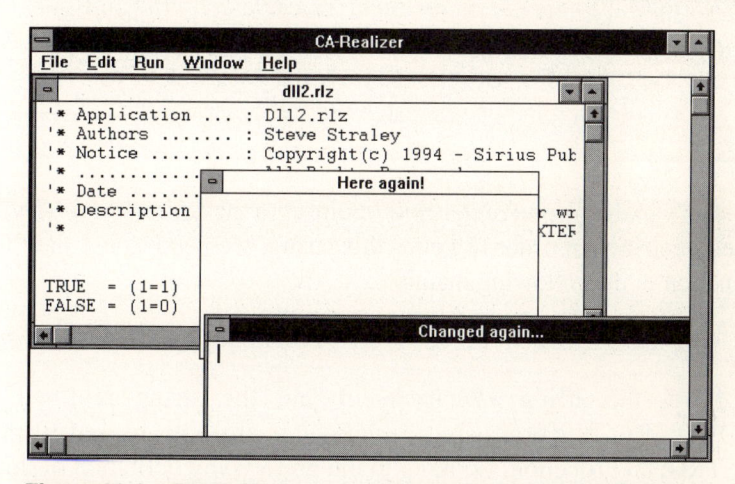

Figure 11-1. DLL2.rlz running with open and active windows.

Figure 11-1 shows how the log's title (foreground) was changed as well as the form's title (background). The focus of the log does not change, since the message to make the move was accomplished outside of Realizer's control and made directly to Windows API.

The POINTER() Function

Another function that works in conjunction with the EXTERNAL command and calls to the Windows API is the POINTER() function. By definition, this function returns a value of the given numeric pointer which, in turn, is to be used as a parameter for other EXTERNAL procedures and functions. Some EXTERNAL operations are prototyped to return a LONG data type. In most cases, this variable will then "point" to a memory address that holds the actual information. Once we have that pointer, we need to use Realizer's POINTER() function to get at it. So in the case of the following:

```
external "kernel" func GetDOSEnvironment() as long
```

the function can be called and the return value stored to a variable that is expecting a LONG data type:

```
local nEnvPointer  as long
nEnvPointer   = GETDOSENVIRONMENT()
```

> **Note:** Make sure the return data type declared in the prototyping instructions used along with the EXTERNAL command is the same data type declared with the LOCAL statement. Otherwise, a run-time error indicating a type mismatch will be generated.

The variable *nEnvPointer* now "points" to the address of the DOS environmental string. In order to get to this string, we need to use the POINTER() function in the following manner:

```
nTempPointer = LSTRCPY(sEnvironment, pointer(nEnvPointer))
```

Here, the string *sEnvironment* and the string returned from the POINTER() function using *nEnvPointer* are both passed to the internal LSTRCPY() function. Looking to the prototyping definition of this function, we can see that it does expect to receive two strings and will return yet another LONG pointer:

```
external "kernel" func Lstrcpy(POINTER sString1, POINTER sString2) as long
```

In this EXTERNAL function, two string pointers are passed and one LONG pointer will be returned. The point is that the data types of parameters passed to EXTERNAL operations and the information returned must match exactly. There is no shortcut without serious ramifications. To see this entire operation in effect, here are three functions from the CARTools library with a simple test found in *Dl13.rlz*:

```
'* Application ... : Dl13.rlz
'* Authors ....... : Steve Straley
'* Notice ........ : Copyright(c) 1994 - Sirius Press, Inc.
'* ............... : All Rights Reserved
'* Date .......... : January 1, 1994
```

External Routines, Windows API, and User-Defined Types

```
'* Description ... : This shows the use of the POINTER function used in
'*                   conjunction with the EXTERNAL command and the use
'*                   of DLL's

external "kernel" func GetDOSEnvironment() as long
external "kernel" func Lstrcpy(POINTER  sString1, POINTER  sString2) \\
                                            as long

func  GetDOSVars(nElement)

  local sReturn       as string     'Buffer to hold environment block
  local nNextVar      as integer    'Indices to step through variables in block
  local sDOSValue     as string     'Buffer holds return value of each variable
  local sEnvironment  as string     'Allocate space for environment block
  local nEnvPointer   as long
  local nTempPointer  as long

  if not qvar(nElement, _REAL + _SCALAR)
    nElement = 1
  else
    if (nElement < 1)
      nElement = 1
    end if
  end if

  sEnvironment = space$(4096)     '* Potential buffer space
  nNextVar     = 0
  sDOSValue    = ""
  nEnvPointer  = GETDOSENVIRONMENT()
  nTempPointer = LSTRCPY(sEnvironment, pointer(nEnvPointer))

  'Step through DOS variables found.  This will stop when
  '* the end of the block is found

  while (nNextVar < nElement)

    'Look for NULL char delimiting each variable
    nPosition = instr(sEnvironment, chr$(0))
    sDOSValue = mid$(sEnvironment,1,nPosition-1)

    'step to new variable
    nEnvPointer  = nEnvPointer + nPosition
    nTempPointer = LSTRCPY(sEnvironment, pointer(nEnvPointer))

    nNextVar = nNextVar + 1
    if (nNextVar = nElement)
      exit while
    end if
```

```
   end while

   if (asc(sDOSValue) = 0)
     sReturn = chr$(0)
   else
     sReturn = ltrim$( rtrim$(sDOSValue))
   end if

   return( sReturn )

end func

func DOSVarList()

   local nCounter as integer
   local aData    as array

   nCounter = 1
   aData    = {""}

       'loop through all variables in environment block
   while (GetDOSVars(nCounter) <> chr$(0))
     aData    = { aData, GetDOSVars(nCounter) }
     nCounter = nCounter + 1
   end while

   return( aData[ startvalid( aData ) + 1 : endvalid(aData) ] )

end func

func DOSVarFind( sName )

   local aData     as array
   local nCounter  as integer
   local sData     as string
   local nPos      as integer
   local nLength   as integer
   local sReturn   as string
   local sVarName  as string

   aData   = DOSVarList()
   sReturn = chr$(0)

   for nCounter = startvalid( aData ) to endvalid( aData )
     sData = aData[nCounter]

     '* Now, begin the parsing!
     nPos     = instr(sData,"=")
```

External Routines, Windows API, and User-Defined Types 551

```
    nLength = len(sData)
    sVarName = ucase$(mid$(sData, 1, nPos-1))

    if (ucase$( sName) = sVarName )
      sReturn = ucase$(mid$(sData, nPos+1, nLength))
      exit for
    end if

  next

  return( sReturn )

end func

'************ MAIN BODY OF THE PROGRAM *************
'***************************************************

print DOSVarList()

print
print "————————"
print DOSVarFind("PATH")

'* End of File: Dll3.rlz
```

If the Print Log window were open when this file is executed, you would see something like Figure 11-2.

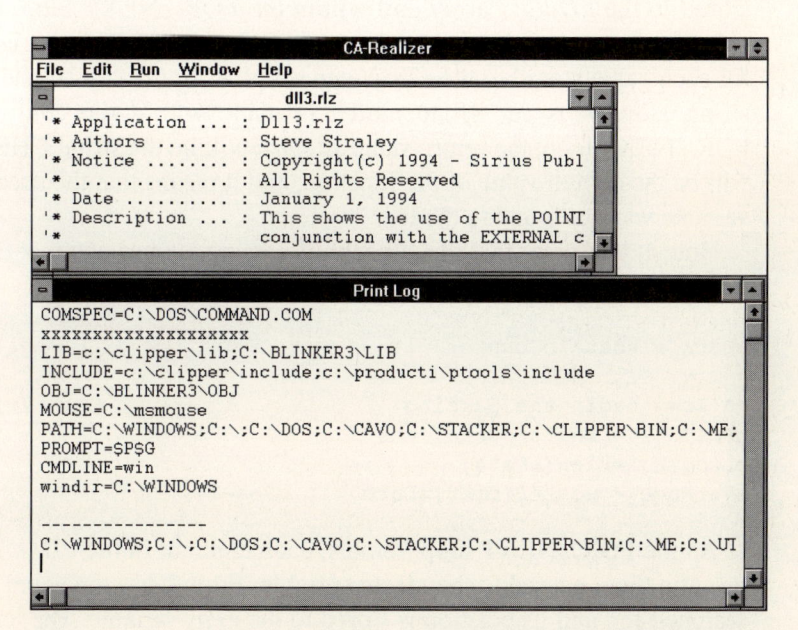

```
╔═══════════════════════ CA-Realizer ═══════════════════════╗
  File  Edit  Run  Window  Help
  ┌──────────────────────── dll3.rlz ────────────────────────┐
  │ '* Application ... : Dll3.rlz                            │
  │ '* Authors ....... : Steve Straley                       │
  │ '* Notice ........ : Copyright(c) 1994 - Sirius Publ     │
  │ '* .............. : All Rights Reserved                  │
  │ '* Date .......... : January 1, 1994                     │
  │ '* Description ... : This shows the use of the POINT     │
  │ '*                   conjunction with the EXTERNAL c     │
  └──────────────────────────────────────────────────────────┘
  ┌──────────────────────── Print Log ───────────────────────┐
  │ COMSPEC=C:\DOS\COMMAND.COM                               │
  │ xxxxxxxxxxxxxxxxxxxx                                     │
  │ LIB=c:\clipper\lib;C:\BLINKER3\LIB                       │
  │ INCLUDE=c:\clipper\include;c:\producti\ptools\include    │
  │ OBJ=C:\BLINKER3\OBJ                                      │
  │ MOUSE=C:\msmouse                                         │
  │ PATH=C:\WINDOWS;C:\;C:\DOS;C:\CAVO;C:\STACKER;C:\CLIPPER\BIN;C:\ME; │
  │ PROMPT=$P$G                                              │
  │ CMDLINE=win                                              │
  │ windir=C:\WINDOWS                                        │
  │                                                          │
  │ ----------------                                         │
  │ C:\WINDOWS;C:\;C:\DOS;C:\CAVO;C:\STACKER;C:\CLIPPER\BIN;C:\ME;C:\UT │
  │ |                                                        │
  └──────────────────────────────────────────────────────────┘
```

Figure 11-2. Running application of DLL3.RLZ with PRINT LOG.

This example program holds three unique and generic functions that use the Windows API. Note, in particular, the "KERNEL" file, which on my machine is named `Krn1386.exe`. Internally, Windows "converts" the name and looks for the appropriate file. The two functions in this file are important: GETDOSENVIRONMENT() and LSTRCPY(). The main wrapper function is called *GetDOSVars()*. It is designed to find individual DOS environmental strings based on the numeric position passed as the variable *nElement*. However, sometimes, the ordinal position of the string is not known, so to make life easier, the *DOSVarList()* function is a wrapper function for the wrapper function, meaning this function uses the *GetDOSVars()* function to build an array of DOS environment variables found by the EXTERNAL GETDOSENVIRONMENT() function. The items found in the environment are separated by a CHR$(0) character. In the *DOSVarList()* function, the array *aData[]* starts off with one element (which is an empty string). As each element passes through the WHILE loop, the string returned from the *GetDOSVars()* function will be added to the *aData[]* array. In the end, however, the first element is skipped in the return value for the *DOSVarList()* function, meaning that only an array of DOS environment values will be returned as part of this function.

The *DOSVarFind()* function is yet another wrapper, but this time, it is a wrapper for the wrapper for the wrapper. (Confused?) This function will find the appropriate DOS environment variable in the list of values generated by the *DOSVarList()* function. In this function, the list of variables is initially stored to the *aData[]* array and within the FOR...NEXT loop, the passed string parameter of *sName* is checked against the parsed out variable named for each value stored to the *sVarName* variable. If a match is made, then the string *sReturn* is set. If no match is made within the confines of the FOR...NEXT loop, the return value *sReturn* will be the string CHR$(0). This will be the default value of the function, and it means that the specified DOS variable was not found in the list.

Note at this point that the concept of parsing is once again at the heart of this function:

```
sData = aData[nCounter]

'* Now, begin the parsing!
nPos     = instr(sData,"=")
nLength  = len(sData)
sVarName = ucase$(mid$(sData, 1, nPos-1))
```

As the FOR...NEXT loop iterates, each element in the *aData[]* array is, one at a time, passed to the *sData* variable. From here, the equal sign (=) is searched for, and its position is stored to the *nPos* variable. The length of the

External Routines, Windows API, and User-Defined Types

individual DOS variable is then stored to the *nLength* name and eventually, everything on the right side of the equal sign is stored to the *sVarName* variable. Keep in mind that the test on this variable is made in UCASE$( ) format. This makes a match more probable, regardless of how the environment keeps the variable or how the call is made to this function.

> **Note:** Even if a return variable from an EXTERNAL function is not needed, it must be declared and the assignment made (for example) to prevent a run-time error message.

Windows and Messages

Windows is an event-oriented operating system. This means that rather than the conventional approach to requesting an action and seeing that action to its logical and linear conclusion, Windows is based on a messaging system. This requires a different approach to problem solving and to acquiring information from the operating system. Consider the idea of a drawing tablet on the screen in a form. Realizer is a layer between you and the operating system, and only a few of the messages from the operating system are directly translated in the language. If, for example, the mouse is moved within the tablet after a button is pressed, there is no way in the language to detect the movement of the cursor. To do this, a call to the Windows API is needed, and specifically to the GETMESSAGE( ) function.

Before getting into the substance of what a message looks like in Windows, a brief word on events and messages is needed. Everything is a message: objects, forms, data, and so on. All of these items send messages to the grand communicator known as Windows, which doesn't just receive messages from the various items, but interprets the meaning of the messages and sends back appropriate messages to all in the proper domains. This means that, to the conventional way of thinking, there is no direct linear pattern or trail from the beginning of a request to the end of that request. Instead, with every request, Windows is the dispatcher of the news and not the item being clicked on or the form in view.

There is a specific format for the messages received from Windows. The prototype of the function in question looks like this:

```
external "User" function GetMessage(POINTER, INTEGER, INTEGER, INTEGER) \\
              as dword
```

The return value of this function is not as important as the first parameter, which is a string pointer. This string will contain the contents of the message sent by Windows and will be changed by the Windows event system. Once the GETMESSAGE() function has been called, our job is to parse the string into the various components of the message. This means that we have to know the structure of the message. The following table outlines this structure:

HWND	hwnd	(2 bytes)
WORD	message	(2 bytes)
WORD	wParam	(2 bytes)
LONG	lParam	(4 bytes)
DWORD	time	(4 bytes)
POINT	pt	(remaining)

The message received from the function starts with the third byte of the passed pointer.

The example in the file named *Dl14.rlz* uses the GETMESSAGE() function to determine the row and column position of a mouse click in the middle of a tablet:

```
'* Application ... : Dl14.rlz
'* Authors ....... : Steve Straley
'* Notice ........ : Copyright(c) 1994 - Sirius Press, Inc.
'* .............. : All Rights Reserved
'* Date .......... : January 1, 1994
'* Description ... : Working with Windows API and the internal message
'*                   system

external "User" function GetMessage(POINTER, INTEGER, INTEGER, INTEGER) \\
                        as dword

WM_LBUTTONDOWN = 513
WM_MOUSEMOVE   = 512
WM_LBUTTONUP   = 514

proc Attached( aParms )

   local nXPosition as integer
   local nYPosition as integer
   local sMessage   as string
   local nMessage   as integer
   local dTheREsult as dword

   formselect( aParms[_FORMNUM])
   select case aParms[ _ITEMNUM ]
```

```
      case 10                              'the tablet
         sMessage = string$(255,0)
         nMessage = 0
         messagebox( "The tablet was clicked on at: " + \\
                     numtostr( tabletmousex ) +   "," +     \\
                     numtostr( tabletmousey ) + chr$(10) + \\
                     chr$(13), "Sirius Press, Inc.", _MB_OK )

         while nMessage <> WM_LBUTTONUP
           dTheResult = getmessage( sMessage, formqobject(10)[_FQO_HWND],0,0)

           '* Start the conversion with the passed message pointer
           nMessage   = cvi( mid$( sMessage, 3, 2) )       'start at byte 3
           nXPosition = cvi( mid$( sMessage, 7, 2))
           nYPosition = cvi( mid$( sMessage, 9, 2))

           print "Mouse movement: ", nMessage, nXPosition, nYPosition
         end while

   end select

end proc

logselect( _PRINTLOG )      '* Open the print log window automatically
logcontrol( _SHOW )         '* Show the log

formnew(100; "Sirius Form with Tablet on Fresca", _TITLE+_CLOSE )
formcontrol( _SIZE; 200, 10 )
formsetobject(10, _TABLET, "", 10 pct, 10 pct, 80 pct, 80 pct)
tabletsetcolor( _BLUE; _BACKGROUND )
tablettext("", 0, 0)
formsetproc( Attached )
formcontrol( _SHOW )

'* End of File
```

As can be expected, the EXTERNAL command and the definition of the *Attached()* procedure attached to the form is standard. Following this, the Print Log window is selected and opened, and a new form is created. This form is positioned and a _TABLET object is attached with a _BLUE hue as the _BACKGROUND color. When the user clicks the mouse anywhere on the _TABLET object (which has an ID marker of 10), the form will be selected and the SELECT CASE statement will be processed. Since the mouse button was clicked in order to get to the CASE 10 statement inside the *Attached()* routine, the values of TABLETMOUSEX and TABLETMOUSEY will be known to Realizer. However, the real test will take place once the OK button is pressed within the MESSAGEBOX().

The WHILE loop continues to process until the left mouse button is pressed again. This value is held in the constant *WM_LBUTTONUP* declared at the top of the file. When that takes place, the GETMESSAGE() API call will be made. At the start of this look, the variable *sMessage* will hold a blank string pointer which will be passed to the GETMESSAGE() function. After each call to that function, we have to parse out the Window message based on the structure outlined earlier. The first item we parse out will start at byte 3 of *sMessage* and go for 2 bytes. This will be converted to an INTEGER using the CVI() function, and the results will be stored to the *nMessage* variable. This variable will hold the mouse button that was pressed and should be one of the three constant values declared at the top of the file. You could also declare 516 and 517 (right mouse button down and right mouse button up respectively). And we could have made a further test for an *nMessage* value of 512, which is for mouse movement. The values for the row and column position of the mouse are also stored in the *sMessage* variable at the prescribed structure points. To start, the value of *nXPosition* should be the same as TABLETMOUSEX, and the value of *nYPosition* should be the same as TABLETMOUSEY.

User-Defined Types

The reason that this section is placed in between the sections on EXTERNAL routines and the Windows API is to show the importance of user-defined types in relation to the preceding discussion. So this first example will continue on the current theme. Toward the end of the chapter, we will look at other reasons for using user-defined TYPEs.

A user-defined type is a structure that is defined by the programmer. Once defined, variables can be initialized based on that type. Ironically, this is a very object-oriented concept, in which code and structures bound together effect a certain behavior. For example, if we wanted to start thinking about boxes, we know that every box has four corners. To help define this, we might build a special data type called BOX. The code might look something like this:

```
type Box
   top      as integer
   left     as integer
   bottom   as integer
   right    as integer
end type
```

Now we can build variables using this structure:

```
local myBox as box
myBox.top    = 0
myBox.left   = 0
```

External Routines, Windows API, and User-Defined Types

```
myBox.bottom = 200
myBox.right  = 200
```

Expanding on this, we could create an array of 100 boxes with this structure:

```
local aBoxes(1 to 100) as box
local temp as box
for nCount = 1 to 100
   temp.top         = 0
   temp.left        = 0
   temp.bottom      = 200
   temp.right       = 200
   aBoxes[nCount]   = temp
next
```

Both the array of *aBoxes[ ]* and the variable *temp* have the same structure, so when the individual members of the type are added to the *temp* variable, they will match perfectly within the array of structures stored in *aBoxes[ ]*.

So what does that have to do with Windows and the API system? In the previous section, I outlined how the message from Windows had a particular, constant structure. By joining that fact with the notion of user-defined types, it is not too much of a stretch to build a special structure that is geared to the Windows API message system. Here, we could build a special type that has all of the elements of that message broken down into smaller components. The advantage is twofold. First, we would not have to use the MID$() function (seen in the previous example) to parse out the individual bytes from the return message. The structure of the message would break this down for us. Second, and more subtle, the pointer of structure or pointer of string can be passed to the Windows GETMESSAGE() function. Consider a generic function that makes a specific call to the API:

```
func MessageGet( nHandle )

   if not qvar( msgStruct, _DEFINED )
      type msgStruct
         hwnd    as string*2       '* 2 Bytes
         msg     as string*2       '* 2 Bytes
         wParam  as string*2       '* 2 Bytes
         xPos    as string*2       '* 2 Bytes
         yPos    as string*2       '* 2 Bytes
         time    as string*4       '* 4 Bytes
         pntr    as string*241     '* Remaining
      end type
   end if
```

```
    local dTheResult    as dWord
    local nStarting     as integer
    local nEnding       as integer
    local aReturn       as array
    local message       as msgStruct

    aReturn = {0}

    message.hwnd    = mki$(0)         ' ------+>
    message.msg     = mki$(0)         '       |>
    message.wParam  = mki$(0)         '       |>
    message.XPos    = mki$(0)         '       |> 255 Bytes of Information
    message.YPos    = mki$(0)         '       |>
    message.time    = mkl$(0)         '       |>
    message.pntr    = string$(241,0)  ' ------+>

    dTheResult = getmessage( message, nHandle, 0, 0 )

    aReturn = { aReturn, cvi( message.hwnd ),   cvi( message.msg ), \\
                         cvi( message.wParam ), cvi( message.xPos ), \\
                         cvi( message.yPos ),   cvl( message.time ) }

    nStarting = startvalid( aReturn ) + 1
    nEnding   = endvalid( aReturn )

    return( aReturn[ nStarting:nEnding ] )

end func
```

This function requires the Windows handle for the object that is being worked on. This remains the same from the preceding example, in that `formqobject(10)[_FQO_HWND]` is passed as a parameter to this function. This function checks to see if the TYPE has already been defined. If not, it defines this structure and gives it the name *msgStruct*. Within the TYPE command, the individual member names of the TYPE are specified as well as their individual data type.

> **Note:** It is possible to mix data types within a structure.

Since the GETMESSAGE() function takes a string pointer as the first parameter, these elements will be of String data type. In addition, their lengths will be fixed. If we were to total up all of the bytes allocated within the defined TYPE structure, they would add up to 255, which is the same

External Routines, Windows API, and User-Defined Types

length as the string passed to the GETMESSAGE( ) function in the first example. Once the type is defined to the system, all we need to do is declare a variable based on that structure. Here, the *message* variable is that entity.

The next step is to fill the individual members with an empty string pointer. The length of the fixed string for each member dictates whether the MKI$( ) function (for those with just 2 bytes in length) or the MKL$( ) function (for those with 4 bytes in length) will be used. For the member in the structure which is something like a filler member, the remaining 241 bytes are filled using the conventional STRING$( ) function, which is the same trick used in the previous example. Now, with our variable message declared, our TYPE initialized, and the individual members filled with a starting value, the GETMESSAGE( ) function may be called, passing to it the variable *message*. We do not have to send a flat string; the string structure known as *msgStruct* will do just as well. In fact, since the structure breaks out all the individual pieces, it is easier to work with `msgStruct` than to pass one long string and parse it with the MID$( ) function. Having the structure in place makes that parsing job easier.

The final stages of this function show just how easy it is once the structure is built and in place. The return array *aReturn[ ]* is simply the reverse of the MKI$( ) or MKL$( ) function. Here, the return array will contain the converted CVI$( ) or CVL$( ) values for the individual members; again, the length of the string of the member dictates which of the two functions will be called. The array *aReturn[ ]* is a message stack of the individual pieces of the Windows message, which can and does get printed in the remaining part of the example file `D115.rlz`:

```
'* Application ... : Dl15.rlz
'* Authors ....... : Steve Straley
'* Notice ........ : Copyright(c) 1994 - Sirius Press, Inc.
'* .............. : All Rights Reserved
'* Date .......... : January 1, 1994
'* Description ... : Working with Windows API and the internal message
'*                   system and adds a user defined type to make the whole
'*                   thing jive.

external "User" function GetMessage(POINTER, INTEGER, INTEGER, INTEGER) \\
                         as dword

WM_LBUTTONDOWN = 513
WM_MOUSEMOVE   = 512
WM_LBUTTONUP   = 514


func MessageGet( nHandle )     '* The same seen above*
end func
```

```
proc Attached( aParms )

  local nXPosition as integer
  local nYPosition as integer
  local sMessage    as string
  local nMessage    as integer
  local dTheREsult as dword

   formselect( aParms[_FORMNUM])
   select case aParms[ _ITEMNUM ]
     case 2
       logselect( _PRINTLOG )
       logcontrol( _CLOSE )
       formselect( aParms[_FORMNUM] )
       formcontrol( _CLOSE )

     case 10                              'the tablet
       sMessage = string$(255,0)
       nMessage = 0
       messagebox( "The tablet was clicked on at: " + numtostr( TabletMouseX ) + \\
            "," + numtostr(TabletMouseY) + Chr$(10) + Chr$(13), \\
            "Sirius Press, Inc.", _MB_OK )

       loop

          aData = MessageGet( formqobject(10)[_FQO_HWND] )

          if aData[3] = WM_MOUSEMOVE
            print "Mouse movement: ", aData[2], aData[3], aData[4], aData[5], aData[6]
          end if

          if aData[4] = 1 '* Mouse left button clicked
            exit loop
          end if

       end loop

   end select

end proc

logselect( _PRINTLOG )    '* Open the print log window automatically
logcontrol( _SHOW )       '* Show the log

formnew(100; "Sirius Form with Tablet on Fresca", _TITLE+_CLOSE )
formcontrol( _SIZE; 200, 10 )
formsetobject(10, _TABLET, "", 10 pct, 10 pct, 80 pct, 80 pct)
formsetobject(2, _BUTTON, "Quit", _LEFT, _BOTTOM, 20 pct, 10 pct )
```

```
tabletsetcolor( _BLUE; _BACKGROUND )
tablettext("", 0, 0)
formsetproc( Attached )
formcontrol( _SHOW )

'* End of File
```

The rest of the file is pretty much the same code seen in *Dll4.rlz*, with the addition of a _BUTTON object to shut down the example and the use of a few more of the return values from the *MessageGet()* function.

More API Calls

Turning our attention back to simple API calls, there are even calls to see what the keyboard is doing while in a form or a Windows application. So, if those nasty icons for the CAPS LOCK key do not work, this example program shows you how a simple API call can do the trick:

```
'* Application ... : Dll6.rlz
'* Authors ....... : Steve Straley
'* Notice ........ : Copyright(c) 1994 - Sirius Press, Inc.
'* .............. : All Rights Reserved
'* Date .......... : January 1, 1994
'* Description ... : Simple API calls to see the keyboard

external "User.exe" Func GetKeyState(WORD) as byte

' Scroll     = _VK_SCROLL
' Caps       = _VK_CAPITAL
' Numlock    = _VK_NUMLOCK

function IsScrollOn()

   return( GetKeyState( _VK_SCROLL ) )

end func

function IsCapsOn()

   return( GetKeyState( _VK_CAPITAL ) )

end func

function IsNumLockOn()

   return( GetKeyState( _VK_NUMLOCK ) )

end func
```

```
'*********** MAIN MODULE **********'

logselect( _PRINTLOG )
logcontrol( _SHOW )

loop
  print IsCapsOn(), IsNumLockOn(), IsScrollOn()
end loop

'* End of File: Dll6.rlz
```

Each wrapper function returns a 1 or a 0, depending on whether the associated key is pressed or not. To exit this program, press the CTRL+ALT+F2 key combination.

Complex Calls

Some API calls can be very complex and, in their complexity, provide interesting results. Detecting mouse movement, as seen in previous examples, can be important in an application. In game software, for example, mouse movement is usually a very important part of the supporting code. Mouse movement can also be used to turn on specific pixels within a framed area of the screen. Many professional drawing packages, such as Corel Draw, rely on this extensively. The file named *Rll7.rlz* demonstrates this technique, and Figure 11-3 shows what the resulting screen might look like.

```
'* Application ... : Dll7.rlz
'* Authors ....... : David C. Ullrich
'* Modified ...... : Steve Straley
'* Base Code ..... : Public Domain material
'* Notice ........ : modified code Copyright(c) 1994 - Sirius Press, Inc.
'* .............. : All Rights Reserved
'* Date .......... : January 1, 1994
'* Description ... : This shows an extended use of the Windows API to make a
'*                   drawing tablet that, if not overused (which will cause
'*                   a run-time error message out of memory), will show
'*                   how to draw in Windows and Realizer.

external "User" func GetMessage(POINTER,INTEGER,INTEGER,INTEGER) as dword
external "User" proc ClipCursor(POINTER rectorlong)

if not qvar(rectangle, _DEFINED)
  type rectangle
    left   as integer
    top    as integer
```

```
      right      as integer
      bottom     as integer
   end type
end if

WM_LBUTTONDOWN = 513
WM_MOUSEMOVE   = 512
WM_LBUTTONUP   = 514

proc Attached(aParms)

   local tabrect        as rectangle
   local undoclip       as long
   local cMessage       as string*255
   local nMessage       as integer
   local nOldXPosition  as integer
   local nOldYPosition  as integer
   local nNewXPosition  as integer
   local nNewYPosition  as integer
   local dResult        as dword

   formselect(aParms[_FORMNUM])
   select case aParms[_ITEMNUM]
     case 10                        'the tablet
       tabrect.left   = qsys(_sizeinside)[1] + formq(_sizeinside)[1] +\\
                                             formqobject(10)[_FQO_LEFT]
       tabrect.top    = qsys(_sizeinside)[2] + formq(_sizeinside)[2] + \\
                                             formqobject(10)[_FQO_TOP]
       tabrect.right  = tabrect.left + formqobject(10)[_FQO_WIDTH]
       tabrect.bottom = tabrect.top + formqobject(10)[_FQO_HEIGHT]
       clipcursor(tabrect)

       cMessage      = string$(255,0)
       nMessage      = 0
       nOldXPosition = tabletmousex
       nOldYPosition = tabletmousey

       while nMessage <> WM_LBUTTONUP
         dResult       = getmessage(cMessage, formqobject(10)[_FQO_HWND], 0, 0)
         nMessage      = cvi(mid$(cMessage,3,2))    'start at byte 3
         nNewXPosition = cvi(mid$(cMessage,7,2))
         nNewYPosition = cvi(mid$(cMessage,9,2))

         tabletline(nOldXPosition, nOldYPosition, nNewXPosition, nNewYPosition)
         nOldXPosition = nNewXPosition
         nOldYPosition = nNewYPosition

       end while
       clipcursor(pointer(undoclip))
```

```
    case 20
      tabletcontrol(_CLEAR)
      tablettext("",0,0)
      tabletsetcolor(_CYAN;_BACKGROUND)
      tabletcontrol(_SHOW)

    case 2
      formcontrol(_CLOSE)

  end select
end proc

'*************** MAIN PIECE OF CODE ***************'
'**************************************************'

formnew(100; "Dave's Drawing Program, Clipped", _TITLE + _CLOSE)
formsetobject(10, _TABLET, "",12 pct, 9 pct, 75 pct,75 pct)
formsetobject(20, _BUTTON, "CLEAR", _LEFT,  _BOTTOM)
formsetobject(2,  _BUTTON, "EXIT",  _RIGHT, _BOTTOM)
tabletsetcolor( _CYAN; _BACKGROUND)
tablettext("",0,0)
formcontrol(_SHOW)
formsetproc( Attached )

'* End of File: Dll7.rlz
```

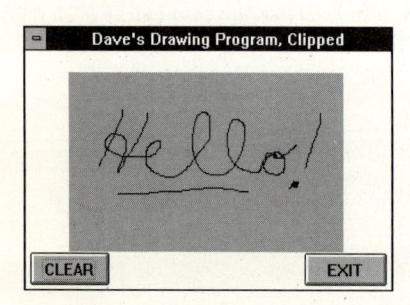

Figure 11-3. Running drawing program using TABLETLINE().

Most of the code builds on what we already know about a few of the API calls available to us. The new API call is to the CLIPCURSOR() function, which holds the image of the _TABLET region before and after the image has been drawn. Once a mouse click is detected in the _TABLET, the procedure *Attached( )* takes over, and as long as the left mouse button is pressed, the WHILE loop will continue to process and call the GETMESSAGE() function. In that loop, the values of the variables *nNewXPosition* and *nNewYPosition* will be updated with new coordinates, and the TABLETLINE( ) function will draw a line between the old coordinates stored to *nOldXPosition* and *nOldYPosition*. This means, in essence, that the "dots" between the old coordinates and the new coordinates are connected. Since this difference is at best fractional, the TABLETLINE( ) function will appear not to be drawing a line, but rather drawing dots on the screen to create the "drawing" effect.

Other Possibilities?

What this should then imply is that sometimes, for the sake of simplicity and extendability, wrapper functions work in conjunction with most EXTERNAL function calls. For example, in the CARTools Library, a series of wrapper functions are made around EXTERNAL function calls to a special .DLL file that allows for both database and indexing updates and queries.

Conclusion

We have see the benefits of making EXTERNAL calls to existing custom controls, tools, and subroutines. We have seen more examples of reusable code, this time outside of the Realizer environment. In addition, we have extended the concepts of structure to allow the programmer to build that structure "as is" and to allow the program to be tailored to a Windows API message or even a file format. These simple techniques can allow us to attach database engines to Realizer to achieve the final goal: a powerful database and graphical BASIC-oriented language.

Chapter 12

Frequently Asked Questions

This section, which contains the top 20 Realizer questions, is a rough compilation inspired by a variety of sources, including Gary Zimak and Michael Massaro.

Q: Will all applications built in CA-Realizer have the same root window?

A: When you build an application using Project Builder, select EXE Options and mark the Application Invisible check box. Once the application is invisible, it may be restored using the following line of code:

```
setsys(_SIZE, {_RESTORE} )
```

Another way to open an invisible application is to use a `_POPUP` form instead of a regular form. A `_POPUP` form will appear even though the main window is still invisible. This allows you to make the form and application look exactly the way you want (except for a menu, which can be attached only to a main window).

Q: Can I change the font in CA-Realizer's editor?

A: Yes. As a matter of fact, I wanted a nonproportional, or monospaced, font for the examples in this book, so making the change in the editor was very important. In the `\WINDOWS` subdirectory, there should be a file called `Realizer.ini`. This is the initialization file for Realizer. In that text file, there should be an entry for `EDITFONT` under the [CA-REALIZER] title. (Do not modify the section called [REALIZER].) You can change this to any font you have available to your system. I selected Courier-12. In my system, the `Realizer.ini` file looks like this:

```
[CA-Realizer]
Maximized=1
CaretRoot=c:\realizer\caret\
ShowDebugger=0
MaxNum SavedBreakpoints=10
NumSavedBreakpoints=0
MaxNumSavedWatchpoints=10
NumSavedWatchpoints=0
RecentFile1=c:\realizer\sirius\trya.rlz
RecentFile2=c:\realizer\sirius\tryh.rlz
RecentFile3=c:\realizer\sirius\samples\dll6.rlz
RecentFile4=c:\realizer\sirius\samples\dll5.rlz
RecentFile5=c:\realizer\sirius\samples\dll4.rlz
WindowSymList=30 171 516 331
RecentFile6=c:\realizer\sirius\tryg.rlz
RecentFile7=c:\realizer\sirius\trye.rlz
WindowCalltree=310 201 330 139
WindowBreakpoint=154 276 408 267
Breakpoint1=MenuLoop
RecentFile8=c:\realizer\sirius\tryf.rlz
WindowWatchpoint=312 125 408 267
EditFont=Courier-12
WindowValShow1=70 229 498 335
```

Q: Why is it that when NUMTOSTR() is used to convert a number like 2.33 to a string representation, the result is 2.0. How can this be corrected?

A: This answer is simple: Use SPRINT() instead of NUMTOSTR(). The NUMTOSTR() function is a quick function to make those integer-related conversions. The SPRINT() function allows you to choose a pattern or template for the conversion, including how many digits to allow.

In addition, there is a function in this book (see Chapter 2) and in our CARTools library that makes conversions like this, including the addition of commas for the American currency format.

Q: How do I declare an EXTERNAL function?

A: Chapter 11 in this book that deals extensively with subject. The basic answer lies in what you are trying to call. If it is, for example, a Windows API call, then you must prototype the function in advance of it being called. This is accomplished via the EXTERNAL command, which tells Realizer, before the actual call, where to look for the specified operation, what the item is (a function or a procedure), what the parameter list will be (if any), the data types of those parameters, and the expected return value of the call if it is declared to be a FUNCTION and not a PROCEDURE.

Q: What does "height" mean to a drop-down box? There never seems to be enough room for them.

A: The term "height" means how far the object will drop down whenever it is selected, not how it should appear in its initial state. You need to allow enough room for the listbox to drop down properly within a screen region, starting from the base of the object.

Q: Is it possible to tell if a procedure or a function is available in an application?

A: The QVAR() function works for procedure and function names as well as for variables. Try the following code:

```
clear MyProc
print qvar(MyProc)

proc MyProc
end proc

print qvar(MyProc)
clear MyProc
print qvar(MyProc)
```

Q: Can an OLE object be a bitmap?

A: Yes. When the object is created on the form, continue to use _OLE as the definition; however, when referring to the object, use the name of the bitmap file, including the file extension:

```
formnew(100; "The Form", _TITLE + _CLOSE )
formcontrol(_SIZE;10 pct, 10 pct, 85 pct, 85 pct)
formsetcolor( _GRAY; _BACKGROUND )
formsetobject(10, _OLE, "C:\WINDOWS\REDBRICK.BMP",\\
                    10 pct, 10 pct, 80 pct, 80 pct )
formcontrol( _SHOW )
```

Q: When a _BITMAP object is created on a form, it appears to have a narrow outline. Is there any way to eliminate this?

A: Yes, use the FORMMODIFYOBJECT() function on that object, and use the _GRAY internal variable. This will eliminate the outline from the bitmap.

Q: Other than through API calls, is there a way to change the title of a window?

A: There are some undocumented internal variables that may be called with some of the forms. Because these are undocumented, they may not appear in future versions, so be careful. However, the _SETTITLE internal variable seems to work quite nicely:

```
local nCount as integer
local nForm  as integer

nForm = formqunique
formnew( nForm; "FIRST TITLE", _CLOSE + _TITLE + _SIZE)
formcontrol( _SHOW )

for nCount = 1 to 5
  idle 5
  formcontrol( _SETTILE; sprint("Title P(0)", nCount))
next

idle 5
formcontrol( _CLOSE )
```

Q: Are there any other undocumented internal variables or values that may be beneficial?

A: More are discovered each day. Keep in mind that an undocumented variable or feature may not be supported in the future. This is a risk each programmer must face. Here is a short list of known internal variables that "do something":

_SETTITLE	Changes the title of a form on the screen
_HEAVYFRAME	Creates a heavy frame around a form's perimeter.
_ALL	Works with FORMWAIT() function; returns the same array of parameters automatically passed to an attached form procedure.
_PEEKGET	Similar to the _PEEK option for a FORMWAIT() function, except this will retrieve a message from the event queue whereas the _PEEK function will indicate only if there is a message to process.

Q: Is there a utility that allows you to create and add buttons with pictures or icons to create, say, a button bars in an application?

A: The FORMNEW(...., + _PALETTE) or FORMNEW(...., _TOOLBAR) commands allow you to create forms that generally work the way a button bar should. You may add objects like BitmapButtons and OptionBitmaps to these forms.

Remember to adjust the MDI region, if necessary, to ensure that other forms created do not cover up the newly created button bars. To do this, the SETSYS(_SIZEMDI) function needs to be called.

Q: Is there a book that lists information on the various API calls that may be made within Realizer?

A: Ziff-Davis publishes The Visual Basic Programmer's Guide to the Windows API. Most of the API calls listed in this book may be used in Realizer.

Q: Is or will Realizer be compatible with .VBX files, and if so, how will these be incorporated into an OS/2 application?

A: CA-Realizer 2.0 cannot use .VBX files, and as of the date of this publication, there are no plans to add this capability. Future versions may have independent database controls, as will the CARTools library published by Sirius Press, Inc.

Q: Is there a way to control the LFLUSH command, specifically to print single labels?

A: There is no way to control LFLUSH and the text it prints out. It is strictly a form-feed dumping its buffer. For this, the CA-RET report writer should be used instead.

Q: If there is an edit control set with the notify style flag, the form seems to be notified on both entering and leaving the control. Is there a way to control it to notify only upon leaving?

A: The following example shows how a form is notified when the user attempts to leave an edit control created via the _NOTIFY attribute. Note that a _CLICK message will also appear in the form when the ENTER key is pressed.

```
proc Attached( aParam )

  formselect( aParam[ _FORMNUM ] )
  select case aParam[ _ITEMNUM ]
    case 10
      select case aParam[ _INVOKE ]
        case _CLICK
          input "Exiting Box #1", "Sirius Publishing, Inc" ;
      end select

    case 20
      select case aParam[ _INVOKE ]
        case _CLICK
          input "Exiting Box #2", "Sirius Publishing, Inc" ;

      end select
  end select
end proc
```

```
formnew( 100; "A new Form", _TITLE + _CLOSE)
formsetobject( 10, _TEXTBOX, "Some text", 10 pct, 20 pct; _NOTIFY )
formsetobject( 10, _TEXTBOX, "More text", 10 pct, 50 pct; _NOTIFY )
formcontrol( _SHOW )
formsetproc( Attached )
```

Q: If a user tabs to an edit control that already contains text, the text is automatically highlighted, as long as the _SETFOCUS attribute is not set. If it is, then the text is not highlighted. Can this be altered?

A: Yes. Sometimes, a code extract is like a picture: It simplifies the explanation.

```
proc Attached( aParam )

  formselect aParam[_FORMNUM]
  select case aParam[_ITEMNUM]
    case 20
      formmodifyobject(10, _SETFOCUS )
    case 30
      formmodifyobject(15, _SETFOCUS )
  end select

end proc

formnew(100; "The Text Box Form", _TITLE + _CLOSE)
formsetobject(10,_textbox,"the text",25 pct, 20 pct)
formsetobject(15,_textbox,"some more text",25 pct, 40 pct)
formsetobject(20,_button,"Go to 1st Text Box", _LEFT, _BOTTOM)
formsetobject(30,_button,"Go to 2nd Text Box", _RIGHT, _BOTTOM)
formcontrol(_SHOW)
formsetproc( Attached )
```

Q: How can a Realizer-specific feature be executed directly from Realizer application?

A: Check out the MENUDOCMD() function and the various internal variables associated with it. Some other interesting possibilities may be found in that program file, including copying to the Clipboard. Consider the following:

```
'* Application ... : ClipUp.rlz
'* Authors ....... : Steve Straley
'* Notice ........ : Copyright(c) 1994 - Sirius Publishing, Inc.
'* .............. : All Rights Reserved
'* Date .......... : January 1, 1994
'* Description ... : This shows how the MENUDOCMD() might work
'*                   in conjunction with the Clip Board.
```

Chapter 12

```
proc LogAttached( aParam )

  logselect( aParam[ _ITEMNUM ] )
  select case aParam[ _INVOKE ]
    case _CLOSE
    '* Remove these lines to see the image of the FORM
    '* copied to the ClipBoard; otherwise, the contents
    '* of the LOG will be copied to the ClipBoard
'       formselect( 10 )
'       formcontrol( _SHOW )

      menudocmd( _RLZM_COPYWINDOW )
  end select

end proc

proc FormAttached( aParam )

  formselect( aParam[_FORMNUM] )
  select case aParam[_ITEMNUM]
    case 10
      lognew( 10 )
      print #10;  "Look at the clipboard..."
      print #10;  "Type something..."
      print #10;  "Look at the clipboard..."
      print #10;  "Close the log, THEN look at the clipboard..."
      logcontrol( _SHOW )
      logsetproc( LogAttached )
  end select

end proc

'************ BODY OF MAIN PROGRAM ***********'

formnew(10; "Sirius Publishing, Inc.", _TITLE + _CLOSE + _SIZE )
formsetobject(10, _BUTTON, "Make My Log", _CENTER, _CENTER)
formsetproc( FormAttached )
formcontrol( _SHOW )

'* End of File: ClipUp.rlz
```

> **Q:** Can any of the menu items on the main menu bar be _GRAY'd just like the individual menu options?
>
> **A:** Yes and no. The only way in which the top-level menu items can be turned _GRAY is to go through the Windows API system. If you do this, however, beware of two things: First, the _GRAY mechanism through the API looks different from the _GRAY associated with individual menu

items. Second, the "hoops" that the application has to go through in order to achieve this effect will quickly dampen your enthusiasm for implementing it. Consider the following:

```
'* Application ... : Graymenu.rlz
'* Authors ....... : Steve Straley
'* Notice ........ : Copyright(c) 1994 - Sirius Publishing, Inc.
'* ............... : All Rights Reserved
'* Date .......... : January 1, 1994
'* Description ... : Shows how the main menu items may be GRAY'd...but you
'*                   won't like it.

external "User" func GetMenu(WORD) as integer
external "User" func EnableMenuItem(WORD,INTEGER,INTEGER) as integer

__POSITION = hextonum("400")
__ENABLED  = hextonum("0")
__GRAYED   = hextonum("1")

local nHandle as integer

nHandle = getmenu( qsys(_HWND) )

enablemenuitem( nHandle, 4, __POSITION + __GRAYED)
enablemenuitem( nHandle, 2, __POSITION + __GRAYED)
setsys( _SIZE, {_MINIMIZE} )
setsys( _SIZE, {_RESTORE} )

input "The one item is now GRAY'd", "Sirius Publishing, Inc." ;

enablemenuitem( nHandle, 4, __POSITION + __ENABLED)
enablemenuitem( nHandle, 2, __POSITION + __ENABLED)

setsys(_SIZE, {_MINIMIZE} )
setsys(_SIZE, {_RESTORE} )

input "Now it's turned back", "Sirius Publishing, Inc." ;

'* End of File: GrayMenu.rlz
```

Q: How can someone tell what version of Realizer they have?

A: Try running the following lines of code:

```
logselect( _PRINTLOG )
logcontrol( _SHOW )
print qsys( _VERSION )
```

Epilog

This has been a very exciting book to write. It was my first departure from my core language in more than ten years. However, in looking at an ever-expanding world of possibilities, I discovered that power and possibilities are not limited to the implementation of a language, but can reside in many other noncommerical entities. Mostly, I've been driven by the desire to get the computer to "do something." That desire knows not the syntax of a language, the marketing muscle of a company, or even the name of a particular computer. The issue of "the something" starts with an idea or a need from a client. That need or idea is the seedling that needs time to develop and grow. For me, the added task of learning the language and the philosophy behind it has been unexpectedly exciting.

There is much more to the Realizer language that could not be covered in this first book. The issues of working with the scheduler or with the communication ports require extensive chapters of their own. Topics like ODBC, VBXs, database and indexing control, custom controls, complex user-defined data types, file manipulation, and more Windows API calls all need to be explored further. I hope this means that there will be a more advanced book on Realizer in the future. There are certainly enough materials and need for information to warrant such a book.

The BASIC language has been in computing circles for quite some time, and in these times of rapid change and invention, that is an accomplishment. I had to shift my focus and my need to be in total control. I had to learn a new syntax. I had to rediscover what I had, in other languages, taken for granted. However, there was one underlying discovery that transcended everything else. Even though there were many "new" things to consider, there were many old and familiar themes. Code structures seemed to have the same flair. Problem solving seemed to take the same direction. Resources for solutions seemed abundant, which only intensified the creative juices that bubbled up in the spirit of programming. I have often said that programming is more of an art than a science—that when all is said and done, the need to create is paramount.

Realizer is a great tool. The products and services that can be created with it are astounding. The only limitation is that found within oneself, awaiting the burning embers of an idea to flame into a raging bonfire of creativity. If you encounter problems along the way, look not to the language for "the" solution, but look to yourself, your thinking process, and your desire to beat the machine... the beast. The programmer's world is one of increasing possibilities, and creative thought demands that each of us look beyond the traditions of the past to new platforms of possibilities. **Realize** your potential by expanding and taking a leap of faith. You will find, as I did, the excitement of the future!

Appendix

Libraries, Add-On Products, and Third-Party Services

The Realizer language is emerging as a formidable language, complete with a third party to support it. Below is a list of known services and products available for Realizer 2.0a and higher.

Education and Technical Services

> **Sirius Press, Inc.**
> 564 Mission Street - Suite 343
> San Francisco, CA 94105
> 1-800-4-SIRIUS
> Contact: Essor Maso

Source code disk for *Straley's Programming in CA-Realizer* — The source code disk for this book includes technical support via fax and/or CompuServe, example programs, help files, and additional documentation. Also includes a special upgrade price for new versions of Realizer.

Advanced Programming in CA-Realizer — The follow-up book to this edition includes many useful examples for building front-end utilities as well as drag & drop possibilities, data communications, custom controls, and integration with CA-Visual Objects, CA-Visual Express, and other products in the CA product line.

CAR and Programmer Magazine™ — This monthly magazine for Realizer programmers contains current tricks and tips, hints, technical support issues, new products, and up-to-minute information on the expanding Realizer market.

Add-On Libraries

Sirius Press, Inc.
564 Mission Street - Suite 343
San Francisco, CA 94105
1-800-4-SIRIUS
Contact: Essor Maso

CARTools™ — A software library of tools, .DLL files, source code files, example programs, documentation, source code documentor, and support services that show how Realizer can connect to CA-Clipper and Xbase database files (.DBF) and indexes. All files come with the Steve Straley seal of approval.

Databases

Coromandel Industries, Inc.
70-15 Austin Street, Third Floor
Forest Hills, NY 11375
(800) 535-3267
Contact: Narayan Laksham

ObjecTrieve — A powerful data manager that provides ISAM support and allows Realizer applications to store Binary Large Objects and ASCII data. Users can store bitmaps, images, rule sets, or any large data stream and retrieve them, using attributes. It also provides support for multiple variable-length fields in the same record, container file support, unlimited index support, transactions, and locking.

Integra SQL A powerful SQL database DLL for Realizer, supporting SQL calls, Microsoft SQL Server–compatible calls, and DDE. Developers can build a wide variety of applications ranging from corporatewide business solutions to specific vertical-market products.

ETN Corporation
RD4 Box 659
Montoursville, PA 17754
(717) 435-2202
Contact: Wynne Yoder

PowerLibW A library of functions that provide Realizer users true, native-mode I/O access to dBASE III Plus/IV- and Clipper-compatible database files. More than 90 PowerLibW functions are provided to support expressions, filters, indexes, memos, relations, multiple database and index file access, and more.

Gupta Technologies
1040 Marsh Road
Menlo Park, CA 94025
(415) 321-9500
Contact: Linda Roos

SQLBase Server An SQL database server for Realizer optimized for graphical applications, on-line transaction processing, and decision support. Its standard automatic crash recovery, password protection, on-line backup, remote monitoring, and diagnostic tools duplicate features found on minicomputer and mainframe database servers. Supports multiple users and background reporting.

> **Novell**
> 5918 West Courtyard Drive
> Austin, TX 78730
> (512) 346-8380
> Contact: Bruce McFarland

Btrieve	A complete key indexed record manager for Realizer designed for high-performance file handling and improved programming productivity. It uses b-tree indexing algorithms with extensive caching and automatic balancing to provide fast, maintenance-free operation and can be invoked with simple subroutine calls.

NetWare SQL	A high-performance relational database engine for Realizer optimized for the NetWare environment. NetWare SQL reduces LAN traffic, speeding applications and increasing LAN throughput. NetWare SQL applications can share data with Btrieve, XQL, and Xtrieve Plus.

> **Pioneer Software**
> 5540 Centerview Drive, Suite 324
> Raleigh, NC 27606
> (919) 859-2220
> Contact: Pamela Atkinson

Q+E Database Library	Allows Realizer applications easily to incorporate relational databases using a common call-level interface for most database types. With QELIB and Realizer you can create complete database applications to generate reports, build customized data-entry forms, perform batch updates, or any other database operations. Supports dBase, Paradox, Sybase, Oracle, Netware SQL, EE Database Manager, DB2, SQL Server, text files, and Excel files.

Quadbase Systems Inc.
790 Lucerne Drive, Suite 51
Sunnyvale, CA 94086
(408) 738-6989
Contact: Fred Luk

Quadbase-SQL/Win A fast and compact database engine for Realizer designed to manage large amounts of data efficiently. Up to 16 instances can be supported by the DLL. The system supports an updateable scroll cursor for interactive data browsing. SQL features are fully compliant with ANSI SQL-86 Level 2 and feature many additional extensions. Also features multi-user concurrency control, crash recovery, and transaction processing.

Raima Corporation
3245 148th Place SE
Bellevue, WA 98007
(206) 747-5570
Contact: Paul Mitchell

db_VISTA III The db_VISTA Database Management System provides powerful, flexible, high-performance capabilities for Realizer database application development. By combining the strengths of two proven database technologies, db_VISTA III gives performance and efficiency not achievable with a single model. Features fast update and retrieval almost independent of database size, efficient use of memory and disk storage, minimal data redundancy, and inherent referential integrity.

> **Sirius Press, Inc.**
> 564 Mission Street - Suite 343
> San Francisco, CA 94105
> 1-800-4-SIRIUS
> Contact: Essor Maso

CARTools™ — A library collection of tools, .DLL files, source code files, example programs, documentation, and support services that show how Realizer can connect to CA-Clipper and Xbase database files (.DBF) and indexes.

> **Software Source**
> 42808 Christy Street, Suite 222
> Fremont, CA 94538
> (510) 623-7854
> Contact: Don Wanless

VB/ISAM — A powerful Realizer extension for indexed sequential file handling (ISAM)—flexible, fast, and clean. An easy, straightforward way to read and write data file records by alphanumeric key, pre-integrated in the BASIC style. Supports variable-length keys and records, random and sequential data, range positioning, multiple record formats, very large files, and much more.

> **SQLSoft**
> 10635 NE 36th Place, Building 24, Suite B
> Kirkland, WA 98033
> (206) 822-1287
> Contact: James O'Farrell

SQL SoftLink — SQL SoftLink provides an easy-to-use DDE link between Realizer and Microsoft's SQL Server.

Connectivity/Communications

> **CNA Computer Systems Engineering, Inc.**
> P.O. Box 70248
> Bellevue, WA 98007
> (800) 235-4091
> Contact: Doug Wright

ConnX — Provides record-level communication between Realizer applications and VAX RMS files. It includes a VAX-resident file server and a PC-resident API. The file server provides complete VMS user-level security, RMS file security, RMS file-sharing support, and support of indexed, relative, and sequential files.

> **DCA**
> 1000 Alderman Drive
> Alpharetta, GA 30202
> (404) 442-4979

Crosstalk for Windows — This product enhances Realizer communications abilities by providing a broad range of terminal emulations, including VT220 and VT320, and transfer protocols, including XModem and ZModem. Includes support for network modem sharing and high-speed modems.

> **Eicon Technology Corporation**
> 2196-32nd Ave. (Lachine)
> Montreal, Quebec H8T 3H7
> Canada
> (514) 631-2592
> Contact: Alex Gostin

SNA and OSI LAN Gateways, Terminal Emulators, Multiprotocol Routers, Developer Toolkits	Eicon provides a wide variety of products for Realizer for PC and LAN connection to SNA and OSI distributed host environments. Toolkits provide entry points to various layers of the SNA and OSI protocol stacks without requiring detailed knowledge of the underlying communications protocols. The Windows-based emulators support DDE. Interfaces supported include X.25 Network Level, OSI Transport Level, SNA Function Management, SNA Path Control, APPC (LU6.2), EHLLAPI, EEHLLAPI, Presentation Space API, and a variety of proprietary interfaces.

> **FutureSoft**
> 1001 S. Dairy Ashford Rd., Suite 101
> Houston, TX 77077
> (713) 496-9400
> Contact: Marjorie Fowler

DynaComm Asynchronous 3.0Z	Provides Realizer applications with 14 terminal emulations, 7 file transfers, and LAN access.
DynaComm/Open Connect	Provides IBM 3270 and 5250 support to Realizer applications on TCP/IP LANs.

HI-Q International
1142 Pelican Bay Drive
Daytona Beach, FL 32119
(904) 756-8988
Contact: Gary Lenz

Mission Control — Communications software that provides Realizer applications with event-driven multiple simultaneous scripts, modular script library (with canned scripts), major LAN interfaces, DDE support with ad-hoc hotlinks definable by screen area (for mainframe hotlinking), database-style dialing directory, learn mode, and major terminal emulations.

MicroHelp, Inc.
4636 Huntridge Drive
Roswell, GA 30075
(404) 552-0565
Contact: Tim O'Pry

MicroHelp Communications Library — The MicroHelp Communications library for Realizer will support up to eight ports simultaneously on PS/2 systems or non-PS/2s with add-in boards. Other systems are limited by the bus to two ports simultaneously. There are six different transfer protocols, including XModem, YModem, and ZModem. The TTY windowing routines allow you to have a separate terminal window for each open COM port. All scrolling and word wrap is handled automatically by the routines. Additional routines provide automatic data filtering.

> **Saros Corporation**
> 700 Plaza Center Building
> 10900 NE 8th Street
> Bellevue, WA 98004
> (206) 646-1066
> Contact: Rod Hoffman

Saros Mezzanine A document engine for Realizer that organizes, manages, and provides relational access to unstructured data (such as text, spreadsheets, scanned images, and presentation graphics). Mezzanine acts as a platform for integrated PC LAN-based solutions by providing network independent storage management and retrieval capabilities across multiple disks and/or servers.

Data Acquisition

> **National Instruments**
> 6504 Bridge Point Parkway
> Austin, TX 78730-5039
> (800) 433-3488
> Contact: Laura Golla

NI-488.2 Windows National Instruments NI-488.2 Windows software adds IEEE-488 instrument control to Realizer. This software is shipped free of charge with the IEEE-488.2 AT-GPIB, GPIB-PCII/IIA, MC-GPIB, and GD-DPIB hardware interface kits. NI-488.2 Windows and GPIB hardware transform a PC or PS/2 into a full-function IEEE-488.2 Controller, which can be used to control a wide variety of IEEE-488 instruments. The GPIB DLL for Realizer is available. A C interface is currently available.

> **Scientific Software Tools, Inc.**
> Penn State Technology Development Center
> 30 E. Swedesford Road
> Malvern, PA 19355
> (215) 889-1354
> Contact: Elise C. Furman

DriverLINX for Realizer

The DriverLINX series for Realizer are real-time, multitasking, data-acquisition drivers for third-party, high-speed analog and digital I/O boards. DriverLINX for Realizer provides scientists and engineers who use data-acquisition hardware with a unique solution for building sophisticated data-acquisition applications. Users can choose from over 100 functions for creating foreground and background tasks to perform analog input and output, digital input and output, time and frequency measurement, event counting, pulse output, and period measurements. These functions implement the most common data-acquisition tasks without sacrificing the high-speed data-acquisition capabilities of the hardware. Supports hardware from Keithley Metrabyte, Data Translation, Advantech, Computer Boards, Scientific Solutions, and ADAC.

Graphics

> **Adonis Corporation**
> 12310 NE 8th Street
> Bellevue, WA 98005
> (800) 234-9497
> Contact: Paul Travis

Clip-Art Window Shopper

An on-line service that provides access to 20,000 clip art images for inclusion in Realizer programs.

> **The Crossley Group, Inc.**
> PO Box 921759
> Norcross, GA 30092
> (404) 751-3703
> Contact: Jim Crossley

The Developer's Business Graphics Toolkit

A toolkit for Realizer that helps application developers integrate two- and three-dimensional business graphics into their application programs. Data can be displayed in real-time applications without repainting the graphic chart. Hot-spot resolution, y- and z-axis manual and automatic scaling for positive and negative data, x-axis application-specific elements, and programmer-defined string and floating point values are supported.

> **ETN Corporation**
> RD4 Box 659
> Montoursville, PA 17754
> (717) 435-2202
> Contact: Wynne Yoder

PowerShoW

PowerShoW functions allow Realizer applications to retrieve, manipulate, display, and manage DIB, TIFF, and TARGA images. It adds complete graphical image retrieval and display capabilities, including colorization, zoom-in/zoom-out, and dynamic image compression.

Libraries, Add-On Products, and Third-Party Services

> **WISE Software**
> Seelandstr. 3
> 2400 Lubeck 14
> Germany
> (49) 451-3909-413
> Contact: Werner Knauss

Z-PHIGS for MS-Windows Provides a library of over 300 functions for creating and displaying three-dimensional graphics using the PHIGS imaging standard. Includes 3-D picking and cursoring, Phong and Gouraud shading, transparency, texture mapping, hidden surface removal, and support for non-rational B-Splines and multiple light sources.

Multimedia

> **American Caribbean Trading, Inc.**
> O'Neill Street #113
> Hato Rey, Puerto Rico 00918
> (809) 756-7280
> Contact: Rolando E. Cruz Marshall

The Animator 1.0 Allows the creation and maintenance of animation sequences being developed with Realizer. You can position the animation control within forms created by FormDev, control the animation speed and direction, preview the animation sequence, and create sequence files for use with Realizer's animation commands. Includes a large set of bitmap sequence files.

> **Aristosoft**
> 6920 Coal Center Parkway
> Pleasanton, CA 94566
> (415) 426-5571
> Contact: Ernest Priestly

Wired for Sound   Adds Mac-like sound capability to Realizer. Using the internal PC speaker, it allows users to attach sounds to specific messages in dialog boxes and alert boxes (and upon sign-on and exit). Users can personalize their desktops with over 50 sound effects and voices, including a talking clock.

> **VideoLogic, Inc.**
> 245 First Street
> Cambridge, MA 02142
> (617) 494-0530
> Contact: Karyn Scott

MIC System Software, DVA-4000/ISA, DVA-4000/MCA   MIC System software and development tools, in conjunction with DVA-4000 full-motion video adapters, allow Realizer applications to incorporate full-motion video.

> **Videomail, Inc.**
> 568-4 Weddell Drive
> Sunnyvale, CA 94089
> (408) 747-0223
> Contact: David Moore

VMC-1E, VMC-1J, VMC-2, VMC-2J   Videomail's software and hardware allow Realizer applications to incorporate full-motion video. Features include zoom, freeze, save (TIFF, TARGA, YUV, JPEG, BMP, etc.), display, chroma key, and full video control. The hardware and software are auto-sensing for NTSC and PAL. Live video can play in a window without detracting from other Windows applications.

> **Voyetra Technologies**
> 333 Fifth Avenue
> Pelham, NY 10803
> (914) 738-4500
> Contact: Carmine J. Bonanno

Voyetra Multimedia Lite for Windows — A set of audio DLLs that add digital audio and MIDI playback to Realizer applications. Includes drivers for every major PC sound platform, including Sound Blaster and Sound Blaster Pro, MediaVision Pro Audio Spectrum, ATI VGAudio FX and Audio FX, IBM PS/1 audio adapter, as well as other MIDI and digital audio cards.

Voyetra MusiClips MIDI song files — Includes over 150 songs in MIDI format that can be incorporated into Realizer applications, using Multimedia Lite.

Other

> **Sirius Press, Inc.**
> 564 Mission Street - Suite 343
> San Francisco, CA 94105
> 1-800-4-SIRIUS
> Contact: Essor Maso

CARTools™ — A library collection of tools, .DLL files, source code files, example programs, documentation, source code documentor, and support services that show how Realizer can connect to CA-Clipper and Xbase database files (.DBF) and indexes. All files come with the Steve Straley seal of approval.

Symbologic Corporation
15379 NE 90th Street
Redmond, WA 98052
(206) 881-3938
Contact: Craig Chelius

Symbologic Adept 2.0   Symbologic Adept 2.0 adds interactive expert-system design to Realizer applications, using a simple DDE interface. Adept allows engineers, managers, trainers, and developers to create expert-system applications by creating and connecting visual objects called nodes. Nodes can display customized screens, access external functions, or call procedures. Adept provides an innovative approach to expert-system design that avoids the headache of writing hundreds of if/then rules.

Index

& (ampersand), 49, 63, 75, 79
' (apostrophe), 48, 385
\ (backslash), 16
, (comma), 16, 95, 156, 218
{ } (curly brackets), 119
... (ellipsis), 76
= (equal sign), 29, 114, 552
( ) (parentheses), 30, 104–6, 119
. (period), 152
; (semicolon), 95, 106, 218
[ ] (square brackets), 118–19
_ (underscore), 27, 44

A

aAnother, 128
aBaseArray, 131, 133–34, 137, 140, 144
aBoxes[ ], 557
aBytes, 125
Accelerator keys, 47, 96
   adding, 62–63
   forms and, 212
aData[ ], 424, 428, 429, 430, 552
aDaysOfWeek, 118–19, 120, 124
AddData( ), 313, 511
ADD_DATE, 113
AddMenu( ), 442–44, 445
AddRecord( ), 153, 155
ADel( ), 136–37
Adonis Corporation, 584–85
_ADVISE, 524–27, 529

aFebruary[ ], 359, 360, 361
aFields[ ], 435
aFirstArray, 131
After button, 73, 75, 77, 78
aGrid, 146
aGroups[ ], 363, 364
AIns( ), 136–38
aIntern, 128, 129
aJanuary( ), 359
aLabels[ ], 349, 509
ALIAS, 540
aLine[ ], 384–85, 390
_ALL, 53, 144, 250, 569
_ALLFORMATS, 519
_ALPHA, 23–24, 26, 380, 534
_ALPHAFORMAT, 264
aMarch[ ], 361
aMatrix, 147, 148
aMenuIDStack[ ], 444, 445
aMenuRoot[ ], 445
American Caribbean Trading, 586
aMonthArray, 133, 134
ampersand (&), 49, 63, 75, 79
aNames[ ], 342, 343
AND operator, 30–31
aNew, 147, 148
aNewArray, 128
aNewDays, 123
aNewOne, 128
aNewValue, 146
_ANIMATE, 492

ANIMATECELLS( ), 494
ANIMATECONTROL( ), 494
Animate.rlz, 492–94, 518
Animator, 491–94, 586
ANSI (command), 460
aParams, 52, 55, 257, 262, 268, 280, 287, 315, 319, 338, 353, 354, 358
API (Application Programming Interface), 538–65, 568–69
   calls, getting information on, 570
   complex calls, 562–65
   graying menu items and, 442, 572–73
   messages and, 553–57, 559, 561
   using, overview of, 543–47
aPositions[ ], 428
apostrophe, 48, 385
aReturn[ ], 559
Aristosoft, 587
_ARRAY, 23–24
Array1.rlz, 121–22
Array2a.rlz, 126–29
Array3.rlz, 130–35
Array4.rlz, 132–33
Array5.rlz, 138–40
Array5a.rlz, 136–37
Array6.rlz, 138–43
Array6a.rlz, 140, 144
Array data type, 13–14, 135

Index

Array fixed data type, 13–14
Arrays, 118–49
  creating (declaring), 119–25
  deleting elements in, 135–38
  finding elements in, 138–44
  functions returning, 126–30
  inserting elements in, 135–38
  menu-building and, 52
  multi-dimensional, 118–19, 145–49
  shifting elements in, 135–38
  sorting elements in, 138–44
AS, 540
aSales[ ], 366, 368
ASC( ), 403–6, 409, 413
ASCII code, 29, 195, 201, 319, 321, 373
  carriage return/line feed (CR/LF) combination, 373, 375
  end-of-file markers and, 385
  RTF files and, 460
  string parsing and, 385, 403–6, 408–9, 413–14
aSecondArray, 131
ASeek( ), 144
ASort( ), 140–43
AssignNamesWine( ), 315
aStrings, 125
aStuff, 152, 157
ASum( ), 410, 413
ATN( ), 27–28
Attached( ), 441, 442, 555, 564
aValues[ ], 335, 338, 340, 342–43, 356–57, 358, 363, 441
aVar, 383
aWineries, 153
aWords[ ], 390

B

_BACKGROUND, 163, 168, 277, 555
Background button, 292
backslash (\), double (\\), 16
BASIC, 375, 565
Basic Color palette, 181
BEFORE button, 75, 77, 79

BIN$( ), 406, 408, 409
Binary notation, 12–13
BINTONUM( ), 406, 409
_BITMAP, 174, 187
_BITMAPBUTTON, 244, 263, 268, 272, 275, 277–78
Bitmap images, 170–74, 184–87. See also .BMP (bitmapped) files
  OLE objects as, 568
  option buttons and, 244–47, 296–97
  toolbars and, 263–64, 268, 269, 271
_BLUE, 424, 555
.BMP (bitmapped) files, 414–17. See also Bitmap images
  the animator and, 491–94
  help and, 458, 466, 478
BMROOT, 479
Board1.rlz, 325–26
Board3.rlz, 327
Board4.rlz, 333–34
BOARDCONTROL( ), 328–29, 333
BOARDNEW( ), 323–27, 362
Boards, 322–34
  creating, 323–26
  modeless, 329–34
BOARDSETPROC( ), 329, 330
BoardTest( ), 329, 330
BOARDUPDATE( ), 331–32, 333
_BOLD, 173, 179
_BORDERLESS, 159, 160, 263, 269, 277, 282
_BOTTOM, 167, 169, 212, 257, 280
_BOTTOMTITLE, 346, 347
BOX data type, 556
brackets, 118–19
\BRDRB, 469
Breakpoints option, 47
BrowseDB( ), 507, 508
Browsing, 462, 503–10
Btrieve, 577
BuildStructure( ), 153
_BUTTON, 351–53, 441–42, 507, 561

Buttons, option, 244–47, 296–97
Buttons.bmp, 244, 246, 296
Byte data type, 8, 135

C

C (high-level language), 14, 31, 371
CA-Clipper, 26–27, 31
Call Tree window, 12
CallSirius( ), 430
CAPS LOCK key, 561–62
_CAPTION, 179, 182, 193, 201, 293–94, 295, 317
_CAPTIONCENTER, 167, 173, 175, 423
_CAPTIONLEFT, 167, 193, 196, 296, 317, 320, 387
_CAPTIONRIGHT, 167, 211–12, 295, 296, 314, 342, 423
CA-RET( ), 456
CARTools: A DLL Library for Realizer, 136, 144, 216, 374, 377, 382, 385, 389, 409, 435, 446, 502, 543, 548, 565, 575, 589
CASE, 31, 95, 96, 268, 487, 508
_CASESENSITIVE, 264
CEIL( ), 358
Cellar Rack Designer, 77–79
_CENTER, 212, 295
_CENTURYSPLIT, 264
\CF, 468
_CHANGE, 250, 316, 369
Char data type, 8, 17
Chart1.rlz, 334–42
Chart2.rlz, 337–38, 341
Chart3.rlz, 338–39
Chart4.rlz, 338
Chart5.rlz, 340
Chart6.rlz, 341
Chart7.rlz, 341
Chart8.rlz, 342
Chart9.rlz, 344
Chart10.rlz, 344, 351
Chart11.rlz, 345
Chart12.rlz, 347–49
Chart13.rlz, 350–51, 358–59

Index

Chart14.rlz, 351
Chart17.rlz, 356
Chart19.rlz, 360–61
CHARTBAR( ), 335, 338–39
CHARTCONTROL( ), 336, 349, 352, 454
CHARTCONTROLKEY( ), 344, 350
CHARTCONTROLPANE( ), 349
CHARTLINE( ), 340, 341
CHARTMARK( ), 341
CHARTNEW( ), 335, 342, 343, 362
CHARTPIE( ), 335, 342
CHARTQPTINFO( ), 359–61
CHARTQUNIQUE( ), 342
charts, 334–61
   adding text to, 342–47
   attaching procedures to, 353–61
   controlling colors in, 344–45, 346
   displaying multiple, 347–51
   printing, 351–53
   setting titles for, 346–47
CHARTSELECT( ), 342, 343
CHARTSELECTPANE( ), 349, 350
CHARTSETCOLOR( ), 344–45, 346
CHARTSETFONT( ), 345–46, 347
CHARTSETKEY( ), 350
CHARTSETPROC( ), 353–54, 357
CHARTSETTITLE( ), 346
CHARTSETXGRID( ), 351
CHARTTEXT( ), 349
CHARTUPDATE( ), 338, 340, 341, 361
_CHECK, 95, 96, 106
_CHECKBOX, 204, 206
Check marks, 95–96
CHR$( ), 319, 364, 373, 403–6, 408, 414, 439, 552
CLEAR, 13, 16, 22–23, 28, 422–23
ClearConstant( ), 144

ClearMenus( ), 36, 51, 53, 60, 63, 94–95
_CLICK, 250, 257, 330, 358
Client1.rlz, 521–23
Client2.rlz, 523
Client3.rlz, 524, 526
Client4.rlz, 527
Client5.rlz, 531–33
ClientAttached( ), 527, 533, 535
Clip art, 184–85, 585
Clip-Art Window Shopper, 585
Clipboard, 288, 289
CLIPCURSOR( ), 564
Clipper, 216, 315, 384
   add-on function libraries, 418
   coding conventions, 44
   file manipulation and, 371, 373
   VALTYPE( ), 434
_CLOSE, 159, 278, 282, 314, 316, 338, 386, 424, 528, 529, 535
CLOSE button, 83
CloseLog( ), 284
_CMDLINE, 264
CNA Computer Systems Engineering, 580
cName, 16
Code button, 82, 300
Coding conventions, for data types, 7–8, 14
Coding standards, used in this book, 44
_COLBUTTON, 368
Color
   charts and, 344–45, 346
   forms and, 162–63, 180–83, 186, 277–78, 292–93, 294
   help files and, 468–73
   sheets and, 363–68
_COLRANGE, 368, 509
Combo boxes, 179
_COMBOLIST, 296
COMMDLG.DLL, 539
Comma (,), 16, 95, 156, 218
Comments, menu-building and, 50, 58
Communications services, 580–83

COMPRESS, 459, 460
Concatenation, 131–34
Confirmation dialog boxes, 81
Connectivity services, 580–83
ConnX, 580
CONST, 27–28
Constant.rlz, 27–28
Constants, 4, 26–28
   internal, 97
   menu-building and, 95
   modifiers and, 107–9, 113
   values of, used to define more constants, 116
_CONTEXENTER, 160
_CONTROLHELD, 251, 354
Conversion, data, 410–14
   of files, 414–17
   of numbers to string representations, 567
Corel Draw, 170, 183, 244, 269–70, 491–92
Coromandel Industries, 576
Count( ), 39
cPassword, 319–21
CR/LF (carriage return/line feed) combination, 373, 375
Crossley Group, 585
Crosstalk for Windows, 581–82
cString, 283, 284
_CTPOS_LEFT, 349
CTRL_HOME, 58
CTRL_INS, 58
CUA (Common User Access) menu types, 47, 73
Curly brackets ({}), 119
_CUSTOM, 250, 316
_CUSTOMLP, 251, 354
_CUSTOMNOW, 250, 316
_CUSTOMWP, 251, 354
CVI( ), 414, 556
CVI$( ), 559

D

_DARKPURPLE, 346, 365
_DATA, 529, 530, 534

Index

Data. *See also* Data type(s)
  acquisition, software for, 583–84
  conversion, 410–17, 567
  encryption, 403–9
  -entry screens, 192, 207–18, 262–72, 290–317
Database(s), 145, 192. *See also* .DBF (database) files
  browsing, 503–10
  data types and, 13, 14
  importing/exporting data and, 495–503
  records, 149–52, 510–12
  software, list of, 575–80
DataEntry( ), 199–201, 204, 206, 208–10, 217, 219–21, 223–24, 234–35, 256–58
DataTools( ), 268, 269
DataType( ), 434
Data type(s). *See also* specific data types
  coding conventions for, 7–8, 14
  complex, 4, 13–17
  declaring, 14–17
  "logical," as nonexistent, 106
  meta symbols for, 8, 14
  modifiers and, 108
  simple, 4–13
  weak vs. strong typing and, 15
DATE$( ), 113, 449, 453
_DATEFORMAT, 264
_DATELINE, 23–24, 375
DateTime data type, 7, 12, 27, 135, 149–50
Date-Time Table template, 451–52
dBASE, 281
_DBF, 495
.DBF (database) files, 417, 509, 575. *See also* Database(s)
  file manipulation and, 371, 373
  importing/exporting data and, 495–503
DBUPLUS.EXE, 499
db_VISTA III, 579
DCA (company), 581–82
Dcanter.rlz, 457–58

DDE (Dynamic Data Exchange), 456, 491, 516–37
  client applications, 527–37
  server applications, 524–26
DDECONTROL( ), 525–34
DDENEW( ), 518–22
DDEQ( ), 520–23, 527
DDEQUNIQUE, 519, 520, 524
DDESELECT( ), 521
DDESETPROC( ), 523–24, 526, 527, 529
Debug window, 3, 9, 11–12, 17, 25, 27, 104
  arrays and, 132–33
  DLLs and, 539
  forms and, 161, 163, 171, 253, 273
  menu-building and, 45–46, 48, 50, 55
  modifiers and, 109
  passing parameters and, 100, 101
DecanterMenuProc( ), 95
Decanter.rfm, 82–84
Decanter.rlz, 85, 89–90, 95, 177, 304, 313
DECREMENT, 116, 117
Decrypt( ), 405, 408, 409, 414
_DEFAULT, 172, 173, 190, 203, 328, 379
Default Object Color radio button, 183
_DEFBUTTON, 212
_DEFINED, 23–24, 26, 128, 333, 444
DELETE button, 75, 79, 81
deleting
  elements in arrays, 135–38
  items from menus, 75, 79, 81
Developer's Business Graphics Toolkit, 585
Developer Toolkits, 581
DFuncs.rlz, 313
Dialog boxes
  definition of, 96
  standard file, 56–57
_DIGITALCLOCK, 212, 277

DIM, 15, 18, 20, 22, 26, 39, 121, 125, 127–29
Directories, moving menus to, 89
DispExam.rlz, 420–22
DisplayBox( ), 382, 385–87, 420–23, 424
DisplayBoxClose( ), 385, 386, 420, 422
Display boxes, 382, 385–87, 419–23
DisplayMake( ), 387, 422
DispText( ), 283
Dll1.rlz, 540–42
Dll2.rlz, 547
Dll3.rlz, 548–52
Dll4.rlz, 554–55, 561
Dll5.rlz, 559–61
Dll7.rlz, 562–63
DLLs (Dynamic Link Libraries), 538–56, 565, 575. *See also* CARTools: A DLL Library for Realizer
  advantages/disadvantages of, 539
  DOS and, 538
  using, 539–43
DLogo.rlz, 176–77
Dmenu.rlz, 89–94
DO( ), 449
DOS (Disk Operating System)
  DDE and, 518
  DLLs and, 538
  environmental strings, 548, 552–53
  File Handles, 49
  help files and, 457, 468, 469
  program editors, 89
DosDiskFreeSpace( ), 542
Double data type, 27, 135
DOWN_ARROW, 202
_DRAGFORM, 251, 354
_DRAGITEM, 251, 354
_DRAGNDROP, 250, 316
DriverLINX for Realizer, 584
Drop-down boxes, height of, 568
_DROPDOWNCOMBO, 203, 204

Index

_DROPDOWNLIST, 202, 203, 223, 262, 296, 317
_DROPDOWNLISTBOX, 204
DToS( ), 436, 439, 453
DWineDat.rlz , 315
Dword data type, 8, 135
DynaComm, 581–82

E

EditLog( ), 286–87
Edit Menu dialog box, 81
editor, source code, 2–3, 8–12, 25
EditTastedLog( ), 314
Education services, 574–75
Eicon Technology Corporation, 581
Ellipsis (...), 76
ELSE, 509
Empty( ), 223, 236, 287, 385, 387
Encrypt( ), 405, 408, 409, 413
Encryption, 403–9, 413
END FUNC, 38
End-of-file markers, 373, 385
END PROC, 35–36, 50, 53, 258
END SELECT, 53
ENDVALID( ), 123–25, 128
EnterTastedLog( ), 314
EnterText( ), 286
Equal sign (=), 29, 114, 552
EQV operator, 30–31
ERF, 483
ERL, 483
ERR, 481–88
_ERR_Control, 488
Error1.rlz, 479–80
Error2.rlz, 482–83
Error3.rlz, 483
Error4.rlz, 483–85
Error5.rlz, 486–87
Error6.rlz, 488–90
Error(s), 447, 479–90. *See also* Error Log window
 altering variables and, 20–21
 appending records and, 512
 arrays and, 128–29
 clearing variables and, 22
 data-entry screens and, 192

forms and, 192, 207, 225
ON ERROR GOTO and, 479–83, 488–89
passing parameters and, 100, 102
reserved words and, 225
tables, 434–35
"Unable to Load Program," 539
variable declarations and, 16–17
_ERRORLOG, 264, 287
Error Log window, 17, 21, 100–101, 281
 API calls and, 545
 arrays and, 125, 128
ErrorTable( ), 434–35
_ERR_TypeMismatch, 488
ETN Corporation, 576, 585
Event-driven programming, 252–53
_EXECUTE, 456, 528, 533, 534
EXECUTE, 423, 430, 431, 435, 438, 439, 503–7
.EXE (executable) files, 128, 538
 building, 66–69
 installing, 69–71
_EXISTS, 375, 502, 507, 522, 527
EXIT LOOP, 34, 320
EXIT MACRO, 488
Exit option, 49–50, 52, 55, 62
EXIT PROC, 36, 37
EXIT PROGRAM, 53, 70, 485
EXIT SYSTEM, 70, 96
EXIT WHILE, 218
_EXPORT, 512
Exporting data, 495–503
Expressions, 30, 104–6
EXTERNAL, 442, 495, 538–65, 567–68

F

Families, 149, 156–57
 help files and, 461
 importing/exporting data and, 496–97, 500, 507, 512–13
 replacing elements of, 430–39

_FAMILY, 23–24
Family data type, 13–14, 135
Family1.rlz, 156–57
fAmount, 16
FamRecs.rlz, 431–32
fData, 434, 495–98, 500, 502, 507–8, 511, 512
fData.InStock, 206
fData1, 332–34
fDisplay.member, 324–25, 327
fDisplay.title, 327
.FDV files, 291
Fever bars. *See* Gauges
FExam1.rlz, 497–98, 502–3
FExam2.rlz, 500–502, 511
FExam3.rlz, 503–7
FExam4.rlz, 510–12
FExam5.rlz, 515–16
fFile, 500
FHeader, 500, 507, 509
fIdMarker, 107
_FIELD, 163, 181, 183, 277
Field button, 292
fields, modeless data-entry, 192
_FILE*, 371
FileCreate( ), 374, 375
FILEDB( ), 495–97, 500, 502, 503, 509–12
FileExists( ), 374, 375
FILEEXPORT( ), 512–16
File extensions
 .BMP, 244
 .DLL, 539
 .HPJ, 458
 .ICO, 68
 .RLZ, 48, 56–57, 67
 .TMP, 384
File handles, 49, 371
FILEIMPORT( ), 265, 512–16
FILEMAKENAME( ), 384, 385
File manipulation, 371–417
 building temporary files, 383–403
 converting data, 410–17
 encryption and, 403–9
 low-level file control, 371–75
 writing files, 410–14
_FILEMENU, 51

File menu, 25, 55–56, 62, 75, 83, 187, 284
   three options on, 49–50
FILEOPEN( ), 371, 374, 375, 384, 385
File option, 47, 50, 59, 69, 75, 76, 83
FILEQ( ), 375, 502, 507
FILEQUNIQUE( ), 371
FILEREAD( ), 373, 375, 380, 384, 432
FILEWRITE( ), 375, 385, 413, 431, 432
FILEXPORT( ), 265
fInfo, 495, 513, 514
fInfo.fields, 496, 497
FirstPass( ), 41
fItems, 225, 235
fItems.winery, 234
Fixed-string data type, 8
Flag, notify style, 570
Float-double data type, 8
Floating data type, 7, 8
FLOOR( ), 358
fModifier, 108, 113
fObjs.Button_Accept, 317
fObjs.Get_Quantity, 317
fObjs.Get_Size, 317
fObjs.Get_WineType, 317
Font(s), 3, 173–80, 461, 539
   in the CA-Realizer editor, changing, 566–67
   charts and, 345–47
   sheets and, 364, 366
FONTNEW( ), 173, 179–80, 346, 364
FONTQUNIQUE( ), 173
FONTSELECT( ), 281
Footnotes, 462–63, 466, 478
FOPEN( ), 371
Form1.rlz, 161, 164–65, 167
Form2.rlz, 163, 168–69
Form3.rlz, 171–72
Form4.rlz, 175–77
Form5.rlz, 187, 188–90
Form6.rlz, 195
Form7.rlz, 198–99
Form8.rlz, 207, 219
Form9.rlz, 220–21
Form9a.rlz, 221–23

Form9b.rlz, 223, 226–33
Form10.rlz, 237–41
Form11.rlz, 242–44, 253–56
Form12.rlz, 245
Form13.rlz, 246–47
Form14.rlz, 253, 257
Form15.rlz, 258–62
Form(s), 249–321. *See also* FormDev
   building data-entry screens and, 191–207
   color and, 162–63, 180–83, 186, 277–78, 292–93, 294
   data-entry, 158–248
   fonts and, 173–76, 179–80
   logs and, 281–90
   MDI (multiple document interface), 263–73, 314
   passwords and, 317–21
   pixel settings and, 169–70, 173–74, 183, 195–96, 203, 211–12, 267, 269–74
   pop-up, 277–81
   radio buttons and, 241–47
   warning messages and, 235–41
_FORMAT, 368
FormBrowse( ), 507, 508
FORMCONTROL( ), 161, 170, 197, 205, 217, 267, 271, 277, 319, 336, 352
FormDev, 207, 224–25, 290–98, 321
   building menus with, 45–46, 50, 71–76
   changing colors with, 292–93, 294
   generating source code and, 297, 300–313
   help for, 76
   radio buttons and, 241
FORMMODIFYOBJECT( ), 168–69, 234, 236, 258, 262, 317, 319–20, 441–42
FORMNEW( ), 159–61, 163, 178, 191, 193, 263, 266, 271, 277–78, 281, 319, 569
_FORMNUM, 251, 257, 287, 354
FORMQ( ), 197, 428, 546, 547

FORMQOBJECT( ), 197, 199, 206, 207
FORMQSTR( ), 206, 216, 245, 262, 338
FORMQSTRING( ), 197
FORMQUNIQUE( ), 178, 319
FORMSELECT( ), 159, 161, 206, 257, 268, 281, 338, 442
FORMSET( ), 250
FORMSETCOLOR( ), 163, 167–68, 183
FORMSETOBJECT( ), 166–67, 169, 172, 190, 204, 224–25, 245, 268–69, 272, 508
FORMSETPROC( ), 249–50, 257, 258, 262, 267, 317, 507
FormValue( ), 243
FORMWAIT( ), 196, 205, 207, 210–11, 213, 214, 234, 236, 237, 249, 258, 262, 320, 429
FOR...NEXT loops, 33–34, 39, 117, 123, 130–35, 165–66, 204, 206, 552–53
   the animator, 494
   errors and, 481, 482
   importing/exporting data and, 507
   reusable code and, 429, 435, 438, 445
   string parsing and, 405, 406
_FQO_VALUE, 206
_FRAME, 159, 195, 282
FREAD( ), 371, 373
fRecord1, 322–26, 330
fRecord2, 322–26
fRecord3, 322–26
fRecord4, 322–26
fRecord5, 322–26
fRecord, 200, 205, 207, 217–18, 224–25, 235, 257, 258, 313, 314
fRecord.Notes, 314
FreeSpace, 542
\FS, 464
fSays, 225
fSelected, 330, 332
fStructure, 514
fStructure.variable, 513
fStyle, 106, 107
FUNC, 539

Index

FuncAndProc( ), 391
FUNC...END FUNC, 35
FUNCNEW( ), 391
Functions
  availability of, determining, 568
  calling, 38
  generic, rules for, 420
  introduction to, 35–43
  the one-exit rule and, 37
  procedures and, comparison of, 48
  for producing reports, 448–56
  returning arrays and, 126–30
  setting up, 219–35
  template, 448–56
  wrapper, 453, 542–46, 562, 565
FutureSoft, 581
fWine, 201
fWine.bin, 439
fWine.BinNumber, 217
fWine.LotNumber, 217
fWine.Style, 201, 225
fWine.Type, 225

G

GasGauge( ), 429
Gateways, 581
GatherNext( ), 438
GatherRecord( ), 432–36, 439
GaugeBox( ), 424, 440, 442
GaugeBoxClose( ), 424, 442
Gauges, building, 423–30
GaugExam.rlz, 423–26, 440–41
GetCurrentDrive( ), 542
GETDOSENVIRONMENT( ), 552
GetDOSVars( ), 552
_GETFOCUS, 250, 258, 262, 316
GetIt( ), 128, 129
GetIt2( ), 128
GetMenu( ), 442
GETMESSAGE( ), 553–57, 559
GETs, 304, 313, 315
Go icon, 10, 17, 163
Go option, 20, 46

GOTO, 321, 389, 390
Grapes.bmp, 184
Graphics software, 584–86
_GRAY, 64, 106, 439, 442, 445, 446, 572–73
Grayed-out menu options, 63–66, 439–46, 572–73
_GROUPBOX, 173–74, 185, 191, 294
GUI (Graphical User Interface), 192, 263
Gupta Technologies, 577

H

Handles
  file, 49, 371
  selection, 185
Headers, creating standard, 47–48
HeaderSheet( ), 509
_HEAVYFRAME, 569
Height, of drop-down boxes, 568
HELP( ), 466, 473, 475
Help1.hlp, 466
Help1.txt, 465
Help2.hlp, 472
Help2.hpj, 471
Help3.txt, 477–78
Help (help files), 447, 456–79
  adding color and, 468–73
  context-sensitive help and, 473–79
  for the FormDev utility program, 76
  improving on main files, 468–69
  source files and, 460–66
  the Windows Help Compiler and, 457–59
HELPSETPROC( ), 466, 473, 475
HEX$( ), 406, 408, 409, 414
Hexadecimal notation, 12–13
HEXTONUM( ), 406, 409
_HIDE, 51, 197, 320, 386, 508
Highlighting, automatic, 571
HI-Q International, 582
_HOTCLICK, 160, 263, 269, 271, 282

Hot keys. See Accelerator keys
Hour glasses, adding, 56, 63
.HPJ (Help Project) files, 459–60, 466, 471, 478, 479
Htest1.rlz, 466–67
HTest2.rlz, 467–68, 472
Htest3.rlz, 473–75
Hungarian notation, 7, 14, 20, 44, 152
  menu-building and, 95, 96
  forms and, 199
_HWND, 546
Hypertext links, 458

I

iBoard, 323
Icofile.rlz, 414–17
.ICO (icon) files, 414–17
iCount, 42, 131
iCounter, 257, 258
iDirection, 143–44
IDLE, 144, 177, 207, 221, 287, 520, 546
iDrive, 542
IEEE floating-point standards, 7
IF command, 111, 320–21, 388–89, 480
IF...END IF loops, 32, 41, 113, 234, 434
iFont, 284
iFont1, 175
iForm, 206
iForm1, 161
iForm2, 167
iFormNumber, 219
IF statements, 31–32, 113, 213
iItem, 8
iLog, 283, 314
iMainMenu, 49
IMP operator, 30–31
_IMPORT, 499, 502
Importing/exporting data, 491, 495–503
_INACTIVE, 518, 520
INCREMENT, 116, 117
INDEX( ), 119–20, 124–25, 138
iNewLength, 320, 321
_INFO, 500, 502, 509, 511, 512

InitSession( ), 521, 523–24
INPUT, 234, 236, 243, 256, 262, 277–78, 281, 313, 317, 319–20, 330, 432, 546
  boards and, 333, 334
  charts and, 352, 358, 359
  errors and, 480, 485
  reusable code and, 432, 433, 436
  string parsing and, 377, 382, 404
INPUT_TITLE, 313
INSTR$( ), 375–78, 391
Integer data type, 7, 8, 125, 165, 556
Integra SQL, 576
Interpreters, definition of, 97
Interpretive environments, 66
_INVOKE, 251, 280, 316, 330, 354
iPassWordLength, 319, 321
iSelection, 213
_ISLOG, 546
iStart, 34, 39
_ITALICS, 173, 179
iTasted, 247
_ITEMNUM, 52, 252, 262, 287, 315, 316, 338, 354
iTemp, 34
_ITEMTYPE, 252, 354
iTextSize, 287
iUpdate, 215, 217
iValue, 99, 100
iValue1, 103
iValue2, 103, 104
iVar, 102
iVar1, 103
iVar2, 103
iVariable, 99–100
iWindowWidth, 328–29

K

\KEEPN, 465–66, 472
Krnl386.exe, 552

L

Labels, 363–65
_LANDSCAPE, 456

LBOUND( ), 123, 125
_LEFT, 167, 169, 295, 336
LEFT$( ), 41, 42, 375, 376, 385
LEN( ), 41, 319, 406
LFLUSH, 352, 454, 456, 570
Libraries. *See also* CARTools: A DLL Library for Realizer; DLLs (Dynamic Link Libraries)
  add-on, 575
  as collections of routines, 36
  MicroHelp Communications Library, 582
  Q+E Database Library, 578
_LISTBOX, 258, 263
List boxes, 97, 258, 263
_LISTFAMS, 202, 204
_LISTFILES, 202
_LISTFONTS, 202
Lists, drop-down, 56–57, 96
lLineContinue, 389, 390
LOAD button, 82
_LOADDIR, 265
LoadMenus( ), 53, 60, 63
LOCAL, 18–20, 39, 195, 219–20, 224, 234, 258, 268–69, 281, 286–87, 424, 434, 445
Log1.rlz, 282–83
Log2.rlz, 284–86
Log3.rlz, 288–89
Log4.rlz, 289–90
LOG, 542
LOGCONTROL( ), 281, 284, 286, 314, 456
LoggedDrive( ), 542–43
LOGNEW( ), 281, 287, 314, 546
LogProc( ), 288
LOGQ( ), 546
LOGQDATA( ), 281, 313, 314
LOGQSIZE( ), 281, 287
Logs, 281–90. *See also* Error Log window; Print Log window
LOGSELECT( ), 281, 287
LOGSETPROC( ), 281, 314
Long data type, 8, 27, 547–48
LOOP, 34, 249–50, 319, 320. *See also* Loops

Loops, 32–36, 39. *See also* FOR...NEXT loops; IF...END IF loops; LOOP; WHILE loops
  reusable code and, 423, 424, 429
  string parsing and, 382, 385
Lotus 1-2-3, 361
LPRINT, 454
LROWPRINT, 454
LSTRCPY( ), 548, 552
LTRIM$( ), 382

M

_MACRODIR, 265
Macros, 265, 457, 462
MainMenu( ), 50, 52, 53, 62
MakeData( ), 498–99
MakeDataEntryForm_Wine( ), 314
MakeFamily( ), 200–201, 223, 224–25
MakeForm( ), 223, 226
MakeInputItems( ), 223, 224
MakeSayItems( ), 223
Markers, end-of-file, 373, 385
Massaro, Michael, 566
MATINVERT( ), 148
MATMULTI( ), 148
Matrix1.rlz, 146–47
Matrixes, 13–14, 145–49, 155
_MAXIMIZE, 265
_MB_EXCLAMATION, 214
MDI (multiple document interface), 263–73, 314
_MEMBERS, 23–24
Memory
  arrays and, 135
  DLLs and, 540
  forms and, 183, 190
  menu-building and, 60
  POINTER( ) and, 547–53
  toolbars and, 269
  variable scoping and, 18–20
Menu2.rlz, 59–62, 64–66, 67, 94
Menu3.rlz, 442–43

Index

Menu(s), 44–97. *See also* Menu-building
  accessing, 50
  adding options to, 56–66
  bar, 47, 96
  "child," 76
  clearing, 51–52
  deleting items from, 75, 79, 81
  grayed-out options on, 63–66, 439–46, 572–73
  pull-down, 47, 49–50, 81, 97
  saving, 82, 83, 84
  separators, 62, 78–79
  trees, building, 58–59
  two types of, 47
Menu-building
  building executable files, 66–69
  building main menus, from scratch, 45–56
  installing executable files, 69–71
  using FormDev for, 45–46, 50, 71–76
MENUCONTROL( ), 50, 51
MENUDOCMD( ), 288, 289–90, 571–72
Menu Editor, 50, 71, 74, 75, 76, 83
MENUNEW( ), 49, 73, 95, 443
_MENUNUM, 52, 252, 354
MENUQ( ), 444
MENUQUNIQUE, 49
MenusChange( ), 444, 446
MENUSELECT( ), 51, 52, 281, 445
MENUSETCMD( ), 49, 62, 64, 95, 106, 107, 443, 444
MENUSETPROC( ), 50, 475
Menu Stack, 75, 77, 78, 80, 81
MESSAGEBOX( ), 213–14, 382–83, 385, 417, 482–83, 485, 488, 502, 520–22, 531, 533–34, 543, 555–56
MessageGet( ), 561
Messages, 553–56, 561. *See also* DDE (Dynamic Data Exchange); MESSAGEBOX( )
Meta symbols, 8, 14, 20, 108

MicroHelp, 582
MicroHelp Communications Library, 582
MIC System Software, 587
MID$( ), 375, 376, 403–6, 410, 413, 557, 559
_MIDDLECLICK, 250, 257, 316
_MINIMIZE, 160, 163, 164, 191, 193, 265, 282
Mission Control, 582
MKDMBF$( ), 414
MKI$( ), 410, 413, 414
MKIRead( ), 414
MKIWrite( ), 413
MKL$( ), 410, 413–14
MKS$( ), 414
MKSMBF$( ), 414
Modal systems, 192, 248, 249, 290, 298
Modeless systems, 192–93, 248, 249–62, 298, 317
Modif1.rlz, 109
Modif2.rlz, 109–11
Modif3.rlz, 111–13
Modif4.rlz, 115–16
Modifiers, 106–18
  basic format for, 113
  missing, 113–18
  rules about, 109–13
Modify Colors dialog box, 181, 183, 292–93
Modularity, 19
Mouse
  vs. accelerator keys, 47
  accessing menus and, 50, 52
  cursor, changing, 56, 63
  movement, detecting, 562–64
msgStruct, 557
_MULTILINE, 193
Multimedia software, 586–88
Multiprotocol routers, 581
MyHelpMenuProc( ), 466, 475

N

_NAME, 23–24, 41, 370, 375, 434
_NAMED, 512, 514, 515–16
Name field, 190

National Instruments, 583
nBase, 406, 409
nChart, 342, 343
nCompFont, 347
nCondition, 111
nCount, 384, 385, 389, 390, 435, 438, 481
nDirection, 445
nDispHandle, 422
nDispSize, 423
nElement, 361, 552
nEnd, 503, 507
nEnvPointer, 548
NetWare SQL, 577
NEW, 47, 48, 50, 59, 69
NewAssignment( ), 524, 526, 528, 534
NewGauge.rlz, 440–41
New option, 25, 49–50
NEXT, 34
nFile, 413
nFile1, 385
nFont2, 364
nForm, 428
nHeaderSheet, 508–9
NI-488.2 Windows, 583
nLength, 553
nLevel, 389
nLong, 343
nMessage, 526, 528
nNewXPosition, 564
nNewYPosition, 564
_NOBORDER, 193
_NOFAMILYHEADERS, 327
_NOFOOTER, 454
_NOHEADER, 353, 454
nOldPosition, 565
nOldYPosition, 565
_NOMAX, 160, 277–78, 282
_NONMDI, 160, 263, 269, 271, 277–78
_NORMAL, 64, 106, 196, 213, 439, 440, 442, 445, 446
notDeclared, 481, 483, 487, 488
Notifications, 235–41
_NOTIFY, 193, 235–36, 237, 242, 247, 249, 262, 316, 336
Notify style flag, 570
NOT operator, 30–31

602 Index

NotTaste.bmp, 246
Novell, 577
nPaneNumber, 361
nPlot, 340, 341
nPos, 428, 429, 552
nReturn, 117
nSession, 520, 524
nStart, 503, 507
nTimes, 435, 494
nTripped, 480–81, 485
_NUMDIMS, 23–24
Numeric data types, 5–6, 125, 149–50
NUMTOSTR( ), 567
nValue1, 117
nValue2, 117
nVar, 159

O

OCT$( ), 406, 408, 409, 414
Octal notation, 12–13
OCTONUM( ), 406, 409
ODBC (Open Database Connectivity), 417, 517
OLE (Object Linking and Embedding), 568
ON ERROR GOTO, 35, 479–83, 488–89
OOP (Object Oriented Programming), 168, 290
OPEN dialog window, 57
Operators, 28–31
  arrays and, 131–34
  logical, six basic, 30–31
  mathematical, 28–30
OPTION BASE, 120, 124, 125, 138, 356
_OPTIONBITMAP, 244–47
OR operator, 30–31
OS/2, 570
_OUTPUTWIDTH, 265

P

\PAGE, 478
_PALETTE, 160, 275, 277–78
Panes, 347–51

\PAR, 469
Parameters. *See also* Passing parameters
  introduction to, 35–43
  menu-building and, 52
  missing, 113–18
  rules for, 109–13
Params1.rlz, 40–41
Params2.rlz, 101
Params3.rlz, 102–3, 104
\PARD, 464–65, 466, 478
Parentheses, 30, 104–6, 119
Parse.prg, 373
Parse1.rlz, 372
Parse2.rlz, 374
Parse3.rlz, 379
Parse4.rlz, 383–403
Parse5.rlz, 387–89, 391–403
Parse6.rlz, 376, 377
Parse7.rlz, 377–78
Parse8.rlz, 403–6
Parse10.rlz, 406
Parse11.rlz, 409, 410–13
Parsing. *See* String parsing
Pass.rlz, 317
Passing parameters, 39–43
  forms and, 170, 213, 235
  by reference, 43, 98–101, 104, 438
  rules for, 109–13
  sorting arrays and, 143–44
  by value, 43, 100, 101–4
PassWordProc( ), 319, 320
Passwords, 317–321
_PEEK, 196, 237, 262
_PEEKGET, 569
period (.), 152
_PICK, 213
_PICKDRAG, 196
Pioneer Software, 578
Pixel settings, 169–70, 173–74, 183, 195–96, 203, 211–12, 267, 269–74
_PLAIN, 513–16
Pleiades Software and Training Kit, 499
POINTER( ), 547–53
Pointing systems, 49–50

_POKE, 528–34
_POPUP, 160, 280, 281
Pop-up boxes, 278–81
PopUp.rlz, 278–80
PopUpProc( ), 281
_PORTRAIT, 456
_POWDERBLUE, 181, 183, 277, 292
PowerLibW, 576
PowerShoW, 585
_PRINT, 352, 454, 456
Print2.rlz, 454–55
PRINT, 13, 19, 26, 32, 38–42, 99, 104, 108, 152, 155, 448, 452–54, 521–23, 533
  API calls and, 546
  arrays and, 123–24, 128, 133, 134, 146–47
  ASum( ) and, 413
  DDE and, 526, 527, 534
  errors and, 481–83, 487
  forms and, 192, 206–7, 218, 281, 284, 313, 314
  importing/exporting data and, 499, 502–3
  reusable code and, 439
  writing files and, 413
PRINTBEST, 265
PRINTERCONTROL( ), 456
Printing. *See also* PRINT; Print Log window
  charts, 351–53
  formatting data for, 448–56
PrintIt( ), 19, 20, 108, 109, 111, 113
_PRINTLOG, 265, 287, 480, 521–22
Print Log window, 3, 9–12, 17, 25, 27, 29, 38, 41, 104
  arrays and, 123–24, 128, 131–34, 137, 139–40, 144, 146–48
  building strings and, 439
  charts and, 357
  databases and, 512
  DDE and, 522, 526, 533
  Dll3.rlz and, 551
  errors and, 481

file manipulation and, 373
forms and, 197, 218, 281, 287
importing/exporting data and, 499
menu-building and, 45–46, 48
modifiers and, 109, 111
passing parameters and, 99, 101, 100, 103, 117–18, 117
records and, 152, 156
reusable code and, 424
string parsing and, 378, 408, 410
PrintRecord( ), 214, 223, 235
PROC, 35–36, 539
Procedures
  attaching, to charts, 353–61
  availability of, determining, 568
  attaching, to sheets, 369–70
  definition of, 97
  introduction to, 35–43
  menu-building and, 48–49
  naming, 36
  rules for using, 251
  setting up, 219–35
  terminating, 36–37
ProcessWineData( ), 315–16
PRODUCT( ), 148
Program Group window, 70–71
Program Manager, 69–71, 73, 96, 278, 457, 527
Project Builder, 67–69
Protocols. *See* DDE (Dynamic Data Exchange)
Prototyping, 540
Push buttons, 56–57, 97, 207–18

Q

\QC, 464
QDATE, 113, 449
Q+E Database Library, 578
QNOPTMODS, 114, 115, 117, 143–44, 387, 422
QNOPTPARAMS, 114
QOPTMOD( ), 114, 115
QOPTPARAM( ), 114, 405, 423, 547
Quadbase-SQL/Win, 578

Quadbase Systems, 578
QVAR( ), 23–27, 32, 41, 128, 330, 333, 370, 429, 434, 435, 444, 445, 534, 568
QVar.rlz, 24–25

R

Radio buttons, 241–47
Raima Corporation, 579
rDataSet, 155
_READ, 373
ReadFile( ), 388
_READONLY, 367, 369, 509
_REALFORMAT, 265
Realizer menu, 47, 55
Reals, 7
_RECORD, 23–24
Record1.rlz, 150–52, 157
Record2.rlz, 152–55, 157
Record data type, 13–14, 135
Records, 149–56, 191
  appending, 510–12
  groups of, 152–56
_RED, 181
REM, 48
Remarks, making, 48
_REMOVE, 64, 106
Reports, techniques for producing, 447–56
_REQUEST, 456, 524–25, 527, 529, 533
Reserved words, 225
RESET( ), 144
RESET, 53, 128, 129, 218, 485
RESETHOURGLASS( ), 63, 494
_RESTORE, 265
RESUME, 482, 483, 485
RESUME NEXT, 488
RETURN, 27, 31, 36, 38, 42, 113, 127, 129, 444
REVERSE$( ), 403–6
_RIGHT, 295, 351
RIGHT$( ), 375–77, 390
RIGHT_ARROW, 74
_RIGHTCLICK, 250, 316
_RIGHTCLICKED, 257
_RIGHTTITLE, 346, 347
_RLZM_COPYWINDOW, 288

Root windows, 566
ROUND( ), 217, 358
ROWPRINT, 133, 137, 138, 140, 448, 452
_ROWRANGE, 367, 368
.RTF (Rich Text Format) files, 457, 460, 466
RUN, 19, 38, 60, 127, 128, 140, 144, 153, 207, 221, 269
Run menu, 45–46, 62, 66–68, 177–78, 291
rWine, 152, 153, 155, 191

S

Samples directory, 57
sApplication, 521, 526
Saros Corporation, 583
Saros Mezzanine, 583
SAVE AS dialog window, 55
Saving
  forms, 187
  menus, 82, 83, 84
SAYs, 304, 315
_SCALAR, 23–24, 534
Scientific Software Tools, 584
sCommand, 428–30, 507
Scoping, 18–20
_SCREEN, 349
Screen resolution, 291
sData, 405, 406, 408, 432, 435, 437
sDisplay, 423
sDoIt, 438, 439
SecondPass( ), 41, 42
SELECT CASE, 31–33, 117, 338, 446, 555
  charts and, 343
  DDE and, 526, 534
  errors and, 487
  forms and, 213, 214, 236, 243, 257, 316
  menu-building and, 52, 53, 55, 62, 96
  modifiers and, 106–7
Selection handles, 185
Semicolon (;), 95, 106, 218
sEnvironment, 548
_SEPARATOR, 62, 265

Separator radio button, 78
Server1.rlz, 520–23
Server3.rlz, 525–26
Server4.rlz, 528
Server5.rlz, 531, 534, 536–37
_SETCOLOR, 365
SETCONTROL( ), 509
_SETFOCUS, 234, 262, 317, 423, 571
SETFORMAT( ), 366, 368, 453
SETHOURGLASS( ), 63, 494
SETPROC, 329
SETSYS( ), 264–65, 268–69, 271–73, 466, 475, 516
_SETTITLE, 569
SetWindowText( ), 545, 546
SetWindowTitle( ), 546, 547
\SF, 468–69
sFile, 502
sFileName, 385
Shadow effects, 185–86, 191
_SHEET, 507, 508
Sheet2.rlz, 366–67
SheetBrowse, 508
SHEETCONTROL( ), 364, 365, 367, 368, 383, 385, 454
SHEETCONTROLLABELS( ), 508
SHEETNEW( ), 362, 363, 366, 508, 509
Sheets, 361–70
  attaching procedures to, 369–70
  buttons and, 368–69
  color in, 365–68
  column/row restrictions for, 365–68
  headings and, 363–65
  labels and, 363–65
  string parsing and, 382–83
SHEETSELECT( ), 509
SHEETSETCOLLABELS( ), 363–64, 507, 509
SHEETUPDATE( ), 365, 508
Shell1.rlz, 517–18
SHELL, 499, 517, 518, 520, 521
_SHIFTHELD, 252, 354
_SHOW, 284, 286, 321, 337, 344, 386, 509

Show Debugger option, 9
SHOW_DATE, 108
ShowLogo( ), 176–77
SHOW_NUMBER, 108
SHOW_STRING, 108
_SIDETRACK, 328
SimpVar.rlz, 8–13
sInformation, 533, 534
SINGLE, 166
Single data type, 135
Sirius1.bmp, 494
Sirius directory, 57
Sirius Press, 570, 574, 575, 589
Sirius Software Development, 499
sItem, 42, 281
_SIZE, 159–60, 170, 250, 265, 267, 271, 277–78, 282, 284, 287, 316, 329, 330, 336, 349, 353, 369, 375, 423
_SIZEINSIDE, 265
_SIZEMDI, 264, 265, 266, 272
sLine, 373, 390, 391
sLoc, 268, 269
sMainString, 378, 379
sMessage, 488, 556
smgStruct, 559
SNA, 581
sName, 20, 21, 26, 41, 195, 197, 507, 552
Software Source, 579
Sorting, elements in arrays, 138–44
Source code editor, 2–3, 8–12, 25
Space( ), 201
Spreadsheets
  arrays and, 145
  data-entry screens and, 192
  data types and, 13, 14
SPRINT( ), 436, 448, 449, 452–55
SQLBase Server, 577
SQL Soft, 580
SQL SoftLink, 580
Square brackets ([ ]), 118–19
sReturn, 32, 41–43, 405, 552
sStatement, 435
sString, 41, 444
sString1, 413

sString2, 413
sString3, 413
Standard.exe, 542
_START, 494
STARTVALID( ), 123–25, 128
Statements, 31–35
STATNORM( ), 149
STATPERCENT( ), 149
STATRANK( ), 149
STATSORT( ), 149
STDOPEN( ), 389, 417, 454, 456, 507
STDSAVEAS( ), 417
STDTOK( ), 382
sTemp, 382
STEP, 34, 165
Step icon, 10
sText, 287
sTitle, 423, 424, 533
sTopic, 525, 526
STRDELETE$( ), 378
STRING$( ), 195, 201, 319, 321, 559
String(s). See also String parsing
  concatenation, 131–34
  literal, 101–2
  null, 127
  rules for, 29
String data types, 6–8, 12, 21, 26, 120–21, 135, 149–50, 216, 439, 558
String parsing
  building temporary files and, 383–403
  converting data and, 410–14
  encryption and, 403–6
  low-level file control and, 371–75
  overview of, 375–403
STRKEYWORD( ), 391
Strong typing, 15
STRTODATE( ), 13
STRTOK( ), 375, 378–79, 382, 390, 437
STRTONUM( ), 217, 338
_STYLE, 523
Sub Menu radio button, 79
Subranging, 131, 136
Subroutines

Index

definition of, 35, 97
  passing parameters and, 39, 98–99
SUBSTR$( ), 375, 378, 429
Subsystems, 418–46
SUM( ), 148, 410
SuperCalc, 361
sVarName, 552, 553
SVGA resolution, 291
SWAP, 21, 22
SWITCH, 31
Symbologic Adept 2.0, 589
Symbologic Corporation, 589
System menu, 284

T

\TAB, 478
_TABLET, 428, 430, 555, 564
TABLETBRUSH( ), 428
TABLETLINE( ), 564, 565
TABLETPEN( ), 428
Tasted.bmp, 246
Technical services, 574–75
Templates, 448–56
  Date-Time Table, 451–52
  Fractional Table, 451
  Numeric Table, 450
  String Table, 449–50
Terminal emulators, 581
Test1.rlz, 55–56, 58–59, 66
Test2.rlz, 58–60, 62, 66–68, 89, 94
TestChart( ), 335, 336–38, 341–42, 352, 357, 361
TestForm( ), 257, 258, 262
TestProc( ), 250, 251, 258
TestSheet( ), 380–81, 382, 383
TestThis( ), 116, 117
TestToolBar( ), 267–68, 277–78
_TEXT, 163, 197, 516
_TEXTBOX, 192–97, 201, 212, 216, 225, 262–63, 296–98, 314, 317, 319–21, 336, 338, 340–42
TextChar( ), 353

Texture, added to forms, 162–63
TheYears( ), 203–4, 223
ThisTest( ), 99, 100, 103, 104
3-D (three-dimensional) effects, 183
_TITLE, 159, 160, 191, 193, 201, 265, 277–78, 281, 282, 284, 471, 522, 533
Titles, changing, 568–69. See also _TITLE
_TO_GRAY, 446
Tool1.rlz, 266–67, 271
Tool2.rlz, 269
Tool3.rlz, 270–71
Tool4.rlz, 275–77
_TOOLBAR, 160, 263, 264, 266–69, 275, 277–78
Toolbars, 186–87, 262–72
  clip art, 184
  definition of, 97
  group boxes and, 294–95
  non-MDI forms and, 275–76
Topic tags, 458, 462
TopOfLoop, 390
_TOPTITLE, 346, 347
Transaction files, 77, 80
TRUE/FALSE values, 111, 116, 215, 243, 244, 247, 389, 390
Twips, 464–65
\TX, 465
TYPE, 150, 153, 156, 225, 557

U

UBOUND( ), 123, 125
UCASE$( ), 41, 553
_UNADVISE, 524–25, 526, 528–29
_UNCHECK, 96, 106
Underscore character (_), 27, 44
Unions, 131–34
_UPDATE, 338, 343
UpdateRecord( ), 205, 206, 213–17, 223, 235–36
User-defined types, 538, 556–61
User.exe, 543–44

_USERREALIZER, 252, 315, 355
USING, 218, 453
Utilities menu, 71
Utility window, 83

V

ValidEntries( ), 223, 234
ValidEntry( ), 234–35
VALTYPE( ), 434
Var2.rlz, 18–20
Var3a.rlz, 19–20
_VAR, 129
Variable(s), 3–28. See also specific variables
  acquiring information on, 23–26
  clearing, 17, 20–23, 28, 129
  declaring data types and, 14–17
  examples using, 8–12
  internal, 23–24, 27, 44
  names, 4–5
  scoping, 18–20
  undocumented, 569
VB/ISAM, 579
.VBX files, 570
VideoLogic, 587
Videomail, 587–88
View menu, 298
VisiCalc, 361
Visual items, building, 418–30
Visual Objects, 290, 420
VMC-1E, 588
VMC-1J, 588
VMC-2, 588
VMC-2J, 588
Voyetra Technologies, 588

W

Warning messages, 235–41
WHILE loops, 210, 213, 214, 556, 564
WHILE statements, 34
_WHITE, 351
Whole numbers, 7

Index

Windows (Microsoft). *See also*
   API (Application
   Programming Interface)
  Help Manager, 466
  Program Manager, 69–71, 73,
   96, 278, 457, 527
  standards for menus, 73
WineDatEntry( ), 315
WineList( ), 202–4, 223
Winhelp.exe, 457
Winhelp.hlp, 457
Wired for Sound, 587
WISE Software, 586
WM_LBUTTONUP, 556

Word data type, 8, 135
Word (Microsoft), 173, 192
Wrapper functions, 453, 542–46,
  562, 565
_WRITE, 373, 374

X

xBASE, 456, 495
xData, 435, 436, 438, 530,
  531, 534
XOR operator, 30–31
_XPOS, 252, 355–56, 358,
  359, 361

xReturn, 108
xValue, 429

Y

YES button, 84
_YPOS, 252, 355–56, 358,
  359, 361

Z

Zimak, Gary, 566
Z-PHIGS for MS-Windows, 586

The CARTools Library

1. .DBF-.CDX-.NDX-.NTX Support
2. Multiple Work Areas
3. Directory & file functions
4. Gas Gauges, New Tools, and MORE!
5. Over 100 Functions and Tools that add the final PUNCH to CA-Realizer!

Only...... $59.95!

U.S. Funds Only
$ 5.00 Domestic Shipping
$ 15.00 Foreign Shipping
Overnight is extra

Sirius Press, Inc.
564 Mission St
Suite 343
San Francisco CA, 94105
415-399-9857 (FAX)
76220,3620 CIS

Name _____
Address _____
City, State, Zip _____
Phone _____
Country _____
Credit Card Number __
Expiration _____

MasterCard ORDER NOW! VISA

Source Code Companion Disk Offer!

Sirius Press, Inc.

→ The Complete Source Code and sample files for the first and ONLY book on CA-Realizer! ←

→ Over 400K of source code that shows every step outlined in the definitive guide! ←

Only...... $19.95!

or include CARTools for $69.95

U.S. Funds Only $5.00 Domestic Shipping / $15.00 Foreign Shipping / Overnight is extra

---

564 Mission St
Suite 343
San Francisco CA, 94105
415-399-9810
415-399-9857 (FAX)
76220,3620 CIS

Name
Address
City, State, Zip
Phone
Country
Credit Card Number
Expiration

MasterCard   **ORDER NOW!**   VISA